THE BIOGRAPHICAL EDITION

THE WORKS OF

WILLIAM MAKEPEACE THACKERAY

WITH BIOGRAPHICAL INTRODUCTIONS BY
HIS DAUGHTER, ANNE RITCHIE

IN THIRTEEN VOLUMES

VOLUME XIII.

BALLADS AND MISCELLANIES

Samuel Lawrence
Delt. 1864

Joseph Brown. sc.

WMThackeray

Published by Harper Brothers New York.

BALLADS
CRITICAL REVIEWS, TALES
VARIOUS ESSAYS, LETTERS
SKETCHES, ETC.

BY

WILLIAM MAKEPEACE THACKERAY

WITH A LIFE OF THE AUTHOR
BY
LESLIE STEPHEN
AND A BIBLIOGRAPHY

WITH ILLUSTRATIONS BY THE AUTHOR
GEORGE CRUIKSHANK, AND JOHN LEECH

HARPER & BROTHERS PUBLISHERS
NEW YORK AND LONDON
1900

THE BIOGRAPHICAL EDITION OF
W. M. THACKERAY'S COMPLETE WORKS

Edited by Mrs. ANNE THACKERAY RITCHIE

The volumes are issued as far as possible in order of original publication

1. VANITY FAIR
2. PENDENNIS
3. YELLOWPLUSH PAPERS, ETC.
4. BARRY LYNDON, ETC.
5. SKETCH BOOKS
6. CONTRIBUTIONS TO "PUNCH," ETC.
7. HENRY ESMOND, ETC.
8. THE NEWCOMES
9. CHRISTMAS BOOKS, ETC.
10. THE VIRGINIANS
11. PHILIP, ETC.
12. DENIS DUVAL, ETC.
13. BALLADS & MISCELLANIES

Illustrated. Crown 8vo, Cloth, Ornamental, Uncut Edges and Gilt Tops,
$1 75 per volume

HARPER & BROTHERS, PUBLISHERS,

NEW YORK AND LONDON

CONTENTS

LOVE-SONGS MADE EASY

FIVE GERMAN DITTIES

FOUR IMITATIONS OF BÉRANGER

IMITATION OF HORACE

OLD FRIENDS WITH NEW FACES

CRITICAL REVIEWS

TALES

VARIOUS ESSAYS, LETTERS, SKETCHES, ETC.

LIST OF ILLUSTRATIONS

CRITICAL REVIEWS

VARIOUS ESSAYS, LETTERS, SKETCHES

INTRODUCTION

TO

MISCELLANIES

1840–1863

I

BALLADS

WHEN my father first published his "Ballads and Poems," he wrote a preface, dated Boston, October 27, 1855, saying: "These ballads have been written during the past fifteen years, and are now gathered by the author from his own books and the various periodicals in which the pieces appeared originally. They are published simultaneously in England and America, where a public which has been interested in the writer's prose stories, he hopes, may be kindly disposed to his little volume of verses."

The next edition of the "Ballads" was that of 1861, when Messrs. Bradbury & Evans published the "Miscellanies."

"The Chronicle of the Drum" came out in a little volume in 1841, and was published with the "Second Funeral of Napoleon." It was a cheap little book, costing a few pence; but I see that by one of those curious freaks of fashion, with which it is difficult to sympathise, a copy was sold lately at Sotheby's for £19; and another, so *The Times* states, realised forty guineas a little while ago. The "Second Funeral of Napoleon" was reprinted in *The Cornhill Magazine* for January 1866, two years after my father's death, with a prefatory note by Mr. Greenwood. He writes: "The intelligent public of the time

refused to read it. The gentleman who sends us the original
MS. from which we reprint the long-forgotten narrative, says :
' I had the pleasure of editing the tiny volume for Mr. Titmarsh,
and saw it through the press, and after a while, on the dismal

THE SECOND FUNERAL

OF

AND

THE CHRONICLE OF THE DRUM.

BY MR. M. A. TITMARSH.

COVER OF " SECOND FUNERAL OF NAPOLEON."

tidings that the little effort made no impression on the public,
Mr. Titmarsh wrote to me from Paris a pretty little note, com-
mencing, "So your poor Titmarsh has made another fiasco.
How are we to take this great stupid public by the ears ? Never

mind, I think I have something which will surprise them yet." '
He had just begun ' Vanity Fair.' "

The story of " Little Billee " is told by Mr. Samuel Bevan in
a book called " Sand and Canvas," in which that ballad was first
printed under the title of " The Three Sailors." It was in the
autumn of 1844, at Rome, that Mr. Bevan met my father, who
was then on his way back from the East. " I met Titmarsh,"
Mr. Bevan writes, " at many of the evening parties which were
held by the artists at this season. '. . .

" Perhaps the greatest display of this sort was made on a certain holiday, when the whole of us dined together at Bertini's,
and he was voted into the chair. . . . Just at this time there
was a schism among the members of the English Academy in
Rome, and an important question was fresh on the tapis ; it was
no wonder, therefore, that a considerable portion of the evening was consumed in long-winded speeches, and had it not been
for a proposal on the part of our friend Beardman ' to take the
basso part in a glee,' a harmonious feeling would hardly have
been arrived at. His instigation was succeeded by a call for a
song from the chair, amid a vociferous shout of ' Viva Titmarsh !' and a deafening clatter of dessert furniture.

" Our great friend assured us he was unable to sing, but would
endeavour to make amends by a recitation, if some one in the
meantime would make a beginning. Whilst a few, therefore, on
the right of the chair were tantalising the company by a tortured
version of one of Calcott's glees, Titmarsh, busy with his tablets,
produced the affecting narrative of the Three Sailors, of which he
soon after delivered himself in a fittingly lugubrious tone of voice."

Next to Little Billee, Policeman X is perhaps one of the most
popular of incarnations.

The great constable seems to have been made for *Punch* and
Punch for him, as he treads his

> " Beat with steady steps and slow,
> All huppandownd—of Ranelagh Street;
> Ranelagh Street, Pimlico.
>
> While marching huppandownd—
> Upon that fair May morn—
> Beold the booming cannings sound,
> A Royal child is born !"

Had Policeman X been still among us there is no knowing what different awards might not have been made of certain honours lately distributed ; as he himself justly observes—

> "The Poit-Laureat's crownd,
>   I think in some respex,
> Egstremely shootable might be found,
>   For honest Pleaseman X."

The ballads of Policemen X are in the "Miscellanies," all except "The Organ Boy's Appeal," which was my father's last poetical contribution to *Punch*. "Jacob Omnium's Hoss" interested and amused us all at the time it came out. In this ballad, Pleaseman X exclaims—

> "Who was this master good,
>   Of whomb I makes these rhymes?
> His name is Jacob Homnium Exquire;
>   And if I'd committed crimes,   .
> Good Lord! I wouldn't 'ave that man,
>   Attack me in the *Times!*"

As I quote from Pleaseman X there comes before me the well-remembered stately figure of Jacob Omnium, so dignified, so gallant, that keen, handsome face, so significant with sense and wit. I can think of no one very easily comparable in looks or in manner with Mr. Higgins, that most lovable and most fearable gentleman. Nor can I imagine how any average jury of the usual stature ever found courage to give a verdict against him. "I would give half-a-crown an hour," my father used to say, "if only Higgins would stand outside in the garden and let me make studies from his figure."

One morning—it must have been on the 1st of May 1851—my father was sitting at breakfast in the bow-windowed dining-room in Young Street, when we came in and found him reading *The Times*. He held out the sheet and pointed to his name at the foot of a long column of verses, the Ode upon the Great Exhibition—

> "But yesterday a naked sod,
>   The dandies sneered from Rotten Row,
> And cantered o'er it to and fro;
>   And see 'tis done!
> As though 'twere by a wizard's rod,
>   A blazing arch of lucid glass
> Leaps like a fountain from the grass
>   To meet the sun!"

He said he liked the simile of the fountain, it was so simple and yet it described the building exactly.

Our old friend Sir Henry Cole was one of the chief originators of the Great Exhibition of '51, and he used often to come and talk about the scheme to my father, who greatly admired it, and who has written more than one account of that wonderful building. Besides the ode in the *Times* there is also the poem by Mr. Malony of Malony, which was published in *Punch*—

> " With janial foire
> Thransfuse me loyre,
> Ye sacred nymphs of Pindus,
> The whoile I sing
> That wondthrous thing.
> The Palace made o' windows !"

The " Legend of St. Sophia of Kioff " provided its author with an unexpected little experience when he was lecturing on the " Four Georges " in Scotland. He wrote from Aberdeen :—

" I wonder if sneering is of the devil and laughter is not wicked ? At a delightful industrial school at Aberdeen (where the children's faces and voices choked me and covered my spectacles with salt water) the founder of the school, Sheriff Watson, pulled my ' Ballads ' out of his pocket, and bade one of the little ones read out, ' A hundred years ago and more, a city built by burghers stout, and fenced with ramparts round about,' which the little man did in an innocent voice, and a strong Scotch accent of course ; but the tone of levity in the ballad pained me coming from guileless lips, and I turned away ashamed and said to myself, ' Pray God I may be able some day to write something good for children.' That will be better than glory or Parliament. We must try and do it, mustn't we ? As soon as we have made a competence for the two young ones, we must see if we can do anything for the pleasure of young ones in general. That truth suggested itself to me in the industrial schools in Aberdeen."

The lines to K. E. P. are well known—" The Pen and the Album "—

> "Stranger, I never writ a flattery,
> Nor signed the page that registered a lie."

Miss Perry has given her own notes about my father, and

tioned here, the ballad of " Catherine Hayes," to which allusion
was made in the preface to " Barry Lyndon." The original
version has only just been sent me through the kindness of my
old friend Dr. Weir Mitchell of New York, and it is republished
for the first time, in this volume.

In that preface I told the story of the confusion which arose
in the mind of the Irish public between the murderess Catherine
Hayes and the popular singer of that name, and how my father
sent the ballad on the subject to Adelaide Procter.

One of the letters to Miss Procter shows that my father had
time to read other people's verses as well as to rewrite his own—

"36 Onslow Square, *June* 4 (1860).

" My dear Adelaide,—Thank you for the little book with
the kind little inscription on the first page. There will always
be an " a——" between us, won't there? and we shall like each
other out of our books and melancholies and satires, and poetries
and proses. Why are your verses so very, very grey and sad?
I have been reading them this morning till the sky has got a
crape over it—other folks' prose I have heard has sometimes a
like dismal effect, one man's specially I mean, with whom I am
pretty intimate, and who writes very glumly, though I believe
he is inwardly a cheerful, wine-bibbing, easy-going person, liking
the wicked world pretty well in spite of all his grumbling. We
can't help what we write though ; an unknown something works
within us and makes us write so and so. I'm putting this case
de me (as usual) and *de te*. I don't like to think you half so sad
as your verses. I like some of them very much indeed, especially
the little tender bits. All the allusions to children are full of a
sweet, natural compassionateness ; and you sit in your poems
like a grey nun with three or four little prattlers nestling round
your knees, and smiling at you, and a thin hand laid upon the
golden heads of one or two of them ; and having smoothed them
and patted them, and told them a little story, and given them a
bonbon, the grey nun walks into the grey twilight, taking up
her own sad thoughts and leaving the *parvulos* silent and wist-
ful. There goes the Angelus ! There they are, lighting up the
chapel. Go home, little children, to your bread and butter and
teas, and kneel at your bedside in crisp little nightgowns.

THERE ARE NO MAIDS.

EDITOR AND AUTHOR.

The pictures and sketches from which we have been drawing are not yet exhausted. Among those which are here published some tell their own stories, some have to do with things belonging to many long-agos of fun and youthful impression. Take, for instance, the illustration to the old song, " There are no Maids like English Maids," or the sketches from wood blocks or the Irish Ballads, or the notes from abroad, such as Mon Cheval Boit and La Pluie, and the pretty group of the Soldier and the Peasant Girl. The Buck seems of English extraction, but the Musicians and Yssengiettery certainly come from the land of Caran d'Ache, who was not yet in existence. Tom Fool's country, who shall divine ?

Besides these sketches we give others, such as the portraits of the Dobus family, in their different avocations.

Here, also, are the adventures of " Vivaldi," with their delightful horrors, which have never yet been put before the public, and of which a more elaborate version is in the British Museum. The MS. was sent to us for verification, a discriminating little schoolboy having bartered his collection of stamps for it with another little schoolboy, who had become the lawful possessor of the picture by inheritance, I think. The family of the stamp-collector demurred, if I remember rightly, and thought the stamps far too valuable to part with for mere sketches ; but Professor Colvin, at the British Museum, finally settled the controversy by offering a sum of money, which was accepted, and the pictures are now safely in their niche in the British Museum.

TOM FOOL'S PORTFOLIO.

"I wonder whether this has anything on earth to do with Adelaide Anne Procter's poems? I wish the tunes she sang were gayer; but *que voulez vous?* The Lord has made a multitude of birds and fitted them with various pipes (there goes —— singing in her room, with a voice that is not so good as Adelaide Sartorises', but which touches me inexpressibly when I hear it), and the chorus of all is Laus Domino.

"I am writing in this queer way, I suppose, because I went to St. Paul's yesterday—Charity Children's day, miss, and the sight and sound immensely moved and charmed yours affectionately, dear Adelaide,   W. M. THACKERAY."

When my father wrote a poem he used to be more agitated than when he wrote in prose. He would come into the room worried and excited, saying, "Here are two more days wasted. I have done nothing at all. It has taken me four mornings' work to produce six lines." Then, after a further struggle, all would go well.

There is some such account given in the life of Lady Blessington concerning the little poem called "Piscator and Piscatrix." He nearly gave it up in despair, but finally the pretty verses came to him.

I have still some of his poems torn down the centre. They are as often as not in pencil.

The volume of "Ballads" finishes with "The End of the Play," of which the last verses might seem almost to speak of his own history—

> "My song save this is little worth;
>   I lay the weary pen aside,
> And wish you health, and love, and mirth,
>   As fits the solemn Christmas-tide,
>   As fits the holy Christmas birth.
>   Be this, good friends, our carol still,
> Be peace on earth, be peace on earth,
>   To men of gentle will."

If ever peace came at Christmas-time to a man of gentle will, it was to the writer of those lines. "Good Will" was the name some one gave him in some verses written after his death.

SKETCHES—IRISH BALLADS.

MON CHEVAL BOIT.

LA PLUIE.

Vivaldi escaping from the Bandits tower.

The Fury of the Bandit Chief!.

Wounded & overpowered by numbers he is carried back to the Tower.

The Bandits Tower a Tale for young persons uniting Instruction with amusement & blending Terror with delight!

His uncomfortable condition in the DUNGEON.

VIVALDI.

The Gaoler on bringing to Vivaldi
his monthly portion of bread & water.
is so struck by his appearance
that he gives him the means to escape.

he escapes on the Captain's
favorite mule.

The effects of the anger of
the Bandit chief! —

Vivaldi in the arms of
his Matilda! —

VIVALDI.

Captain & Lt. Colonel the Honble Wellesly Dobus

Dobus the Poet

Sir John Dobus M.P.
In his place in Parliament.

The Celebrated (though Unapprecia
ted) Painter Dobus

SOLDIER AND PEASANT GIRL.

BUCK AND NURSEMAID

MUSICIANS.

YSSENGIETTERY.

FAMILY GROUP.

NAVAL COURTESY.

P.S.—CONCERNING GRANDFATHERS AND GRANDMOTHERS

THE author of " Vanity Fair " was always very much interested in his grandfathers and grandmothers—long before the present fashion for heredity had set in. I have often heard him describe the Thackerays as a race, though he did not seem exactly to belong to it himself. They were tall, thin people, with marked eyebrows, and clear dark eyes, simple, serious. They were schoolmasters, parsons, doctors, Indian Civil Servants, and some officers thrown in to give us an air. My father once went to see the place in Yorkshire—Hampsthwaite, near Harrogate— from whence his ancestors first came, and he took me with him. We walked through the village and down a steep road, until we came to an old grey bridge across the rushing Nidd, beyond which rolls a long line of hills. (Visiting the place again with my own children after a lifetime, it seemed even prettier to me than I remembered it. The waters were fuller, the ash trees had spread their branches, starting from between the rocks and hanging over the stream.) I have been told that there is a brook called the Thackwray not far from Hampsthwaite (wray means running water). After walking through the village my father went into the old church. The clergyman came out to meet him, and showed us the Parish Registers, kept in an ancient, worm-eaten chest, where Dorothys and Cicelys and Timothys and Timotheas were inscribed from 1660 downwards. We were told that the Thackeray farm was an old Elizabethan dwelling, which had only lately been pulled down, and which had stood on the slope on the other side of the stream. For two hundred years or more generations of farmers had dwelt among these hills and breathed the life-giving Yorkshire air, before the first of their race came to the front.

This worthy was Elias Thackeray of Hampsthwaite, a handsome man and a good scholar, who went to Cambridge, took orders, and was appointed to the living of Hawkhurst in his native Yorkshire. Elias Thackeray never married, but his brother Timothy, the farmer, had a well-favoured son called Thomas, who also distinguished himself at his books, and was finally ordained and became a schoolmaster. He was then successively

ARCHDEACON THACKERAY

a master at Eton, Headmaster of Harrow in 1746, Chaplain to the Prince of Wales in 1748. In the Whitehall *Evening Post* for Tuesday the 28th of June of that year we read : " On Sunday last the Rev. Dr. Thackeray, master of the school at Harrow on the Hill, kissed H. R. H. the Prince of Wales's hand on being appointed one of his Chaplains-in-Ordinary." This piece of news appears among other more important facts, such as the Return of the French from the Netherlands, Conferences between Marshal Saxe and the Envoy-Extraordinary of the King of Poland, Account of Admiral Byng's successful encounter in the Mediterranean with a convoy of eighty ships. Dr. Thackeray was Archdeacon of Surrey at his death in 1760.

The Archdeacon is described as a dignified person, with a charming manner, dark eyes, and a powdered wig ; he must have been a good Headmaster, for he more than doubled the numbers at Harrow. He was just about to be made a bishop when he died, but none of his descendants, although there were a great many of them, ever reached to such a dignity. He was also distinguished as an apparition, and is said to have been seen walking into his own house a few hours after his death.

We have a picture kindly given to us by the Rennell Rodds ; it is that of an old lady sitting in a red velvet chair. She wears long white gloves up to her elbows, a grey dress with short frilled sleeves made in the fashion of George the Third's time, a white kerchief folded and tucked away into black velvet bands, a quaint cap with a frill to it tied under her chin. She also wears a big black silk apron, and sits demurely with her hands folded. Her face is pleasant but determined, as should be that of the mother of sixteen children and the wife of a Headmaster of Harrow. When Miss Anne Woodward married Dr. Thackeray, a family historian declares that they were the handsomest couple of their time. Their grandchildren certainly were very good-looking people, and I can trace a look of many of the old lady's descendants in her own spirited, smiling face. William Makepeace, Mrs. Thackeray's sixteenth child, was my father's grandfather. He went to India, and soon after his return home, still a young man, but already somewhat broken in health, he settled with his wife, Amelia Richmond Webb, at Hadley, in Middlesex, where were born many sons and daughters.

The story of William Makepeace Thackeray the first, as well as of his seven sons, has been told by Sir William Hunter in his delightful and spirited records of the history of an empire, with the story of the making of which he has interwoven the lives of these good, self-respecting, and public-spirited young men.

In Sir William's pages we find the earlier history of the father of them all, William Makepeace Thackeray, the "elephant hunter" as he is called, "arriving in India on his seventeenth birthday with his mother's Bible in his trunk." We hear of his rapid promotion under Mr. Cartier, the predecessor of Warren Hastings as Governor of Bengal; of the wild territories he was set to govern, of his adventurous wanderings, his speculations in elephants and tigers, his audacious disputes with the Court of Directors—all happening within the ten years he remained in India. He was not unlike the hero of a fairy tale, somewhat limited, but brave and single-minded. Family feeling was strong in this enterprising young civilian. He sailed for India in 1766; in 1768, at the age of nineteen, he had sent home for his sisters, Jane, ten years his senior, and Henrietta, who was a little younger and very beautiful. Sir William quotes the old family story of Mrs. Thackeray's exclamation, "If there is a sensible man in India, he will find out my Jane."

This is a copy of the petition of the sisters:

"To the Honble the Court of Directors—
"For the Honble East India Company.
"The humble petition of Jane and Henrietta Thackeray—
"Sheweth
"That your Petitioner having a Brother in your Service, a writer in Bengal, who is desirous of their going there, and an invitation being also sent them by John Cartier Esqr. they therefore humbly beg permission so to do, by one of the Ships bound thither, and the Security required will be duly given by

Your Honours' most obedient Servants
(signed)   JANE THACKERAY.
                HENRIETTA THACKERAY.

"Endorsed:
"Request of Misses Jane and Henrietta Thackeray to go to their friends at Bengal.   Read in Court.
"Granted.   2 Nov. 1768."

MRS. THACKERAY

Widow of Archdeacon Thackeray

Eventually under their young brother's auspices the two sisters both married, Jane became the wife of Major Rennell, and Henrietta married Mr. Harris, chief of the Council of Dacca.

William Makepeace Thackeray in Calcutta also married about this time. His wife was Amelia Richmond Webb, a daughter of Colonel Richmond Webb, who commanded a company at the battle of Culloden, and lies buried in the East Cloister of West-minster Abbey.* Colonel Webb was a kinsman of the General Webb who appears in "Esmond."

A letter from Colonel Webb to his son still exists, and is characteristic enough to be inserted here:—

Col. R. Webb *to his* Son.

"Bath, *August* 25, 1765.

"My dear Richmond,—I have received a letter this day, by which I perceive that there is no likelyhood of getting you to the East Indies (in the fair and genteel prospect I would send you) *this* next year. . . . In the meantime, you have time enough; you may keep at your college, and as I shall be in London I will procure a master to instruct you in arithmetic, that you may not go abroad ignorant of what every man must know, and every mechanic does know. You shall be taught under my eye, and will not have it to learn among little boys when you go abroad, but be immediately able to enter on merchant's accounts. As to the Church, it does not seem to be your choice, and therefore I'll not name it.

"If the two new pair of shoes and two new pair pumps are not made, forbid them, and only bespeak one pair of each; which will serve you to wear in college. Pray, are your new clothes made? Write me word by return of post. . . .

"I do not doubt of your readiness to acquiesce in whatever I propose, that you will make a figure in whatever way of life fortune shall put you in. I am convinced that you will conduct

---

* His name is recorded on a tablet on the cloister wall. The inscription on the gravestone below has been worn away by the steps of the congregations passing into the Abbey, but the tablet has been restored quite lately by one of the family of the Moores: it records Colonel Webb's virtues in the language of the day, and tells of the death of his wife Sarah Webb, who could not long survive her loss.

yourself with honour and good, and keep clear of vice and idleness, these rocks which so many youths split upon; and for my part, if Heaven spares my life, I will do my utmost to protect, encourage, and support you in anything that's praiseworthy.

"Be honest and good, you have a good stock of learning which I hope you won't neglect. Make yourself master of your pen and your sword, and you will be enabled to serve your king, country, yourself and friends, and there's nothing that you, who are born a gentleman and educated like one, may not pretend to. . . .

"I must now busy myself with putting all your sisters out, and Mama and you and I spend the winter in London.—Adieu, my dear boy.   R. WEBB."

The younger Richmond subsequently entered the army and was killed in the American War.

Apparently the poor Webb sisters were all " put out," as their father says, and shipped off to India. Three of them married there. Amelia met Mr. Thackeray at Calcutta, at the age of seventeen. Another, Augusta, became Mrs. Evans; a third, Sarah, married Mr. Peter Moore. On the unmarried daughter, Charlotte, some sad tragedy seems to have fallen; although her start in life was happy. After the Thackerays' departure for England she made her home with Mrs. Moore. One of this lively lady's letters describing her sister's adventures has been preserved, and reads like a page out of " Evelina " or " Cecilia."

From Mrs. Moore *in Calcutta to* Mrs. Thackeray
in England.

" The day following Dr. Williams being discarded as a lover came Mr. Wodsworth, who had teased us with his company almost incessantly for some time before. He took Mr. Moore aside and declared a most violent love for Charlotte, entreating that P. M. should give him his interest. Mr. Moore replied with great coolness that she was at her own disposal, and that he did not mean to interfere. Mr. Wodsworth then came to me and told me that Mr. Moore had something to say to me. I accordingly went out, and was a little astonished at Wodsworth's as-

W. M. THACKERAY, THE GRANDFATHER (1749-1813)

surance. I rejoined the company with a very grave aspect, and took no further notice, but saw that Mr. W., *agreeable to his bold and constant custom*, had stayed supper without being asked. We had not an opportunity to mention the matter to Charlotte, so that you may guess her surprise when, as we were walking with the Auriols to the door, Mr. W. laid hold on her, and without further preface began with, ' O dear Miss Webb, don't distract me, I love you to distraction.' Poor Charlotte, who was thunderstruck at so abrupt and indelicate a declaration, was much provoked, and turning short on him only said, ' Bless me, sir, you're mad, sure !' and immediately joined us in the verandah. Notwithstanding this rebuff he had the boldness to come the next day to tea, and joined us in our walk ; but we received him very coolly, and hardly spoke to him, and Mr. Moore took this opportunity of telling him he must be much less frequent in his visits. He expressed great concern lest Mr Thomson should have overheard his speech to Charlotte. Mr. Moore told him he might well be ashamed of it, for he never heard anything like it in his life, and added that he spoke so loud, that not only Mr Thomson, but the two Mr. Auriols must have heard it. You know P. M. loves a little mischief. Here endeth the chapter of Mr. Wodsworth.

" Auriol of late has paid her very great and constant attention, which she seems to receive with much pleasure." . . .

Mrs. Moore goes on to hope that Charlotte will soon make up her mind, as Augusta,—still wearing short frocks, and with her hair over her forehead,—is also beginning to receive verses and offers, which she refuses with great spirit.

The following pathetic letter from the mother in England to Warren Hastings—which was found in the British Museum and given us by Mr. Malcolm Low—comes in vivid contrast to all the merriment and feasting :—

From Mrs. Webb *to* Warren Hastings, Esq.

" London, High Street, Marylebone,
" *December* 20, 1781.

" Sir,—Distracted with the sufferings of our dear beloved and unfortunate daughter, Charlotte Webb, I hope, will plead my excuse for the liberty of thus addressing you on her behalf. Apprehending Mr. Evans may possibly be absent from Calcutta, as (or?) fearing any other accident should put it out of his power to convey our dear child to England, in compliance to most earnest and repeated request. If, therefore, she is not already on her passage home, I beg and implore that you, Sir, will have the great goodness and compassion to her wretched state, and ours, as to have her conveyed home with all possible speed and safety, which shall ever be esteemed as the greatest obligation, which favour I should never have presumed to ask, but that urgent necessity prompts me to it; the miserys she has already suffered, and the great loss of time past *owing to Mrs. Moore's imprudence in keeping her summer after summer since her first illness,* which has perhaps rendered all our future endeavour to recover her, lost. These dreadful considerations, together with their completing her tradgedy by a sham marriage, all which shocking events makes her poor father and I really fear that *even murder* may be the next cruel scene with which we may be presented. Our troubles and reflections are of the bitterest kind, that so *good,* so fine a girl should meet with such a load of woes, for, if there are Truth, Innocence, and Honour in the Humane breast, our dear Charlotte Webb had her full portion. Such was her character from infancy while in England, but that fatal period in which I unhappily suffered her to depart from under the protection of her parents has ruined her, and I am the innocent cause, for which I shall never forgive myself.

" Pardon, Sir, my thus trespassing on your time and patience, but I trust your humanity will consider this comes from an unhappy mother, who weeps over every line as she writes, so full is my heart of sorrow for my dear Charlotte, that I am almost frantic. Her father and I have both wrote long letters to Mr. Evans pressing him to send our poor girl home, we likewise got a friend to convey a small letter to the same purpose over land. But she has suffered so very much and so have we, on her account, which has obliged us to try every method to convey our wishes to Mr. Evans, and even (here a word or two blurred) feeling heart, and which I hope will apologise for the freedom.—I have the honor to be, Sir, your most obliged and most humble servant, SARAH WEBB."

This letter makes us realise, as indeed does many another instance, what a remarkable rôle Warren Hastings was called on to perform. He seems to have been Father Confessor as well as Dictator to the whole colony. They turn to him in every difficulty, invariably counting on his help and good offices.

Seven or eight years later we find Amelia Thackeray and Sarah Moore and their husbands settled on Hadley Green, where they are afterwards joined by Henrietta, now Mrs. Harris, a widow, and visited by Jane and her distinguished husband, Major James Rennell.

Some volumes of old letters were lately found at a second-hand bookseller's; they are from Great-grandpapa Thackeray, the elephant-hunter, and chiefly addressed to his solicitor. Mr. Thackeray seems fond of business, and is deputed to look after investments for his brothers and sisters. He has also wards who have been left to his guardianship. They had been sent by their dying father in India to Mr. Thackeray's care, and to that of Mr. Morgan Thomas the friendly man of business. They arrived with a patrimony consisting among other things of diamonds and cashmere shawls, to be disposed of for their benefit. Mrs. Rennell is prepared to buy some of the treasures. Mr. Thackeray's family is so large, he cannot have his wards to stay with him, he says. The family preoccupies him very much. One year he is engaged in having it " occulated," another year he and his wife have just returned from France, to find Mrs. Moore and her little family established on the Green. There is a story of a black boy, who has stolen Mrs. Thackeray's purse with " a guinea " in it, the year in which my grandfather, Richmond Thackeray, was born. Great-grandpapa Thackeray wishes the black boy out of the house, and begs Mr. Thomas to find him a lodging at a hairdresser's until he can be sent on board ship. One might be puzzled by this cure for dishonesty, but the writer goes on to explain that at the barber's the boy might make some progress in hairdressing, which would be of service to him in India, and enable him to earn an honest living there, without stealing purses. Parents nowadays might envy Mr. Thackeray's complaints of the expenses of education. " I can speak from experience," he says, " it is to me a most serious matter. My son's bills at Eton for the last year came to near

£80." Incidentally some of the family names occur—the other dwellers upon Hadley Green are mentioned. Mr. Peter Moore arrives from India, brothers and sisters cross the scene; so does Mr. Cartier, his former chief, and a Mr. Baronneau, who lends Mrs. Thackeray his carriage.

Mrs. Bayne, the family historian, tells us how Mr. Thackeray alternately wore a pepper and salt suit, and a blue one with brass buttons, and that Mrs. Thackeray used to dress in white, and lie upon a sofa, rather to the scandal of her more energetic contemporaries.

Among the various letters bound up with Mr. Thackeray's is a very unexpected epistle addressed to one of the wards by Miss Amelia Alderson, better known as Mrs. Opie. They had met on some country visit. It is as long as letters seemed to be in those days, and a somewhat ponderous mixture of heavy flirtation and lively good advice.

It was from this family home on Hadley Green that the sons started one by one—never to return.

Six of them followed their father's example, and went to India; William, Richmond, Tom, Webb, St. John, Charles, each one in turn, some soldiers, some civil servants. Richmond, my own grandfather, went out at sixteen, in the Company's Civil Service, and held various appointments. He was the only one of the Indian brothers who married, and my own father was his only son. The history of William is also told—the handsomest and foremost of them all. He was the friend of Sir Thomas Munro, the Governor of Madras, and he worked with him for many years. The task, says Sir William, assigned to Munro and his assistants was to bring order to chaos, and substitute a fair revenue system for extortion by the sword. "They spent their days in the saddle, and their nights in tents, in ruined forts, and Hindu temples, or under the shadow of some crumbling town gate. One by one each hamlet was visited, and the people were assured that the British Government only asked for a moderate rental, and would protect them in the undisturbed possession of their homesteads." William Thackeray was famous for his horses and horsemanship, as well as for being an authority on financial subjects. He was President of the Board of Revenue in the Madras Government when he died, January 11, 1823, aged forty-four.

St. John Thackeray was also in the Civil Service; he was chosen to help to bring into order the territories just won from the Mahrattas, and we read that he lost his life as he advanced unguarded with a flag of truce to a Kittur fort which the insurgents had seized. Webb, who had a special gift for languages, lived but a year after his arrival as a Madras civilian, but he lived long enough to make his mark.

Then there is the story of Thomas, killed in action in the Nepal War of 1814, after showing "extraordinary valour." We have a letter dated from the camp, "On ye banks of the Jumna." It is docketed in a sister's handwriting, "My beloved brother Thomas's last letter, written fourteen days before he fell."

"The appearance of a left-hand epistle," he says, "will not alarm you, my dear Charlotte, even though you should not have been apprised of the trifling accident which gives me no pain and little uneasiness, except that it will for a time put it out of my power to write to you. I trust," he continues, "I shall soon have occasion to address you again, to thank you for the Hadley news, and very shortly my right hand will be able to apologise for this awkward attempt of my left to express my affection."

It is odd to read letters in the familiar family phraseology, *almost* not *quite* in the familiar handwriting—letters full of the doings of people who are *almost* not *quite* those one has known. Here is a letter of 1801 ; it is written to his sister by my grandfather at the age of nineteen from the college at Calcutta. It is very like one of my father's early letters.

"I hope to be out of this in ten months," he says; "I am almost sorry I entered it, as the people begin to give themselves airs, and you know I always hated a jack in office. I could make Mater laugh with a few anecdotes, but I believe it is dangerous, and therefore will not indulge myself. Should I leave college next December I shall hope to see you here, but I suppose you won't come without a formal invitation.

A CARD.

MR. THACKERAY *requests the honour of Miss Thackeray's company at his house in Calcutta.*

"Joking apart, I think, my dear Emily, should I leave college by that time, and you have no great fears, you had better come. . . . For next to our dear father and mother you have no better friend than me."

My kind young grandfather goes on making plans for his family at home, just as my own father used to do. "Should any accident, which God forbid, happen in England, this would be a good situation for the whole family." Then he speculates about his father being appointed to some place at home. "But I could not see him attending a levée of a lord, whose highest good quality would be totally obscured by the least conspicuous one of Pater's." "Go down the Grove," he says in a postscript, "and read this on the bench by yourself, and then perhaps you will have patience to make out the epistle."

There are some brotherly jokes in it; he is sending his letter by the hand of a friend, " a good sort of man ; indeed, I intend him for either an admirer of yours or one of the Moores *i.e.* if you are not already married." The Moore cousins lived next door to the Thackerays at Hadley. Mr. Peter Moore was named my father's guardian in my grandfather's will. He was an interesting and brilliant man, the friend of Sheridan, who indeed died in Mr. Moore's house in Westminster. He was M.P. for Coventry for twenty-one years.* Fortune deserted him in later life.

There is a second letter from Richmond Thackeray to his mother, urging that his sister when she comes to India should bring letters of introduction, "for to tell you the truth," he says, "I am very far from a lady's man. It will be my and William's business to see that Emily is as well provided with everything as possible. I find economy will carry a small salary a great way, and am in hopes of having at least 800 rupees a month before she arrives." Emily accepted the invitation, and my grandfather then writes to beg that another of his sisters may come out. It is Charlotte he wishes for, beautiful Charlotte, barely sixteen. Augusta he loves quite as well, he says, but he has set his heart on Charlotte.

Parents in those days were less influenced by their children's wishes than they are now. Charlotte remained at Hadley, Augusta

---

* Mr. Richmond Moore of Guildford has a fine oil painting of Mr. Peter Moore.

was sent out to her brother, being next in rotation.   She was a very stately, and, when I knew her, a most alarming old lady. I just came up to her knees, and used to gaze in awe at her white stockings and sandalled shoes, as she walked along the Champs Elysées, where so many of our relations had congregated by that time.   Among these was Charlotte, my Great-aunt Ritchie ; and I loved her, as who did not love that laughing, loving, romantic, handsome, humorous, indolent old lady.   Shy, expansive in turn, she was big and sweet looking, with a great look of my father. Though she was old when I knew her, she would still go off into peals of the most delightful laughter, just as if she were a girl. When she was still quite young, soon after her parents' death (both of whom she had devotedly nursed with the help of her brother Charles), she came out of the house at Hadley one day dressed in the deepest mourning, and got into the London coach which passed through the village.   She looked so blooming, and so beautiful in her crape veils, that Mr. John Ritchie, a well-to-do merchant of a suitable age, who was travelling in the coach, fell in love with her then and there.   He inquired who she was, " paid his addresses," and was accepted very soon after.

One autumn day, just before his second visit to America, my father sent for an open carriage and a pair of horses, and we drove to Hadley, near Barnet, to see the early Thackeray home. It was a square family house, upon a green.   It was not high, but spread comfortably, with many windows, and it was to let. The Thackerays were gone from it long since, the seven sons and the many daughters.

My father seemed to know it all, though he had never been there before.   He went into the garden exclaiming, There was the old holly tree that *his* father used to write about.   Half the leaves were white on the branches that spread across the path ; that gravel path, which my grandfather, Richmond Thackeray, used to roll as a boy, and which he longed for in India some-times.   At the back of the drawing-room was a study, with a criss-cross network of wire bookcase along the walls ; it was here that Amelia Thackeray was sitting when her husband came in agitated and very pale ; he said there was terrible news from India, and as she started, terrified, from her seat, he exclaimed, "Not William, not William, but Webb."   "O Webb, my Webb," cried the poor mother, and dropped senseless on the ground. She never quite recovered the use of her limbs, though she regained consciousness. Until then she had never told anybody that she loved Webb the best of all her children. We have but one record of her own, a letter written to her son St. John, aged sixteen, at the East India College, Hertford, written with very motherly and touching expressions :—

MRS. W. M. THACKERAY *to* ST. JOHN THACKERAY.

"*December* 12, 1807.

" I feel impatient to wish my dear boy every success, at the same time not to feel discouraged should it prove otherwise than my anxious wishes would have it. If you do but profit by the past, which can't be recalled, it will still prove beneficial by affording you experience for the future; for, as you most justly observe, 'the loss of time in youth is certainly most unfortunate, because irreparable.' But, thank God, my dear boy has still left enough of early youth to redeem all past neglect, and since, thank God, he has sense and true understanding to enable him to perceive the mighty advantages of diligence in order to sow in due season to make *sure* of a good harvest. . . . I feel much for your approaching trial on Saturday, and can't forbear recommending you, my dearest St. John, still to exert your utmost until that day in getting by heart the parts you have to exhibit in as perfectly as possible. Do your best and leave the rest to Providence. Be sure on no account to neglect your precious health. Remember that a cheerful, open countenance and fine, graceful carriage is the *characteristic* of a gentleman and a young man of sense. To feel quite well—and to be so— are quite essential requisites towards succeeding. Pray be at the trouble to *peruse* this with *attention*, and forget not the hints of your most affectionate mother,

"A. T.

" *P.S.*—Be as neatly dressed as possible on Saturday, and with your own pleasing, manly, yet modest, open countenance you need not fear that any one will excel my dear boy; and the next year I am, please God, at least *certain* that in *superiority* of talents and abilities, as well as person, *none* will surpass you. God ever bless you."

Amelia Thackeray was only a little over fifty when she died; she and her husband were both buried at Hadley in the churchyard. I can remember my own father as he stood by the stone which was half hidden in the ivy at his feet. "Do you see what is written there," he said gravely, and with his finger he pointed to William Makepeace Thackeray carved upon the slab.

I have never seen any picture of Mrs. Amelia Thackeray, but there are pretty miniatures of Mrs. Peter Moore, gay, and sprightly, and of another sister, Mrs. Evans, a very charming person to look at. The Webbs, if they took after my father's favourite hero, General Webb, must have been an audacious, outspoken race. Any reserve in the family comes from the Thackeray side of the house. My father used to say that it was through his grandmother that the wits had come into the family, for certainly Great-grandpapa Thackeray was a practical but not at all a clever man.

There is a picture we used to look at in the nursery at home, and which my own children look at now as it hangs upon the wall. It is a water-colour sketch delicately pencilled and tinted, done in India some three quarters of a century ago by Chinnery, a well-known artist of those days, who went to Calcutta and drew the people there with charming skill. This picture represents a family group; father, mother, infant child, a subject which has been popular with painters ever since they first began their craft. Long before Raphael's wondrous art was known this particular composition was a favourite with artists and spectators, as I think it will ever be from generation to generation, while mothers continue to clasp their little ones in their arms. This special group of Thackerays is almost the only glimpse we have of my father's earliest childhood, but it gives a vivid passing impression of that first home which lasted so short a time. My long, lean young grandfather sits at such ease as people allowed themselves in those classic days, propped in a stiff chair with tight white ducks and pumps, and with a kind grave face. He was at that time collector of the district called the 24 Pergunnahs. My grandmother, a beautiful young woman of some two-and-twenty summers, stands draped in white, and beside her, perched upon half-a-dozen big piled books, with his arms round his mother's neck, is her little son, William Makepeace Thackeray, a round-eyed boy of three years old, dressed in a white muslin frock. He has curly dark hair, and a very sweet look and smile. This look was almost the same indeed after a lifetime. Neither long years of work and trouble, nor pain nor chill anxiety ever dimmed its clear simplicity, though the gleam of his spectacles may have sometimes come between his eyes and those who did not know him very well.*

My father would take his spectacles off when he looked at this old water-colour. "It is a pretty drawing," he used to say, but he added that if his father in the picture had risen from the chair in which he sat, he would have been above nine feet high from the length of the legs there depicted. My father could just remember him, a very tall thin man rising out of a bath. He could also remember the crocodiles floating on the Ganges, and that was almost all he ever described of India, though in his writings there are many allusions to Indian life. A year after this sketch was painted the poor young collector died of a fever on board a ship, where he had been carried from the shore for fresher air. Forty years afterwards my father described a visit he paid to Paris to his aunt Mrs. Halliday, the Augusta who was sent to India in the place of Charlotte. The old lady was ill, and wandering in her mind, and she imagined herself still on board that ship on the Ganges beside her dying brother. Richmond Thackeray was little over thirty when he died. The account of his solid and lasting work in India is given by Sir William Hunter, and must not be altogether omitted here. He seems to have had the family gift for administration, for brilliant and conscientious public work. His tastes and amusements curiously recall my father's—his drawings, his love of art, the paint box with the silver clasps, the horses, the portfolios of prints, the bric-à-brac, his collections of various kinds, and his pleasure in hospitality. Richmond Thackeray was a

* Much of this is reprinted, by the permission of Messrs. Scribner, from the *St. Nicholas Magazine*.

Walker & Boutall ph.sc.

Richmond Thackeray, his wife and child.
(W. M. Thackeray at three years of age.)
From a drawing by Chinnery in 1814.

Published by Harper and Bros New York.

reserved man, but he was no recluse. He was a great road maker, I have been told. As for his love of drawing, it will be seen from the facsimiles here given how great his taste was, and

THE COURSE.

PEOPLE AT TABLE.

from whom my own father inherited his love of drawing. His grave * is in the old cemetery at Calcutta, where he was laid

* An Indian correspondent has sent me the photograph of the tall obelisk put up to the memory of Richmond Thackeray.

with all sympathy and respect. Richmond Thackeray's widow
remained out in India with her mother and sisters. She must
have been about twenty-five when she married for the second
time.

Meanwhile her little son had come back to England with a
cousin of his own age, both returning under the care of a
civilian, Mr. James Macnab, who had promised to befriend the
children on the journey home, and of whose kindness we have
often heard in after times.

There was an officer called Reed on board the ship, whom

GENTLEMAN PROPOSING.   THE WILL.

my father met long after when lecturing in the North, and with
whom he talked over those almost forgotten days. In one of
the "Roundabout Papers" there is a mention of this coming
home, and of the cousin Richmond Shakespear, who had been
his little playfellow and friend from the time of their birth;
there is a description of a ghaut or river stair in Calcutta, and
of the day "when down those steps to a boat which was waiting, came two children whose mothers remained on the shore."
One of these ladies was never to see her boy more, he says,
speaking of his aunt Mrs. Shakespear — the Emily to whom
Richmond Thackeray's letter had been written. My grandmother's was a happier fate, for she returned to make a home

for her son, and to see him grow up and prosper, and set his mark upon the time.

"When I first saw England," my father writes in his lecture upon George III., "she was in mourning for the young Princess Charlotte, the hope of the Empire. I came from India as a child, and our ship touched at an island on the way home, where my black servant took me a long walk over rocks and hills until

NAPOLEON AND MAJOR GAHAGAN.

we reached a garden, where we saw a man walking. 'That is he,' said the black man, 'that is Buonaparte; he eats three sheep every day, and all the little children he can lay hands on.'"

The traveller was six years old when he landed. He was sent to Fareham, in Hampshire, to the care of his mother's aunt and grandmother in the same quiet old house where his mother also had lived as a child. "Trix's house" it was called in those days, and still may be for all I know. It stood in Fareham High Street, with pretty old-fashioned airs and graces, with a high sloping roof and narrow porch. The front windows looked across a flower bed into the village roadway, the back windows opened into a pleasant fruit garden sloping to the river. It was from this house that my grandmother had started to go to India when she was about sixteen, dressed for the journey in a green cloth riding-habit, so she used to tell us. She was destined to be married, to be a mother, and a widow, and to be married again, before a decade had gone by.

It was to Fareham my father returned in thought at the end of his life, and where he meant to place the closing scenes of "Denis Duval."

* These drawings of Lord Bateman were found by Mrs. Julia Stephen in
an old drawer, where they had been forgotten for a quarter of a century, and
were given to me by her. The sketches here reproduced are a reduced fac-
simile of the originals. This particular page is very carefully coloured, the
rest of the drawings are in pen and ink.

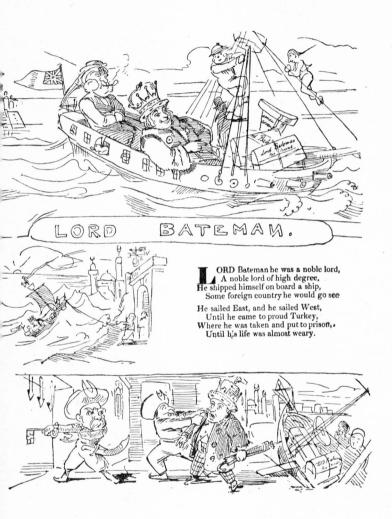

LORD Bateman he was a noble lord,
   A noble lord of high degree,
He shipped himself on board a ship,
   Some foreign country he would go see

He sailed East, and he sailed West,
   Until he came to proud Turkey,
Where he was taken and put to prison,
   Until his life was almost weary.

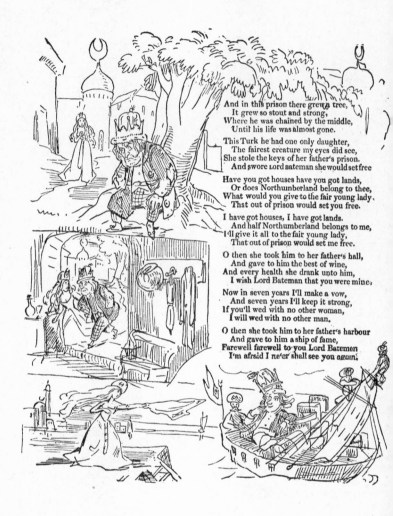

And in this prison there grew a tree,
  It grew so stout and strong,
Where he was chained by the middle,
  Until his life was almost gone.

This Turk he had one only daughter,
  The fairest creature my eyes did see,
She stole the keys of her father's prison.
  And swore Lord Bateman she would set free

Have you got houses have you got lands,
  Or does Northumberland belong to thee,
What would you give to the fair young lady,
  That out of prison would set you free.

I have got houses, I have got lands.
  And half Northumberland belongs to me,
I'll give it all to the fair young lady,
  That out of prison would set me free.

O then she took him to her father's hall,
  And gave to him the best of wine,
And every health she drank unto him,
  I wish Lord Bateman that you were mine.

Now in seven years I'll make a vow,
  And seven years I'll keep it strong,
If you'll wed with no other woman,
  I will wed with no other man.

O then she took him to her father's harbour
  And gave to him a ship of fame,
Farewell farewell to you Lord Bateman
  I'm afraid I ne'er shall see you again.

Now seven long years are gone and past,
    And fourteen days well known to thee,
She packed up all her gay cloathing,
    And swore Lord Bateman she would go see,

But when she came to Lord Bateman's castle
    So boldly she rang the bell,   (porter
Who's there, whose there cry'd the proud
    Who's there come tell unto me.
O is this Lord Bateman's castle,
    Or is his Lordship here within,
O yes, O yes, cried the young porter,
    He's just now taken his new bride in.

O tell him to send me a slice of bread,
    And a bottle of the best wine,
And not forgetting the fair young lady,
    Who did release him when close confin'd.

Away away went this young proud porter,
    Away away, and away went he,
Until he came to Lord Bateman's chamber,
    Down on his bended knees fell he.

What news what news, my proud young por-
   What news hast thou brought unto me (ter
There is the fairest of all young creatures,
   That e'er my two eyes did see.

She has got rings on every finger,
   And round one of them she has got three,
And as much gay cloathing round her mid-
   As would buy all Northumberland. (dle

She bids you send her a slice of bread,
   And a bottle of the best wine,
And not forgetting the fair young lady,
   Who did release you when close confin'd.

Lord Bateman he then in a passion flew,
   And broke his sword in splinters three,
Saying I will give all my father's riches,
   That if Sophia has crossed the sea.

Then up spoke the young bride's mother,
   Who never was heard to speak so free,
You'll not forget my only daughter,
   That if Sophia has crossed the sea.

I own I made a bride of your daughter,
 She's neither the better nor worse for me
She came to me with her horse and saddle,
 She may go back in her coach and three.

Lord Bateman prepared another marriage,
 With both their hearts so full of glee.
I'll range no more in foreign countries,
 Now since Sophia has crossed the sea.

II

DRAMATIC FUND SPEECH

MR. BRAM STOKER kindly obtained for me the report of a speech delivered on the thirteenth anniversary festival of the General Theatrical Fund, held at the Freemason's Tavern on the 29th of March 1858, W. M. Thackeray in the chair, and all the Vice-Presidents, with well-known names, such as Dickens, Landseer, Lytton, Milnes, Macready, &c., present on the occasion. The chairman's speech was as follows:—

"You are not perhaps aware—I only became acquainted with the fact this very day—that the celebrated Solon was born 592 years before the present era. He was one of the Seven Sages of Greece. He invented a saying, as each of the wise men are said to have done. He was a warrior, a statesman, a philosopher, of considerable repute. I make these statements to you, being anxious to give you a favourable idea of my learning, and also pleased to think of the perplexity of some ingenuous persons here present who are asking themselves, 'What on earth does he mean by dragging in old Solon, neck and heels, to preface the toast of the evening.' Solon once attended one of Thespis's dramatic entertainments—a professional godfather to professional gentlemen here present, the inventor of the drama, who used to go about from place to place, as we read, and act his plays out of a waggon; I suppose a stage waggon. Well, the great Solon having attended one of poor Thespis's performances, sent for that wandering manager when the piece was over, and it is recorded flapped his cane down upon the ground and said to Thespis, 'How dare you utter such a number of lies as I have heard you tell from your waggon?'

"The first manager of the world humbly interceded with the great magistrate, beak, or Mayor before whom he stood, and represented that his little interludes were mere harmless fictions intended to amuse or create laughter or sympathy, that they were not to be taken as matter-of-fact at all. Solon again banged his stick upon the ground, ordered the poor vagrant about his business, saying that the man who will tell fibs in a play will forge a contract. Plutarch relates the anecdote in his celebrated Life of Solon. . . . Thespis and Solon, who were alive twenty-four hundred years ago, have left their descendants : Thespis continues to this time, and there are Solons too. Solon has a little not illegitimate suspicion regarding Thespis, or Solon is a pompous old humbug, and calls out to his children to keep away from that wicked man, passes the door of his booth with horror, and thanks Heaven he is so much more virtuous than that vagrant. Or finally, and this is the more charitable and natural supposition, Solon is simply stupid, can't understand a joke when it is uttered ; and when the artist sings before him, or plays his harmless interlude, slaps his great stupid stick on the ground and says, ' I never heard such lies and nonsense in my life.' Suppose Solon says that because he is virtuous there should be no more cakes and ale, all youth, all life, all pleasure, all honest humour laugh in the pompous old dotard's face, and continue their fun. The curtain shall rise, the dance shall go on ; Harlequin shall take Columbine round the waist, clowns shall prig the sausages. Hamlet shall kill his wicked old Uncle ; Pauline shall walk up and down the garden with Claude Melnotte ; William shall rescue Susan from the hands of the amatory but kind-hearted Crosstree. We will have our provision of pleasure, wonder, laughter, tears, in spite of old Solon, though he flourish a stick as big as a beadle's.

" Now I take it be a most encouraging sign for Thespis that he is becoming orderly, frugal, prosperous, a good accountant, a good father to his children, a provider against a rainy day, a subscriber to such an admirable institution as this which we have all met to-night to support."

Mr. Dickens winds the proceedings up with a pretty compliment, saying " That none of the present company can have studied life from the stage waggons of Thespis downwards to greater advantage, to greater profit, and to greater contentment than in the airy books of ' Vanity Fair.'

" To this skilful showman, who has so much delighted us, and whose words have so charmed us to-night, . . . we will now, if you please, join in drinking a bumper toast. To the chairman's health."

13   3

III

NOTE-BOOKS

There is almost material for another lecture in the note-books which remain for "The Four Georges," of which notes a certain number are here reproduced as they stand. Some of the quotations are so interesting that they are given verbatim, even though they may be familiar to many of our readers.

Most of the annotations to the "Lectures on the Humourists" were added by Mr. Hannay at my father's request, as the publication only took place after his start for America. Of the note-books which served for these I have no trace.* The extracts here given all concern the Four Georges. These first pages were evidently intended to make part of the lecture on George the First.

The Königsmarks.—Count Philip of Königsmark descended from an ancient noble family of Brandenburg, where there is a place of that name. The Königsmarks had also passed over into Sweden, where they had acquired property, and this Swedish branch especially distinguished itself by producing several powerful men. Philip's grandfather, Hans Christoff, was first page at the court of Frederic Ulric of Brunswick, and in the storm of the Thirty Years War rose to·be a famous general; was a partisan of Gustavus Adolphus of Torstensohn, stormed Prague, and contributed to the Peace of Westphalia. By this peace the principalities of Verden and Bremen were ceded to the Swedes, over which Hans Christoff became governor, building a castle near Stade, which he named after his wife, Agathenburg. In 1651 he received the title of Count, and died a field-marshal at Stockholm in 1663. He left his children an income

---

* Nor have I any of the notes for "Esmond," except one very small memorandum-book. Mr. Andrew Lang, who has read my father to such good purpose, would have liked him to give another version of the character of the Old Pretender. Mr. Lang has his authorities for defending the morals of James Stuart, and for rehabilitating those of the lady mentioned as Queen Oglethorpe. He has written an interesting account of her as the member of a respectable family who lived and died in loyal devotion to the Stuarts in their misfortunes.

of 130,000 dollars, so that his sons were enabled to marry into the first Swedish houses, with the daughters of lords who had espoused German princesses. No one understood how to levy booty better than this bold partisan of the Thirty Years War. In Lower Saxony he cut down whole forests, and sold the wood to the merchants of Hamburg and Bremen. In Prague he took an immense plunder, having seized no less than twelve barrels of gold in the house of Count Collorado, the Commandant. He was a fierce, passionate man, of herculean build and giant strength. When he was angry his hair bristled on his head like that of a boar, so that his friends and foes were frightened at him. In his castle of Agathenburg he had his portrait paint-ed after this fashion, jokingly bidding the painter so to depict him that the world might see the fierce countenance which had frightened the enemy in the Thirty Years War.

(Part of the next paragraph is given in the Lecture itself.)

One of his sons was Otto Wilhelm, a notable lion in the great society of the seventeenth century, and a great traveller to for-eign lands and courts. He had for tutor Esaias Puffendorff, brother of the famous philosopher who was afterwards Swedish Envoy to Vienna. With this leader the young bear frequented various German universities; learnt to ride at Blois and An-gers; made the grand tour of France, Spain, Portugal, and Eng-land; and in 1667, being then twenty-six years old, appeared as ambassador at the Court of Louis XIV. He had to make a Swedish speech at his reception before the most Christian king, and forgetting his speech recited the *Paternoster* and several other prayers in Swedish to the edification of the Court at Versailles, not one of whom understood a word of his lingo with the exception of his own suite, who had to keep their gravity as best they might.

Subsequently he entered into the French service, raising for the king the regiment of Royal Allemand. He died, finally, in 1688, before Negropont, in Morea—generalissimo of the Vene-tian army against the Turks.

Count Philip Königsmark, Otto's nephew, the lover of the an-cestress of the Brunswick kings of England, was born in 1662. He inherited from his mother the beauty of the noble Swedish house of Wrangel, and was as handsome a gallant, and as dis-

solute a cavalier as any of his time. In youth he had been bred
up with the Electress of Hanover at her father's court of Zell,
and vowed to her Electoral Highness that he had loved her from
those early days, though not daring at this modest period to declare his passion. From Zell the young gentleman came over
to one Faubert's Academy in London, perfecting his education
in the neighbourhood of the polite court, of which the Chevalier
de Grammont has left such an edifying history. And here the
lad was implicated in that notorious adventure of which his
elder brother, Carl Johann, was the chief actor, and which ended
in a murder and a criminal trial.

Carl Johann had the fierceness of his grandfather the Boar,
and the accomplishments of his uncle the Field-Marshal and
pretty fellow. He began his life at fifteen in gaming and all
sorts of adventures in love and war. His uncle introduced him
to the world at Paris, whence he shipped himself for Malta, and
took part with the knights of the Order in a crusade against the
Barbaresques. He fought so bravely that he won the Malta
Cross, though he was only eighteen years old, and a Protestant
to boot. Returning from this campaign he visited Leghorn,
Rome, Venice, Iona, Madrid, Lisbon, and Paris again finally;
and it was on this journey that he was accompanied by the
Countess of Southampton, who was so desperately in love with
him, that she followed him everywhere in page's clothes. In
1680 he sought service in the English army, and performed
wonders at the siege of Tangiers, whence returning covered with
laurels, and forgetting my Lady Southampton, his page, who subsided into a convent with her little daughter, Königsmark fell
in love with the rich and lovely Elizabeth Percy, heiress of the
Earls of Northumberland and widow of the Lord Ogle, last son
of the Cavendish Dukes of Newcastle. Charming as Königsmark was, the widow preferred to him another pretty fellow,
Thomas Thynne of Longleat, "Tom of Ten Thousand," as he
was called in those days—a gentleman of the highest fashion,
who had the friendship of Rochester, and royally entertained
the Duke of Monmouth at his princely Wiltshire mansion. Lord
Ogle's widow was but sixteen years old when she espoused the
Lord of Longleat, and it was agreed that she should pass a year
on the Continent away from her husband ere they dwelt together.

Königsmark, indignant at this preference shown to " Tom of Ten Thousand," engaged three gentlemen to murder Mr. Thynne, who accordingly was shot in his carriage on the night of the 12th of February 1682. Both the Königsmarks were taken up for this murder, the actors in which, stoutly refusing to peach against their employers, were duly hanged, and the Königsmarks left England to finish their brilliant careers elsewhere.

The young gentleman from Faubert's Academy entered the service of the Elector Ernest Augustus of Hanover, and became lieutenant-colonel in a regiment of his Electoral Highness' dragoons, and here he renewed the relations with the fair young Princess of Zell, which ended so lucklessly for the pair.

Crisett calls Sophia Dorothea's father, the Duke of Zell, an old Trojan, and an excellent huntsman. He kept some famous champagne for King William's tasting, and gave his minister, Lord Lexington, a bottle of it.

George I. assisted at the raising of the siege of Vienna and the defeat of the Turks in 1684 ; he made three campaigns in Austria and Hungary, where he commanded a body of 1000 men of Brunswick. In 1689 he was with 8000 before Bonn ; in 1690 he commanded 11,000 with the Spaniards ; and in '92, '93, a like number being with his father's troops under King William.

The Royal Household.—A Dean of the Chapel Royal, five other Almoners and Clerks of the Closet, forty-eight Chaplains-in-Ordinary, six Chaplains at Whitehall, and Household Chaplains at Kensington and Hampton Court, twenty-seven gentlemen and ten children of the Chapel ; besides Organist, Lutenist, Violist, and Tuner of the Regals, Confessor of the Household, Organ-blower, Bell-ringer, and Surplice-washers; one officer, whose salary is £18, is called the " Cock and Cryet." Add to these three French, two Dutch, and three German Lutheran chaplains. And fancy King George, who did not care a fig for any religion, with this prodigious train of professional theologians.

Then come His Majesty's Household officers (under command of his Grace William, Duke of Devonshire, Lord Steward), attending in the several offices below stairs. These begin with the ten noblemen and gentlemen forming the supervisional Board of Green Cloth, with salaries varying from £1300 to £500

C

a year. After these follow the officers of the Accompting House, Bakehouse, Pantry, Cellar, Buttery, Spicery, Confectionery, Ewry, Laundry, King's Kitchen (in which there are thirty-five male persons, such as cooks, yeomen, scourers, turn-broaches, &c.). After the Kitchen comes the Larder, Acatery, Poultery, Scalding-house, Pastry, Scullery, and Woodyard; then the Almoners, Gate Porters, Cartakers, Tailcartakers, Officers of the Hall, Marshals, Vergers, and Breadbearers, Wine Porters, Clerks and Purveyors, in all 174 in number, with salaries amounting altogether to £1300.

Now we come to the King's servants upstairs under my Lord Chamberlain, the most noble Charles, Duke of Bolton: he has a Vice Chamberlain, 45 Gentlemen of the Privy chamber, 4 Cup-bearers, 4 Sewers, 18 Gentlemen Ushers, 14 Grooms of the Chambers, 4 Pages of the Presence Chamber, 6 of the Bed Chambers and Back Stairs, 8 Servers, 28 Officers of the Wardrobe and Armoury, a Treasurer and Comptroller of the Chamber, a Master of the Ceremonies and Assistants, 10 Serjeants-at-Arms, a Groom Porter, a Master of the Revels, a Knight Harbinger and a Secretary to the Lord Chamberlain, 44 Messengers and 2 Clerks of the Cheque, 30 Musicians, a Physician-in-Ordinary, 3 Apothecaries, 2 Surgeons, 30 Housekeepers, Warders, Surveyors, Rangers, Woodwards, 13 Trumpeters, 4 Kettle Drums and a Drum-major, a Repairer of Bridges, a Master of the Tennis Court, a Master of the Barges, and 48 Watermen.

The Court.—Our first Georges' Court was rather a dull one. "Their Majesties don't seem to be fond of noisy pleasures," says Mr. Pöllnitz, a peripatetic fortune-hunter and ambulatory court-newsman of the last century, whose works were very eagerly read by our great-great-grandfathers.

Any gentleman who wished to go to Court had but to send his name to the King's Lord Chamberlain, or Queen Caroline's Master of the Horse, and the interview was granted. The Queen's Drawing-room was held at 10 o'clock at night in those days, and thrice in a week; this reception took place in three great saloons of St. James's, made by the direction of Queen Anne the only tolerable rooms in the palace. The King came attended by the Queen, who was led by the Prince of Wales when he was not in disgrace, and accompanied by her royal daughters. Their Majesties conversed for a few moments with such persons as they were pleased to distinguish, after which the Queen made a profound curtsey to the King, and went to cards for about an hour, retiring at midnight. On other days their Majesties partook of the delights of the opera or the play-house. The former was a very splendid and costly aristocratic resort. A seat in the gallery cost five shillings, and the boxes a guinea. The theatre was illuminated with a multiplicity of expensive wax candles; and as for the singers, some of those warbling sopranos from the Pope's chapel were paid no less a sum than £1500 a year.

"You will observe, amongst the livery-servants of the King and their Royal Highnesses, a most remarkable circumstance which you will not encounter in your visits in any other court of Europe, viz.: that the footmen when they are in waiting wear, instead of a hat, plain caps of black velvet, made like the caps of running footmen. His Majesty preferred a chair, slow as that conveyance was—doubtless because the city of London was one of the worst paved in Europe." That queer traveller, Pöllnitz, from whom I have extracted the invaluable informa-tion just given regarding the habits of the European courts and footmen, deplores pathetically the state of his bones after a ride in a London hackney-coach of the year 1725. The horses galloped, it appears, over those abominable roads, but the wretched coaches had no springs, and the story goes that the French king offered to make a bargain with the English king some years previous, and to provide London with paving stones, if his Britannic Majesty would lay down Versailles with gravel.

The Town.—My friend Peter Cunningham has a print of Piccadilly planted with trees and thick heavy railings before them, about the time of King William III.; a few boys, beggars, and dogs sauntering about the countrified place, and my Lord Duke of Albemarle bolt upright in jack-boots, a mounted servant with saddle-bags following him, riding forth from his great gate at Clarendon House, which the porter and other servants are closing behind his Grace. The porter is in a long tasseled gown, with a mace in his hand. Such figures you still see amongst Roman and Prussian noblemen.

All beyond Pall Mall is country. Chesterfield House was

not built until sixty years afterwards, nor the great Mayfair district northward, where London has now dwelt for some six score years.

The grand house-warming of Chesterfield House took place in 1751. The lovely Gunnings—those stars of beauty—were present, and it was there that Duke Hamilton fell so rapturously in love with the younger sister, that he called for a parson and married her with a curtain-ring at midnight on the night after.

At Oxford and Tyburn Road began country again. There were fields then all the way to Hampstead—fields profusely ornamented by cut-throats and footpads. Fields stretched all the way eastward to Montague House and Bedford House; the Foundling Hospital lay pleasantly in the country; it has taken about a century to build the most genteel district of spacious squares and broad streets which run northwards to the foot of Hampstead Hill and westward across hundreds of once pleasant acres to Bayswater. I can myself remember the sublime Belgravia a marshy flat; snipes have been shot in it quite within the memory of man; and amiable footpads sprang out of the hedges, as gentlefolk knew to their cost in their journeys from Chelsea to town.

The *Spectator* and *Tatler* are full of delightful glimpses of the town-life of those days. . . . Under the arm of that charming guide one can go to the opera, the puppet-show, or the cock-pit. We can see Broughton and Figg set to, we can listen to Robinson and Senesino, we can appraise the different merits of Pinkerman and Bullock. " Mr. William Bullock and Mr. William Pinkerman are of the same age, profession, and sex. They both distinguished themselves in a very particular manner under the discipline at Crabtree's, with this only difference, that Mr. Bullock has the most agreeable squall and Mr. Pinkerman the most graceful shrug. Pinkerman devours a cold chick with great applause; Bullock's talent lies chiefly in asparagus. Pinkerman is very dextrous at conveying himself under a table, Bullock is no less active in leaping over a stick; and Pinkerman has a great deal of money, but Mr. Bullock is the taller man." Delightful kindly humour, how it lives and smiles yet, after a hundred and fifty years—with gentle sympathy, with true loving-kindness, with generous laughter.

Shall we take a boat and go in company with two of the finest gentlemen in the world, Sir Roger de Coverley and Mr.

Spectator, to Spring Garden? There is another Spring Garden
in the town, near to where Mrs. Centlivre lives, the jolly widow
of Queen Anne's Jolly Yeoman of the Month, where Colley Cibber has a house near to the Bull Head Tavern; come, let us go
take water with Sir Roger and take a turn in this delightful
place. We can have other amusements if we like, and my be-
fore-quoted friend, Baron de Pöllnitz, will conduct us to those.
I warrant me that old rogue knew every haunt of pleasure in
every city in the world, and that he would not have been shocked by some of the company from whom Sir Roger's noble eyes
turned away with such a sweet, simple rebuke.

From Pöllnitz.—" At the chocolate house, where I go every
morning, there are dukes and other peers mixed with gentlemen;
to be admitted there needs nothing more than to dress like a
gentleman. At one o'clock they go to Court to the King's levee,
and from thence to the Queen's apartments, where is commonly
a great number of ladies very well dressed. At three o'clock
they all retire to their several apartments. Dinners here are
very expensive, and parties at taverns very much in fashion.

" When the company breaks up from table, if it be fine weather they go out again for the air, either in a coach to Hyde Park,
where the ring is, or else on foot to St. James's Park. In the
winter they make visits till the plays begin. After the opera or
plays the company goes to the assemblies, or else they repair to
the drawing-room. At midnight they go to supper; the companies formed at the taverns are the merriest, and at daylight
the jolly carouser returns home. Judge now, after what I have
said, whether a young gentleman has not enough to amuse himself at London, as at Paris or Rome. Believe me, that they who
say this city is too melancholy for them only say so to give themselves an air."

Queen Caroline.—There are some curious specimens of Queen
Caroline's spelling. She wrote to Leibnitz: " Nous panson à
faire tradevuire votre Déodisé "; and to a contemporary monarch, " Le ciel, chalou de notre bonheur, nous vien d'enlever notre
adorable reine; le coup fadalle m'a plougée dans une affliction
mordelle, et il y a rien qui ne puise consoller. Je vous plaint de
tout mon cœur Monsieur et suis avec un parfait adachement.—
Votre servant,   CAROLINE."

The King was always talking of her when she was gone, and judging what *she* would have thought had she been alive regarding events of the day. He ordered payment to be continued to all her officers and servants, and of all her contributions to benevolent societies, in order that nobody should suffer by her death but himself. Baron Bourkman had a portrait of his wife, which the King asked to see, and bade the Baron leave it with him till he rang. At the end of two hours the Baron was called, and found the King in tears, who said, " Take it away—take it away."

Prince Frederick of Wales.—Without being such a wretch as his fond papa and mamma held him to be, the Prince Frederick of Wales was not, it must be confessed, a very virtuous character, quarrelled with papa, made debts, sowed wild oats as Princes of Wales will do, and died but little lamented except by his Princess, who was balked of her natural wish to be Queen of England. They say she was in an awful state for some days after that tragic disappointment. Let us throw a respectful curtain over that royal anguish.

Mackay, Bute's Secretary.—The peace of 1763 was made with money : there was no other way of conquering the opposition. The money went through my hands : £80,000 was the sum employed. Forty M.P.'s had lost £1000 apiece, eighty others £500. A regular counting-house was opened in the Treasury, where members came and received the price of their treason in bank-notes.

When the peace of '63 was made, the Princess of Wales cried : " Now my son is King of England."

Murphy dedicated a play to Lord Bute, and narrating the circumstance at Holland House, Lord Hillsborough asked Murphy whether his lordship had invited him to sit down. " No," said Murphy, " he walked me up and down a long gallery during the whole time." " I thought so," said Lord Hillsborough.

From the Correspondence between Lady Hertford and Lady Pomfret.—"Mrs. Purcell sent to me yesterday to ask if I would see the Princess Mary's clothes and laces. They were all laid in order on the two tables, which are the whole length of the poor Queen's state bedchamber, from whence the bed is removed. There are four nightgowns, three trimmed, and one blue tabby embroidered with silver. Four sacks or robes, all trimmed—

that for the wedding night in silver tissue, faced and doubled
to the bottom with pink coloured satin, and trimmed with a
silver point-d'Espagne.   The stiff-bodiced gown she is to be
married in is very nearly the same as the Princess Royal's was.
There is an embroidery upon white, with gold and colours very
rich, and a stuff on a gold ground, prodigiously fine, with
flowers shaded up the middle of the breadths like painting, and
a kind of embossed work of blue and silver towards the edges.
Mrs. Purcell assured me that she bought the gold by itself before the stuff was woven, and that there was in it no less than
eighteen pounds weight."

Atterbury.—Macaulay in the *Encyclopædia* has hit some
awfully damaging blows at the reputation of Pope's friend Atterbury, at the scantiness of his scholarship, the blunders of his
Greek, the duplicity of his life as a priest and politician.   Was
selfishness more undisguised, were principles looser, were temptations greater for public men in those days than ours ?   They
certainly lied more broadly and boldly than nowadays, and their
friends were not so much shocked at discovered treason.   Atterbury went off to exile, putting a Bible into Pope's hand,
giving him a parting blessing, and telling him a parting fib.
The year 1721, in Atterbury's opinion, was the hour of darkness and the power thereof.

Here is a paragraph contrasting Lord Chesterfield's character
of George I. with Addison's.   " George I. was an honest, dull
German gentleman, as unfit as he was unwilling to act the part
of king, which is to shine and to oppress," says Lord Chesterfield.   " Lazy and inactive in his pleasures, which were therefore lowly sensual, he was coolly intrepid, and indolently benevolent.   He was diffident of his own parts, which made him speak
little in public, and prefer, in his social, which were his favourite, hours the company of wags and buffoons.   Even his
mistress, the Duchess of Kendal, with whom he passed most of
his time, was very little above an idiot."   Addison declares
him, on the contrary, " to be the most amiable monarch that
ever filled a throne."

From Reliquiæ Hearnianæ.—" George, Duke of Northumberland, Charles the Second's son, being at King George's court,
by chance touched the Prince of Wales, who turned round

fiercely and said, 'One can't move here for bastards!' 'Sir,' said Northumberland, 'my father was as great a king as yours, and as for our mothers, the less we say about them the better.'"

From the same source comes the following character of George II. :—

"George II. was very well-bred, but in a stiff and formal manner. He spoke French and Italian well, English very properly, but with something of a foreign accent. He had a contempt for the belles lettres, which he denominated trifling. He troubled himself little about religion, but jogged on in that which he had been bred, without scruples, doubts, zeal, or inquiry."

Chatham, writhing under the "malign influence" which had turned him out of George III.'s confidence, ruefully recalled the superior frankness of the King's grandfather. "Among his many royal virtues," says Chatham, "was eminently that of sincerity. He had something about him which made it possible to know whether he liked or disliked you."

George II. was prejudiced against his father's minister, but wisely kept him. George III., who would be a king, disliked Chatham, and dismissed him.

George III.—My father had an old kinswoman for whom he had a great regard. She was the widow of a well-known admiral, who presented Nelson at Court after the battle of the Nile. "Lady Rodd told me" (my father writes) "that all that George III. said to Nelson was, 'My lord, this is very rainy weather. I heard you were too ill to come out in rainy weather.'" Moore mentions a similar story of Nelson's mortification at the King's treatment of him.

The King asked the Duchess of Gordon how she liked London. "Not much, sir; it is knock, knock all day; and friz, friz all night."

A Scotch lady saw the King robing for Parliament. Two peers put his robes on, but he lifted his crown with his own hands; and, placing it on himself, he looked round to us all a perfect king, and *his tongue never lay.*

Boots.—Mr. Frost, of Hull, remembers going on the terrace at Windsor about 1803–4, and seeing the royal family walking there. He was obliged to take off his boots before going on the terrace, and people at the gate supplied shoes or slippers to strangers.

Lord North.—Having made up a quarrel between the King and the Prince, Lord North besought the latter to conduct himself differently in future. " Do so on all accounts," said Lord North ; " do so for your own sake—do so for your excellent father's sake—do so for the sake of that good-natured man Lord North, and don't oblige him again to tell the King, your good father, so many lies as he has been obliged to tell him this morning."

Drink.—The pulse of pleasure beat more strongly a hundred years since than it appears to do in our languid century. There was more amusement and more frolicking, more commerce among mankind, a very great deal more idleness, so much so indeed that one wonders how business was done. I knew a Scotch judge, a famous *bon-vivant*, who was forced to drink water for two months, and being asked what was the effect of the régime, owned that he saw the world really as it was for the first time for twenty years. For a quarter of a century he had never been quite sober. The fumes of the last night's three bottles and whisky-toddy inflamed all the day's thought and business. He transacted his business, got up his case, made his speech as an advocate, or delivered his charge as a judge with great volubility and power ; but his argument was muzzy with dreams ; he never saw the judge before him except through a film of whisky. I wonder how much claret went to inflame the judgment of the orator and the auditors of the House of Commons which debated the American War ? Men dined at three o'clock, and regaled themselves with beer, wine, and quantities of punch after. What business were they good for after such a diet ? The best thing they could do was to play at cards perhaps, and then about ten or eleven, you know, they would be hungry again and behold, broiled bones and Madeira and more punch—quantities more punch—and to bed after midnight, and plenty of rest required to sleep off all that feasting ; and compute the mere time for pleasure, and there remain really but three or four hours for work, with a headache. A lady of little more than my own age has told me that at her father's table—he was a peer of ancient name and large estates in the Midland counties—dinner was served at two or three, the old nobleman sitting with such company as the county afforded, and strong ale went on all dinner time, then port, then punch, then supper, and so forth. People in those days were continually carried away drunk and put to bed, and I suppose had no shame in meeting their families the next morning. No wonder the pulse of pleasure beat with all this liquor to inflame it!

Pather of Whitstable.—There was a parson who, if any of his congregation held up a lemon whilst he was preaching, could not resist, but finished his discourse and went to the public-house for punch.

1777. A rencontre at the Adelphi Tavern between the Rev. Mr. Bate of the *Morning Post* and Captain Andrew Robinson Stony, in consequence of a paragraph reflecting upon a lady; after firing a case of pistols without effect they fought with swords, and each received a wound; but they were interrupted, and the Captain on the following Sunday married the lady.

Cards.—The soldier pulled out of his pocket the pack of cards, which he spread before the Mayor. "When I see the ace," he said, "it puts me in mind that there is one God only; when I see the deuce, it puts me in mind of the F. and the S.; when I see the tray, it puts me in mind of F., S., and H. G.; when I see the four, it puts me in mind of the four Evangelists that penned the Gospel, viz., Matthew, Mark, Luke, and John; when I see the five, it puts me in mind of the five wise virgins who trimmed the lamps—there were ten, but five were shut out; when I see the six, it puts me in mind that in six days heaven and earth were made; when I see the seven, it puts me in mind of Sunday; when I see the eight, it puts me in mind of the eight righteous persons who were in the ark; when I see the nine, it puts me in mind of the nine lepers that were healed— there were ten, but nine never returned thanks; when I see the ten, it puts me in mind of the ten commandments; when I see the king and queen, I think of their Majesties, and long life to them; and when I see the knave, of the rogue who brought me before your worship.

"When I count how many spots there are in a pack of cards, I find 365; how many cards in a pack, 52; how many tricks in a pack, 13. Thus you see this pack of cards is Bible, almanac, Common Prayer-book, and pack of cards to me."

Then the Mayor called for a loaf of bread, a piece of good

cheese, and a pot of good beer, and giving the soldier a piece of money, bid him go about his business, saying he was the cleverest man he had ever seen.

In 1793, Dr. Rennell of the Temple wrote a sermon against card-playing, and put it under Fox's door in South Street.

A friend of mine, one of the few great whist-players still extant in London, told me that he knew a few years since at the Portland Club a very agreeable old Irish gentleman of the old school, who had come to London of late, had a good house, gave excellent dinners, and told a hundred pleasant anecdotes of the great world of fifty years ago. It came out after a while that the poor old gentleman had been of this great world himself, and had been detected hiding "nines" at the game of Macao with Charles Fox, and had been forced to retire. He returned, and was found out again after fifty years of exile. Poor old Punter! The second discovery killed him. He went home to Ireland and presently died.

There was a certain Jones said to have borrowed £10,000 in half-crowns; these little debts were not debts of honour, and not, therefore, necessarily to be repaid. It was different with debts of honour. This same Jones having lost £5 to the Colonel Dash at the Admiralty Coffee-house (fancy two gentlemen gambling in the forenoon at a coffee-house now!), and it being near dinner-time, the Colonel declined playing any longer. Mr. Jones whispered that he was a little out of cash, and hoped the Colonel would give him credit. "How is that, sir?" cries the Colonel; "when I saw you come out of Drummond's an hour ago?" "It was because I went to pay in all my money, and have not a shilling left," says Jones. "So much the better, give me your draft." "Sir, I have not a cheque about me." "Then, by Jove! you must go out of the window and get one." Half-crown Jones pleaded for being kicked out of doors and not thrown out of window — and kicked out he accordingly was.

Sir Fletcher Norton had the reputation of not adhering strictly to truth. It was imputed to him that he said, "My dear lady is the most unfortunate player of cards that ever was known. She has played at whist for twenty years, and never had a trump." "Nay," said somebody, "how can that be? She

must have had a trump when she dealt ?"   "Oh, as to that," said
he, "she lost every deal during the whole twenty years !"

Queen Charlotte.—At her marriage Queen Charlotte was
dressed in white and silver, an endless mantle of violet-coloured
velvet, lined with ermine, and attempted to be fastened on her
shoulder by a bunch of large pearls, dragged itself and the rest
of her clothes half down her waist.   On her head was a beautiful little tiara of diamonds ; she had a diamond necklace and a
stomacher worth £60,000, which she is to wear at her coronation.   Besides, she had hired diamonds for £9000.

The Queen said of the "Sorrows of Werther," "It is very
finely writ in German, and I can't bear it."

Nelson apud Collingwood.—"My friend Nelson, whose spirit
is equal to all undertakings, and whose resources are fitted to all
occasions, was sent with three sail of the line and some other
ships to Teneriffe to surprise and capture it.   After a series of
adventures, tragic and comic, that belong to romance, they were
obliged to abandon their enterprise.   Nelson was shot in the
right arm when landing, and was obliged to be carried on board.
He himself hailed the ship and desired the surgeon would get
his instruments ready to disarm him.   And in half-an-hour after
it was off he gave all the orders necessary for carrying on their
operations, as if nothing had happened to him."

Successors of Brummell. — Mr. Ball Hughes, called the
"Golden Ball," may be mentioned first for his taste in dress,
equipages, appointments.   The papers rang with his doings : he
was a man of exceedingly good taste, and in whatever he did he
never lost sight of the appearance and character of a gentleman.
Coaching was the rage of his day, and those who saw his well-
built, dark chocolate-coloured coach, with the four white horses
and two neat grooms in brown liveries behind, saw that it was
possible for a gentleman to drive four-in-hand without adopting the dress and manners of a stage-coachman.   Mr. Ball was
a beautiful dresser: his colours were quiet—chiefly black or
white—and he was the only man we ever saw who could carry off a
white waistcoat in a morning.   He was the introducer of the
large black-fronted cravats which helped to set off the otherwise difficult attire.   No man, it has been said, is a hero to his
valet-de-chambre, but the illustrious Ball was an exception to this

rule, for we heard his valet publicly declare at a *table d'hôte* in a continental town, that he was the handsomest man in the place, except his master.

Him Pea-Green Hayne followed, conspicuous for the colour of his coat and his dressing-case, which cost £1500. Lord Wellesley also must be mentioned as a dandy of eminence, and one of the first that turned back the wristbands of his shirts; and after him Mr. Bayley's name must be recorded. Mr. Bayley was a dandy of the butterfly order, a patron of bright colours, light-blue coats, coloured silk cravats, and fancy waistcoats. To have seen him cantering up Rotten Row of a summer's evening on his well-groomed hack, perfuming the air as he fanned the flies from his noble horse with his well-scented handkerchief, and to observe him in the crush-room of the opera with gauze silk stockings, thin pumps, and silver buckles, his hair hanging in ringlets over his ears, with a waistcoat of pink and blue satin embroidered with silver and gold—a stranger would have set him down as an effeminate puppy, and yet this languid dandy, one night single-handed, actually thrashed all the watchmen in Bond Street!

.It is sad to be obliged to own that all these heroes came to misfortune like Brummell. The paper from which I quote says "Ball has for some time resided in Paris; Hayne, we believe, lives at Brussels; Mr. Wellesley is also abroad; and the last time we saw Mr. Bailey he was vegetating on the beach at Ostend." (*Fraser*, 1837.)

The Prince drove a beautiful phaeton and six, the leaders guided by a diminutive postilion and the rest driven by himself, and is to be revered as one of the latest supporters of hair powder. The Princess, his consort, said that he looked like a great serjeant-major with his powdered ears; which speech, when it reached the powdered ears, offended their royal owner.

In 1794 the Stadtholder who had fled from Holland was the guest of the Prince of Wales, and amused his host and the public by his great alacrity in sleeping. The Princess commanded a play for him; he slept and snored in the box beside her, and was only awakened with difficulty. He was invited to a ball, fell asleep whilst eating his supper, and snored so loud as to vie with the music. Other celebrated sleepers were Lord North,

13   4

Selwyn, and the Duke of Norfolk, regarding whom Eldon is delighted to record the circumstance that the Duke was performing his usual music when a paper was read from the village of Great Snorham, in Norfolk.

"Jockey of Norfolk" had a clergyman who was a valuable friend to him. The Duke, when drunk, lost his voice, but retained the use of his limbs; his friend retained his power of speech, but could not stand. So the Duke who could not speak rang the bell, and the parson who could not move ordered more wine.

In 1798, at the Crown and Anchor, Norfolk drank "the people, the only scource of legitimate power," for which the King removed him from the Lieutenancy of the West Riding and the Colonelcy of the West York Militia. Fox repeated the toast at Brooks's, and the King struck his name off the list of Privy Councillors. You remember what uniform he wore, blue and buff, and who wore it on their side of the Atlantic?

George IV.—Mr. Milnes, who knew him well, says he never was in a house with twenty people but he fascinated them all. He (Mr. M.) gives a counter-story to Jesse's of Brummell, as told by Brummell himself, that on arrival at Calais the King sent Lord Blomfield to Mr. Brummell with his snuff-box, saying, "No one knew how to mix snuff so well in old times, would Brummell fill his box!" And at the same time the King told Blomfield to inquire what the poor dandy's circumstances were. Brummell may have told both stories, pro and con the King, his lies were constant, and at the end of his time he was utterly untrustworthy.

Lady Hertford said the reason George IV. broke from the Whigs was that, being on terms of "entire confidence" with a celebrated lady, he went one day to visit her, and found Lord Grey in possession already, from which time, Lady Hertford said, he never could bear the sight of a Whig.

"The Prince was a very plain dresser—nothing flaunting in his attire at all." How does this accord with the sale of his wondrous wardrobe at his death?

We read that three waggons were needed to bring the royal wardrobe from Windsor to London. It was displayed in two chambers in Mount Street at the King's cabinetmakers. In the former were the coronation robes, regimentals, British and foreign, covered with a profusion of lace, robes of the various orders of which the late King was a member, ermine and silken hose; the other room contained the habiliment of ordinary wear —coats, waistcoats, trousers, and especially boots, shoes, and hats enough to equip a regiment. One spectator purchased 150 hats, 200 whips, and a great portion of the contents of this room. Among the buyers we hear of Prince Esterhazy, Lord Londonderry a cane at the price of 30 guineas, and Lord Chesterfield purchased for 220 a cloak lined with sable, the original cost of which was 800. Hamlet, the jeweller, bought the whole of the gold-headed canes.

Gray's description of Southampton Row in 1759.—" I am now settled in my new territories commanding Bedford Gardens and all the fields as far as Highgate and Hampstead, with such a concourse of moving pictures as would astonish you—so *rus in urbe*-ish that I believe I shall stay here, except little excursions and vagaries, for a year to come. What though I am separated from the fashionable world by the broad St. Giles's and many a dirty court and alley, yet here is quiet and air and sunshine. However, to comfort you, I shall confess that I am basking with heat all the summer, and, I suppose, shall be blown down all the winter, besides being robbed every night. I trust, how- ever, that the Museum, with all its manuscripts and rarities by the cartload, will make amends for the aforesaid inconveniences. I this day passed through the jaws of the great leviathan super- intendent of the Reading-room."

Johnsoniana.—Besides his household, Johnson had a score of outdoor dependants on his bounty, " People who didn't like to see him," he said, " unless he brought 'em money." He called upon his rich friends to help them, making it his duty to urge their charity upon them.

He excused himself for turning his back upon a lord because his lordship was ... his rank.

Rude...   rnard wrote:

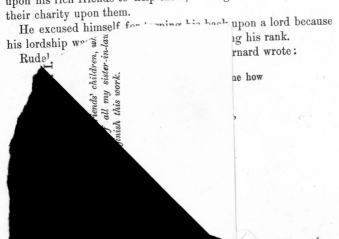

ends' children, ... all my sister-in-law ... finish this work.

he how

Johnson always praised Addison, though he did not seem really to like him.

He was greatly disgusted with the coarse language used on board a man-of-war. He asked an officer what was the name of some part of the ship, and was answered it was the place where the loblolly man kept his loblolly. The reply he considered as "disrespectful, gross, and ignorant." I should like to have seen his face when the officer spoke.

He said of a pious man, "I should as soon have thought of contradicting a Bishop."

He once saw Chesterfield's son in Dodsley's shop, and was so much struck by his awkward manner and appearance, he could not help asking who the gentleman was.

Johnson's Funeral.—His body was brought out of Bolt Court preceded by two clergymen, to a hearse and six in Fleet Street. This was followed by the executors, Reynolds, Sir W. Scott, &c., in a coach and four; by the Literary Club in eight coaches and four; by two coaches and four containing the pall-bearers, Burke, Windham, Bunbury, &c. After these followed two other mourning-coaches and four, and thirteen gentlemen's carriages closed the procession. He was deposited in the Abbey by the side of Mr. Garrick, with the feet opposite Shakespeare's monument.

Not far from Johnson's grave, by the monument to Addison, stands the bust which was put up by some of my father's friends to his memory. It is not in marble that he is best portrayed, but in the constant impressions of his life and words and ways, and in these collected fragments enough has been given to show what he was in himself, something more than a writer and master of his art.

13th February 1899.

A. R.

I have to thank those old and new friends, and old f[...] *have assisted me to put these notes together; most o[...]* *Emily Ritchie, whose help has alone enabled me to [...]*

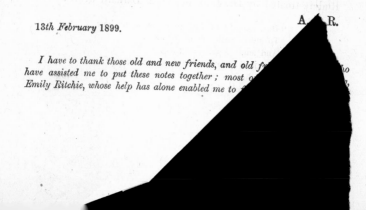

BALLADS

BALLADS

SONG OF THE VIOLET

A HUMBLE flower long time I pined
    Upon the solitary plain,
    And trembled at the angry wind,
And shrank before the bitter rain.
And oh! 'twas in a blessed hour
    A passing wanderer chanced to see,
And, pitying the lonely flower,
    To stoop and gather me.

I fear no more the tempest rude,
    On dreary heath no more I pine,
But left my cheerless solitude,
    To deck the breast of Caroline.
Alas! our days are brief at best,
    Nor long, I fear, will mine endure,
Though sheltered here upon a breast
    So gentle and so pure.

It draws the fragrance from my leaves,
    It robs me of my sweetest breath,
And every time it falls and heaves,
    It warns me of my coming death.
But one I know would glad forego
    All joys of life to be as I;
An hour to rest on that sweet breast,
    And then, contented, die.

THE CHRONICLE OF THE DRUM

Part I.

AT Paris, hard by the Maine barriers,
 Whoever will choose to repair,
 Midst a dozen of wooden-legged warriors
May haply fall in with old Pierre.
On the sunshiny bench of a tavern
 He sits and he prates of old wars,
And moistens his pipe of tobacco
 With a drink that is named after Mars.

The beer makes his tongue run the quicker,
 And as long as his tap never fails,
Thus over his favourite liquor
 Old Peter will tell his old tales.
Says he, "In my life's ninety summers
 Strange changes and chances I've seen,—
So here's to all gentlemen drummers
 That ever have thumped on a skin.

"Brought up in the art military
 For four generations we are;
My ancestors drumm'd for King Harry,
 The Huguenot lad of Navarre.
And as each man in life has his station
 According as Fortune may fix,
While Condé was waving the bâton,
 My grandsire was trolling the sticks.

"Ah! those were the days for commanders!
 What glories my grandfather won,
Ere bigots, and lacqueys, and panders
 The fortunes of France had undone!

In Germany, Flanders, and Holland,—
    What foeman resisted us then?
No; my grandsire was ever victorious,
    My grandsire and Monsieur Turenne.

" He died: and our noble battalions
    The jade fickle Fortune forsook;
And at Blenheim, in spite of our valiance,
    The victory lay with Malbrook.
The news it was brought to King Louis;
    Corbleu! how His Majesty swore
When he heard they had taken my grandsire:
    And twelve thousand gentlemen more.

" At Namur, Ramillies, and Malplaquet
    Were we posted, on plain or in trench:
Malbrook only need to attack it,
    And away from him scamper'd we French.
Cheer up! 'tis no use to be glum, boys,—
    'Tis written, since fighting begun,
That sometimes we fight and we conquer,
    And sometimes we fight and we run.

To fight and to run was our fate:
    Our fortune and fame had departed.
And so perish'd Louis the Great,—
    Old, lonely, and half broken-hearted.
His coffin they pelted with mud,
    His body they tried to lay hands on;
And so having buried King Louis,
    They loyally served his great grandson.

" God save the beloved King Louis!
    (For so he was nicknamed by some),
And now came my father to do his
    King's orders and beat on the drum.
My grandsire was dead, but his bones
    Must have shaken, I'm certain, for joy,
To hear daddy drumming the English
    From the meadows of famed Fontenoy.

" So well did he drum in that battle
    That the enemy showed us their backs;
Corbleu! it was pleasant to rattle
    The sticks and to follow old Saxe!

We next had Soubise as a leader,
   And as luck hath its changes and fits,
At Rossbach, in spite of dad's drumming
   'Tis said we were beaten by Fritz.

" And now daddy cross'd the Atlantic,
   To drum for Montcalm and his men ;
Morbleu ! but it makes a man frantic
   To think we were beaten again !
My daddy he cross'd the wide ocean,
   My mother brought me on her neck,
And we came in the year fifty-seven
   To guard the good town of Quebec.

" In the year fifty-nine came the Britons,—
   Full well I remember the day,—
They knocked at our gates for admittance,
   Their vessels were moor'd in our bay.
Says our general, ' Drive me yon red coats
   Away to the sea whence they come !'
So we march'd against Wolfe and his bull-dogs,
   We marched at the sound of the drum.

" I think I can see my poor mammy
   With me in her hand as she waits,
And our regiment, slowly retreating,
   Pours back through the citadel gates.
Dear mammy she looks in their faces,
   And asks if her husband has come ?—
He is lying all cold on the glacis,
   And will never more beat on the drum.

" Come, drink, 'tis no use to be glum, boys !
   He died like a soldier in glory ;
Here's a glass to the health of all drum-boys,
   And now I'll commence my own story.
Once more did we cross the salt ocean,
   We came in the year eighty-one ;
And the wrongs of my father the drummer
   Were avenged by the drummer his son.

" In Chesapeak Bay we were landed.
   In vain strove the British to pass :
Rochambeau our armies commanded,
   Our ships they were led by De Grasse

Morbleu ! how, I rattled the drumsticks
 The day we march'd into Yorktown ;
Ten thousand of beef-eating British
 Their weapons we caused to lay down.

" Then homewards returning victorious,
 In peace to our country we came,
And were thanked for our glorious actions
 By Louis, Sixteenth of the name.
What drummer on earth could be prouder
 Than I, while I drumm'd at Versailles
To the lovely Court ladies in powder,
 And lappets, and long satin-tails ?

" The princes that day pass'd before us,
 Our countrymen's glory and hope ;
Monsieur, who was learned in Horace,
 D'Artois, who could dance the tight-rope
One night we kept guard for the Queen
 At Her Majesty's opera box,
While the King, that majestical monarch,
 Sat filing at home at his locks.

" Yes, I drumm'd for the fair Antoinette,
 And so smiling she look'd and so tender,
That our officers, privates, and drummers,
 All vow'd they would die to defend her.
But she cared not for us honest fellows,
 Who fought and who bled in her wars,
She sneer'd at our gallant Rochambeau,
 And turned Lafayette out of doors.

" Ventrebleu ! then I swore a great oath,
 No more to such tyrants to kneel ;
And so, just to keep up my drumming,
 One day I drumm'd down the Bastille.
Ho, landlord ! a stoup of fresh wine.
 Come, comrades, a bumper we'll try,
And drink to the year eighty-nine
 And the glorious fourth of July !

" Then bravely our cannon it thunder'd
 As onwards our patriots bore.
Our enemies were but a hundred,
 And we twenty thousand or more.

They carried the news to King Louis.
　　He heard it as calm as you please,
And, like a majestical monarch,
　　Kept filing his locks and his keys.

"We show'd our Republican courage,
　　We storm'd and we broke the great gate in,
And we murder'd the insolent governor
　　For daring to keep us a-waiting.
Lambesc and his squadrons stood by :
　　They never stirr'd finger or thumb.
The saucy aristocrats trembled
　　As they heard the republican drum.

"Hurrah ! what a storm was a-brewing !
　　The day of our vengeance was come !
Through scenes of what carnage and ruin
　　Did I beat on the patriot drum !
Let's drink to the famed tenth of August :
　　At midnight I beat the tattoo,
And woke up the pikemen of Paris
　　To follow the bold Barbaroux.

"With pikes, and with shouts, and with torches
　　March'd onwards our dusty battalions,
And we girt the tall castle of Louis,
　　A million of tatterdemalions !
We storm'd the fair gardens where tower'd
　　The walls of his heritage splendid.
Ah, shame on him, craven and coward,
　　That had not the heart to defend it !

"With the crown of his sires on his head,
　　His nobles and knights by his side,
At the foot of his ancestors' palace
　　'Twere easy, methinks, to have died.
But no : when we burst through his barriers,
　　Mid heaps of the dying and dead,
In vain through the chambers we sought him—
　　He had turn'd like a craven and fled.

　　　　·　　　　·　　　　·　　　　·

"You all know the Place de la Concorde ?
　　'Tis hard by the Tuileries wall.
Mid terraces, fountains, and statues,
　　There rises an obelisk tall.

There rises an obelisk tall,
   All garnish'd and gilded the base is :
'Tis surely the gayest of all
   Our beautiful city's gay places.

" Around it are gardens and flowers,
   And the Cities of France on their thrones
Each crown'd with his circlet of flowers,
   Sits watching this biggest of stones !
I love to go sit in the sun there,
   The flowers and fountains to see,
And to think of the deeds that were done **there**
   In the glorious year ninety-three.

" 'Twas here stood the Altar of Freedom ;
   And though neither marble nor gilding
Was used in those days to adorn
   Our simple republican building,
Corbleu ! but the MÈRE GUILLOTINE
   Cared little for splendour or show,
So you gave her an axe and a beam,
   And a plank and a basket or so.

" Awful, and proud, and erect,
   Here sat our republican goddess.
Each morning her table we deck'd
   With dainty aristocrats' bodies.
The people each day flocked around
   As she sat at her meat and her wine :
'Twas always the use of our nation
   To witness the sovereign dine.

" Young virgins with fair golden tresses,
   Old silver-hair'd prelates and priests,
Dukes, marquises, barons, princesses,
   Were splendidly served at her feasts.
Ventrebleu ! but we pampered our ogress
   With the best that our nation could bring,
And dainty she grew in her progress,
   And called for the head of a King !

" She called for the blood of our King,
   And straight from his prison we drew him ;
And to her with shouting we led him,
   And took him, and bound him, and slew him

'The monarchs of Europe against me
    Have plotted a godless alliance:
I'll fling them the head of King Louis,'
    She said, 'as my gage of defiance.'

"I see him as now, for a moment,
    Away from his gaolers he broke;
And stood at the foot of the scaffold,
    And linger'd, and fain would have spoke.
'Ho, drummer! quick, silence yon Capet,'
    Says Santerre, 'with a beat of your drum.
Lustily then did I tap it,
    And the son of Saint Louis was dumb."

· · · · ·

Part II.

"The glorious days of September
    Saw many aristocrats fall;
'Twas then that our pikes drank the blood
    In the beautiful breast of Lamballe.
Pardi, 'twas a beautiful lady!
    I seldom have look'd on her like;
And I drumm'd for a gallant procession,
    That marched with her head on a pike.

"Let's show the pale head to the Queen,
    We said—she'll remember it well.
She looked from the bars of her prison,
    And shriek'd as she saw it, and fell.
We set up a shout at her screaming,
    We laugh'd at the fright she had shown
At the sight of the head of her minion—
    How she'd tremble to part with her own!

"We had taken the head of King Capet,
    We called for the blood of his wife;
Undaunted she came to the scaffold,
    And bared her fair neck to the knife.
As she felt the foul fingers that touch'd her,
    She shrank, but she deigned not to speak:
She look'd with a royal disdain,
    And died with a blush on her cheek!

" 'Twas thus that our country was saved ;
    So told us the safety committee !
But psha ! I've the heart of a soldier,
    All gentleness, mercy, and pity.
I loathed to assist at such deeds,
    And my drum beat its loudest of tunes
As we offered to justice offended
    The blood of the bloody tribunes.

" Away with such foul recollections !
    No more of the axe and the block ;
I saw the last fight of the sections,
    As they fell 'neath our guns at Saint Roch.
Young BONAPARTE led us that day ;
    When he sought the Italian frontier,
I follow'd my gallant young captain,
    I follow'd him many a long year.

" We came to an army in rags,
    Our general was but a boy
When we first saw the Austrian flags
    Flaunt proud in the fields of Savoy.
In the glorious year ninety-six,
    We march'd to the banks of the Po ;
I carried my drum and my sticks,
    And we laid the proud Austrian low.

" In triumph we enter'd Milan,
    We seized on the Mantuan keys ;
The troops of the Emperor ran,
    And the Pope he fell down on his knees."—
Pierre's comrades here call'd a fresh bottle,
    And clubbing together their wealth,
They drank to the Army of Italy,
    And General Bonaparte's health.

The drummer now bared his old breast,
    And show'd us a plenty of scars,
Rude presents that Fortune had made him
    In fifty victorious wars.
" This came when I follow'd bold Kleber—
    'Twas shot by a Mameluke gun ;
And this from an Austrian sabre,
    When the field of Marengo was won.

" My forehead has many deep furrows,
    But this is the deepest of all :
A Brunswicker made it at Jena,
    Beside the fair river of Saal.
This cross, 'twas the Emperor gave it ;
    (God bless him !) it covers a blow ;
I had it at Austerlitz fight,
    As I beat on my drum in the snow.

" 'Twas thus that we conquer'd and fought ;
    But wherefore continue the story ?
There's never a baby in France
    But has heard of our chief and our glory,—
But has heard of our chief and our fame,
    His sorrows and triumphs can tell,
How bravely Napoleon conquer'd,
    How bravely and sadly he fell.

" It makes my old heart to beat higher,
    To think of the deeds that I saw ;
I follow'd bold Ney through the fire,
    And charged at the side of Murat."
And so did old Peter continue
    His story of twenty brave years ;
His audience follow'd with comments—
    Rude comments of curses and tears.

He told how the Prussians in vain
    Had died in defence of their land ;
His audience laugh'd at the story,
    And vow'd that their captain was grand !
He had fought the red English, he said,
    In many a battle of Spain ;
They cursed the red English, and prayed
    To meet them and fight them again.

He told them how Russia was lost,
    Had winter not driven them back ;
And his company cursed the quick frost,
    And doubly they cursed the Cossack.
He told how the stranger arrived ;
    They wept at the tale of disgrace ;
And they long'd but for one battle more,
    The stain of their shame to efface.

" Our country their hordes overrun,
    We fled to the fields of Champagne,
And fought them, though twenty to one,
    And beat them again and again !
Our warrior was conquer'd at last ;
    They bade him his crown to resign ;
To fate and his country he yielded
    The rights of himself and his line.

' He came, and among us he stood,
    Around him we press'd in a throng :
We could not regard him for weeping,
    Who had led us and loved us so long.
' I have led you for twenty long years,'
    Napoleon said ere he went ;
' Wherever was honour I found you,
    And with you, my sons, am content !

" ' Though Europe against me was arm'd,
    Your chiefs and my people are true ;
I still might have struggled with fortune,
    And baffled all Europe with you.

" ' But France would have suffer'd the while,
    'Tis best that I suffer alone ;
I go to my place of exile,
    To write of the deeds we have done.

" ' Be true to the king that they give you.
    We may not embrace ere we part ;
But, General, reach me your hand,
    And press me, I pray, to your heart.'

" He call'd for our battle standard ;
    One kiss to the eagle he gave.
' Dear eagle !' he said, ' may this kiss
    Long sound in the hearts of the brave !'
'Twas thus that Napoleon left us ;
    Our people were weeping and mute,
As he passed through the lines of his guard
    And our drums beat the notes of salute.

"I look'd when the drumming was o'er,
  I look'd, but our hero was gone;
We were destined to see him once more,
  When we fought on the Mount of St. John.
The Emperor rode through our files;
  'Twas June, and a fair Sunday morn.
The lines of our warriors for miles
  Stretch'd wide through the Waterloo corn.

"In thousands we stood on the plain,
  The red-coats were crowning the height;
'Go scatter yon English,' he said;
  'We'll sup, lads, at Brussels to-night.'
We answer'd his voice with a shout;
  Our eagles were bright in the sun;
Our drums and our cannon spoke out,
  And the thundering battle begun.

"One charge to another succeeds,
  Like waves that a hurricane bears;
All day do our galloping steeds
  Dash fierce on the enemy's squares.
At noon we began the fell onset:
  We charged up the Englishman's hill;
And madly we charged it at sunset—
  His banners were floating there still.

" —Go to! I will tell you no more;
  You know how the battle was lost.
Ho! fetch me a beaker of wine,
  And, comrades, I'll give you a toast,
I'll give you a curse on all traitors,
  Who plotted our Emperor's ruin;
And a curse on those red-coated English,
  Whose bayonets helped our undoing.

"A curse on those British assassins,
  Who order'd the slaughter of Ney;
A curse on Sir Hudson, who tortured
  The life of our hero away.
A curse on all Russians—I hate them—
  On all Prussian and Austrian fry;
And oh! but I pray we may meet them,
  And fight them again ere I die."

'Twas thus old Peter did conclude
   His chronicle with curses fit.
He spoke the tale in accents rude,
   In ruder verse I copied it.

Perhaps the tale a moral bears
   (All tales in time to this must come),
The story of two hundred years
   Writ on the parchment of a drum.

What Peter told with drum and stick,
   Is endless theme for poet's pen :
Is found in endless quartos thick,
   Enormous books by learned men.

And ever since historian writ,
   And ever since a bard could sing,
Doth each exalt with all his wit
   The noble art of murdering.

We love to read the glorious page,
   How bold Achilles kill'd his foe ;
And Turnus, fell'd by Trojans' rage,
   Went howling to the shades below.

How Godfrey led his red-cross knights,
   How mad Orlando slash'd and slew ;
There's not a single bard that writes
   But doth the glorious theme renew.

And while, in fashion picturesque,
   The poet rhymes of blood and blows,
The grave historian at his desk
   Describes the same in classic prose.

Go read the works of Reverend Coxe,
   You'll duly see recorded there
The history of the self-same knocks
   Here roughly sung by Drummer Pierre.

Of battles fierce and warriors big,
   He writes in phrases dull and slow,
And waves his cauliflower wig,
   And shouts " Saint George for Marlborow ! *

Take Doctor Southey from the shelf,
    An LL.D.,—a peaceful man ;
Good Lord, how doth he plume himself
    Because we beat the Corsican !

From first to last his page is filled
    With stirring tales how blows were struck.
He shows how we the Frenchmen kill'd,
    And praises God for our good luck.

Some hints, 'tis true, of politics
    The Doctor gives and statesman's art :
Pierre only bangs his drum and sticks,
    And understands the bloody part.

He cares not what the cause may be,
    He is not nice for wrong and right ;
But show him where's the enemy,
    He only asks to drum and fight.

They bid him fight,—perhaps he wins ;
    And when he tells the story o'er,
The honest savage brags and grins,
    And only longs to fight once more.

But luck may change, and valour fail,
    Our drummer, Peter, meet reverse,
And with a moral points his tale—
    The end of all such tales—a curse.

Last year, my love, it was my hap
    Behind a grenadier to be,
And, but he wore a hairy cap,
    No taller man, methinks, than me.

Prince Albert and the Queen, God wot
    (Be blessings on the glorious pair !),
Before us passed.   I saw them not—
    I only saw a cap of hair.

Your orthodox historian puts
    In foremost rank the soldier thus,
The red-coat bully in his boots,
    That hides the march of men from us.

He puts him there in foremost rank,
    You wonder at his cap of hair :
You hear his sabre's cursed clank,
    His spurs are jingling everywhere.

Go to ! I hate him and his trade :
    Who bade us so to cringe and bend,
And all God's peaceful people made
    To such as him subservient ?

Tell me what find we to admire
    In epaulets and scarlet coats—
In men, because they load and fire,
    And know the art of cutting throats ?

Ah, gentle, tender lady mine !
    The winter wind blows cold and shrill ;
Come, fill me one more glass of wine,
    And give the silly fools their will.

And what care we for war and wrack,
    How kings and heroes rise and fall ?
Look yonder,* in his coffin black
    There lies the greatest of them all !

To pluck him down, and keep him up,
    Died many million human souls.—
'Tis twelve o'clock and time to sup ;
    Bid Mary heap the fire with coals.

He captured many thousand guns ;
    He wrote " The Great " before his name ;
And dying, only left his sons
    The recollection of his shame.

* This ballad was written at Paris at the time of the Second Funeral of
Napoleon.

E

Though more than half the world was his,
    He died without a rood his own ;
And borrow'd from his enemies
    Six foot of ground to lie upon.

He fought a thousand glorious wars,
    And more than half the world was his ;
And somewhere now, in yonder stars,
    Can tell, mayhap, what greatness is.

1841.

THE KING OF BRENTFORD'S TESTAMENT

THE noble King of Brentford
   Was old and very sick,
   He summon'd his physicians
To wait upon him quick;
They stepp'd into their coaches
   And brought their best physick.

They cramm'd their gracious master
   With potion and with pill;
They drench'd him and they bled him:
   They could not cure his ill.
" Go fetch," says he, " my lawyer;
   I'd better make my will."

The monarch's royal mandate
   The lawyer did obey;
The thought of six-and-eightpence
   Did make his heart full gay.
" What is't," says he, " your Majesty
   Would wish of me to-day?"

" The doctors have belabour'd me
   With potion and with pill:
My hours of life are counted,
   O man of tape and quill!
Sit down and mend a pen or two;
   I want to make my will.

" O'er all the land of Brentford
   I'm lord, and eke of Kew:
I've three-per-cents and five-per-cents;
   My debts are but a few;
And to inherit after me
   I have but children two.

" Prince Thomas is my eldest son ;
 A sober prince is he,
And from the day we breech'd him
 Till now—he's twenty-three—
He never caused disquiet
 To his poor mamma or me.

" At school they never flogg'd him ;
 At college, though not fast,
Yet his little-go and great-go
 He creditably pass'd,
And made his year's allowance
 For eighteen months to last.

" He never owed a shilling,
 Went never drunk to bed,
He has not two ideas
 Within his honest head—
In all respects he differs
 From my second son, Prince Ned.

" When Tom has half his income
 Laid by at the year's end,
Poor Ned has ne'er a stiver
 That rightly he may spend,
But sponges on a tradesman,
 Or borrows from a friend.

" While Tom his legal studies
 Most soberly pursues,
Poor Ned must pass his mornings
 A-dawdling with the Muse :
While Tom frequents his banker,
 Young Ned frequents the Jews.

" Ned drives about in buggies,
 Tom sometimes takes a 'bus ;
Ah, cruel fate, why made you
 My children differ thus ?
Why make of Tom a *dullard*,
 And Ned a *genius ?* "

" You'll cut him with a shilling,"
    Exclaimed the man of wits :
" I'll leave my wealth," said Brentford,
    " Sir Lawyer, as befits,
And portion both their fortunes
    Unto their several wits."

" Your Grace knows best," the lawyer said ;
    " On your commands I wait."
" Be silent, sir," says Brentford,
    " A plague upon your prate !
Come take your pen and paper,
    And write as I dictate."

The will as Brentford spoke it
    Was writ and signed and closed ;
He bade the lawyer leave him,
    And turn'd him round and dozed ;
And next week in the churchyard
    The good old King reposed.

Tom, dressed in crape and hatband,
    Of mourners was the chief ;
In bitter self-upbraidings
    Poor Edward showed his grief :
Tom hid his fat white countenance
    In his pocket-handkerchief.

Ned's eyes were full of weeping,
    He falter'd in his walk ;
Tom never shed a tear,
    But onwards he did stalk,
As pompous, black, and solemn
    As any catafalque.

And when the bones of Brentford—
    That gentle King and just—
With bell and book and candle
    Were duly laid in dust,
" Now, gentlemen," says Thomas,
    " Let business be discussed.

" When late our sire beloved
    Was taken deadly ill,
Sir Lawyer, you attended him
    (I mean to tax your bill) ;
And, as you signed and wrote it,
    I prithee read the will."

The lawyer wiped his spectacles,
    And drew the parchment out ;
And all the Brentford family
    Sat eager round about :
Poor Ned was somewhat anxious,
    But Tom had ne'er a doubt.

" My son, as I make ready
    To seek my last long home,
Some cares I had for Neddy,
    But none for thee, my Tom :
Sobriety and order
    You ne'er departed from.

" Ned hath a brilliant genius,
    And thou a plodding brain ;
On thee I think with pleasure,
    On him with doubt and pain."
(" You see, good Ned," says Thomas,
    " What he thought about us twain.")

" Though small was your allowance,
    You saved a little store ;
And those who save a little
    Shall get a plenty more."
As the lawyer read this compliment,
    Tom's eyes were running o'er.

" The tortoise and the hare, Tom,
    Set out at each his pace ;
The hare it was the fleeter,
    The tortoise won the race ;
And since the world's beginning
    This ever was the case.

" Ned's genius, blithe and singing,
    Steps gaily o'er the ground ;
As steadily you trudge it,
    He clears it with a bound ;
But dulness has stout legs, Tom,
    And wind that's wondrous sound

" O'er fruits and flowers alike, Tom,
    You pass with plodding feet ;
You heed not one nor t'other,
    But onwards go your beat ;
While genius stops to loiter
    With all that he may meet ;

" And ever as he wanders,
    Will have a pretext fine
For sleeping in the morning,
    Or loitering to dine,
Or dozing in the shade,
    Or basking in the shine.

" Your little steady eyes, Tom,
    Though not so bright as those
That restless round about him
    His flashing genius throws,
Are excellently suited
    To look before your nose.

" Thank Heaven, then, for the blinkers
    It placed before your eyes ;
The stupidest are strongest,
    The witty are not wise ;
Oh, bless your good stupidity !
    It is your dearest prize.

" And though my lands are wide,
    And plenty is my gold,
Still better gifts from Nature,
    My Thomas, do you hold—
A brain that's thick and heavy,
    A heart that's dull and cold.

" Too dull to feel depression,
    Too hard to heed distress,
Too cold to yield to passion
    Or silly tenderness.
March on—your road is open
    To wealth, Tom, and success.

" Ned sinneth in extravagance,
    And you in greedy lust."
(" I' faith," says Ned, " our father
    Is less polite than just.")
" In you, son Tom, I've confidence,
    But Ned I cannot trust.

" Wherefore my lease and copyholds,
    My lands and tenements,
My parks, my farms, and orchards,
    My houses and my rents,
My Dutch stock and my Spanish stock,
    My five and three per cents,

" I leave to you, my Thomas "
    (" What, all ? " poor Edward said.
" Well, well, I should have spent them,
    And Tom's a prudent head ")—
" I leave to you, my Thomas,—
    To you IN TRUST for Ned."

The wrath and consternation
    What poet e'er could trace
That at this fatal passage
    Came o'er Prince Tom his face ;
The wonder of the company,
    And honest Ned's amaze ?

" 'Tis surely some mistake,"
    Good-naturedly cries Ned ;
The lawyer answered gravely,
    " 'Tis even as I said ;
'Twas thus his gracious Majesty
    Ordain'd on his death-bed.

" See, here the will is witness'd.
    And here's his autograph."
" In truth, our father's writing,"
    Says Edward, with a laugh ;
" But thou shalt not be a loser, Tom ;
    We'll share it half and half."

" Alas ! my kind young gentleman,
    This sharing cannot be ;
'Tis written in the testament
    That Brentford spoke to me,
' I do forbid Prince Ned to give
    Prince Tom a halfpenny.

' He hath a store of money,
    But ne'er was known to lend it ;
He never helped his brother ;
    The poor he ne'er befriended ;
He hath no need of property
    Who knows not how to spend it.

" ' Poor Edward knows but how to spend,
    And thrifty Tom to hoard ;
Let Thomas be the steward then,
    And Edward be the lord ;
And as the honest labourer
    Is worthy his reward,

" ' I pray Prince Ned, my second son,
    And my successor dear,
To pay to his intendant
    Five hundred pounds a year ;
And to think of his old father,
    And live and make good cheer.' "

Such was old Brentford's honest testament,
    He did devise his moneys for the best,
    And lies in Brentford church in peaceful rest.
Prince Edward lived, and money made and spent ;
    But his good sire was wrong, it is confess'd,
To say his son, young Thomas, never lent.
    He did.   Young Thomas lent at interest,
And nobly took his twenty-five per cent.

Long time the famous reign of Ned endured
  O'er Chiswick, Fulham, Brentford, Putney, Kew,
But of extravagance he ne'er was cured.
  And when both died, as mortal men will do,
'Twas commonly reported that the steward
  Was very much the richer of the two.

FAIRY DAYS

B ESIDE the old hall-fire—upon my nurse's knee,
    Of happy fairy days—what tales were told to me !
    I thought the world was once—all peopled with princesses,
And my heart would beat to hear—their loves and their distresses ;
And many a quiet night,—in slumber sweet and deep,
The pretty fairy people—would visit me in sleep.

I saw them in my dreams—come flying east and west,
With wondrous fairy gifts—the new-born babe they bless'd ;
One has brought a jewel—and one a crown of gold,
And one has brought a curse—but she is wrinkled and old.
The gentle Queen turns pale—to hear those words of sin,
But the King he only laughs—and bids the dance begin.

The babe has grown to be—the fairest of the land,
And rides the forest green—a hawk upon her hand,
An ambling palfrey white—a golden robe and crown :
I've seen her in my dreams—riding up and down :
And heard the ogre laugh—as she fell into his snare,
At the little tender creature—who wept and tore her hair !

But ever when it seemed—her need was at the sorest,
A prince in shining mail—comes prancing through the forest,
A waving ostrich-plume—a buckler burnished bright ;
I've seen him in my dreams—good sooth ! a gallant knight.
His lips are coral red—beneath a dark moustache ;
See how he waves his hand—and how his blue eyes flash !

" Come forth, thou Paynim knight ! "—he shouts in accents clear.
The giant and the maid—both tremble his voice to hear.
Saint Mary guard him well !—he draws his falchion keen,
The giant and the knight—are fighting on the green.
I see them in my dreams—his blade gives stroke on stroke,
The giant pants and reels—and tumbles like an oak !

With what a blushing grace—he falls upon his knee
And takes the lady's hand—and whispers, "You are free!"
Ah! happy childish tales—of knight and faërie!
I waken from my dreams—but there's ne'er a knight for me!
I waken from my dreams—and wish that I could be
A child by the old hall-fire—upon my nurse's knee!

PEG OF LIMAVADDY

R IDING from Coleraine
    (Famed for lovely Kitty),
    Came a Cockney bound
Unto Derry city;
Weary was his soul,
    Shivering and sad, he
Bumped along the road
    Leads to Limavaddy.

Mountains stretch'd around,
    Gloomy was their tinting,
And the horse's hoofs
    Made a dismal clinting;
Wind upon the heath
    Howling was and piping,
On the heath and bog,
    Black with many a snipe in.
Mid the bogs of black,
    Silver pools were flashing,
Crows upon their sides
    Pecking were and splashing.
Cockney on the car
    Closer folds his plaidy,
Grumbling at the road
    Leads to Limavaddy.

Through the crashing woods
    Autumn brawl'd and bluster'd,
Tossing round about
    Leaves the hue of mustard;
Yonder lay Lough Foyle,
    Which a storm was whipping,
Covering with mist
    Lake, and shores, and shipping

Up and down the hill
  (Nothing could be bolder),
Horse went with a raw
  Bleeding on his shoulder.
" Where are horses changed ? "
  Said I to the laddy
Driving on the box :
  " Sir, at Limavaddy."

Limavaddy inn's
  But a humble bait-house,
Where you may procure
  Whisky and-potatoes ;
Landlord at the door
  Gives a smiling welcome
To the shivering wights
  Who to his hotel come.
Landlady within
  Sits and knits a stocking,
With a wary foot
  Baby's cradle rocking.

To the chimney nook
  Having found admittance,
There I watch a pup
  Playing with two kittens ;
(Playing round the fire,
  Which of blazing turf is,
Roaring to the pot
  Which bubbles with the murphies.)
And the cradled babe
  Fond the mother nursed it,
Singing it a song
  As she twists the worsted !

Up and down the stair
  Two more young ones patter
(Twins were never seen
  Dirtier or fatter).
Both have mottled legs,
  Both have snubby noses,
Both have——Here the host
  Kindly interposes :

"Sure you must be froze
    With the sleet and hail, sir :
So will you have some punch,
    Or will you have some ale, sir ?"

Presently a maid
    Enters with the liquor
(Half-a-pint of ale
    Frothing in a beaker).
Gads ! I didn't know
    What my beating heart meant :
Hebe's self, I thought,
    Entered the apartment.
As she came she smiled,
    And the smile bewitching,
On my word and honour,
    Lighted all the kitchen !

With a curtsey neat
    Greeting the new comer,
Lovely, smiling Peg
    Offers me the rummer ;
But my trembling hand
    Up the beaker tilted,
And the glass of ale
    Every drop I spilt it :
Spilt it every drop
    (Dames, who read my volumes,
Pardon such a word)
    On my what-d'ye-call-'ems !

Witnessing the sight
    Of that dire disaster,
Out began to laugh
    Missis, maid, and master ;
Such a merry peal
    'Specially Miss Peg's was
(As the glass of ale
    Trickling down my legs was),
That the joyful sound
    Of that mingling laughter
Echoed in my ears
    Many a long day after.

Such a silver peal!
   In the meadows listening,
You who've heard the bells
   Ringing to a christening;
You who ever heard
   Caradori pretty,
Smiling like an angel,
   Singing "Giovinetti";
Fancy Peggy's laugh,
   Sweet, and clear, and cheerful,
At my pantaloons
   With half-a-pint of beer full!

When the laugh was done,
   Peg, the pretty hussy,
Moved about the room
   Wonderfully busy;
Now she looks to see
   If the kettle keep hot;
Now she rubs the spoons,
   Now she cleans the teapot;
Now she sets the cups
   Trimly and secure:
Now she scours a pot,
   And so it was I drew her.

Thus it was I drew her
   Scouring of a kettle
(Faith! her blushing cheeks
   Redden'd on the metal!)
Ah! but 'tis in vain
   That I try to sketch it;
The pot perhaps is like,
   But Peggy's face is wretched.
No! the best of lead
   And of india-rubber
Never could depict
   That sweet kettle-scrubber!

See her as she moves,
   Scarce the ground she touches
Airy as a fay,
   Graceful as a duchess:

Bare her rounded arm,
   Bare her little leg is,
Vestris never show'd
   Ankles like to Peggy's.
Braided is her hair,
   Soft her look and modest,
Slim her little waist
   Comfortably bodiced.

This I do declare,
   Happy is the laddy
Who the heart can share
   Of Peg of Limavaddy.
Married if she were
   Blest would be the daddy
Of the children fair
   Of Peg of Limavaddy.
Beauty is not rare
   In the land of Paddy,
Fair beyond compare
   Is Peg of Limavaddy.

Citizen or Squire,
   Tory, Whig, or Radi-
cal would all desire
   Peg of Limavaddy.
Had I Homer's fire,
   Or that of Serjeant Taddy,
Meetly I'd admire
   Peg of Limavaddy.
And till I expire,
   Or till I grow mad, I
Will sing unto my lyre
   Peg of Limavaddy!

TITMARSH'S CARMEN LILLIENSE

LILLE: *Sept.* **2, 1843.**

My heart is weary, my peace is gone,
How shall I e'er my woes reveal ?
I have no money, I lie in pawn,
A stranger in the town of Lille.

I.

WITH twenty pounds but three weeks since
   From Paris forth did Titmarsh wheel,
   I thought myself as rich a prince
As beggar poor I'm now at Lille.

Confiding in my ample means—
   In troth, I was a happy chiel !
I passed the gates of Valenciennes,
   I never thought to come by Lille.

I never thought my twenty pounds
   Some rascal knave would dare to steal ;
I gaily passed the Belgic bounds
   At Quiévrain, twenty miles from Lille.

To Antwerp town I hastened post,
   And as I took my evening meal,
I felt my pouch,—my purse was lost,
   O Heaven !   Why came I not by Lille ?

I straightway called for ink and pen,
   To Grandmamma I made appeal ;
Meanwhile a loan of guineas ten
   I borrowed from a friend so leal.

I got the cash from Grandmamma
    (Her gentle heart my woes could feel),
But where I went, and what I saw,
    What matters?   Here I am at Lille.

My heart is weary, my peace is gone,
    How shall I e'er my woes reveal?
I have no cash, I lie in pawn,
    A stranger in the town of Lille.

II.

To stealing I can never come,
    To pawn my watch I'm too genteel:
Besides, I left my watch at home—
    How could I pawn it then at Lille?

" *La note*," at times the guests will say
    I turn as white as cold boil'd veal;
I turn and look another way,
    I dare not ask the bill at Lille.

I dare not to the landlord say,
    "Good sir, I cannot pay your bill;"
He thinks I am a Lord Anglais,
    And is quite proud I stay at Lille.

He thinks I am a Lord Anglais,
    Like Rothschild or Sir Robert Peel,
And so he serves me every day
    The best of meat and drink in Lille.

Yet when he looks me in the face
    I blush as red as cochineal;
And think, did he but know my case,
    How changed he'd be, my host of Lille

My heart is weary, my peace is gone,
    How shall I e'er my woes reveal?
I have no money, I lie in pawn,
    A stranger in the town of Lille.

III.

The sun bursts out in furious blaze,
  I perspirate from head to heel;
I'd like to hire a one-horse chaise—
  How can I, without cash at Lille?

I pass in sunshine burning hot
  By cafés where in beer they deal;
I think how pleasant were a pot,
  A frothing pot of beer of Lille!

What is yon house with walls so thick,
  All girt around with guard and grille?
O gracious gods! it makes me sick,
  It is the *prison-house* of Lille!

O cursed prison strong and barred,
  It does my very blood congeal!
I tremble as I pass the guard,
  And quit that ugly part of Lille.

The church-door beggar whines and prays,
  I turn away at his appeal:
Ah, church-door beggar! go thy ways!
  You're not the poorest man in Lille.

My heart is weary, my peace is gone,
  How shall I e'er my woes reveal?
I have no money, I lie in pawn,
  A stranger in the town of Lille.

IV.

Say, shall I to yon Flemish church,
  And at a Popish altar kneel?
Oh, do not leave me in the lurch,—
  I'll cry, ye patron-saints of Lille!

Ye virgins dressed in satin hoops,
  Ye martyrs slain for mortal weal,
Look kindly down! before you stoops
  The miserablest man in Lille.

And lo! as I beheld with awe
    A pictured saint (I swear 'tis real),
It smiled, and turned to Grandmamma!—
    It did! and I had hope in Lille!

'Twas five o'clock, and I could eat,
    Although I could not pay my meal:
I hasten back into the street
    Where lies my inn, the best in Lille.

What see I on my table stand,—
    A letter with a well-known seal?
'Tis Grandmamma's! I know her hand,—
    "To Mr. M. A. Titmarsh, Lille."

I feel a choking in my throat,
    I pant and stagger, faint and reel!
It is—it is—a ten-pound note,
    And I'm no more in pawn at Lille!

[He goes off, by the diligence that evening, and is restored to the bosom of
his happy family.]

JEAMES OF BUCKLEY SQUARE

A HELIGY

COME all ye gents vot cleans the plate,
 Come all ye ladies' maids so fair—
 Vile I a story vill relate
Of cruel Jeames of Buckley Square.
A tighter lad, it is confest,
 Neer valked with powder in his air,
Or vore a nosegay in his breast,
 Than andsum Jeames of Buckley Square.

O Evns! it vas the best of sights,
 Behind his Master's coach and pair,
To see our Jeames in red plush tights,
 A driving hoff from Buckley Square.
He vel became his hagwilletts,
 He cocked his at with *such* a hair;
His calves and viskers *vas* such pets,
 That hall loved Jeames of Buckley Square.

He pleased the hupstairs folks as vell,
 And o! I vithered vith despair,
Missis *vould* ring the parler bell,
 And call up Jeames in Buckley Square.
Both beer and sperrits he abhord
 (Sperrits and beer I can't a bear),
You would have thought he vas a lord
 Down in our All in Buckley Square.

Last year he visper'd, "Mary Ann,
 Ven I've an under'd pound to spare,
To take a public is my plan,
 And leave this hojous Buckley Square."

O how my gentle heart did bound,
 To think that I his name should bear !
" Dear Jeames," says I, " I've twenty pound,"
 And gev them him in Buckley Square.

Our master vas a City gent,
 His name's in railroads everywhere,
And lord, vot lots of letters vent
 Betwigst his brokers and Buckley Square :
My Jeames it was the letters took,
 And read them all (I think it's fair),
And took a leaf from Master's book,
 As *hothers* do in Buckley Square.

Encouraged with my twenty pound,
 Of which poor *I* was unavare,
He wrote the Companies all round,
 And signed hisself from Buckley Square.
And how John Porter used to grin,
 As day by day, share after share,
Came railvay letters pouring in,
 " J. Plush, Esquire, in Buckley Square."

Our servants' All was in a rage—
 Scrip, stock, curves, gradients, bull and bear,
Vith butler, coachman, groom and page,
 Vas all the talk in Buckley Square.
But O ! imagine vot I felt
 Last Vensday veek as ever were ;
I gits a letter, which I spelt
 " Miss M. A. Hoggins, Buckley Square."

He sent me back my money true—
 He sent me back my lock of air,
And said, " My dear, I bid ajew
 To Mary Hann and Buckley Square.
Think not to marry, foolish Hann,
 With people who your betters are :
James Plush is now a gentleman,
 And you—a cook in Buckley Square.

"I've thirty thousand guineas won,
 In six short months, by genus rare;
You little thought what Jeames was on,
 Poor Mary Hann, in Buckley Square.
I've thirty thousand guineas net,
 Powder and plush I scorn to vear;
And so, Miss Mary Hann, forget
 For hever Jeames of Buckley Square."

LINES UPON MY SISTER'S PORTRAIT

BY THE LORD SOUTHDOWN

THE castle towers of Bareacres are fair upon the lea,
    Where the cliffs of bonny Diddlesex rise up from out the sea :
    I stood upon the donjon keep and view'd the country o'er,
I saw the lands of Bareacres for fifty miles or more.
I stood upon the donjon keep—it is a sacred place,—
Where floated for eight hundred years the banner of my race ;
Argent, a dexter sinople, and gules an azure field ;
There ne'er was nobler cognisance on knightly warrior's shield.

The first time England saw the shield 'twas round a Norman neck,
On board a ship from Valery, King William was on deck.
A Norman lance the colours wore, in Hastings' fatal fray—
St. Willibald for Bareacres ! 'twas double gules that day !
O Heaven and sweet Saint Willibald ! in many a battle since
A loyal-hearted Bareacres has ridden by his Prince !
At Acre with Plantagenet, with Edward at Poictiers,
The pennon of the Bareacres was foremost on the spears !

'Twas pleasant in the battle-shock to hear our war-cry ringing :
Oh grant me, sweet Saint Willibald, to listen to such singing !
Three hundred steel-clad gentlemen, we drove the foe before us,
And thirty score of British bows kept twanging to the chorus !
O knights, my noble ancestors ! and shall I never hear
Saint Willibald for Bareacres through battle ringing clear?
I'd cut me off this strong right hand a single hour to ride,
And strike a blow for Bareacres, my fathers, at your side !
Dash down, dash down yon mandolin, beloved sister mine !
Those blushing lips may never sing the glories of our line :
Our ancient castles echo to the clumsy feet of churls,
The spinning-jenny houses in the mansion of our Earls.
Sing not, sing not, my Angeline ! in days so base and vile,
'Twere sinful to be happy, 'twere sacrilege to smile.
I'll hie me to my lonely hall, and by its cheerless hob
I'll muse on other days, and wish—and wish I were—A SNOB.

A DOE IN THE CITY

LITTLE KITTY LORIMER,
  Fair, and young, and witty,
   What has brought your ladyship
 Rambling to the City?

All the Stags in Capel Court
 Saw her lightly trip it;
All the lads of Stock Exchange
 Twigg'd her muff and tippet.

With a sweet perplexity,
 And a mystery pretty,
Threading through Threadneedle Street,
 Trots the little KITTY.

What was my astonishment—
 What was my compunction,
When she reached the Offices
 Of the Didland Junction!

Up the Didland stairs she went,
 To the Didland door, Sir;
Porters, lost in wonderment,
 Let her pass before, Sir.

"Madam," says the old chief Clerk,
 "Sure we can't admit ye."
"Where's the Didland Junction deed?"
 Dauntlessly says KITTY.

"If you doubt my honesty,
 Look at my receipt, Sir."
Up then jumps the old chief Clerk,
 Smiling as he meets her.

KITTY at the table sits
  (Whither the old Clerk leads her),
" *I deliver this*," she says,
  " *As my act and deed, Sir.*"

When I heard these funny words
  Come from lips so pretty,
This, I thought, should surely be
  - Subject for a ditty.

What! are ladies stagging it?
  Sure, the more's the pity;
But I've lost my heart to her,—
  Naughty little KITTY.

RONSARD TO HIS MISTRESS

"Quand vous serez bien vieille, au soir à la chandelle,
     Assise auprès du feu devisant et filant,
        Direz, chantant mes vers en vous esmerveillant:
Ronsard me célébroit du temps que j'étois belle."

SOME winter night, shut snugly in
        Beside the faggot in the hall,
    I think I see you sit and spin,
Surrounded by your maidens all.
Old tales are told, old songs are sung,
    Old days come back to memory ;
You say, "When I was fair and young,
    A poet sang of me ! "

There's not a maiden in your hall,
    Though tired and sleepy ever so,
But wakes, as you my name recall,
    And longs the history to know.
And, as the piteous tale is said,
    Of lady cold and lover true,
Each, musing, carries it to bed,
    And sighs and envies you !

" Our lady's old and feeble now,"
    They'll say ; " she once was fresh and fair,
And yet she spurn'd her lover's vow,
    And heartless left him to despair :
The lover lies in silent earth,
    No kindly mate the lady cheers :
She sits beside a lonely hearth,
    With threescore and ten years ! "

Ah ! dreary thoughts and dreams are those.
    But wherefore yield me to despair,

While yet the poet's bosom glows,
   While yet the dame is peerless fair?
Sweet lady mine! while yet 'tis time
   Requite my passion and my truth,
And gather in their blushing prime
   The roses of your youth!

THE WHITE SQUALL

ON deck, beneath the awning,
  I dozing lay and yawning;
  It was the grey of dawning,
Ere yet the sun arose;
And above the funnel's roaring,
And the fitful winds deploring,
I heard the cabin snoring
 With universal nose.
I could hear the passengers snorting,
I envied their disporting—
Vainly I was courting
 The pleasure of a doze!

So I lay, and wondered why light
Came not, and watched the twilight,
And the glimmer of the skylight,
 That shot across the deck
And the binnacle pale and steady,
And the dull glimpse of the dead-eye,
And the sparks in fiery eddy
 That whirled from the chimney neck.
In our jovial floating prison
There was sleep from fore to mizen,
And never a star had risen
 The hazy sky to speck.

Strange company we harboured;
We'd a hundred Jews to larboard;
Unwashed, uncombed, unbarbered—
 Jews black, and brown, and grey;
With terror it would seize ye,
And make your souls uneasy,
To see those Rabbis greasy,
 Who did nought but scratch and pray:

Their dirty children puking—
Their dirty saucepans cooking—
Their dirty fingers hooking
    Their swarming fleas away.

To starboard, Turks and Greeks were—
Whiskered and brown their cheeks were—
Enormous wide their breeks were,
    Their pipes did puff alway;
Each on his mat allotted
In silence smoked and squatted,
Whilst round their children trotted
    In pretty, pleasant play.
He can't but smile who traces
The smiles on those brown faces,
And the pretty prattling graces
    Of those small heathens gay.

And so the hours kept tolling,
And through the ocean rolling
Went the brave *Iberia* bowling
    Before the break of day——
When A SQUALL, upon a sudden,
Came o'er the waters scudding;
And the clouds began to gather,
And the sea was lashed to lather,
And the lowering thunder grumbled,
And the lightning jumped and tumbled,
And the ship, and all the ocean,
Woke up in wild commotion.
Then the wind set up a howling,
And the poodle dog a yowling,
And the cocks began a crowing,
And the old cow raised a lowing,
As she heard the tempest blowing;
And fowls and geese did cackle,
And the cordage and the tackle
Began to shriek and crackle;
And the spray dashed o'er the funnels,
And down the deck in runnels;
And the rushing water soaks all,
From the seamen in the fo'ksal
To the stokers whose black faces
Peer out of their bed-places;

And the captain he was bawling,
And the sailors pulling, hauling,
And the quarter-deck tarpauling
Was shivered in the squalling;
And the passengers awaken,
Most pitifully shaken;
And the steward jumps up, and hastens
For the necessary basins.

Then the Greeks they groaned and quivered,
And they knelt, and moaned, and shivered,
As the plunging waters met them,
And splashed and overset them;
And they call in their emergence
Upon countless saints and virgins;
And their marrowbones are bended,
And they think the world is ended.
And the Turkish women for'ard
Were frightened and behorror'd;
And shrieking and bewildering,
The mothers clutched their children;
The men sang "Allah! Illah!
Mashallah Bismillah!"
As the warring waters doused them
And splashed them and soused them,
And they called upon the Prophet,
And thought but little of it.

Then all the fleas in Jewry
Jumped up and bit like fury;
And the progeny of Jacob
Did on the main-deck wake up
(I wot those greasy Rabbins
Would never pay for cabins);
And each man moaned and jabbered in
His filthy Jewish gaberdine,
In woe and lamentation,
And howling consternation.
And the splashing water drenches
Their dirty brats and wenches;
And they crawl from bales and benches
In a hundred thousand stenches.

This was the White Squall famous,
Which latterly o'ercame us,
And which all will well remember
On the 28th September;
When a Prussian captain of Lancers
(Those tight-laced, whiskered prancers)
Came on the deck astonished,
By that wild squall admonished,
And wondering cried, "Potztausend!
Wie ist der Sturm jetzt brausend?"
And looked at Captain Lewis,
Who calmly stood and blew his
Cigar in all the bustle,
And scorned the tempest's tussle.
And oft we've thought thereafter
How he beat the storm to laughter;
For well he knew his vessel
With that vain wind could wrestle;
And when a wreck we thought her,
And doomed ourselves to slaughter,
How gaily he fought her,
And through the hubbub brought her,
And as the tempest caught her,
Cried, "GEORGE! SOME BRANDY-AND-WATER!'

And when, its force expended,
The harmless storm was ended,
And as the sunrise splendid
    Came blushing o'er the sea,
I thought, as day was breaking,
My little girls were waking,
And smiling, and making
    A prayer at home for me.

1844.

THE AGE OF WISDOM

HO, pretty page, with the dimpled chin,
　　That never has known the barber's shear,
　　All your wish is woman to win,
This is the way that boys begin,—
　　Wait till you come to Forty Year.

Curly gold locks cover foolish brains,
　　Billing and cooing is all your cheer;
Sighing and singing of midnight strains,
Under Bonnybell's window panes,—
　　Wait till you come to Forty Year.

Forty times over let Michaelmas pass,
　　Grizzling hair the brain doth clear—
Then you know a boy is an ass,
Then you know the worth of a lass,
　　Once you have come to Forty Year.

Pledge me round, I bid ye declare,
　　All good fellows whose beards are grey,
Did not the fairest of the fair
Common grow and wearisome ere
　　Ever a month was passed away?

The reddest lips that ever have kissed,
　　The brightest eyes that ever have shone,
May pray and whisper, and we not list,
Or look away, and never be missed,
　　Ere yet ever a month is gone.

Gillian's dead, God rest her bier,
　　How I loved her twenty years syne!
Marian's married, but I sit here
Alone and merry at Forty Year,
　　Dipping my nose in the Gascon wine.

THE MAHOGANY TREE

CHRISTMAS is here:
　　Winds whistle shrill,
　　Icy and chill,
Little care we:
Little we fear
Weather without,
Sheltered about
The Mahogany Tree.

Once on the boughs
Birds of rare plume
Sang, in its bloom;
Night-birds are we:
Here we carouse,
Singing like them,
Perched round the stem
Of the jolly old tree.

Here let us sport,
Boys, as we sit;
Laughter and wit
Flashing so free.
Life is but short—
When we are gone,
Let them sing on
Round the old tree.

Evenings we knew,
Happy as this;
Faces we miss,
Pleasant to see.

Kind hearts and true,
Gentle and just,
Peace to your dust!
We sing round the tree.

Care, like a dun,
Lurks at the gate:
Let the dog wait;
Happy we'll be!
Drink, every one;
Pile up the coals,
Fill the red bowls,
Round the old tree!

Drain we the cup.—
Friend, art afraid?
Spirits are laid
In the Red Sea.
Mantle it up;
Empty it yet;
Let us forget,
Round the old tree.

Sorrows, begone!
Life and its ills,
Duns and their bills,
Bid we to flee.
Come with the dawn,
Blue-devil sprite,
Leave us to-night,
Round the old tree

THE CANE-BOTTOM'D CHAIR

IN tattered old slippers that toast at the bars,
    And a ragged old jacket perfumed with cigars,
    Away from the world and its toils and its cares,
I've a snug little kingdom up four pair of stairs.

To mount to this realm is a toil, to be sure,
But the fire there is bright and the air rather pure ;
And the view I behold on a sunshiny day
Is grand through the chimney-pots over the way.

This snug little chamber is cramm'd in all nooks
With worthless old nicknacks and silly old books,
And foolish old odds and foolish old ends,
Crack'd bargains from brokers, cheap keepsakes from friends.

Old armour, prints, pictures, pipes, china (all crack'd),
Old rickety tables, and chairs broken-backed ;
A twopenny treasury, wondrous to see ;
What matter ? 'tis pleasant to you, friend, and me.

No better divan need the Sultan require,
Than the creaking old sofa that basks by the fire ;
And 'tis wonderful, surely, what music you get
From the rickety, ramshackle, wheezy spinet.

That praying-rug came from a Turcoman's camp ;
By Tiber once twinkled that brazen old lamp ;
A Mameluke fierce yonder dagger has drawn :
'Tis a murderous knife to toast muffins upon.

Long long through the hours, and the night, and the chimes,
Here we talk of old books, and old friends, and old times ;
As we sit in a fog made of rich Latakie
This chamber is pleasant to you, friend, and me.

But of all the cheap treasures that garnish my nest,
There's one that I love and I cherish the best:
For the finest of couches that's padded with hair
I never would change thee, my cane-bottom'd chair.

'Tis a bandy-legg'd, high-shoulder'd, worm-eaten seat,
With a creaking old back, and twisted old feet;
But since the fair morning when Fanny sat there,
I bless thee and love thee, old cane-bottom'd chair.

If chairs have but feeling, in holding such charms,
A thrill must have pass'd through your wither'd old arms!
I look'd, and I long'd, and I wish'd in despair;
I wish'd myself turn'd to a cane-bottom'd chair.

It was but a moment she sat in this place,
She'd a scarf on her neck, and a smile on her face!
A smile on her face, and a rose in her hair,
And she sat there, and bloom'd in my cane-bottom'd chair.

And so I have valued my chair ever since,
Like the shrine of a saint, or the throne of a prince;
Saint Fanny, my patroness sweet I declare,
The queen of my heart and my cane-bottom'd chair.

When the candles burn low, and the company's gone,
In the silence of night as I sit here alone—
I sit here alone, but we yet are a pair—
My Fanny I see in my cane-bottom'd chair.

She comes from the past and revisits my room;
She looks as she then did, all beauty and bloom;
So smiling and tender, so fresh and so fair,
And yonder she sits in my cane-bottom'd chair.

"AH, BLEAK AND BARREN WAS THE MOOR"

AH! bleak and barren was the moor,
    Ah! loud and piercing was the storm,
    The cottage roof was sheltered sure,
The cottage hearth was bright and warm.
An orphan-boy the lattice pass'd,
    And, as he marked its cheerful glow,
Felt doubly keen the midnight blast,
    And doubly cold the fallen snow.

They marked him as he onward press'd,
    With fainting heart and weary limb;
Kind voices bade him turn and rest,
    And gentle faces welcomed him.
The dawn is up—the guest is gone,
    The cottage hearth is blazing still:
Heaven pity all poor wanderers lone!
    Hark to the wind upon the hill!

THE ROSE UPON MY BALCONY

THE rose upon my balcony the morning air perfuming,
    Was leafless all the winter time and pining for the spring ;
    You ask me why her breath is sweet, and why her cheek is
        blooming :
It is because the sun is out and birds begin to sing.

The nightingale, whose melody is through the greenwood ringing,
Was silent when the boughs were bare and winds were blowing
    keen :
And if, Mamma, you ask of me the reason of his singing,
It is because the sun is out and all the leaves are green.

Thus each performs his part, Mamma : the birds have found their
    voices,
The blowing rose a flush, Mamma, her bonny cheek to dye ;
And there's sunshine in my heart, Mamma, which wakens and
    rejoices,
And so I sing and blush, Mamma, and that's the reason why.

ABD-EL-KADER AT TOULON;

NO more, thou lithe and long-winged hawk, of desert life for
    thee ;
    No more across the sultry sands shalt thou go swooping
      free :
Blunt idle talons, idle beak, with spurning of thy chain,
Shatter against thy cage the wing thou ne'er mayst spread again.

Long, sitting by their watchfires, shall the Kabyles tell the tale
Of thy dash from Ben Halifa on the fat Metidja vale ;
How thou swept'st the desert over, bearing down the wild
    El Riff,
From eastern Beni Salah to western Ouad Shelif ;

How thy white burnous went streaming, like the storm-rack o'er
    the sea,
When thou rodest in the vanward of the Moorish chivalry ;
How thy razzia was a whirlwind, thy onset a simoom,
How thy sword-sweep was the lightning, dealing death from out
    the gloom !

Nor less quick to slay in battle than in peace to spare and save,
Of brave men wisest counsellor, of wise counsellors most brave ;
How the eye that flashed destruction could beam gentleness and
    love ;
How lion in thee mated lamb, how eagle mated dove !

Availèd not or steel or shot 'gainst that charmed life secure,
Till cunning France, in last resource, tossed up the golden lure ;
And the carrion buzzards round him stooped, faithless, to the
    cast,
And the wild hawk of the desert is caught and caged at last.

Weep, maidens of Zerifah, above the laden loom !
Scar, chieftains of Al Elmah, your cheeks in grief and gloom !
Sons of the Beni Snazam, throw down the useless lance,
And stoop your necks and bare your backs to yoke and scourge of
     France !

'Twas not in fight they bore him down : he never cried *amàn ;*
He never sank his sword before the PRINCE OF FRANGHISTAN ;
But with traitors all around him, his star upon the wane,
He heard the voice of ALLAH, and he would not strive in vain.

They gave him what he asked them : from king to king he spake,
As one that plighted word and seal not knoweth how to break :
"Let me pass from out my deserts, be't mine own choice where
     to go ;
I brook no fettered life to live, a captive and a show."

And they promised, and he trusted them, and proud and calm he
     came,
Upon his black mare riding, girt with his sword of fame.
Good steed, good sword, he rendered both unto the Frankish throng ;
He knew them false and fickle—but a Prince's word is strong.

How have they kept their promise ?   Turned they the vessel's prow
Unto Acre, Alexandria, as they have sworn e'en now ?
Not so : from Oran northwards the white sails gleam and glance,
And the wild hawk of the desert is borne away to France !

Where Toulon's white-walled lazaret looks southward o'er the wave,
Sits he that trusted in the word a son of LOUIS gave.
O noble faith of noble heart !   And was the warning vain,
The text writ by the BOURBON in the blurred black book of Spain ?

They have need of thee to gaze on, they have need of thee to grace
The triumph of the Prince, to gild the pinchbeck of their race.
Words are but wind ; conditions must be construed by GUIZOT ;
Dash out thy heart, thou desert hawk, ere thou art made a show !

AT THE CHURCH GATE

ALTHOUGH I enter not,
    Yet round about the spot
       Ofttimes I hover;
And near the sacred gate,
With longing eyes I wait,
       Expectant of her.

The Minster bell tolls out
Above the city's rout,
       And noise and humming:
They've hush'd the Minster bell:
The organ 'gins to swell:
       She's coming, she's coming!

My lady comes at last,
Timid, and stepping fast,
       And hastening hither,
With modest eyes downcast:
She comes—she's here—she's past—
       May Heaven go with her!

Kneel, undisturbed, fair Saint!
Pour out your praise or plaint
       Meekly and duly;
I will not enter there,
To sully your pure prayer
       With thoughts unruly.

But suffer me to pace
Round the forbidden place,
       Lingering a minute
Like outcast spirits who wait
And see through heaven's gate
       Angels within it.

THE END OF THE PLAY

THE play is done; the curtain drops,
    Slow falling to the prompter's bell:
    A moment yet the actor stops,
And looks around, to say farewell.
It is an irksome word and task;
    And, when he's laughed and said his say,
He shows, as he removes the mask,
    A face that's anything but gay.

One word, ere yet the evening ends,
    Let's close it with a parting rhyme,
And pledge a hand to all young friends,
    As fits the merry Christmas time.*
On life's wide scene you, too, have parts,
    That Fate ere long shall bid you play;
Good night! with honest gentle hearts
    A kindly greeting go alway!

Good night!—I'd say, the griefs, the joys,
    Just hinted in this mimic page,
The triumphs and defeats of boys,
    Are but repeated in our age.
I'd say, your woes were not less keen,
    Your hopes more vain, than those of men;
Your pangs or pleasures of fifteen
    At forty-five played o'er again.

I'd say, we suffer and we strive,
    Not less nor more as men than boys;
With grizzled beards at forty-five,
    As erst at twelve in corduroys.

These verses were printed at the end of a Christmas book (1848-9), " Dr.
Birch and his Young Friends."

And if, in time of sacred youth,
   We learned at home to love and pray,
Pray Heaven that early Love and Truth
   May never wholly pass away.

And in the world, as in the school,
   I'd say, how fate may change and shift;
The prize be sometimes with the fool,
   The race not always to the swift.
The strong may yield, the good may fall,
   The great man be a vulgar clown,
The knave be lifted over all,
   The kind cast pitilessly down.

Who knows the inscrutable design?
   Blessed be He who took and gave!
Why should your mother, Charles, not mine,
   Be weeping at her darling's grave? *
We bow to Heaven that will'd it so,
   That darkly rules the fate of all,
That sends the respite or the blow,
   That's free to give, or to recall.

This crowns his feast with wine and wit:
   Who brought him to that mirth and state?
His betters, see, below him sit,
   Or hunger hopeless at the gate.
Who bade the mud from Dives' wheel
   To spurn the rags of Lazarus?
Come, brother, in that dust we'll kneel,
   Confessing Heaven that ruled it thus.

So each shall mourn, in life's advance,
   Dear hopes, dear friends, untimely killed;
Shall grieve for many a forfeit chance,
   And longing passion unfulfilled.
Amen! whatever fate be sent,
   Pray God the heart may kindly glow,
Although the head with cares be bent,
   And whitened with the winter snow.

* C. B. ob. 29th November 1848, æt. 42.

Come wealth or want, come good or ill,
    Let young and old accept their part,
And bow before the Awful Will,
    And bear it with an honest heart,
Who misses or who wins the prize.
    Go, lose or conquer as you can ;
But if you fail, or if you rise,
    Be each, pray God, a gentleman.

A gentleman, or old or young !
    (Bear kindly with my humble lays) ;
The sacred chorus first was sung
    Upon the first of Christmas days :
The shepherds heard it overhead—
    The joyful angels raised it then :
Glory to Heaven on high, it said,
    And peace on earth to gentle men.

My song, save this, is little worth ;
    I lay the weary pen aside,
And wish you health, and love, and mirth,
    As fits the solemn Christmastide.
As fits the holy Christmas birth,
    Be this, good friends, our carol still—
Be peace on earth, be peace on earth,
    To men of gentle will.

THE BALLAD OF BOUILLABAISSE

A STREET there is in Paris famous,
     For which no rhyme our language yields,
     Rue Neuve des Petits Champs its name is—
The New Street of the Little Fields.
And here's an inn, not rich and splendid,
     But still in comfortable case;
The which in youth I oft attended,
     To eat a bowl of Bouillabaisse.

This Bouillabaisse a noble dish is—
     A sort of soup or broth, or brew,
Or hotchpotch of all sorts of fishes,
     That Greenwich never could outdo:
Green herbs, red peppers, mussels, saffron,
     Soles, onions, garlic, roach, and dace:
All these you eat at TERRÉ's tavern
     In that one dish of Bouillabaisse.

Indeed, a rich and savoury stew 'tis;
     And true philosophers, methinks,
Who love all sorts of natural beauties,
     Should love good victuals and good drinks.
And Cordelier or Benedictine
     Might gladly, sure, his lot embrace,
Nor find a fast-day too afflicting,
     Which served him up a Bouillabaisse.

I wonder if the house still there is?
     Yes, here the lamp is, as before;
The smiling red-cheeked *écaillère* is
     Still opening oysters at the door.
Is TERRÉ still alive and able?
     I recollect his droll grimace:
He'd come and smile before your table,
     And hope you liked your Bouillabaisse.

We enter—nothing's changed or older.
 " How's Monsieur TERRÉ, waiter, pray ? "
The waiter stares, and shrugs his shoulder—
 " Monsieur is dead this many a day."
" It is the lot of saint and sinner,
 So honest TERRÉ's run his race."
" What will Monsieur require for dinner ? "
 " Say, do you still cook Bouillabaisse ? "

" Oh, oui, Monsieur," 's the waiter's answer ;
 " Quel vin Monsieur désire-t-il ? "
" Tell me a good one."—" That I can, Sir :
 The Chambertin with yellow seal."
" So TERRÉ's gone," I say, and sink in
 My old accustom'd corner-place ;
" He's done with feasting and with drinking,
 With Burgundy and Bouillabaisse."

My old accustom'd corner here is,
 The table still is in the nook ;
Ah ! vanished many a busy year is
 This well-known chair since last I took.
When first I saw ye, *cari luoghi*,
 I'd scarce a beard upon my face,
And now a grizzled, grim old fogy,
 I sit and wait for Bouillabaisse.

Where are you, old companions trusty
 Of early days here met to dine ?
Come, waiter ! quick, a flagon crusty—
 I'll pledge them in the good old wine.
The kind old voices and old faces
 My memory can quick retrace ;
Around the board they take their places,
 And share the wine and Bouillabaisse.

There's JACK has made a wondrous marriage ;
 There's laughing TOM is laughing yet ;
There's brave AUGUSTUS drives his carriage ;
 There's poor old FRED in the *Gazette ;*
On JAMES's head the grass is growing :
 Good Lord ! the world has wagged apace
Since here we set the claret flowing,
 And drank, and ate the Bouillabaisse.

Ah me! how quick the days are flitting!
  I mind me of a time that's gone,
When here I'd sit, as now I'm sitting,
  In this same place—but not alone.
A fair young form was nestled near me,
  A dear dear face looked fondly up,
And sweetly spoke and smiled to cheer me
  —There's no one now to share my cup.

.   .   .   .   .

I drink it as the Fates ordain it.
  Come, fill it, and have done with rhymes:
Fill up the lonely glass, and drain it
  In memory of dear old times.
Welcome the wine, whate'er the seal is;
  And sit you down and say your grace
With thankful heart, whate'er the meal is.
  —Here comes the smoking Bouillabaisse!

High Sovereign, in your Royal state,
  Captains, and chiefs, and councillors,
  Before the lofty palace doors
              Are open set,—
Hush ! ere you pass the shining gate ;
  Hush ! ere the heaving curtain draws,
  And let the Royal pageant pause
              A moment yet.

People and prince a silence keep !
  Bow coronet and kingly crown,
  Helmet and plume, bow lowly down,
              The while the priest,
Before the splendid portal step
  (While still the wondrous banquet stays),
  From Heaven supreme a blessing prays
              Upon the feast.

Then onwards let the triumph march ;
  Then let the loud artillery roll,
  And trumpets ring, and joy-bells toll,
              And pass the gate.
Pass underneath the shining arch,
  'Neath which the leafy elms are green ;
  Ascend unto your throne, O Queen !
              And take your state.

Behold her in her Royal place ;
  A gentle lady ; and the hand
  That sways the sceptre of this land,
              How frail and weak !
Soft is the voice, and fair the face :
  She breathes amen to prayer and hymn ;
  No wonder that her eyes are dim,
              And pale her cheek.

This moment round her empire's shores
  The winds of Austral winter sweep,
  And thousands lie in midnight sleep
              At rest to-day.
Oh ! awful is that crown of yours,
  Queen of innumerable realms
  Sitting beneath the budding elms
              Of English May !

MAY-DAY ODE

B UT yesterday a naked sod
  The dandies sneered from Rotten Row,
  And cantered o'er it to and fro :
      And see 'tis done !
As though 'twere by a wizard's rod
  A blazing arch of lucid glass
  Leaps like a fountain from the grass
      To meet the sun !

A quiet green but few days since,
  With cattle browsing in the shade :
  And here are lines of bright arcade
      In order raised !
A palace as for fairy prince,
  A rare pavilion, such as man
  Saw never since mankind began,
      And built and glazed !

A peaceful place it was but now,
  And lo ! within its shining streets
  A multitude of nations meets ;
      A countless throng
I see beneath the crystal bow,
  And Gaul and German, Russ and Turk,
  Each with his native handiwork
      And busy tongue.

I felt a thrill of love and awe
  To mark the different garb of each,
  The changing tongue, the various speech
      Together blent :
A thrill, methinks, like His who saw
  " All people dwelling upon earth
  Praising our God with solemn mirth
      And one consent."

A wondrous sceptre 'tis to bear :
  Strange mystery of God which set
  Upon her brow yon coronet,—
                    The foremost crown
Of all the world, on one so fair !
  That chose her to it from her birth,
  And bade the sons of all the earth
                • To her bow down.

The representatives of man
  Here from the far Antipodes,
  And from the subject Indian seas,
                    In congress meet ;
From Afric and from Hindustan,
  From Western continent and isle,
  The envoys of her empire pile
                    Gifts at her feet ;

Our brethren cross the Atlantic tides,
  Loading the gallant decks which once
  Roared a defiance to our guns,
                    With peaceful store ;
Symbol of peace, their vessel rides ! *
  O'er English waves float Star and Stripe,
  And firm their friendly anchors gripe
                    The father shore !

From Rhine and Danube, Rhone and Seine,
  As rivers from their sources gush,
  The swelling floods of nations rush,
                    And seaward pour :
From coast to coast in friendly chain,
  With countless ships we bridge the straits,
  And angry ocean separates
                    Europe no more.

From Mississippi and from Nile—
  From Baltic, Ganges, Bosphorus,
  In England's ark assembled thus
                    Are friend and guest.
Look down the mighty sunlit aisle,
  And see the sumptuous banquet set,
  The brotherhood of nations met
                    Around the feast !

    * The U.S. frigate *St. Lawrence.*

Along the dazzling colonnade,
  Far as the straining eye can gaze,
  Gleam cross and fountain, bell and vase,
      In vistas bright;
And statues fair of nymph and maid,
  And steeds and pards and Amazons,
  Writhing and grappling in the bronze,
      In endless fight.

To deck the glorious roof and dome,
  To make the Queen a canopy,
  The peaceful hosts of industry
      Their standards bear.
Yon are the works of Brahmin loom;
  On such a web of Persian thread
  The desert Arab bows his head
      And cries his prayer.

Look yonder where the engines toil:
  These England's arms of conquest are,
  The trophies of her bloodless war:
      Brave weapons these.
Victorious over wave and soil,
  With these she sails, she weaves, she tills,
  Pierces the everlasting hills
      And spans the seas.

The engine roars upon its race,
  The shuttle whirrs along the woof,
  The people hum from floor to roof,
      With Babel tongue.
The fountain in the basin plays,
  The chanting organ echoes clear,
  An awful chorus 'tis to hear,
      A wondrous song!

Swell, organ, swell your trumpet blast,
  March, Queen and Royal pageant, march
  By splendid aisle and springing arch
      Of this fair Hall:
And see! above the fabric vast,
  God's boundless heaven is bending blue,
  God's peaceful sunlight's beaming through,
      And shines o'er all.

May 1851.

THE PEN AND THE ALBUM

" I AM Miss Catherine's book," the Album speaks ;
    " I've lain among your tomes these many weeks ;
    I'm tired of their old coats and yellow cheeks.

" Quick, Pen ! and write a line with a good grace :
    Come ! draw me off a funny little face ;
    And, prithee, send me back to Chesham Place."

PEN.

" I am my master's faithful old Gold Pen ;
    I've served him three long years, and drawn since then
    Thousands of funny women and droll men.

" O Album ! could I tell you all his ways
    And thoughts, since I am his, these thousand days,
    Lord, how your pretty pages I'd amaze ! "

ALBUM.

" His ways ? his thoughts ?   Just whisper me a few ;
    Tell me a curious anecdote or two,
    And write 'em quickly off, good Mordan, do ! "

PEN.

" Since he my faithful service did engage
    To follow him through his queer pilgrimage,
    I've drawn and written many a line and page.

" Caricatures I scribbled have, and rhymes,
    And dinner-cards, and picture pantomimes,
    And merry little children's books at times.

" I've writ the foolish fancy of his brain ;
  The aimless jest that, striking, hath caused pain ;
  The idle word that he'd wish back again.

  .   .   .   .   .   .

" I've help'd him to pen many a line for bread ;
  To joke, with sorrow aching in his head ;
  And make your laughter when his own heart bled.

" I've spoke with men of all degree and sort—
  Peers of the land, and ladies of the Court ;
  Oh, but I've chronicled a deal of sport !

" Feasts that were ate a thousand days ago,
  Biddings to wine that long hath ceased to flow,
  Gay meetings with good fellows long laid low ;

" Summons to bridal, banquet, burial, ball,
  Tradesmen's polite reminders of his small
  Account due Christmas last—I've answer'd all.

" Poor Diddler's tenth petition for a half-
  Guinea ; Miss Bunyan's for an autograph ;
  So I refuse, accept, lament, or laugh,

" Condole, congratulate, invite, praise, scoff,
  Day after day still dipping in my trough,
  And scribbling pages after pages off.

" Day after day the labour's to be done,
  And sure as come the postman and the sun,
  The indefatigable ink must run.

  .   .   .   .   .   .

" Go back, my pretty little gilded tome,
  To a fair mistress and a pleasant home,
  Where soft hearts greet us whensoe'er we come !

" Dear friendly eyes, with constant kindness lit,
  However rude my verse, or poor my wit,
  Or sad or gay my mood, you welcome it.

" Kind lady ! till my last of lines is penn'd,
  My master's love, grief, laughter, at an end,
  Whene'er I write your name, may I write friend !

" Not all are so that were so in past years ;
Voices, familiar once, no more he hears ;
Names, often writ, are blotted out in tears.

" So be it :—joys will end and tears will dry——
Album ! my master bids me wish good-bye,
He'll send you to your mistress presently.

" And thus with thankful heart he closes you :
Blessing the happy hour when a friend he knew
So gentle, and so generous, and so true.

" Nor pass the words as idle phrases by ;
Stranger ! I never writ a flattery,
Nor sign'd the page that register'd a lie."

LUCY'S BIRTHDAY

SEVENTEEN rose-buds in a ring,
　　Thick with sister flowers beset,
　　In a fragrant coronet,
Lucy's servants this day bring.
Be it the birthday wreath she wears
Fresh and fair, and symbolling
The young number of her years,
The sweet blushes of her spring.

Types of youth and love and hope!
Friendly hearts your mistress greet,
Be you ever fair and sweet,
And grow lovelier as you ope!
Gentle nurseling, fenced about
With fond care, and guarded so,
Scarce you've heard of storms without,
Frosts that bite, or winds that blow!

Kindly has your life begun,
And we pray that Heaven may send
To our floweret a warm sun,
A calm summer, a sweet end.
And where'er shall be her home,
May she decorate the place;
Still expanding into bloom,
And developing in grace.

THE YANKEE VOLUNTEERS

"A surgeon of the United States army says, that on inquiring of
the Captain of his company, he found that *nine-tenths* of the men had en-
listed on account of some female difficulty."—*Morning Paper*.

YE Yankee volunteers!
    It makes my bosom bleed
    When I your story read,
        Though oft 'tis told one.
So—in both hemispheres
The women are untrue,
And cruel in the New,
        As in the Old one!

What—in this company
Of sixty sons of Mars,
Who march 'neath Stripes and Stars,
        With fife and horn,
Nine-tenths of all we see
Along the warlike line
Had but one cause to join
        This Hope Forlorn?

Deserters from the realm
Where tyrant Venus reigns,
You slipp'd her wicked chains,
        Fled and outran her.
And now, with sword and helm,
Together banded are
Beneath the Stripe and Star-
        Embroider'd banner!

And is it so with all
The warriors ranged in line,
With lace bedizen'd fine
        And swords gold-hilted?

Yon lusty córporal,
Yon colour-man who gripes
The flag of Stars and Stripes—
    Has each been jilted?

Come, each man of this line,
The privates strong and tall,
" The pioneers and all,"
    The fifer nimble—
Lieutenant and Ensign,
Captain with epaulets,
And Blacky there, who beats
    The clanging cymbal.—

O cymbal-beating black,
Tell us, as thou canst feel,
Was it some Lucy Neal
    Who caused thy ruin?
O nimble fifing Jack,
And drummer making din
So deftly on the skin,
    With thy rat-tat-tooing—

Confess, ye volunteers,
Lieutenant and Ensign,
And Captain of the line,
    As bold as Roman—
Confess, ye grenadiers,
However strong and tall,
The Conqueror of you all
    Is Woman, Woman!

No corselet is so proof
But through it from her bow
The shafts that she can throw
    Will pierce and rankle.
No champion e'er so tough
But 's in the struggle thrown,
And tripp'd and trodden down
    By her slim ankle.

Thus always it was ruled :
And when a woman smiled,
The strong man was a child,
  The sage a noodle.
Alcides was befool'd,
And silly Samson shorn,
Long long ere you were born,
  Poor Yankee Doodle !

PISCATOR AND PISCATRIX

LINES WRITTEN TO AN ALBUM PRINT

A S on this pictured page I look,
This pretty tale of line and hook
As though it were a novel-book
　　Amuses and engages :
I know them both, the boy and girl ;
She is the daughter of the Earl,
The lad (that has his hair in curl)
　　　　My Lord the County's page is.

A pleasant place for such a pair !
The fields lie basking in the glare ;
No breath of wind the heavy air
　　　　Of lazy summer quickens.
Hard by you see the castle tall ;
The village nestles round the wall,
As round about the hen its small
　　　　Young progeny of chickens.

It is too hot to pace the keep ;
To climb the turret is too steep ;
My Lord the Earl is dozing deep,
　　　　His noonday dinner over :
The postern-warder is asleep
(Perhaps they've bribed him not to peep) :
And so from out the gate they creep,
　　　　And cross the fields of clover.

Their lines into the brook they launch ;
He lays his cloak upon a branch,
To guarantee his Lady Blanche
　　　　's delicate complexion :

He takes his rapier from his haunch,
That beardless doughty champion staunch;
He'd drill it through the rival's paunch
    That question'd his affection!

O heedless pair of sportsmen slack!
You never mark, though trout or jack,
Or little foolish stickleback,
    Your baited snares may capture.
What care has *she* for line and hook?
She turns her back upon the brook,
Upon her lover's eyes to look
    In sentimental rapture.

O loving pair! as thus I gaze
Upon the girl who smiles always,
The little hand that ever plays
    Upon the lover's shoulder;
In looking at your pretty shapes,
A sort of envious wish escapes
(Such as the Fox had for the Grapes)
    The Poet your beholder.

To be brave, handsome, twenty-two;
With nothing else on earth to do,
But all day long to bill and coo:
    It were a pleasant calling.
And had I such a partner sweet;
A tender heart for mine to beat,
A gentle hand my clasp to meet;—
I'd let the world flow at my feet,
    And never heed its brawling.

SORROWS OF WERTHER

WERTHER had a love for Charlotte
    Such as words could never utter;
      Would you know how first he met her?
She was cutting bread and butter.

Charlotte was a married lady,
    And a moral man was Werther,
And, for all the wealth of Indies,
    Would do nothing for to hurt her.

So he sighed and pined and ogled,
    And his passion boiled and bubbled,
Till he blew his silly brains out,
    And no more was by it troubled.

Charlotte, having seen his body
    Borne before her on a shutter,
Like a well-conducted person,
    Went on cutting bread and butter.

THE LAST OF MAY

BY fate's benevolent award,
    Should I survive the day,
  I'll drink a bumper with my lord
    Upon the last of May.

That I may reach that happy time
    The kindly gods I pray,
For are not ducks and peas in prime
    Upon the last of May ?

At thirty boards, 'twixt now and then,
    My knife and fork shall play ;
But better wine and better men
    I shall not meet in May.

And though, good friend, with whom I dine,
    Your honest head is grey,
And, like this grizzled head of mine,
    Has seen its last of May ;

Yet, with a heart that's ever kind,
    A gentle spirit gay,
You've spring perennial in your mind,
    And round you make a May !

AN EPIC POEM, IN TWENTY BOOKS

I.

The Poet describes the city and spelling of Kiow, Kioff, or Kiova.

A THOUSAND years ago, or more,
    A city filled with burghers stout,
    And girt with ramparts round about,
Stood on the rocky Dnieper shore.
In armour bright, by day and night,
    The sentries they paced to and fro.
Well guarded and walled was this town, and calle
    By different names, I'd have you to know;
For if you looks in the g'ography books,
In those dictionaries the name it varies,
And they write it off Kieff or Kioff,
                        Kiova or Kiow.

II.

Its buildings, public works, and ordinances, religious and civil.

Thus guarded without by wall and redoubt,
    Kiova within was a place of renown,
With more advantages than in those dark ages
    Were commonly known to belong to a town.
There were places and squares, and each year four
And regular aldermen and regular lord mayors;
And streets, and alleys, and a bishop's palace;
And a church with clocks for the orthodox—
With clocks and with spires, as religion desires;
And beadles to whip the bad little boys
Over their poor little corduroys,
In service-time, when they *didn't* make a noise;
And a chapter and dean, and a cathedral-green
With ancient trees, underneath whose shades
Wandered nice young nursery-maids.
Ding-dong, ding-dong, ding-ding-a ring-ding,
The bells they made a merry merry ring

From the tall tall steeple ; and all the people
(Except the Jews) came and filled the pews—
   Poles, Russians, and Germans,
    To hear the sermons
Which HYACINTH preached to those Germans and Poles
   For the safety of their souls.

The poet shows how a certain priest dwelt at Kioff, a godly clergyman, and one that preached rare good sermons.

III.

A worthy priest he was and a stout—
 You've seldom looked on such a one ;
For, though he fasted thrice in a week,
Yet nevertheless his skin was sleek ;
His waist it spanned two yards about,
 And he weighed a score of stone.

How this priest was short and fat of body.

IV.

A worthy priest for fasting and prayer
 And mortification most deserving,
And as for preaching beyond compare :
He'd exert his powers for three or four hours
With greater pith than Sydney Smith
 Or the Reverend Edward Irving.

And like unto the author of "Plymley's Letters."

V.

He was the Prior of Saint Sophia
(A Cockney rhyme, but no better I know)—
Of Saint Sophia, that Church in Kiow,
 Built by missionaries I can't tell when ;
Who by their discussions converted the Russians,
 And made them Christian men.

Of what convent he was prior, and when the convent was built.

VI.

Sainted Sophia (so the legend vows)
With special favour did regard this house ;
 And to uphold her converts' new devotion
Her statue (needing but her legs for *her* ship)
 Walks of itself across the German Ocean ;
  And of a sudden perches
  In this the best of churches,
Whither all Kiovites come and pay it grateful worship.

Of Saint Sophia of Kioff ; and how her statue miraculously travelled thither.

I

VII.

And how Kioff
should have
been a happy
city ; but that

Thus with her patron-saints and pious preachers
   Recorded here in catalogue precise,
A goodly city, worthy magistrates,
You would have thought in all the Russian states
The citizens the happiest of all creatures,—
   The town itself a perfect Paradise.

VIII.

Certain wicked
Cossacks did
besiege it,

No, alas ! this well-built city
   Was in a perpetual fidget ;
For the Tartars, without pity,
   Did remorselessly besiege it.

Tartars fierce, with swords and sabres,
   Huns and Turks, and such as these,
Envied much their peaceful neighbours
   By the blue Borysthenes.

Murdering the
citizens,

Down they came, these ruthless Russians,
   From their steppes, and woods, and fens,
For to levy contributions
   On the peaceful citizens.

Winter, Summer, Spring, and Autumn,
   Down they came to peaceful Kioff,
Killed the burghers when they caught 'em,
   If their lives they would not buy off.

Until they
agreed to pay a
tribute yearly.

Till the city, quite confounded
   By the ravages they made,
Humbly with their chief compounded,
   And a yearly tribute paid.

How they paid
the tribute, and
then suddenly
refused it,

Which (because their courage lax was)
   They discharged while they were able :
Tolerated thus the tax was,
   Till it grew intolerable,

To the wonder
of the Cossack
envoy.

And the Calmuc envoy sent,
   As before to take their dues all,
Got, to his astonishment,
   A unanimous refusal !

"Men of Kioff!" thus courageous
   Did the stout Lord Mayor harangue them,
"Wherefore pay these sneaking wages
   To the hectoring Russians? hang them!

Of a mighty gallant speech

"Hark! I hear the awful cry of
   Our forefathers in their graves;
"'Fight, ye citizens of Kioff!
   Kioff was not made for slaves.'

That the Lord Mayor made,

'All too long have ye betrayed her;
   Rouse, ye men and aldermen,
Send the insolent invader—
   Send him starving back again."

Exhorting the burghers to pay no longer.

IX.

He spoke and he sat down; the people of the town,
   Who were fired with a brave emulation,
Now rose with one accord, and voted thanks unto the Lord
   Mayor for his oration:

Of their thanks and heroic resolves.

The envoy they dismissed, never placing in his fist
   So much as a single shilling;
And all with courage fired, as his Lordship he desired,
   At once set about their drilling.

They dismiss the envoy, and set about drilling.

Then every city ward established a guard,
   Diurnal and nocturnal:
Militia volunteers, light dragoons, and bombardiers,
   With an alderman for colonel.

Of the City guard: viz. militia, dragoons, and bombardiers, and their commanders.

There was muster and roll-calls, and repairing city walls,
   And filling up of fosses:
And the captains and the majors, so gallant and courageous,
   A-riding about on their hosses.

Of the majors and captains;

To be guarded at all hours they built themselves watch-towers,
   With every tower a man on;
And surely and secure, each from out his embrasure,
   Looked down the iron cannon!

The fortifications and artillery.

A battle-song was writ for the theatre, where it
 Was sung with vast enérgy

Of the conduct
of the actors and
the clergy.
And rapturous applause ; and besides, the public cause
 Was supported by the clergy.

The pretty ladies'-maids were pinning of cockades,
 And tying on of sashes ;
And dropping gentle tears, while their lovers bluster'd fie
 About gunshot and gashes ;

Of the ladies,
The ladies took the hint, and all day were scraping lint,
 As became their softer genders ;
And got bandages and beds for the limbs and for the hea
 Of the city's brave defenders.

The men, both young and old, felt resolute and bold,
 And panted hot for glory ;

And, finally, of
the taylors.
Even the tailors 'gan to brag, and embroidered on their fl
 "AUT WINCERE AUT MORI."

X.

Of the Cossack
chief,—his
stratagem ;
Seeing the city's resolute condition,
 The Cossack chief, too cunning to despise it,
Said to himself, " Not having ammunition
Wherewith to batter the place in proper form,
Some of these nights I'll carry it by storm,
 And sudden escalade it or surprise it.

And the bur-
ghers' sillie
victorie.
" Let's see, however, if the cits stand firmish."
 He rode up to the city gates ; for answers,
Out rushed an eager troop of the town *élite*,
 And straightway did begin a gallant skirmish :
The Cossack hereupon did sound retreat,
 Leaving the victory with the city lancers.

What prisoners
they took,
They took two prisoners and as many horses,
 And the whole town grew quickly so elate
With this small victory of their virgin forces,
 That they did deem their privates and commanders
So many Cæsars, Pompeys, Alexanders,
 Napoleons, or Fredericks the Great.

nd puffing with inordinate conceit
  They utterly despised these Cossack thieves ;
nd thought the ruffians easier to beat
han porters carpets think, or ushers boys.
eanwhile, a sly spectator of their joys,
  The Cossack captain giggled in his sleeves.

And how con-
ceited they were

Whene'er you meet yon stupid city hogs "
  (He bade his troops precise this order keep),
Don't stand a moment—run away, you dogs ! "
was done ; and when they met the town battalions,
he Cossacks, as if frightened at their valiance,
  Turned tail, and bolted like so many sheep.

Of the Cossack
chief,—his
orders ;

hey fled, obedient to their captain's order :
  And now this bloodless siege a month had lasted,
When, viewing the country round, the city warder
Who, like a faithful weathercock, did perch
pon the steeple of Saint Sophy's church),
  Sudden his trumpet took, and a mighty blast he blasted.

And how he
feigned a
retreat.

is voice it might be heard through all the streets
  (He was a warder wondrous strong in lung),
Victory, victory ! the foe retreats ! "
The foe retreats ! " each cries to each he meets ;
The foe retreats ! " each in his turn repeats.
  Gods ! how the guns did roar, and how the joy-bells rung !

The warder pro-
clayms the Cos-
sacks' retreat,
and the citie
greatly rejoyces.

rming in haste his gallant city lancers,
  The Mayor, to learn if true the news might be,
league or two out issued with his prancers.
he Cossacks (something had given their courage a damper)
astened their flight, and 'gan like mad to scamper ;
  Blessed be all the saints, Kiova town was free !

XI.

ow, puffed with pride, the Mayor grew vain,
ought all his battles o'er again ;
nd thrice he routed all his foes, and thrice he slew the
    slain.
Tis true he might amuse himself thus,
nd not be very murderous ;

For as of those who to death were done
The number was exactly *none,*
His Lordship, in his soul's elation,
Did take a bloodless recreation—

The manner of
the citie's
rejoycings, Going home again, he did ordain
A very splendid cold collation
For the magistrates and the corporation ;
Likewise a grand illumination
For the amusement of the nation.

That night the theatres were free,
The conduits they ran Malvoisie ;
Each house that night did beam with light
And sound with mirth and jollity :

And its impiety. But shame, O shame ! not a soul in the town,
Now the city was safe and the Cossacks flown,
Ever thought of the bountiful saint by whose care
      The town had been rid of these terrible Turks—
Said ever a prayer to that patroness fair
      For these her wondrous works !

How the priest,
Hyacinth,
waited at
church, and
nobody came
thither. Lord Hyacinth waited, the meekest of priors—
He waited at church with the rest of his friars ;
He went there at noon and he waited till ten,
Expecting in vain the Lord Mayor and his men.

He waited and waited from mid-day to dark ;
But in vain—you might search through the whole of th
      church,
Not a layman, alas ! to the city's disgrace,
From mid-day to dark showed his nose in the place.

The pew-woman, organist, beadle, and clerk,
Kept away from their work, and were dancing like mad
Away in the streets with the other mad people,
Not thinking to pray, but to guzzle and tipple
      Wherever the drink might be had.

XII.

How he went
forth to bid
them to prayer. Amidst this din and revelry throughout the city roaring,
The silver moon rose silently, and high in heaven soaring ;
Prior Hyacinth was fervently upon his knees adoring :
" Towards my precious patroness this conduct sure unfair is
I cannot think, I must confess, what keeps the dignitaries
And our good Mayor away, unless some business them con
      traries."

puts his long white mantle on, and forth the Prior
  sallies—
s pious thoughts were bent upon good deeds and not on
  malice):
avens! how the banquet lights they shone about the
  Mayor's palace!
out the hall the scullions ran with meats both fresh and
  potted;
pages came with cup and can, all for the guests
  allotted;
, how they jeered that good fat man as up the stairs he
  trotted!

How the grooms
and lacqueys
jeered him.

entered in the ante-rooms where sat the Mayor's
  court in;
found a pack of drunken grooms a-dicing and a-sporting;
e horrid wine and 'bacco fumes, they set the Prior
  a-snorting!
e Prior thought he'd speak about their sins before he
  went hence,
d lustily began to shout of sin and of repentance;
e rogues, they kicked the Prior out before he'd done a
  sentence!

d having got no portion small of buffeting and tussling,
t last he reached the banquet-hall, where sat the Mayor
  a-guzzling,
nd by his side his lady tall dressed out in white sprig
  muslin.
round the table in a ring the guests were drinking
  heavy;
ney drank the Church, and drank the King, and the Army
  and the Navy;
a fact they'd toasted everything. The Prior said, "God
  save ye!"

And the mayor,
mayoress, and
aldermen, being
tipsie, refused
to go to church.

he Mayor cried, "Bring a silver cup—there's one upon
  the buffet;
nd, Prior, have the venison up—it's capital *réchauffé*.
nd so, Sir Priest, you've come to sup? And pray you,
  how's Saint Sophy?"

The Prior's face quite red was grown with horror and wi
    anger ;
He flung the proffered goblet down—it made a hideo
    clangour ;
And 'gan a-preaching with a frown — he was a fier
    haranguer.

He tried the Mayor and aldermen—they all set up a-jeerin₃
He tried the common-councilmen — they too began
    sneering :
He turned towards the May'ress then, and hoped to get
    hearing.
He knelt and seized her dinner-dress, made of the musl
    snowy,
" To church, to church, my sweet mistress ! " he cried : " t₁
    way I'll show ye."
Alas, the Lady Mayoress fell back as drunk as Chloe !

XIII.

How the Prior
went back alone,
Out from this dissolute and drunken Court
    Went the good Prior, his eyes with weeping dim :
He tried the people of a meaner sort—
They too, alas, were bent upon their sport,
    And not a single soul would follow him !
But all were swigging schnapps and guzzling beer.

He found the cits, their daughters, sons, and spouses,
Spending the live-long night in fierce carouses :
    Alas, unthinking of the danger near !
One or two sentinels the ramparts guarded,
    The rest were sharing in the general feast :
" God wot, our tipsy town is poorly warded ;
    Sweet Saint Sophia help us ! " cried the priest.

Alone he entered the cathedral gate,
    Careful he locked the mighty oaken door ;
Within his company of monks did wait,
    A dozen poor old pious men—no more.
    Oh, but it grieved the gentle Prior sore,
To think of those lost souls, given up to drink and fate ₃

The mighty outer gate well barred and fast,
   The poor old friars stirred their poor old bones,
   And pattering swiftly on the damp cold stones,
They through the solitary chancel passed.
The chancel walls looked black and dim and vast,
   And rendered, ghost-like, melancholy tones.

And shut himself into Saint Sophia's chapel with his brethren.

Onward the fathers sped, till coming nigh a
   Small iron gate, the which they entered quick at,
   They locked and double-locked the inner wicket
And stood within the chapel of Sophia.
Vain were it to describe this sainted place,
   Vain to describe that celebrated trophy,
   The venerable statue of Saint Sophy,
Which formed its chiefest ornament and grace.

Here the good Prior, his personal griefs and sorrows
   In his extreme devotion quickly merging,
At once began to pray with voice sonorous ;
The other friars joined in pious chorus,
   And passed the night in singing, praying, scourging,
   In honour of Sophia, that sweet virgin.

XIV.

   Leaving thus the pious priest in
      Humble penitence and prayer,
   And the greedy cits a-feasting,
      Let us to the walls repair.

The episode Sneezoff and Katinka.

   Walking by the sentry-boxes,
      Underneath the silver moon,
   Lo ! the sentry boldly cocks his—
      Boldly cocks his musketoon.

   Sneezoff was his designation.
      Fair-haired boy, for ever pitied ;
   For to take his cruel station,
      He but now Katinka quitted.

   Poor in purse were both, but rich in
      Tender love's delicious plenties ;
   She a damsel of the kitchen,
      He a haberdasher's 'prentice.

'Tinka, maiden tender-hearted,
    Was dissolved in tearful fits,
On that fatal night she parted
    From her darling fair-haired Fritz.

Warm her soldier lad she wrapt in
    Comforter and muffettee ;
Called him " general " and " captain,"
    Though a simple private he.

" On your bosom wear this plaster,
    'Twill defend you from the cold ;
In your pipe smoke this canaster—
    Smuggled 'tis, my love, and old.

" All the night, my love, I'll miss you."
    Thus she spoke ; and from the door
Fair-haired Sneezoff made his issue,
    To return, alas, no more.

He it is who calmly walks his
    Walk beneath the silver moon ;
He it is who boldly cocks his
    Detonating musketoon.

He the bland canaster puffing,
    As upon his round he paces,
Sudden sees a ragamuffin
    Clambering swiftly up the glacis.

" Who goes there ? " exclaims the sentry ;
    " When the sun has once gone down
No one ever makes an entry
    Into this here fortified town ! "

How the sentrie
Sneezoff was
surprised and
slayn.

Shouted thus the watchful Sneezoff ;
    But, ere any one replied,
Wretched youth ! he fired his piece off,
    Started, staggered, groaned, and died !

XV.

Ah, full well might the sentinel cry, " Who goes there ? "
But echo was frightened too much to declare.
Who goes there ? who goes there ?   Can any one swear
To the number of sands *sur les bords de la mer*,
Or the whiskers of D'Orsay count down to a hair ?
As well might you tell of the sands the amount,
Or number each hair in each curl of the Count,
As ever proclaim the number and name
Of the hundreds and thousands that up the wall came !
Down, down the knaves poured with fire and with
    sword :
There were thieves from the Danube and rogues from the
    Don ;
There were Turks and Wallacks, and shouting Cossacks ;
Of all nations and regions, and tongues and religions—
Jew, Christian, idolater, Frank, Mussulman :
Ah, a horrible sight was Kioff that night !
The gates were all taken—no chance e'en of flight ;
And with torch and with axe the bloody Cossacks
Went hither and thither a-hunting in packs :
They slashed and they slew both Christian and Jew—
Women and children, they slaughtered them too.
Some, saving their throats, plunged into the moats,
Or the river—but oh, they had burned all the boats !

.   .   .   .   .   .

But here let us pause—for I can't pursue further
This scene of rack, ravishment, ruin, and murther.
Too well did the cunning old Cossack succeed !
His plan of attack was successful indeed !
The night was his own—the town it was gone ;
'Twas a heap still a-burning of timber and stone.
One building alone had escaped from the fires,
Saint Sophy's fair church, with its steeples and spires.
          Calm, stately, and white,
          It stood in the light ;
And as if 'twould defy all the conqueror's power,—
          As if nought had occurred,
          Might clearly be heard
The chimes ringing soberly every half-hour !

Marginal notes:

How the Cossacks rushed in suddenly and took the citie.

Of the Cossack troops,

And of their manner of burning, murdering, and ravishing.

How they burned the whole citie down, save the church,

Whereof the bells began to ring.

XVI.

The city was defunct—silence succeeded
    Unto its last fierce agonising yells ;
And then it was the conqueror first heeded
    The sound of these calm bells.

How the Cossack
chief bade them
burn the church
too.

Furious towards his aides-de-camp he turns,
    And (speaking as if Byron's works he knew)
" Villains ! " he fiercely cries, " the city burns,
    Why not the temple too ?
Burn me yon church, and murder all within ! "
    The Cossacks thundered at the outer door ;

How they
stormed it ;
and of Hyacinth,
his anger
thereat,

And Father Hyacinth, who heard the din,
(And thought himself and brethren in distress,
Deserted by their lady patroness)
    Did to her statue turn, and thus his woes outpour.

XVII.

His prayer to the
Saint Sophia.

" And is it thus, O falsest of the saints,
    Thou hearest our complaints ?
Tell me, did ever my attachment falter
    To serve thy altar ?
Was not thy name, ere ever I did sleep,
    The last upon my lip ?
Was not thy name the very first that broke
    From me when I awoke ?
Have I not tried with fasting, flogging, penance,
    And mortified counténance
For to find favour, Sophy, in thy sight ?
    And lo ! this night,
Forgetful of my prayers and thine own promise,
    Thou turnest from us ;
Lettest the heathen enter in our city,
    And, without pity,
Murder our burghers, seize upon their spouses,
    Burn down their houses !
Is such a breach of faith to be endured ?
    See what a lurid
Light from the insolent invader's torches
    Shines on your porches !
E'en now, with thundering battering-ram and hammer
    And hideous clamour,

With axemen, swordsmen, pikemen, billmen, bowmen,
    The conquering foemen,
O Sophy! beat your gate about your ears,
    Alas! and here's
A humble company of pious men,
    Like muttons in a pen,
Whose souls shall quickly from their bodies be thrusted,
    Because in you they trusted.
Do you not know the Calmuc chief's desires—
    KILL ALL THE FRIARS!
And you, of all the saints most false and fickle,
    Leave us in this abominable pickle."

"RASH HYACINTHUS!"   *The statue sud-*
    (Here, to the astonishment of all her backers,   *denlie speaks*
Saint Sophy, opening wide her wooden jaws,
    Like to a pair of German walnut-crackers,
Began), "I did not think you had been thus,—
O monk of little faith! Is it because
A rascal scum of filthy Cossack heathen
Besiege our town, that you distrust in *me*, then?
Think'st thou that I, who in a former day
Did walk across the sea of Marmora
(Not mentioning, for shortness, other seas),—
That I, who skimmed the broad Borysthenes,
Without so much as wetting of my toes,
Am frightened at a set of men like *those?*
I have a mind to leave you to your fate:
Such cowardice as this my scorn inspires."

    Saint Sophy was here   *But is inter-*
      Cut short in her words,—   *rupted by the*
For at this very moment in tumbled the gate,   *breaking in of*
      And with a wild cheer,   *the Cossacks.*
        And a clashing of swords,
    Swift through the church porches,
      With a waving of torches,
      And a shriek and a yell
    Like the devils of hell,
      With pike and with axe
      In rushed the Cossacks,—
In rushed the Cossacks, crying, "MURDER THE FRIARS!"

Ah ! what a thrill felt Hyacinth,
    When he heard that villanous shout Calmuc !
Now, thought he, my trial beginneth ;
    Saints, O give me courage and pluck !
" Courage, boys, 'tis useless to funk ! "
    Thus unto the friars he began :
" Never let it be said that a monk
    Is not likewise a gentleman.
Though the patron saint of the church,
    Spite of all that we've done and we've pray'd,
Leaves us wickedly here in the lurch,
    Hang it, gentlemen, who's afraid ? "

As thus the gallant Hyacinthus spoke,
    He, with an air as easy and as free as
If the quick-coming murder were a joke,
    Folded his robes around his sides, and took
Place under sainted Sophy's legs of oak,
    Like Cæsar at the statue of Pompeius.
The monks no leisure had about to look
    (Each being absorbed in his particular case),
Else had they seen with what celestial grace
    A wooden smile stole o'er the saint's mahogany face.

" Well done, well done, Hyacinthus, my son ! "
    Thus spoke the sainted statue,
" Though you doubted me in the hour of need,
And spoke of me very rude indeed,
You deserve good luck for showing such pluck,
    And I won't be angry at you."

The monks bystanding, one and all,
    Of this wondrous scene beholders,
To this kind promise listened content,
And couldn't contain their astonishment,
When Saint Sophia moved and went
Down from her wooden pedestal,
    And twisted her legs, sure as eggs is eggs,
    Round Hyacinthus's shoulders !

" Ho ! forwards," cries Sophy, " there's no time for waiting,
The Cossacks are breaking the very last gate in :
See, the glare of their torches shines red through the grating;
We've still the back door, and two minutes or more.

Now, boys, now or never, we must make for the river,
  For we only are safe on the opposite shore.
Run swiftly to-day, lads, if ever you ran,—
Put out your best leg, Hyacinthus, my man ;
And I'll lay five to two that you carry us through,
  Only scamper as fast as you can."

XVIII.

Away went the priest through the little back door,   He runneth
And light on his shoulders the image he bore :
  The honest old priest was not punished the least,
Though the image was eight feet, and he measured four.
Away went the Prior, and the monks at his tail
Went snorting, and puffing, and panting full sail ;
  And just as the last at the back door had passed,
In furious hunt behold at the front
The Tartars so fierce, with their terrible cheers ;
With axes, and halberts, and muskets, and spears,
With torches a-flaming the chapel now came in.
They tore up the mass-book, they stamped on the psalter,
They pulled the gold crucifix down from the altar ;
The vestments they burned with their blasphemous fires,
And many cried, " Curse on them ! where are the friars ? "
When loaded with plunder, yet seeking for more,
One chanced to fling open the little back door,
Spied out the friars' white robes and long shadows
In the moon, scampering over the meadows,
And stopped the Cossacks in the midst of their arsons,
By crying out lustily, " THERE GO THE PARSONS ! "
With a whoop and a yell, and a scream and a shout,   And the Tartars
At once the whole murderous body turned out ;   after him.
And swift as the hawk pounces down on the pigeon,
Pursued the poor short-winded men of religion.

When the sound of that cheering came to the monks' How the friars
    hearing,   sweated,
  O Heaven ! how the poor fellows panted and blew !
At fighting not cunning, unaccustomed to running,
  When the Tartars came up, what the deuce should they
    do ?
" They'll make us all martyrs, those bloodthirsty Tartars ! "
  Quoth fat Father Peter to fat Father Hugh.

The shouts they came clearer, the foe they drew nearer ;
     Oh, how the bolts whistled, and how the lights shone !
" I cannot get further, this running is murther ;
     Come carry me, some one ! " cried big Father John.
And even the statue grew frightened : " Od rat you ! "
     It cried, " Mr. Prior, I wish you'd get on ! "
On tugged the good friar, but nigher and nigher
Appeared the fierce Russians, with sword and with fire.
On tugged the good prior at Saint Sophy's desire,—
A scramble through bramble, through mud, and through
     mire,
The swift arrows' whizziness causing a dizziness.
Nigh done his business, fit to expire,
Father Hyacinth tugged, and the monks they tugged
     after :
The foemen pursued with a horrible laughter,

And the pursuers fixed arrows into their tayls.

And hurl'd their long spears round the poor brethren's ears
So true, that next day in the coat of each priest,
Though never a wound was given, there were found
     A dozen arrows at least.

How, at the last gasp,

     Now the chase seemed at its worst,
     Prior and monks were fit to burst ;
     Scarce you knew the which was first,
         Or pursuers or pursued ;
     When the statue, by Heaven's grace,
     Suddenly did change the face
     Of this interesting race,
         As a saint, sure, only could.

For as the jockey who at Epsom rides,
     When that his steed is spent and punished sore,
Diggeth his heels into the courser's sides,
     And thereby makes him run one or two furlongs more ;
     Even thus, betwixt the eighth rib and the ninth,
The saint rebuked the Prior, that weary creeper ;
     Fresh strength into his limbs her kicks imparted,
     One bound he made, as gay as when he started.

The friars won, and jumped into Borysthenes fluvius.

Yes, with his brethren clinging at his cloak,
The statue on his shoulders—fit to choke—
One most tremendous bound made Hyacinth,
And soused friars, statue, and all, slapdash into the Dnieper !

XIX.

nd when the Russians, in a fiery rank,
  Panting and fierce, drew up along the shore ;
  (For here the vain pursuing they forbore,
or cared they to surpass the river's bank) ;
hen, looking from the rocks and rushes dank,
  A sight they witnessed never seen before,
nd which, with its accompaniments glorious,
  writ i' the golden book, or *liber aureus*.

And how the
Russians saw

lump in the Dnieper flounced the friar and friends,—
  They dangling round his neck, he fit to choke,
  When suddenly his most miraculous cloak
ver the billowy waves itself extends,
own from his shoulders quietly descends
  The venerable Sophy's statue of oak ;
hich, sitting down upon the cloak so ample,
ids all the brethren follow its example !

The statue get
off Hyacinth his
back, and sit
down with the
friars on
Hyacinth his
cloak.

ach at her bidding sat, and sat at ease ;
  The statue 'gan a gracious conversation,
  And (waving to the foe a salutation)
ail'd with her wondering happy protégés
aily adown the wide Borysthenes,
  Until they came unto some friendly nation.
nd when the heathen had at length grown shy of
heir conquest, she one day came back again to Kioff.

How in this
manner of boat
they sayled
away.

XX.

HINK NOT, O READER, THAT WE'RE LAUGHING AT YOU ;
OU MAY GO TO KIOFF NOW AND SEE THE STATUE !

Finis, or the
end.

POCAHONTAS

WEARIED arm and broken sword
  Wage in vain the desperate fight:
  Round him press a countless horde,
He is but a single knight.
Hark! a cry of triumph shrill
  Through the wilderness resounds,
  As, with twenty bleeding wounds,
Sinks the warrior, fighting still.

Now they heap the fatal pyre,
  And the torch of death they light;
Ah! 'tis hard to die of fire!
  Who will shield the captive knight?
Round the stake with fiendish cry
  Wheel and dance the savage crowd,
  Cold the victim's mien, and proud,
And his breast is bared to die.

Who will shield the fearless heart?
  Who avert the murderous blade?
From the throng, with sudden start,
  See there springs an Indian maid.
Quick she stands before the knight:
  "Loose the chain, unbind the ring;
  I am daughter of the King,
And I claim the Indian right!"

Dauntlessly aside she flings
  Lifted axe and thirsty knife;
Fondly to his heart she clings,
  And her bosom guards his life!
In the woods of Powhattan,
  Still 'tis told by Indian fires,
  How a daughter of their sires
Saved the captive Englishman.

FROM POCAHONTAS

RETURNING from the cruel fight
　　How pale and faint appears my knight!
　　He sees me anxious at his side;
"Why seek, my love, your wounds to hide?
Or deem your English girl afraid
To emulate the Indian maid?"

Be mine my husband's grief to cheer,
In peril to be ever near;
Whate'er of ill or woe betide,
To bear it clinging at his side;
The poisoned stroke of fate to ward,
His bosom with my own to guard:
Ah! could it spare a pang to his,
It could not know a purer bliss!
'Twould gladden as it felt the smart,
And thank the hand that flung the dart!

VANITAS VANITATUM

HOW spake of old the Royal Seer?
   (His text is one I love to treat on.)
  This life of ours, he said, is sheer
Mataiotes Mataioteton.

O Student of this gilded Book,
  Declare, while musing on its pages,
If truer words were ever spoke
  By ancient or by modern sages?

The various authors' names but note,*
  French, Spanish, English, Russians, Germans .
And in the volume polyglot,
  Sure you may read a hundred sermons!

What histories of life are here,
  More wild than all romancers' stories;
What wondrous transformations queer,
  What homilies on human glories!

What theme for sorrow or for scorn!
  What chronicle of Fate's surprises—
Of adverse fortune nobly borne,
  Of chances, changes, ruins, rises!

Of thrones upset, and sceptres broke,
  How strange a record here is written!
Of honours, dealt as if in joke;
  Of brave desert unkindly smitten.

* Between a page by Jules Janin, and a poem by the Turkish Ambassador,
in Madame de R——'s album, containing the autographs of kings, princes,
poets, marshals, musicians, diplomatists, statesmen, artists, and men of letters
of all nations.

How low men were, and how they rise !
   How high they were, and how they tumble !
O vanity of vanities !
   O laughable, pathetic jumble !

Here between honest Janin's joke
   And his Turk Excellency's firman,
I write my name upon the book :
   I write my name—and end my sermon.

O Vanity of vanities !
   How wayward the decrees of Fate are ;
How very weak the very wise,
   How very small the very great are !

What mean these stale moralities,
   Sir Preacher, from your desk you mumble ?
Why rail against the great and wise,
   And tire us with your ceaseless grumble ?

Pray choose us out another text,
   O man morose and narrow-minded !
Come turn the page—I read the next,
   And then the next, and still I find it.

Read here how Wealth aside was thrust,
   And Folly set in place exalted ;
How Princes footed in the dust,
   While lacqueys in the saddle vaulted.

Though thrice a thousand years are past
   Since David's son, the sad and splendid,
The weary King Ecclesiast,
   Upon his awful tablets penned it,—

Methinks the text is never stale,
   And life is every day renewing
Fresh comments on the old old tale
   Of Folly, Fortune, Glory, Ruin.

Hark to the Preacher, preaching still
　　He lifts his voice and cries his sermon,
Here at St. Peter's on Cornhill,
　　As yonder on the Mount of Hermon :

For you and me to heart to take
　　(O dear beloved brother readers)
To-day as when the good King spake
　　Beneath the solemn Syrian cedars.

LITTLE BILLEE *

Air—" Il y avait un petit navire."

THERE were three sailors of Bristol city
Who took a boat and went to sea.
But first with beef and captain's biscuits
And pickled pork they loaded she.

There was gorging Jack and guzzling Jimmy,
And the youngest he was little Billee.
Now when they got as far as the Equator
They'd nothing left but one split pea.

Says gorging Jack to guzzling Jimmy,
" I am extremely hungaree."
To gorging Jack says guzzling Jimmy,
" We've nothing left, us must eat we."

Says gorging Jack to guzzling Jimmy,
" With one another we shouldn't agree !
There's little Bill, he's young and tender,
We're old and tough, so let's eat he.

" Oh ! Billy, we're going to kill and eat you,
So undo the button of your chemie."
When Bill received this information
He used his pocket-handkerchie.

" First let me say my catechism,
Which my poor mammy taught to me."
' Make haste, make haste," says guzzling Jimmy,
While Jack pulled out his snickersnee.

---

* As different versions of this popular song have been set to music and sung, no apology is needed for the insertion in these pages of what is considered to be the correct version.

So Billy went up to the main-top gallant mast,
And down he fell on his bended knee.
He scarce had come to the twelfth commandment
When up he jumps. "There's land I see:

"Jerusalem and Madagascar,
And North and South Amerikee:
There's the British flag a-riding at anchor,
With Admiral Napier, K.C.B."

So when they got aboard of the Admiral's
He hanged fat Jack and flogged Jimmee;
But as for little Bill he made him
The Captain of a Seventy-three.

MRS. KATHERINE'S LANTERN

WRITTEN IN A LADY'S ALBUM

COMING from a gloomy court,
   Place of Israelite resort,
    This old lamp I've brought with me.
Madam, on its panes you'll see
The initials K and E."

" An old lantern brought to me?
Ugly, dingy, battered, black ! "
(Here a lady I suppose
Turning up a pretty nose)—
" Pray, sir, take the old thing back.
I've no taste for *bric-à-brac*."

" Please to mark the letters twain "—
(I'm supposed to speak again)—
" Graven on the lantern pane.
Can you tell me who was she,
Mistress of the flowery wreath,
And the anagram beneath—
The mysterious K E ?

Full a hundred years are gone
Since the little beacon shone
From a Venice balcony :
There, on summer nights, it hung,
And her lovers came and sung
To their beautiful K E.

" Hush ! in the canal below
Don't you hear the splash of oars
Underneath the lantern's glow,

And a thrilling voice begins
To the sound of mandolins?—
Begins singing of amore
And delire and dolore—
O the ravishing tenore!

" Lady, do you know the tune?
Ah, we all of us have hummed it!
I've an old guitar has thrummed it,
Under many a changing moon.
Shall I try it? *Do* RE MI . . .
What is this? *Ma foi*, the fact is,
That my hand is out of practice,
And my poor old fiddle cracked is,

" And a man—I let the truth out,—
Who's had almost every tooth out,
Cannot sing as once he sung,
When he was young as you are young,
When he was young and lutes were strung,
And love-lamps in the casement hung."

CATHERINE HAYES

Part I.

IN the reign of King George and Queen Anne,
    In Swift's and in Marlborough's days,
    There lived an unfortunate man,
A man by the name of John Hayes.

A decent respectable life,
    And rather deserving of praise,
Lived John, but his curse was his wife
    —His horrible wife Mrs. Hayes.

A heart more atrociously foul
    Never beat under any one's stays:
As eager for blood as a ghoul
    Was Catherine the wife of John Hayes.

By marriage and John she was bored
    (He'd many ridiculous traits) ;
And she hated her husband and lord,
    This infamous, false Mrs. Hayes.

When madness and fury begin,
    The senses they utterly craze ;
She called two accomplices in,
    And the three of 'em killed Mr. Hayes.

And when they'd completed the act,
    The old *Bailey Chronicle* says,
In several pieces they hacked
    The body of poor Mr. Hayes.

The body and limbs of the dead
    They buried in various ways,
And into the Thames flung his head,
    And there seemed an end of John Hayes.

The head was brought back by the tide,
　　And what was a bargeman's amaze
One day, in the mud, when he spied
　　The horrible head of John Hayes !

In the front of St. Margaret's church
　　(Where the Westminster Scholars act plays)
They stuck the pale head on a perch,
　　None knew 'twas the head of John Hayes.

Long time at the object surprised,
　　Did all the metropolis gaze,
Till some one at last recognised
　　The face of the late Mr. Hayes.

And when people knew it was he
　　They went to his widow straightways,
For who could the murderess be,
　　They said, but the vile Mrs. Hayes ?

As sooner or later 'tis plain
　　For wickedness every one pays.
They hanged the accomplices twain,
　　And burned the foul murderess Hayes.

And a writer who scribbles in prose,
　　And sometimes poetical lays,
The terrible tale did compose
　　Of Mr. and Mrs. John Hayes.

Part II.

Where Shannon's broad wathers pour down
　　And rush to the Imerald seas,
A lady in Limerick Town
　　Was bred, and her name it was Hayes.

Her voice was so sweet and so loud,
　　So favoured her faytures to playse,
No wonder that Oireland was proud
　　Of her beautiful singer, Miss Hayes.

At Neeples and Doblin the fair
  (In towns with whose beautiful bays
I'd loike to see England compare)
  Bright laurils were awarded Miss Hayes.

When she'd dthrive in the Phaynix for air,
  They'd take out the horse from her chaise,
For we honour the gentle and fair,
  And gentle and fair was Miss Hayes.

When she gracefully stepped on the steage
  Our thayatre boomed with huzzays :
And each man was glad to obleege,
  And longed for a look of Miss Hayes.

A Saxon who thinks that he dthraws
  Our porthraits as loike as two pays,
Insulted one day without cause,
  Our innocent singer, Miss Hayes.

And though he meant somebody else
  (At layst so the raycreant says.
Declaring that history tells
  Of another, a wicked Miss Hayes),

Yet Ireland, the free and the brave,
  Says, what's that to do with the case ?
How dare he, the cowardly slave,
  To mintion the name of a Hayes ?

In vain let him say he forgot,
  What base hypocritical pleas !
The miscreant ought to be shot :
  How dare he forget our Miss Hayes !

The *Freeman* in language refined,
  The *Post* whom no prayer can appayse,
Lashed fiercely the wretch who maligned
  The innocent name of a Hayes.

And Grattan upraises the moight
    Of his terrible arrum, and flays
The sides of the shuddering wight
    That ventured to speak of a Hayes.

Accursed let his memory be,
    Who dares to say aught in dispraise
Of Oireland, the land of the free,
    And of beauty and janius and Hayes.

LOVE-SONGS MADE EASY

LOVE-SONGS MADE EASY

SERENADE

N OW the toils of day are over,
  And the sun hath sunk to rest,
  Seeking, like a fiery lover,
The bosom of the blushing West—

The faithful night keeps watch and ward,
  Raising the moon her silver shield,
And summoning the stars to guard
  The slumbers of my fair Mathilde!

The faithful night! Now all things lie
  Hid by her mantle dark and dim,
In pious hope I hither hie,
  And humbly chant mine evening hymn.

Thou art my prayer, my saint, my shrine!
  (For never holy pilgrim kneel'd
Or wept at feet more pure than thine),
  My virgin love, my sweet Mathilde!

THE MINARET BELLS

TINK-A-TINK, tink-a-tink,
    By the light of the star,
    On the blue river's brink,
I heard a guitar.

I heard a guitar
    On the blue waters clear,
And knew by its music
    That Selim was near!

Tink-a-tink, tink-a-tink,
    How the soft music swells,
And I hear the soft clink
    Of the minaret bells!

COME TO THE GREENWOOD TREE

COME to the greenwood tree,
Come where the dark woods be,
Dearest, O come with me!
Let us rove—O my love—O my love!

Come—'tis the moonlight hour:
Dew is on leaf and flower:
Come to the linden bower,—
Let us rove—O my love—O my love!

Dark is the wood, and wide;
Dangers, they say, betide;
But, at my Albert's side,
Nought I fear, O my love—O my love!

Welcome the greenwood tree,
Welcome the forest free,
Dearest, with thee, with thee,
Nought I fear, O my love—O my love!

TO MARY

I SEEM, in the midst of the crowd,
  The lightest of all;
 My laughter rings cheery and loud
In banquet and ball.
My lip hath its smiles and its sneers,
  For all men to see;
But my soul, and my truth, and my tears,
  Are for thee, are for thee!

Around me they flatter and fawn—
  The young and the old,
The fairest are ready to pawn
  Their hearts for my gold.
They sue me—I laugh as I spurn
  The slaves at my knee;
But in faith and in fondness I turn
  Unto thee, unto thee!

WHAT MAKES MY HEART TO THRILL AND GLOW?

THE MAYFAIR LOVE-SONG

WINTER and summer, night and morn,
  I languish at this table dark;
  My office window has a corn-
er looks into St. James's Park.
I hear the foot-guards' bugle horn,
  Their tramp upon parade I mark;
I am a gentleman forlorn,
  I am a Foreign-Office Clerk.

My toils, my pleasures, every one,
  I find are stale, and dull, and slow;
And yesterday, when work was done,
  I felt myself so sad and low,
I could have seized a sentry's gun
  My wearied brains out out to blow.
What is it makes my blood to run?
  What makes my heart to beat and glow?

My notes of hand are burnt, perhaps?
  Some one has paid my tailor's bill?
No: every morn the tailor raps;
  My I O U's are extant still.
I still am prey of debt and dun;
  My elder brother's stout and well.
What is it makes my blood to run?
  What makes my heart to glow and swell?

I know my chief's distrust and hate;
  He says I'm lazy, and I shirk.
Ah! had I genius like the late
  Right Honourable Edmund Burke!

My chance of all promotion's gone,
    I know it is,—he hates me so.
What is it makes my blood to run,
    And all my heart to swell and glow?

Why, why is all so bright and gay?
    There is no change, there is no cause;
My office-time I found to-day
    Disgusting as it ever was.
At three, I went and tried the Clubs,
    And yawned and saunter'd to and fro;
And now my heart jumps up and throbs,
    And all my soul is in a glow.

At half-past four I had the cab;
    I drove as hard as I could go.
The London sky was dirty drab,
    And dirty brown the London snow.
And as I rattled in a cant-
    er down by dear old Bolton Row,
A something made my heart to pant,
    And caused my cheek to flush and glow.

What could it be that made me find
    Old Jawkins pleasant at the Club?
Why was it that I laughed and grinned
    At whist, although I lost the rub?
What was it made me drink like mad
    Thirteen small glasses of Curaçao?
That made my inmost heart so glad,
    And every fibre thrill and glow?

She's home again! she's home, she's home!
    Away all cares and griefs and pain;
I knew she would—she's back from Rome;
    She's home again! she's home again!
"The family's gone abroad," they said,
    September last—they told me so;
Since then my lonely heart is dead,
    My blood, I think's forgot to flow.

She's home again ! away all care !
  O fairest form the world can show !
O beaming eyes ! O golden hair !
  O tender voice, that breathes so low !
O gentlest, softest, purest heart !
  O joy, O hope !—" My tiger, ho ! "
Fitz-Clarence said ; we saw him start—
  He galloped down to Bolton Row.

THE GHAZUL, OR ORIENTAL LOVE-SONG

THE ROCKS

I WAS a timid little antelope ;
   My home was in the rocks, the lonely rocks.

I saw the hunters scouring on the plain ;
I lived among the rocks, the lonely rocks.

I was a-thirsty in the summer-heat ;
I ventured to the tents beneath the rocks.

Zuleikah brought me water from the well ;
Since then I have been faithless to the rocks.

I saw her face reflected in the well ;
Her camels since have marched into the rocks.

I look to see her image in the well :
I only see my eyes, my own sad eyes.
My mother is alone among the rocks.

THE MERRY BARD

ZULEIKAH! The young Agas in the bazaar are slim-waisted and wear yellow slippers. I am old and hideous. One of my eyes is out, and the hairs of my beard are mostly grey. Praise be to Allah! I am a merry bard.

There is a bird upon the terrace of the Emir's chief wife. Praise be to Allah! He has emeralds on his neck, and a ruby tail. I am a merry bard. He deafens me with his diabolical screaming.

There is a little brown bird in the basket-maker's cage. Praise be to Allah! He ravishes my soul in the moonlight. I am a merry bard.

The peacock is an Aga, but the little bird is a Bulbul.

I am a little brown Bulbul. Come and listen in the moonlight. Praise be to Allah! I am a merry bard.

THE CAÏQUE

YONDER to the kiosk, beside the creek,
    Paddle the swift caïque.
    Thou brawny oarsman with the sunburnt cheek,
Quick ! for it soothes my heart to hear the Bulbul speak.

Ferry me quickly to the Asian shores,
Swift bending to your oars.
Beneath the melancholy sycamores,
Hark ! what a ravishing note the love-lorn Bulbul pours !

Behold, the boughs seem quivering with delight,
The stars themselves more bright,
As mid the waving branches out of sight
The Lover of the Rose sits singing through the night.

Under the boughs I sat and listened still,
I could not have my fill.
" How comes," I said, " such music to his bill ?
Tell me for whom he sings so beautiful a trill."

" Once I was dumb," then did the Bird disclose,
" But looked upon the Rose ;
And in the garden where the loved one grows,
I straightway did begin sweet music to compose."

" O bird of song, there's one in this caïque
The Rose would also seek,
So he might learn like you to love and speak."
Then answered me the bird of dusky beak,
" The Rose, the Rose of Love blushes on Leilah's cheek."

MY NORA

BENEATH the gold acacia buds
　　My gentle Nora sits and broods,
　　Far, far away in Boston woods,
　　　　　　　My gentle Nora !

I see the tear-drop in her e'e,
Her bosom's heaving tenderly ;
I know—I know she thinks of me,
　　　　　　　My darling Nora !

And where am I ?　My love, whilst thou
Sitt'st sad beneath the acacia bough,
Where pearl's on neck, and wreath on brow,
　　　　　　　I stand, my Nora !

Mid carcanet and coronet,
Where joy-lamps shine and flowers are set—
Where England's chivalry are met,
　　　　　　　Behold me, Nora !

In this strange scene of revelry,
Amidst this gorgeous chivalry,
A form I saw was like to thee,
　　　　　　　My love, my Nora !

She paused amidst her converse glad ;
The lady saw that I was sad,
She pitied the poor lonely lad,—
　　　　　　　Dost love her, Nora ?

In sooth, she is a lovely dame,
A lip of red, and eye of flame,
And clustering golden locks, the same
　　　　　　　As thine, dear Nora !

Her glance is softer than the dawn's,
Her foot is lighter than the fawn's,
Her breast is whiter than the swan's,
                    Or thine, my Nora!

Oh, gentle breast to pity me!
Oh, lovely Ladye Emily!
Till death—till death I'll think of thee—
                    Of thee and Nora!

FIVE GERMAN DITTIES

FIVE GERMAN DITTIES

A TRAGIC STORY

BY ADELBERT VON CHAMISSO

" ——'s war Einer, dem's zu Herzen gieng."

THERE lived a sage in days of yore,
   And he a handsome pigtail wore;
   But wondered much and sorrowed more
      Because it hung behind him.

He mused upon this curious case,
And swore he'd change the pigtail's place,
And have it hanging at his face,
      Not dangling there behind him

Says he, " The mystery I've found,—
I'll turn me round,"—he turned him round;
      But still it hung behind him.

Then round, and round, and out and in,
All day the puzzled sage did spin;
In vain—it mattered not a pin,—
      The pigtail hung behind him.

And right, and left, and round about,
And up, and down, and in, and out,
He turned; but still the pigtail stout
      Hung steadily behind him.

And though his efforts never slack,
And though he twist, and twirl, and tack,
Alas! still faithful to his back
      The pigtail hangs behind him.

THE CHAPLET

FROM UHLAND

"Es pflückte Blümlein mannigfalt."

A LITTLE girl through field and wood
　　Went plucking flowerets here and there,
　　When suddenly beside her stood
A lady wondrous fair.

The lovely lady smiled, and laid
　　A wreath upon the maiden's brow :
" Wear it ; 'twill blossom soon," she said,
　　" Although 'tis leafless now."

The little maiden older grew
　　And wandered forth of moonlight eves,
And sighed and loved as maids will do ;
　　When, lo ! her wreath bore leaves.

Then was our maid a wife, and hung
　　Upon a joyful bridegroom's bosom ;
When from the garland's leaves there sprung
　　Fair store of blossom.

And presently a baby fair
　　Upon her gentle breast she reared ;
When midst the wreath that bound her hair
　　Rich golden fruit appeared.

But when her love lay cold in death,
　　Sunk in the black and silent tomb,
All sere and withered was the wreath
　　That wont so bright to bloom.

Yet still the withered wreath she wore ;
　　She wore it at her dying hour ;
When, lo ! the wondrous garland bore
　　Both leaf, and fruit, and flower !

THE KING ON THE TOWER

FROM UHLAND

"Da liegen sie alle, die grauen Höhen."

THE cold grey hills they bind me around,
　　The darksome valleys lie sleeping below,
　　But the winds, as they pass o'er all this ground,
　Bring me never a sound of woe.

Oh! for all I have suffered and striven,
　Care has embittered my cup and my feast;
But here is the night and the dark blue heaven,
　And my soul shall be at rest.

O golden legends writ in the skies!
　I turn towards you with longing soul,
And list to the awful harmonies
　Of the Spheres as on they roll.

My hair is grey and my sight nigh gone;
　My sword it rusteth upon the wall;
Right have I spoken, and right have I done;
　When shall I rest me once for all?

O blessed rest! O royal night!
　Wherefore seemeth the time so long
Till I see yon stars in their fullest light,
　And list to their loudest song?

TO A VERY OLD WOMAN

LA MOTTE FOUQUÉ

"Und Du gingst einst, die Myrt' im Haare."

AND thou wert once a maiden fair,
    A blushing virgin warm and young:
    With myrtles wreathed in golden hair,
And glossy brow that knew no care—
    Upon a bridegroom's arm you hung.

The golden locks are silvered now,
    The blushing cheek is pale and wan;
The spring may bloom, the autumn glow,
All's one—in chimney corner thou
    Sitt'st shivering on.–

A moment—and thou sink'st to rest!
To wake perhaps an angel blest
    In the bright presence of thy Lord.
Oh, weary is life's path to all!
Hard is the strife, and light the fall,
    But wondrous the reward!

A CREDO

I.

FOR the sole edification
  Of this decent congregation,
    Goodly people, by your grant
I will sing a holy chant—
    I will sing a holy chant.
If the ditty sound but oddly,
'Twas a father, wise and godly,
    Sang it so long ago—
Then sing as Martin Luther sang,
As Doctor Martin Luther sang:
"Who loves not wine, woman, and song,
He is a fool his whole life long!"

II.

He, by custom patriarchal,
Loved to see the beaker sparkle;
And he thought the wine improved,
Tasted by the lips he loved—
    By the kindly lips he loved.
Friends, I wish this custom pious
Duly were observed by us,
    To combine love, song, wine,
And sing as Martin Luther sang,
As Doctor Martin Luther sang:
"Who loves not wine, woman, and song,
He is a fool his whole life long!"

III.

Who refuses this our Credo,
And who will not sing as we do,
Were he holy as John Knox,
I'd pronounce him heterodox!
  I'd pronounce him heterodox,
And from out this congregation,
With a solemn commination,
  Banish quick the heretic,
Who will not sing as Luther sang,
As Doctor Martin Luther sang:
"Who loves not wine, woman, and song,
He is a fool his whole life long!"

FOUR IMITATIONS OF
BÉRANGER

FOUR IMITATIONS OF
BÉRANGER

LE ROI D'YVETOT

IL était un roi d'Yvetot,
    Peu connu dans l'histoire,
    Se levant tard, se couchant tôt,
    Dormant fort bien sans gloire,
Et couronné par Jeanneton
D'un simple bonnet de coton.
        Dit-on.
    Oh! oh! oh! oh! ah! ah! ah! ah!
    Quel bon petit roi c'était là!
        La, la.

Il fesait ses quatre repas
    Dans son palais de chaume,
Et sur un âne, pas à pas,
    Parcourait son royaume.
Joyeux, simple, et croyant le bien,
Pour toute garde il n'avait rien
        Qu'un chien.
    Oh! oh! oh! oh! ah! ah! ah! ah! &c

Il n'avait de goût onéreux
    Qu'une soif un peu vive ;
Mais, en rendant son peuple heureux,
    Il faut bien qu'un roi vive ;
Lui-même à table, et sans suppôt,
Sur chaque muid levait un pot
        D'impôt.
    Oh! oh! oh! oh! ah! ah! ah! ah! &c.

Aux filles de bonnes maisons
Comme il avait su plaire,
Ses sujets avaient cent raisons
De le nommer leur père :
D'ailleurs il ne levait de ban
Que pour tirer quatre fois l'an
Au blanc.
  Oh! oh! oh! oh! ah! ah! ah! ah! &c.

Il n'agrandit point ses états,
Fut un voisin commode,
Et, modèle des potentats,
Prit le plaisir pour code.
Ce n'est que lorsqu'il expira,
Que le peuple qui l'enterra
Pleura.
  Oh! oh! oh! oh! ah! ah! ah! ah! &c.

On conserve encor le portrait
De ce digne et bon prince ;
C'est l'enseigne d'un cabaret
Fameux dans la province.
Les jours de fête, bien souvent,
La foule s'écrie en buvant
Devant :
  Oh! oh! oh! oh! ah! ah! ah! ah! &c.

THE KING OF YVETOT

THERE was a king of Yvetot,
　　Of whom renown hath little said,
　　Who let all thoughts of glory go,
And dawdled half his days abed ;
And every night, as night came round,
By Jenny with a nightcap crowned,
　　　　Slept very sound :
　　　Sing ho, ho, ho! and he, he, he!
　　　That's the kind of king for me.

And every day it came to pass,
　　That four lusty meals made he ;
And, step by step, upon an ass,
　　Rode abroad, his realms to see ;
And wherever he did stir,
What think you was his escort, sir ?
　　　　Why, an old cur.
　　　Sing ho, ho, ho! &c.

If e'er he went into excess,
　　'Twas from a somewhat lively thirst ;
But he who would his subjects bless,
　　Odd's fish !—must wet his whistle first ;
And so from every cask they got,
Our king did to himself allot
　　　　At least a pot.
　　　Sing ho, ho! &c.

To all the ladies of the land,
　　A courteous king, and kind, was he—
The reason why, you'll understand,
　　They named him Pater Patriæ.
Each year he called his fighting men,
And marched a league from home, and then
　　　　Marched back again.
　　　· Sing ho, ho! &c.

Neither by force nor false pretence,
  He sought to make his kingdom great,
And made (O princes, learn from hence)—
  "Live and let live," his rule of state.
'Twas only when he came to die,
That his people who stood by,
        Were known to cry.
    Sing ho, ho! &c.

The portrait of this best of kings
  Is extant still, upon a sign
That on a village tavern swings,
  Famed in the country for good wine.
The people in their Sunday trim,
Filling their glasses to the brim,
        Look up to him,
      Singing ha, ha, ha! and he, he, **he**
      That's the sort of king for me.

THE KING OF BRENTFORD

ANOTHER VERSION

THERE was a king in Brentford,—of whom no legends tell,
But who, without his glory,—could eat and sleep right well.
His Polly's cotton nightcap,—it was his crown of state,
He slept of evenings early,—and rose of mornings late.

All in a fine mud palace,—each day he took four meals,
And for a guard of honour—a dog ran at his heels ;
Sometimes, to view his kingdoms,—rode forth this monarch good,
And then a prancing jackass—he royally bestrode.

There were no costly habits—with which this king was curst,
Except (and where's the harm on't ?)—a somewhat lively thirst ;
But people must pay taxes,—and kings must have their sport,
So out of every gallon—His Grace he took a quart.

He pleased the ladies round him,—with manners soft and bland ;
With reason good, they named him—the father of his land.
Each year his mighty armies—marched forth in gallant show ;
Their enemies were targets,—their bullets they were tow.

He vexed no quiet neighbour,—no useless conquest made,
But by the laws of pleasure—his peaceful realm he swayed.
And in the years he reigned,—through all this country wide,
There was no cause for weeping,—save when the good man died.

The faithful men of Brentford—do still their king deplore,
His portrait yet is swinging—beside an alehouse door.
And topers, tender-hearted,—regard his honest phiz,
And envy times departed,—that knew a reign like his.

LE GRENIER

JE viens revoir l'asile où ma jeunesse
    De la misère a subi les leçons.
  J'avais vingt ans, une folle maîtresse,
De francs amis et l'amour des chansons.
Bravant le monde et les sots et les sages,
Sans avenir, riche de mon printemps,
Leste et joyeux je montais six étages.
Dans un grenier qu'on est bien à vingt ans !

C'est un grenier, point ne veux qu'on l'ignore.
Là fut mon lit, bien chétif et bien dur ;
Là fut ma table ; et je retrouve encore
Trois pieds d'un vers charbonnés sur le mur.
Apparaissez, plaisirs de mon bel âge,
Que d'un coup d'aile a fustigés le temps :
Vingt fois pour vous j'ai mis ma montre en gage.
Dans un grenier qu'on est bien à vingt ans !

Lisette ici doit surtout apparaître,
Vive, jolie, avec un frais chapeau ;
Déjà sa main à l'étroite fenêtre
Suspend son schal, en guise de rideau.
Sa robe aussi va parer ma couchette ;
Respecte, Amour, ses plis longs et flottans.
J'ai su depuis qui payait sa toilette.
Dans un grenier qu'on est bien à vingt ans !

A table un jour, jour de grande richesse,
De mes amis les voix brillaient en chœur,
Quand jusqu'ici monte un cri d'allégresse :
A Marengo Bonaparte est vainqueur.
Le canon gronde ; un autre chant commence ;
Nous célébrons tant de faits éclatans.
Les rois jamais n'envahiront la France.
Dans un grenier qu'on est bien à vingt ans !

Quittons ce toit où ma raison s'enivre.
Oh ! qu'ils sont loin ces jours si regrettés !
J'échangerais ce qu'il me reste à vivre
Contre un des mois qu'ici Dieu m'a comptés,
Pour rêver gloire, amour, plaisir, folie,
Pour dépenser sa vie en peu d'instans,
D'un long espoir pour la voir embellie.
Dans un grenier qu'on est bien à vingt ans !

THE GARRET

WITH pensive eyes the little room I view,
 Where, in my youth, I weathered it so long,
 With a wild mistress, a staunch friend or two,
And a light heart still breaking into song:
Making a mock of life and all its cares,
 Rich in the glory of my rising sun,
Lightly I vaulted up four pair of stairs,
 In the brave days when I was twenty-one.

Yes ; 'tis a garret—let him know't who will—
 There was my bed—full hard it was and small ;
My table there—and I decipher still
 Half a lame couplet charcoaled on the wall.
Ye joys, that Time hath swept with him away,
 Come to mine eyes, ye dreams of love and fun ;
For you I pawned my watch how many a day,
 In the brave days when I was twenty-one.

And see my little Jessy, first of all ;
 She comes with pouting lips and sparkling eyes :
Behold, how roguishly she pins her shawl
 Across the narrow casement, curtain-wise ;
Now by the bed her petticoat glides down,
 And when did woman look the worse in none ?
I have heard since who paid for many a gown,
 In the brave days when I was twenty-one.

One jolly evening, when my friends and I
 Made happy music with our songs and cheers,
A shout of triumph mounted up thus high,
 And distant cannon opened on our ears :
We rise,—we join in the triumphant strain,—
 Napoleon conquers—Austerlitz is won—
Tyrants shall never tread us down again,
 In the brave days when I was twenty-one.

Let us begone—the place is sad and strange—
　　How far, far off, these happy times appear;
All that I have to live I'd gladly change
　　For one such month as I have wasted here—
To draw long dreams of beauty, love, and power,
　　From founts of hope that never will outrun,
And drink all life's quintessence in an hour,
　　Give me the days when I was twenty-one.

ROGER-BONTEMPS

AUX gens atrabilaires
    Pour exemple donné,
    En un temps de misères
Roger-Bontemps est né.
Vivre obscur à sa guise,
Narguer les mécontens ;
Eh, gai ! c'est la devise
Du gros Roger-Bontemps.

Du chapeau de son père
Coiffé dans les grands jours ;
De roses ou de lierre
Le rajeunir toujours ;
Mettre un manteau de bure,
Vieil ami de vingt ans ;
Eh, gai ! c'est la parure
Du gros Roger-Bontemps.

Posséder dans sa hutte
Une table, un vieux lit,
Des cartes, une flûte,
Un broc que Dieu remplit ;
Un portrait de maîtresse,
Un coffre et rien dedans ;
Eh, gai ! c'est la richesse
Du gros Roger-Bontemps.

Aux enfans de la ville
Montrer de petits jeux ;
Etre feseur habile
De contes graveleux ;
Ne parler que de danse
Et d'almanachs chantans :
Eh, gai ! c'est la science
Du gros Roger-Bontemps.

Faute de vins d'élite,
Sabler ceux du canton :
Préférer Marguerite
Aux dames du grand ton :
De joie et de tendresse
Remplir tous ses instans :
Eh, gai ! c'est la sagesse
Du gros Roger-Bontemps.

Dire au ciel : Je me fie,
Mon père, à ta bonté ;
De ma philosophie
Pardonne la gaîté :
Que ma saison dernière
Soit encore un printemps ;
Eh, gai ! c'est la prière
Du gros Roger-Bontemps.

Vous pauvres, pleins d'envie,
Vous riches, désireux,
Vous, dont le char dévie
Après un cours heureux ;
Vous, qui perdrez peut-être
Des titres éclatans,
Eh, gai ! prenez pour maître
Le gros Roger-Bontemps.

JOLLY JACK

WHEN fierce political debate
  Throughout the isle was storming,
  And Rads attacked the throne and state,
And Tories the reforming,
To calm the furious rage of each,
 And right the land demented,
Heaven send us Jolly Jack, to teach
 The way to be contented.

Jack's bed was straw, 'twas warm and soft,
 His chair, a three-legged stool;
His broken jug was emptied oft,
 Yet, somehow, always full.
His mistress' portrait decked the wall,
 His mirror had a crack;
Yet, gay and glad, though this was all
 His wealth, lived Jolly Jack.

To give advice to avarice,
 Teach pride its mean condition,
And preach good sense to dull pretence,
 Was honest Jack's high mission.
Our simple statesman found his rule
 Of moral in the flagon,
And held his philosophic school
 Beneath the " George and Dragon."

When village Solons cursed the Lords,
 And called the malt-tax sinful,
Jack heeded not their angry words,
 But smiled and drank his skinful.
And when men wasted health and life
 In search of rank and riches,
Jack marked aloof the paltry strife,
 And wore his threadbare breeches.

" I enter not the church," he said,
    " But I'll not seek to rob it ; "
So worthy Jack Joe Miller read,
    While others studied Cobbett.
His talk it was of feast and fun ;
    His guide the Almanack ;
From youth to age thus gaily run
    The life of Jolly Jack.

And when Jack prayed, as oft he would,
    He humbly thanked his Maker ;
" I am," said he, " O Father good !
    Nor Catholic nor Quaker :
Give each his creed, let each proclaim
    His catalogue of curses ;
I trust in Thee, and not in them,
    In Thee and in Thy mercies !

" Forgive me if, midst all Thy works,
    No hint I see of damning ;
And think there's faith among the Turks,
    And hope for e'en the Brahmin.
Harmless my mind is, and my mirth,
    And kindly is my laughter ;
I cannot see the smiling earth,
    And think there's hell hereafter."

Jack died ; he left no legacy,
    Save that his story teaches :—
Content to peevish poverty ;
    Humility to riches.
Ye scornful great, ye envious small,
    Come follow in his track ;
We all were happier, if we all
    Would copy JOLLY JACK.

IMITATION OF HORACE

IMITATION OF HORACE

TO HIS SERVING BOY

PERSICOS odi,
    Puer, apparatus ;
    Displicent nexæ
Philyrâ coronæ :
Mitte sectari,
Rosa quo locorum
Sera moretur.

Simplici myrto
Nihil allabores,
Sedulus, curo :
Neque te ministrum
Dedecet myrtus,
Neque me sub arctâ
Vite bibentem.

AD MINISTRAM

DEAR Lucy, you know what my wish is,—
    I hate all your Frenchified fuss :
    Your silly entrées and made dishes
    Were never intended for us.
No footman in lace and in ruffles
    Need dangle behind my arm-chair ;
And never mind seeking for truffles,
    Although they be ever so rare.

But a plain leg of mutton, my Lucy,
    I prithee get ready at three :
Have it smoking, and tender, and juicy,
    And what better meat can there be ?
And when it has feasted the master,
    'Twill amply suffice for the maid ;
Meanwhile I will smoke my canaster,
    And tipple my ale in the shade.

OLD FRIENDS WITH
NEW FACES

OLD FRIENDS WITH
NEW FACES

OLD FRIENDS WITH
NEW FACES

FRIAR'S SONG

SOME love the matin-chimes, which tell
    The hour of prayer to sinner:
    But better far's the mid-day bell,
Which speaks the hour of dinner;
For when I see a smoking fish,
    Or capon drown'd in gravy,
Or noble haunch on silver dish,
    Full glad I sing my ave.

My pulpit is an alehouse bench,
    Whereon I sit so jolly;
A smiling rosy country wench
    My saint and patron holy.
I kiss her cheek so red and sleek,
    I press her ringlets wavy,
And in her willing ear I speak
    A most religious ave.

And if I'm blind, yet Heaven is kind,
    And holy saints forgiving;
For sure he leads a right good life
    Who thus admires good living.
Above, they say, our flesh is air,
    Our blood celestial ichor:
Oh, grant! mid all the changes there,
    They may not change our liquor!

KING CANUTE

KING CANUTE was weary-hearted; he had reigned for years a score,
Battling, struggling, pushing, fighting, killing much and robbing more;
And he thought upon his actions, walking by the wild sea-shore.

'Twixt the Chancellor and Bishop walked the King with steps sedate,
Chamberlains and grooms came after, silversticks and goldsticks great,
Chaplains, aides-de-camp, and pages,—all the officers of state.

Sliding after like a shadow, pausing when he chose to pause,
If a frown his face contracted, straight the courtiers dropped their jaws;
If to laugh the King was minded, out they burst in loud hee-haws.

But that day a something vexed him, that was clear to old and young:
Thrice his Grace had yawned at table, when his favourite gleemen sung,
Once the Queen would have consoled him, but he bade her hold her tongue.

"Something ails my gracious master," cried the Keeper of the Seal.
"Sure, my Lord, it is the lampreys served to dinner, or the veal?"
"Psha!" exclaimed the angry monarch. "Keeper, 'tis not that I feel.

"'Tis the *heart*, and not the dinner, fool, that doth my rest impair:
Can a king be great as I am, prithee, and yet know no care?
Oh, I'm sick, and tired, and weary."—Some one cried, "The King's arm-chair!"

Then towards the lacqueys turning, quick my Lord the Keeper
    nodded,
Straight the King's great chair was brought him by two footmen
    able-bodied ;
Languidly he sank into it : it was comfortably wadded.

"Leading on my fierce companions," cried he, "over storm and
    brine,
I have fought and I have conquered ! Where was glory like to
    mine ?"
Loudly all the courtiers echoed : "Where is glory like to thine ?"

"What avail me all my kingdoms ? Weary am I now and old ;
Those fair sons I have begotten long to see me dead and cold ;
Would I were, and quiet buried underneath the silent mould !

"Oh, remorse, the writhing serpent ! at my bosom tears and bites ;
Horrid horrid things I look on, though I put out all the lights ;
Ghosts of ghastly recollections troop about my bed at nights.

"Cities burning, convents blazing, red with sacrilegious fires ;
Mothers weeping, virgins screaming vainly for their slaughtered
    sires."—
"Such a tender conscience," cries the Bishop, "every one admires.

"But for such unpleasant bygones cease, my gracious lord, to
    search,
They're forgotten and forgiven by our Holy Mother Church ;
Never, never does she leave her benefactors in the lurch.

"Look ! the land is crowned with minsters, which your Grace's
    bounty raised ;
Abbeys filled with holy men, where you and Heaven are daily
    praised :
You, my Lord, to think of dying? on my conscience I'm amazed !"

"Nay, I feel," replied King Canute, "that my end is drawing near."
"Don't say so," exclaimed the courtiers (striving each to squeeze
    a tear).
"Sure your Grace is strong and lusty, and may live this fifty year."

"Live these fifty years !" the Bishop roared, with actions made
    to suit.
"Are you mad, my good Lord Keeper, thus to speak of King Canute?
Men have lived a thousand years, and sure His Majesty will do't.

"Adam, Enoch, Lamech, Cainan, Mahaleel, Methuselah,
Lived nine hundred years apiece, and mayn't the King as well
    as they?"
"Fervently," exclaimed the Keeper, "fervently I trust he may."

"*He* to die?" resumed the Bishop.   "He a mortal like to *us?*
Death was not for him intended, though *communis omnibus:*
Keeper, you are irreligious for to talk and cavil thus.

"With his wondrous skill in healing ne'er a doctor can compete,
Loathsome lepers, if he touch them, start up clean upon their feet;
Surely he could raise the dead up, did his Highness think it meet.

"Did not once the Jewish captain stay the sun upon the hill,
And, the while he slew the foemen, bid the silver moon stand still?
So, no doubt, could gracious Canute, if it were his sacred will."

"Might I stay the sun above us, good Sir Bishop?" Canute cried;
"Could I bid the silver moon to pause upon her heavenly ride?
If the moon obeys my orders, sure I can command the tide.

"Will the advancing waves obey me, Bishop, if I make the sign?"
Said the Bishop, bowing lowly, "Land and sea, my Lord, are thine."
Canute turned towards the ocean—"Back!" he said, "thou foaming
    brine.

"From the sacred shore I stand on, I command thee to retreat;
Venture not, thou stormy rebel, to approach thy master's seat:
Ocean, be thou still!   I bid thee come not nearer to my feet!"

But the sullen ocean answered with a louder deeper roar,
And the rapid waves drew nearer, falling sounding on the shore;
Back the Keeper and the Bishop, back the King and courtiers bore.

And he sternly bade them never more to kneel to human clay,
But alone to praise and worship That which earth and seas obey;
And his golden crown of empire never wore he from that day.
King Canute is dead and gone: Parasites exist alway.

THE WILLOW-TREE

KNOW ye the willow-tree
  Whose grey leaves quiver,
  Whispering gloomily
 To yon pale river?
Lady, at eventide
 Wander not near it:
They say its branches hide
 A sad, lost spirit!

Once to the willow-tree
 A maid came fearful;
Pale seemed her cheek to be,
 Her blue eye tearful.
Soon as she saw the tree,
 Her step moved fleeter;
No one was there—ah me!
 No one to meet her!

Quick beat her heart to hear
 The far bells' chime
Toll from the chapel-tower
 The trysting time:
But the red sun went down
 In golden flame,
And though she looked round,
 Yet no one came!

Presently came the night,
 Sadly to greet her,—
Moon in her silver light,
 Stars in their glitter;
Then sank the moon away
 Under the billow,
Still wept the maid alone—
 There by the willow!

Through the long darkness,
    By the stream rolling,
Hour after hour went on
    Tolling and tolling.
Long was the darkness,
    Lonely and stilly;
Shrill came the night-wind,
    Piercing and chilly.

Shrill blew the morning breeze,
    Biting and cold,
Bleak peers the grey dawn
    Over the wold.
Bleak over moor and stream
    Looks the grey dawn,
Grey, with dishevelled hair,
Still stands the willow there—
    THE MAID IS GONE!

Domine, Domine!
    Sing we a litany,
Sing for poor maiden-hearts broken and weary;
    Domine, Domine!
    Sing we a litany,
Wail we and weep we a wild Miserere!

THE WILLOW-TREE

I.

LONG by the willow-trees
    Vainly they sought her,
    Wild rang the mother's screams
O'er the grey water :
"Where is my lovely one ?
    Where is my daughter ?

II.

"Rouse thee, Sir Constable—
    Rouse thee and look ;
Fisherman, bring your net,
    Boatman, your hook.
Beat in the lily-beds,
    Dive in the brook ! "

III.

Vainly the constable
    Shouted and called her ;
Vainly the fisherman
    Beat the green alder ;
Vainly he flung the net,
    Never it hauled her !

IV.

Mother beside the fire
    Sat, her nightcap in ;

Father, in easy chair,
    Gloomily napping,
When at the window-sill
    Came a light tapping!

v.

And a pale countenance
    Looked through the casement,
Loud beat the mother's heart,
    Sick with amazement,
And at the vision which
    Came to surprise her,
Shrieked in an agony—
    "Lor! it's Elizar!"

vi.

Yes, 'twas Elizabeth—
    Yes, 'twas their girl;
Pale was her cheek, and her
    Hair out of curl.
"Mother!" the loving one,
    Blushing, exclaimed,
"Let not your innocent
    Lizzy be blamed.

vii.

"Yesterday, going to Aunt
    Jones's to tea,
Mother, dear mother, I
    Forgot the door-key!
And as the night was cold,
    And the way steep,
Mrs. Jones kept me to
    Breakfast and sleep."

viii.

Whether her Pa and Ma
    Fully believed her,
That we shall never know,
    Stern they received her;

And for the work of that
 Cruel, though short, night,
Sent her to bed without
 Tea for a fortnight.

IX.

MORAL

Hey diddle diddlety,
* Cat and the Fiddlety,*
Maidens of England, take caution by she !
* Let love and suicide*
* Never tempt you aside,*
And always remember to take the door-key.

WHEN MOONLIKE ORE THE
HAZURE SEAS

WHEN moonlike ore the hazure seas
    In soft effulgence swells,
     When silver jews and balmy breaze
Bend down the Lily's bells;
When calm and deap, the rosy sleap
    Has lapt your soal in dreems,
R Hangeline! R lady mine!
    Dost thou remember Jeames?

I mark thee in the Marble All,
    Where England's loveliest shine—
I say the fairest of them hall
    Is Lady Hangeline.
My soul, in desolate eclipse,
    With recollection teems—
And then I hask, with weeping lips,
    Dost thou remember Jeames?

Away! I may not tell thee hall
    This soughring heart endures—
There is a lonely sperrit-call
    That Sorrow never cures;
There is a little, little Star,
    That still above me beams;
It is the Star of Hope—but ar!
    Dost thou remember Jeames?

ATRA CURA

B EFORE I lost my five poor wits,
   I mind me of a Romish clerk,
   Who sang how Care, the phantom dark,
Beside the belted horseman sits.
Methought I saw the grisly sprite
Jump up but now behind my Knight.

And though he gallop as he may,
I mark that cursèd monster black
Still sits behind his honour's back,
Tight squeezing of his heart alway.
Like two black Templars sit they there
Beside one crupper, Knight and Care.

No knight am I with pennoned spear
To prance upon a bold destrere :
I will not have black Care prevail
Upon my long-eared charger's tail ;
For lo, I am a witless fool,
And laugh at Grief and ride a mule.

COMMANDERS OF THE FAITHFUL

THE Pope he is a happy man,
 His Palace is the Vatican,
 And there he sits and drains his can:
The Pope he is a happy man.
I often say when I'm at home,
I'd like to be the Pope of Rome.

And then there's Sultan Saladin,
That Turkish Soldan full of sin;
He has a hundred wives at least,
By which his pleasure is increased:
I've often wished, I hope no sin,
That I were Sultan Saladin.

But no, the Pope no wife may choose,
And so I would not wear his shoes;
No wine may drink the proud Paynim,
And so I'd rather not be him:
My wife, my wine, I love, I hope,
And would be neither Turk nor Pope.

REQUIESCAT

U NDER the stone you behold,
Buried, and coffined, and cold,
Lieth Sir Wilfrid the Bold.

Always he marched in advance,
Warring in Flanders and France,
Doughty with sword and with lance.

Famous in Saracen fight,
Rode in his youth the good knight,
Scattering Paynims in flight.

Brian, the Templar untrue,
Fairly in tourney he slew,
Saw Hierusalem too.

Now he is buried and gone,
Lying beneath the grey stone :
Where shall you find such a one ?

Long time his widow deplored,
Weeping the fate of her lord,
Sadly cut off by the sword.

When she was eased of her pain,
Came the good Lord Athelstane,
When her Ladyship married again.

DEAR JACK

DEAR Jack, this white mug that with Guinness I fill,
   And drink to the health of Sweet Nan of the Hill,
   Was once Tommy Tosspot's, as jovial a sot
As e'er drew a spigot, or drain'd a full pot—
In drinking all round 'twas his joy to surpass,
And with all merry tipplers he swigg'd off his glass.

One morning in summer, while seated so snug,
In the porch of his garden, discussing his jug,
Stern Death, on a sudden, to Tom did appear,
And said, " Honest Thomas, come take your last bier."
We kneaded his clay in the shape of this can,
From which let us drink to the health of my Nan.

WHEN THE GLOOM IS ON THE GLEN

WHEN the moonlight's on the mountain
       And the gloom is on the glen,
          At the cross beside the fountain
There is one will meet thee then.
At the cross beside the fountain,
    Yes, the cross beside the fountain,
There is one will meet thee then!

I have braved, since first we met, love,
    Many a danger in my course;
But I never can forget, love,
    That dear fountain, that old cross,
Where, her mantle shrouded o'er her—
    For the winds were chilly then—
First I met my Leonora,
    When the gloom was on the glen.

Many a clime I've ranged since then, love,
    Many a land I've wandered o'er;
But a valley like that glen, love,
    Half so dear I never sor!
Ne'er saw maiden fairer, coyer,
    Than wert thou, my true love, when
In the gloaming first I saw yer,
    In the gloaming of the glen!

THE RED FLAG

W HERE the quivering lightning flings
　　His arrows from out the clouds,
　　And the howling tempest sings
And whistles among the shrouds,
'Tis pleasant, 'tis pleasant to ride
　Along the foaming brine—
Wilt be the Rover's bride?
　Wilt follow him, lady mine?
　　　　Hurrah!
　For the bonny bonny brine.

Amidst the storm and rack,
　You shall see our galley pass,
As a serpent, lithe and black,
　Glides through the waving grass.
As the vulture, swift and dark,
　Down on the ring-dove flies,
You shall see the Rover's bark
　Swoop down upon his prize.
　　　　Hurrah!
　For the bonny bonny prize

Over her sides we dash,
　We gallop across her deck—
Ha! there's a ghastly gash
　On the merchant-captain's neck—
Well shot, well shot, old Ned!
　Well struck, well struck, black James!
Our arms are red, and our foes are dead,
　And we leave a ship in flames!
　　　　Hurrah!
　For the bonny bonny flames!

THE KNIGHTLY GUERDON *

UNTRUE to my Ulric I never could be,
I vow by the saints and the blessed Marie,
Since the desolate hour when we stood by the
shore,
And your dark galley waited to carry you o'er :
My faith then I plighted, my love I confess'd,
As I gave you the BATTLE-AXE marked with your
crest !

When the bold barons met in my father's old hall,
Was not Edith the flower of the banquet and ball ?
In the festival hour, on the lips of your bride,
Was there ever a smile save with THEE at my side ?
Alone in my turret I loved to sit best,
To blazon your BANNER and broider your crest.

* "WAPPING OLD STAIRS

"Your Molly has never been false, she declares,
Since the last time we parted at Wapping Old Stairs ;
When I said that I would continue the same,
And gave you the 'bacco-box marked with my name.
When I passed a whole fortnight between decks with you,
Did I e'er give a kiss, Tom, to one of your crew ?
To be useful and kind to my Thomas I stay'd,
For his trousers I washed, and his grog too I made.

Though you promised last Sunday to walk in the Mall
With Susan from Deptford and likewise with Sall,
In silence I stood your unkindness to hear,
And only upbraided my Tom with a tear.
Why should Sall, or should Susan, than me be more prized ?
For the heart that is true, Tom, should ne'er be despised.
Then be constant and kind, nor your Molly forsake ;
Still your trousers I'll wash, and your grog too I'll make."

The knights were assembled, the tourney was gay !
Sir Ulric rode first in the warrior-mêlée.
In the dire battle-hour, when the tourney was done,
And you gave to another the wreath you had won !
Though I never reproached thee, cold cold was my breast,
As I thought of that BATTLE-AXE, ah ! and that crest !

But away with remembrance, no more will I pine
That others usurped for a time what was mine !
There's a FESTIVAL HOUR for my Ulric and me :
Once more, as of old, shall he bend at my knee ;
Once more by the side of the knight I love best
Shall I blazon his BANNER and broider his crest.

THE ALMACK'S ADIEU

YOUR Fanny was never false-hearted,
    And this she protests and she vows,
    From the *triste moment* when we parted
On the staircase of Devonshire House !
I blushed when you asked me to marry,
    I vowed I would never forget ;
And at parting I gave my dear Harry
    A beautiful vinegarette !

We spent *en province* all December,
    And I ne'er condescended to look
At Sir Charles, or the rich county member,
    Or even at that darling old Duke.
You were busy with dogs and with horses ;
    Alone in my chamber I sat,
And made you the nicest of purses,
    And the smartest black satin cravat !

At night with that vile Lady Frances
    (*Je faisais moi tapisserie*)
You danced every one of the dances,
    And never once thought of poor me ;
Mon pauvre petit cœur ! what a shiver
    I felt as she danced the last set ;
And you gave, *O mon Dieu !* to revive her
    My beautiful vinegarette !

Return, love ! away with coquetting ;
    This flirting disgraces a man !
And ah ! all the while you're forgetting
    The heart of your poor little Fan !
Reviens ! break away from those Circes,
    Reviens, for a nice little chat ;
And I've made you the sweetest of purses,
    And a lovely black satin cravat !

LYRA HIBERNICA

IE POEMS OF THE MOLONY OF KILBALLYMOLONY

LYRA HIBERNICA

THE POEMS OF THE MOLONY OF KILBALLYMOLONY

THE ROSE OF FLORA

SENT BY A YOUNG GENTLEMAN OF QUALITY TO MISS
BR—DY, OF CASTLE BRADY

O N Brady's tower there grows a flower,
  It is the loveliest flower that blows,—
  At Castle Brady there lives a lady,
(And how I love her no one knows);
Her name is Nora, and the goddess Flora
  Presents her with this blooming rose.

" O Lady Nora," says the goddess Flora,
  " I've many a rich and bright parterre ;
In Brady's towers there's seven more flowers,
  But you're the fairest lady there :
Not all the county, nor Ireland's bounty,
  Can projuice a treasure that's half so fair ! "

What cheek is redder ? sure roses fed her !
  Her hair is maregolds, and her eye of blew
Beneath her eyelid, is like the vi'let,
  That darkly glistens with gentle jew !
The lily's nature is not surely whiter
  Than Nora's neck is,—and her arrums too.

" Come, gentle Nora," says the goddess Flora
  " My dearest creature, take my advice :
There is a poet, full well you know it,
  Who spends his lifetime in heavy sighs,—
Young Redmond Barry, 'tis him you'll marry,
  If rhyme and raisin you'd choose likewise."

P

THE PIMLICO PAVILION

YE pathrons of janius, Minerva and Vanius,
 Who sit on Parnassus, that mountain of snow,
 Descind from your station and make observation
Of the Prince's pavilion in sweet Pimlico.

This garden, by jakurs, is forty poor acres
 (The garner he tould me, and sure ought to know)
And yet greatly bigger, in size and in figure,
 Than the Phanix itself, seems the Park Pimlico.

O 'tis there that the spoort is, when the Queen and the Court
 Walking magnanimous all of a row,
Forgetful what state is among the pataties
 And the pine-apple gardens of sweet Pimlico.

There in blossoms odorous the birds sing a chorus
 Of " God save the Queen " as they hop to and fro ;
And you sit on the binches and hark to the finches,
 Singing melodious in sweet Pimlico.

There shuiting their phanthasies, they pluck polyanthuses
 That round in the gardens resplindently grow,
Wid roses and jessimins, and other sweet specimins,
 Would charm bould Linnayus in sweet Pimlico.

You see when you inther, and stand in the cinther,
 Where the roses, and necturns, and collyflowers blow,
A hill so tremindous, it tops the top-windows
 Of the elegant houses of famed Pimlico.

And when you've ascinded that precipice splindid
 You see on its summit a wondtherful show—
A lovely Swish building, all painting and gilding,
 The famous Pavilion of sweet Pimlico.

Prince Albert of Flandthers, that Prince of Commandthers
   (On whom my best blessings hereby I bestow),
With goold and vermilion has decked that Pavilion,
    Where the Queen may take tay in her sweet Pimlico.

There's lines from John Milton the chamber all gilt on,
   And pictures beneath them that's shaped liked a bow;
I was greatly astounded to think that that Roundhead
    Should find an admission to famed Pimlico.

O lovely's each fresco, and most picturesque O;
   And while round the chamber astonished I go,
I think Dan Maclise's it baits all the pieces
    Surrounding the cottage of famed Pimlico.

Eastlake has the chimney (a good one to limn he),
   And a vargin he paints with a sarpent below;
While bulls, pigs, and panthers, and other enchanthers,
    Are painted by Landseer in sweet Pimlico.

And nature smiles opposite, Stanfield he copies it;
   O'er Claude or Poussang sure 'tis he that may crow:
But Sir Ross's best faiture is small miniáture—
    He shouldn't paint frescoes in famed Pimlico.

There's Leslie and Uwins has rather small doings;
   There's Dyce, as brave masther as England can show;
And the flowers and the sthrawberries, sure he no dauber is,
    That painted the panels of famed Pimlico.

In the pictures from Walther Scott, never a fault there's got,
   Sure the marble's as natural as thrue Scaglio;
And the Chamber Pompayen is sweet to take tay in,
    And ait butther'd muffins in sweet Pimlico.

There's landscapes by Gruner, both solar and lunar,
   Them two little Doyles, too, deserve a bravo;
Wid de piece by young Townsend, (for janius abounds in't;)
    And that's why he's shuited to paint Pimlico.

That picture of Severn's is worthy of rever'nce,
  But some I won't mintion is rather so so ;
For sweet philosóphy, or crumpets and coffee,
  O where's a Pavilion like sweet Pimlico ?

O to praise this Pavilion would puzzle Quintilian,
  Daymosthenes, Brougham, or young Cicero ;
So, heavenly Goddess, d'ye pardon my modesty,
  And silence, my lyre ! about sweet Pimlico.

LARRY O'TOOLE

YOU'VE all heard of Larry O'Toole,
    Of the beautiful town of Drumgoole;
      He had but one eye,
      To ogle ye by—
Oh, murther, but that was a jew'l!
      A fool
He made of de girls, dis O'Toole.

'Twas he was the boy didn't fail,
That tuck down pataties and mail;
      He never would shrink
      From any sthrong dthrink,
Was it whisky or Drogheda ale;
      I'm bail
This Larry would swallow a pail.

Oh, many a night at the bowl,
With Larry I've sot cheek by jowl;
      He's gone to his rest,
      Where there's dthrink of the best,
And so let us give his old sowl
      A howl,
For 'twas he made the noggin to rowl.

THE BATTLE OF LIMERICK

YE Genii of the nation,
    Who look with veneration,
    And Ireland's desolation onsaysingly deplore
Ye sons of General Jackson,
Who thrample on the Saxon,
Attend to the thransaction upon Shannon shore.

When William, Duke of Schumbug,
    A tyrant and a humbug,
With cannon and with thunder on our city bore,
    Our fortitude and valliance
    Insthructed his battalions
To rispict the galliant Irish upon Shannon shore.

Since that capitulation,
    No city in this nation
So grand a reputation could boast before,
    As Limerick prodigious,
    That stands with quays and bridges,
And the ships up to the windies of the Shannon shore.

A chief of ancient line,
    'Tis William Smith O'Brine,
Reprisints this darling Limerick, this ten years or more :
    O the Saxons can't endure
    To see him on the flure,
And thrimble at the Cicero from Shannon shore !

This valiant son of Mars
    Had been to visit Par's,
That land of Revolution, that grows the tricolor ;
    And to welcome his returrn
    From pilgrimages furren,
We invited him to tay on the Shannon shore !

Then we summoned to our board
Young Meagher of the Sword ;
'Tis he will sheathe that battle-axe in Saxon gore :
And Mitchil of Belfast
We bade to our repast,
To dthrink a dish of coffee on the Shannon shore.

Convaniently to hould
These patriots so bould,
We tuck the opportunity of Tim Doolan's store ;
And with ornamints and banners
(As becomes gintale good manners)
We made the loveliest tay-room upon Shannon shore.

'Twould binifit your sowls,
To see the butthered rowls,
The sugar-tongs and sangwidges and craim galyore,
And the muffins and the crumpets,
And the band of harps and thrumpets,
To celebrate the sworry upon Shannon shore.

Sure the Imperor of Bohay
Would be proud to dthrink the tay
That Misthress Biddy Rooney for O'Brine did pour ;
And, since the days of Strongbow,
There never was such Congo—
Mitchil dthrank six quarts of it—by Shannon shore.

But Clarndon and Corry
Connellan beheld this sworry
With rage and imulation in their black hearts' core ;
And they hired a gang of ruffins
To interrupt the muffins
And the fragrance of the Congo on the Shannon shore.

When full of tay and cake,
O'Brine began to spake ;
But juice a one could hear him, for a sudden roar
Of a ragamuffin rout
Began to yell and shout,
And frighten the propriety of Shannon shore.

As Smith O'Brine harangued,
They batthered and they banged:
Tim Doolan's doors and windies down they tore;
They smashed the lovely windies
(Hung with muslin from the Indies),
Purshuing of their shindies upon Shannon shore.

With throwing of brickbats,
Drowned puppies and dead rats,
These ruffin democrats themselves did lower;
Tin kettles, rotten eggs,
Cabbage-stalks, and wooden legs,
They flung among the patriots of Shannon shore.

O the girls began to scrame
And upset the milk and crame;
And the honourable gintlemin, they cursed and swore:
And Mitchil of Belfast,
'Twas he that looked aghast,
When they roasted him in effigy by Shannon shore.

O the lovely tay was spilt
On that day of Ireland's guilt;
Says Jack Mitchil, "I am kilt! Boys, where's the back door
'Tis a national disgrace:
Let me go and veil me face;"
And he boulted with quick pace from the Shannon shore.

" Cut down the bloody horde!"
Says Meagher of the Sword,
" This conduct would disgrace any blackamore;"
But the best use Tommy made
Of his famous battle blade
Was to cut his own stick from the Shannon shore.

Immortal Smith O'Brine
Was raging like a line;
'Twould have done your sowl good to have heard him roar;
In his glory he arose,
And he rush'd upon his foes,
But they hit him on the nose by the Shannon shore.

Then the Futt and the Dthragoons
In squadthrons and platoons,
With their music playing chunes, down upon us bore ;
And they bate the rattatoo,
But the Peelers came in view,
And ended the shaloo on the Shannon shore.

MR. MOLONY'S ACCOUNT OF THE BALL

GIVEN TO THE NEPAULESE AMBASSADOR BY THE PENINSULAR AND ORIENTAL COMPANY

O WILL ye choose to hear the news,
 Bedad I cannot pass it o'er :
 I'll tell you all about the Ball
To the Naypaulase Ambassador.
Begor ! this fête all balls does bate
 At which I've worn a pump, and I
Must here relate the splendthor great
 Of th' Oriental Company.

These men of sinse dispoised expinse,
 To fête these black Achilleses.
" We'll show the blacks," says they, " Almack's,
 And take the rooms at Willis's."
With flags and shawls, for these Nepauls,
 They hung the rooms of Willis up,
And decked the walls, and stairs, and halls,
 With roses and with lilies up.

And Jullien's band it tuck its stand
 So sweetly in the middle there,
And soft bassoons played heavenly chunes,
 And violins did fiddle there.
And when the Coort was tired of spoort,
 I'd lave you, boys, to think there was
A nate buffet before them set,
 Where lashins of good dthrink there was.

At ten before the ballroom door,
 His moighty Excelléncy was,
He smoiled and bowed to all the crowd,
 So gorgeous and immense he was.

His dusky shuit, sublime and mute,
    Into the doorway followed him ;
And O the noise of the blackguard boys,
    As they hurrood and hollowed him !

The noble Chair * stud at the stair,
    And bade the dthrums to thump ; and he
Did thus evince, to that Black Prince,
    The welcome of his Company.
O fair the girls, and rich the curls,
    And bright the oys you saw there was,
And fixed each oye, ye there could spoi,
    On Gineral Jung Bahawther, was !

This Gineral great then tuck his sate,
    With all the other ginerals
(Bedad his troat, his belt, his coat,
    All bleezed with precious minerals) ;
And as he there, with princely air,
    Recloinin on his cushion was,
All round about his royal chair
    The squeezin and the pushin was.

O Pat, such girls, such Jukes, and Earls,
    Such fashion and nobilitee !
Just think of Tim, and fancy him
    Amidst the hoigh gentilitee !
There was Lord De L'Huys, and the Portygeese
    Ministher and his lady there,
And I reckonised, with much surprise,
    Our messmate, Bob O'Grady, there ;

There was Baroness Brunow, that looked like Juno,
    And Baroness Rehausen there,
And Countess Roullier, that looked peculiar
    Well, in her robes of gauze in there.
There was Lord Crowhurst (I knew him first,
    When only Mr. Pips he was),
And Mick O'Toole, the great big fool,
    That after supper tipsy was.

* James Matheson, Esquire, to whom, and the Board of Directors of the
Peninsular and Oriental Company, I, Timotheus Molony, late stoker on board
the *Iberia*, the *Lady Mary Wood*, the *Tagus*, and the Oriental steamships,
humbly dedicate this production of my grateful muse.

There was Lord Fingall, and his ladies all,
    And Lords Killeen and Dufferin,
And Paddy Fife, with his fat wife;
    I wondther how he could stuff her in.
There was Lord Belfast, that by me past,
    And seemed to ask how should *I* go there?
And the Widow Macrae, and Lord A. Hay,
    And the Marchioness of Sligo there.

Yes, Jukes, and Earls, and diamonds, and pearls,
    And pretty girls, was spoorting there;
And some beside (the rogues!) I spied,
    Behind the windies, coorting there.
O, there's one I know, bedad, would show
    As beautiful as any there,
And I'd like to hear the pipers blow,
    And shake a fut with Fanny there!

THE LAST IRISH GRIEVANCE

ON reading of the general indignation occasioned in Ireland by the appointment of a Scotch Professor to one of HER MAJESTY'S Godless Colleges, MASTER MOLLOY MOLONY, brother of THADDEUS MOLONY, Esq., of the Temple, a youth only fifteen years of age, dashed off the following spirited lines :—

AS I think of the insult that's done to this nation,
    Red tears of rivinge from me faytures I wash,
      And uphold in this pome, to the world's daytistation,
  The sleeves that appointed PROFESSOR MACCOSH.

I look round me counthree, renowned by exparience,
    And see midst her childthren, the witty, the wise,—
Whole hayps of logicians, potes, schollars, grammarians,
    All ayger for pleeces, all panting to rise ;

I gaze round the world in its utmost diminsion ;
    LARD JAHN and his minions in Council I ask,
Was there ever a Government-pleece (with a pinsion)
    But children of Erin were fit for that task ?

What, Erin beloved, is thy fetal condition ?
    What shame in aych boosom must rankle and burrun,
To think that our countree has ne'er a logician
    In the hour of her deenger will surrev her turrun !

On the logic of Saxons there's little reliance,
    And, rather from Saxon than gather its rules,
I'd stamp under feet the base book of his science,
    And spit on his chair as he taught in the schools !

O false SIR JOHN KANE ! is it thus that you praych me ?
    I think all your Queen's Universitees Bosh ;
And if you've no neetive Professor to taych me,
    I scawurn to be learned by the Saxon MACCOSH.

There's WISEMAN and CHUME, and his Grace the Lord Primate,
 That sinds round the box, and the world will subscribe;
'Tis they'll build a College that's fit for our climate,
 And taych me the saycrets I burn to imboibe!

'Tis there as a Student of Science I'll enther,
 Fair Fountain of Knowledge, of Joy, and Contint!
SAINT PATHRICK'S sweet Statue shall stand in the centher,
 And wink his dear oi every day during Lint.

And good DOCTOR NEWMAN, that praycher unwary,
 'Tis he shall preside the Academee School,
And quit the gay robe of ST. PHILIP of Neri,
 To wield the soft rod of ST. LAWRENCE O'TOOLE!

THE CRYSTAL PALACE

WITH ganial foire
 Thransfuse me loyre,
  Ye sacred nympths of Pindus,
The whoile I sing
That wondthrous thing,
The Palace made o' windows!

 Say, Paxton, truth,
 Thou wondthrous youth,
What sthroke of art celistial,
 What power was lint
 You to invint
This combineetion cristial.

 O would before
 That Thomas Moore,
Likewoise the late Lord Boyron,
 Thim aigles sthrong
 Of godlike song,
Cast oi on that cast oiron!

 And saw thim walls,
 And glittering halls,
Thim rising slendther columns,
 Which I, poor pote,
 Could not denote,
No, not in twinty vollums.

 My Muse's words
 Is like the bird's
That roosts beneath the panes there;
 Her wings she spoils
 'Gainst them bright toiles,
And cracks her silly brains there.

This Palace tall,
This Cristial Hall,
Which Imperors might covet,
Stands in High Park,
Like Noah's Ark,
A rainbow bint above it.

The towers and fanes,
In other scaynes,
The fame of this will undo,
Saint Paul's big doom,
Saint Payther's Room,
And Dublin's proud Rotundo.

'Tis here that roams,
As well becomes
Her dignitee and stations,
Victoria Great,
And houlds in state
The Congress of the Nations.

Her subjects pours
From distant shores,
Her Injians and Canajians;
And also we,
Her kingdoms three,
Attind with our allagiance.

Here come likewise
Her bould allies,
Both Asian and Europian;
From East and West
They send their best
To fill her Coornucopean.

I seen (thank Grace!)
This wondthrous place
(His Noble Honour Misther
H. Cole it was
That gave the pass,
And let me see what is there).

With conscious proide
I stud insoide
And look'd the World's Great Fair in,
Until me sight
Was dazzled quite,
And couldn't see for staring.

There's holy saints
And window paints,
By Maydiayval Pugin;
Alhamborough Jones
Did paint the tones
Of yellow and gambouge in.

There's fountains there
And crosses fair;
There's water-gods with urrns:
There's organs three,
To play, d'ye see?
"God save the Queen," by turrns.

There's statues bright
Of marble white,
Of silver, and of copper;
And some in zinc,
And some, I think,
That isn't over proper.

There's staym ingynes,
That stands in lines,
Enormous and amazing,
That squeal and snort
Like whales in sport,
Or elephants a-grazing.

There's carts and gigs,
And pins for pigs,
There's dibblers and there's harrows,
And ploughs like toys
For little boys,
And iligant wheelbarrows.

For thim genteels
Who ride on wheels,
There's plenty to indulge 'em:
There's droskys snug
From Paytersbug,
And vayhycles from Bulgium.

There's cabs on stands
And shandthrydanns;
There's waggons from New York here;
There's Lapland sleighs
Have cross'd the seas,
And jaunting cyars from Cork here.

Amazed I pass
From glass to glass,
Deloighted I survey 'em;
Fresh wondthers grows
Before me nose
In this sublime Musayum!

Look, here's a fan
From far Japan,
A sabre from Damasco:
There's shawls ye get
From far Thibet,
And cotton prints from Glasgow.

There's German flutes,
Marocky boots,
And Naples macaronies;
Bohaymia
Has sent Bohay;
Polonia her polonies.

There's granite flints
That's quite imminse,
There's sacks of coals and fuels,
There's swords and guns,
And soap in tuns,
And gingerbread and jewels.

There's taypots there,
And cannons rare ;
There's coffins fill'd with roses ;
There's canvas tints,
Teeth insthrumints,
And shuits of clothes by MOSES.

There's lashins more
Of things in store,
But thim I don't remimber ;
Nor could disclose
Did I compose
From May time to Novimber !

Ah, JUDY thru !
With eyes so blue,
That you were here to view it !
And could I screw
But tu pound tu,
'Tis I would thrait you to it !

So let us raise
Victoria's praise,
And Albert's proud condition,
That takes his ayse
As he surveys
This Cristial Exhibition.

1851.

MOLONY'S LAMENT

O TIM, did you hear of thim Saxons,
  And read what the peepers report?
  They're goan to recal the Liftinant,
 And shut up the Castle and Coort!
Our desolate counthry of Oireland
 They're bint, the blagyards, to desthroy,
And now having murdthered our counthry,
 They're goin to kill the Viceroy,
   Dear boy ;
  'Twas he was our proide and our joy!

And will we no longer behould him,
  Surrounding his carriage in throngs,
As he waves his cocked-hat from the windies,
  And smiles to his bould aid-de-congs?
I liked for to see the young haroes,
  All shoining with sthripes and with stars,
A horsing about in the Phaynix,
  And winking the girls in the cyars,
    Like Mars,
  A smokin' their poipes and cigyars.

Dear Mitchell exoiled to Bermudies,
  Your beautiful oilids you'll ope,
And there'll be an abondance of croyin'
  From O'Brine at the Keep of Good Hope,
When they read of this news in the peepers,
  Acrass the Atlantical wave,
That the last of the Oirish Liftinints
  Of the oisland of Seents has tuck lave.
    God save
  The Queen—she should betther behave.

And what's to become of poor Dame Sthreet,
    And who'll ait the puffs and the tarts,
Whin the Coort of imparial splindor
    From Doblin's sad city departs?
And who'll have the fiddlers and pipers,
    When the deuce of a Coort there remains?
And where'll be the bucks and the ladies,
    To hire the Coort-shuits and the thrains?
        In sthrains,
    It's thus that ould Erin complains!

There's Counsellor Flanagan's leedy,
    'Twas she in the Coort didn't fail,
And she wanted a plinty of popplin,
    For her dthress, and her flounce, and her tail;
She bought it of Misthress O'Grady,
    Eight shillings a yard tabinet,
But now that the Coort is concluded,
    The divvle a yard will she get;
        I bet,
    Bedad, that she wears the old set.

There's Surgeon O'Toole and Miss Leary,
    They'd daylings at Madam O'Riggs';
Each year at the dthrawing-room sayson,
    They mounted the neatest of wigs.
When Spring, with its buds and its dasies,
    Comes out in her beauty and bloom,
Thim tu'll never think of new jasies,
    Becase there is no dthrawing-room,
        For whom
    They'd choose the expense to ashume.

There's Alderman Toad and his lady,
    'Twas they gave the Clart and the Poort,
And the poine-apples, turbots, and lobsters,
    To feast the Lord Liftinint's Coort.
But now that the quality's goin,
    I warnt that the aiting will stop,
And you'll get at the Alderman's teeble
    The devil a bite or a dthrop,
        Or chop;
    And the butcher may shut up his shop.

Yes, the grooms and the ushers are goin,
   And his Lordship, the dear honest man,
And the Duchess, his eemiable leedy,
   And Corry, the bould Connellan,
And little Lord Hyde and the childthren,
   And the Chewter and Governess tu ;
And the servants are packing their boxes,—
   Oh, murther, but what shall I due
          Without you ?
   O Meery, with ois of the blue !

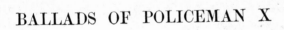

BALLADS OF POLICEMAN X

THE

BALLADS OF POLICEMAN X

JACOB HOMNIUM'S HOSS

A NEW PALLICE COURT CHAUNT

ONE sees in Viteall Yard,
  Vere pleacemen do resort,
  A wenerable hinstitute,
'Tis called the Pallis Court.
A gent as got his i on it,
  I think 'twill make some sport.

The natur of this Court
  My hindignation riles :
A few fat legal spiders
  Here set & spin their viles ;
To rob the town theyr privlege is,
  In a hayrea of twelve miles.

The Judge of this year Court
  Is a mellitary beak,
He knows no more of Lor
  Than praps he does of Greek,
And prowides hisself a deputy
  Because he cannot speak.

Four counsel in this Court—
  Misnamed of Justice—sits ;
These lawyers owes their places to
  Their money, not their wits ;
And there's six attornies under them,
  As here their living gits.

These lawyers, six and four,
    Was a livin at their ease,
A sendin of their writs abowt,
    And droring in the fees,
When there erose a cirkimstance
    As is like to make a breeze.

It now is some monce since
    A gent both good and trew
Possest an ansum oss vith vich
    He didn know what to do ;
Peraps he did not like the oss,
    Peraps he was a scru.

This gentleman his oss
    At Tattersall's did lodge ;
There came a wulgar oss-dealer,
    This gentleman's name did fodge,
And took the oss from Tattersall's :
    Wasn that a artful dodge ?

One day this gentleman's groom
    This willain did spy out,
A mounted on this oss
    A ridin him about ;
" Get out of that there oss, you rogue,"
    Speaks up the groom so stout.

The thief was cruel whex'd
    To find himself so pinn'd ;
The oss began to whinny,
    The honest groom he grinn'd ;
And the raskle thief got off the oss
    And cut avay like vind.

And phansy with what joy
    The master did regard
His dearly bluvd lost oss again
    Trot in the stable yard !

Who was this master good
　　Of whomb I makes these rhymes?
His name is Jacob Homnium, Exquire;
　　And if *I*'d committed crimes,
Good Lord! I wouldn't ave that **mann**
　　Attack me in the *Times!*

Now shortly after the groomb
　　His master's oss did take up,
There came a livery-man
　　This gentleman to wake up;
And he handed in a little bill,
　　Which hangered Mr. Jacob.

For two pound seventeen
　　This livery-man eplied,
For the keep of Mr. Jacob's oss,
　　Which the thief had took to ride.
"Do you see anythink green in me?"
　　Mr. Jacob Homnium cried.

"Because a raskle chews
　　My oss away to robb,
And goes tick at your Mews
　　For seven-and-fifty bobb,
Shall *I* be call'd to pay?—It is
　　A iniquitious Jobb."

Thus Mr. Jacob cut
　　The conwasation short;
The livery-man went ome,
　　Detummingd to ave sport,
And summingsd Jacob Homnium, Exquire,
　　Into the Pallis Court.

Pore Jacob went to Court,
　　A Counsel for to fix,
And choose a barrister out of the four,
　　An attorney of the six:
And there he sor these men of Lor,
　　And watch'd 'em at their tricks.

The dreadful day of trile
   In the Pallis Court did come;
The lawyers said their say,
   The Judge look'd wery glum,
And then the British Jury cast
   Pore Jacob Hom-ni-um.

O a weary day was that
   For Jacob to go through;
The debt was two seventeen
   (Which he no mor owed than you),
And then there was the plaintives costs,
   Eleven pound six and two.

And then there was his own,
   Which the lawyers they did fix
At the wery moderit figgar
   Of ten pound one and six.
Now Evins bless the Pallis Court,
   And all its bold ver-dicks!

I cannot settingly tell
   If Jacob swaw and cust,
At aving for to pay this sumb;
   But I should think he must,
And av drawn a cheque for £24 4s. 8d.
   With most igstreme disgust.

O Pallis Court, you move
   My pitty most profound.
A most emusing sport
   You thought it, I'll be bound,
To saddle hup a three-pound debt
   With two-and-twenty pound.

Good sport it is to you
   To grind the honest pore,
To pay their just or unjust debts
   With eight hundred per cent. for Lor;
Make haste and get your costes in,
   They will not last much mor!

Come down from that tribewn,
    Thou shameless and Unjust;
Thou Swindle, picking pockets in
    The name of Truth august:
Come down, thou hoary Blasphemy,
    For die thou shalt and must.

And go it, Jacob Homnium,
    And ply your iron pen,
And rise up, Sir John Jervis,
    And shut me up that den;
That sty for fattening lawyers in
    On the bones of honest men.

PLEACEMAN X.

THE THREE CHRISTMAS WAITS

M Y name is Pleaceman X;
 Last night I was in bed,
 A dream did me perplex,
Which came into my Edd.
I dreamed I sor three Waits
 A playing of their tune,
At Pimlico Palace gates,
 All underneath the moon.
One puffed a hold French horn,
 And one a hold Banjo,
And one chap seedy and torn
 A Hirish pipe did blow.
They sadly piped and played,
 Dexcribing of their fates;
And this was what they said,
 Those three pore Christmas Waits:—

"When this black year began,
 This Eighteen-forty-eight,
I was a great great man,
 And king both vise and great,
And Munseer Guizot by me did show
 As Minister of State.

"But Febuwerry came,'
 And brought a rabble rout,
And me and my good dame
 And children did turn out,
And us, in spite of all our right,
 Sent to the right about.

"I left my native ground,
 I left my kin and kith,

I left my Royal crownd,
   Vich I couldn't travel vith,
And without a pound came to English ground
   In the name of Mr. Smith.

" Like any anchorite
   I've lived since I came here,
I've kep myself quite quite,
   I've drank the small small beer,
And the vater, you see, disagrees vith me
   And all my famly dear.

" O Tweeleries so dear,
   O darling Pally Royl,
Vas it to finish here
   That I did trouble and toyl ?
That all my plans should break in my ands,
   And should on me recoil ?

" My state I fenced about
   Vith baynicks and vith guns ;
My gals I portioned hout,
   Rich vives I got my sons ;
O varn't it crule to lose my rule,
   My money and lands at once ?

" And so, vith arp and woice,
   Both troubled and shagreened,
I bid you to rejoice,
   O glorious England's Queend !
And never have to veep, like pore Louis-Phileep,
   Because you out are cleaned.

" O Prins, so brave and stout,
   I stand before your gate ;
Pray send a trifle hout
   To me, your pore old Vait ;
For nothink could be vuss than it's been along vith us
   In this year Forty-eight."

" Ven this bad year began,"
    The nex man said, saysee,
" I vas a Journeyman,
    A taylor black and free,
And my wife went out and chaired about,
    And my name's the bold Cuffee.

" The Queen and Halbert both
    I swore I would confound,
I took a hawfle hoath
    To drag them to the ground;
And sevral more with me they swore
    Aginst the British Crownd.

" Aginst her Pleaceman all
    We said we'd try our strenth;
Her scarlick soldiers tall
    We vow'd we'd lay full lenth:
And out we came, in Freedom's name,
    Last Aypril was the tenth.

" Three 'undred thousand snobs
    Came out to stop the vay,
Vith sticks vith iron knobs,
    Or else we'd gained the day.
The harmy quite kept out of sight,
    And so ve vent avay.

" Next day the Pleacemen came—
    Rewenge it was their plann—
And from my good old dame
    They took her tailor-mann:
And the hard hard beak did me bespeak
    To Newgit in the Wann.

" In that etrocious Cort
    The Jewry did agree;
The Judge did me transport,
    To go beyond the sea:
And so for life, from his dear wife
    They took poor old Cuffee.

"O Halbert, Appy Prince!
    With children round your knees,
  Ingraving ansum Prints,
    And taking hoff your hease;
  O think of me, the old Cuffee,
    Beyond the solt solt seas!

"Although I'm hold and black,
    My hanguish is most great;
  Great Prince, O call me back,
    And I vill be your Vait!
  And never no more vill break the Lor,
    As I did in 'Forty-eight."

The tailer thus did close
    (A pore old blackymore rogue),
  When a dismal gent uprose,
    And spoke with Hirish brogue:
  "I'm Smith O'Brine, of Royal Line,
    Descended from Rory Ogue.

"When great O'Connle died,
    That man whom all did trust,
  That man whom Henglish pride
    Beheld with such disgust,
  Then Erin free fixed eyes on me,
    And swoar I should be fust.

" 'The glorious Hirish Crown,'
    Says she, 'it shall be thine:
  Long time, it's wery well known,
    You kep it in your line;
  That diadem of hemerald gem
    Is yours, my Smith O'Brine.

" 'Too long the Saxon churl
    Our land encumbered hath;
  Arise, my Prince, my Earl,
    And brush them from thy path:
  Rise, mighty Smith, and sveep 'em vith
    The besom of your wrath.'

R

" Then in my might I rose,
    My country I surveyed,
I saw it filled with foes,
    I viewed them undismayed ;
' Ha, ha ! ' says I, ' the harvest's high,
    I'll reap it with my blade.'

" My warriors I enrolled,
    They rallied round their lord ;
And cheafs in council old
    I summoned to the board—
Wise Doheny and Duffy bold,
    And Meagher of the Sword.

" I stood on Slievenamaun,
    They came with pikes and bills ;
They gathered in the dawn,
    Like mist upon the hills,
And rushed adown the mountain side
    Like twenty thousand rills.

" Their fortress we assail ;
    Hurroo ! my boys, hurroo !
The bloody Saxons quail
    To hear the wild shaloo :
Strike, and prevail, proud Innesfail,
    O'Brine aboo, aboo !

" Our people they defied ;
    They shot at 'em like savages,
Their bloody guns they plied
    With sanguinary ravages :
Hide, blushing Glory, hide
    That day among the cabbages !

" And so no more I'll say,
    But ask your Mussy great,
And humbly sing and pray,
    Your Majesty's poor Wait :
Your Smith O'Brine in 'Forty-nine
    Will blush for 'Forty-eight."

THE BALLAD OF ELIZA DAVIS

GALLIANT gents and lovely ladies,
    List a tail vich late befel,
    Vich I heard it, bein on duty,
At the Pleace Hoffice, Clerkenwell.

Praps you know the Fondling Chapel,
    Vere the little children sings :
(Lor ! I likes to hear on Sundies
    Them there pooty little things !)

In this street there lived a housemaid,
    If you particklarly ask me where—
Vy, it vas at four-and-tventy
    Guilford Street, by Brunsvick Square.

Vich her name was Eliza Davis,
    And she went to fetch the beer :
In the street she met a party
    As was quite surprized to see her.

Vich he vas a British Sailor,
    For to judge him by his look :
Tarry jacket, canvass trowsies,
    Ha-la Mr. T. P. Cooke.

Presently this Mann accostes
    Of this hinnocent young gal—
" Pray," saysee, " excuse my freedom,
    You're so like my Sister Sal !

" You're so like my Sister Sally,
    Both in valk and face and size,
Miss, that—dang my old lee scuppers,
    It brings tears into my heyes !

" I'm a mate on board a wessel,
    I'm a sailor bold and true ;
Shiver up my poor old timbers,
    Let me be a mate for you !

" What's your name, my beauty, tell me ;"
    And she faintly hansers, " Lore,
Sir, my name's Eliza Davis,
    And I live at tventy-four."

Hofttimes came this British seaman,
    This deluded gal to meet ;
And at tventy-four was welcome,
    Tventy-four in Guilford Street.

And Eliza told her Master
    (Kinder they than Missuses are),
How in marridge he had ast her,
    Like a galliant Brittish Tar.

And he brought his landlady vith him
    (Vich vas all his hartful plan),
And she told how Charley Thompson
    Reely vas a good young man ;

And how she herself had lived in
    Many years of union sweet
Vith a gent she met promiskous,
    Valkin in the public street.

And Eliza listened to them,
    And she thought that soon their bands
Vould be published at the Fondlin,
    Hand the clergyman jine their ands.

And he ast about the lodgers
    (Vich her master let some rooms),
Likevise vere they kep their things, and
    Vere her master kep his spoons.

Hand this vicked Charley Thompson
    Came on Sundy veek to see her ;
And he sent Eliza Davis
    Hout to fetch a pint of beer.

Hand while pore Eliza vent to
    Fetch the beer, dewoid of sin,
This etrocious Charley Thompson
    Let his wile accomplish hin.

To the lodgers, their apartments,
    This abandingd female goes,
Prigs their shirts and umberellas ;
    Prigs their boots, and hats, and clothes.

Vile the scoundrle Charley Thompson,
    Lest his wictim should escape,
Hocust her with rum and vater,
    Like a fiend in huming shape.

But a hi was fixt upon 'em
    Vich these raskles little sore ;
Namely, Mr. Hide, the landlord
    Of the house at tventy-four.

He vas valking in his garden,
    Just afore he vent to sup ;
And on looking up he sor the
    Lodgers' vinders lighted hup.

Hup the stairs the landlord tumbled ;
    " Something's going wrong," he said ;
And he caught the vicked voman
    Underneath the lodgers' bed.

And he called a brother Pleaseman,
    Vich vas passing on his beat,
Like a true and galliant feller,
    Hup and down in Guilford Street.

And that Pleaseman able-bodied
    Took this voman to the cell ;
To the cell vere she was quodded,
    In the Close of Clerkenwell.

And though vicked Charley Thompson
    Boulted like a miscrant base,
Presently another Pleaseman
    Took him to the self-same place.

And this precious pair of raskles
   Tuesday last came up for doom;
By the beak they was committed,
   Vich his name was Mr. Combe.

Has for poor Eliza Davis,
   Simple gurl of tventy-four,
She, I ope, vill never listen
   In the streets to sailors moar.

But if she must ave a sweet-art
   (Vich most every gurl expex),
Let her take a jolly pleaseman;
   Vich his name peraps is—X.

THE LAMENTABLE BALLAD OF THE
FOUNDLING OF SHOREDITCH

COME all ye Christian people, and listen to my tail,
    It is all about a doctor was travelling by the rail,
        By the Heastern Counties Railway (vich the shares I
           don't desire),
rom Ixworth town in Suffolk, vich his name did not transpire.

 travelling from Bury this Doctor was employed
Vith a gentleman, a friend of his, vich his name was Captain Loyd,
nd on reaching Marks Tey Station, that is next beyond Colchest-
r, a lady entered in to them most elegantly dressed.

he entered into the Carriage all with a tottering step,
nd a pooty little Bayby upon her bussum slep;
he gentlemen received her with kindness and siwillaty,
itying this lady for her illness and debillaty.

he had a fust-class ticket, this lovely lady said;
ecause it was so lonesome she took a secknd instead.
etter to travel by secknd class, than sit alone in the fust,
nd the pooty little Baby upon her breast she nust.

seein of her cryin, and shiverin and pail,
o her spoke this surging, the Ero of my tail;
aysee "You look unwell, ma'am; I'll elp you if I can,
nd you may tell your case to me, for I'm a meddicle man."

"Thank you, sir," the lady said, "I only look so pale,
ecause I ain't accustom'd to travelling on the Rale;
shall be better presnly, when I've ad some rest:"
nd that pooty little Baby she squeeged it to her breast.

So in conwersation the journey they beguiled,
Capting Loyd and the meddicle man, and the lady and the child,
Till the warious stations along the line was passed,
For even the Heastern Counties' trains must come in at last.

When at Shoreditch tumminus at lenth stopped the train,
This kind meddicle gentleman proposed his aid again.
"Thank you, sir," the lady said, "for your kyindness dear ;
My carridge and my osses is probibbly come here.

"Will you old this baby, please, vilst I step and see ? "
The Doctor was a famly man : "That I will," says he.
Then the little child she kist, kist it very gently,
Vich was sucking his little fist, sleeping innocently.

With a sigh from her art, as though she would have bust it,
Then she gave the Doctor the child—wery kind he nust it :
Hup then the lady jumped hoff the bench she sat from,
Tumbled down the carridge steps and ran along the platform.

Vile hall the other passengers vent upon their vays,
The Capting and the Doctor sat there in a maze ;
Some vent in a Homminibus, some vent in a Cabby,
The Capting and the Doctor vaited vith the babby.

There they sat looking queer, for an hour or more,
But their feller passinger neather on 'em sore :
Never, never back again did that lady come
To that pooty sleeping Hinfnt a suckin of his Thum !

What could this pore Doctor do, bein treated thus,
When the darling Baby woke, cryin for its nuss ?
Off he drove to a female friend, vich she was both kind and mild,
And igsplained to her the circumstance of this year little child.

That kind lady took the child instantly in her lap,
And made it very comfortable by giving it some pap ;
And when she took its close off, what d'you think she found ?
A couple of ten pun notes sewn up, in its little gownd !

Also in its little close, was a note which did conwey,
That this little baby's parents lived in a handsome way
And for its Headucation they reglarly would pay,
And sirtingly like gentlefolks would claim the child one day,
If the Christian people who'd charge of it would say,
Per adwertisement in the *Times*, where the baby lay.

'ity of this bayby many people took,
t had such pooty ways and such a pooty look;
nd there came a lady forrard (I wish that I could see
ny kind lady as would do as much for me;

nd I wish with all my art, some night in *my* night gownd,
  could find a note stitched for ten or twenty pound)—
'here came a lady forrard, that most honorable did say,
he'd adopt this little baby, which her parents cast away.

Vhile the Doctor pondered on this hoffer fair,
'omes a letter from Devonshire, from a party there,
Iordering the Doctor, at its Mar's desire,
'o send the little Infant back to Devonshire.

.ost in apoplexity, this pore meddicle man,
.ike a sensable gentleman, to the Justice ran;
Vhich his name was Mr. Hammill, a honorable beak,
'hat takes his seat in Worship Street four times a week.

'O Justice!" says the Doctor, "instrugt me what to do.
've come up from the country, to throw myself on you;
My patients have no doctor to tend them in their ills
There they are in Suffolk without their draffts and pills!).

'I've come up from the country, to know how I'll dispose
)f this pore little baby, and the twenty pun note, and the close,
.nd I want to go back to Suffolk, dear Justice, if you please,
.nd my patients wants their Doctor, and their Doctor wants
        his feez.

Jp spoke Mr. Hammill, sittin at his desk,
'This year application does me much perplesk;
Vhat I do adwise you, is to leave this babby
'n the Parish where it was left by its mother shabby."

'he Doctor from his Worship sadly did depart—
Ie might have left the baby, but he hadn't got the heart
'o go for to leave that Hinnocent, has the laws allows,
'o the tender mussies of the Union House.

Mother, who left this little one on a stranger's knee,
'hink how cruel you have been, and how good was he!
'hink, if you've been guilty, innocent was she;
And do not take unkindly this little word of me:
Ieaven be merciful to us all, sinners as we be!

LINES ON A LATE HOSPICIOUS EWENT*

BY A GENTLEMAN OF THE FOOT-GUARDS (BLUE).

I PACED upon my beat
  With steady step and slow,
All huppandownd of Ranelagh Street;
  Ran'lagh St. Pimlico.

While marching huppandownd
  Upon that fair May morn,
Beold the booming cannings sound,
  A royal child is born!

The Ministers of State
  Then presnly I sor,
They gallops to the Pallis gate,
  In carridges and for.

With anxious looks intent,
  Before the gate they stop,
There comes the good Lord President,
  And there the Archbishopp.

Lord John he next elights;
  And who comes here in haste?
'Tis the ero of one underd fights,
  The caudle for to taste.

Then Mrs. Lily, the nuss,
  Towards them steps with joy;
Says the brave old Duke, "Come tell to us,
  Is it a gal or a boy?"

* The birth of Prince Arthur.

Says Mrs. L. to the Duke,
   "Your Grace, it is *a Prince.*"
And at that nuss's bold rebuke
   He did both laugh and wince.

He vews with pleasant look
   This pooty flower of May,
Then says the wenerable Duke,
   "Egad, it's my buthday."

By memory backards borne,
   Peraps his thoughts did stray
To that old place where he was born
   Upon the first of May.

Perhaps he did recal
   The ancient towers of Trim;
And County Meath and Dangan Hall
   They did rewisit him.

I phansy of him so
   His good old thoughts employin';
Fourscore years and one ago
   Beside the flowin' Boyne.

His father praps he sees,
   Most musicle of Lords,
A playing maddrigles and glees
   Upon the Arpsicords.

Jest phansy this old Ero
   Upon his mother's knee!
Did ever lady in this land
   Ave greater sons than she?

And I shoudn be surprize
   While this was in his mind,
If a drop there twinkled in his eyes
   Of unfamiliar brind.

  .   .   .   .   .

To Hapsly Ouse next day
   Drives up a Broosh and for,
A gracious prince sits in that Shay
   (I mention him with Hor!).

They ring upon the bell,
　　The Porter shows his Ed,
(He fought at Vaterloo as vell,
　　And vears a Veskit red).

To see that carriage come,
　　The people round it press :
"And is the galliant Duke at ome?"
"Your Royal Ighness, yes."

He stepps from out the Broosh
　　And in the gate is gone ;
And X, although the people push,
　　Says wery kind, "Move hon."

The Royal Prince unto
　　The galliant Duke did say,
"Dear Duke, my little son and you
　　Was born the self-same day.

"The Lady of the land,
　　My wife and Sovring dear,
It is by her horgust command
　　I wait upon you here.

"That lady is as well
　　As can expected be ;
And to your Grace she bid me tell
　　This gracious message free.

"That offspring of our race,
　　Whom yesterday you see,
To show our honour for your Grace,
　　Prince Arthur he shall be.

"That name it rhymes to fame ;
　　All Europe knows the sound :
And I couldn't find a better name
　　If you'd give me twenty pound.

"King Arthur had his knights
　　That girt his table round,
But you have won a hundred fights,
　　Will match 'em, I'll be bound.

" You fought with Bonypart,
   And likewise Tippoo Saib ;
I name you then with all my heart
   The Godsire of this babe."

That Prince his leave was took,
   His hinterview was done.
So let us give the good old Duke
   Good luck òf his god-son,

And wish him years of joy
   In this our time of Schism,
And hope he'll hear the Royal boy
   His little catechism.

And my pooty little Prince
   That's come our arts to cheer,
Let me my loyal powers ewince
   A welcomin of you ere.

And the Poit-Laureat's crownd,
   I think, in some respex,
Egstremely shootable might be found
   For honest Pleaseman X.

THE WOFLE NEW BALLAD OF JANE RONEY
AND MARY BROWN

AN igstrawnary tail I vill tell you this veek—
    I stood in the Court of A'Beckett the Beak,
    Vere Mrs. Jane Roney, a vidow, I see,
Who charged Mary Brown with a robbin of she.

This Mary was pore and in misery once,
And she came to Mrs. Roney it's more than twelve monce.
She adn't got no bed, nor no dinner nor no tea,
And kind Mrs. Roney gave Mary all three.

Mrs. Roney kep Mary for ever so many veeks
(Her conduct disgusted the best of all Beax),
She kep her for nothink, as kind as could be,
Never thinkin that this Mary was a traitor to she.

"Mrs. Roney, O Mrs. Roney, I feel very ill;
Will you just step to the Doctor's for to fetch me a pill?"
"That I will, my pore Mary," Mrs. Roney says she;
And she goes off to the Doctor's as quickly as may be.

No sooner on this message Mrs. Roney was sped,
Than hup gits vicked Mary, and jumps out a bed;
She hopens all the trunks without never a key—
She bustes all the boxes, and vith them makes free.

Mrs. Roney's best linning, gownds, petticoats, and close,
Her children's little coats and things, her boots, and her hose,
She packed them, and she stole 'em, and avay vith them did flee.
Mrs. Roney's situation—you may think vat it vould be!

Of Mary, ungrateful, who had served her this vay,
Mrs. Roney heard nothink for a long year and a day.
Till last Thursday, in Lambeth, ven whom should she see
But this Mary, as had acted so ungrateful to she?

She was leaning on the helbo of a worthy young man,
They were going to be married, and were walkin hand in hand;
And the Church bells was a ringin for Mary and he,
And the parson was ready, and a waitin for his fee.

When up comes Mrs. Roney, and faces Mary Brown,
Who trembles, and castes her eyes upon the ground.
She calls a jolly pleaseman, it happens to be me; .
" I charge this young woman, Mr. Pleaseman," says she.

" Mrs. Roney, o, Mrs. Roney, o, do let me go,
I acted most ungrateful I own, and I know,
But the marriage bell is a ringin, and the ring you may see,
And this young man is a waitin," says Mary says she.

" I don't care three fardens for the parson and clark,
And the bell may keep ringin from noon day to dark.
Mary Brown, Mary Brown, you must come along with me;
And I think this young man is lucky to be free."

So, in spite of the tears which bejew'd Mary's cheek,
I took that young gurl to A'Beckett the Beak;
That exlent Justice demanded her plea—
But never a sullable said Mary said she.   •

On account of her conduck so base and so vile,
That wicked young gurl is committed for trile,
And if she's transpawted beyond the salt sea,
It's a proper reward for such willians as she.

Now you young gurls of Southwark for Mary who veep,
From pickin and stealin your ands you must keep,
Or it may be my dooty, as it was Thursday veek,
To pull you all hup to A'Beckett the Beak.

DAMAGES, TWO HUNDRED POUNDS

SPECIAL Jurymen of England! who admire your country's laws,
 And proclaim a British Jury worthy of the realm's applause ;
 Gaily compliment each other at the issue of a cause
Which was tried at Guildford 'sizes this day week as ever was.

Unto that august tribunal comes a gentleman in grief
(Special was the British Jury, and the Judge, the Baron Chief),
Comes a British man and husband—asking of the law relief,
For his wife was stolen from him—he'd have vengeance on the
 thief.

Yes, his wife, the blessed treasure with the which his life was crowned,
Wickedly was ravished from him by a hypocrite profound.
And he comes before twelve Britons, men for sense and truth re-
 nowned,
To award him for his damage twenty hundred sterling pound.

He by counsel and attorney there at Guildford does appear,
Asking damage of the villain who seduced his lady dear :
But I can't help asking, though the lady's guilt was all too clear,
And though guilty the defendant, wasn't the plaintiff rather queer ?

First the lady's mother spoke, and said she'd seen her daughter cry
But a fortnight after marriage : early times for piping eye.
Six months after, things were worse, and the piping eye was black,
And this gallant British husband caned his wife upon the back.

Three months after they were married, husband pushed her to the
 door,
Told her to be off and leave him, for he wanted her no more.
As she would not go, why *he* went : thrice he left his lady dear ;
Left her, too, without a penny, for more than a quarter of a
 year.

Mrs. Frances Duncan knew the parties very well indeed,
She had seen him pull his lady's nose and make her lip to bleed;
If he chanced to sit at home not a single word he said:
Once she saw him throw the cover of a dish at his lady's head.

Sarah Green, another witness, clear did to the jury note
How she saw this honest fellow seize his lady by the throat,
How he cursed her and abused her, beating her into a fit,
Till the pitying next-door neighbours crossed the wall and wit-
    nessed it.

Next door to this injured Briton Mr. Owers a butcher dwelt;
Mrs. Owers's foolish heart towards this erring dame did melt
(Not that she had erred as yet, crime was not developed in her);
But being left without a penny, Mrs. Owers supplied her dinner—
God be merciful to Mrs. Owers, who was merciful to this sinner!

Caroline Naylor was their servant, said they led a wretched life,
Saw this most distinguished Briton fling a teacup at his wife;
He went out to balls and pleasures, and never once, in ten months'
    space,
Sat with his wife or spoke her kindly.   This was the defendant's
    case.

Pollock, C.B., charged the Jury; said the woman's guilt was
    clear:
That was not the point, however, which the Jury came to hear;
But the damage to determine which, as it should true appear,
This most tender-hearted husband, who so used his lady dear—

Beat her, kicked her, caned her, cursed her, left her starving, year
    by year,
Flung her from him, parted from her, wrung her neck, and boxed
    her ear—
What the reasonable damage this afflicted man could claim
By the loss of the affections of this guilty graceless dame?

Then the honest British Twelve, to each other turning round,
Laid their clever heads together with a wisdom most profound:
And towards his Lordship looking, spoke the foreman wise and
    sound;—
"My Lord, we find for this here plaintiff, damages two hundred
    pound."
13

So, God bless the Special Jury ! pride and joy of English ground,
And the happy land of England, where true justice does abound !
British jurymen and husbands, let us hail this verdict proper :
If a British wife offends you, Britons, you've a right to whop her.

Though you promised to protect her, though you promised to
    defend her,
You are welcome to neglect her : to the devil you may send her :
You may strike her, curse, abuse her ; so declares our law
    renowned ;
And if after this you lose her,—why, you're paid two hundred
    pound.

A WOEFUL NEW BALLAD

OF THE

PROTESTANT CONSPIRACY TO TAKE THE POPE'S LIFE

BY A GENTLEMAN WHO HAS BEEN ON THE SPOT

COME all ye Christian people, unto my tale give ear;
    'Tis about a base consperracy, as quickly shall appear;
    'Twill make your hair to bristle up, and your eyes to start
        and glow,
When of this dread consperracy you honest folks shall know.

The news of this consperracy and villianous attempt,
  read it in a newspaper, from Italy it was sent:
t was sent from lovely Italy, where the olives they do grow,
And our Holy Father lives, yes, yes, while his name it is No NO.

And 'tis there our English noblemen goes that is Puseyites no longer,
Because they finds the ancient faith both better is and stronger.
And 'tis there I knelt beside my Lord when he kiss'd the POPE
    his toe,
And hung his neck with chains at Saint Peter's Vinculo.

And 'tis there the splendid churches is, and the fountains playing
    grand,
And the palace of PRINCE TORLONIA, likewise the Vatican;
And there's the stairs where the bagpipe-men and the piffararys
    blow.
And it's there I drove my Lady and Lord in the Park of Pincio.

And 'tis there our splendid churches is in all their pride and glory,
Saint Peter's famous Basilisk and Saint Mary's Maggiory;
And them benighted Prodestants, on Sunday they must go
Outside the town to the preaching-shop by the gate of Popolo.

Now in this town of famous Room, as I dessay you have heard,
There is scarcely any gentleman as hasn't got a beard.
And ever since the world began it was ordained so,
That there should always barbers be wheresumever beards do grow

And as it always has been so since the world it did begin,
The POPE, our Holy Potentate, has a beard upon his chin;
And every morning regular when cocks begin to crow,
There comes a certing party to wait on POPE PIO.

There comes a certing gintleman with razier, soap, and lather,
A shaving most respectfully the POPE, our Holy Father.
And now the dread consperracy I'll quickly to you show,
Which them sanguinary Prodestants did form against NONO.

Them sanguinary Prodestants, which I abore and hate,
Assembled in the preaching-shop by the Flaminian gate;
And they took counsel with their selves to deal a deadly blow
Against our gentle Father, the Holy POPE PIO.

Exhibiting a wickedness which I never heerd or read of;
What do you think them Prodestants wished? to cut the go
        POPE'S head off!
And to the kind POPE'S Air-dresser the Prodestant Clark did go,
And proposed him to decapitate the innocent PIO.

"What hever can be easier," said this Clerk—this Man of Sin,
"When you are called to hoperate on His Holiness's chin,
Than just to give the razier a little slip—just so?—
And there's an end, dear barber, of innocent PIO!"

This wicked conversation it chanced was overerd
By an Italian lady; she heard it every word:
Which by birth she was a Marchioness, in service forced to go
With the parson of the preaching-shop at the gate of Popolo.

When the lady heard the news, as duty did obleege,
As fast as her legs could carry her she ran to the Poleege.
"O Polegia," says she (for they pronounts it so),
"They're going for to massyker our Holy POPE PIO.

"The ebomminable Englishmen, the Parsing and his Clark,
His Holiness's Air-dresser devised it in the dark!
And I would recommend you in prison for to throw
These villians would esassinate the Holy POPE PIO!

" And for saving of His Holiness and his trebble crownd
  humbly hope your Worships will give me a few pound;
Because I was a Marchioness many years ago,
Before I came to service at the gate of Popolo."

That sackreligious Air-dresser, the Parson and his man,
Wouldn't, though ask'd continyally, own their wicked plan—
And so the kind Authoraties let those villians go
That was plotting of the murder of the good Pio Nono.

Now isn't this safishnt proof, ye gentlemen at home,
How wicked is them Prodestants, and how good our Pope at Rome;
So let us drink confusion to Lord John and Lord Minto,
And a health unto His Eminence, and good Pio Nono.

THE ORGAN-BOY'S APPEAL

"WESTMINSTER POLICE COURT.—POLICEMAN X brought a paper of doggerel verses to the MAGISTRATE, which had been thrust into his hands, X said, by an Italian boy, who ran away immediately afterwards.

"The MAGISTRATE, after perusing the lines, looked hard at X, and said he did not think they were written by an Italian.

"X, blushing, said he thought the paper read in court last week, and which frightened so the old gentleman to whom it was addressed, was also not of Italian origin."

O SIGNOR BRODERIP, you are a wickid ole man,
You wexis us little horgin-boys whenever you can:
How dare you talk of Justice, and go for to seek
To pussicute us horgin-boys, you senguinary Beek?

Though you set in Vestminster surrounded by your crushers,
Harrogint and habsolute like the Hortacrat of hall the Rushers,
Yet there is a better vurld I'd have you for to know,
Likewise a place vere the henimies of horgin-boys will go.

O you vickid HEROD without any pity!
London vithout horgin-boys vood be a dismal city.
Sweet SAINT CICILY who first taught horgin-pipes to blow
Soften the heart of this Magistrit that haggerywates us so!

Good Italian gentlemen, fatherly and kind,
Brings us over to London here our horgins for to grind;
Sends us out vith little vite mice and guinea-pigs also
A poppin of the Veasel and a Jumpin of JIM CROW.

And as us young horgin-boys is grateful in our turn
We gives to these kind gentlemen hall the money we earn,
Because that they vood vop us as wery wel we know
Unless we brought our hurnings back to them as loves us so.

O Mr. Broderip ! wery much I'm surprise,
Ven you take your valks abroad where can be your eyes?
If a Beak had a heart then you'd compryend
Us pore little horgin-boys was the poor man's friend.

Don't you see the shildren in the droring-rooms
Clapping of their little ands when they year our toons?
On their mothers' bussums don't you see the babbies crow
And down to us dear horgin-boys lots of apence throw?

Don't you see the ousemaids (pooty Pollies and Maries),
Ven ve bring our urdigurdis, smiling from the hairies?
Then they come out vith a slice o' cole puddn or a bit o' bacon or so
And give it us young horgin-boys for lunch afore we go.

Have you ever seen the Hirish children sport
When our velcome music-box brings sunshine in the Court?
To these little paupers who can never pay
Surely all good horgin-boys, for God's love, will play.

Has for those proud gentlemen, like a serting B—k
(Vich I von't be pussonal and therefore vil not speak),
That flings their parler-vinders hup ven ve begin to play
And cusses us and swears at us in such a wiolent way,

Instedd of their abewsing and calling hout Poleece,
Let em send out John to us vith sixpence or a shillin apiece.
Then like good young horgin-boys avay from there we'll go,
Blessing sweet Saint Cicily that taught our pipes to blow.

THE KNIGHT AND THE LADY

THERE'S in the Vest a city pleasant
    To vich King Bladud gev his name,
    And in that city there's a Crescent
Vere dwelt a noble knight of fame.

Although that galliant knight is oldish,
    Although Sir John as grey grey air,
Hage has not made his busum coldish,
    His Art still beats tewodds the Fair!

'Twas two years sins, this knight so splendid,
    Peraps fateagued with Bath's routines,
To Paris towne his phootsteps bended
    In sutch of gayer folks and seans.

His and was free, his means was easy,
    A nobler, finer gent than he
Ne'er drove about the Shons-Eleesy,
    Or paced the Roo de Rivolee.

A brougham and pair Sir John prowided,
    In which abroad he loved to ride;
But ar! he most of all enjyed it,
    When some one helse was sittin' inside!

That "some one helse" a lovely dame was,
    Dear ladies, you will heasy tell—
Countess Grabrowski her sweet name was,
    A noble title, ard to spell.

This faymus Countess ad a daughter
    Of lovely form and tender art;
A nobleman in marridge sought her,
    By name the Baron of Saint Bart.

Their pashn touched the noble Sir John,
    It was so pewer and profound ;
Lady Grabrowski he did urge on
    With Hyming's wreeth their loves to crownd.

" O, come to Bath, to Lansdowne Crescent,"
    Says kind Sir John, " and live with me ;
The living there's uncommon pleasant—
    I'm sure you'll find the hair agree.

" O, come to Bath, my fair Grabrowski,
    And bring your charming girl," sezee ;
" The Barring here shall have the ouse-key,
    Vith breakfast, dinner, lunch, and tea.

" And when they've passed an appy winter,
    Their opes and loves no more we'll bar ;
The marridge-vow they'll enter inter,
    And I at church will be their Par."

To Bath they went to Lansdowne Crescent,
    Where good Sir John he did provide
No end of teas and balls incessant,
    And hosses both to drive and ride.

He was so Ospitably busy,
    When Miss was late, he'd make so bold
Upstairs to call out, " Missy, Missy,
    Come down, the coffy's getting cold ! "

But O ! 'tis sadd to think such bounties
    Should meet with such return as this ;
O Barring of Saint Bart, O Countess
    Grabrowski, and O cruel Miss !

He married you at Bath's fair Habby,
    Saint Bart he treated like a son—
And wasn't it uncommon shabby
    To do what you have went and done !

My trembling And amost refewses
    To write the charge which Sir John swore,
Of which the Countess he ecuses,
    Her daughter and her son-in-lore.

My Mews quite blushes as she sings of
    The fatle charge which now I quote :
He says Miss took his two best rings off,
    And pawned 'em for a tenpun note.

" Is this the child of honest parince,
    To make away with folks' best things ?
Is this, pray, like the wives of Barrins,
    To go and prig a gentleman's rings ? "

Thus thought Sir John, by anger wrought on,
    And to rewenge his injured cause,
He brought them hup to Mr. Broughton,
    Last Vensday veek as ever waws.

If guiltless, how she have been slandered !
    If guilty, wengeance will not fail :
Meanwhile the lady is remanded
    And gev three hundred pouns in bail.

THE SPECULATORS

THE night was stormy and dark, The town was shut up in sleep : Only those were abroad who were out on a lark, Or those who'd no beds to keep.

I pass'd through the lonely street, The wind did sing and blow ; I could hear the policeman's feet Clapping to and fro.

There stood a potato-man In the midst of all the wet ; He stood with his 'tato can In the lonely Haymarket.

Two gents of dismal mien, And dank and greasy rags, Came out of a shop for gin, Swaggering over the flags :

Swaggering over the stones, These shabby bucks did walk ; And I went and followed those seedy ones, And listened to their talk.

Was I sober or awake ? Could I believe my ears ? Those dismal beggars spake Of nothing but railroad shares.

I wondered more and more : Says one—" Good friend of mine, How many shares have you wrote for, In the Diddlesex Junction line ? "

"I wrote for twenty," says Jim, "But they wouldn't give me one ; " His comrade straight rebuked him For the folly he had done :

"O Jim, you are unawares Of the ways of this bad town ; *I* always write for five hundred shares, And *then* they put me down."

"And yet you got no shares," Says Jim, "for all your boast ; " "I *would* have wrote," says Jack, "but where Was the penny to pay the post ? "

"I lost, for I couldn't pay   That first instalment up;   But here's taters smoking hot—I say,   Let's stop, my boy, and sup."

And at this simple feast   The while they did regale,   I drew each ragged capitalist   Down on my left thumb-nail.

Their talk did me perplex,   All night I tumbled and tost,   And thought of railroad specs,   And how money was won and lost.

"Bless railroads everywhere,"   I said, "and the world's advance ;   Bless every railroad share   In Italy, Ireland, France ; For never a beggar need now despair,   And every rogue has a chance."

CRITICAL REVIEWS

CRITICAL REVIEWS

CARLYLE'S FRENCH REVOLUTION *

[1837]

SINCE the appearance of this work, within the last two months, it has raised among the critics and the reading public a strange storm of applause and discontent. To hear one arty you would fancy the author was but a dull madman, indulg-g in wild vagaries of language and dispensing with common sense d reason, while, according to another, his opinions are little short ' inspiration, and his eloquence unbounded as his genius. We nfess, that in reading the first few pages, we were not a little clined to adopt the former opinion, and yet, after perusing the hole of this extraordinary work, we can allow, almost to their llest extent, the high qualities with which Mr. Carlyle's idolaters dow him.

But never did a book sin so grievously from outward appear-ce, or a man's style so mar his subject and dim his genius. It stiff, short, and rugged, it abounds with Germanisms and Latin-ns, strange epithets, and choking double words, astonishing to the mirers of simple Addisonian English, to those who love history it gracefully runs in Hume, or struts pompously in Gibbon—no ch style is Mr. Carlyle's. A man, at the first onset, must take eath at the end of a sentence, or, worse still, go to sleep in the dst of it. But these hardships become lighter as the traveller ows accustomed to the road, and he speedily learns to admire and mpathise; just as he would admire a Gothic cathedral in spite of e quaint carvings and hideous images on door and buttress.

There are, however, a happy few of Mr. Carlyle's critics and ders to whom these very obscurities and mysticisms of style are

* "The French Revolution : A History." In three volumes. By Thomas rlyle. London: James Fraser, 1837.

welcome and almost intelligible; the initiated in metaphysics, the sages who have passed the veil of Kantian philosophy, and discovered that the "critique of pure reason" is really that which it purports to be, and not the critique of pure nonsense, as it seems to worldly men: to these the present book has charms unknown to us, who can merely receive it as a history of a stirring time, and a skilful record of men's worldly thoughts and doings. Even through these dim spectacles a man may read and profit much from Mr. Carlyle's volumes.

He is not a party historian like Scott, who could not, in his benevolent respect for rank and royalty, see duly the faults of either: he is as impartial as Thiers, but with a far loftier and nobler impartiality.

No man can have read the admirable history of the French ex-Minister who has not been struck with this equal justice which he bestows on all the parties or heroes of his book. He has completely mastered the active part of the history: he has no more partiality for court than for regicide—scarcely a movement of intriguing king or republican which is unknown to him or undescribed. He sees with equal eyes Madame Roland or Marie Antoinette—bullying Brunswick on the frontier, or Marat at his butcher's work or in his cellar—he metes to each of them justice, and no more, finding good even in butcher Marat or bullying Brunswick, and recording what he finds. What a pity that one gains such a complete contempt for the author of all this cleverness. Only a rogue could be so impartial, for Thiers but views this awful series of circumstances in their very meanest and basest light, like a petty, clever statesman as he is, watching with wonderful accuracy all the moves of the great game, but looking for no more, never drawing a single moral from it, or seeking to tell aught beyond it.

Mr. Carlyle, as we have said, is as impartial as the illustrious Academician and Minister; but with what different eyes he looks upon the men and the doings of this strange time! To the one the whole story is but a hustling for places—a list of battles and intrigues—of kings and governments rising and falling; to the other, the little actors of this great drama are striving but towards a great end and moral. It is better to view it loftily from afar like our mystic poetic Mr. Carlyle, than too nearly with sharp-sighted and prosaic Thiers. Thiers is the *valet de chambre* of this history, he is too familiar with its dishabille and off-scourings: it can never be a hero to him.

It is difficult to convey to the reader a fair notion of Mr. Carlyle's powers or his philosophy, for the reader has not grown familiar with the strange style of this book, and may laugh perhaps

t the grotesqueness of his teacher: in this some honest critics of
he present day have preceded him, who have formed their awful
udgments after scanning half-a-dozen lines, and damned poor Mr.
Carlyle's because they chanced to be lazy. Here, at hazard, however, we fall upon the story of the Bastille capture; the people
re thundering at the gates, but Delaunay will receive no terms,
aises his drawbridge and gives fire. Now, cries Mr. Carlyle with
n uncouth Orson-like shout:—

"Bursts forth Insurrection, at sight of its own blood, into
ndless explosion of musketry, distraction, execration;—and over-
ead, from the Fortress, let one great gun go booming, to show
what we *could* do. The Bastille is besieged!

"On, then, all Frenchmen that have hearts in their bodies!
Roar with all your throats, of cartilage and metal, ye Sons of
Liberty; stir spasmodically whatsoever of utmost faculty is in
ou, soul, body, or spirit; for it is the hour! Smite, thou Louis
Tournay, cartwright of the Marais, old-soldier of the Regiment
Dauphiné; smite at that Outer Drawbridge-chain, though the fiery
ail whistles round thee! Never, over nave or felloe, did thy axe
trike such a stroke. Down with it, man; down with it to Orcus:
et the whole accursed Edifice sink thither, and Tyranny be
wallowed up for ever! Mounted, some say, on the roof of the
uard-room, Louis Tournay smites, brave Aubin Bonnemère (also
n old soldier) seconding him: the chain yields, breaks; the huge
Drawbridge slams down, thundering. Glorious: and yet, alas, it
s still but the outworks. The eight grim Towers, with their In-
alides, musketry, their paving stones and cannon-mouths, still soar
loft intact;—Ditch yawning impassable, stone-faced; the inner
Drawbridge with its *back* towards us: the Bastille is still to take!"

Did "Savage Rosa" ever "dash" a more spirited battle sketch?
The two principal figures of the pieces, placed in skilful relief, the
aging multitude and sombre fortress admirably laid down! In
he midst of this writhing and wrestling, "the line too labours (Mr.
Carlyle's line labours perhaps too often), and the words move slow."
The whole story of the fall of the fortress and its defenders is told
a a style similarly picturesque and real.

"The poor Invalides have sunk under their battlements, or
se only with reversed muskets: they have made a white flag of
apkins; go beating the *chamade*, or seeming to beat, for one can
ear nothing. The very Swiss at the Portcullis look weary of
ring; disheartened in the fire-deluge; a porthole at the draw-
ridge is opened, as by one that would speak. See Huissier
Maillard, the shifty man! On his plank, swinging over the abyss
f that stone-Ditch; plank resting on parapet, balanced by weight

T

of Patriots,—he hovers perilous: such a Dove towards such a
Ark! Deftly, thou shifty Usher: one man already fell; and lie
smashed, far down there against the masonry! Usher Maillar
falls not: deftly, unerring he walks, with outspread palm. Th
Swiss holds a paper through his porthole; the shifty Usher snatche
it, and returns. Terms of surrender: Pardon, immunity to all
Are they accepted? '*Foi d'officier*, on the word of an officer
answers half-pay Hulin,—or half-pay Elie, for men do not agre
on it, 'they are.' Sinks the drawbridge,—Usher Maillard boltin
it when down; rushes in the living deluge: the Bastille is fallen
Victoire! La Bastille est prise!"

This is prose run mad—no doubt of it—according to our notior
of the sober gait and avocations of homely prose; but is there no
method in it, and could sober prose have described the incident i
briefer words, more emphatically, or more sensibly? And th
passage, which succeeds the picture of storm and slaughter, oper
(grotesque though it be), not in prose, but in noble poetry; tl
author describes the rest of France during the acting of this Par
tragedy—and by this peaceful image admirably heightens the gloo
and storm of his first description:—

"O evening sun of July, how, at this hour, thy beams fall slar
on reapers amid peaceful woody fields; on old women spinning i
cottages; on ships far out in the silent main; on Balls at tl
Orangerie of Versailles, where high-rouged Dames are even no
dancing with double-jacketted Hussar-Officers, and also on this roa
ing Hell-porch of a Hôtel-de-Ville! One forest of distracted stee
bristles, in front of an Electoral Committee; points itself, in horri
radii, against this and the other accused breast. It was the Titar
warring with Olympus; and they, scarcely crediting it, hav
conquered." The reader will smile at the double-jackets and roug
which never would be allowed entrance into a polite modern epi
but, familiar though they be, they complete the picture, and giv
it reality, that gloomy rough Rembrandt-kind of reality which
Mr. Carlyle's style of historic painting.

In this same style Mr. Carlyle dashes off the portraits of h
various characters as they rise in the course of the history. Tak
for instance, this grotesque portrait of vapouring Tonneau Mirabea
his life and death; it follows a solemn, almost awful picture of tl
demise of his great brother:—

"Here, then, the wild Gabriel Honoré drops from the tissue
our History; not without a tragic farewell. He is gone: tl
flower of the wild Riquetti kindred; which seems as if in him
had done its best, and then expired, or sunk down to the undi
tinguished level. Crabbed old Marquis Mirabeau, the Friend

en, sleeps sound. Barrel Mirabeau gone across the Rhine; his
egiment of Emigrants will drive nigh desperate. 'Barrel Mira-
au,' says a biographer of his, 'went indignantly across the Rhine,
d drilled Emigrant Regiments. But as he sat one morning in
s tent, sour of stomach doubtless and of heart, meditating in
artarean humour on the turn things took, a certain Captain or
ubaltern demanded admittance on business. Such Captain is
fused; he again demands, with refusal; and then again, till
olonel Viscount Barrel-Mirabeau, blazing up into a mere brandy
arrel, clutches his sword and tumbles out on this *canaille* of an
truder,—alas, on the *canaille* of an intruder's sword's point, who
d drawn with swift dexterity; and dies, and the Newspapers
me it *apoplexy* and *alarming accident*. So die the Mirabeaus."

Mr. Carlyle gives this passage to "a biographer," but he himself
ust be the author of this History of a Tub; the grim humour
d style belong only to him. In a graver strain he speaks of
abriel:—

"New Mirabeaus one hears not of: the wild kindred, as we
id, is gone out with this its greatest. As families and kindreds
metimes do; producing, after long ages of unnoted notability,
me living quintessence of all they had, to flame forth as a man
orld-noted; after whom they rest, as if exhausted; the sceptre
ssing to others. The chosen Last of the Mirabeaus is gone; the
osen man of France is gone. It was he who shook old France
om its basis; and, as if with his single hand, has held it toppling
ere, still unfallen. What things depended on that one man!
e is as a ship suddenly shivered on sunk rocks: much swims on
e waste waters, far from help."

Here is a picture of *the* heroine of the Revolution :—" Radiant
ith enthusiasm are those dark eyes, is that strong Minerva-face,
oking dignity and earnest joy; joyfullest she where all are joyful.
eader, mark that queen-like burgher-woman : beautiful, Amazonian-
aceful to the eye; more so to the mind. Unconscious of her
orth (as all worth is), of her greatness, of her crystal clearness;
nuine, the creature of Sincerity and Nature in an age of Artifici-
ty, Pollution, and Cant; there, in her still completeness, in her
ll invincibility, *she*, if thou knew it, is the noblest of all living
renchwomen,—and will be seen, one day."

The reader, we think, will not fail to observe the real beauty
hich lurks among all these odd words and twisted sentences,
ving, as it were, in spite of the weeds; but we repeat, that no
ere extracts can do justice to the book; it requires time and
udy. A first acquaintance with it is very unprepossessing; only
miliarity knows its great merits, and values it accordingly.

We would gladly extract a complete chapter or episode from the work—the flight to Varennes, for instance, the huge coach bearing away the sleepy, dawdling, milk-sop royalty of France, fiery Bouillé spreading abroad his scouts and Hussars, "his electric thunder-chain of military outposts," as Mr. Carlyle calls them with one of his great similes. Paris in tremendous commotion, the country up and armed, to prevent the King's egress, the chance of escape glimmering bright until the last moment, and only extinguished by bewildered Louis himself, too pious and too out-of-breath, too hungry and sleepy, to make one charge at the head of those gallant dragoons—one single blow to win crown and kingdom and liberty again! We never read this hundred-times told tale with such a breathless interest as Mr. Carlyle has managed to instil into it. The whole of the sad story is equally touching and vivid, from the mean ignominious return down to the fatal 10th of August, when the sections beleaguered the King's palace, and King Louis with arms, artillery, and 2000 true and gallant men, flung open the Tuileries gates and said "*Marchons! marchons!*" whither? No, with *vive le Roi*, and roaring guns, and bright bayonets, sheer through the rabble who barred the gate, swift through the broad Champs Elysées, and the near barrier,—not to conquer or fall like a King and gentleman, but to the reporters' box in the National Assembly, to be cooped and fattened until killing time; to be trussed and tranquil like a fat capon. What a son for St. Louis! What a husband for brave Antoinette!

Let us, however, follow Mr. Carlyle to the last volume, and passing over the time, when, in Danton's awful image, "coalized Kings made war upon France, and France, as a gage of battle, flung the head of a King at their feet," quote two of the last scenes of that awful tragedy, the deaths of bold Danton and "sea-green Robespierre, as Carlyle delights to call him.

"On the night of the 30th of March, Juryman Pâris came rushing in; haste looking through his eyes : a clerk of the Salut Committee had told him Danton's warrant was made out, he is to be arrested this very night! Entreaties there are and trepidation of poor Wife, of Pâris and Friends : Danton sat silent for a while, then answered, '*Ils n'oseraient*, They dare not;' and would take no measures. Murmuring 'They dare not,' he goes to sleep as usual.

"And yet, on the morrow morning, strange rumour spread over Paris city : Danton, Camille, Phélippeaux, Lacroix, have been arrested over night! It is verily so : the corridors of the Luxembourg were all crowded, Prisoners crowding forth to see this giant of the Revolution enter among them. 'Messieurs,' said Danton politely, 'I hoped soon to have got you all out of this;

but here I am myself; and one sees not where it will end.'—
Rumour may spread over Paris : the Convention clusters itself into
groups ; wide-eyed, whispering, 'Danton arrested!' Who then is
safe? Legendre, mounting the Tribune, utters, at his own peril, a
feeble word for him ; moving that he be heard at that bar before
indictment ; but Robespierre frowns him down : 'Did you hear
Chabot, or Bazire? Would you have two weights and measures?'
Legendre cowers low ; Danton, like the others, must take his doom.

"Danton's Prison-thoughts were curious to have ; but are not
given in any quantity : indeed, few such remarkable men have
been left so obscure to us as this Titan of the Revolution. He
was heard to ejaculate : 'This time twelvemonth, I was moving
the creation of that same Revolutionary Tribunal. I crave pardon
for it of God and man. They are all Brothers Cain : Briscot
would have had me guillotined as Robespierre now will. I leave
the whole business in a frightful welter (*gâchis épouvantable*) : not
one of them understands anything of government. Robespierre
will follow me ; I drag down Robespierre. Oh, it were better to
be a poor fisherman than to meddle with governing of men.'—
Camille's young beautiful Wife, who had made him rich not in
money alone, hovers round the Luxembourg, like a disembodied
spirit, day and night. Camille's stolen letters to her still exist ;
stained with the mark of his tears. 'I carry my head like a
Saint-Sacrament?' So Saint Just was heard to mutter : 'Perhaps
he will carry his like a Saint-Dennis.'

"Unhappy Danton, thou still unhappier light Camille, once
light *Procureur de la Lanterne,* ye also have arrived, then, at the
Bourne of Creation, where, like Ulysses Polytlas at the limit and
utmost Gades of his voyage, gazing into that dim Waste beyond
Creation, a man does see *the Shade of his Mother,* pale, ineffectual ;
—and days when his Mother nursed and wrapped him are all
too sternly contrasted with this day ! Danton, Camille, Hérault,
Westermann, and the others, very strangely massed up with Bazires,
Swindler Chabots, Fabre d'Eglantines, Banker Freys, a most
motley Batch, '*Fournée*' as such things will be called, stand
ranked at the bar of Tinville. It is the 2nd of April, 1794.
Danton has had but three days to lie in prison ; for the time
presses.

"'What is your name? place of abode?' and the like, Fouquier
asks ; according to formality. 'My name is Danton,' answers he ;
'a name tolerably known in the Revolution : my abode will soon
be Annihilation (*dans le Néant*) ; but I shall live in the Pantheon
of History.' A man will endeavour to say something forcible, be
it by nature or not ! Hérault mentions epigrammatically that he

'sat in this Hall, and was detested of Parlementeers.' Camill
makes answer, ' My age is that of the *bon Sansculotte Jésus; a*
age fatal to Revolutionists.' O Camille, Camille! And yet i
that Divine Transaction, let us say, there did lie, among othe
things, the fatallest Reproof ever uttered here below to Worldly
Right-honourableness; ' the highest Fact,' so devout Novalis call
it, ' in the Rights of Man.' Camille's real age, it would seem, i
thirty-four. Danton is one year older.

"Some five months ago, the Trial of the Twenty-two Girondin
was the greatest that Fouquier had then done. But here is a stil
greater to do; a thing which tasks the whole faculty of Fouquier
which makes the very heart of him waver. For it is the voice o
Danton that reverberates now from these domes; in passionate
words, piercing with their wild sincerity, winged with wrath
Your best Witnesses he shivers into ruin at one stroke. He
demands that the Committee-men themselves come as Witnesses
as Accusers; he ' will cover them with ignominy.' He raises his
huge stature, he shakes his huge black head, fire flashes from the
eyes of him,—piercing to all Republican hearts: so that the very
Galleries, though we filled them by ticket, murmur sympathy; and
are like to burst down, and raise the People, and deliver him
He complains loudly that he is classed with Chabots, with swindling
Stockjobbers; that his Indictment is a list of platitudes and horrors.
' Danton hidden on the Tenth of August?' reverberates he, with
the roar of a lion in the toils: 'Where are the men that had to
press Danton to show himself, that day? Where are these high-
gifted souls of whom he borrowed energy? Let them appear, these
Accusers of mine: I have all the clearness of my self-possession
when I demand them. I will unmask the three shallow scoundrels,
les trois plats coquins, Saint-Just, Couthon, Lebas, ' who fawn on
Robespierre, and lead him towards his destruction. Let them
produce themselves here; I will plunge them into Nothingness,
out of which they ought never to have risen.' The agitated President agitates his bell; enjoins calmness, in a vehement manner:
' What is it to thee how I defend myself?' cries the other; ' the
right of dooming me is thine always. The voice of a man speaking
for his honour and his life may well drown the jingling of thy
bell!' Thus Danton, higher and higher; till the lion voice of him
' dies away in his throat:' speech will not utter what is in that
man. The Galleries murmur ominously; the first day's Session
is over."

. . . .

"Danton carried a high look in the Death-cart. Not so
Camille: it is but one week, and all is so topsy-turvied; ange

Wife left weeping; love, riches, Revolutionary fame, left all at the Prison-gate; carnivorous Rabble now howling round. Palpable, and yet incredible; like a madman's dream! Camille struggles and writhes; his shoulders shuffle the loose coat off hem, which hangs knotted, the hands tied: ' Calm, my friend,' said Danton, 'heed not that vile canaille (*laissez là cette vile canaille*).' At the foot of the Scaffold, Danton was heard to ejaculate, 'O my Wife, my well-beloved, I shall never see thee more then!'—but, interrupting himself: 'Danton, no weakness!' He said to Hérault-Sechelles stepping forward to embrace him: Our heads will meet *there*,' in the Headsman's sack. His last words were to Samson the Headsman himself, 'Thou wilt show my head to the people; it is worth showing.'

"So passes, like a gigantic mass of valour, ostentation, fury, affection, and wild revolutionary manhood, this Danton, to his unknown home. He was of Arcis-sur-Aube; born of ' good farmer-people' there. He had many sins; but one worst sin he had not, that of Cant. No hollow Formalist, deceptive and self-deceptive, *ghastly* to the natural sense, was this; but a very Man: with all his dross he was a Man; fiery-real, from the great fire-bosom of Nature herself. He saved France from Brunswick; he walked straight his own wild road, whither it led him. He may live for some generations in the memory of men."

This noble passage requires no comment, nor does that in which the poor wretched Robespierre shrieks his last shriek, and dies his pitiful and cowardly death. Tallien has drawn his theatrical dagger, and made his speech, trembling Robespierre has fled to the Hôtel de Ville, and Henriot, of the National Guard, clatters through the city, summoning the sections to the aid of the people's friend.

" About three in the morning, the dissident Armed-forces have *met*. Henriot's Armed Force stood ranked in the Place de Grève; and now Barras's, which he has recruited, arrives there; and they front each other, cannon bristling against cannon. Citoyens! cries the voice of Discretion loudly enough. Before coming to bloodshed, to endless civil war, hear the Convention Decree read :—' Robespierre and all rebels Out of Law!' Out of Law? There is terror in the sound: unarmed Citoyens disperse rapidly home; Municipal Cannoneers range themselves on the Convention side, with shouting. At which shout, Henriot descends from his upper room, far gone in drink as some say; finds his Place de Grève empty; the cannons' mouth turned *towards* him; and, on the whole,—that it is now the catastrophe!

"Stumbling in again, the wretched drunk-sobered Henriot announces: ' All is lost!' ' *Miserable!* it is thou that hast lost it,'

cry they; and fling him, or else he flings himself, out of window
far enough down; into masonwork and horror of cesspool; not into
death but worse. Augustin Robespierre follows him; with the
like fate. Saint-Just called on Lebas to kill him; who would not.
Couthon crept under a table; attempting to kill himself; not doing
it.—On entering that Sanhedrim of Insurrection, we find all as
good as extinct! undone, ready for seizure. Robespierre was sitting
on a chair, with pistol-shot blown through, not his head, but his
under jaw; the suicidal hand had failed. With prompt zeal, not
without trouble, we gather these wrecked Conspirators; fish up even
Henriot and Augustin, bleeding and foul; pack them all, rudely
enough, into carts; and shall, before sunrise, have them safe under
lock and key. Amid shoutings and embracings.

"Robespierre lay in an ante-room of the Convention Hall, while
his Prison-escort was getting ready; the mangled jaw bound up
rudely with bloody linen: a spectacle to men. He lies stretched
on a table, a deal-box his pillow; the sheath of the pistol is still
clenched convulsively in his hand. Men bully him, insult him:
his eyes still indicate intelligence; he speaks no word. 'He had
on the sky-blue coat he had got made for the Feast of the *Être
Supreme*'—O reader, can thy hard heart hold out against that?
His trousers were nankeen; the stockings had fallen down over the
ankles. He spake no word more in this world."

.   .   .   .

"The Death-tumbrils, with their motley Batch of Outlaws,
some Twenty-three or so, from Maximilien to Mayor Fleuriot and
Simon the Cordwainer, roll on. All eyes are on Robespierre's
Tumbril, where he, his jaw bound in dirty linen, with his half-dead
Brother, and half-dead Henriot, lie shattered, their 'seventeen hours'
of agony about to end. The Gendarmes point their swords at him,
to show the people which is he. A woman springs on the Tumbril;
clutching the side of it with one hand; waving the other Sibyl-
like; and exclaims, 'The death of thee gladdens my very heart,
m'enivre de joie;' Robespierre opened his eyes; '*Scélérat*, go down
to Hell, with the curses of all wives and mothers!'—At the foot of
the Scaffold, they stretched him on the ground till his turn came.
Lifted aloft, his eyes again opened; caught the bloody axe. Samson
wrenched the coat off him; wrenched the dirty linen from his jaw;
the jaw fell powerless, there burst from him a cry;—hideous to
hear and see. Samson, thou canst not be too quick!

"Samson's work done, there bursts forth shout on shout of
applause. Shout, which prolongs itself not only over Paris, but
over France, but over Europe, and down to this Generation. De-

servedly, and also undeservedly. Oh, unhappiest Advocate of Arras, wert thou worse than other Advocates? Stricter man, according to his Formula, to his Credo, and his Cant, of probities, benevolences, pleasures-of-virtue, and such like, lived not in that age. A man fitted, in some luckier settled age, to have become one of those incorruptible barren Pattern-Figures, and have had marble-tablets and funeral-sermons! His poor landlord, the Cabinetmaker in the Rue Saint-Honoré, loved him; his Brother died for him. May God be merciful to him, and to us!"

The reader will see in the above extracts most of the faults, and a few of the merits, of this book. He need not be told that it is written in an eccentric prose, here and there disfigured by grotesque conceits and images; but, for all this, it betrays most extraordinary powers—learning, observation, and humour. Above all, it has no CANT. It teems with sound, hearty philosophy (besides certain transcendentalisms which we do not pretend to understand), it possesses genius, if any book ever did. It wanted no more for keen critics to cry fie upon it! Clever critics who have such an eye for genius, that when Mr. Bulwer published his forgotten book concerning Athens, they discovered that no historian was like to him; that he, on his Athenian hobby, had quite out-trotted stately Mr. Gibbon; and with the same creditable unanimity they cried down Mr. Carlyle's history, opening upon it a hundred little piddling sluices of small wit, destined to wash the book sheer away; and lo! the book remains, it is only the poor wit which has run dry.

We need scarcely recommend this book and its timely appearance, now that some of the questions solved in it seem almost likely to be battled over again. The hottest Radical in England may learn by it that there is something more necessary for him even than his mad liberty—the authority, namely, by which he retains his head on his shoulders and his money in his pocket, which privileges that by-word "liberty" is often unable to secure for him. It teaches (by as strong examples as ever taught any-thing) to rulers and to ruled alike moderation, and yet there are many who would react the same dire tragedy, and repeat the experiment tried in France so fatally. "No Peers—no Bishops—no property qualification—no restriction of suffrage." Mr. Leader bellows it out at Westminster and Mr. Roebuck croaks it at Bath. Pert quacks at public meetings joke about hereditary legislators, journalists gibe at them, and moody starving labourers, who do not know how to jest, but can hate lustily, are told to curse crowns and coronets as the origin of their woes and their poverty,—and so did the clever French spouters and journalists gibe at royalty, until royalty fell poisoned under their satire; and so did the screaming hungry French mob curse royalty until they overthrew it : and to what end? To bring tyranny and leave starvation, battering down Bastilles to erect guillotines, and murdering kings to set up emperors in their stead.

We do not say that in our own country similar excesses are to be expected or feared; the cause of complaint has never been so great, the wrong has never been so crying on the part of the rulers, as to bring down such fearful retaliation from the governed. Mr. Roebuck is not Robespierre, and Mr. Attwood, with his threatened legion of fiery Marseillois, is at best but a Brummagem Barbaroux. But men alter with circumstances; six months before the kingly *decheance*, the bitter and bilious advocate of Arras spake with tears in his eyes about good King Louis, and the sweets and merits of constitutional monarchy and hereditary representation : and so he spoke, until his own turn came, and his own delectable guillotining system had its hour. God forbid that we should pursue the simile with Mr. Roebuck so far as this; God forbid, too, that he ever should have the trial.

True; but we have no right, it is said, to compare the Republicanism of England with that of France, no right to suppose that such crimes would be perpetrated in a country so enlightened as ours. Why is there peace and liberty and a republic in America? No guillotining, no ruthless Yankee tribunes retaliating for bygone tyranny by double oppression? Surely the reason is obvious—because there was no hunger in America; because there were easier ways of livelihood than those offered by ambition. Banish Queen, and Bishops, and Lords, seize the lands, open the ports, or shut them (according to the fancy of your trades' unions and democratic clubs, who have each their freaks and hobbies), and are you a whit richer in a month, are your poor Spitalfields men vending their silks, or your poor Irishmen reaping their harvests at home? Strong interest keeps Americans quiet, not Government; here there is always a party which is interested in rebellion. People America like England, and the poor weak rickety republic is jostled to death in the crowd. Give us this republic to-morrow and it would share no better fate; have not all of us the power, and many of us the interest, to destroy it?

FASHNABLE FAX AND POLITE ANNYGOATS

BY CHARLES YELLOWPLUSH, ESQ.

No. —, Grosvenor Square : 10th October.
(N.B. Hairy Bell.)

MY DEAR Y.—Your dellixy in sending me "My Book"*
does you honour; for the subjick on which it treats
cannot, like politix, metafizzix, or other silly sciences, be
criticised by the common writin creaturs who do your and other
Magazines at so much a yard. I am a chap of a different sort.
I have lived with some of the first families in Europe, and I
say it, without fear of contradistinction, that, since the death of
George the IV., and Mr. Simpson of Voxall Gardens, there doesn't,
praps, live a more genlmnly man than myself. As to figger, I beat
Simpson all to shivers ; and know more of the world than the late
George. He did things in a handsome style enough, but he lived
always in one set, and got narrow in his notions. How could he
be otherwise? Had he my opportunities, I say he would have
been a better dressed man, a better dined man (poor angsy deer,
as the French say), and a better furnitured man. These qualities
an't got by indolence, but by acute hobservation and foring travel,
as I have had. But a truce to heggotism, and let us proceed
with bisness.

Skelton's "Anatomy" (or Skeleton's, which, I presume, is his
real name) is a work which has been long wanted in the littery
world. A reglar slap-up, no-mistake, out-an'-out account of the
manners and usitches of genteel society, will be appreciated in
every famly from Buckly Square to Whitechapel Market. Ever
since you sent me the volum, I have read it to the gals in our
hall, who are quite delighted of it, and every day grows genteeler
and genteeler. So is Jeames, coachman ; so is Sam and George,
and little Halfred, the sugar-loafed page:—all 'xcept old Hufly,
the fat veezy porter, who sits all day in his hall-chair, and never
reads a word of anythink but that ojus Hage newspaper. "Hufly,"

* "My Book ; or, The Anatomy of Conduct." By John Henry Skelton
London : Simpkin & Marshall. 1837.

I often say to him, "why continue to read that blaggerd print Want of decency, Huffy, becomes no man in your high situation a genlman without morallity, is like a liv'ry-coat without a shoulder-knot." But the old-fashioned beast reads on, and don't care for a syllable of what I say. As for the *Sat'rist*, that's different : I read it myself, reg'lar; for it's of uncompromising Raddicle principils, and lashes the vices of the arristoxy. But again I am diverging from Skeleton.

What I like about him so pertiklerly is his moddisty. Be fore you come to the book, there is, fust, a Deddication ; then, a Preface ; and nex', a Prolygomeny. The fust is about hisself the second about hisself, too ; and, cuss me ! if the Prolygoly gominy an't about hisself again, and his schoolmaster, the Rev. John Finlay, late of Streatham Academy. I shall give a few extrax from them :—

"Graceful manners are not intuitive : so he, who, through industry or the smiles of fortune, *would emulate a polite carriage*, must be *taught* not to outrage propriety. Many topics herein considered have been discussed, more or less gravely or jocosely, according as the subject-matter admitted the varying treatment. I would that with propriety much might be expunged, but that I felt it is all required from the nature of the work. The public is the tribunal to which I appeal : not friendship, but public attestation, must affix the signet to 'My Book's' approval or con-demnation. Sheridan, when manager of Drury, was known to say, he had solicited and received the patronage of friends, but from the public only had he found support. So may it be with me !"

There's a sentence for you, Mr. Yorke ! * We disputed about it, for three-quarters of an hour, in the servants' hall. Miss Simkins, my Lady's *feel de chamber*, says it's complete ungramatticle, as so it is. " I would that," &c., " but that," and so forth : what can be the earthly meaning of it ? " Graceful manners," says Skeleton, " is not intuitive." Nor more an't grammar, Skelton ; sooner than make a fault in which, I'd knife my fish, or malt after my cheese.

As for " emulating a genteel carriage," not knowing what that might mean, we at once asked Jim Coachman ; but neither he nor his helpers could help us. Jim thinks it was a baroosh ; cook says, a brisky ; Sam, the stable-boy (who, from living chiefly among the hosses and things, has got a sad low way of talking), said it was all dicky, and bid us drive on to the nex' page.

---

* Oliver Yorke was the well-known pseudonym of the editor of *Fraser's Magazine.*

"For years, when I have observed anything in false taste, I have remarked that, when 'My Book' makes its appearance, such an anomaly will be discontinued; and, instead of an angry reply, it has ever been, 'What! are *you* writing such a work?' till at length, in several societies, 'My Book' has been referred to whenever *une méprise* has taken place. As thus: '"My Book" is, indeed, wanted;' or, 'If "My Book" were here;' or, 'We shall never be right without "My Book";' which led me to take minutes of the barbarisms I observed. I now give them to the world, from a conviction that a rule of conduct should be studied, and impressed upon the mind. Other studies come occasionally into play; but the conduct, the deportment, and the manner are ever in view, and should be a primary consideration, and by no means left to chance (as at present), 'whether it be good, or whether it be evil.'

"Most books that have appeared on this vital subject have generally been of a trashy nature; intended, one would imagine— if you took the trouble to read them—as advertisements to this trade, or for that man, this draper, or that dentist, instead of attempting to form the mind, and leaving the judgment to act.

"To Lord Chesterfield other remarks apply: but Dr. Johnson has so truly and so wittily characterised, in few words, that heartless libertine's advice to his son, that, without danger of corrupting the mind, you cannot place his works in the hands of youth.

"It should ever be kept in our recollection, that a graceful carriage—a noble bearing, and a generous disposition to sit with ease and grace, must be enthroned 'in the mind's eye' on every virtuous sentiment."

There it is, the carriage again! But never mind that—to the nex' sentence it's nothink: "to sit with ease and grace must be enthroned 'in the mind's eye' on every virtuous sentiment!" Heaven bless your bones, Mr. Skeleton! where are you driving us? I say, this sentence would puzzle the very Spinx himself! How *can* a man sit in his eye? If the late Mr. Finlay, of Streatham Academy, taught John Henry Anatomy Skeleton to do this, he's a very wonderful pupil, and no mistake! as well as a finominy in natural history, quite exceeding that of Miss Mackavoy. Sich *peculiar* opportunities for hobservation must make his remarks really valuable.*

Well, he observes on every think that is at all observable, and

* I canot refrain from quattin, in a note, the following extract, from page 8:—

"To be done with propriety, everything must be done quietly. When the cards are dealt round do not sort them in all possible haste, and, having performed it in a most hurried manner, clap your cards on the table, looking can make a gen'l'man fit for gen'l'manly society. His beayviour at dinner and brexfast, at bawls and swarries, at chuch, at vist, at skittles, at drivin' cabs, at gettin' in an' out of a carriage, at his death and burill—givin', on every one of these subjicks, a plenty of ex'lent maxums ; as we shall very soon see. Let's begin about dinner—it's always a pleasant thing to hear talk of. Skeleton (who is a slap-up heppycure) says :—

"Earn the reputation of being a good carver ; it is a weakness to pretend superiority to an art in such constant requisition, and on which so much enjoyment depends. You must not crowd the plate—send only a moderate quantity, with fat and gravy ; in short, whatever you may be carving, serve others as if you were helping yourself : this may be done with rapidity, if the carver takes pleasure in his province, and endeavours to excel. It is cruel and disgusting to send a lump of meat to any one : if at the table of a friend, it is offensive ; if at your own, unpardonable. No refined appetite can survive it."

Taken in general, I say this remark is admiral. I saw an instance, only last wick, at our table. There was, first, Sir James and my Lady, in course, at the head of their own table ; then there was Lord and Lady Smigsmag right and left of my Lady ; Captain Flupp, of the huzzas (huzza he may be ; but he looks, to my thinkin, much more like a bravo) ; and the Bishop of Biffeter, with his lady ; Haldermin Snodgrass, and me—that is, I waited.

Well, the haldermin, who was helpin the tuttle, puts on Biffeter's plate a wad of green fat, which might way a pound and three-quarters. His Ludship goes at it very hearty ; but not likin to seprate it, tries to swallow the lump at one go. I recklect Lady Smigsmag saying gaily, "What, my Lord, are you goin that whole hog at once ? " The bishop looked at her, rowled his eyes, and tried to spick ; but between the spickin and swallerin, and the green fat, the consquinsies were fatle ! He sunk back on his chair, his spoon dropt, his face became of a blew colour, and down he fell as dead as a nit. He recovered, to be sure, nex day ; but not till after a precious deal of bleedin and dosin, which Dr. Drencher described for him.

proudly round, conscious of your own superiority. I speak to those in good society,—not to him who, making cards his trade, has his motives for thus hurrying,—that he may remark the countenances of those with whom he plays —that he may make observations in *his mind's eye*, from what passes around, and use those observations to *suit ulterior ends.*"

This, now, is what I call a reg'lar parrylel passidge, and renders quite clear Mr. Skeltonses notin of the situation of the mind's eye.—CHAS. YLPLSH.

This would never have happened, had not the haldermin given him such a plate-full; and to Skeleton's maxim let me add mine.

Dinner was made for eatin, not for talkin: never pay compliments with your mouth full.

"The person carving must bear in mind that a knife is a saw, by which means it will never slip; and should it be blunt, or the meat overdone, he will succeed neatly and expertly, while others are unequal to the task. For my part, I have been accustomed to think I could carve any meat, with any knife; but lately, in France, I have found my mistake—for the meat was so overdone, and the knives so blunt, that the little merit I thought I possessed completely failed me. Such was never the case with any knife I ever met with in England.

"Pity that there is not a greater reciprocity in the world! How much would France be benefited by the introduction of our cutlery and woollens; and we by much of its produce!

"When the finger-glass is placed before you, you must not drink the contents, or even rinse your mouth, and spit it back; although this has been done by some inconsiderate persons. Never, in short, do that of which, on reflection, you would be ashamed; for instance, never help yourself to salt with your knife—a thing which is not unfrequently done in la belle France in the 'perfumed chambers of the great.' We all have much to unlearn, ere we can learn much that we should. My effort is 'to gather up the tares, and bind them in bundles to destroy them,' and then to 'gather the wheat into the barn.'

"When the rose-water is carried round after dinner, dip into it the corner of your napkin lightly; touch the tips of your fingers, and press the napkin on your lips. Forbear plunging into the liquid as into a bath."

This, to be sure, would be diffiklt, as well as ungenlmnly; and I have something to say on this head, too.

About them blue water bowls which are brought in after dinner, and in which the company makes such a bubblin and spirtin; people should be very careful in usin them, and mind how they hire short-sighted servants. Lady Smigsmag is a melancholy instance of this. Her Ladyship wears two rows of false teeth (what the French call a *rattler*), and is, every body knows, one of the most absint of women. After dinner one day (at her own house), she whips out her teeth, and puts them into the blue bowl, as she always did, when the squirtin time came. Well, the conversation grew hanimated; and so much was Lady Smigsmag interested, that she clean forgot her teeth, and wen to bed without them.

Nex morning was a dreadful disturbance in the house : sumbady had stolen my Lady's teeth out of her mouth ! But this is a loss which a lady don't like positively to advertise ; so the matter was hushed up, and my Lady got a new set from Parkison's. But nobody ever knew who was the thief of the teeth.

A fortnight after, another dinner was given. Lady Smigsmag only kep a butler and one man, and this was a chap whom we used to call, professionally, Lazy Jim. He never did nothing but when he couldn't help it ; he was as lazy as a dormus, and as blind as a howl. If the plate was dirty, Jim never touched it until the day it was wanted, and the same he did by the glas ; you might go into his pantry, and see dozens on 'em with the water (he drenk up all the wind) which had been left in 'em since last dinner party. How such things could be allowed in a house, I don't know ; it only shewed that Smigsmag was an easy master, and that Higgs, the butler, didn't know his bisniss.

Well, the day kem for the sek'nd party. Lazy Jim's plate was all as dutty as pos'bil, and his whole work to do ; he cleaned up the plate, the glas, and everythink else, as he thought, and set out the trays and things on the sideboard. " Law, Jim, you jackass," cried out the butler, at half-past seven, jist as the people was a comen down to dinner ; " you've forgot the washand basins."

Jim spun down into his room,—for he'd forgotten 'em, sure enough ; there they were, however, on his shelf, and full of water : so he brought 'em up, and said nothink ; but gev 'em a polishin wipe with the tail of his coat.

Down kem the company to dinner, and set to it like good uns. The society was reg'lar *distangy* (as they say) : there was the Duke of Haldersgit, Lord and Lady Barbikin, Sir Gregory Jewin, and Lady Suky Smithfield, asides a lot of commontators. The dinner was removed, and the bubble and squeakers (as I call 'em) put down ; and all the people began a washin themselves, like any-think. " Whrrrrr !" went Lady Smigsmag ; "Clooclooclooloophizz ! " says Lady Barbikin ; " Goggleoggleoggleblrrawaw ! " says Jewin (a very fat g'n'l'm'n), " Blobblobgob ! " began his Grace of Haldersgit, who has got the widest mouth in all the peeridge, when all of a sudden he stopped, down went his washand-basin, and he gev such a piercing shrick ! such a bust of agony as I never saw, excep when the prince sees the ghost in " Hamlick " : down went his basin, and up went his eyes ; I really thought he was going to vomick !

I rushed up to his Grace, squeeging him in the shoulders, and patting him on the back. Everybody was in alarm ; the duke as ale as hashes, grinding his teeth, frowning, and makin the most rightful extortions : the ladis were in astarrix ; and I observed Lazy Jim leaning against the sideboard, and looking as white as hock.

I looked into his Grace's plate, and, on my honour as a gnlmn, mong the amins and reasons, there was two rows of TEETH !

" Law !—heavens !—what !—your Grace !—is it possible ? " said Lady Smigsmag, puttin her hand into the duke's plate. " Dear Duke of Aldersgate ! as I live, they are my lost teeth ! "

Flesh and blud coodn't stand this, and I bust out laffin, till I hought I should split ; a footman's a man, and as impregnable as any other to the ridiklous. *I* bust, and every body bust after me —lords and ladies, duke and butler, and all—every body excep Lazy Jim.

Would you blieve it ? *He hadn't cleaned out the glasses, and he company was a washin themselves in second-hand water, a ortnit old !*

I don't wish to insinuate that this kind of thing is general ; only people had better take warnin by me and Mr. Skeleton, and wash heirselves at home. Lazy Jeames was turned off the nex morning, ook to drinkin and evil habits, and is now, in consquints, a leftenant-general in the Axillary Legend. Let's now get on to what Skelton alls his " Derelictions "—here's some of 'em, and very funny one's hey are too. What do you think of Number 1, by way of a dereliction ?

" 1. A knocker on the door of a lone house in the country.

" 2. When on horseback, to be followed by a groom in a fine ivery ; or, when in your gig or cab, with a ' tiger ' so adorned y your side. George IV., whose taste was never excelled, if ver equalled, always, excepting on state occasions, exhibited his etinue in plain liveries—a grey frock being the usual dress of his grooms.

" 4. To elbow people as you walk is rude. For such uncouth beings, perhaps, a good thrashing would be the best monitor ; only here might be disagreeables attending the correction, in the shape f legal functionaries.

" 9. When riding with a companion, be not two or three horse-engths before or behind.

" 10. When walking with one friend, and you encounter another, although you may stop and speak, never introduce the strangers, unless each expresses a wish to that effect.

" 13. Be careful to check vulgarities in children ; for instance : Tom, did you get wet ? '—' No ; Bob did, but I cut away.' You

13

should also affectionately rebuke an unbecoming tone and manne
in children.

"18. To pass a glass, or any drinking vessel, by the brim, o
to offer a lady a bumper, are things equally in bad taste.

"19. To look from the window to ascertain who has knocked
whilst the servant goes to the door, must not be done.

"26. Humming, drumming, or whistling, we must avoid, a
disrespectful to our company.

"27. Never whisper in company, nor make confidants of mer
acquaintance.

"28. Vulgar abbreviations, such as gent for gentleman, or bus
for omnibus, &c., must be shunned.

"29. Make no noise in eating: as, when you masticate wit
the lips unclosed, the action of the jaw is heard. It is equally ba
in drinking. Gulping loudly is abominable—it is but habit—unre
strained, no more ; but enough to disgust.

"30. To do anything that might be obnoxious to censure, o
even bear animadversion from eccentricity, you must take care no
to commit.

"31. Be especially cautious not to drink while your plate i
sent to be replenished.

"32. A bright light in a dirty lamp * is not to be endured.

"33. The statue of the Achilles in Hyde Park is in bad taste
To erect a statue in honour of a hero in a defensive attitude, whe
his good sword has carved his renown—Ha, ha, ha ! "

Ha, ha, ha ! isn't that reg'lar ridiklous ? Not the statute]
mean, but the *dereliction*, as Skillyton calls it. Ha, ha, ha
indeed ! *D*efensive hattitude ! He may call that nasty nake
figger *d*efensive—I say it's *ho*ffensive, and no mistake. But rea
the whole bunch of remarx, Mr. YORKE; a'nt they *rich ?*—a'n
they what you may call a perfect gallixy of derelictions ?

Take, for instance, twenty-nine and thutty-one—gulpins, masti
gatin, and the haction of the jaw ! Why, sich things a'nt done, no
by the knife-boy, and the skillery-made, who dine in the back kitchi
after we've done ! And nex appeal to thutty-one. *Why* shouldn'
a man drink, when his plate's taken away ? Is it unnatral ? is i
ungen'm'n'ly ? is it unbecomin ? If he'd said that a chap shouldn'
drink when his *glass* is taken away, that would be a reason, and
good one. Now let's read "hayteen." Pass a glass *by the brim*
Put your thum and fingers, I spose. The very notin makes me a

* "If in the hall, or in your cab, this, if seen a second time, admits n
excuse : *turn away the man.*"

over uncomfrble ; and, in all my experience of society, I never saw no not a coalheaver do such a thing.   Nex comes :—

"The most barbarous modern introduction is the habit of wearing the hat in the 'salon,' as now practised even in the presence of the ladies.

"When, in making a morning call, you give your card at the door, the servant should be instructed to do his duty, and not stand looking at the name on the card while you speak to him."

There's two rules for you !   Who *does* wear a hat in the salong ? Nobody,. as I ever saw.   And as for Number 40, I can only say, on my own part individiwidiwally, and on the part of the perfession, that if ever Mr. Skelton comes to a house where I am the gen'l'm'n to open the door, and instrux me about doing my duty, I'll instruct him about the head, I will.   No man should instruct other people's servants.   No man should bully or talk loud to a gen'l'm'n who, from his wery situation, is hincapable of defense or reply.   I've known this cistim to be carried on by low swaggerin fellars in clubbs and privit houses, but never by reel gen'l'm'n.   And now for the last maxum, or dereliction :—

"The custom of putting the knife in the mouth is so repulsive to our feelings as men, is so entirely at variance with the manners of gentlemen, that I deem it unnecessary to inveigh against it here. The very appearance of the act is—

'A monster of so odious mien,
That to be hated, needs but to be seen.' "

Oh, heavens ! the notion is overpowerin !   I once see a gen'l'm'n cut his head off eatin peez that way.   Knife in your mouth !—oh !—fawgh !—it makes me all over.   Mrs. Cook, do have the kindniss to git me a basin !

. . . .

In this abrupt way Mr. Yellowplush's article concludes.   The notion conveyed in the last paragraph was too disgusting for his delicate spirit, and caused him emotions that are neither pleasant to experience nor to describe.

It may be objected to his communicatibn, that it contains some orthographic eccentricities, and that his acuteness surpasses considerably his education.   But a gentleman of his rank and talent was the exact person fitted to criticise the volume which forms the subject of his remarks.   We at once saw that only Mr. Yellowplush was fit for Mr. Skelton, Mr. Skelton for Mr. Yellowplush.   There

is a luxury of fashionable observation, a fund of apt illustration, an
intimacy with the first leaders of the *ton*, and a richness of authentic
anecdote, which is not to be found in any other writer of any other
periodical. He who looketh from a tower sees more of the battle
than the knights and captains engaged in it; and, in like manner,
he who stands behind a fashionable table knows more of society
than the guests who sit at the board. It is from this source that
our great novel-writers have drawn their experience, retailing the
truths which they learned.

It is not impossible that Mr. Yellowplush may continue his
communications, when we shall be able to present the reader with
the only authentic picture of fashionable life which has been given
to the world in our time. All the rest are stolen and disfigured
copies of that original piece, of which we are proud to be in
possession.

After our contributor's able critique, it is needless for us to
extend our remarks upon Mr. Skelton's book. We have to thank
that gentleman for some hours' extraordinary amusement; and shall
be delighted at any further productions of his pen.   O. Y.

STRICTURES ON PICTURES

A LETTER FROM MICHAEL ANGELO TITMARSH, ESQUIRE, TC
MONSIEUR ANATOLE VICTOR ISIDOR HYACINTHE ACHILLE
HERCULE DE BRICABRAC, PEINTRE D'HISTOIRE, RUE MOUF-
FETARD, À PARIS

LORD'S HOTEL, NEW STREET, COVENT GARDEN:
Tuesday, 15th May.

I PROPOSE to be both learned and pleasant in my remarks
upon the exhibitions here; for I know, my dear Bricabrac, that
it is your intention to translate this letter into French, for the
benefit of some of your countrymen, who are anxious about the
progress of the fine arts—when I say some, I mean all, for, thanks
to your Government patronage, your magnificent public galleries,
and, above all, your delicious sky and sunshine, there is not a
scavenger in your nation who has not a feeling for the beauty of
Nature, which is, my dear Anatole, neither more nor less than Art.

You know nothing about art in this country—almost as little
as we know of French art. One Gustave Planche, who makes visits
to London, and writes accounts of pictures in your reviews, is,
believe me, an impostor. I do not mean a private impostor, for
I know not whether Planche is a real or assumed name, but simply a
quack on matters of art. Depend on it, my dear young friend, that
there is nobody like Titmarsh: you will learn more about the arts
in England from this letter than from anything in or out of print.

Well, then, every year, at the commencement of this blessed
month of May, wide open the doors of three picture galleries, in
which figure all the works of genius which our brother artists have
produced during the whole year. I wish you could see my historical
picture of " Heliogabalus in the Ruins of Carthage," or the full-
length of Sir Samuel Hicks and his Lady,—sitting in a garden
light, Lady H. reading the " Book of Beauty," Sir Samuel catching
a butterfly which is settling on a flower-pot. This, however, is all
egotism. I am not going to speak of *my* works, which are pretty
well known in Paris already, as I flatter myself, but of other artists
—some of them men of merit—as well as myself.

Let us commence, then, with the commencement—the Royal

Academy. That is held in one wing of a little building like a gin-shop, which is near Saint Martin's Church. In the other wing is our National Gallery. As for the building, you must not take *that* as a specimen of our skill in the fine arts; come down the Seven Dials, and I will show you many modern structures of which the architect deserves far higher credit.

But, bad as the place is—a pigmy abortion, in lieu of a noble monument to the greatest school of painting in the greatest country of the modern world (you may be angry, but I'm right in *both* cases)—bad as the outside is, the interior, it must be confessed, is marvellously pretty and convenient for the reception and exhibition of the pictures it will hold. Since the old pictures have got their new gallery, and their new scouring, one hardly knows them. O Ferdinand, Ferdinand, that *is* a treat, that National Gallery, and no mistake! I shall write to you fourteen or fifteen long letters about it some day or other. The apartment devoted to the Academy exhibition is equally commodious : a small room for miniatures and aquarelles, another for architectural drawings, and three saloons for pictures—all very small, but well lighted and neat; no interminable passage, like your five hundred yards at the Louvre, with a slippery floor, and tiresome straggling cross-lights. Let us buy a catalogue, and walk straight into the gallery, however :—we have been a long time talking, *de omnibus rebus,* at the door.

Look, my dear Isidor, at the first names in the catalogue, and thank your stars for being in such good company. Bless us and save us, what a power of knights is here !

Sir William Beechey.
Sir Martin Shee.
Sir David Wilkie.
Sir Augustus Callcott.
Sir W. J. Newton.
Sir Geoffrey Wyattville.
Sir Francis Chantrey.
Sir Richard Westmacott.
Sir Michael Angelo Titmarsh—

not yet, that is; but I shall be, in course, when our little liege lady—Heaven bless her !—has seen my portrait of Sir Sam and Lady Hicks.

If all these gentlemen in the list of Academicians and Associates are to have titles of some sort or other, I should propose :—

1. Baron Briggs. (At the very least, he is out and out the best portrait-painter of the set.)

2. Daniel, Prince Maclise. (His Royal Highness's pictures place him very near to the throne indeed.)

3. Edwin, Earl of Landseer.
4. The Lord Charles Landseer.
5. The Duke of Etty.
6. Archbishop Eastlake.
7. His Majesty KING MULREADY.

King Mulready, I repeat, in double capitals; for, if this man has not the crowning picture of the exhibition, I am no better than a Dutchman. His picture represents the "Seven Ages," as described by a poet whom you have heard of—one Shakspeare, a Warwick-shire man : and there they are, all together ; the portly justice and the quarrelsome soldier ; the lover leaning apart, and whispering sweet things in his pretty mistress's ear ; the baby hanging on her gentle mother's bosom ; the schoolboy, rosy and lazy ; the old man crabbed and stingy ; and the old old man of all, sans teeth, sans eyes, sans ears, sans everything—but why describe them ? You will find the thing better done in Shakspeare, or possibly translated by some of your Frenchmen. I can't say much about the drawing of this picture, for here and there are some queer-looking limbs ; but—oh, Anatole !—the intention is godlike. Not one of those figures but has a grace and a soul of his own ; no conventional copies of the stony antique ; no distorted caricatures, like those of your "classiques," David, Girodet and Co. (the impostors!)—but such expressions as a great poet would draw, who thinks profoundly and truly, and never forgets (he could not if he would) grace and beauty withal. The colour and manner of this noble picture are neither of the Venetian school, nor the Florentine, nor the English, but of the Mulready school. Ah ! my dear Floridor ! I wish that you and I, ere we die, may have erected such a beautiful monument to hallow and perpetuate our names. Our children—my boy, Sebastian Piombo Titmarsh, will see this picture in his old age, hanging by the side of the Raffaelles in our National Gallery. I sometimes fancy, in the presence of such works of genius as this, that my picture of Sir Sam and Lady Hicks is but a magnificent error after all, and that it will die away, and be forgotten.

Near to "All the world's a stage" is a charming picture, by Archbishop Eastlake ; so denominated by me, because the rank is very respectable, and because there is a certain purity and religious feeling in all Mr. Eastlake does, which eminently entitles him to the honours of the prelacy. In this picture, Gaston de Foix (he whom Titian painted, his mistress buckling on his armour) is part-ing from his mistress. A fair peaceful garden is round about them ; and here his lady sits and clings to him, as though she would cling for ever. But, look ! yonder stands the page and the horse pawing ; and, beyond the wall which bounds the quiet garden and flowers,

you see the spears and pennons of knights, the banners of Kin
Louis and De Foix " the thunderbolt of Italy." Long shining row
of steel-clad men are marching stately by; and with them mus
ride Count Gaston—to conquer and die at Ravenna. You can rea
his history, my dear friend, in Lacretelle, or Brantôme; only
perhaps, not so well expressed as it has just been by me.

Yonder is Sir David Wilkie's grand picture, "Queen Victori
holding her First Council." A marvellous painting, in which on
admires the exquisite richness of the colour, the breadth of ligl
and shadow, the graceful dignity and beauty of the principal figur
and the extraordinary skill with which all the figures have bee
grouped, so as to produce a grand and simple effect. What ca
one say more but admire the artist who has made, out of suc
unpoetical materials as a table of red cloth, and fifty unoccupie
middle-aged gentlemen, a beautiful and interesting picture? S
David has a charming portrait, too, of Mrs. Maberly, in dar
crimson velvet, and delicate white hat and feathers : a marvel
colour, though somewhat askew in the drawing.

The Earl of Landseer's best picture, to my thinking, is tha
which represents her Majesty's favourite dogs and parrot. He ha
in painting, an absolute mastery over

$$K\acute{\upsilon}\nu\epsilon\sigma\sigma\iota\nu$$
$$O\grave{\iota}\omega\nuo\hat{\iota}\sigma\acute{\iota} \; \tau\epsilon \; \pi\hat{a}\sigma\iota:$$

this is, he can paint all manner of birds and beasts as nobody el
can. To tell you a secret I do not think he understands how 1
paint the great beast, man, quite so well; or, at least, to do wha
is the highest quality of an artist, to place *a soul* under the ribs a
he draws them. They are, if you like, the most dexterous pictur
that ever were painted, but not *great* pictures. I would muc
rather look at yonder rough Leslie than at all the wonderf
painting of parrots or greyhounds, though done to a hair or
feather.

Leslie is the only man in this country who translates Shakspea
into form and colour. Old Shallow and Sir Hugh, Slender and h
man Simple, pretty Anne Page and the Merry Wives of Windso
are here joking with the fat knight; who, with a monstrous gravit
and profound brazen humour, is narrating some tale of his fea
with the wild Prince and Poins. Master Brooke is offering
tankard to Master Slender, who will not drink, forsooth.

This picture is executed with the utmost simplicity, and almo
rudeness; but is charming, from its great truth of effect and e
pression. Wilkie's pictures (in his latter style) seem to begin whe
Leslie's end ; the former's men and women look as if *the bodies ha*

been taken out of them, and only the surface left. Lovely as the Queen's figure is, for instance, it looks like a spirit, and not a woman ; one may almost see through her into the waistcoat of Lord Lansdowne, and so on through the rest of the transparent heroes and statesmen of the company.

Opposite the Queen is another charming performance of Sir David—a bride dressing, amidst a rout of bridesmaids and relations. Some are crying, some are smiling, some are pinning her gown ; a back door is open, and a golden sun shines into a room which contains a venerable-looking bed and tester, probably that in which the dear girl is to—but *parlons d'autres choses.* The colour of this picture is delicious, and the effect faultless : Sir David does everything for a picture nowadays but the *drawing.* Who knows ? Perhaps it is as well left out.

Look yonder, down to the ground, and admire a most beautiful fantastic Ariel.

> "On the bat's back do I fly,
> After sunset merrily.'

Merry Ariel lies at his ease, and whips with gorgeous peacock's feather his courser, flapping lazy through the golden evening sky. This exquisite little picture is the work of Mr. Severn, an artist who has educated his taste and his hand in the early Roman school. He has not the dash and dexterity of the latter which belong to some of our painters, but he possesses that solemn earnestness and simplicity of mind and purpose which make a religion of art, and seem to be accorded only to a few in our profession. I have heard a pious pupil of Mr. Ingres (the head of your academy at Rome) aver stoutly that, in matters of art, Titian was Antichrist, and Rubens, Martin Luther. They came with their brilliant colours, and dashing worldly notions, upsetting that beautiful system of faith in which art had lived hitherto. Portraits of saints and martyrs, with pure eyes turned heavenward ; and (as all true sanctity will) making those pure who came within their reach, now gave way to wicked likenesses of men of blood, or dangerous, devilish, sensual portraits of tempting women. Before Titian, a picture was the labour of years. Why did this reformer ever come among us, and show how it might be done in a day ? He drove the good angels away from painters' easels, and called down a host of voluptuous spirits instead, who ever since have held the mastery there.

Only a few artists of our country (none in yours, where the so-called Catholic school is a mere theatrical folly), and some among the Germans, have kept to the true faith, and eschewed the tempta-

tions of Titian and his like. Mr. Eastlake is one of these. Who
does not recollect his portrait of Miss Bury ? Not a simple woman
—the lovely daughter of the authoress of "Love," "Flirtation,"
and other remarkable works—but a glorified saint. Who does no
remember his Saint Sebastian ; his body bare, his eyes cast melan
choly down ; his limbs, as yet untouched by the arrows of his perse
cutors, tied to the fatal tree ? Those two pictures of Mr. Eastlake
would merit to hang in a gallery where there were only Raffaelle
besides. Mr. Severn is another of the school. I don't know wha
hidden and indefinable charm there is in his simple pictures ; bu
I never can look at them without a certain emotion of awe—with
out that thrill of the heart with which one hears country childre
sing the Old Hundredth, for instance. The singers are rude, per
haps, and the voices shrill ; but the melody is still pure and goc
like. Some such majestic and pious harmony is there in thes
pictures of Mr. Severn, Mr. Mulready's mind has lately gained th
same kind of inspiration. I know no one else who possesses i
except, perhaps, myself. Without flattery, I may say, that m
picture of "Heliogabalus at Carthage" is *not* in the popular tast
and has about it some faint odour of celestial incense.

Do not, my dear Anatole, consider me too great an ass for pe
sisting upon this point, and exemplifying Mr. Severn's picture o
the "Crusaders catching a First View of Jerusalem" as an instance
Godfrey and Tancred, Raymond and Ademar, Beamond and Rinald
with Peter and the Christian host, behold at length the da
dawning.

> " E quando il sol gli aridi campi fiede
>   Con raggi assai ferventi, e in alto sorge,
> Ecco apparir Gerusalem si vede,
>   Ecco additar Gerusalem si scorge,
> Ecco da mille voci unitamente
>   Gerusalemme salutar si sente ! "

Well, Godfrey and Tancred, Peter, and the rest, look like litt
wooden dolls ; and as for the horses belonging to the crusadin
cavalry, I have seen better in gingerbread. But, what then
There is a higher ingredient in beauty than mere form ; a skilf
hand is only the second artistical quality, worthless, my Anatol
without the first, which is *a great heart*. This picture is beautifu
in spite of its defects, as many women are. Mrs. Titmarsh i
beautiful, though she weighs nineteen stone.

Being on the subject of religious pictures, what shall I say o
Mr. Ward's ? Anything so mysteriously hideous was never see
before now ; they are worse than all the horrors in your Spanis
Gallery at Paris. As Eastlake's are of the Catholic, these ma

be called of the Muggletonian, school of art; monstrous, livid, and dreadful, as the dreams of a man in the scarlet fever. I would much sooner buy a bottled baby with two heads as a pleasing ornament for my cabinet; and should be afraid to sit alone in a room with "ignorance, envy, and jealousy filling the throat, and widening the mouth of calumny endeavouring to bear down truth!"

Mr. Maclise's picture of "Christmas" you will find excellently described in the May number of a periodical of much celebrity among us, called *Fraser's Magazine*. Since the circulation of that miscellany is almost as extensive in Paris as in London, it is need-less in this letter to go over beaten ground, and speak at length of the plot of this remarkable picture. There are five hundred merry figures painted on this canvas, gobbling, singing, kissing, carousing. A line of jolly serving men troop down the hall stairs, and bear the boar's head in procession up to the daïs, where sits the good old English gentleman, and his guests and family; a set of mummers and vassals are crowded round a table gorging beef and wassail; a bevy of blooming girls and young men are huddled in a circle, and play at hunt the slipper. Of course, there are plenty of stories told at the huge hall fire, and kissing under the glistening mistletoe-bough. But I wish you could see the wonderful accuracy with which all these figures are drawn, and the extraordinary skill with which the artist has managed to throw into a hundred different faces a hundred different characters and individualities of joy. Every one of these little people is smiling, but each has his own particular smile. As for the colouring of the picture, it is, between ourselves, atrocious; but a man cannot have all the merits at once. Mr. Maclise has for his share humour such as few painters ever possessed, and a power of drawing such as never was possessed by *any other;* no, not by one, from Albert Dürer downwards. His scene from the "Vicar of Wakefield" is equally charming. Moses's shining grinning face; the little man in red who stands on tiptoe, and painfully scrawls his copy; and the youngest of the family of the Primroses, who learns his letters on his father's knee, are perfect in design and expression. What might not this man do, if he would read and meditate a little, and profit by the works of men whose taste and education were superior to his own.

Mr. Charles Landseer has two *tableaux de genre*, which possess very great merit. His characters are a little too timid, perhaps, as Mr. Maclise's are too bold; but the figures are beautifully drawn, the colouring and effect excellent, and the accessories painted with great faithfulness and skill. "The Parting Benison" is, perhaps, the more interesting picture of the two.

And now we arrive at Mr. Etty, whose rich luscious pencil has covered a hundred glowing can'vases, which every painter must love. I don't know whether the Duke has this year produced anything which one might have expected from a man of his rank and consequence. He is, like great men, lazy, or indifferent, perhaps, about public approbation; and also, like great men, somewhat too luxurious and fond of pleasure. For instance, here is a picture of a sleepy nymph, most richly painted; but tipsy-looking, coarse, and so naked as to be unfit for appearance among respectable people at an exhibition. You will understand what I mean. There are some figures without a rag to cover them, which look modest and decent for all that; and others, which may be clothed to the chin, and yet are not fit for modest eyes to gaze on. *Verbum sat*—this naughty "Somnolency" ought to go to sleep in her nightgown.

But here is a far nobler painting,—the prodigal kneeling down lonely in the stormy evening, and praying to Heaven for pardon. It is a grand and touching picture; and looks as large as if the three-foot canvas had been twenty. His wan wretched figure and clasped hands are lighted up by the sunset; the clouds are livid and heavy; and the wind is howling over the solitary common, and numbing the chill limbs of the poor wanderer. A goat and a boar are looking at him with horrid obscene eyes. They are the demons of Lust and Gluttony, which have brought him to this sad pass. And there seems no hope, no succour, no ear for the prayer of this wretched, wayworn, miserable man who kneels there alone, shuddering. Only above, in the gusty blue sky, you see a glistening, peaceful, silver star, which points to home and hope, as clearly as if the little star were a signpost, and home at the very next turn of the road.

Away, then, O conscience-stricken prodigal! and you shall find a good father, who loves you; and an elder brother, who hates you —but never mind that; and a dear, kind, stout old mother, who liked you twice as well as the elder, for all his goodness and psalm-singing, and has a tear and a prayer for you night and morning; and a pair of gentle sisters, maybe; and a poor young thing down in the village, who has never forgotten your walks in the quiet nut-woods, and the birds' nests you brought her, and the big boy you thrashed, because he broke the eggs: he is squire now, the big boy, and would marry her, but she will not have him—not she!—her thoughts are with her dark-eyed, bold-browed, devil-may-care play-mate, who swore she should be his little wife—and then went to college—and then came back sick and changed—and then got into debt—and then—— But never mind, man! down to her at once. She will pretend to be cold at first, and then shiver and turn red and deadly pale; and then she tumbles into your arms, with a gush of sweet tears, and a pair of rainbows in her soft eyes, welcoming the sunshine back to her bosom again! To her, man!—never fear, miss! Hug him, and kiss him, as though you would draw the heart from his lips.

When she has done, the poor thing falls stone-pale and sobbing on young Prodigal's shoulder; and he carries her, quite gently, to that old bench where he carved her name fourteen years ago, and steals his arm round her waist, and kisses her hand, and soothes her. Then comes but the poor widow, her mother, who is pale and tearful too, and tries to look cold and unconcerned. She kisses her daughter, and leads her trembling into the house. "You will come to us to-morrow, Tom?" says she, as she takes his hand at the gate.

To-morrow! To be sure he will; and this very night, too, after supper with the old people. (Young Squire Prodigal never sups; and has found out that he must ride into town, to arrange about a missionary meeting with the Reverend Doctor Slackjaw.) To be sure, Tom Prodigal will go: the moon will be up, and who knows but Lucy may be looking at it about twelve o'clock. At one, back trots the young squire, and he sees two people whispering at a window; and he gives something very like a curse, as he digs into the ribs of his mare, and canters, clattering, down the silent road.

Yes—but, in the meantime, there is the old housekeeper, with "Lord bless us!" and "Heaven save us!" and "Who'd have thought ever again to see his dear face? And master to forget it all, who swore so dreadful that he would never see him!—as for missis, she always loved him." There, I say, is the old housekeeper, logging the fire, airing the sheets, and flapping the feather beds—for Master Tom's room has never been used this many a day; and the young ladies have got some flowers for his chimney-piece, and put back his mother's portrait, which they have had in their room ever since he went away and forgot it, woe is me! And old John, the butler, coachman, footman, valet, factotum, consults with master about supper.

"What can we have?" says master; "all the shops are shut, and there's nothing in the house."

John. "No, no more there isn't; only Guernsey's calf. Butcher kill'd'n yesterday, as your honour knowth."

Master. "Come, John, a calf's enough. Tell the cook to *send us up that.*"

And he gives a hoarse haw! haw! at his wit; and Mrs. Prodigal smiles too, and says, "Ah, Tom Prodigal, you were always a merry fellow!"

Well, John Footman carries down the message to cook, who is

a country wench, and takes people at their word; and what do you think she sends up?

Top Dish.

Fillet of veal, and bacon on the side-table.

Bottom Dish.

Roast ribs of veal.

In the Middle.

Calves'-head soup (à la tortue).
Veal broth.

Between.

Boiled knuckle of veal, and parsley sauce.
Stewed veal, with brown sauce and forced-meat balls.

Entremets.

Veal olives (for sauce, see stewed veal).
Veal cutlets (panées, sauce piquante).
Ditto (en papillote).
Scotch collops.
Fricandeau of veal (piqué au lard à la chicorée).
Minced veal.
Blanquet of veal.

Second Course.

Curry of calves'-head.
Sweetbreads.
Calves'-foot jelly.

See, my dear Anatole, what a world of thought can be conjured up out of a few inches of painted canvas.

And now we come to the great and crowning picture of the exhibition, my own historical piece, namely, "Heliogabalus in the Ruins of Carthage." In this grand and finished perform——

*** Mr. Titmarsh's letter stops, unfortunately, here. We found it at midnight, the 15th–16th May, in a gutter of Saint Martin's Lane, whence a young gentleman had been just removed by the police. It is to be presumed that intoxication could be his only cause for choosing such a sleeping-place, at such an hour; and it had probably commenced as he was writing the above fragment. We made inquiries at Lord's Coffee House, of Mr. Moth (who, from being the active and experienced head-waiter, is now the obliging landlord of that establishment), and were told that a gentleman unknown had dined there at three, and had been ceaselessly occupied in writing and drinking until a quarter to twelve, when he abruptly left the house. Mr. Moth regretted to add, that the

tranger had neglected to pay for thirteen glasses of gin-and-water,
ιalf-a-pint of porter, a bottle of soda-water, and a plate of ham-
andwiches, which he had consumed in the course of the day.

We have paid Mr. Moth (whose very moderate charges, and ex-
ellent stock of wines and spirits, cannot be too highly commended),
nd shall gladly hand over to Mr. Titmarsh the remaining sum
vhich is his due.   Has he any more of his rhapsody ?—O. Y.

STRICTURES ON PICTURES

A SECOND LECTURE ON THE FINE ARTS, B
MICHAEL ANGELO TITMARSH, ESQUIRE

THE EXHIBITIONS

JACK STRAW'S CASTLE, HAMPSTEAD.

MY DEAR BRICABRAC,—You, of course, remember th letter on the subject of our exhibitions which I addresse to you this time last year. As you are now lying at th Hôtel Dieu, wounded during the late unsuccessful *émeute* (which think, my dear friend, is the seventeenth you have been engage in), and as the letter which I wrote last year was received wit unbounded applause by the people here, and caused a sale of thre or four editions of this Magazine,* I cannot surely, my dear Bricabra do better than send you another sheet or two, which may consol you under your present bereavement, and at the same time amus the British public, who now know their friend Titmarsh as well a you in France know that little scamp Thiers.

Well, then, from "Jack Straw's Castle," an hotel on Hamp stead's breezy heath, which Keats, Wordsworth, Leigh Hun F. W. N. Bayly, and others of our choicest spirits, have ofte patronised, and a heath of which every pool, bramble, furze-bush with-clothes-hanging-on-it-to-dry, steep, stock, stone, tree, lodging house, and distant gloomy background of London city, or brigh green stretch of sunshiny Hertfordshire meadows, has been depicte by our noble English landscape-painter, Constable, in his own Con stabulary way—at "Jack Straw's Castle," I say, where I at th present moment am located (not that it matters in the least, bu the world is always interested to know where men of genius ar accustomed to disport themselves), I cannot do better than loo over the heap of picture-gallery catalogues which I brought with m from London, and communicate to you, my friend in Paris, m remarks thereon.

A man, with five shillings to spare, may at this presen moment half kill himself with pleasure in London town, and i the neighbourhood of Pall Mall, by going from one picture galler

* *Fraser's Magazine.*

to another, and examining the beauties and absurdities which are to be found in each. There is first the National Gallery (entrance, nothing), in one wing of the little gin-shop of a building so styled near Saint Martin's Church; in another wing is the exhibition of the Royal Academy (entrance, one shilling; catalogue, one ditto). After having seen this, you come to the Water-Colour Exhibition in Pall Mall East; then to the gallery in Suffolk Street; and, finally, to the New Water-Colour Society in Pall Mall,—a pretty room, which formerly used to be a gambling-house, where many a bout of seven's-the-main, and iced champagne, has been had by the dissipated in former days. All these collections (all the modern ones, that is) deserve to be noticed, and contain a deal of good, bad, and indifferent wares, as is the way with all other institutions in this wicked world.

Commençons donc avec le commencement—with the exhibition of the Royal Academy, which consists, as everybody knows, of thirty-eight knight and esquire Academicians, and nineteen simple and ungenteel Associates, who have not so much as a shabby Mister before their names. I recollect last year facetiously ranging these gentlemen in rank according to what I conceived to be their merits, —King Mulready, Prince Maclise, Lord Landseer, Archbishop Eastlake (according to the best of my memory, for "Jack Straw," strange to say, does not take in *Fraser's Magazine*), and so on. At present, a great number of new-comers, not Associates even, ought to be elevated to these aristocratic dignities; and, perhaps, the order ought to be somewhat changed. There are many more good pictures (here and elsewhere) than there were last year. A great stride has been taken in matters of art, my dear friend. The young painters are stepping forward. Let the old fogies look to it; let the old Academic Olympians beware, for there are fellows among the rising race who bid fair to oust them from sovereignty. They have not yet arrived at the throne, to be sure, but they are near it. The lads are not so good as the best of the Academicians; but many of the Academicians are infinitely worse than the lads, and are old, stupid, and cannot improve, as the younger and more active painters will.

If you are particularly anxious to know what is the best picture in the room, not the biggest (Sir David Wilkie's is the biggest, and exactly contrary to the best), I must request you to turn your attention to a noble river-piece by J. W. M. Turner, Esquire, R.A., "The Fighting *Téméraire*"—as grand a painting as ever figured on the walls of any Academy, or came from the easel of any painter. The old *Téméraire* is dragged to her last home by a little, spiteful, diabolical steamer. A mighty red sun,

x

amidst a host of flaring clouds, sinks to rest on one side of the picture, and illumines a river that seems interminable, and a count less navy that fades away into such a wonderful distance as never was painted before. The little demon of a steamer is belching out volume (why do I say a volume? not a hundred volumes could express it) of foul, lurid, red-hot, malignant smoke, paddling furiously, and lashing up the water round about it; while behind it (a cold grey moon looking down on it), slow, sad, and majestic follows the brave old ship, with death, as it were, written on her I think, my dear Bricabrac (although, to be sure, your nation would be somewhat offended by such a collection of trophies), that we ought not, in common gratitude, to sacrifice entirely these noble old champions of ours, but that we should have somewhere a museum of their skeletons, which our children might visit, and think of the brave deeds which were done in them. The bones of the *Agamemnon* and the *Captain*, the *Vanguard*, the *Culloden* and the *Victory* ought to be sacred relics, for Englishmen to worship almost. Think of them when alive, and braving the battle and the breeze, they carried Nelson and his heroes vic torious by the Cape of Saint Vincent, in the dark waters of Aboukir, and through the fatal conflict of Trafalgar. All these things, my dear Bricabrac, are, you will say, absurd, and not to th purpose. Be it so; but Bowbellites as we are, we Cockneys fee our hearts leap up when we recall them to memory; and every clerk in Threadneedle Street feels the strength of a Nelson, when he thinks of the mighty actions performed by him.

It is absurd, you will say (and with a great deal of reason) for Titmarsh, or any other Briton, to grow so politically enthusiasti about a four-foot canvas, representing a ship, a steamer, a river, and a sunset. But herein surely lies the power of the great artist. He makes you see and think of a great deal more than the object before you; he knows how to soothe or intoxicate, to fire or t depress, by a few notes, or forms, or colours, of which we canno trace the effect to the source, but only acknowledge the power I recollect some years ago, at the theatre at Weimar, hearing Beethoven's "Battle of Vittoria," in which, amidst a storm of glorious music, the air of "God save the King" was introduced The very instant it began, every Englishman in the house was bolt upright, and so stood reverently until the air was played out Why so? From some such thrill of excitement as makes us glow and rejoice over Mr. Turner and his "Fighting *Téméraire*" which I am sure, when the art of translating colours into music or poetry shall be discovered, will be found to be a magnificent national ode or piece of music.

I must tell you, however, that Mr. Turner's performances are for the most part quite incomprehensible to me; and that his other pictures, which he is pleased to call "Cicero at his Villa," "Agrippina with the Ashes of Germanicus," "Pluto carrying off Proserpina," or what you will, are not a whit more natural, or less mad, than they used to be in former years, since he has forsaken nature, or attempted (like your French barbers) to embellish it. On n'embellit pas la nature, my dear Bricabrac; one may make pert caricatures of it,. or mad exaggerations like Mr. Turner in his fancy pieces. O ye gods! why will he not stick to copying her majestical countenance, instead of daubing it with some absurd antics and fard of his own? Fancy pea-green skies, crimson-lake trees, and orange and purple grass—fancy cataracts, rainbows, suns, moons, and thunderbolts—shake them well up, with a quantity of gamboge, and you will have an idea of a fancy picture by Turner. It is worth a shilling alone to go and see "Pluto and Proserpina." Such a landscape! such figures! such a little red-hot coal-scuttle of a chariot! As Nat Lee sings—

> " Methought I saw a hieroglyphic bat
> Skim o'er the surface of a slipshod hat ;
> While, to increase the tumult of the skies,
> A damned potato o'er the whirlwind flies."

If you can understand these lines, you can understand one of Turner's landscapes ; and I recommend them to him, as a pretty subject for a piece for next year.

Etty has a picture on the same subject as Turner's, "Pluto carrying off Proserpina;" and if one may complain that in the latter the figures are not indicated, one cannot at least lay this fault to Mr. Etty's door. His figures are drawn, and a deuced deal too much drawn. A great large curtain of fig-leaves should be hung over every one of this artist's pictures, and the world should pass on, content to know that there are some glorious colours painted beneath. His colour, indeed, is sublime : I doubt if Titian ever knew how to paint flesh better—but his taste! Not David or Girodet ever offended propriety so—scarcely ever Peter Paul himself, by whose side, as a colourist and a magnificent heroic painter, Mr. Etty is sometimes worthy to stand. I wish he would take Ariosto in hand, and give us a series of designs from him. His hand would be the very one for those deep luscious landscapes, and fiery scenes of love and battle. Besides " Proserpine," Mr. Etty has two more pictures, " Endymion," with a dirty, affected, beautiful, slatternly Diana, and a portrait of the " Lady Mayoress of York," which is a curiosity in its way. The line of

her Ladyship's eyes and mouth (it is a front face) are made
meet at a point in a marabou feather which she wears in h
turban, and close to her cheekbone; while the expression of t
whole countenance is so fierce, that you would imagine it a La
Macbeth, and not a lady mayoress. The picture has, neverth
less, some very fine painting about it—as which of Mr. Etty
pieces has not?

The artists say there is very fine painting, too, in Sir Dav
Wilkie's great "Sir David Baird"; for my part, I think very littl
You see a great quantity of brown paint; in this is a great flashi
of torches, feathers, and bayonets. You see in the foregroun
huddled up in a rich heap of corpses and drapery, Tippoo Sahi
and swaggering over him on a step, waving a sword for no earth
purpose, and wearing a red jacket and buckskins, the figure of S
David Baird. The picture. is poor, feeble, theatrical; and I wou
just as soon have Mr. Hart's great canvas of "Lady Jane Grey
(which is worth exactly twopence-halfpenny) as Sir David's po
picture of "Seringapatam." Some of Sir David's portraits a
worse even than his historical compositions—they seem to
painted with snuff and tallow-grease: the faces are merely indicate
and without individuality; the forms only half-drawn, and almo
always wrong. What has come to the hand that painted "T
Blind Fiddler" and "The Chelsea Pensioners"? Who would ha
thought that such a portrait as that of "Master Robert Donne
or the composition entitled "The Grandfather," could ever ha
come from the author of "The Rent Day" and "The Reading
the Will"? If it be but a contrast to this feeble, flimsy, tran
parent figure of Master Donne, the spectator cannot do better tha
cast his eyes upwards, and look at Mr. Linnell's excellent portra
of "Mr. Robert Peel." It is real substantial nature, carefully ar
honestly painted, and without any flashy tricks of art. It ma
seem ungracious in "us youth" thus to fall foul of our better
but if Sir David has taught us to like good pictures, by paintin
them formerly, we cannot help criticising if he paints bad on
now: and bad they most surely are.

From the censure, however, must be excepted the picture
"Grace before Meat," which, a little misty and feeble, perhap
in drawing and substance, in colour, feeling, composition, a
expression is exquisite. The eye loves to repose upon this pictur
and the heart to brood over it afterwards. When, as I said befor
lines and colours come to be translated into sounds, this pictur
I have no doubt, will turn out to be a sweet and touching hym
tune, with rude notes of cheerful voices, and peal of soft melodio
organ, such as one hears stealing over the meadows on sunshi

Sabbath-days, while waves under cloudless blue the peaceful golden
corn. Some such feeling of exquisite pleasure and content is to be
had, too, from Mr. Eastlake's picture of "Our Lord and the Little
Children." You never saw such tender white faces, and solemn
eyes, and sweet forms of mothers round their little ones bending
gracefully. These pictures come straight to the heart, and then
all criticism and calculation vanishes at once,—for the artist has
attained his great end, which is, to strike far deeper than the sight;
and we have no business to quarrel about defects in form and colour,
which are but little parts of the great painter's skill.

Look, for instance, at another piece of Mr. Eastlake's, called,
somewhat affectedly, "La Svegliarina." The defects of the painter,
which one does not condescend to notice when he is filled with a
great idea, become visible instantly when he is only occupied with
a small one; and you see that the hand is too scrupulous and finikin,
the drawing weak, the flesh chalky, and unreal. The very same
objections exist to the other picture, but the subject and the genius
overcome them.

Passing from Mr. Eastlake's pictures to those of a greater
genius, though in a different line,—look at Mr. Leslie's little pieces.
Can anything be more simple—almost rude—than their manner,
and more complete in their effect upon the spectator? The very
soul of comedy is in them; there is no coarseness, no exaggeration;
but they gladden the eye, and the merriment which they excite
cannot possibly be more pure, gentlemanlike, or delightful. Mr.
Maclise has humour, too, and vast powers of expressing it; but
whisky is not more different from rich burgundy than his fun from
Mr. Leslie's. To our thinking, Leslie's little head of "Sancho" is
worth the whole picture from "Gil Blas," which hangs by it. In
point of workmanship, this is, perhaps, the best picture that Mr.
Maclise ever painted; the colour is far better than that usually
employed by him, and the representation of objects carried to such
an extent as we do believe was never reached before. There is a
poached egg, which one could swallow; a trout, that beats all the
trout that was ever seen; a copper pan, scoured so clean that you
might see your face in it; a green blind, through which the sun
comes; and a wall, with the sun shining on it, that De Hooghe
could not surpass. This young man has the greatest power of
hand that was ever had, perhaps, by any painter in any time or
country. What does he want? Polish, I think; thought, and
cultivation. His great picture of "King Richard and Robin Hood"
is a wonder of dexterity of hand; but coarse, I think, and inefficient
in humour. His models repeat themselves too continually. Allen
Dale, the harper, is the very counterpart of Gil Blas; and Robin

Hood is only Apollo with whiskers : the same grin, the same display of grinders,—the same coarse luscious mouth, belongs to both. In the large picture, everybody grins, and shows his whole *râtelier* , and you look at them and say, " These people seem all very jolly.' Leslie's characters do not laugh themselves, but they make *you* laugh ; and this is where the experienced American artist beats the dashing young Irish one. We shall say nothing of the colour of Mr. Maclise's large picture ; some part appears to us to be excellent, and the whole piece, as far as execution goes, is worthy of his amazing talents and high reputation. Mr. Maclise has but one portrait ; it is, perhaps, the best in the exhibition : sober in colour, wonderful for truth, effect, and power of drawing.

In speaking of portraits, there is never much to say ; and they are fewer, and for the most part more indifferent, than usual. Mr. Pickersgill has a good one, a gentleman in a green chair ; and one or two outrageously bad. Mr. Phillips's " Doctor Sheppard " is a finely painted head and picture ; his Lady Dunraven, and her son, as poor, ill drawn, and ill coloured a performance as can possibly be. Mr. Wood has a pretty head ; Mr. Stone a good portrait of a very noble-looking lady, the Hon. Mrs. Blackwood ; Mr. Bewick a good one ; and there are, of course, many others whose names might be mentioned with praise or censure, but whom we will, if you please, pass over altogether.

The great advance of the year is in the small historical compositions, of which there are many that deserve honourable mention. Redgrave's " Return of Olivia to the Vicar " has some very pretty painting and feeling in it ; " Quentin Matsys," by the same artist, is tolerably good. D. Cowper's " Othello relating his Adventures,' really beautiful ; as is Cope's " Belgian Family." All these are painted with grace, feeling, and delicacy ; as is E. M. Ward's " Cimabue and Giotto " (there is in Tiepolo's etchings the self-same composition, by the way) ; and Herbert's elegant picture of the " Brides of Venice." Mr. Severn's composition from the " Ancient Mariner " is a noble performance ; and the figure of the angel with raised arm awful and beautiful too. It does good to see such figures in pictures as those and the above, invented and drawn —for they belong, as we take it, to the best school of art, of which one is glad to see the daily spread among our young painters.

Mr. Charles Landseer's " Pillage of a Jew's House " is a very well and carefully painted picture, containing a great many figures and good points ; but we are not going to praise it : it wants vigour to our taste, and what you call *actualité*. The people stretch their arms and turn their eyes the proper way, but as if they were in a tableau and paid for standing there; one longs to see them all in motion and naturally employed.

I feel, I confess, a kind of delight in finding out Mr. Edwin Landseer in a bad picture ; for the man paints so wonderfully well, that one is angry that he does not paint better, which he might with half his talent, and without half his facility. "Van Amburgh and the Lions" *is* a bad picture, and no mistake ; dexterous, of course, but flat and washy : the drawing even of the animals is careless ; that of the man bad, though the head is very like, and very smartly painted. Then there are other dog-and-man portraits ; "Miss Peel with Fido," for instance. Fido is wonderful, and so are the sponges, and hair-brushes, and looking-glass, prepared for the dog's bath ; and the drawing of the child's face, as far as the lines and expression go, is very good ; but the face is covered with flesh-coloured paint, and not flesh, and the child looks like a wonderful doll, or imitation child, and not a real young lady, daughter of a gentleman who was prime minister last week (by-the-bye, my dear Bricabrac, did you ever read of such a pretty Whig game as that, and such a nice *coup d'état ?*). There, again, is the beautiful little Princess of Cambridge, with a dog, and a piece of biscuit : the dog and the biscuit are just perfection ; but the princess is no such thing—only a beautiful apology for a princess, like that which Princess Penelope *didn't* send the other day to the Lord Mayor of London.

We have to thank you (and not our Academy, which has hung the picture in a most scurvy way) for Mr. Scheffer's "Prêche Protestante." This fine composition has been thrust down on the ground, and trampled under foot, as it were, by a great number of worthless Academics ; but it merits one of the very best places in the gallery ; and I mention it to hint an idea to your worship, which only could come from a great mind like that of Titmarsh,— to have, namely, some day a great European congress of paintings, which might be exhibited at one place,—Paris, say, as the most central ; or, better still, travel about, under the care of trusty superintendents, as they might, without fear of injury. I think such a circuit would do much to make the brethren known to one another, and we should hear quickly of much manly emulation, and stout training for the contest. If you will mention this to Louis Philippe the next time you see that *roi citoyen* (mention it soon,— for, egad ! the next *émeute* may be successful ; and who knows when it will happen?)—if you will mention this at the Tuileries, *we* will take care of Saint James's ; for I suppose that you know, in spite of the Whigs, her most sacred Majesty reads every word of *Fraser's Magazine*, and will be as sure to see this on the first of next month, as Lord Melbourne will be to dine with her on that day.

But let us return to our muttons. I think there are few more of the oil pictures about which it is necessary to speak ; and besides them, there are a host of miniatures, difficult to expatiate upon, but pleasing to behold. There are Chalon's ogling beauties, half-a-dozen of them ; and the skill with which their silks and satins are dashed in by the painter is a marvel to the beholder. There are Ross's heads, that to be seen must be seen through a microscope. There is Saunders, who runs the best of the miniature men very hard ; and Thorburn, with Newton, Robertson, Rochard, and a host of others : and, finally, there is the sculpture-room, containing many pieces of clay and marble, and, to my notions, but two good things, a sleeping child (ridiculously called the Lady Susan Somebody), by Westmacott ; and the bust of Miss Stuart, by Macdonald : never was anything on earth more exquisitely lovely.

These things seen, take your stick from the porter at the hall door, cut it, and go to fresh picture galleries ; but ere you go, just by way of contrast, and to soothe your mind, after the glare and bustle of the modern collection, take half-an-hour's repose in the National Gallery ; where, before the "Bacchus and Ariadne," you may see what the magic of colour is ; before "Christ and Lazarus" what is majestic, solemn, grace and awful beauty ; and before the new "Saint Catherine" what is the real divinity of art. Oh, Eastlake and Turner !—Oh, Maclise and Mulready ! you are all very nice men ; but what are you to the men of old ?

. . . . . .

Issuing then from the National Gallery—you may step over to Farrance's by the way, if you like, and sip an ice, or bolt a couple of dozen forced-meat balls in a basin of mock-turtle soup—issuing, I say, from the National Gallery, and after refreshing yourself or not, as your purse or appetite permits, you arrive speedily at the Water-Colour Exhibition, and cannot do better than enter. I know nothing more cheerful or sparkling than the first *coup d'œil* of this little gallery. In the first place, you never can enter it without finding four or five pretty women, that's a fact ; pretty women with pretty pink bonnets peeping at pretty pictures, and with sweet whispers vowing that Mrs. Seyffarth is a dear delicious painter, and that her style is "so soft" ; and that Miss Sharpe paints every bit as well as her sister ; and that Mr. Jean Paul Frederick Richter draws the loveliest things, to be sure, that ever were seen. Well, very likely the ladies are right, and it would be unpolite to argue the matter ; but I wish Mrs. Seyffarth's gentlemen and ladies were not so dreadfully handsome, with such white pillars of necks, such long eyes and lashes, and such dabs of carmine at the mouth and nostrils. I wish Miss Sharpe would not paint Scripture subjects, and Mr. Richter great goggle eyed, red-cheeked, simpering wenches, whose ogling has become odious from its repetition. However, the ladies like it, and, of course, must have their way.

If you want to see *real* nature, now, real expression, real startling home poetry, look at every one of Hunt's heads. Hogarth never painted anything better than these figures, taken singly. That man rushing away frightened from the beer-barrel is a noble head of terror; that Miss Jemima Crow, whose whole body is a grin, regards you with an ogle that all the race of Richters could never hope to imitate. Look at yonder card-players; they have a penny pack of the devil's books, and one has just laid down the king of trumps! I defy you to look at him without laughing, or to examine the wondrous puzzled face of his adversary without longing to hug the greasy rogue. Come hither, Mr. Maclise, and see what genuine comedy is; you who can paint better than all the Hunts and Leslies, and yet not near so well. If I were the Duke of Devonshire, I would have a couple of Hunts in every room in all my houses; if I had the blue-devils (and even their graces are, I suppose, occasionally so troubled), I would but cast my eyes upon these grand good-humoured pictures, and defy care. Who does not recollect "Before and After the Mutton Pie," the two pictures of that wondrous boy? Where Mr. Hunt finds his models, I cannot tell; they are the very flower of the British youth; each of them is as good as "Sancho"; blessed is he that has his portfolio full of them.

There is no need to mention to you the charming landscapes of Cox, Copley Fielding, De Wint, Gastineau, and the rest. A new painter, somewhat in the style of Harding, is Mr. Callow; and better, I think, than his master or original, whose colours are too gaudy to my taste, and effects too glaringly theatrical.

Mr. Cattermole has, among others, two very fine drawings; a large one, the most finished and the best coloured of any which have been exhibited by this fine artist; and a smaller one, "The Portrait," which is charming. The portrait is that of Jane Seymour or Anne Boleyn; and Henry VIII. is the person examining it, with the Cardinal at his side, the painter before him, and one or two attendants. The picture seems to me a perfect masterpiece, very simply coloured and composed, but delicious in effect and tone, and telling the story to a wonder. It is much more gratifying, I think, to let a painter tell his own story in this way, than to bind him down to a scene of "Ivanhoe" or "Uncle Toby"; or worse still, to an illustration of some wretched story in some wretched fribble Annual. Woe to the painter who falls into the hands of Mr. Charles Heath (I speak, of course, not of Mr. Heath personally, but in a Pickwickian sense—of Mr. Heath the Annual-monger); he ruins the young artist, sucks his brains out, emasculates his genius so as to make it fit company for the purchasers of Annuals. Take, for instance, that unfortunate young man, Mr. Corbould, who gave great promise two years since, painted a pretty picture last year, and now—he has been in the hands of the Annual-mongers, and has left well-nigh all his vigour behind him. Numerous Zuleikas and Lalla Rookhs, which are hanging about the walls of the Academy and the New Water-Colour Gallery, give lamentable proofs of this : such handsome Turks and leering sultanas ; such Moors, with straight noses and pretty curled beards ! Away, Mr. Corbould ! away while it is yet time, out of the hands of these sickly heartless Annual sirens ! and ten years hence, when you have painted a good, vigorous, healthy picture, bestow the tear of gratitude upon Titmarsh, who tore you from the lap of your crimson-silk-and-gilt-edged Armida.

Mr. Cattermole has a couple, we will not say of imitators, but of friends, who admire his works very much ; these are, Mr. Nash and Mr. Lake Price ; the former paints furniture and old houses, the latter old houses and furniture, and both very pretty. No harm can be said of these miniature scene-painters ; on the contrary, Mr. Price's " Gallery at Hardwicke " is really remarkably dexterous ; and the chairs, tables, curtains, and pictures are nicked off with extraordinary neatness and sharpness—and then ? why then, no more is to be said. Cobalt, sepia, and a sable pencil will do a deal of work, to be sure ; and very pretty it is, too, when done : and as for finding fault with it, that nobody will and can ; but an artist wants something more than sepia, cobalt, and sable pencils, and the knowledge how to use them. What do you think, my dear Bricabrac, of a little *genius ?—that's* the picture-painter, depend on it.

Being on the subject of water-colours, we may as well step into the New Water-Colour Exhibition : not so good as the old, but very good. You will see here a large drawing by Mr. Corbould of a tournament, which will show at once how clever that young artist is, and how weak and *manièré.* You will see some charming unaffected English landscapes by Mr. Sims ; and a capital Spanish Girl by Hicks, of which the flesh-painting cannot be too much approved. It is done without the heavy white, with which water-colour artists are now wont to belabour their pictures ; and is, therefore, frankly and clearly painted, as all transparent water-colour drawing must be. The same praise of clearness, boldness, and depth of tone must be given to Mr. Absolon, who uses no white, and only just so much stippling as is necessary ; his picture has the force of oil, and we should be glad to see his manner more followed.

Mr. Haghe's "Town Hall of Courtray" has attracted, and deservedly, a great deal of notice. It is a very fine and masterly architectural drawing, rich and sombre in effect, the figures intro-duced being very nearly as good as the rest of the picture. Mr. Haghe, we suppose, will be called to the upper house of water-colour painters, who might well be anxious to receive into their ranks many persons belonging to the new society. We hope, how-ever, the latter will be faithful to themselves ; there is plenty of room for two galleries, and the public must, ere long, learn to appreciate the merits of the new one. Having spoken a word in favour of Mr. Johnston's pleasing and quaintly-coloured South American sketches, we have but to bend our steps to Suffolk Street, and draw this discourse to a close.

Here is a very fine picture, indeed, by Mr. Hurlstone, "Olympia, attacked by Bourbon's Soldiers in Saint Peter's and flying to the Cross." Seen from the further room, this picture is grand in effect and colour, and the rush of the armed men towards the girl finely and vigorously expressed. The head of Olympia has been called too calm by the critics ; it seems to me most beautiful, and the action of the figure springing forward and flinging its arms round the cross nobly conceived and executed. There is a good deal of fine Titianic painting in the soldiers' figures (oh, that Mr. Hurlstone would throw away his lampblack!), and the background of the church is fine, vast, and gloomy. This is the best historical picture to be seen anywhere this year ; perhaps the worst is the one which stands at the other end of the room, and which strikes upon the eye as if it were an immense water-colour sketch of a feeble picture by President West. Speaking of historical paintings, I forgot to mention a large and fine picture by Mr. Dyce, the "Separation of Edwy and Elgiva ;" somewhat crude and odd in colour, with a good deal of exaggeration in the countenances of the figures, but having grandeur in it, and unmistakable genius ; there is a figure of an old woman seated, which would pass muster very well in a group of Sebastian Piombo.

A capitally painted head by Mr. Stone, called the "Sword-bearer," almost as fresh, bright, and vigorous as a Vandyke, is the portrait, we believe, of a brother artist, the clever actor Mr. M'Ian. The latter's picture of "Sir Tristram in the Cave" deserves especial remark and praise; and is really as fine a dramatic composition as one will often see. The figures of the knight and the lady asleep in the foreground are novel, striking, and beautifully easy. The advance of the old King, who comes upon the lovers; the look of the hideous dwarf, who finds them out; and behind, the line of spears that are seen glancing over the rocks, and indicating the march of the unseen troops, are all very well conceived and arranged. The piece deserves engraving; it is wild, poetic, and original. To how many pictures, nowadays, can one apply the two last terms?

There are some more new pictures, in the midst of a great quantity of trash, that deserve notice. Mr. D. Cowper is always good; Mr. Stewart's "Grandfather" contains two excellent like-nesses, and is a pleasing little picture. Mr. Hurlstone's "Italian Boy," and "Girl with a Dog," are excellent; and in this pleasant mood, for fear of falling into an angry fit on coming to look further into the gallery, it will be as well to conclude. Wishing many remembrances to Mrs. Bricabrac, and better luck to you in the next *émeute*, I beg here to bid you farewell, and entreat you to accept the assurances of my distinguished consideration.   M. A. T.

Au CITOYEN BRUTUS NAPOLÉON BRICABRAC, *Réfugié*
    d'Avril, Blessé de Mai, Condamné de Juin, Décoré
    de Juillet, &c. &c. Hôtel Dieu, à Paris.

GEORGE CRUIKSHANK *

ACCUSATIONS of ingratitude, and just accusations no doubt, are made against every inhabitant of this wicked world, and the fact is, that a man who is ceaselessly engaged in its trouble and turmoil, borne hither and thither upon the fierce waves of the crowd, bustling, shifting, struggling to keep himself somewhat above water—fighting for reputation, or more likely for bread, and ceaselessly occupied to-day with plans for appeasing the eternal appetite of inevitable hunger to-morrow—a man in such straits has hardly time to think of anything but himself, and, as in a sinking ship, must make his own rush for the boats, and fight, struggle, and trample for safety. In the midst of such a combat as this, the "ingenious arts, which prevent the ferocity of the manners, and act upon them as an emollient" (as the philosophic bard remarks in the Latin Grammar) are likely to be jostled to death, and then forgotten. The world will allow no such compromises between it and that which does not belong to it—no two gods must we serve ; but (as one has seen in some old portraits) the horrible glazed eyes of Necessity are always fixed upon you ; fly away as you will, black Care sits behind you, and with his ceaseless gloomy croaking drowns the voice of all more cheerful companions. Happy he whose fortune has placed him where there is calm and plenty, and who has the wisdom not to give up his quiet in quest of visionary gain.

Here is, no doubt, the reason why a man, after the period of his boyhood, or first youth, makes so few friends. Want and ambition (new acquaintances which are introduced to him along with his beard) thrust away all other society from him. Some old friends remain, it is true, but these are become as a habit—a part of your selfishness ; and, for new ones, they are selfish as you are. Neither member of the new partnership has the capital of affection and kindly feeling, or can even afford the time that is requisite for the establishment of the new firm. Damp and chill the shades of the prison-house begin to close round us, and that " vision splendid "

* Reprinted from the *Westminster Review* for June 1840 (No. 66).

which has accompanied our steps in our journey daily farther from the east, fades away and dies into the light of common day.

And what a common day ! what a foggy, dull, shivering apology for light is this kind of muddy twilight through which we are about to tramp and flounder for the rest of our existence, wandering farther and farther from the beauty and freshness and from the kindly gushing springs of clear gladness that made all around us green in our youth ! One wanders and gropes in a slough of stock-jobbing, one sinks or rises in a storm of politics, and in either case it is as good to fall as to rise—to mount a bubble on the crest of the wave, as to sink a stone to the bottom.

The reader who has seen the name affixed to the head of this article scarcely expected to be entertained with a declamation upon ingratitude, youth, and the vanity of human pursuits, which may seem at first sight to have little to do with the subject in hand. But (although we reserve the privilege of discoursing upon whatever subject shall suit us, and by no means admit the public has any right to ask in our sentences for any meaning, or any connection whatever) it happens that, in this particular instance, there is an undoubted connection. In Susan's case, as recorded by Wordsworth, what connection had the corner of Wood Street with a mountain ascending, a vision of trees, and a nest by the Dove ? Why should the song of a thrush cause bright volumes of vapour to glide through Lothbury, and a river to flow on through the vale of Cheapside ? As she stood at that corner of Wood Street, a mop and a pail in her hand most likely, she heard the bird singing, and straightway began pining and yearning for the days of her youth, forgetting the proper business of the pail and mop. Even so we are moved by the sight of some of Mr. Cruikshank's works—the " Busen fühlt sich jugendlich erschüttert," the " schwankende Gestalten " of youth flit before one again,—Cruikshank's thrush begins to pipe and carol, as in the days of boyhood ; hence misty moralities, reflections, and sad and pleasant remembrances arise. He is the friend of the young especially. Have we not read all the story-books that his wonderful pencil has illustrated ? Did we not forego tarts, in order to buy his " Breaking-up," or his " Fashionable Monstrosities " of the year eighteen hundred and something ? Have we not before us, at this very moment, a print,—one of the admirable " Illustrations of Phrenology "—which entire work was purchased by a joint-stock company of boys, each drawing lots afterwards for the separate prints, and taking his choice in rotation ? The writer of this, too, had the honour of drawing the first lot, and seized immediately upon " Philoprogenitiveness "—a marvellous print (our copy is not at all improved by being coloured, which operation we per-

rmed on it ourselves)—a marvellous print, indeed,—full of ingenuity and fine jovial humour. A father, possessor of an enormous
ose and family, is surrounded by the latter, who are, some of
em, embracing the former. The composition writhes and twists
out like the Kermes of Rubens. No less than seven little men
d women in nightcaps, in frocks, in bibs, in breeches, are clamber-
g about the head, knees, and arms of the man with the nose ;
eir noses, too, are preternaturally developed—the twins in the
adle have noses of the most considerable kind. The second
ughter, who is watching them ; the youngest but two, who sits
ualling in a certain wicker chair ; the eldest son, who is yawning ;
e eldest daughter, who is preparing with the gravy of two mutton
ops a savoury dish of Yorkshire pudding for eighteen persons ;
e youths who are examining her operations (one a literary gentle-
an, in a remarkably neat nightcap and pinafore, who has just
d his finger in the pudding) ; the genius who is at work on the
ate, and the two honest lads who are hugging the good-humoured
asherwoman, their mother—all, all, save this worthy woman, have
oses of the largest size. Not handsome certainly are they, and
et everybody must be charmed with the picture. It is full of
otesque beauty. The artist has at the back of his own skull,
e are certain, a huge bump of philoprogenitiveness. He loves
ildren in his heart ; every one of those he has drawn is perfectly
ppy, and jovial, and affectionate, and innocent as possible. He
akes them with large noses, but he loves them, and you always
nd something kind in the midst of his humour, and the ugliness
deemed by a sly touch of beauty. The smiling mother reconciles
e with all the hideous family : they have all something of the
other in them—something kind, and generous, and tender.

Knight's, in Sweeting's Alley ; Fairburn's, in a court off Ludgate
ill ; Hone's, in Fleet Street—bright, enchanted palaces, which
eorge Cruikshank used to people with grinning, fantastical imps,
d merry, harmless sprites,—where are they ? Fairburn's shop
nows him no more ; not only has Knight disappeared from
weeting's Alley, but, as we are given to understand, Sweeting's
lley has disappeared from the face of the globe. Slop, the
rocious Castlereagh, the sainted Caroline (in a tight pelisse, with
athers in her head), the "Dandy of Sixty," who used to glance
us from Hone's friendly windows—where are they ? Mr.
ruikshank may have drawn a thousand better things since the
ys when these were ; but they are to us a thousand times more
easing than anything else he has done. How we used to believe
them ! to stray miles out of the way on holidays, in order to
onder for an hour before that delightful window in Sweeting's

Alley! in walks through Fleet Street, to vanish abruptly dow
Fairburn's passage, and there make one at his "charming gratis
exhibition. There used to be a crowd round the window in thos
days, of grinning, good-natured mechanics, who spelt the songs, an
spoke them out for the benefit of the company, and who receive
the points of humour with a general sympathising roar. Wher
are these people now? You never hear any laughing at HB.; hi
pictures are a great deal too genteel for that—polite points of wi1
which strike one as exceedingly clever and pretty, and cause on
to smile in a quiet, gentleman-like kind of way.

There must be no smiling with Cruikshank. A man wh
does not laugh outright is a dullard, and has no heart; even th
old dandy of sixty must have laughed at his own wondrou
grotesque image, as they say Louis Philippe did, who saw all th
caricatures that were made of himself. And there are some c
Cruikshank's designs which have the blessed faculty of creatin
laughter as often as you see them. As Diggory says in the play
who is bidden by his master not to laugh while waiting at table—
"Don't tell the story of Grouse in the Gun-room, master, or I can
help laughing." Repeat that history ever so often, and at th
proper moment, honest Diggory is sure to explode. Every mai
no doubt, who loves Cruikshank, has his "Grouse in the Gui
room." There is a fellow in the "Points of Humour" who
offering to eat up a certain little general, that has made us happ
any time these sixteen years: his huge mouth is a perpetual we
of laughter—buckets full of fun can be drawn from it. We hav
formed no such friendships as that boyish one of the man wit
the mouth. But though, in our eyes, Mr. Cruikshank reache
his apogee some eighteen years since, it must not be imagined tha
such is really the case. Eighteen sets of children have since the
learned to love and admire him, and may many more of the
successors be brought up in the same delightful faith. It is nc
the artist who fails, but the men who grow cold—the men, fro
whom the illusions (why illusions? realities) of youth disappe
one by one; who have no leisure to be happy, no blessed holiday
but only fresh cares at Midsummer and Christmas, being th
inevitable seasons which bring us bills instead of pleasures. Ton
who comes bounding home from school, has the doctor's account i
his trunk, and his father goes to sleep at the pantomime to whic
he takes him. *Pater infelix*, you too have laughed at clown, an
the magic wand of spangled harlequin; what delightful enchan
ment did it wave around you, in the golden days "when Georg
the Third was king!" But our clown lies in his grave; and o
harlequin, Ellar, prince of how many enchanted islands, was

ot at Bow Street the other day,* in his dirty, tattered, faded
motley—seized as a law-breaker, for acting at a penny theatre,
fter having well-nigh starved in the streets, where nobody would
isten to his old guitar! No one gave a shilling to bless him : not
one of us who owe him so much.

We know not if Mr. Cruikshank will be very well pleased at
inding his name in such company as that of Clown and Harlequin ;
out he, like them, is certainly the children's friend. His drawings
abound in feeling for these little ones, and hideous as in the course
of his duty he is from time to time compelled to design them, he
never sketches one without a certain pity for it, and imparting to
the figure a certain grotesque grace. In happy schoolboys he
revels ; plum-pudding and holidays his needle has engraved over
and over again ; there is a design in one of the comic almanacs of
some young gentlemen who are employed in administering to a
schoolfellow the correction of the pump, which is as graceful and
elegant as a drawing of Stothard. Dull books about children George
Cruikshank makes bright with illustrations—there is one published
by the ingenious and opulent Mr. Tegg. It is entitled " Mirth and
Morality," the mirth being, for the most part, on the side of the
designer — the morality, unexceptionable certainly, the author's
capital. Here are then, to these moralities, a smiling train of
mirths supplied by George Cruikshank. See yonder little fellows
butterfly-hunting across a common ! Such a light, brisk, airy,
gentlemanlike drawing was never made upon such a theme. Who,
cries the author—

> " Who has not chased the butterfly,
> And crushed its slender legs and wings,
> And heaved a moralising sigh :
> Alas ! how frail are human things ! '

A very unexceptionable morality truly ; but it would have puzzled
another than George Cruikshank to make mirth out of it as he has
done. Away, surely not on the wings of these verses, Cruikshank's
imagination begins to soar ; and he makes us three darling little
men on a green common, backed by old farm-houses, somewhere
about May. A great mixture of blue and clouds in the air, a strong
fresh breeze stirring, Tom's jacket flapping in the same, in order to
bring down the insect queen or king of spring that is fluttering
above him,—he renders all this with a few strokes on a little block
of wood not two inches square, upon which one may gaze for hours,
so merry and lifelike a scene does it present. What a charming
creative power is this, what a privilege to be a god, and create little

* This was written in 1840.

13

worlds upon paper, and whole generations of smiling, jovial men, women, and children half inch high, whose portraits are carried abroad, and have the faculty of making us monsters of six feet curious and happy in our turn. Now, who would imagine that an artist could make anything of such a subject as this ? The writer begins by stating—

> " I love to go back to the days of my youth,
>   And to reckon my joys to the letter,
>   And to count o'er the friends that I have in the world,
>   *Ay, and those who are gone to a better.*"

This brings him to the consideration of his uncle. "Of all the men I have ever known," says he, "my uncle united the greatest degree of cheerfulness with the sobriety of manhood. Though a man when I was a boy, he was yet one of the most agreeable companions I ever possessed. . . . He embarked for America, and nearly twenty years passed by before he came back again ; . . . but oh, how altered !—he was in every sense of the word an old man, his body and mind were enfeebled, and second childishness had come upon him. How often have I bent over him, vainly endeavouring to recall to his memory the scenes we had shared together : and how frequently, with an aching heart, have I gazed on his vacant and lustreless eye, while he has amused himself in clapping his hands and singing with a quavering voice a verse of a psalm." Alas ! such are the consequences of long residences in America, and of old age even in uncles ! Well, the point of this morality is, that the uncle one day in the morning of life vowed that he would catch his two nephews and tie them together, ay, and actually did so, for all the efforts the rogues made to run away from him ; but he was so fatigued that he declared he never would make the attempt again, whereupon the nephew remarks,—" Often since then, when engaged in enterprises beyond my strength, have I called to mind the determination of my uncle."

Does it not seem impossible to make a picture out of this ? And yet George Cruikshank has produced a charming design, in which the uncle and nephews are so prettily portrayed that one is reconciled to their existence, with all their moralities. Many more of the mirths in this little book are excellent, especially a great figure of a parson entering church on horseback,—an enormous parson truly, calm, unconscious, unwieldy. As Zeuxis had a bevy of virgins in order to make his famous picture—his express virgin— a clerical host must have passed under Cruikshank's eyes before he sketched this little, enormous parson of parsons.

Being on the subject of children's books, how shall we enough

praise the delightful German nursery-tales, and Cruikshank's illustrations of them? We coupled his name with pantomime awhile
since, and sure never pantomimes were more charming than these.
Of all the artists that ever drew, from Michael Angelo upwards
and downwards, Cruikshank was the man to illustrate these tales,
and give them just the proper admixture of the grotesque, the
wonderful, and the graceful. May all Mother Bunch's collection
be similarly indebted to him; may "Jack the Giant Killer," may
'Tom Thumb," may "Puss in Boots," be one day revivified by his
pencil. Is not Whittington sitting yet on Highgate Hill, and poor
Cinderella (in that sweetest of all fairy stories) still pining in her
lonely chimney nook? A man who has a true affection for these
delightful companions of his youth is bound to be grateful to them
f he can, and we pray Mr. Cruikshank to remember them.

It is folly to say that this or that kind of humour is too good
for the public, that only a chosen few can relish it. The best
humour that we know of has been as eagerly received by the public
as by the most delicate connoisseur. There is hardly a man in
England who can read but will laugh at Falstaff and the humour of
Joseph Andrews; and honest Mr. Pickwick's story can be felt and
loved by any person above the age of six. Some may have a keener
enjoyment of it than others, but all the world can be merry over it,
and is always ready to welcome it. The best criterion of good
humour is success, and what a share of this has Mr. Cruikshank
had! how many millions of mortals has he made happy! We
have heard very profound persons talk philosophically of the
marvellous and mysterious manner in which he has suited himself
to the time—*fait vibrer la fibre populaire* (as Napoleon boasted
of himself), supplied a peculiar want felt at a peculiar period, the
simple secret of which is, as we take it, that he, living amongst the
public, has with them a general wide-hearted sympathy, that he
laughs at what they laugh at, that he has a kindly spirit of enjoyment, with not a morsel of mysticism in his composition; that
he pities and loves the poor, and jokes at the follies of the great,
and that he addresses all in a perfectly sincere and manly way. To
be greatly successful as a professional humourist, as in any other
calling, a man must be quite honest, and show that his heart is in
his work. A bad preacher will get admiration and a hearing with
this point in his favour, where a man of three times his acquirements
will only find indifference and coldness. Is any man more remarkable than our artist for telling the truth after his own manner?
Hogarth's honesty of purpose was as conspicuous in an earlier time,
and we fancy that Gilray would have been far more successful and
more powerful but for that unhappy bribe, which turned the whole

course of his humour into an unnatural channel. Cruikshank would
not for any bribe say what he did not think, or lend his aid to
sneer down anything meritorious, or to praise any thing or person
that deserved censure. When he levelled his wit against the
Regent, and did his very prettiest for the Princess, he most certainly
believed, along with the great body of the people whom he represents, that the Princess was the most spotless, pure-mannered
darling of a Princess that ever married a heartless debauchee of a
Prince Royal. Did not millions believe with him, and noble and
learned lords take their oaths to her Royal Highness's innocence
Cruikshank would not stand by and see a woman ill-used, and so
struck in for her rescue, he and the people belabouring with all
their might the party who were making the attack, and determining
from pure sympathy and indignation, that the woman must be
innocent because her husband treated her so foully.

To be sure we have never heard so much from Mr. Cruikshank's
own lips, but any man who will examine these odd drawings, which
first made him famous, will see what an honest, hearty hatred the
champion of woman has for all who abuse her, and will admire
the energy with which he flings his wood-blocks at all who side
against her. Canning, Castlereagh, Bexley, Sidmouth, he is at
them, one and all; and as for the Prince, up to what a whipping
post of ridicule did he tie that unfortunate old man! And do not
let squeamish Tories cry out about disloyalty; if the crown does
wrong, the crown must be corrected by the nation, out of respect
of course, for the crown. In those days, and by those people who
so bitterly attacked the son, no word was ever breathed against the
father, simply because he was a good husband, and a sober, thrifty,
pious, orderly man.

This attack upon the Prince Regent we believe to have been
Mr. Cruikshank's only effort as a party politician. Some early
manifestoes against Napoleon we find, it is true, done in the regular
John Bull style, with the Gilray model for the little upstart
Corsican : but as soon as the Emperor had yielded to stern fortune
our artist's heart relented (as Béranger's did on the other side
of the water), and many of our readers will doubtless recollect
fine drawing of " Louis XVIII. trying on Napoleon's boots," which
did not certainly fit the gouty son of Saint Louis. Such satirical
hits as these, however, must not be considered as political, or as
anything more than the expression of the artist's national British
idea of Frenchmen.

It must be confessed that for that great nation Mr. Cruikshank
entertains a considerable contempt. Let the reader examine the
" Life in Paris," or the five hundred designs in which Frenchmen

re introduced, and he will find them almost invariably thin, with idicrous spindle-shanks, pigtails, outstretched hands, shrugging houlders, and queer hair and mustachios. He has the British idea of a Frenchman; and if he does not believe that the inhabitants of France are for the most part dancing-masters and barbers, et takes care to depict such in preference, and would not speak so well of them. It is curious how these traditions endure. In rance, at the present moment, the Englishman on the stage is he caricatured Englishman at the time of the war, with a shock ed head, a long white coat, and invariable gaiters. Those who rish to study this subject should peruse Monsieur Paul de Kock's istories of "Lord Boulingrog" and "Lady Crockmilove." On he other hand, the old *émigré* has taken his station amongst us, nd we doubt if a good British gallery would understand that such nd such a character *was* a Frenchman unless he appeared in the ncient traditional costume."

A curious book, called "Life in Paris," published in 1822, ontains a number of the artist's plates in the aquatint style; nd though we believe he had never been in that capital, the esigns have a great deal of life in them, and pass muster very rell. A villainous race of shoulder-shrugging mortals are his renchmen indeed. And the heroes of the tale, a certain Mr.)ick Wildfire, Squire Jenkins, and Captain O'Shuffleton, are made o show the true British superiority on every occasion when Britons nd French are brought together. This book was one among the nany that the designer's genius has caused to be popular; the lates are not carefully executed, but, being coloured, have a leasant, lively look. The same style was adopted in the once amous book called "Tom and Jerry, or Life in London," which nust have a word of notice here, for, although by no means Mr. Jruikshank's best work, his reputation was extraordinarily raised by it. Tom and Jerry were as popular twenty years since as Mr. 'ickwick and Sam Weller now are; and often have we wished, rhile reading the biographies of the latter celebrated personages, hat they had been described as well by Mr. Cruikshank's pencil as by Mr. Dickens's pen.

As for Tom and Jerry, to show the mutability of human affairs nd the evanescent nature of reputation, we have been to the British Museum and no less than five circulating libraries in quest of the book, and "Life in London," alas, is not to be found at any one of hem. We can only, therefore, speak of the work from recollection, ut have still a very clear remembrance of the leather-gaiters of Terry Hawthorn, the green spectacles of Logic, and the hooked nose of Corinthian Tom. They were the schoolboy's delight; and in

the days when the work appeared we firmly believed the thr
heroes above named to be types of the most elegant, fashionab
young fellows the town afforded, and thought their occupatio
and amusements were those of all high-bred English gentleme
Tom knocking down the watchman at Temple Bar; Tom and Jer
dancing at Almack's ; or flirting in the saloon at the theatre ;
the night-houses, after the play; at Tom Cribb's, examining t
silver cup then in the possession of that champion; at the chambe
of Bob Logic, who, seated at a cabinet piano, plays a waltz to whic
Corinthian Tom and Kate are dancing ; ambling gallantly in Rotte
Row; or examining the poor fellow at Newgate who was having b
chains knocked off before hanging : all these scenes remain indelib.
engraved upon the mind, and so far we are independent of all t
circulating libraries in London.

As to the literary contents of the book, they have passed she
away.   It was, most likely, not particularly refined; nay, t
chances are that it was absolutely vulgar.   But it must have h
some merit of its own, that is clear ; it must have given striki
descriptions of life in some part or other of London, for all Lond
read it, and went to see it in its dramatic shape.   The artist, it
said, wished to close the career of the three heroes by bringing the
all to ruin, but the writer, or publishers, would not allow any su
melancholy subjects to dash the merriment of the public, and v
believe Tom, Jerry, and Logic were married off at the end of t
tale, as if they had been the most moral personages in the worl
There is some goodness in this pity, which authors and the pub
are disposed to show towards certain agreeable, disreputab
characters of romance.   Who would mar the prospects of hone
Roderick Random, or Charles Surface, or Tom Jones ? only a ve
stern moralist indeed.   And in regard of Jerry Hawthorn and th
hero without a surname, Corinthian Tom, Mr. Cruikshank, we ma
little doubt, was glad in his heart that he was not allowed to ha
his own way.

Soon after the " Tom and Jerry " and the " Life in Paris," M
Cruikshank produced a much more elaborate set of prints, in a wo
which was called " Points of Humour." These " Points " we
selected from various comic works, and did not, we believe, exte
beyond a couple of numbers, containing about a score of copp
plates.   The collector of humorous designs cannot fail to ha
them in his portfolio, for they contain some of the very best effor
of Mr. Cruikshank's genius, and though not quite so highly labour
as some of his later productions, are none the worse, in our opinio
for their comparative want of finish.   All the effects are perfect
given, and the expression is as good as it could be in the mo

delicate engraving upon steel. The artist's style, too, was then completely formed ; and, for our parts, we should say that we pre- ferred his manner of 1825 to any other which he has adopted since. The first picture, which is called "The Point of Honour," illustrates the old story of the officer who, on being accused of cowardice for refusing to fight a duel, came among his brother officers and flung a lighted grenade down upon the floor, before which his comrades fled ignominiously. This design is capital, and the outward rush of heroes, walking, trampling, twisting, scuffling at the door, is in the best style of the grotesque. You see but the back of most of these gentlemen ; into which, nevertheless, the artist has managed to throw an expression of ludicrous agony that one could scarcely have expected to find in such a part of the human figure. The next plate is not less good. It represents a couple who, having been found one night tipsy, and lying in the same gutter, were, by a charitable though misguided gentleman, supposed to be man and wife, and put comfortably to bed together. The morning came ; fancy the surprise of this interesting pair when they awoke and discovered their situation. Fancy the manner, too, in which Cruikshank has depicted them, to which words cannot do justice. It is needless to state that this fortuitous and temporary union was followed by one more lasting and sentimental, and that these two worthy persons were married, and lived happily ever after.

We should like to go through every one of these prints. There is the jolly miller, who, returning home at night, calls upon his wife to get him a supper, and falls to upon rashers of bacon and ale. How he gormandises, that jolly miller ! rasher after rasher, how they pass away frizzling and smoking from the gridiron down that immense grinning gulf of a mouth. Poor wife ! how she pines and frets, at that untimely hour of midnight to be obliged to fry, fry, fry perpetually, and minister to the monster's appetite. And yonder in the clock : what agonised face is that we see ? By heavens, it is the squire of the parish. What business has he there ? Let us not ask. Suffice it to say, that he has, in the hurry of the moment, left upstairs his br—— ; his—psha ! a part of his dress, in short, with a number of bank-notes in the pockets. Look in the next page, and you will see the ferocious, bacon-devouring ruffian of a miller is actually causing this garment to be carried through the village and cried by the town-crier. And we blush to be obliged to say that the demoralised miller never offered to return the bank- notes, although he was so mighty scrupulous in endeavouring to find an owner for the corduroy portfolio in which he had found them.

Passing from this painful subject, we come, we regret to
state, to a series of prints representing personages not a whit
more moral. Burns's famous "Jolly Beggars" have all had
their portraits drawn by Cruikshank. There is the lovely
"hempen widow," quite as interesting and romantic as the famous
Mrs. Sheppard, who has at the lamented demise of her husband
adopted the very same consolation.

> " My curse upon them every one,
> They've hanged my braw John Highlandman;
>
> .   .   .   .   .
>
> And now a widow I must mourn,
> Departed joys that ne'er return ;
> No comfort but a hearty can
> When I think on John Highlandman."

Sweet "raucle carlin," she has none of the sentimentality of the
English highwayman's lady ; but being wooed by a tinker and

> " A pigmy scraper wi' his fiddle
> Wha us'd to trystes and fairs to driddle,"

prefers the practical to the merely musical man. The tinker sing
with a noble candour, worthy of a fellow of his strength of body
and station in life—

> " My bonnie lass, I work in brass,
> A tinker is my station ;
> I've travell'd round all Christian ground
> In this my occupation.
> I've taen the gold, I've been enroll'd
> In many a noble squadron ;
> But when they search'd when off I march'd
> To go an' clout the caudron."

It was his ruling passion. What was military glory to him, forsooth
He had the greatest contempt for it, and loved freedom and his
copper kettle a thousand times better—a kind of hardware Diogenes
Of fiddling he has no better opinion. The picture represents the
" sturdy caird" taking " poor gut-scraper" by the beard,—drawing
his " roosty rapier," and swearing to " speet him like a pliver
unless he would relinquish the bonnie lassie for ever—

> " Wi' ghastly ee, poor tweedle-dee
> Upon his hunkers bended,
> An' pray'd for grace wi' ruefu' face,
> An' so the quarrel ended."

Hark how the tinker apostrophises the violinist, stating to the

widow at the same time the advantages which she might expect
from an alliance with himself :—

> " Despise that shrimp, that withered imp,
>   Wi' a' his noise and caperin' ;
> And take a share with those that bear
>   The budget and the apron !
>
> And by that stowp, my faith an' houpe,
>   An' by that dear Kilbaigie !
> If e'er ye want, or meet wi' scant,
>   May I ne'er weet my craigie."

Cruikshank's caird is a noble creature; his face and figure show
him to be fully capable of doing and saying all that is above written
of him.

In the second part, the old tale of " The Three Hunchbacked
Fiddlers " is illustrated with equal felicity. The famous classical
dinners and duel in " Peregrine Pickle " are also excellent in their
way ; and the connoisseur of prints and etchings may see in the
latter plate, and in another in this volume, how great the artist's
mechanical skill is as an etcher. The distant view of the city in
the duel, and of a market-place in " The Quack Doctor," are delightful specimens of the artist's skill in depicting buildings and backgrounds. They are touched with a grace, truth, and dexterity
of workmanship that leave nothing to desire. We have before
mentioned the man with the mouth, which appears in this number
emblematical of gout and indigestion, in which the artist has shown
all the fancy of Callot. Little demons, with long saws for noses,
are making dreadful incisions into the toes of the unhappy sufferer;
some are bringing pans of hot coals to keep the wounded member
warm ; a huge, solemn nightmare sits on the invalid's chest, staring
solemnly into his eyes ; a monster, with a pair of drumsticks, is banging a devil's tattoo on his forehead ; and a pair of imps are nailing
great tenpenny nails into his hands to make his happiness complete.

The late Mr. Clark's excellent work, " Three Courses and a
Dessert," was published at a time when the rage for comic stories
was not so great as it since has been, and Messrs. Clark and
Cruikshank only sold their hundreds where Messrs. Dickens and
Phiz dispose of their thousands. But if our recommendation can in
any way influence the reader, we would enjoin him to have a copy
of the " Three Courses," that contains some of the best designs
of our artist, and some of the most amusing tales in our language.
The invention of the pictures, for which Mr. Clark takes credit to
himself, says a great deal for his wit and fancy. Can we, for instance,
praise too highly the man who invented that wonderful oyster?

Examine him well : his beard, his pearl, his little round stomach, and his sweet smile. Only oysters know how to smile in this way : cool, gentle, waggish, and yet inexpressibly innocent and winning. Dando himself must have allowed such an artless native to go free, and consigned him to the glassy, cool, translucent wave again.

In writing upon such subjects as these with which we have been furnished, it can hardly be expected that we should follow any fixed plan and order—we must therefore take such advantage as we may, and seize upon our subject when. and wherever we can lay hold of him.

For Jews, sailors, Irishmen, Hessian boots, little boys, beadles, policemen, tall life-guardsmen, charity children, pumps, dustmen, very short pantaloons, dandies in spectacles, and ladies with aquiline noses, remarkably taper waists, and wonderfully long ringlets, Mr. Cruikshank has a special predilection. The tribe of Israelites he has studied with amusing gusto ; witness the Jew in Mr. Ainsworth's "Jack Sheppard," and the immortal Fagin of "Oliver Twist." Whereabouts lies the comic *vis* in these persons and things ? Why should a beadle be comic, and his opposite a charity boy ? Why should a tall life-guardsman have something in him essentially absurd ? Why are short breeches more ridiculous than long ? What is there particularly jocose about a pump, and wherefore does a long nose always provoke the beholder to laughter ? These points may be metaphysically elucidated by those who list. It is probable that Mr. Cruikshank could not give an accurate definition of that which is ridiculous in these objects, but his instinct has told him that fun lurks in them, and cold must be the heart that can pass by the pantaloons of his charity boys, the Hessian boots of his dandies, and the fan-tail hats of his dustmen, without respectful wonder.

He has made a complete little gallery of dustmen. There is, in the first place, the professional dustman, who having, in the enthusiastic exercise of his delightful trade, laid hands upon property not strictly his own, is pursued, we presume, by the right owner, from whom he flies as fast as his crooked shanks will carry him.

What a curious picture it is—the horrid rickety houses in some dingy suburb of London, the grinning cobbler, the smothered butcher, the very trees which are covered with dust—it is fine to look at the different expressions of the two interesting fugitives. The fiery charioteer who belabours the poor donkey has still a glance for his brother on foot, on whom punishment is about to descend. And not a little curious is it to think of the creative power of the man who has arranged this little tale of low life. How logically it is conducted, how cleverly each one of the accessories is made to contribute to the effect of the whole. What a deal of thought and humour has the artist expended on this little block of wood ; a large picture might have been painted out of the very same materials, which Mr. Cruikshank, out of his wondrous fund of merriment and observation, can afford to throw away upon a drawing not two inches long. From the practical dustmen we pass to those purely poetical. There are three of them who rise on clouds of their own raising, the very genii of the sack and shovel.

Is there no one to write a sonnet to these ?—and yet a whole poem was written about Peter Bell the Waggoner, a character by no means so poetic.

And lastly, we have the dustman in love : the honest fellow having seen a young beauty stepping out of a gin-shop on a Sunday morning, is pressing eagerly his suit.

Gin has furnished many subjects to Mr. Cruikshank, who labours in his own sound and hearty way to teach his countrymen the dangers of that drink. In the " Sketch-Book " is a plate upon the subject, remarkable for fancy and beauty of design ; it is called the " Gin Juggernaut," and represents a hideous moving palace, with a reeking still at the roof and vast gin-barrels for wheels, under which unhappy millions are crushed to death. An immense black cloud of desolation covers over the country through which the gin monster has passed, dimly looming through the darkness whereof you see an agreeable prospect of gibbets with men dangling, burnt houses, &c. The vast cloud comes sweeping on in the wake of this horrible body-crusher ; and you see, by way of contrast, a distant, smiling, sunshiny track of old English country, where gin as yet is not known. The allegory is as good, as earnest, and as fanciful as one of John Bunyan's, and we have often fancied there was a similarity between the men.

The reader will examine the work called " My Sketch-Book " with not a little amusement, and may gather from it, as we fancy, a good deal of information regarding the character of the individual man, George Cruikshank : what points strike his eye as a painter ; what move his anger or admiration as a moralist ; what classes he seems most especially disposed to observe, and what to ridicule. There are quacks of all kinds, to whom he has a mortal hatred : quack dandies, who assume under his pencil, perhaps in his eye, the most grotesque appearance possible— their hats grow larger, their legs infinitely more crooked and lean ; the tassels of their canes swell out to a most preposterous size ; the tails of their coats dwindle away, and finish where coat-tails generally begin. Let us lay a wager that Cruikshank, a man of the people if ever there was one, heartily hates and despises these supercilious, swaggering young

gentlemen ; and his contempt is not a whit the less laudable becaus
there may be *tant soit peu* of prejudice in it.   It is right an
wholesome to scorn dandies, as Nelson said it was to hate Frenchmen
in which sentiment (as we have before said) George Cruikshan
undoubtedly shares.   In the "Sunday in London," * Monsieur th

---

* The following lines—ever fresh—by the author of "Headlong Hall,
published years ago in the *Globe and Traveller*, are an excellent comment o
several of the cuts from the "Sunday in London" :—

I.

" The poor man's sins are glaring ;
In the face of ghostly warning
   He is caught in the fact
   Of an overt act
Buying greens on Sunday morning.

II.

The rich man's sins are hidden
In the pomp of wealth and station,
   And escape the sight
   Of the children of light,
Who are wise in their generation.

III.

The rich man has a kitchen,
And cooks to dress his dinner ;
   The poor who would roast,
   To the baker's must post,
And thus becomes a sinner.

IV.

The rich man's painted windows
Hide the concerts of the quality ;
   The poor can but share
   A crack'd fiddle in the air,
Which offends all sound morality.

V.

The rich man has a cellar
And a ready butler by him ;
   The poor must steer
   For his pint of beer
Where the saint can't choose but spy him.

VI.

The rich man is invisible
In the crowd of his gay society ;
   But the poor man's delight
   Is a sore in the sight
And a stench in the nose of piety."

Chef is instructing a kitchen-maid how to compound some rascally French kickshaw or the other—a pretty scoundrel truly! with what an air he wears that nightcap of his, and shrugs his lank shoulders, and chatters, and ogles, and grins : they are all the same, these mounseers ; there are other two fellows—*morbleu !* one is putting his dirty fingers into the saucepan ; there are frogs cooking in it, no doubt ; and just over some other dish of abomination, another dirty rascal is taking snuff ! Never mind, the sauce won't be hurt by a few ingredients more or less. Three such fellows as these are not worth one Englishman, that's clear. There is one in the very midst of them, the great burly fellow with the beef : he could beat all three in five minutes. We cannot be certain that such was the process going on in Mr. Cruikshank's mind when he made the design ; but some feelings of the sort were no doubt entertained by him.

Against Dandy footmen he is particularly severe. He hates idlers, pretenders, boasters, and punishes these fellows as best he may. Who does not recollect the famous picture, "What *is* Taxes, Thomas?" What is taxes indeed? well may that vast, over-fed, lounging flunkey ask the question of his associate Thomas : and yet not well, for all that Thomas says in reply is, "*I don't know.*" "O beati *plushicolæ,*" what a charming state of ignorance is yours ! In the "Sketch-Book," many footmen make their appearance : one is a huge fat Hercules of a Portman Square porter, who calmly surveys another poor fellow, a porter likewise, but out of livery, who comes staggering forward with a box that Hercules might lift with his little finger. Will Hercules do so? not he. The giant can carry nothing heavier than a cocked-hat note on a silver tray, and his labours are to walk from his sentry-box to the door, and from the door back to his sentry-box, and to read the Sunday paper, and to poke the hall fire twice or thrice, and to make five meals a day. Such a fellow does Cruikshank hate and scorn worse even than a Frenchman.

The man's master, too, comes in for no small share of our artist's wrath. There is a company of them at church, who humbly designate themselves "miserable sinners !" Miserable sinners indeed ! Oh, what floods of turtle-soup, what tons of turbot and lobster-sauce must have been sacrificed to make those sinners properly miserable. My lady with the ermine tippet and draggling feather, can we not see that she lives in Portland Place, and is the wife of an East India Director? She has been to the Opera over-night (indeed, her husband, on her right, with his fat hand dangling over the pew door, is at this minute thinking of Mademoiselle Léocadie, whom he saw behind the scenes)—she has been at the Opera over-

z

night, which with a trifle of supper afterwards—a white-and-brown soup, a lobster salad, some woodcocks, and a little champagne—sent her to bed quite comfortable. At half-past eight her maid brings her chocolate in bed, at ten she has fresh eggs and muffins, with, perhaps, a half-hundred of prawns for breakfast, and so can get over the day and the sermon till lunch-time pretty well. What an odour of musk and bergamot exhales from the pew!—how it is wadded, and stuffed, and spangled over with brass nails! what hassocks are there for those who are not too fat to kneel! what a flustering and flapping of gilt prayer-books : and what a pious whirring of Bible leaves one hears all over the church, as the doctor blandly gives out the text! To be miserable at this rate you must, at the very least, have four thousand a year : and many persons are there so enamoured of grief and sin, that they would willingly take the risk of the misery to have a life-interest in the consols that accompany it, quite careless about consequences, and sceptical as to the notion that a day is at hand when you must fulfil *your share of the bargain.*

Our artist loves to joke at a soldier; in whose livery there appears to him to be something almost as ridiculous as in the uniform of the gentleman of the shoulder-knot. Tall life-guardsmen and fierce grenadiers figure in many of his designs, and almost always in a ridiculous way. Here again we have the honest popular English feeling which jeers at pomp or pretension of all kinds, and is especially jealous of all display of military authority. " Raw Recruit," " ditto dressed," ditto " served up," as we see them in the " Sketch-Book," are so many satires upon the army : Hodge with his ribbons flaunting in his hat, or with red coat and musket, drilled stiff and pompous, or at last, minus leg and arm, tottering about on crutches, does not fill our English artist with the enthusiasm that follows the soldier in every other part of Europe. Jeanjean, the conscript in France, is laughed at to be sure, but then it is because he is a bad soldier : when he comes to have a huge pair of mustachios and the *croix-d'honneur* to *briller* on his *poitrine cicatrisée,* Jean-jean becomes a member of a class that is more respected than any other in the French nation. The veteran soldier inspires our people with no such awe—we hold that democratic weapon the fist in much more honour than the sabre and bayonet, and laugh at a man tricked out in scarlet and pipe-clay.

That regiment of heroes is " marching to divine service," to the tune of the " British Grenadiers." There they march in state, and a pretty contempt our artist shows for all their gimcracks and trumpery. He has drawn a perfectly English scene—the little blackguard boys are playing pranks round about the men, and

Please your Honor Tom Towzer has tied my tail so tight that I can't shut my eyes!

shouting, "Heads up, soldier," "Eyes right, lobster," as little British urchins will do. Did one ever hear the like sentiments expressed in France? Shade of Napoleon, we insult you by asking the question. In England, however, see how different the case is: and designedly or undesignedly, the artist has opened to us a piece of his mind. In the crowd the only person who admires the soldiers is the poor idiot, whose pocket a rogue is picking. There is another picture, in which the sentiment is much the same, only, as in the former drawing we see Englishmen laughing at the troops of the line, here are Irishmen giggling at the militia.

We have said that our artist has a great love for the drolleries of the Green Island. Would any one doubt what was the country of the merry fellows depicted in his group of Paddies?

> " Place me amid O'Rourkes, O'Tooles,
> The ragged royal race of Tara;
> Or place me where Dick Martin rules
> The pathless wilds of Connemara."

We know not if Mr. Cruikshank has ever had any such good luck as to see the Irish in Ireland itself, but he certainly has obtained a knowledge of their looks, as if the country had been all his life familiar to him. Could Mr. O'Connell himself desire anything more national than the scene of a drunken row, or could Father Mathew have a better text to preach upon? There is not a broken nose in the room that is not thoroughly Irish.

We have then a couple of compositions treated in a graver manner, as characteristic too as the other. We call attention to the comical look of poor Teague, who has been pursued and beaten by the witch's stick, in order to point out also the singular neatness of the workmanship, and the pretty, fanciful little glimpse of landscape that the artist has introduced in the background. Mr. Cruikshank has a fine eye for such homely landscapes, and renders them with great delicacy and taste. Old villages, farm-yards, groups of stacks, queer chimneys, churches, gable-ended cottages, Elizabethan mansion-houses, and other old English scenes, he depicts with evident enthusiasm.

Famous books in their day were Cruikshank's " John Gilpin " and " Epping Hunt "; for though our artist does not draw horses very scientifically,—to use a phrase of the atelier, he *feels* them very keenly ; and his queer animals, after one is used to them, answer quite as well as better. Neither is he very happy in trees, and such rustical produce ; or rather, we should say, he is very original, his trees being decidedly of his own make and composition, not imitated from any master.

But what then ? Can a man be supposed to imitate everything ? We know what the noblest study of mankind is, and to this Mr. Cruikshank has confined himself. That postillion with the people in the broken-down chaise roaring after him is as deaf as the post by which he passes. Suppose all the accessories were away, could not one swear that the man was stone-deaf, beyond the reach of trumpet ? What is the peculiar character in a deaf man's physiognomy ?—can any person define it satisfactorily in words ?—not in pages ; and Mr. Cruikshank has expressed it on a piece of paper not so big as the tenth part of your thumb-nail. The horses of John Gilpin are much more of the equestrian order ; and as here the artist has only his favourite suburban buildings to draw, not a word is to be said against his design. The inn and old buildings are charmingly designed, and nothing can be more prettily or playfully touched.

> " At Edmonton his loving wife
> From the balcony spied
> Her tender husband, wond'ring much
> To see how he did ride.
>
> ' Stop, stop, John Gilpin ! Here's the house !'
> They all at once did cry ;
> ' The dinner waits, and we are tired—'
> Said Gilpin—' So am I !'
>
> Six gentlemen upon the road
> Thus seeing Gilpin fly,
> With post-boy scamp'ring in the rear,
> They raised the hue and cry :—
>
> ' Stop thief ! stop thief !—a highwayman !'
> Not one of them was mute ;
> And all and each that passed that way
> Did join in the pursuit.
>
> And now the turnpike gates again
> Flew open in short space ;
> The toll-men thinking, as before,
> That Gilpin rode a race."

The rush, and shouting, and clatter are excellently depicted by the artist ; and we, who have been scoffing at his manner of designing animals, must here make a special exception in favour of the hens and chickens ; each has a different action, and is curiously natural.

Happy are children of all ages who have such a ballad and such pictures as this in store for them ! It is a comfort to think that

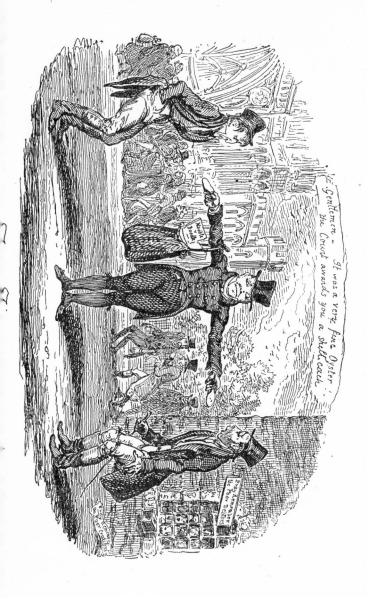

"Gentlemen — It was a very fine Oyster the Court awards you a shell each ..."

wood-cuts never wear out, and that the book still may be had for a shilling, for those who can command that sum of money.

In the "Epping Hunt," which we owe to the facetious pen of Mr. Hood, our artist has not been so successful. There is here too much horsemanship and not enough incident for him ; but the portrait of Roundings the huntsman is an excellent sketch, and a couple of the designs contain great humour. The first represents the Cockney hero, who, "like a bird, was singing out while sitting on a tree."

And in the second the natural order is reversed. The stag having taken heart, is hunting the huntsman, and the Cheapside Nimrod is most ignominiously running away.

The Easter Hunt, we are told, is no more ; and as the *Quarterly Review* recommends the British public to purchase Mr. Catlin's pictures, as they form the only record of an interesting race now rapidly passing away, in like manner we should exhort all our friends to purchase Mr. Cruikshank's designs of *another* interesting race, that is run already and for the last time.

Besides these, we must mention, in the line of our duty, the notable tragedies of "Tom Thumb" and "Bombastes Furioso," both of which have appeared with many illustrations by Mr. Cruikshank. The "brave army" of Bombastes exhibits a terrific display of brutal force, which must shock the sensibilities of an English radical. And we can well understand the caution of the general, who bids this *soldatesque effrénée* to begone, and not to kick up a row.

Such a troop of lawless ruffians let loose upon a populous city would play sad havoc in it ; and we fancy the massacres of Birmingham renewed, or at least of Badajoz, which, though not quite so dreadful, if we may believe his Grace the Duke of Wellington, as the former scenes of slaughter, were nevertheless severe enough : but we must not venture upon any ill-timed pleasantries in presence of the disturbed King Arthur and the awful ghost of Gaffer Thumb.

We are thus carried at once into the supernatural, and here we find Cruikshank reigning supreme. He has invented in his time a little comic pandemonium, peopled with the most droll, good-natured fiends possible. We have before us Chamisso's "Peter Schlemihl," with Cruikshank's designs translated into German, and gaining nothing by the change. The "Kinder und Hans-Maerchen" of Grimm are likewise ornamented with a frontispiece, copied from that one which appeared to the amusing version of the English work. The books on Phrenology and Time have been imitated by the same nation ; and even in France, whither reputation travels slower than to any country except China, we have seen copies of the works of George Cruikshank.

He in return has complimented the French by illustrating a couple of Lives of Napoleon, and the " Life in Paris " before mentioned. He has also made designs for Victor Hugo's " Hans of Iceland." Strange wild etchings were those, on a strange, mad subject; not so good in our notion as the designs for the German books, the peculiar humour of which latter seemed to suit the artist exactly. There is a mixture of the awful and the ridiculous in these, which perpetually excites and keeps awake the reader's attention ; the German writer and the English artist seem to have an entire faith in their subject. The reader, no doubt, remembers the awful passage in " Peter Schlemihl," where the little gentleman purchases the shadow of that hero—" Have the kindness, noble sir, to examine and try this bag." " He put his hand into his pocket, and drew thence a tolerably large bag of Cordovan leather, to which a couple of thongs were fixed. I took it from him, and immediately counted out ten gold pieces, and ten more, and ten more, and still other ten, whereupon I held out my hand to him. Done, said I, it is a bargain ; you shall have my shadow for your bag. The bargain was concluded ; he knelt down before me, and I saw him with a wonderful neatness take my shadow from head to foot, lightly lift it up from the grass, roll and fold it up neatly, and at last pocket it. He then rose up, bowed to me once more, and walked away again, disappearing behind the rose-bushes. I don't know, but I thought I heard him laughing a little. I, however, kept fast hold of the bag. Everything around me was bright in the sun, and as yet I gave no thought to what I had done."

This marvellous event, narrated by Peter with such a faithful circumstantial detail, is painted by Cruikshank in the most wonderful poetic way, with that happy mixture of the real and supernatural that makes the narrative so curious, and like truth. The sun is shining with the utmost brilliancy in a great quiet park or garden ; there is a palace in the background, and a statue basking in the sun quite lonely and melancholy ; there is a sun-dial, on which is a deep shadow, and in the front stands Peter Schlemihl, bag in hand : the old gentleman is down on his knees to him, and has just lifted off the ground the *shadow of one leg ;* he is going to fold it back neatly, as one does the tails of a coat, and will stow it, without any creases or crumples, along with the other black garments that lie in that immense pocket of his. Cruikshank has designed all this as if he had a very serious belief in the story ; he laughs, to be sure, but one fancies that he is a little frightened in his heart, in spite of all his fun and joking.

The German tales we have mentioned before. " The Prince riding on the Fox," " Hans in Luck," " The Fiddler and his

Goose," "Heads off," are all drawings which, albeit not before us now, nor seen for ten years, remain indelibly fixed on the memory. "*Heisst du etwa Rumpelstilzchen?*" There sits the Queen on her throne, surrounded by grinning beef-eaters, and little Rumpelstiltskin stamps his foot through the floor in the excess of his tremendous despair. In one of these German tales, if we remember rightly, there is an account of a little orphan who is carried away by a pitying fairy for a term of seven years, and passing that period of sweet apprenticeship among the imps and sprites of fairy-land. Has our artist been among the same company, and brought back their portraits in his sketch-book? He is the only designer fairy-land has had. Callot's imps, for all their strangeness, are only of the earth earthy. Fuseli's fairies belong to the infernal regions; they are monstrous, lurid, and hideously melancholy. Mr. Cruikshank alone has had a true insight into the character of the "little people." They are something like men and women, and yet not flesh and blood; they are laughing and mischievous, but why we know not. Mr. Cruikshank, however, has had some dream or the other, or else a natural mysterious instinct (as the Seherin of Prevorst had for beholding ghosts), or else some preternatural fairy revelation, which has made him acquainted with the looks and ways of the fantastical subjects of Oberon and Titania.

We have, unfortunately, no fairy portraits; but, on the other hand, can descend lower than fairy-land, and have seen some fine specimens of devils. One has already been raised, and the reader has seen him tempting a fat Dutch burgomaster, in an ancient gloomy market-place, such as George Cruikshank can draw as well as Mr. Prout, Mr. Nash, or any man living. There is our friend once more; our friend the burgomaster, in a highly excited state, and running as hard as his great legs will carry him, with our mutual enemy at his tail.

What are the bets; will that long-legged bond-holder of a devil come up with the honest Dutchman? It serves him right: why did he put his name to stamped paper? And yet we should not wonder if some lucky chance should turn up in the burgomaster's favour, and his infernal creditor lose his labour; for one so proverbially cunning as yonder tall individual with the saucer eyes, it must be confessed that he has been very often outwitted.

There is, for instance, the case of "The Gentleman in Black," which has been illustrated by our artist. A young French gentleman, by name M. Desonge, who having expended his patrimony in a variety of taverns and gaming-houses, was one day pondering upon the exhausted state of his finances, and utterly at a loss to think how he should provide means for future support, exclaimed, very naturally, "What the devil shall I do?" He had no sooner spoken than a GENTLEMAN IN BLACK made his appearance, whose authentic portrait Mr. Cruikshank has had the honour to paint. This gentleman produced a black-edged book out of a black bag, some black-edged papers tied up with black crape, and sitting down familiarly opposite M. Desonge, began conversing with him on the state of his affairs.

It is needless to state what was the result of the interview. M. Desonge was induced by the gentleman to sign his name to one of the black-edged papers, and found himself at the close of the conversation to be possessed of an unlimited command of capital. This arrangement completed, the Gentleman in Black posted (in an extraordinarily rapid manner) from Paris to London, there found a young English merchant in exactly the same situation in which M. Desonge had been, and concluded a bargain with the Briton of exactly the same nature.

The book goes on to relate how these young men spent the money so miraculously handed over to them, and how both, when the period drew near that was to witness the performance of *their* part of the bargain, grew melancholy, wretched, nay, so absolutely dishonourable as to seek for every means of breaking through their agreement. The Englishman living in a country where the lawyers are more astute than any other lawyers in the world, took the advice of a Mr. Bagsby, of Lyon's Inn; whose name, as we cannot find it in the "Law List," we presume to be fictitious. Who could it be that was a match for the devil? Lord —— very likely ; we shall not give his name, but let every reader of this Review fill up the blank according to his own fancy, and on comparing it with the copy purchased by his neighbours, he will find that fifteen out of twenty have written down the same honoured name.

Well, the Gentleman in Black was anxious for the fulfilment of his bond. The parties met at Mr. Bagsby's chambers to consult, the Black Gentleman foolishly thinking that he could act as his own counsel, and fearing no attorney alive. But mark the superiority of British law, and see how the black pettifogger was defeated.

Mr. Bagsby simply stated that he would take the case into Chancery, and his antagonist, utterly humiliated and defeated, refused to move a step farther in the matter.

And now the French gentleman, M. Desonge, hearing of his friend's escape, became anxious to be free from his own rash engagements. He employed the same counsel who had been successful in the former instance, but the Gentleman in Black was a great deal

George Cruikshank

MAY.

iser by this time, and whether M. Desonge escaped, or whether he
s now in that extensive place which is paved with good intentions,
re shall not say. Those who are anxious to know had better
urchase the book wherein all these interesting matters are duly
et down. There is one more diabolical picture in our budget,
ngraved by Mr. Thompson, the same dexterous artist who has
endered the former *diableries* so well.

We may mention Mr. Thompson's name as among the first of
he engravers to whom Cruikshank's designs have been entrusted ;
nd next to him (if we may be allowed to make such arbitrary
istinctions) we may place Mr. Williams ; and the reader is not
ossibly aware of the immense difficulties to be overcome in the
endering of these little sketches, which, traced by the designer in
few hours, require weeks' labour from the engraver. Mr. Cruik-
hank has not been educated in the regular schools of drawing (very
uckily for him, as we think), and consequently has had to make
manner for himself, which is quite unlike that of any other
raftsman. There is nothing in the least mechanical about it ; to
roduce his particular effects he uses his own particular lines, which
re queer, free, fantastical, and must be followed in all their
ufinite twists and vagaries by the careful tool of the engraver.
hose three lovely heads, for instance, imagined out of the rinds
f lemons, are worth examining, not so much for the jovial humour
nd wonderful variety of feature exhibited in these darling counte-
ances as for the engraver's part of the work. See the infinite
elicate cross-lines and hatchings which he is obliged to render ;
t him go, not a hair's breadth, but the hundredth part of a hair's
readth, beyond the given line, and the *feeling* of it is ruined. He
ceives these little dots and specks, and fantastical quirks of the
encil, and cuts away with a little knife round each, not too much
or too little. Antonio's pound of flesh did not puzzle the Jew so
uch ; and so well does the engraver succeed at last, that we
ver remember to have met with a single artist who did not vow
at the wood-cutter had utterly ruined his design.

Of Messrs. Thompson and Williams we have spoken as the first
gravers in point of rank ; however, the regulations of professional
ecedence are certainly very difficult, and the rest of their brethren
e shall not endeavour to class. Why should the artists who
ecuted the cuts of the admirable " Three Courses " yield the *pas*
any one ?

There, for instance, is an engraving by Mr. Landells, nearly as
od in our opinion as the very best wood-cut that ever was made
ter Cruikshank, and curiously happy in rendering the artist's
culiar manner : this cut does not come from the facetious publica-

tions which we have consulted; but is a contribution by M
Cruikshank to an elaborate and splendid botanical work upon t
Orchidaceæ of Mexico, by Mr. Bateman. Mr. Bateman despatche
some extremely choice roots of this valuable plant to a friend
England, who, on the arrival of the case, consigned it to h
gardener to unpack. A great deal of anxiety with regard to t
contents was manifested by all concerned, but on the lid of the b
being removed, there issued from it three or four fine specimens
the enormous Blatta beetle that had been preying upon the plan
during the voyage; against these the gardeners, the grooms, t
porters, and the porters' children issued forth in arms, and th
scene the artist has immortalised.

We have spoken of the admirable way in which Mr. Cruikshar
has depicted Irish character and Cockney character : English count
character is quite as faithfully delineated in the person of the sto
porteress and her children, and of the "Chawbacon" with t
shovel, on whose face is written "Zummerzetsheer." Chawbac
appears in another plate, or else Chawbacon's brother. He h
come up to Lunnan, and is looking about him at raaces.

How distinct are these rustics from those whom we have ju
been examining! They hang about the purlieus of the metropoli
Brook Green, Epsom, Greenwich, Ascot, Goodwood, are the
haunts. They visit London professionally once a year, and that
at the time of Bartholomew fair. How one may speculate up
the different degrees of rascality, as exhibited in each face of t
thimblerigging trio, and form little histories for these worthi
charming Newgate romances, such as have been of late the fashio
Is any man so blind that he cannot see the exact face that is writ
ing under the thimblerigged hero's hat? Like Timanthes of o
our artist expresses great passions without the aid of the hum
countenance. There is another specimen—a street row of inebriat
bottles. Is there any need of having a face after this? "Cor
on!" says Claret-bottle, a dashing, genteel fellow, with his hat
one ear—"Come on! has any man a mind to tap me?" Clar
bottle is a little screwed (as one may see by his legs), but full
gaiety and courage; not so that stout, apoplectic Bottle-of-ru
who has staggered against the wall, and has his hand upon l
liver : the fellow hurts himself with smoking, that is clear, and
as sick as sick can be. See, Port is making away from the stor
and Double X is as flat as ditch-water. Against these, awful
their white robes, the sober watchmen come.

Our artist then can cover up faces, and yet show them qui
clearly, as in the thimblerig group; or he can do without fac
altogether; or he can, at a pinch, provide a countenance for

George Cruikshank

M A Y. — Beating the Bounds.

gentleman out of any given object—a beautiful Irish physiognomy
being moulded upon a keg of whisky; and a jolly English countenance frothing out of a pot of ale (the spirit of brave Toby
Philpot come back to reanimate his clay); while in a fungus may
be recognised the physiognomy of a mushroom peer. Finally, if
he is at a loss, he can make a living head, body, and legs out of
steel or tortoise-shell, as in the case of the vivacious pair of spectacles
that are jockeying the nose of Caddy Cuddle.

Of late years Mr. Cruikshank has busied himself very much
with steel-engraving, and the consequences of that lucky invention
have been, that his plates are now sold by thousands, where they
could only be produced by hundreds before. He has made many
a bookseller's and author's fortune (we trust that in so doing he
may not have neglected his own). Twelve admirable plates,
furnished yearly to that facetious little publication, the *Comic
Almanac*, have gained for it a sale, as we hear, of nearly twenty
thousand copies. The idea of the work was novel; there was, in
the first number especially, a great deal of comic power, and Cruikshank's designs were so admirable that the *Almanac* at once became
a vast favourite with the public, and has so remained ever since.

Besides the twelve plates, this almanac contains a prophetic
wood-cut, accompanying an awful Blarneyhum Astrologicum that
appears in this and other almanacs. There is one that hints in
pretty clear terms that with the Reform of Municipal Corporations
the ruin of the great Lord Mayor of London is at hand. His
lordship is meekly going to dine at an eightpenny ordinary,—his
giants in pawn, his men in armour dwindled to "one poor knight,"
his carriage to be sold, his stalwart aldermen vanished, his sheriffs,
alas! and alas! in gaol! Another design shows that Rigdum, if
a true, is also a moral and instructive prophet. John Bull is
asleep, or rather in a vision; the cunning demon, Speculation,
blowing a thousand bright bubbles about him. Meanwhile the
rooks are busy at his fob, a knave has cut a cruel hole in his
pocket, a rattlesnake has coiled safe round his feet, and will in a
trice swallow Bull, chair, money, and all; the rats are at his corn-
bags (as if, poor devil, he had corn to spare); his faithful dog is
bolting his leg-of-mutton—nay, a thief has gotten hold of his very
candle, and there, by way of moral, is his ale-pot, which looks and
winks in his face, and seems to say, O Bull, all this is froth, and a
cruel satirical picture of a certain rustic who had a goose that laid
certain golden eggs, which goose the rustic slew in expectation of
finding all the eggs at once. This is goose and sage too, to borrow
the pun of "learned Doctor Gill;" but we shrewdly suspect that
Mr. Cruikshank is becoming a little conservative in his notions.

We love these pictures so that it is hard to part us, and we still fondly endeavour to hold on, but this wild word, farewell, must be spoken by the best friends at last, and so good-bye, brave wood-cuts : we feel quite a sadness in coming to the last of our collection.

In the earlier numbers of the *Comic Almanac* all the manners and customs of Londoners that would afford food for fun were noted down ; and if during the last two years the mysterious personage who, under the title of " Rigdum Funnidos," compiles this ephemeris, has been compelled to resort to romantic tales, we must suppose that he did so because the great metropolis was exhausted, and it was necessary to discover new worlds in the cloud land of fancy. The character of Mr. Stubbs, who made his appearance in the *Almanac* for 1839, had, we think, great merit, although his adventures were somewhat of too tragical a description to provoke pure laughter.

We should be glad to devote a few pages to the " Illustrations of Time," the " Scraps and Sketches," and the " Illustrations of Phrenology," which are among the most famous of our artist's publications ; but it is very difficult to find new terms of praise, as find them one must, when reviewing Mr. Cruikshank's publications, and more difficult still (as the reader of this notice will no doubt have perceived for himself long since) to translate his design into words, and go to the printer's box for a description of all that fun and humour which the artist can produce by a few skilful turns of his needle. A famous article upon the " Illustrations of Time " appeared some dozen years since in *Blackwood's Magazine,* of which the conductors have always been great admirers of our artist, as became men of honour and genius. To these grand qualities do not let it be supposed that we are laying claim, but, thank heaven, Cruikshank's humour is so good and benevolent that any man must love it, and on this score we may speak as well as another.

Then there are the " Greenwich Hospital " designs, which must not be passed over. " Greenwich Hospital " is a hearty, good-natured book, in the Tom Dibdin school, treating of the virtues of British tars, in approved nautical language. They maul Frenchmen and Spaniards, they go out in brigs and take frigates, they relieve women in distress, and are yard-arm and yard-arming, athwart-hawsing, marlinspiking, binnacling, and helm's-a-leeing, as honest seamen invariably do, in novels, on the stage, and doubtless on board ship. This we cannot take upon us to say, but the artist, like a true Englishman as he is, loves dearly these brave guardians of Old England, and chronicles their rare or fanciful exploits with the greatest goodwill. Let any one look at the noble head of Nelson in the " Family Library," and they will, we are sure, think with us that the designer must have felt and loved what he drew.

There are to this abridgment of Southey's admirable book many
more cuts after Cruikshank ; and about a dozen pieces by the same
hand will be found in a work equally popular, Lockhart's excellent
"Life of Napoleon." Among these the retreat from Moscow is
very fine ; the Mamlouks most vigorous, furious, and barbarous,
as they should be. At the end of these three volumes Mr. Cruikshank's contributions to the "Family Library" seem suddenly to
have ceased.

We are not at all disposed to undervalue the works and genius
of Mr. Dickens, and we are sure that he would admit as readily as
any man the wonderful assistance that he has derived from the
artist who has given us the portraits of his ideal personages, and
made them familiar to all the world. Once seen, these figures
remain impressed on the memory, which otherwise would have had
no hold upon them, and the heroes and heroines of Boz become
personal acquaintances with each of us. Oh, that Hogarth could
have illustrated Fielding in the same way ! and fixed down on paper
those grand figures of Parson Adams, and Squire Allworthy, and
the great Jonathan Wild.

With regard to the modern romance of "Jack Sheppard," in
which the latter personage makes a second appearance, it seems
to us that Mr. Cruikshank really created the tale, and that Mr.
Ainsworth, as it were, only put words to it. Let any reader of
the novel think over it for awhile, now that it is some months since
he has perused and laid it down—let him think, and tell us what
he remembers of the tale ? George Cruikshank's pictures—always
George Cruikshank's pictures. The storm in the Thames, for instance : all the author's laboured description of that event has passed
clean away—we have only before the mind's eye the fine plates of
Cruikshank : the poor wretch cowering under the bridge arch, as
the waves come rushing in, and the boats are whirling away in the
drift of the great swollen black waters. And let any man look
at that second plate of the murder on the Thames, and he must
acknowledge how much more brilliant the artist's description is than
the writer's, and what a real genius for the terrible as well as for
the ridiculous the former has ; how awful is the gloom of the old
bridge, a few lights glimmering from the houses here and there, but
not so as to be reflected on the water at all, which is too turbid and
raging : a great heavy rack of clouds goes sweeping over the bridge,
and men with flaring torches, the murderers, are borne away with
the stream.

The author requires many pages to describe the fury of the
storm, which Mr. Cruikshank has represented in one. First, he
has to prepare you with the something inexpressibly melancholy in

sailing on a dark night upon the Thames : "the ripple of th
water," "the darkling current," "the indistinctively seen craft,
"the solemn shadows," and other phenomena visible on rivers a
night are detailed (with not unskilful rhetoric) in order to brin
the reader into a proper frame of mind for the deeper gloom an
horror which is to ensue. Then follow pages of description. " A
Roland sprang to the helm, and gave the signal for pursuit, a wa
like a volley of ordnance was heard aloft, and the wind again burs
its bondage. A moment before the surface of the stream was a
black as ink. It was now whitening, hissing, and seething, like a
enormous cauldron. The blast once more swept over the agitate
river, whirled off the sheets of foam, scattered them far and wide i
rain-drops, and left the raging torrent blacker than before. Destruc
tion everywhere marked the course of the gale. Steeples topple
and towers reeled beneath its fury. All was darkness, horror, con
fusion, ruin. Men fled from their tottering habitations and returne
to them, scared by greater danger. The end of the world seeme
at hand. . . . The hurricane had now reached its climax. Th
blast shrieked, as if exulting in its wrathful mission. Stunnin
and continuous, the din seemed almost to take away the power o
hearing. He who had faced the gale *would have been instantl
stifled*," &c. &c. See with what a tremendous war of words (an
good loud words too ; Mr. Ainsworth's description is a good an
spirited one) the author is obliged to pour in upon the reader befor
he can effect his purpose upon the latter, and inspire him with
proper terror. The painter does it at a glance, and old Wood'
dilemma in the midst of that tremendous storm, with the littl
infant at his bosom, is remembered afterwards, not from the words
but from the visible image of them that the artist has left us.

It would not, perhaps, be out of place to glance through th
whole of the "Jack Sheppard" plates, which are among the mos
finished and the most successful of Mr. Cruikshank's performances
and say a word or two concerning them. Let us begin wit
finding fault with No. 1, "Mr. Wood offers to adopt little Jac
Sheppard." A poor print, on a poor subject; the figure of th
woman not as carefully designed as it might be, and the expressio
of the eyes (not an uncommon fault with our artist) much carica
tured. The print is cut up, to use the artist's phrase, by th
number of accessories which the engraver has thought proper, afte
the author's elaborate description, elaborately to reproduce. Th
plate of "Wild discovering Darrell in the loft" is admirable–
ghastly, terrible, and the treatment of it extraordinarily skilfu
minute, and bold. The intricacies of the tile-work, and the my
terious twinkling of light among the beams, are excellently fel

JUNE

George Cruikshank

and rendered; and one sees here, as in the two next plates of the storm and murder, what a fine eye the artist has, what a skilful hand, and what a sympathy for the wild and dreadful. As a mere imitation of nature, the clouds and the bridge in the murder picture may be examined by painters who make far higher pretensions than Mr. Cruikshank. In point of workmanship they are equally good, the manner quite unaffected, the effect produced without any violent contrast, the whole scene evidently well and philosophically arranged in the artist's brain, before he began to put it upon copper.

The famous drawing of " Jack carving the name on the beam," which has been transferred to half the play-bills in town, is over-loaded with accessories, as the first plate; but they are much better arranged than in the last-named engraving, and do not injure the effect of the principal figure. Remark, too, the conscientiousness of the artist, and that shrewd pervading idea of *form* which is one of his principal characteristics. Jack is surrounded by all sorts of implements of his profession; he stands on a regular carpenter's table : away in the shadow under it lie shavings and a couple of carpenter's hampers. The glue-pot, the mallet, the chisel-handle, the planes, the saws, the hone with its cover, and the other para-phernalia are all represented with extraordinary accuracy and forethought. The man's mind has retained the exact *drawing* of all these minute objects (unconsciously perhaps to himself), but we can see with what keen eyes he must go through the world, and what a fund of facts (as such a knowledge of the shape of objects is in his profession) this keen student of nature has stored away in his brain. In the next plate, where Jack is escaping from his mistress, the figure of that lady, one of the deepest of the βαθυκόλποι, strikes us as disagreeable and unrefined; that of Winifred is, on the contrary, very pretty and graceful; and Jack's puzzled, slinking look must not be forgotten. All the accessories are good, and the apartment has a snug, cosy air; which is not remarkable, except that it shows how faithfully the designer has performed his work, and how curiously he has entered into all the particulars of the subject.

Master Thames Darrell, the handsome young man of the book, is, in Mr. Cruikshank's portraits of him, no favourite of ours. The lad seems to wish to make up for the natural insignificance of his face by frowning on all occasions most portentously. This figure, borrowed from the compositor's desk, will give a notion of what we mean. Wild's face is too violent for the great man of history (if we may call Fielding history), but this is in consonance with the ranting, frowning, braggadocio character that Mr. Ainsworth has given him.

The "Interior of Willesden Church" is excellent as a composition, and a piece of artistical workmanship; the groups are well arranged; and the figure of Mrs. Sheppard looking round alarmed, as her son is robbing the dandy Kneebone, is charming, simple, and unaffected. Not so "Mrs. Sheppard ill in bed," whose face is screwed up to an expression vastly too tragic. The little glimpse of the church seen through the open door of the room is very beautiful and poetical : it is in such small hints that an artist especially excels ; they are the morals which he loves to append to his stories and are always appropriate and welcome. The boozing-ken is not to our liking; Mrs. Sheppard is there with her horrified eyebrows again. Why this exaggeration—is it necessary for the public ? We think not, or if they require such excitement, let our artist, like a true painter as he is, teach them better things.*

The "Escape from Willesden Cage" is excellent; the "Burglary in Wood's house" has not less merit ; "Mrs. Sheppard in Bedlam,' a ghastly picture indeed, is finely conceived, but not, as we fancy, so carefully executed ; it would be better for a little more careful drawing in the female figure.

"Jack sitting for his picture" is a very pleasing group, and savours of the manner of Hogarth, who is introduced in the company. The "Murder of Trenchard" must be noticed too as remarkable for the effect and terrible vigour which the artist has given to the scene. The "Willesden Churchyard" has great merit too, but the gems of the book are the little vignettes illustrating the escape from Newgate. Here, too, much anatomical care or drawing is not required ; the figures are so small that the outline and attitude need only to be indicated, and the designer has produced a series of figures quite remarkable for reality and poetry too. There are no less than ten of Jack's feats so described by Mr Cruikshank. (Let us say a word here in praise of the excellent manner in which the author has carried us through the adventure. Here is Jack clattering up the chimney, now peering into the lonely red room, now opening "the door between the red room and the chapel." What a wild, fierce, scared look he has, the young

* A gentleman (whose wit is so celebrated that one should be very cautious in repeating his stories) gave the writer a good illustration of the philosophy of exaggeration. Mr. —— was once behind the scenes at the Opera when the scene-shifters were preparing for the ballet. Flora was to sleep under a bush, whereon were growing a number of roses, and amidst which was fluttering a gay covey of butterflies. In size the roses exceeded the most expansive sun flowers, and the butterflies were as large as cocked hats ;—the scene-shifter explained to Mr. ——, who asked the reason why everything was so magnified that the galleries could never see the objects unless they were enormously ex aggerated. How many of our writers and designers work for the galleries?

George Cruikshank

ıffian, as cautiously he steps in, holding light his bar of iron. You
ın see by his face how his heart is beating! If any one were
ıere! but no! And this is a very fine characteristic of the prints,
ıe extreme *loneliness* of them all. Not a soul is there to disturb
im—woe to him who should—and Jack drives in the chapel gate,
ıd shatters down the passage door, and there you have him on
ıe leads. Up he goes! it is but a spring of a few feet from the
ɪanket, and he is gone—*abiit, evasit, erupit!* Mr. Wild must
ıtch him again if he can.

We must not forget to mention "Oliver Twist," and Mr.
ruikshank's famous designs to that work.* The sausage scene at
ıagin's, Nancy seizing the boy; that capital piece of humour, Mr.
umble's courtship, which is even better in Cruikshank's version
ıan in Boz's exquisite account of the interview; Sykes's farewell
ɔ the dog; and the Jew,—the dreadful Jew—that Cruikshank
ew! What a fine touching picture of melancholy desolation is
ıat of Sykes and the dog! The poor cur is not too well drawn,
ıe landscape is stiff and formal; but in this case the faults, if
ults they be, of execution rather add to than diminish the effect
ʳthe picture: it has a strange, wild, dreary, broken-hearted look;
e fancy we see the landscape as it must have appeared to Sykes,
ɪen ghastly and with bloodshot eyes he looked at it. As for the
ɪw in the dungeon, let us say nothing of it—what can we say to
ɪscribe it? What a fine homely poet is the man who can produce
is little world of mirth or woe for us! Does he elaborate his
ʳects by slow process of thought, or do they come to him by
ɪstinct? Does the painter ever arrange in his brain an image so
mplete, that he afterwards can copy it exactly on the canvas, or
es the hand work in spite of him?

A great deal of this random work of course every artist has done
his time; many men produce effects of which they never dreamed,
d strike off excellences, haphazard, which gain for them reputa-
ɔn; but a fine quality in Mr. Cruikshank, the quality of his
ccess, as we have said before, is the extraordinary earnestness and
od faith with which he executes all he attempts—the ludicrous,
e polite, the low, the terrible. In the second of these he often,
our fancy, fails, his figures lacking elegance and descending to
ricature; but there is something fine in this too: it is good that
  should fail, that he should have these honest *naïve* notions
garding the *beau monde*, the characteristics of which a namby-
mby tea-party painter could hit off far better than he. He is
great deal too downright and manly to appreciate the flimsy

* Or his new work, "The Tower of London," which promises even to sur-
ıs Mr. Cruikshank's former productions.

2 B

delicacies of small society—you cannot expect a lion to roar yc
like any sucking dove, or frisk about a drawing-room like a lady
little spaniel.

If then, in the course of his life and business, he has bee
occasionally obliged to imitate the ways of such small animals, b
has done so, let us say it at once, clumsily, and like as a lion shoul
Many artists, we hear, hold his works rather cheap; they pra
about bad drawing, want of scientific knowledge;—they would ha
something vastly more neat, regular, anatomical.

Not one of the whole band most likely but can paint an Academ
figure better than himself; nay, or a portrait of an alderman's lae
and family of children. But look down the list of the painters and t
us who are they? How many among these men are *poets* (maker
possessing the faculty to create, the greatest among the gifts wi
which Providence has endowed the mind of man? Say how mai
there are, count up what they have done, and see what in the cour
of some nine-and-twenty years has been done by this indefatigal
man.

What amazing energetic fecundity do we find in him! As
boy he began to fight for bread, has been hungry (twice a day
trust) ever since, and has been obliged to sell his wit for his bre
week by week. And his wit, sterling gold as it is, will find no su
purchasers as the fashionable painter's thin pinchbeck, who can li
comfortably for six weeks, when paid for and painting a portra
and fancies his mind prodigiously occupied all the while. The
was an artist in Paris, an artist hairdresser, who used to be fatigu
and take restoratives after inventing a new coiffure. By no su
gentle operation of head-dressing has Cruikshank lived: time w
(we are told so in print) when for a picture with thirty heads in
he was paid three guineas—a poor week's pittance truly, and a d
week's labour. We make no doubt that the same labour would
present bring him twenty times the sum; but whether it be ill-pa
or well, what labour has Mr. Cruikshank's been. Week by wee
for thirty years, to produce something new; some smiling offspri
of painful labour, quite independent and distinct from its t
thousand jovial brethren; in what hours of sorrow and ill-hea
to be told by the world, "Make us laugh or you starve—Give
fresh fun; we have eaten up the old and are hungry." And
this has he been obliged to do—to wring laughter day by da
sometimes, perhaps, out of want, often certainly from ill-health
depression—to keep the fire of his brain perpetually alight: for t
greedy public will give it no leisure to cool. This he has done a
done well. He has told a thousand truths in as many stran
and fascinating ways; he has given a thousand new and pleas

ioughts to millions of people; he has never used his wit dis-
onestly; he has never, in all the exuberance of his frolicsome
umour, caused a single painful or guilty blush : how little do we
iink of the extraordinary power of this man, and how ungrateful
e are to him!

Here, as we are come round to the charge of ingratitude, the
tarting-post from which we set out, perhaps we had better con-
lude. The reader will perhaps wonder at the high-flown tone in
hich we speak of the services and merits of an individual, whom
e considers a humble scraper on steel, that is wonderfully popular
lready. But none of us remember all the benefits we owe him;
iey have come one by one, one driving out the memory of the
ther : it is only when we come to examine them altogether, as
ie writer has done, who has a pile of books on the table before
im—a heap of personal kindnesses from George Cruikshank (not
resents, if you please, for we bought, borrowed, or stole every one
f them)—that we feel what we owe him. Look at one of Mr.
'ruikshank's works, and we pronounce him an excellent humourist.
.ook at all : his reputation is increased by a kind of geometrical
rogression ; as a whole diamond is a hundred times more valuable
ian the hundred splinters into which it might be broken would
e. A fine rough English diamond is this about which we have
een writing.

A PICTORIAL RHAPSODY BY MICHAEL ANGELO TITMARSH

WITH AN INTRODUCTORY LETTER TO MR. YORKE

MY DEAR YORKE,—Do you remember the orders whic
you gave me at the close of our dinner last week at th
Clarendon?—that dinner which you always provide upon m
arrival in town from my country-seat; knowing full well that Ti
marsh before he works must dine, and when he dines, must dine wel
Do you, I say, remember the remarks which you addressed to me
Probably not; for that third bottle of Clos-Vougeot had evidentl
done your business, and you were too tipsy, even to pay the bill.

Well, let bills be bills, and what care we? There is Mr. Jame
Fraser, our employer, master, publisher, purse-bearer, and frien
who has such a pleasure in paying that it is a pity to baulk him
and I never saw a man look more happy than he when he lugge
out four five-pound notes to pay for that dinner of ours. Wh:
a scene it was! You asleep with your head in a dish of melte
raspberry-ice; Mr. Fraser calm, beneficent, majestic, counting o
the thirteens to the waiters; the Doctor and Mr. John Abraha
Heraud singing "Suoni la tromba intrepida," each clutching th
other's hand, and waving a punch-ladle or a dessert-knife in th
unemployed paw, and the rest of us joining in chorus when the
came to "gridando liberta."—But I am wandering from the poin
the address which you delivered to me on drinking my health wa
in substance this:—

"Mr. Michael Angelo Titmarsh, the splendid feast of whic
you have partaken, and the celebrated company of individuals who
you see around you, will show you in what estimation myself an
Mr. Fraser hold your talents,—not that the latter point is of a
consequence, as I am the sole editor of the Magazine. Sir, yo
have been called to the metropolis from a very distant part of t
country, your coach-hire and personal expenses have been defraye
you have been provided with a suit of clothes that *ought* to becom
you, for they have been for at least six months the wonder of t
town while exhibited on my own person; and you may well fan

hat all these charges have not been incurred on our parts, without
n expectation of some corresponding return from you. You are
devilish bad painter, sir; but never mind, Hazlitt was another,
nd old Peter Pindar was a miserable dauber; Mr. Alexander Pope,
who wrote several pretty poems, was always busy with brush and
palette, and made sad work of them. You, then, in common with
hese before-named illustrations, as my friend, Lady Morgan, calls
hem [Sir Charles returned thanks], are a wretched artist; but a
olerable critic—nay, a good critic—nay, let me say to your face,
he best critic, the clearest, the soundest, the gayest, the most
loquent, the most pathetic, and, above all, the most honest critic
n matters of art that is to be found in her Majesty's dominions.
And therefore, Mr. Titmarsh, for we must give the deuce his due,
ou have been brought from your cottage near John O'Groat's or
Land's End,—I forget which,—therefore you have been summoned
o London at the present season.

"Sir, there are at this moment no less than five public exhibi-
ions of pictures in the metropolis; and it will be your duty
arefully to examine every one of them during your residence here,
nd bring us a full and accurate report upon all the pieces exhibited
which are remarkable for goodness, badness, or mediocrity."

I here got up; and, laying my hand on my satin waistcoat,
ooked up to heaven, and said, "Sir, I——"

"Sit down, sir, and keep your eternal wagging jaws quiet!
Waiter! whenever that person attempts to speak, have the good-
ess to fill his mouth with olives or a damson cheese.—To proceed.
ir, and you, gentlemen, and you, O intelligent public of Great
Britain! (for I know that every word I say is in some way carried
o you) you must all be aware, I say, how wickedly,—how foully,
asely, meanly—how, in a word, with every-deteriorating-adverb
hat ends in *ly*—in *ly*, gentlemen [here Mr. Yorke looked round,
nd myself and Mr. Fraser, rather alarmed lest we should have let
ip a pun, began to raise a low faint laugh]—you have all of you
een how the world has been imposed upon by persons calling
hemselves critics, who, in daily, weekly, monthly prints, protrude
heir nonsense upon the town. What are these men? Are they
ducated to be painters?—No! Have they a taste for painting?—
fo! I know of newspapers in this town, gentlemen, which send
heir reporters indifferently to a police-office or a picture gallery,
nd expect them to describe Correggio or a fire in Fleet Street
with equal fidelity. And, alas! it must be confessed that our
natter-of-fact public of England is itself but a dull appreciator of
he arts, and is too easily persuaded by the dull critics who lay
own their stupid laws.

13   X

"But we cannot expect, Mr. Titmarsh, to do any good to ou beloved public by telling them merely that their instructors ar impostors. Abuse is no argument, foul words admit of no pretenc (you may have remarked that I never use them myself, but alway employ the arts of gentlemanly persuasion), and we must endeavou to create a reform amongst the nations by simply preaching a pure and higher doctrine. Go you among the picture galleries, as yo have done in former years, and prattle on at your best rate; don' philosophise, or define, or talk big, for I will cut out every line o such stuff, but speak in a simple natural way,—without fear, an without favour.

"Mark that latter word 'favour' well; for you are a grea deal too tender in your nature, and too profuse of compliments Favour, sir, is the curse of the critical trade; and you will observ how a spirit of *camaraderie* and partisanship prevails in matter of art especially. The picture-critics, as I have remarked, ar eminently dull—dull and loud; perfectly ignorant upon all subject connected with art, never able to guess at the name of an artis without a catalogue and a number, quite unknowing whether a pictur be well or ill drawn, well or ill painted : they must prate nevertheless about light and shade, warm and cool colour, keeping, chiaroscurc and such other terms, from the Painters' Cant Dictionary, a they hear bandied about among the brethren of the brush.

"You will observe that such a critic has ordinarily his one c two idols that he worships; the one or two painters, namely, int whose studios he has free access, and from•whose opinions he form his own. There is Dash, for instance, of the Star newspaper; no and anon you hear him discourse of the fine arts, and you may tak your affidavit that he has just issued from Blank's *atelier :* a Blank's opinions he utters—utters and garbles, of course; all h likings are founded on Blank's dicta, and all his dislikings : 't probable that Blank has a rival, one Asterisk, living over the way In Dash's eye Asterisk is the lowest of creatures. At every fres exhibition you read how 'Mr. Blank has transcended his alread transcendent reputation;' 'Myriads are thronging round his glorioi canvases ;' 'Billions have been trampled to death while rushing t examine his grand portrait of Lady Smigsmag ;' 'His picture c Sir Claude Calipash is a gorgeous representation of aldermani dignity and high chivalric grace !' As for Asterisk, you are tolc 'Mr. Asterisk has two or three pictures—pretty, but weak, repeti tions of his old faces and subjects in his old namby-pamby styl(The Committee, we hear, rejected most of his pictures : the Con mittee are very compassionate. How *dared* they reject Mr. Blank' stupendous historical picture of So-and-so ?' "

[Here, my dear sir, I am sorry to say that there was a general more heard from the guests round the table, which rather disturbed the flow of your rhetoric. You swallowed down two or three pints of burgundy, however, and continued.]

"But I must conclude. Michael Angelo Titmarsh, you know our duty. You are an honest man [loud cheers, the people had wakened during the pause]. You must go forth determined to tell the truth, the whole truth, and nothing but the truth; as far as you, a fallible creature [cries of 'No, no!'], know it. If you see a good picture, were it the work of your bitterest enemy—and you have hundreds—praise it."

"I will," gasped I.

"Hold your tongue, sir, and don't be interrupting me with your perpetual orations! If you see a bad picture, were it the work of your dearest associate, your brother, the friend of your bosom, your benefactor—cut, slash, slaughter him without mercy. Strip off humbug, sir, though it cover your best boon-companion. Praise merit, though it belong to your fiercest foe, your rival in the affections of your mistress, the man from whom you have borrowed money, or taken a beating in private!"

"Mr. Yorke," said I, clenching my fists and starting up, "this passes endurance, were you not intox—— ;" but two waiters here seized and held me down, luckily for you.

"Peace, Titmarsh" (said you); "'twas but raillery. Be honest, my friend, is all that I would say; and if you write a decent article on the exhibitions, Mr. Fraser will pay you hand-somely for your trouble; and, in order that you may have every facility for visiting the picture galleries, I myself will give you a small sum in hand. Here are ten shillings. Five exhibitions, five shillings; catalogues, four. You will have twelvepence for yourself, to take refreshments in the intervals."

I held out my hand, for my anger had quite disappeared.

"Mr. Fraser," said you, "give the fellow half-a-sovereign; and, for Heaven's sake, teach him to be silent when a gentleman is speaking!"

What passed subsequently need not be stated here, but the above account of your speech is a pretty correct one; and, in pursuance of your orders, I busied myself with the exhibitions on the following day. The result of my labours will be found in the accompanying report. I have the honour, sir, of laying it at your feet, and of subscribing myself, with the profoundest respect and devotion, Sir, your very faithful and obedient servant,

MICHAEL ANEGLO TITMARSH.

Moreland's Coffee House, Dean Street, Soho.

ΡΑΨΩιΔΙΑ ἤ ΓΡΑΜΜΑ Α΄

The Royal Academy.

Had the author of the following paragraphs the pen of a Sir Walte
Scott or a Lady Morgan, he would write something excessivel
brilliant and witty about the first day of the exhibition, and of th
company which crowd the rooms upon that occasion. On Frida
the Queen comes (Heaven bless her Majesty!) attended by he
courtiers and train; and deigns, with Royal eyes, to examine th
works of her Royal Academicians. Her, as we are given to unde
stand, the President receives, bowing profoundly, awe-stricken; hi
gold chain dangles from his presidential bosom, and sweet smiles o
respectful courtesy light up his venerable face. Walking by he
Majesty's side, he explains to her the wonders of the show. "That
may it please your Majesty, is a picture representing yoursel
painted by the good knight, Sir David Wilkie: deign to remar
how the robes seem as if they were cut out of British oak, and th
figure is as wooden as the figure-head of one of your Majesty's men
of-war. Opposite is your Majesty's Royal consort, by Mr. Patten
We have the honour to possess two more pairs of Pattens in thi
Academy—ha, ha! Round about you will see some of my own
poor works of art. Yonder is Mr. Landseer's portrait of you
Majesty's own cockatoo, with a brace of Havadavats. Please you
Royal Highness to look at the bit of biscuit; no baker could hav
done it more natural. Fair Maid of Honour, look at that lump o
sugar; couldn't one take an affidavit, now, that it cost elevenpenc
a pound? Isn't it sweet? I know only one thing sweeter, an
that's your Ladyship's lovely face!" .

In such lively conversation might we fancy a bland presiden
discoursing. The Queen should make august replies; the lovel
smiling Maids of Honour should utter remarks becoming thei
innocence and station (turning away very red from that corner o
the apartment where hang certain Venuses and Andromedas, painte
by William Etty, Esquire); the gallant prince, a lordly, handsom
gentleman, with a slight foreign accent, should curl the dark mous
tache that adorns his comely lip, and say, "Petztausend! but da
bigture of First Loaf by Herr von Mulready ist wunder schön!
and courtly chamberlains, prim goldsticks, and sly polonaises of th
Court should take their due share in the gay scene, and delive
their portions of the dialogue of the little drama.

All this, I say, might be done in a very sprightly neat way
were poor Titmarsh an Ainsworth or a Lady Morgan; and th

scene might be ended smartly with the knighting of one of the Academicians by her Majesty on the spot. As thus: "The Royal party had stood for three-and-twenty minutes in mute admiration before that tremendous picture by Mr. Maclise, representing the banquet in the hall of Dunsinane. 'Gory shadow of Banquo,' said Lady Almeria to Lady Wilhelmina, 'how hideous thou art!' 'Hideous! hideous yourself, marry!' replied the arch and lovely Wilhelmina. 'By my halidome!' whispered the seneschal to the venerable prime minister, Lord Melborough—'by cock and pie, Sir Count, but it seems to me that yon Scottish kerne, Macbeth, hath a shrewd look of terror!' 'And a marvellous unkempt beard,' answered the Earl; 'and a huge mouth gaping wide for very terror, and a hand palsied with fear.' 'Hoot awa, mon!' cried an old Scots general, 'but the chield's Macbeth (I'm descanded from him leeneally in the saxty-ninth generation) knew hoo to wield a gude claymore!' 'His hand looks as if it had dropped a hot potato!' whispered a roguish page, and the little knave's remark caused a titter to run through the courtly circle, and brought a smile upon the cheek of the President of the Academy; who, sooth to say, had been twiddling his chain of office between his finger and thumb, somewhat jealous of the praise bestowed upon his young rival.

"'My Lord of Wellington,' said her Majesty, 'lend me your sword.' The veteran, smiling, drew forth that trenchant sabre,— that spotless blade of battle that had flashed victorious on the plains of far Assaye, in the breach of storm-girt Badajoz, in the mighty and supreme combat of Waterloo! A tear stood in the hero's eye as he fell on his gartered knee; and holding the blade between his finger and thumb, he presented the hilt to his liege lady. 'Take it, madam,' said he; 'sheathe it in this old breast, if you will, for my heart and sword are my sovereign's. Take it, madam, and be not angry if there is blood upon the steel—'tis the blood of the enemies of my country!' The Queen took it; and, as the young and delicate creature waved that tremendous war-sword, a gentleman near her remarked, that surely never lighted on the earth a more delightful vision. 'Where is Mr. Maclise?' said her Majesty. The blushing painter stepped forward. 'Kneel! kneel!' whispered fifty voices; and frightened, he did as they ordered him. 'Sure, she's not going to cut my head off?' he cried to the good knights, Sir Augustus Callcott and Sir Isaac Newton, who were standing. 'Your name, sir?' said the Ladye of England. 'Sure you know it's Maclise!' cried the son of Erin. 'Your Christian name?' shrieked Sir Martin Shee in agony. 'Christian name, is it? Oh, then it's Daniel Malcolm, your Majesty, and much at your service !' She waved the sword majestically over his head, and said, 'Rise up, Sir Malcolm Maclise !'

.   .   .   .

"The ceremony was concluded, the brilliant *cortège* moved away, the Royal barouches received the illustrious party, the heralds cried, 'Largesse, Largesse !' and flung silver pennies among the shouting crowds in Trafalgar Square ; and when the last man-at-arms that accompanied the Royal train had disappeared, the loud *vivas* of the crowd were heard no more, the shrill song of the silver clarions had died away, his brother painters congratulated the newly-dubbed chevalier, and retired to partake of a slight collation of bread and cheese and porter in the keeper's apartments."

Were we, I say, inclined to be romantic, did we dare to be imaginative, such a scene might be depicted with considerable effect ; but, as it is, we must not allow poor fancy to get the better of reason, and declare that to write anything of the sort would be perfectly uncalled for and absurd. Let it simply be stated that, on the Friday, her Majesty comes and goes. On the Saturday the Academicians have a private view for the great personages ; the lords of the empire and their ladies, the editors of the newspapers and their friends ; and, after they have seen as much as possible, about seven o'clock the Academicians give a grand feed to their friends and patrons.

In the arrangement of this banquet, let us say roundly that Messieurs de l'Académie are vastly too aristocratic. Why were *we* not asked ? The dinner is said to be done by Gunter ; and, though the soup and fish are notoriously cold and uncomfortable, we are by no means squeamish, and would pass over this gross piece of neglect. We long, too, to hear a bishop say grace, and to sit cheek by jowl with a duke or two. Besides, we could make some return ; a good joke is worth a plateful of turtle ; a smart brisk pun is quite as valuable as a bottle of champagne ; a neat anecdote deserves a slice of venison, with plenty of fat and currant jelly, and so on. On such principles of barter we might be disposed to treat. But a plague on this ribaldry and beating about the bush ! let us leave the plates, and come at once to the pictures.

.   .   .   .   .   .

Once or twice before, in the columns of this Magazine,[*] we have imparted to the public our notions about Greek art, and its manifold deadly errors. The contemplation of such specimens of it as we possess hath always, to tell the truth, left us in a state of unpleasant wonderment and perplexity. It carries corporeal beauty

[*] *Fraser's Magazine.*

to a pitch of painful perfection, and deifies the body and bones truly : but, by dint of sheer beauty, it leaves humanity altogether inhuman—quite heartless and passionless. Look at Apollo the divine : there is no blood in his marble veins, no warmth in his bosom, no fire or speculation in his dull awful eyes. Laocoon writhes and twists in an anguish that never can, in the breast of any spectator, create the smallest degree of pity. Diana,

> " La chasseresse
> Blanche, au sein virginal,
> Qui presse
> Quelque cerf matinal," *

may run from this till Doomsday ; and we feel no desire to join the cold passionless huntress in her ghostly chase. Such monsters of beauty are quite out of the reach of human sympathy : they were purposely (by the poor benighted heathens who followed this error, and strove to make their error as grand as possible) placed beyond it. They seemed to think that human joy and sorrow, passion and love, were mean and contemptible in themselves. Their gods were to be calm, and share in no such feelings. How much grander is the character of the Christian school, which teaches that love is the most beautiful of all things, and the first and highest element of beauty in art !

I don't know, madam, whether I make myself clearly understood in saying so much ; but if you will have the kindness to look at a certain little picture by Mr. Eastlake in this gallery, you will see to what the observation applies, and that out of a homely subject, and a few simple figures not at all wonderful for excessive beauty or grandeur, the artist can make something infinitely more beautiful than Mediceean Venuses, and sublimer than Pythian Apollos. Happy are you, Charles Lock Eastlake, Esquire, R.A. ! I think you have in your breast some of that sacred fire that lighted the bosom of Raphael Sanctius, Esquire, of Urbino, he being a young man,—a holy kind of Sabbath repose—a calm that comes not of feeling, but of the overflowing of it—a tender yearning sympathy and love for God's beautiful world and creatures. Impelled by such a delightful sentiment, the gentle spirit of him in whom it dwells (like the angels of old, who first taught us to receive the doctrine that love was the key to the world) breathes always peace on earth and goodwill towards men. And though the privilege of enjoying this happy frame of mind is accorded to the humblest as well as the most gifted genius, yet the latter must remember that the intellect can exercise itself in no higher way than in the practice of this kind

* Alfred de Musset.

of adoration and gratitude. The great artist who is the priest of nature is consecrated especially to this service of praise ; and though it may have no direct relation to religious subjects, the view of a picture of the highest order does always, like the view of stars in a calm night, or a fair quiet landscape in sunshine, fill the mind with an inexpressible content and gratitude towards the Maker who has created such beautiful things for our use.

And as the poet has told us how, not out of a wide landscape merely, or a sublime expanse of glittering stars, but of any very humble thing, we may gather the same delightful reflections (as out of a small flower, that bring us " thoughts that do often lie too deep for tears ")—in like manner we do not want grand pictures and elaborate yards of canvas so to affect us, as the lover of drawing must have felt in looking at the Raphael designs lately exhibited in London. These were little faint scraps, mostly from the artist's pencil—small groups, unfinished single figures, just indicated ; but the divine elements of beauty were as strong in them as in the grandest pieces : and there were many little sketches, not half an inch high, which charmed and affected one like the violet did Wordsworth ; and left one in that unspeakable, complacent, grateful condition, which, as I have been endeavouring to state, is the highest aim of the art.

And if I might be allowed to give a hint to amateurs concerning pictures and their merit, I would say look to have your *heart* touched by them. The best paintings address themselves to the best feelings of it ; and a great many very clever pictures do not touch it at all. Skill and handling are great parts of a painter's trade, but heart is the first ; this is God's direct gift to him, and cannot be got in any academy, or under any master. Look about, therefore, for pictures, be they large or small, finished well or ill, landscapes, portraits, figure-pieces, pen-and-ink sketches, or what not, that contain senti- ment and great ideas. He who possesses these will be sure to express them, more or less well. Never mind about the manner. He who possesses them not may draw and colour to perfection, and yet be no artist. As for telling you what sentiment is, and what it is not, wherein lies the secret of the sublime, there, madam, we must stop altogether ; only, after reading Burke " On the Sublime," you will find yourself exactly as wise as you were before. I cannot tell why a landscape by Claude or Constable should be more beautiful —it is certainly not more dexterous—than a landscape by Mr.—— or Mr.——. I cannot tell why Raphael should be superior to Mr. Benjamin Haydon (a fact which one person in the world may be perhaps inclined to doubt) ; or why " Vedrai, carino," in " Don Juan," should be more charming to me than " Suoni la tromba," before mentioned. The latter has twice as much drumming, trumpeting, and thundering in it. All these points are quite undefinable and inexplicable (I never read a metaphysical account of them that did not seem sheer dulness and nonsense) ; but we can have no doubt about them. And thus we come to Charles Lock Eastlake, Esquire, from whom we started about a page since ; during which we have laid down, first, that sentiment is the first quality of a picture ; second, that to say whether this sentiment exists or no rests with the individual entirely, the sentiment not being capable of any sort of definition. Charles Lock Eastlake, Esquire, possesses, to my thinking, this undefinable arch-quality of sentiment to a very high degree. And, besides him, let us mention William Mulready, Esquire, Cope, Boxall, Redgrave, Herbert (the two latter don't show so much of it this year as formerly), and Richmond.

Mr. Eastlake's picture is as pure as a Sabbath-hymn sung by the voices of children. He has taken a very simple subject— hardly any subject at all ; but such suggestive points are the best, perhaps, that a painter can take ; for with the illustration of a given subject out of a history or romance, when one has seen it, one has commonly seen all, whereas such a piece as this, which Mr. Eastlake calls " The Salutation of the Aged Friar," brings the spectator to a delightful peaceful state of mind, and gives him matter to ponder upon long after. The story of this piece is simply this :—A group of innocent happy-looking Italian peasants are approaching a couple of friars ; a boy has stepped forward with a little flower, which he presents to the elder of these, and the old monk is giving him his blessing.

Now, it would be very easy to find fault with this picture, and complain of excessive redness in the shadows, excessive whiteness in the linen, of repetition in the faces,—the smallest child is the very counterpart of one in the " Christ and the Little Children " by the same artist last year—the women are not only copies of women before painted by Mr. Eastlake, but absolutely copies of one another ; the drawing lacks vigour, the flesh-tints variety (they seem to be produced, by the most careful stippling, with a brilliant composition of lake and burnt sienna, cooled off as they come to the edges with a little blue). But though, in the writer's judgment, there are in the picture every one of these faults, the merits of the performance incomparably exceed them, and these are of the purely sentimental and intellectual kind. What a tender grace and purity in the female heads ! If Mr. Eastlake repeats his model often, at least he has been very lucky in finding or making her : indeed, I don't know in any painter, ancient or modern, such a charming character of female beauty. The countenances of the monks are full of unction ; the children, with their mild-beaming eyes, are fresh with recollections of heaven. There is no affectation of middle-age mannerism, such as silly Germans and silly Frenchmen are wont to call Catholic art ; and the picture is truly Catholic in consequence, having about it what the hymn calls " solemn mirth," and giving the spectator the utmost possible pleasure in viewing it. Now, if we might suggest to Mr. Lane, the lithographer, how he might confer a vast benefit upon the public, we would entreat him to make several large copies of pictures of this class, executing them with that admirable grace and fidelity which are the characteristics of all his copies. Let these be coloured accurately, as they might be, at a small charge, and poor people for a few guineas might speedily make for them-selves delightful picture galleries. The colour adds amazingly to the charm of these pictures, and attracts the eye to them. And they are such placid pious companions for a man's study, that the continual presence of them could not fail to purify his taste and his heart.

I am not here arguing, let it be remembered, that Mr. Eastlake is absolute perfection ; and will concede to those who find fault with him that his works are deficient in power, however remarkable for grace. Be it so. But then, let us admire his skill in choosing such subjects as are best suited to his style of thinking, and least likely to show his faults. In the pieces ordinarily painted by him, grace and tender feeling are the chief requisites ; and I don't recollect a work of his in which he has aimed at other qualities. One more picture besides the old Friar has Mr. Eastlake, a portrait of that beautiful Miss Bury, whom our readers must recollect in the old house, in a black mantle, a red gown, with long golden hair waving over her shoulders, and a lily in her hand. The picture was engraved afterwards in one of the Annuals ; and was one of the most delightful works that ever came from Mr. East-lake's pencil. I can't say as much for the present portrait : the picture wants relief, and is very odd and heavy in colour. The handsome lady looks as if she wanted her stays. O beautiful lily-bearer of six years since ! you should not have appeared like a mortal after having once shone upon us as an angel.

And now we are come to the man whom we delight to honour, Mr. Mulready, who has three pictures in the exhibition that are all charming in their way. The first (" Fair Time," 116) was painted, it is said, more than a score of years since ; and the observer may look into it with some payment for his curiosity, for it contains specimens of the artist's old and new manner. The picture in its first state is somewhat in the Wilkie style of that day (oh for the Wilkie style of that day !), having many greys, and imitating closely the Dutchmen. Since then the painter has been touching up the figures in the foreground with his new and favourite lurid orange-colour; and you may see how this is stippled in upon the faces and hands, and borrow, perhaps, a hint or two regarding the Mulreadian secret.

What is the meaning of this strange colour?—these glowing burning crimsons, and intense blues, and greens more green than the first budding leaves of spring, or the mignonette-pots in a Cockney's window at Brixton. But don't fancy that we are joking or about to joke at Mr. Mulready. These gaudy prismatic colours are wonderfully captivating to the eye: and, amidst a host of pictures, it cannot fail to settle on a Mulready in preference to all. But for consistency's sake, a protest must be put in against the colour; it is pleasant, but wrong; we never saw it in nature—not even when looking through an orange-coloured glass. This point being settled, then, and our minds eased, let us look at the design and conception of "First Love"; and pray, sir, where in the whole works of modern artists will you find anything more exquisitely beautiful? I don't know what that young fellow, so solemn, so tender, is whispering into the ear of that dear girl (she is only fifteen now, but, *sapristie,* how beautiful she will be about three years hence !), who is folding a pair of slim arms round a little baby, and making believe to nurse it, as they three are standing one glowing summer day under some trees by a stile. I don't know, I say, what they are saying ; nor, if I could hear, would I tell—'tis a secret, madam. Recollect the words that the Captain whispered in your ear that afternoon in the shubbery. Your heart throbs, your cheek flushes ; the sweet sound of those words tells clear upon your ear, and you say, "Oh, Mr. Titmarsh, how *can* you ?" Be not afraid, madam —never, never will I peach ; but sing, in the words of a poet who is occasionally quoted in the House of Commons—

> " Est et fideli tuta silentio
> Merces. Vetabo qui Cereris sacrum
>   Vulgarit arcanæ, sub îsdem
>   Sit trabibus, fragilemve mecum
> Solvat phaselum."

Which may be interpreted (with a slight alteration of the name of Ceres for that of a much more agreeable goddess)—

> Be happy, and thy counsel keep,
>   'Tis thus the bard adviseth thee ;
> Remember that the silent lip
>   In silence shall rewarded be.
> And fly the wretch who dares to strip
>   Love of its sacred mystery.

My loyal legs I would not stretch
      Beneath the same mahogany ;
Nor trust myself in Chelsea Reach,
      In punt or skiff, with such as he.
The villain who would kiss and peach,
      I hold him for mine enemy !

But, to return to our muttons, I would not give a fig for the taste of the individual who does not see the exquisite beauty of this little group. Our artist has more passion than the before-lauded Mr. Eastlake, but quite as much delicacy and tenderness ; and they seem to me to possess the poetry of picture-making more than any other of their brethren.

By the way, what is this insane yell that has been raised throughout the public press about Mr. Mulready's other perform-ance, the postage cover, and why are the sages so bitter against it ? The *Times* says it is disgraceful and ludicrous ; the elegant writers of the *Weekly Dispatch* vow it is ludicrous and disgraceful ; the same sweet song is echoed by papers, Radical and Conservative, in London and the provinces, all the literary gentlemen being alive, and smarting under this insult to the arts of the country. Honest gentlemen of the press, be not so thin-skinned ! Take my word for it, there is no cause for such vehement anger—no good oppor-tunity here for you to show off that exquisite knowledge of the fine arts for which you are so celebrated throughout the world. Gentlemen, the drawing of which you complain is *not* bad. The commonest engravers, who would be ashamed to produce such a design, will tell you, if they know anything of their business, that they could not make a better in a hurry. Every man who knows what drawing is will acknowledge that some of these little groups are charmingly drawn ; and I will trouble your commonest en-gravers to design the Chinese group, the American, or the West Indian, in a manner more graceful and more characteristic than that of the much-bespattered post envelope.

I am not holding up the whole affair as a masterpiece—*pas si bête.* The "triumphant hallegory of Britannia ruling the waves," as Mathews used to call it, is a little stale, certainly, nowadays ; but what would you have ? How is the sublime to be elicited from such a subject ? Let some of the common engravers, in their leisure moments, since the thing is so easy, make a better design, or the literary men who are so indignant invent one. The Govern-ment, no doubt, is not bound heart and soul to Mr. Mulready, and is willing to hear reason. *Fiat justitia, ruat cœlum :* though all the world shall turn on thee, O Government, in this instance Titmarsh shall stand by thee—ay, and without any hope of reward.

o be sure, if my Lord Normanby absolutely insists—but that is
either here nor there. I repeat, the Post Office envelope is not
ad, *quoad* design. That very lion, which some of the men of the
ress (the Daniels!) have been crying out about, is finely, carefully,
nd characteristically sketched; those elephants I am sure were
losely studied, before the artist in a few lines laid them down on
is wood-block; and as for the persons who are to imitate the
ngraving so exactly, let them try. It has been done by the best
ood-engraver in Europe. Ask any man in the profession if Mr.
hompson is not at the head of it? He has bestowed on it a vast
eal of time, and skill, and labour; and all who know the diffi-
ulties of wood-engraving—of outline wood-engraving—and of
endering faithfully a design so very minute as this, will smile at
he sages who declare that all the world could forge it. There was
ne provincial paper which declared, in a style peculiarly elegant,
hat a man "with a block of wood and a *bread-and-cheese* knife
ould easily imitate the envelope;" which remark, for its profound
ruth and sagacity, the London journals copied. For shame, gentle-
nen! Do you think you show your knowledge by adopting such
pinions as these, or prove your taste by clothing yourselves in the
econd-hand garments of the rustic who talks about bread and
heese? Try, Tyrotomos, upon whatever block thou choosest to
ractise; or, be wise, and with appropriate bread-and-cheese knife
ut only bread and cheese. Of bread, white and brown, of cheese,
ld, new, mouldy, toasted, the writer of the *Double-Gloster Journal,*
he *Stilton Examiner,* the *Cheddar Champion,* and *North Wilt-
hire Intelligencer,* may possibly be a competent critic, and (with
nouth replete with the delicious condiment) may no doubt eloquently
peak. But let us be cautious before we agree to and admiringly
dopt his opinions upon matters of art. Mr. Thompson is the first
ood-engraver in our country—Mr. Mulready one of the best
ainters in our or any school: it is hard that such men are to be
ssailed in such language, and by such a critic!

This artist's picture of an interior is remarkable for the same
xaggerated colour, and for the same excellences. The landscape
een from the window is beautifully solemn, and very finely painted,
n the clear bright manner of Van Dyck and Cranach, and the
arly German school.

Mr. Richmond's picture of "Our Lord after the Resurrection"
eserves a much better place than it has in the little, dingy, newly-
iscovered octagon closet; and leaves us to regret that he should
ccupy himself so much with water-colour portraits, and so little
vith compositions in oil. This picture is beautifully conceived, and
ery finely and carefully drawn and painted. One of the apostles

is copied from Raphael, and the more is the pity : a man who coul
execute two such grand figures as the other two in the picture nee
surely borrow from no one. A water-colour group, by the sam
artist (547, "The Children of Colonel Lindsay"), contains tw
charming figures of a young lady and a little boy, painted wit
great care and precision of design and colour, with great purity o
sentiment, and without the least affectation. Let our aristocrac
send their wives and children (the handsomest wives and childre
in the world) to be painted by this gentleman, and those who ar
like him. Miss Lindsay, with her plain red dress and modes
looks, is surely a thousand times more captivating than thos
dangerous smiling Delilahs in her neighbourhood, whom Mr. Chalo
has painted. We must not be understood to undervalue this latte
gentleman however ; his drawings are miracles of dexterity ; ever
year they seem to be more skilful and more brilliant. Such satin
and lace, such diamond rings and charming little lapdogs, wer
never painted before,—not by Watteau, the first master of th
genre,—and Lancret, who was scarcely his inferior. A miniatur
on ivory by Mr. Chalon, among the thousand prim, pretty littl
pictures of the same class which all the ladies crowd about, i
remarkable for its brilliancy of colour and charming freedom o
handling ; as is an oil sketch of masquerading figures, by the sam
painter, for the curious coarseness of the painting.

Before we leave the high-class pictures, we must mention Mr
Boxall's beautiful "Hope," which is exquisitely refined and delicat
in sentiment, colour, and execution. Placed close beneath one o
Turner's magnificent tornadoes of colour, it loses none of its ow
beauty. As Uhland writes of a certain king and queen who ar
seated in state side by side,—

> " Der *Turner* furchtbar prächtig wie blut'ger Nordlichtschein,
> Der *Boxall* süss und milde, als blickte Vollmond drein."

Which signifies in English, that

> " As beams the moon so gentle near the sun, that blood-red burner,
> So shineth William Boxall by Joseph Mallord Turner."

In another part of the room, and contrasting their quiet grace
in the same way with Mr. Turner's glaring colours, are a couple o
delightful pictures by Mr. Cope, with mottoes that will explair
their subjects. "Help thy father in his age, and despise him not
when thou art in thy full strength ; " and " Reject not the affliction
of the afflicted, neither turn away thy face from a poor man." The
latter of these pictures is especially beautiful, and the figure of the

female charity as graceful and delicate as may be. I wish I could say a great deal in praise of Mr. Cope's large altar-piece : it is a very meritorious performance ; but here praise stops, and such praise is worth exactly nothing. A large picture must either be splendid, or else naught. This " Crucifixion " has a great deal of vigour, feeling, grace : BUT—the but is fatal ; all minor praises are drowned in it. Recollect, however, Mr. Cope, that Titmarsh, who writes this, is only giving his private opinion ; that he is mortal ; that it is barely possible that he should be in the wrong ; and' with this confession, which I am compelled (for fear you might overlook the circumstance) to make, you will, I daresay, console yourself, and do well. But men must gird themselves, and go through long trainings, before they can execute such gigantic works as altar-pieces. Handel, doubtless, wrote many little pleasing melodies before he pealed out the "Hallelujah" chorus ; and so painters will do well to try their powers, and, if possible, measure and understand them before they use them. There is Mr. Hart, for instance, who took in an evil hour to the making of great pictures ; in the present exhibition is a decently small one ; but the artist has overstretched himself in the former attempts ; as one hears of gentlemen on the rack, the limbs are stretched one or two inches by the process, and the patient comes away by so much the taller : but he can't *walk* near so well as before, and all his strength is stretched out of him.

Let this be a solemn hint to a clever young painter, Mr. Elmore, who has painted a clever picture of " The Murder of Saint Thomas à Becket," for Mr. Daniel O'Connell. Come off your rack, Mr. Elmore, or you will hurt yourself. Much better is it to paint small subjects, for some time at least. " Non cuivis contingit adire Corinthum," as the proverb says ; but there is a number of pleasant villages in this world beside, where we may snugly take up our quarters. By the way, what is the meaning of Tom à Becket's black cassock under his canonicals ? Would John Tuam celebrate mass in such a dress ? A painter should be as careful about his costumes as an historian about his dates, or he plays the deuce with his composition.

Now, in this matter of costume, nobody can be more scrupulous than Mr. Charles Landseer, whose picture of Nell Gwynne is painted with admirable effect, and honest scrupulousness. It is very good in colour, very gay in spirits (perhaps too refined,—for Nelly never was such a hypocrite as to look as modest as that) ; but the gentle-men and ladies do not look as if they were accustomed to their dresses, for all their correctness, but had put them on for the first time. Indeed, this is a very small fault, and the merits of the picture are very great : every one of the accessories is curiously well painted,—some of the figures very spirited (the drawer is excellent); and the picture one of the most agreeable in the whole gallery. Mr. Redgrave has another costume picture, of a rather old subject, from "The Rambler." A poor girl comes to be companion to Mr. and Mrs. Courtly, who are at piquet; their servants are bringing in tea, and the master and mistress are looking at the new-comer with a great deal of easy scorn. The poor girl is charming; Mrs. Courtly not quite genteel, but with a wonderful quilted petticoat; Courtly looks as if he were not accustomed to his clothes; the servants are very good; and as for the properties, as they would be called on the stage, these are almost too good, painted with a daguerréo-typical minuteness that gives this and Mr. Redgrave's other picture of "Paracelsus" a finikin air, if we may use such a disrespectful term. Both performances, however, contain very high merit of expression and sentiment; and are of such a character as we seldom saw in our schools twenty years ago.

There is a large picture by a Scotch artist, Mr. Duncan, representing "The Entry of Charles Edward into Edinburgh," which runs a little into caricature, but contains a vast deal of character and merit; and which, above all, in the article of costume, shows much study and taste. Mr. Duncan seems to have formed his style upon Mr. Allan and Mr. Wilkie—I beg his pardon—Sir David. The former has a pleasing brown picture likewise on the subject of the Pretender. The latter's Maid of Saragossa and Spaniard at the gun, any one may see habited as Irish peasants superintending "A Whisky Still," in the middle room, No. 252.

This picture, I say, any one may see and admire who pleases: to me it seems all rags and duds, and a strange, straggling, misty composition. There are fine things, of course; for how can Sir David help painting fine things? In the "Benvenuto" there is superb colour, with a rich management of lakes especially, which has been borrowed from no master that we know of. The Queen is as bad a likeness and picture as we have seen for many a day. "Mrs. Ferguson, of Raith," a magnificent picture indeed, as grand in effect as a Rubens or Titian, and having a style of its own. The little sketch from Allan Ramsay is delightful; and the nobleman and hounds (with the exception of his own clumsy vermilion robe), as fine as the fellow-sized portrait mentioned before. Allan Ramsay has given a pretty subject, and brought us a pretty picture from another painter, Mr. A. Johnston, who has illustrated those pleasant quaint lines,—

> " Last morning I was gay, and early out;
> Upon a dike I leaned, glow'ring about.
> I saw my Meg come linkan o'er the lea;
> I saw my Meg, but Meggy saw na me."

And here let us mention with praise two small pictures in a style somewhat similar — "The Recruit," and "Herman and Dorothea," by Mr. Poole. The former of these little pieces is very touching and beautiful. There is among the present exhibitioners no lack of this kind of talent; and we could point out many pictures that are equally remarkable for grace and agreeable feeling. Mr. Stone's "Annot Lyle" should not be passed over,—a pretty picture, very well painted, the female head of great beauty and expression.

Now, if we want to praise performances showing a great deal of power and vigour, rather than grace and delicacy, there are Mr. Etty's "Andromeda" and "Venus." In the former, the dim figure of advancing Perseus galloping on his airy charger is very fine and ghostly ; in the latter, the body of the Venus, and indeed the whole picture, is a perfect miracle of colour. Titian may have painted Italian flesh equally well ; but he never, I think, could surpass the skill of Mr. Etty. The trunk of this voluptuous Venus is the most astonishing representation of beautiful English flesh and blood, painted in the grandest and broadest style. It is said that the Academy at Edinburgh has a room full of Etty's pictures ; they could not do better in England than follow the example ; but perhaps the paintings had better be kept *for the Academy only*—for the *profanum vulgus* are scarcely fitted to comprehend their peculiar beauties. A prettily drawn, graceful, nude figure, is "Bathsheba," by Mr. Fisher, of the street and city of Cork.

The other great man of Cork is Daniel Maclise by name ; and if in the riot of fancy he hath by playful Titmarsh been raised to the honour of knighthood, it is certain that here Titmarsh is a true prophet, and that the sovereign will so elevate him, one day or other, to sit with other cavaliers at the Academic round table. As for his pictures,—why as for his pictures, madam, these are to be carefully reviewed in the next number of this Magazine ; for the present notice has noticed scarcely anybody, and yet stretched to an inordinate length. "Macbeth" is not to be hurried off under six pages ; and, for this June number, Mr. Fraser vows that he has no such room to spare.

We have said how Mr. Turner's pictures blaze about the rooms ; it is not a little curious to hear how artists and the public differ in their judgments concerning them ; the enthusiastic wonder of the first-named, the blank surprise and incredulity of the latter. "The new moon ; or, I've lost my boat : you shan't have your hoop," is the ingenious title of one,—a very beautiful picture, too, of a long shining sea-sand, lighted from the upper part of the canvas by the above-named luminary of night, and from the left-hand corner by a wonderful wary boy in a red jacket—the best painted figure that we ever knew painted by Joseph Mallord Turner, Esquire.

He and Mr. Ward vie with each other in mottoes for their pictures. Ward's epigraph to the S——'s nest is wondrous poetic.

277. The S——'s Nest. S. Ward, R.A.

> " Say they that happiness lives with the great,
> On gorgeous trappings mixt with pomp and state ?
> More frequent found upon the simple plain,
> In poorest garb, with Julia, Jess, or Jane ;
> In sport or slumber, as it likes her best,
> Where'er she *lays* she finds it a S——'s nest."

Ay, and a S——'s eggs, too, as one would fancy, were great geniuses not above grammar. Mark the line, too,

> " On gorgeous trappings *mixt* with pomp and state,"

and construe the whole of this sensible passage.

Not less sublime is Mr. Ward's fellow-Academician :—

230. " Slavers throwing overboard the Dead and Dying : Typhon coming on." J. M. W. Turner, R.A.

> " Aloft all hands, strike the topmasts and belay !
> Yon angry setting sun and fierce-edged clouds
> Declare the Typhon's coming.
> Before it sweeps your decks, throw overboard
> The dead and dying—ne'er heed their chains.
> Hope, Hope, fallacious Hope !
> Where is thy market now ?"

> *MS. Fallacies of Hope.*

Fallacies of Hope, indeed : to a pretty mart has she brought her pigs ! How should Hope be hooked on to the slaver ? By the anchor, to be sure, which accounts for it. As for the picture, the R.A.'s rays are indeed terrific ; and the slaver throwing its cargo overboard is the most tremendous piece of colour that ever was seen ; it sets the corner of the room in which it hangs into a flame. Is the picture sublime or ridiculous ? Indeed I don't know which. Rocks of gamboge are marked down upon the canvas ; flakes of white laid on with a trowel ; bladders of vermilion madly spirted here and there. Yonder is the slaver rocking in the midst of a flashing foam of white-lead. The sun glares down upon a horrible sea of emerald and purple, into which chocolate-coloured slaves are plunged, and chains that will not

ink; and round these are floundering such a race of fishes as
never was seen since the *sœculum Pyrrhœ*; gasping dolphins,
redder than the reddest herrings; horrid spreading polypi, like
huge, slimy, poached eggs, in which hapless niggers plunge and
disappear. Ye gods, what a "middle passage"! How Mr. Fowell
Buxton must shudder! What would they say•to this in Exeter
Hall? If Wilberforce's statue downstairs were to be confronted
with this picture, the stony old gentleman would spring off his
chair, and fly away in terror!

And here, as we are speaking of the slave-trade, let us say
a word in welcome to a French artist, Monsieur Biard, and his
admirable picture. Let the friends of the negro forthwith buy
this canvas, and cause a plate to be taken from it. It is the best,
most striking, most pathetic lecture against the trade that ever
was delivered. The picture is as fine as Hogarth; and the artist,
who, as we have heard, right or wrong, has only of late years
adopted the profession of painting, and was formerly in the French
navy, has evidently drawn a great deal of his materials from life
and personal observation. The scene is laid upon the African
coast. King Tom or King Boy has come with troops of slaves
down the Quorra, and sits in the midst of his chiefs and mistresses
(one a fair creature, not much darker than a copper tea-kettle),
bargaining with a French dealer. What a horrible callous brutality
there is in the scoundrel's face, as he lolls over his greasy ledger,
and makes his calculations. A number of his crew are about him;
their boats close at hand, in which they are stowing their cargo.
See the poor wretches, men and women, collared together, drooping
down. There is one poor thing, just parted from her child. On
the ground in front lies a stalwart negro; one connoisseur is
handling his chest, to try his wind; another has opened his mouth,
and examines his teeth, to know his age and soundness. Yonder
is a poor woman kneeling before one of the Frenchmen; her
shoulder is fizzing under the hot iron with which he brands her;
she is looking up, shuddering and wild, yet quite mild and patient:
it breaks your heart to look at her. I never saw anything so
exquisitely pathetic as that face. God bless you, Monsieur Biard,
for painting it! It stirs the heart more than a hundred thousand
tracts, reports, or sermons: it must convert every man who has
seen it. You British Government, who have given twenty millions
towards the good end of freeing this hapless people, give yet a
couple of thousand more to the French painter, and don't let his
work go out of the country, now that it is here. Let it hang along
with the Hogarths in the National Gallery; it is as good as the
best of them. Or, there is Mr. Thomas Babington Macaulay, who

has a family interest in the matter, and does not know how to spend all the money he brought home from India; let the right honourable gentleman look to it. Down with your dust, right honourable sir; give Monsieur Biard a couple of thousand for his picture of the negroes, and it will be the best black act you ever did in your life; and don't go for to be angry at the suggestion, or fancy we are taking liberties. What is said is said from one public man to another, in a Pickwickian sense, *de puissance en puissance*, —from Titmarsh, in his critical *cathedra*, to your father's eminent son, rich with the spoils of Ind, and wielding the bolts of war.

What a marvellous power is this of the painter's! how each great man can excite us at his will! what a weapon he has, if he knows how to wield it! Look for a while at Mr. Etty's pictures, and away you rush, your "eyes on fire," drunken with the luscious colours that are poured out for you on the liberal canvas, and warm with the sight of the beautiful sirens that appear on it. You fly from this (and full time too), and plunge into a green shady landscape of Lee or Creswick, and follow a quiet stream babbling beneath whispering trees, and chequered with cool shade and golden sunshine; or you set the world—nay, the Thames and the ocean— on fire with that incendiary Turner; or you laugh with honest kind-hearted Webster, and his troops of merry children; or you fall a-weeping with Monsieur Biard for his poor blacks; or you go and consult the priests of the place, Eastlake, Mulready, Boxall, Cope, and the like, and straightway your mind is carried off in an ecstasy,—happy thrilling hymns sound in your ears melodious,— sweet thankfulness fills your bosom. How much instruction and happiness have we gained from these men, and how grateful should we be to them!

It is well that Mr. Titmarsh stopped here, and I shall take special care to examine any further remarks which he may think fit to send. Four-fifths of this would have been cancelled, had the printed sheets fallen sooner into our hands. The story about the "Clarendon" is an absurd fiction; no dinner ever took place there. I never fell asleep in a plate of raspberry ice; and though I certainly did recommend this person to do justice by the painters making him a speech to that effect, my opinions were infinitely better expressed, and I would repeat them were it not so late in the month. O. Y.

A PICTORIAL RHAPSODY: CONCLUDED

AND FOLLOWED BY A REMARKABLE STATEMENT OF FACTS BY
MRS. BARBARA

AND now, in pursuance of the promise recorded in the last number of this Magazine, and for the performance of which the public has ever since been in breathless expectation, it hath become Titmarsh's duty to note down his opinions of the remaining pictures in the Academy exhibition; and to criticise such other pieces as the other galleries may show.

In the first place, then, with regard to Mr. Maclise, it becomes us to say our say : and as the *Observer* newspaper, which, though under the express patronage of the Royal family, devotes by far the noblest part of its eloquence to the consideration of dramatic subjects, and to the discussion of the gains, losses, and theatrical conduct of managers,—as, I say, the *Observer* newspaper, whenever Madame Vestris or Mr. Yates adopts any plan that concurs with the notions of the paper in question, does not fail to say that Madame Vestris or Mr. Yates has been induced so to reform in consequence of the *Observer's* particular suggestion ; in like manner, Titmarsh is fully convinced, that all the painters in this town have their eyes incessantly fixed upon his criticisms, and that all the wise ones regulate their opinions by his.

In the language of the *Observer*, then, Mr. Maclise has done wisely to adopt our suggestions with regard to the moral treatment of his pictures, and has made a great advance in his art. Of his four pictures, let us dismiss the scene from "Gil Blas" at once. Coming from a second-rate man, it would be well enough ; it is well drawn, grouped, lighted, shadowed, and the people all grin very comically, as people do in pictures called comic ; but the soul of fun is wanting, as I take it,—the merry, brisk, good-humoured spirit which in Le Sage's text so charms the reader.

"Olivia and Malvolio" is, on the contrary, one of the best and most spiritual performances of the artist. Nothing can be more elegant than the tender languid melancholy of Olivia, nor more poetical than the general treatment of the picture. The long clipped alleys and quaint gardens, the peacocks trailing through the walks, and vases basking in the sun, are finely painted and conceived. Examine the picture at a little distance, and the *ensemble* of the composition and colour is extraordinarily pleasing. The details, too, are, as usual, wonderful for their accuracy. Here are flower-beds, and a tree above Olivia's head, of which every leaf is painted, and painted with such skill, as not in the least to injure the general effect of the picture. Mr. Maclise has a daguerréotypic eye, and a feeling of form stronger, I do believe, than has ever been possessed by any painter before him.

Look at the portrait of Mr. Dickens,—well arranged as a picture, good in colour, and light, and shadow, and as a likeness perfectly amazing; a looking-glass could not render a better fac-simile. Here we have the real identical man Dickens : the artist must have understood the inward Boz as well as the outward before he made this admirable representation of him. What cheerful intelligence there is about the man's eyes and large forehead ! The mouth is too large and full, too eager and active, perhaps; the smile is very sweet and generous. If Monsieur de Balzac, that voluminous physiognomist, could examine this head, he would, no doubt, interpret every tone and wrinkle in it : the nose firm, and well placed; the nostrils wide and full, as are the nostrils of all men of genius (this is Monsieur Balzac's maxim). The past and the future, says Jean Paul, are written in every countenance. I think we may promise ourselves a brilliant future from this one. There seems no flagging as yet in it, no sense of fatigue, or consciousness of decaying power. Long mayest thou, O Boz ! reign over thy comic kingdom; long may we pay tribute, whether of threepence weekly or of a shilling monthly, it matters not. Mighty prince ! at thy imperial feet, Titmarsh, humblest of thy servants, offers his vows of loyalty, and his humble tribute of praise.

And now (as soon as we are off our knees, and have done paying court to sovereign Boz) it behoves us to say a word or two concerning the picture of "Macbeth," which occupies such a conspicuous place in the Academy gallery. Well, then, this picture of "Macbeth" has been, to our notion, a great deal too much praised and abused ; only Titmarsh understands the golden mean, as is acknowledged by all who read his criticisms. Here is a very fine masterly picture, no doubt, full of beauties, and showing extraordinary power ; but not a masterpiece, as I humbly take it,—not a picture to move the beholder as much as many performances that do not display half the power that is here exhibited. I don't pretend to lay down any absolute laws on the sublime (the reader will remember how the ancient satirist hath accused John Dennis of madness, for his vehement preaching of such rules). No, no; Michael Angelo T. is not quite so impertinent as that; but the public and the artist will not mind being told, without any previous definitions, that this picture is not of the highest order: the "Malvolio" is far more spiritual and suggestive, if we may so speak; it tells not only its own tale very charmingly, but creates for the beholder a very pleasant melancholy train of thought, as every good picture does in its kind, from a six-inch canvas by Hobbema or Ruysdael up to a thousand-foot wall of Michael Angelo. If you read over the banquet-scene in words, it leaves an impression far more dreadful and lively. On the stage, it has always seemed to us to fail; and though out of a trap-door in the middle of it Mr. Cooper is seen to rise very solemnly,—his face covered with white, and a dreadful gash of vermilion across his neck; though he nods and waggles his head about in a very quiet ghost-like manner; yet, strange to say, neither this scene, nor this great actor, has ever frightened us, as they both should, as the former does when we read it at home. The fact is, that it is quite out of Mr. Cooper's power to look ghostly enough, or, perhaps, to soar along with us to that sublime height to which our imagination is continually carrying us.

A large part of this vast picture Mr. Maclise has painted very finely. The lords are all there in gloomy state, fierce stalwart men in steel; the variety of attitude and light in which the different groups are placed, the wonderful knowledge and firmness with which each individual figure and feature are placed down upon the canvas will be understood and admired by the public, but by the artist still more, who knows the difficulty of these things, which seem so easy, which are so easy, no doubt, to a man with Mr. Maclise's extraordinary gifts. How fine is yonder group at the farthest table, lighted up by the reflected light from the armour of one of them ! The effect, as far as we know, is entirely new; the figures drawn with exquisite minuteness and clearness, not in the least interrupting the general harmony of the picture. Look at the two women standing near Lady Macbeth's throne, and those beautiful little hands of one of them placed over the state-chair; the science, workmanship, feeling in these figures are alike wonderful. The face, bust, and attitude of Lady Macbeth are grandly designed; the figures to her right, with looks of stern doubt and wonder, are nobly designed and arranged. The main figure of Macbeth, I confess, does not please; nor the object which has occasioned the frightful convulsive attitude in which he stands. He sees not the ghost of Banquo, but a huge, indistinct, gory shadow, which seems to shake its bloody locks, and frown upon him. Through this shade, intercepted only by its lurid transparency, you see the figures of the guests; they are looking towards it, and *through* it. The skill with which this point is made is unquestionable; there is something there, and nothing. The spectators feel this as well as the painted actors of the scene; there are times when, in looking at the picture, one loses sight of the shade altogether, and begins to wonder with Rosse, Lenox, and the rest.

The idea, then, so far as it goes, is as excellently worked out as it is daringly conceived. But is it a just one? I think not. I should say it was a grim piece of comedy rather than tragedy. One is puzzled by this piece of *diablerie*,—not deeply affected and awe-stricken, as in the midst of such heroical characters and circumstances one should be.

> " Avaunt, and quit my sight! Let the earth hide thee!
> Thy bones are marrowless—thy blood is cold ;
> Thou hast no speculation in those eyes
> Which thou dost glare with."

Before the poet's eyes, at least, the figure of the ghost stood complete—an actual visible body, with the life gone out of it; an image far more grand and dreadful than the painter's fantastical shadow, because more simple. The shadow is an awful object,— granted; but the most sublime, beautiful, fearful sight in all nature is, surely, the face of a man; wonderful in all its expressions of grief or joy, daring or endurance, thought, hope, love, or pain. How Shakspeare painted all these; with what careful thought and brooding were all his imaginary creatures made!

I believe we have mentioned the best figure-pieces in the exhibition; for, alas! the "Milton and his Daughters" of Sir Augustus Callcott, although one of the biggest canvases in the gallery, is by no means one of the best; and one may regret that this most *spirituel* of landscape-painters should have forsaken his old style to follow figure-drawing. Mr. Hollins has a picture of "Benvenuto Cellini showing a Trinket to a Lady." A subject of absorbing interest and passionate excitement, painted in a corresponding manner. A prim lady sits smiling in a chair, by a table, on which is a very neat regular tablecloth, drawn at right angles with the picture-frame; parallel with the table is a chest of drawers, secrétaire, cabinet, or *bahut*. Near this stands a waiting-maid, smiling archly; and in front you behold young Benvenuto, spick and span in his very best clothes and silk stockings, looking —as Benvenuto never did in his life. Of some parts of this picture, the colour and workmanship are very pretty; but was there ever such a niminypiminy subject treated in such a niminypiminy way? We can remember this gentleman's picture of "Margaret at the Spinning-wheel" last year, and should be glad to see and laud others that were equally pretty. Mr. Lauder has, in the same room, a pleasing picture from Walter Scott, "The Glee-Maiden;" and a large sketch, likewise from Scott, by a French artist (who has been celebrated in this Magazine as the author of the picture "The Sinking of the *Vengeur*"), is fine in effect and composition.

If Mr. Herbert's picture of "Travellers taking Refreshment at a Convent Gate" has not produced much sensation, it is because it is feeble in tone, not very striking in subject, and placed some-what too high. There is a great deal of beauty and delicacy in all the figures; and though lost here, amidst the glare and bustle of the Academy, it will be an excellent picture for the cabinet, where its quiet graces and merits will be better seen.

Mr. Webster's "Punch," before alluded to, deserves a great deal of praise. The landscape is beautiful, the group of little figures assembled to view the show are delightfully gay and pretty. Mr. Webster has the bump of philoprogenitiveness (as some ninny says of George Cruikshank in the *Westminster Review*); and all mothers of large families, young ladies who hope to be so one day or the other, and honest papas, are observed to examine this picture with much smiling interest. It is full of sunshine and innocent playful good-humour; all Punch's audience are on the grin. John, the squire's footman, is looking on with a protecting air; the old village folk are looking on, grinning with the very youngest; boys are scampering over the common, in order to be in time for the show; Punchman is tootooing on the pipes, and banging away on the drum; potboy has consigned to the earth his precious cargo, and the head of every tankard of liquor is wasting its frothy fragrance in the air; in like manner, the pieman permits his wares to get cold; nurserymaids, schoolboys, happy children in go-carts, are employed in a similar way: indeed, a delightful little rustic comedy.

In respect of portraits, the prettiest, as I fancy, after Wilkie's splendid picture of Mrs. Ferguson, is one by Mr. Grant, of a lady with a scarf of a greenish colour. The whole picture is of the same tone, and beautifully harmonious; nor are the lady's face and air the least elegant and charming part of it. The Duke has been painted a vast number of times, such are the penalties of glory; nor is it possible to conceive anything much worse than that portrait of him in which Colonel Gurwood is represented by his side, in a red velvet waistcoat, offering to his Grace certain despatches. It is in the style of the famous picture in the Regent Circus, representing Mr. Coleby the cigarist, an orange, a pine-apple, a champagne-cork, a little dog, some decanters, and a yellow bandanna, — all which personages appear to be so excessively important, that the puzzled eyes scarcely know upon which to settle. In like manner, in the Wellington-Gurwood testimonial, the accessories are so numerous, and so brilliantly coloured, that it is long before one can look up to the countenances of the Colonel and his Grace; which, it is to be presumed, are the main objects of interest in the piece. And this plan has been not unartfully contrived,—for the heads are by no means painted up to the point of brilliancy which is visible in boots, clocks, bell-pulls, Turkey carpets, arm-chairs, and other properties here painted.

Now, if the artist of the above picture wishes to know how properties may be painted with all due minuteness, and yet conduce to the general effect of the picture, let him examine the noble little portrait of Lord Cottenham, by Leslie,—the only contribution of this great man to the exhibition. Here are a number of accessories introduced, but with that forethought and sense of propriety which, as I fancy, distinguish all the works of Mr. Leslie. They are not here for mere picturesque effect or ornamental huddle; but are made to tell the story of the piece, and indicate the character of the dignified personage who fills the centre of it. The black brocade drapery of the Chancellor's gown is accurately painted, and falls in that majestic grave way in which a chancellor's robe *should* fall. Are not the learned Lord's arms somewhat short and fin-like? This is a query which we put humbly, having never had occasion to remark that part of his person.

Mr. Briggs has his usual pleasant well-painted portraits; and Mr. Patten a long full-length of Prince Albert that is not admired by artists, it is said, but a good downright honest *bourgeois* picture, as we fancy; or, as a facetious friend remarked, good plain *roast-and-boiled* painting. As for the portrait opposite—that of her Majesty, it is a sheer libel upon that pretty gracious countenance, an act of rebellion for which Sir David should be put into York gaol. Parts of the picture are, however, splendidly painted. And here, being upon the subject, let us say a word in praise of those two delightful lithographic heads, after Ross, which appear in the print-shop windows. Our gracious Queen's head is here most charming; and that of the Prince full of such manly frankness and benevolence as must make all men cry "God bless him." I would much sooner possess a copy of the Ross miniature of the Queen, than a cast from her Majesty's bust by Sir Francis Chantrey, which has the place of honour in the sculpture vault.

All Macdonald's busts deserve honourable notice. This lucky sculptor has some beautiful subjects to model, and beautiful and graceful all his marbles are. As much may be said of Mr. M'Dowell's girl,—the only piece of imaginative sculpture in the Academy that has struck us as pleasing. Mr. Behnes, too, should receive many commendations ; an old man's head particularly, that is full of character and goodness ; and "The Bust of a Lady," which may be called "A Lady with a Bust,"—a beautiful bust, indeed, of which the original and the artist have both good right to be proud. Mr. Bell's virgin is not so pleasing in the full size as in the miniature copy of it.

For the matter of landscapes, we confess ourselves to be no very ardent admirers of these performances, clever and dexterous as most of them are. The works of Mr. Stanfield and Mr. Roberts cannot fail to be skilful ; and both of these famous artists show their wonderful power of drawing, as usual. But these skilful pictures have always appeared to us more pleasing in little on the sketching-board than when expanded upon the canvas. A couple of Martins must be mentioned,—huge, queer, and tawdry to our eyes, but very much admired by the public, who is no bad connoisseur, after all ; and also a fine Castle of Chillon, or Chalon, rudely painted, but very poetical and impressive.

[Here Titmarsh exchanges his check at the door for a valuable gingham umbrella, with a yellow horn-head, representing Lord Brougham or Doctor Syntax, and is soon seen, with his hat very much on one side, swaggering down Pall Mall East, to the Water-Colour Gallery. He flings down eighteenpence in the easiest way, and goes upstairs.]

Accident, or, what is worse, ill health, has deprived us of the two most skilful professors of the noble art of water-colour painting ; and, without the works of Messrs. Lewis and Cattermole, the gallery looks empty indeed. Those gentlemen are accustomed to supply the picture-lover with the *pièces de résistance* of the feast, with which, being decently satisfied, we can trifle with an old market-place by Prout, or six cows and four pigs by Hill, or a misty Downs by Copley Fielding, with some degree of pleasure. Discontented, then, with the absence of the substantials, it must be confessed that we have been examining the rest of the pictures in no very good humour. And so, to tell you a secret, I do not care a fig for all the old town-halls in the world, though they be drawn ever so skilfully. How long are we to go on with Venice, Verona, Lago di Soandso, and Ponte di What-d'ye-call-'em ? I am weary of gondolas, striped awnings, sailors with red night (or rather day) caps, cobalt distances, and posts in the water. I have seen so many white palaces standing before dark purple skies, so many black towers with gamboge atmospheres behind them, so many masses of rifle-green trees plunged into the deepest shadow, in the midst of sunshiny plains, for no other reason but because dark and light contrast together, that a slight expression of satiety may be permitted to me, and a longing for more simple nature. On a great staring theatre such pictures may do very well—you are obliged there to seek for these startling contrasts ; and by the aid of blue lights, red lights, transparencies, and plenty of drums and appropriate music, the scene thus presented to one captivates the eye, and calls down thunder from the galleries.

But in little quiet rooms, on sheets of paper of a yard square, such monstrous theatrical effects are sadly painful. You don't mistake patches of brickdust for maidens' blushes, or fancy that tinfoil is diamonds, or require to be spoken to with the utmost roar of the lungs. Why, in painting, are we to have monstrous, flaring, Drury Lane tricks and claptraps put in practice, when a quieter style is, as I fancy, so infinitely more charming?

There is no use in mentioning the names of persons who are guilty of the above crimes; but let us say who is *not* guilty, and that is D. Cox, upon whose quiet landscapes, moist grass, cool trees, the refreshed eye rests with the utmost pleasure, after it has been perplexed and dazzled elsewhere. May we add an humble wish that this excellent painter will remain out of doors, amidst such quiet scenes as he loves, and not busy himself with Gothicism, middleageism, and the painting of quaint interiors? There are a dozen artists, of not a tithe of his genius, who can excel him at the architectural work. There is, for instance, Mr. Nash, who is improving yearly, and whose pictures are not only most dexterously sketched, but contain numberless little episodes, in the shape of groups of figures, that are full of grace and feeling. There is Mr. Haghe, too, of the lower house ; but of him anon.

To show how ill and how well a man may paint at the same time, the public may look at a couple of drawings by J. Nash, —one, the interior of a church ; the other, a plain landscape : both of which are executed with excessive, almost childish rudeness, and are yet excellent, as being close copies of the best of all drawing-masters, Nature : and Mr. Barrett, who has lately written a book for students, tells them very sagaciously *not* to copy the manner of any master, however much he may be in the mode. Some there are, fashionable instructors in the art of water-colouring, of whom, indeed, a man had better not learn at any price; nay, were they to offer a guinea per lesson, instead of modestly demanding the same, the reader should be counselled not to accept of their instructions.

See in what a different school Mr. Hunt works, and what marvellous effects he produces! There is a small picture of an interior by him (to which the blue ticket having the pretty word SOLD written on it is not fixed) that, as a copy of nature, is a perfect miracle. No De Hooghe was ever better, more airy and sunshiny. And the most extraordinary part of this extraordinary picture is, that the artist has not produced his effect of excessive brilliancy by any violent contrasting darkness; but the whole picture is light; the sunshine is in every corner of the room; and this drawing remains unsold, while Dash, and Blank, and Asterisk have got off all theirs. The large head of the black girl is painted with wonderful power; in water-colours we have scarcely seen anything so vigorous. The boys and virgins are, as usual, admirable; the lad with the bottle, he reading ballads in the barn, and the red, ragged, brickdust-coloured, brigand-looking fellow, especially good. In a corner is a most astonishing young gentleman with a pan of milk: he is stepping forward full into your face; and has seen something in it which has caused him to spill his milk and look dreadfully frightened. Every man who is worth a fig, as he comes up to this picture bursts out a-laughing—he can't help himself; you hear a dozen such laughs in the course of your visit. Why does this little drawing so seize hold of the beholder, and cause him to roar? There is the secret: the painter has got the soul of comedy in him—the undefinable humorous genius. Happy is the man who possesses that drawing: a man must laugh if he were taking his last look at it before being hanged.

Mr. Taylor's flowing pencil has produced several pieces of delightful colour; but we are led bitterly to deplore the use of that fatal white-lead pot, that is clogging and blackening the pictures of so many of the water-colour painters nowadays. His large picture contains a great deal of this white mud, and has lost, as we fancy, in consequence, much of that liquid mellow tone for which his works are remarkable. The retreating figures in this picture are beautiful; the horses are excellently painted, with as much dexterous brilliancy of colour as one sees in the oil pictures of Landseer. If the amateur wants to see how far transparent colour will go, what rich effect may be produced by it, how little necessary it is to plaster drawings with flakes of white, let him examine the background of the design representing a page asleep on a chair, than which nothing can be more melodious in colour, or more skilfully and naturally painted.

In the beauty gallery which this exhibition usually furnishes, there is Mr. Richter, who contributes his usual specimens; the fair

2 D

Miss Sharpe, with those languishing-eyed charmers whom the world admires so much ; and still more to our taste, a sweet pretty lady by Mr. Stone, in a hideous dress, with upper-Benjamin buttons ; a couple of very graceful and delicate heads by Wright ; and one beautiful head, a portrait evidently, by Cristall, that is placed very modestly in a corner near the ground—where such a drawing should be placed, of course, being vigorous, honest, natural, and beautiful. This artist's other drawing—a mysterious subject, representing primæval Scotchmen, rocks, waterfalls, a cataract of bulls, and other strange things, looks like a picture painted in a dream. Near it hangs Mr. Mackenzie's view of Saint Denis's Cathedral, that is painted with great carefulness, and is very true to nature. And having examined this, and Mr. Varley's fine gloomy sketches, you shall be no longer detained at this place, but walk on to see what more remains to be seen.

Of the New Water-Colour Society, I think it may be asserted that their gallery contains neither such good nor such bad drawing as may be seen in the senior exhibition ; unless, indeed, we except Mr. Haghe, a gentleman who in architectural subjects has a marvellous skill, and whose work deserves to be studied by all persons who follow the trade of water-colouring. This gentleman appears to have a profound knowledge (or an extraordinary instinct) of his profession as an architectural draughtsman. There are no tricks, no clumsy plastering of white, no painful niggling, nor swaggering affectation of boldness. He seems to understand every single tone and line which he lays down ; and his picture, in my humble judgment, contains some of the very best qualities of which this branch of painting is capable. You cannot produce by any combination of water-colours such effects as may be had from oil, such richness and depth of tone, such pleasing variety of texture, as gums and varnishes will give ; but, on the other hand, there are many beauties peculiar to the art, which the oil-painter cannot arrive at,—such as air, brightness, coolness, and flatness of surface ; points which painters understand and can speak of a great deal better than amateur writers and readers. Why will the practitioners, then, be so ambitious? Why strive after effects that are only to be got imperfectly at best, and at the expense of qualities far more valuable and pleasing? There are some aspiring individuals who will strive to play a whole band of music off a guitar, or to perform the broadsword exercise with a rapier,—monstrous attempts, that the moral critic must lift up his voice to reprehend. Valuable instruments are guitars and small-swords in themselves, the one for making pleasant small music, the other for drilling small holes in the human person ; but

t the professor of each art do his agreeable duty in his own line,
or strive with his unequal weapons to compete with persons who
ave greater advantages. Indeed, I have seldom seen the works of
skilful water-colour painter of figures, without regretting that he
ad not taken to oil, which would allow him to put forth all the
igour of which he was capable. For works, however, like that of
Ir. Haghe, which are not finished pictures, but admirable finished
ketches, water is best; and we wish that his brethren followed his
anner of using it. Take warning by these remarks, O Mr. Absolon!
our interiors have been regarded by Titmarsh with much pleasure,
nd deserve at his hands a great deal of commendation. Mr.
.bsolon, we take it, has been brought up in a French school—there
re many traces of foreign manner in him; his figures, for instance,
re better costumed than those of our common English artists.
ook at the little sketch which goes by the laconic title of "Jump."
et Mrs. Seyffarth come and look at it before she paints Sir Roger
c Coverley's figure again, and she will see what an air of life and
uthenticity the designer has thrown into his work. Several larger
ieces by Mr. Absolon, in which are a face—is it the artist's own,
y any chance?—(We fancy that we have a knack at guessing a
ortrait of an artist by himself, having designed about five thousand
ich in our own experience,—"Portrait of a Painter," "A Gentle-
an in a Vandyke Dress," "A Brigand," "A Turkish Costume,"
nd so on: they are somehow always rejected by those cursed
cademicians)—but to return to Absolon, whom we have left hang-
g up all this time on the branch of a sentence, he has taken
ugely to the body-colour system within the last twelve months,
nd small good has it done him. The accessories of his pictures
re painted with much vigour and feeling of colour, are a great deal
ronger than heretofore—a great deal too strong for the figures
emselves; and the figures being painted chiefly in transparent
lour, will not bear the atmosphere of distemper by which they
e surrounded. The picture of "The Bachelor" is excellent in
oint of effect and justness of colour.

Mr. Corbould is a gentleman who must be mentioned with a
eat deal of praise. His large drawing of the "Canterbury
ilgrims at the Tabard" is very gay and sparkling; and the artist
ows that he possesses a genuine antiquarian or Walter-Scottish
irit. It is a pity that his people are all so uncommon handsome.
is a pity that his ladies wear such uncommonly low dresses—
ey did not wear such (according to the best authorities) in
haucer's time; and even if they did, Mr. Corbould had much
tter give them a little more cloth, which costs nothing, and would
are much painful blushing to modest men like—never mind whom.

But this is a moral truth : nothing is so easy to see in a painter
a certain inclination towards naughtiness, which we press-Josep
are bound to cry fie at. Cover them up, Mr. Corbould—muslin
the word ; but of this no more. Where the painter departs fro
his line of beauty, his faces have considerable humour and charact
The whole of the pilgrim group, as he has depicted it, is exceeding
picturesque. It might be painted with a little more strength, a
a good deal less finical trifling with the pencil ; but of these man
errors the painter will no doubt get the better as his practice a
experience increase.

Here is a large and interesting picture by Mr. Warren, of t
Pasha of Egypt in the middle of the Nubian desert, surrounded
pipe-bearers and camels, and taking his cup of coffee. There
much character both in the figures and scenery. A slight sket
by the same artist, " The King in Thule," is very pretty, and wou
make a very good picture.

Mr. Bright is an artist of whom we do not before remember
have heard. His pictures are chiefly effects of sunset and moonligh
of too *criarde* a colour as regards sun and moon, but pretty a
skilful in other points, and of a style that strikes us as almost ne
The manner of a French artist, Monsieur Collignon, somewl
resembles that of Mr. Bright. The cool parts of his pictures a
excellent ; but he has dangerous dealings with gamboge and oran
pigments with the use of which a painter is bound to be uncommoi
cautious. Look at Mr. Turner, who has taken to them until th
have driven him quite wild. If there be any Emperor of t
Painters, he should issue " a special edict " against the gambo
dealers :—'tis a deleterious drug. " Hasten, hasten," Mr. Brigl
" obey with trembling," and have a care of gamboge henceforth.

For the rest of the artists at this place, it may be said tl
Mr. Hicks has not been quite so active this year as formerly ; N
Boys has some delightful drawings in his style of art ; and for t
curious there is, moreover, a second-hand Cattermole, a sham Pro
a pseudo-Bentley, and a small double of Cox, whose works are
be seen in various parts of the room. Miss Corbould has a pret
picture. Mr. Duncan's drawings exhibit considerable skill a
fidelity to nature. And here we must close our list of the junio
whose exhibition is very well worth the shilling which all must p
who would enter their pretty gallery.

We have been through a number of picture galleries, and can
do better than go and visit a gentleman who has a gallery of
own, containing only one picture. We mean Mr. Danby, with
" Deluge," now visible in Piccadilly. Every person in London w

no doubt go and see this; artists, because the treatment and effect of the picture are extraordinarily skilful and broad; and the rest of the world, who cannot fail of being deeply moved by the awful tragedy which is here laid before them. The work is full of the strongest dramatic interest; a vast performance, grandly treated, and telling in a wonderful way its solemn awful tale. Mr. Danby has given a curious description of it to our hand; and from this the reader will be able to understand what is the design and treatment of the piece.

[Here follows a long description of the picture.]

The episode of the angel is the sole part of the picture with which we should be disposed to quarrel; but the rest, which has been excellently described in the queer wild words of the artist, is really as grand and magnificent a conception as ever we saw. Why Poussin's famous picture of an inundation has been called "The Deluge," I never could understand: it is only a very small and partial deluge. The artist has genius enough, if any artist ever had, to have executed a work far more vast and tremendous; nor does his picture at the Louvre, nor Turner's Deluge, nor Martin's, nor any that we have ever seen, at all stand a competition with this extraordinary performance of Mr. Danby. He has painted *the* picture of "The Deluge"; we have before our eyes still the ark in the midst of the ruin floating calm and lonely, the great black cataracts of water pouring down, the mad rush of the miserable people clambering up the rocks;—nothing can be finer than the way in which the artist has painted the picture in all its innumerable details, and we hope to hear that his room will be hourly crowded, and his great labour and genius rewarded in some degree.

Let us take some rest after beholding this picture, and what place is cooler and more quiet than the Suffolk Street Gallery? If not remarkable for any pictures of extraordinary merit, it is at least to be praised as a place singularly favourable to meditation. It is a sweet calm solitude, lighted from the top with convenient blinds to keep out the sun. If you have an assignation, bid your mistress to come hither, there is only a dumb secretary in the room; and sitting, like the man in the "Arabian Nights," perpetually before a great book, in which he pores. This would be a grand place to hatch a conspiracy, to avoid a dun, to write an epic poem. Something ails the place! What is it?—what keeps the people away, and gives the moneytaker in his box a gloomy lonely sinecure? Alas, and alas! not even Mr. Haydon's "Samson Agonistes" is strong enough to pull the people in.

13

And yet this picture is worth going to see. You may here take occasion to observe the truth of Mr. Yorke's astute remark about another celebrated artist, and see how bad a painter is this great *writer* of historical paintings, Mr. Haydon. There is an account in some of the late papers—from America, of course—of a remarkably fat boy, three years old, five feet six high, with a fine bass voice, and a handsome beard and whiskers. Much such a hero is this Samson—a great red chubby-cheeked monster, looking at you with the most earnest, mild, dull eyes in the world, and twisting about a brace of ropes, as he comes sprawling for-wards. Sprawling backwards is a Delilah—such a Delilah, with such an arm, with such a dress, on such a sofa, with such a set of ruffians behind her! The picture is perfectly amazing! Is this the author of the "Judgment of Solomon"?—the restorer or setter up of the great style of painting in this country? The drawing of the figures is not only faulty, but bad and careless as can be. It never was nor could be in nature; and, such as it is, the drawing is executed in a manner so loose and slovenly, that one wonders to behold it. Is this the way in which a *chef d'école* condescends to send forth a picture to the public? Would he have his scholars finish no more and draw no better? Look at a picture of "Milton and his Daughters," the same subject which Sir A. Callcott has treated in the Academy, which painters will insist upon treating, so profoundly interesting does it seem to be. Mr. Haydon's "Milton" is playing on the organ, and turning his blind eyes towards the public with an expression that is absolutely laughable. A buxom wench in huge gigot sleeves stands behind the chair, another is at a table writing. The draperies of the ladies are mere smears of colour; in the foreground lies a black cat or dog, a smudge of lamp-black, in which the painter has not condescended to draw a figure. The chair of the poetical organ-player is a similar lump of red and brown; nor is the conception of the picture, to our thinking, one whit better than the execution. If this be the true style of art, there is another great work of the kind at the "Saracen's Head," Snow Hill, which had better be purchased for the National Gallery.

Mr. Hurlstone has, as usual, chosen this retired spot to exhibit a very great number of pictures. There is much good in almost all of these. The children especially are painted with great truth and sweetness of expression, but we never shall be able to reconcile ourselves to the extraordinary dirtiness of the colour. Here are ladies' dresses which look as if they had served for May-day, and arms and shoulders such as might have belonged to Cinderella. Once in a way the artist shows he can paint a clean face, such an

one is that of a child in the little room ; it is charming, if the
artist did but know it, how much more charming for being clean !
A very good picture of a subject somewhat similar to those which
Mr. Hurlstone loves to paint is Mr. Buckner's "Peasants of Sora
in the Regno di Napoli." The artist has seen the works of Léopold
Robert, and profited evidently by the study of them.

Concerning other artists whose works appear in this gallery,
we should speak favourably of Mr. O'Neill, who has two pretty
pictures ; of a couple of animal pieces, "A Pony and Cows," by
Mr. Sosi ; and of a pretty picture by Mr. Elmore, a vast deal
better than his great Becket performance before alluded to. Mr.
Tomkins has some skilful street scenes; and Mr. Holland, a large,
raw, clever picture of Milan Cathedral. And so farewell to this
quiet spot, and let us take a peep at the British Gallery, where a
whole room is devoted to the exhibition of Mr. Hilton, the late
Academician.

A man's sketches and his pictures should never be exhibited
together ; the sketches invariably kill the pictures ; are far more
vigorous, masterly, and effective. Some of those hanging here,
chiefly subjects from Spencer, are excellent, indeed ; and fine in
drawing, colour, and composition. The decision and spirit of the
sketch disappear continually in the finished piece, as any one may
see in examining the design for "Comus," and the large picture
afterwards, the "Two Amphitrites," and many others. Were the
sketches, however, removed, the beholder would be glad to admit
the great feeling and grace of the pictures, and the kindly poetical
spirit which distinguishes the works of the master. Besides the
Hiltons, the picture-lover has here an opportunity of seeing a fine
Virgin by Julio Romano, and a most noble one by Sebastian del
Piombo, than which I never saw anything more majestically
beautiful. The simpering beauties of some of the Virgins of the
Raphael school, many painters are successful in imitating. See, O
ye painters ! how in Michael Angelo strength and beauty are here
combined, wonderful chastity and grace, humility, and a grandeur
almost divine. The critic must have a care as he talks of these
pictures, however, for his words straightway begin to grow turgid
and pompous ; and, lo ! at the end of his lines, the picture is not a
whit better described than before.

And now having devoted space enough to the discussion of the
merits of these different galleries and painters, I am come to the important part of this paper—viz. to my Essay on the State of the Fine
Arts in this Kingdom, my Proposals for the General Improvement
of Public Taste, and my Plan for the Education of Young Artists.

In the first place, I propose that Government should endow a college for painters, where they may receive the benefits of a good literary education, without which artists will never prosper. I propose that lectures should be read, examinations held, and prizes and exhibitions given to students; that professorships should be instituted, and—and a president or lord rector appointed, with a baronetcy, a house, and a couple of thousands a year. This place, of course, will be offered to Michael Angelo Tit——

Mr. Titmarsh's paper came to us exactly as the reader here sees it. His contribution had been paid for in advance, and we regret exceedingly that the public should be deprived of what seemed to be the most valuable part of it. He has never been heard of since the first day of June. He was seen on that day pacing Waterloo Bridge for two hours; but whether he plunged into the river, or took advantage of the steamboat and went down it only, we cannot state.

Why this article was incomplete, the following document will, perhaps, show. It is the work of the waiter at Morland's Hotel, where the eccentric and unhappy gentleman resided.

STATEMENT BY MRS. BARBARA.

"On the evening of the 30th of May, Anay Domino 1840, Mr. Mike Titmash came into our house in a wonderful state of delarium, drest in a new coat, a new bloo satting hankysher, a new wite at, and polisht jipannd boots, all of which he'd bot sins he went out after dinner; nor did he bring any of his old cloves back with him, though he'd often said, 'Barbara,' says he to me, 'when Mr. Frasier pays me my money, and I git new ones, you shall have these as your requisites:' that was his very words, thof I must confess I don't understand the same.

"He'd had dinner and coughy before he went; and we all cumjectured that he'd been somewhere particklar, for I heer'd him barging with a cabman from Hollywell Street, of which he said the fair was only hatepence; but being ableeged to pay a shilling, he cust and swoar horrybill.

"He came in, ordered some supper, laft and joakt with the gents in the parlor, and shewed them a deal of money, which some of the gentlemen was so good as to purpose to borry of him.

"They talked about literaryture and the fine harts (which is both much used by our gentlemen); and Mr. Mike was very merry. Specially he sung them a song, which he ancored hisself for twenty minutes ; and ordered a bole of our punch, which is chocked against his skor to this very day.

"About twelve o'clock he went to bed, very comfortable and quiet, only he cooldnt stand on his legs very well, and cooldnt speak much, excep, 'Frasier for ever !' 'All of a York !' and some such nonsense, which neither me nor George nor Mrs. Stoaks could understand.

"'What's the matter ?' says Mrs. Stokes. 'Barbara,' says she to me, 'has he taken any thin ?' says she.

"'Law bless you, mum !' says I (I always says, Law bless you), 'as I am a Christen woman, and hope to be married, he's had nothin out of common.'

"'What had he for dinner ?' says she, as if she didn't know.

"'There was biled salmon,' says I, 'and a half-crown lobster in soss (bless us if he left so much as a clor or tisspunful !), boil pork and peace puddn, and a secknd course of beef steak and onions, cole plumpuddn, maccarony, and afterwards cheese and sallat.'

"'I don't mean that,' says she. 'What was his liquors, or bavyrage ?'

"'Two Guineas's stouts ; old madeira, one pint ; port, half a ditto ; four tumlers of niggus ; and three cole brandy and water, and sigars.'

"'He is a good fellow,' says Mrs. Stokes, 'and spends his money freely, that I declare.'

"'I wish he'd ony *pay* it,' says I to Mrs. Stokes, says I 'He's lived in our house any time these fourteen years and never——'

"'Hush your imperence !' says Mrs. Stokes ; 'he's a gentleman, and pays when he pleases. He's not one of your common sort Did he have any tea ?'

"'No,' says I, 'not a drop ; ony coughy and muffns. I told you so—three on 'em ; and growled preciously, too, because there was no more. But I wasn't a going to fetch him any more, he whose money we'd never——'

"'Barbara,' says Mrs. Stokes, 'leave the room—do. You're always a suspecting every gentleman. Well, what did he have at supper ?'

"'You know,' says I, 'pickled salmon—that chap's a reglar devil at salmon—(those were my very words)—cold pork, and cold peace puddn agin ; toasted chease this time ; and such a lot of hale and rum-punch as I never saw—nine glasses of heach, I do believe, as I am an honest woman.'

"'Barbara,' says mistress, 'that's not the question. *Did he mix his liquors*, Barbara ? That's the pint.'

" 'No,' says I, 'Mrs. Stokes; that indeed he didn't.' And so we agread that he couldnt posbly be affected by drink, and that something wunderfle must have hapned to him, to send him to bed so quear like.

" Nex morning I took him his tea in bed (on the 4th flore back, No. 104 was his number); and says he to me, 'Barbara,' says he, ' you find me in sperrits.'

" 'Find you in sperrits! I believe we do,' says I; 'we've found you in 'em these fifteen year. I wish you'd find us in *money*,' says I; and laft, too, for I thought it was a good un.

" 'Pooh!' says he, 'my dear, that's not what I mean. You find me in spirits bycause my exlent publisher, Mr. Frasier, of Regent Street, paid me handsum for a remarkable harticle I wrote in his Magazine. He gives twice as much as the other publishers,' says he; 'though, if he didn't, I'd write for him just the same— rayther more, I'm so fond of him.'

" 'How much has he gave you?' says I; 'because I hope you'll pay us.'

" 'Oh,' says he, after a bit, 'a lot of money. Here, you, you darling,' says he (he did; upon my word, he did), 'go and git me change for a five-pound note.'

" And when he got up and had his brekfast, and been out, he changed another five-pound note; and after lunch, another five-pound note; and when he came in to dine, another five-pound note, to pay the cabman. Well, thought we, he's made of money, and so he seemed : but you shall hear soon how it was that he had all them notes to change.

" After dinner he was a sitten over his punch, when some of our gents came in : and he began to talk and brag to them about his harticle, and what he had for it; and that he was the best cricket * in Europe; and how Mr. Murray had begged to be intro-juiced to him, and was so pleased with him, and he with Murray; and how he'd been asked to write in the *Quartly Review*, and in bless us knows what; and how, in fact, he was going to carry all London by storm.

" 'Have you seen what the *Morning Poast* says of you?' says Frank Flint, one of them hartist chaps as comes to our house.

" 'No,' say he, 'I aint. Barbara, bring some more punch, do you hear? No, I aint; but that's a fashnable paper,' says he, 'and always takes notice of a fashnable chap like me. What *does* it say?' says he.

" Mr. Flint opened his mouth and grinned very wide; and taking the *Morning Poast* out of his pocket (he was a great friend

* Critic, Mrs. Barbara means, an absurd monomania of Mr. Titmarsh.

of Mr. Titmarsh's, and, like a good-naterd friend as he was, had always a kind thing to say or do)—Frank pulls out a *Morning Poast*, I say (which had cost Frank Phippens *) : 'Here it is,' says he ; 'read for youeself ; it will make you quite happy.' And so he began to grin to all the gents like winkin.

"When he red it, Titmarsh's jor dropt all of a sudn : he turned pupple, and bloo, and violate ; and then, with a mighty effut, he swigg off his rum and water, and staggered out of the room.

"He looked so ill when he went upstairs to bed, that Mrs. Stokes insisted upon making him some grool for him to have warm in bed ; but, Lor bless you ! he threw it in my face when I went up, and rord and swor so dredfle, that I rann downstairs quite frightened.

"Nex morning I knockt at his dor at nine—no anser.

"At ten, tried agin—never a word.

"At eleven, twelve, one, two, up we went, with a fresh cup of hot tea every time. His dor was lockt, and not one sillibaly could we git.

"At for we began to think he'd suasided hisself ; and having called in the policemen, bust open the dor.

"And then we beheld a pretty spactycle ! Fancy him in his gor, his throat cut from hear to hear, his white nightgownd all over blood, his beautiful face all pail with hagny !—well, no such thing. Fancy him hanging from the bedpost by one of his pore dear garters !—well, no such thing. Agin, fancy him flung out of the window, and dasht into ten billium peaces on the minionet-potts in the fust floar ; or else a naked, melumcolly corpse, laying on the hairy spikes !—not in the least. He wasn't dead, nor he wasn't the least unwell, nor he wasn't asleep neither—he only wasn't there ; and from that day we have heard nothen about him. He left on his table the following note as follows :—

" '1st June, 1840. Midnight.

" 'MRS. STOKES,—I am attached to you by the most disin terested friendship. I have patronised your house for fourteen years, and it was my intention to have paid you a part of your bill, but the *Morning Post* newspaper has destroyed that blessed hope for ever.

" 'Before you receive this I shall be—*ask not where ;* my mind shudders to think where ! You will carry the papers directed to Regent Street to that address, and perhaps you will receive in return a handsome sum of money ; but if the bud of my youth is

---

* Fivepence, Mrs. Barbara means.

blighted, the promise of a long and happy career suddenly and cruelly cut short, an affectionate family deprived of its support and ornament, say that the *Morning Post* has done this by its savage criticisms upon me, the last this day. Farewell.'

"This is hall he said. From that day to this we have never seen the poor fellow—we have never heerd of him—we have never known anythink about him. Being halarmed, Mrs. Stoks hadvertized him in the papers; but not wishing to vex his family, we called him by another name, and put hour address diffrent too. Hall was of no use; and I can't tell you what a pang I felt in my busum when, on going to get change for the five-pound notes he'd given me at the public-house in Hoxford Street, the lan'lord laft when he saw them; and said, says he, ' Do you know, Mrs. Barbara, that a queer gent came in here with five sovrings one day, has a glass of hale, and haskes me to change his sovrings for a note? which I did. Then in about two hours he came back with five more sovrings, gets another note, and another glass of hale, and so goes on four times in one blessed day! It's my beleaf that he had only five pound, and wanted you to suppose that he was worth twenty, for you've got all his notes, I see!'

"And so the poor fellow had no money with him after all! I do pity him, I do, from my hart; and I do hate that wicked *Morning Post* for so treating such a kind, sweet, good-nater'd gentleman!

(*Signed*) "Barbara.
"Morland's Hotel: 15 *Jewin*, 1840."

This is conclusive. Our departed friend had many faults, but he is gone, and we will not discuss them now. It appears that, on the 1st of June, the *Morning Post* published a criticism upon him, accusing him of ignorance, bad taste, and gross partiality. His gentle and susceptible spirit could not brook the rebuke; he was not angry; he did not retort; but *his heart broke!*

Peace to his ashes! A couple of volumes of his works, we see by our advertisements, are about immediately to appear.

ON MEN AND PICTURES

À PROPOS OF A WALK IN THE LOUVRE

PARIS : *June* 1841.

IN the days of my youth I knew a young fellow that I shall here call Tidbody, and who, born in a provincial town of respectable parents, had been considered by the drawing-master of the place, and, indeed, by the principal tea-parties there, as a great genius in the painting line, and one that was sure to make his fortune.

When he had made portraits of his grandmother, of the house-dog, of the door-knocker, of the church and parson of the place, and had copied, *tant bien que mal*, most of the prints that were to be found in the various houses of the village, Harry Tidbody was voted to be very nearly perfect; and his honest parents laid out their little savings in sending the lad to Rome and Paris.

I saw him in the latter town in the year '32, before an immense easel, perched upon a high stool, and copying with perfect complacency a Correggio in the gallery, which he thought he had imitated to a nicety. No misgivings ever entered into the man's mind that he was making an ass of himself; he never once paused to consider that his copy was as much like the Correggio as my nose is like the Apollo's. But he rose early of mornings, and scrubbed away all day with his macgilps and varnishes; he worked away through cold and through sunshine; when other men were warming their fingers at the stoves, or wisely lounging on the Boulevard, he worked away, and thought he was cultivating art in the purest fashion, and smiled with easy scorn upon those who took the world more easily than he. Tidbody drank water with his meals—if meals those miserable scraps of bread and cheese, or bread and sausage, could be called, which he lined his lean stomach with; and voted those persons godless gluttons who recreated themselves with brandy and beef. He rose up at daybreak, and worked away with bladder and brush; he passed all night at life-academies, designing life-guardsmen with chalk and stump; he never was known to take any other recreation; and in ten years he had

spent as much time over his drawing as another man spends in
thirty. At the end of his second year of academical studies Harry
Tidbody could draw exactly as well as he could eight years after.
He had visited Florence, and Rome, and Venice, in the interval;
but there he was as he had begun, without one single farther idea,
and not an inch nearer the goal at which he aimed.

One day, at the Life-academy in Saint Martin's Lane, I saw
before me the back of a shock head of hair and a pair of ragged
elbows, belonging to a man in a certain pompous attitude which
I thought I recognised; and when the model retired behind his
curtain to take his ten minutes' repose, the man belonging to the
back in question turned round a little, and took out an old snuffy
cotton handkerchief and wiped his forehead and lank cheekbones,
that were moist with the vast mental and bodily exertions of the
night. Harry Tidbody was the man in question. In ten years he
had spent at least three thousand nights in copying the model.
When abroad, perhaps, he had passed the Sunday evenings too in
the same rigorous and dismal pastime. He had piles upon piles
of grey paper at his lodgings, covered with worthless nudities in
black and white chalk.

At the end of the evening we shook hands, and I asked him
how the arts flourished. The poor fellow, with a kind of dismal
humour that formed a part of his character, twirled round upon
the iron heels of his old patched Blucher boots, and showed me
his figure for answer. Such a lean, long, ragged, fantastical-
looking personage, it would be hard to match out of the drawing-
schools.

"Tit, my boy," said he, when he had finished his pirouette,
"you may see that the arts have not fattened me as yet;
and, between ourselves, I make by my profession something
considerably less than a thousand a year. But, mind you, I
am not discouraged; my whole soul is in my calling; I can't do
anything else if I would; and I will be a painter, or die in the
attempt."

Tidbody is not dead, I am happy to say, but has a snug place
in the Excise of eighty pounds a year, and now only exercises the
pencil as an amateur. If his story has been told here at some
length, the ingenious reader may fancy that there is some reason
for it. In the first place, there is so little to say about the present
exhibition at Paris, that your humble servant does not know how
to fill his pages without some digressions; and, secondly, the
Tidbodian episode has a certain moral in it, without which it
never would have been related, and which is good for all artists
to read.

It came to my mind upon examining a picture of sixty feet by forty (indeed, it cannot be much smaller), which takes up a good deal of space in the large room of the Louvre. But of this picture anon. Let us come to the general considerations.

Why the deuce will men make light of that golden gift of mediocrity which for the most part they possess, and strive so absurdly at the sublime? What is it that makes a fortune in this world but energetic mediocrity? What is it that is so respected and prosperous as good, honest, emphatic, blundering dulness, bellowing commonplaces with its great healthy lungs, kicking and struggling with its big feet and fists, and bringing an awe-stricken public down on its knees before it? Think, my good sir, of the people who occupy your attention and the world's. Who are they? Upon your honour and conscience now, are they not persons with thews and sinews like your own, only they use them with somewhat more activity—with a voice like yours, only they shout a little louder—with the average portion of brains, in fact, but working them more? But this kind of disbelief in heroes is very offensive to the world, it must be confessed. There, now, is the *Times* newspaper, which the other day rated your humble servant for publishing an account of one of the great humbugs of modern days, viz. the late funeral of Napoleon—which rated me, I say, and talked in its own grave roaring way about the flippancy and conceit of Titmarsh.

O you thundering old *Times!* Napoleon's funeral was a humbug, and your constant reader said so. The people engaged in it were humbugs, and this your Michael Angelo hinted at. There may be irreverence in this, and the process of humbug-hunting may end rather awkwardly for some people. But, surely, there is no conceit. The shamming of modesty is the most pert conceit of all, the *précieuse* affectation of deference where you don't feel it, the sneaking acquiescence in lies. It is very hard that a man may not tell the truth as he fancies it, without being accused of conceit: but so the world wags. As has already been prettily shown in that before-mentioned little book about Napoleon, that is still to be had of the publishers, there is a ballad in the volume, which, if properly studied, will be alone worth two-and-sixpence to any man.

Well, the funeral of Napoleon was a humbug; and, being so, what was a man to call it? What do we call a rose? Is it disrespectful to the pretty flower to call it by its own innocent name? And, in like manner, are we bound, out of respect for society, to speak of humbug only in a circumlocutory way—to call it something else, as they say some Indian people do their devil—to wrap it up in riddles and charades? Nothing is easier. Take, for instance, the following couple of sonnets on the subject:—

> The glad spring sun shone yesterday, as Mr.
>   M. Titmarsh wandered with his favourite lassie
>   By silver Seine, among the meadows grassy
> —Meadows, like mail-coach guards new clad at Easter.
> Fair was the sight 'twixt Neuilly and Passy;.
> And green the field, and bright the river's glister.
>
> The birds sang salutations to the spring;
>   Already buds and leaves from branches burst:
>   "The surly winter time hath done its worst,"
> Said Michael; "Lo, the bees are on the wing!"
> Then on the ground his lazy limbs did fling.
>   Meanwhile the bees pass'd by him with my *first*.
> My *second* dare I to your notice bring,
>   Or name to delicate ears that animal accurst?

> To all our earthly family of fools
>   *My whole*, resistless despot, gives the law—
>   Humble and great, we kneel to it with awe;
> O'er camp and court, the senate and the schools,
> Our grand invisible Lama sits and rules,
>   By ministers that are its men of straw.
> Sir Robert utters it in place of wit,
>   And straight the Opposition shouts "Hear, hear!"
>   And, oh! but all the Whiggish benches cheer
> When great Lord John retorts it, as is fit.
> In you, my *Press*,* each day throughout the year,
> On vast broad sheets we find its praises writ.
> O wondrous are the columns that you rear,
> And sweet the morning hymns you roar in praise of it!

Sacred word! it is kept out of the dictionaries, as if the great compilers of those publications were afraid to utter it. Well, then,

-----

* The reader can easily accommodate this line to the name of his favourite paper. Thus:—

> "In you, my $\left\{ \begin{array}{l} Times, \\ Post, \end{array} \right\}$ each day throughout the year."

Or:—

> "In you, my $\left\{ \begin{array}{l} Herald, \\ 'Tiser, \end{array} \right\}$ daily through the year."

Or, in France:—

> "In you, my *Galignani's Messengere;*"

a capital paper, because you have there the very cream of all the others. In the last line, for "morning" you can read "evening," or "weekly," as circumstances prompt.

the funeral of Napoleon was a humbug, as Titmarsh wrote; and a still better proof that it was a humbug was this, that nobody bought Titmarsh's book, and of the 10,000 copies made ready by the publisher not above 3000 went off. It was a humbug, and an exploded humbug. Peace be to it! *Parlons d'autres choses;* and let us begin to discourse about the pictures without further shilly-shally.

I must confess, with a great deal of shame, that I love to go to the picture gallery of a Sunday after church, on purpose to see the thousand happy people of the working sort amusing themselves —not very wickedly, as I fancy—on the only day in the week on which they have their freedom. Genteel people, who can amuse themselves every day throughout the year, do not frequent the Louvre on a Sunday. You can't see the pictures well, and are pushed and elbowed by all sorts of low-bred creatures. Yesterday there were at the very least two hundred common soldiers in the place—little vulgar ruffians, with red breeches and three-halfpence a day, examining the pictures in company with fifteen hundred grisettes, two thousand liberated shop-boys, eighteen hundred and forty-one artist-apprentices, half-a-dozen of livery servants, and many scores of fellows with caps, and jackets, and copper-coloured countenances, and gold earrings, and large ugly hands, that are hammering, or weaving, or filing, all the week. *Fi donc!* what a thing it is to have a taste for low company! Every man of decent breeding ought to have been in the Bois de Boulogne, in white kid gloves and on horseback or on hackback at least. How the dandies just now went prancing and curvetting down the Champs Elysées, making their horses jump as they passed the carriages, with their japanned boots glittering in the sunshine!

The fountains were flashing and foaming, as if they too were in their best for Sunday; the trees are covered all over with little twinkling bright green sprouts; numberless exhibitions of Punch and the Fantoccini are going on beneath them; and jugglers and balancers are entertaining the people with their pranks. I met two fellows the other day, one with a barrel-organ, and the other with a beard, a turban, a red jacket, and a pair of dirty, short, spangled, white trousers, who were cursing each other in the purest Saint Giles's English; and if I had had impudence or generosity enough, I should have liked to make up their quarrel over a chopine of Strasburg beer, and hear the histories of either. Think of these fellows quitting our beloved country, and their homes in some calm nook of Field Lane or Seven Dials, and toiling over to France with their music and their juggling-traps, to balance cart-wheels and swallow knives for the amusement of our natural enemies! They are very likely at work at this minute, with grinning *bonnes* and conscripts staring at their skill. It is pleasant to walk by and see the nurses and the children so uproariously happy. Yonder is one who has got a halfpenny to give to the beggar at the crossing; several are riding gravely in little carriages drawn by goats. Ah, truly, the sunshine is a fine thing; and one loves to see the little people and the poor basking in it, as well as the great in their fine carriages, or their prancing cock-tailed horses.

In the midst of sights of this kind, you pass on a fine Sunday afternoon down the Elysian Fields and the Tuileries, until you reach the before-mentioned low-bred crowd rushing into the Louvre.

Well, then, the pictures of this exhibition are to be numbered by thousands, and these thousands contain the ordinary number of *chefs-d'œuvre;* that is to say, there may be a couple of works of genius, half-a-dozen very clever performances, a hundred or so of good ones, fifteen hundred very decent, good, or bad pictures, and the remainder atrocious. What a comfort it is, as I have often thought, that they are not all masterpieces, and that there is a good stock of mediocrity in this world, and that we only light upon genius now and then, at rare angel intervals, handed round like tokay at dessert, in a few houses, and in very small quantities only! Fancy how sick one would grow of it, if one had no other drink.

Now, in this exhibition there are, of course, a certain number of persons who make believe that they are handing you round tokay—giving you the real imperial stuff, with the seal of genius stamped on the cork. There are numbers of ambitious pictures, in other words, chiefly upon sacred subjects, and in what is called a severe style of art.

The severe style of art consists in drawing your figures in the first place very big and very neat, in which there is no harm; and in dressing them chiefly in stiff, crisp, old-fashioned draperies, such as one sees in the illuminated missals and the old masters. The old masters, no doubt, copied the habits of the people about them; and it has always appeared as absurd to me to imitate these antique costumes, and to dress up saints and virgins after the fashion of the fifteenth century, as it would be to adorn them with hoops and red heels such as our grandmothers wore; and to make a Magdalen, for instance, taking off her patches, or an angel in powder and a hoop.

It is, or used to be, the custom at the theatres for the grave-digger in "Hamlet" always to wear fifteen or sixteen waistcoats, of which he leisurely divested himself, the audience roaring at each change of raiment. Do the Denmark gravediggers always wear ifteen waistcoats? Let anybody answer who has visited the country. But the probability is that the custom on the stage is a very ancient one, and that the public would not be satisfied at a departure from the legend. As in the matters of gravediggers, so it is with angels: they have—and Heaven knows why—a regular costume, which every "serious" painter follows; and which has a great deal more to do with serious art than people at first may imagine. They have large white wings, that fill up a quarter of the picture in which they have the good fortune to be; they have white gowns that fall round their feet in pretty fantastical draperies; they have fillets round their brows, and their hair combed and neatly pomatumed down the middle; and if they have not a sword, have an elegant portable harp of a certain angelic shape. Large rims of gold leaf they have round their heads always,—a pretty business it would be if such adjuncts were to be left out.

Now, suppose the legend ordered that every gravedigger should be represented with a gold-leaf halo round his head, and every angel with fifteen waistcoats, artists would have followed serious art just as they do now most probably, and looked with scorn at the miserable creature who ventured to scoff at the waistcoats. Ten to one but a certain newspaper would have called a man flippant who did not respect the waistcoats—would have said that he was irreverent for not worshipping the waistcoats.* But why talk of it? The fact is I have rather a desire to set up for a martyr, like my neighbours in the literary trade: it is not a little comforting to undergo such persecutions courageously. "O Socrate! je boirai la ciguë avec toi!" as David said to Robespierre. You too were accused of blasphemy in your time; and the world has been treating us poor literary gents in the same way ever since. There, now, is Bulw——

But to return to the painters. In the matter of canvas covering the French artists are a great deal more audacious than ours; and I have known a man starve all the winter through, without fire and without beef, in order that he might have the honour of filling five-and-twenty feet square of canvas with some favourite subject of his.

It is curious to look through the collection, and see how for the most part the men draw their ideas. There are caricatures of the late and early style of Raphael; there are caricatures of Masaccio; there is a picture painted in the very pyramidical form,

* Last year, when our friend published some article in this Magazine [*Fraser's Magazine*], he seemed to be agitated almost to madness by a criticism, and a very just one too, which appeared in the *Morning Post*. At present he is similarly affected by some strictures on a defunct work of his.

and in the manner of Andrea del Sarto ; there is a Holy Family
the exact counterpart of Leonardo da Vinci ; and, finally, there is
Achille Deveria—it is no use to give the names and numbers of
the other artists, who are not known in England—there is Achille
Deveria, who, having nothing else to caricature, has caricatured a
painted window, and designed a Charity, of which all the outlines
are half an inch thick.

Then there are numberless caricatures in colour as in form.
There is a Violet Entombment—a crimson one, a green one ; a
light emerald and gamboge Eve ; all huge pictures, with talent
enough in their composition, but remarkable for this strange mad
love of extravagance, which belongs to the nation. Titian and the
Venetians have loved to paint lurid skies and sunsets of purple and
gold : here, in consequence, is a piebald picture of crimson and
yellow, laid on in streaks from the top to the bottom.

Who has not heard a great, comfortable, big-chested man, with
bands round a sleek double chin, and fat white cushion-squeezers of
hands, and large red whiskers, and a soft roaring voice, the delight
of a congregation, preaching for an hour with all the appearance and
twice the emphasis of piety, and leading audiences captive ? And
who has not seen a humble individual, who is quite confused
to be conducted down the aisle by the big beadle with his silver
staff (the stalwart "drum-major ecclesiastic") ; and when in his
pulpit, saying his say in the simplest manner possible, uttering
what are very likely commonplaces, without a single rhetorical
grace or emphasis ?

The great, comfortable, red-whiskered, roaring cushion-thumper
is most probably the favourite with the public. But there are
some persons who, nevertheless, prefer to listen to the man of timid
mild commonplaces, because the simple words he speaks come from
his heart, and so find a way directly to yours ; where, if perhaps
you can't find belief for them, you still are sure to receive them
with respect and sympathy.

There are many such professors at the easel as well as the
pulpit ; and you see many painters with a great vigour and dexterity,
and no sincerity of heart ; some with little dexterity, but plenty
of sincerity ; some one or two in a million who have both these
qualities, and thus become the great men of their art. I think
there are instances of the two former kinds in this present exhibition
of the Louvre. There are fellows who have covered great swaggering
canvases with all the attitudes and externals of piety ; and some
few whose humble pictures cause no stir, and remain in quiet nooks,
where one finds them, and straightway acknowledges the simple
kindly appeal which they make.

Of such an order is the picture entitled "La Prière," by Monsieur Trimolet. A man and his wife are kneeling at an old-fashioned praying-desk, and the woman clasps a little sickly-looking child in her arms, and all three are praying as earnestly as their simple hearts will let them. The man is a limner, or painter of missals, by trade, as we fancy. One of his works lies upon the praying-desk, and it is evident that he can paint no more that day, for the sun is just set behind the old-fashioned roofs of the houses in the narrow street of the old city where he lives. Indeed, I have had a great deal of pleasure in looking at this little quiet painting, and in the course of half-a-dozen visits that I have paid to it, have become perfectly acquainted with all the circumstances of the life of the honest missal illuminator and his wife, here praying at the end of their day's work in the calm summer evening.

Very likely Monsieur Trimolet has quite a different history for his little personages, and so has everybody else who examines the picture. But what of that? There is the privilege of pictures. A man does not know all that lies in his picture, any more than he understands all the character of his children. Directly one or the other makes its appearance in the world, it has its own private existence, independent of the progenitor. And in respect of works of art, if the same piece inspire one man with joy that fills another with compassion, what are we to say of it, but that it has sundry properties of its own which its author even does not understand? The fact is, pictures "are as they seem to all," as Mr. Alfred Tennyson sings in the first volume of his poems.

Some of this character of holiness and devotion that I fancy I see in Monsieur Trimolet's pictures is likewise observable in a piece by Madame Juillerat, representing Saint Elizabeth, of Hungary, leading a little beggar-boy into her house, where the holy dame of Hungary will, no doubt, make him comfortable with a good plate of victuals. A couple of young ladies follow behind the princess, with demure looks, and garlands in their hair, that hangs straight on their shoulders, as one sees it in the old illuminations. The whole picture has a pleasant, mystic, innocent look ; and one is all the better for regarding it. What a fine instinct or taste it was in the old missal illuminators to be so particular in the painting of the minor parts of their pictures ! the precise manner in which the flowers and leaves, birds and branches, are painted, gives an air of truth and simplicity to the whole performance, and makes nature, as it were, an accomplice and actor in the scene going on. For instance, you may look at a landscape with certain feelings of pleasure ; but if you have pulled a rose, and are smelling it, and if of a sudden a blackbird in a bush hard by begins to sing and chirrup, your feeling of pleasure is very much enhanced most likely; the senses with which you examine the scene become brightened as it were, and the scene itself becomes more agreeable to you. It is not the same place as it was before you smelt the rose, or before the blackbird began to sing. Now, in Madame Juillerat's picture of the Saint of Hungary and the hungry boy, if the flowers on the young ladies' heads had been omitted, or not painted with their pleasing minuteness and circumstantiality, I fancy that the effect of the piece would have been by no means the same. Another artist of the mystical school, Monsieur Servan, has employed the same adjuncts in a similarly successful manner. One of his pictures represents Saint Augustin meditating in a garden; a great cluster of rose-bushes, hollyhocks, and other plants is in the foreground, most accurately delineated; and a fine rich landscape and river stretch behind the saint, round whom the flowers seem to keep up a mysterious waving and whispering that fill one with a sweet, pleasing, indescribable kind of awe—a great perfection in this style of painting.

In Monsieur Aguado's gallery there is an early Raphael (which all the world declares to be a copy, but no matter). This piece only represents two young people walking hand-in-hand in a garden, and looking at you with a kind of "solemn mirth" (the expression of old Sternhold and Hopkins has always struck me as very fine). A meadow is behind them, at the end of which is a cottage, and by which flows a river, environed by certain very prim-looking trees; and that is all. Well; it is impossible for any person who has a sentiment for the art to look at this picture without feeling indescribably moved and pleased by it. It acts upon you—how? How does a beautiful, pious, tender air of Mozart act upon you? What is there in it that should make you happy and gentle, and fill you with all sorts of good thoughts and kindly feelings? I fear that what Doctor Thumpcushion says at church is correct, and that these indulgences are only carnal, and of the earth earthy; but the sensual effort in this case carries one quite away from the earth, and up to something that is very like heaven.

Now the writer of this has already been severely reprehended for saying that Raphael at thirty had lost that delightful innocence and purity which rendered the works of Raphael of twenty so divine; and perhaps it may be the critic's fault, and not the painter's (I'm not proud, and will allow that even a magazine critic may be mistaken). Perhaps by the greatest stretch of the perhaps, it may be that Raphael was every whit as divine at thirty as at eighteen; and that the very quaintnesses and imperfections of manner observable in his early works are the reasons why they appear so singularly pleasing to me. At least among painters of the present day, I feel myself more disposed to recognise spiritual beauties in those whose powers of execution are manifestly incomplete, than in artists whose hands are skilful and manner formed. Thus there are scores of large pictures here, hanging in the Louvre, that represent subjects taken from Holy Writ, or from the lives of the saints,—pictures skilfully enough painted and intended to be religious, that have not the slightest effect upon me, no more than Doctor Thumpcushion's loudest and glibbest sermon.

Here is No. 1475, for instance—a "Holy Family," painted in the antique manner, and with all the accessories before spoken of, viz. large flowers, fresh roses, and white stately lilies; curling tendrils of vines forming fantastical canopies for the heads of the sacred personages, and rings of gold-leaf drawn neatly round the same. Here is the Virgin, with long, stiff, prim draperies of blue, red, and white; and old Saint Anne in a sober dress, seated gravely at her side; and Saint Joseph in a becoming attitude; and all very cleverly treated, and pleasing to the eye. But though this picture is twice as well painted as any of those before mentioned, it does not touch my heart in the least; nor do any of the rest of the sacred pieces. Opposite the "Holy Family" is a great "Martyrdom of Polycarp," and the catalogue tells you how the executioners first tried to burn the saint; but the fire went out, and the executioners were knocked down; then the soldier struck the saint with a sword, and so killed him. The legends recount numerous miracles of this sort, which I confess have not any very edifying effect upon me. Saints are clapped into boiling oil, which immediately turns cool; or their heads are chopped off, and their blood turns to milk; and so on. One can't understand why these continual delays and disappointments take place, especially as the martyr is always killed at the end; so that it would be best at once to put him out of his pain. For this reason, possibly, the execution of Saint Polycarp did not properly affect the writer of this notice.

Monsieur Læmlein has a good picture of the "Waking of Adam," so royally described by Milton, a picture full of gladness, vigour, and sunshine. There is a very fine figure of a weeping woman in a picture of the "Death of the Virgin"; and the Virgin falling in Monsieur Steuben's picture of "Our Saviour going to Execution" is very pathetic. The mention of this gentleman brings us to what is called the *bourgeois* style of art, of which he is one of the chief professors. He excels in depicting a certain kind of sentiment, and in the vulgar, which is often too the true, pathetic.

Steuben has painted many scores of Napoleons; and his picture of Napoleon this year brings numbers of admiring people round it. The Emperor is seated on a sofa, reading despatches; and the little King of Rome, in a white muslin frock, with his hair beautifully curled, slumbers on his papa's knee. What a contrast! The conqueror of the world, the stern warrior, the great giver of laws and ruler of nations, he dare not move because the little baby is asleep; and he would not disturb him for all the kingdoms he knows so well how to conquer. This is not art, if you please; but it is pleasant to see fat good-natured mothers and grandmothers clustered round this picture, and looking at it with solemn eyes. The same painter has an Esmeralda dancing and frisking in her nightgown, and playing the tambourine to her goat, capering likewise. This picture is so delightfully bad, the little gipsy has such a killing ogle, that all the world admires it. Monsieur Steuben should send it to London, where it would be sure of a gigantic success.

Monsieur Grenier has a piece much looked at, in the *bourgeois* line. Some rogues of gipsies, or mountebanks, have kidnapped a fine fat child, and are stripping it of its pretty clothes; and poor baby is crying; and the gipsy-woman holding up her finger, and threatening; and the he-mountebank is lying on a bank, smoking his pipe,—the callous monster! Preciously they will ill-treat that dear little darling, if justice do not overtake them,—if, ay, *if*. But, thank Heaven! there in the corner come the police, and they will have that pipe-smoking scoundrel off to the galleys before five minutes are over.

1056. A picture of the galleys. Two galley-slaves are before you, and the piece is called "A Crime and a Fault." The poor "Fault" is sitting on a stone, looking very repentant and unhappy indeed. The great "Crime" stands grinning you in the face, smoking his pipe. The ruffian! That pipe seems to be a great mark of callosity in ruffians. I heard one man whisper to another, as they were looking at these galley-slaves, "*They are portraits*," and very much affected his companion seemed by the information.

Of a similar virtuous interest is 705, by Monsieur Finart, "A Family of African Colonists carried off by Abd-el-Kader." There is the poor male colonist without a single thing on but a rope round his wrists. His silver skin is dabbled with his golden blood, and he looks up to heaven as the Arabs are poking him on with the tips of their horrid spears. Behind him come his flocks and herds, and other members of his family. In front, principal figure, is his angelic wife, in her nightgown, and in the arms of an odious blackamoor on horseback. Poor thing—poor thing! she is kicking, and struggling, and resisting as hard as she possibly can.

485. "The Two Friends." Debay.

"Deux jeunes femmes se donnent le gage le plus sacré d'une amitié sincère, dans un acte de dévoûment et de reconnaissance.

"L'une d'elles, faible, exténuée d'efforts inutilement tentés pour allaiter, découvre son sein tari, cause du dépérissement de son enfant. Sa douleur est comprise par son amie, à qui la santé permet d'ajouter au bonheur de nourrir son propre enfant, celui de rappeler à la vie le fils mourant de sa compagne."

Monsieur Debay's pictures are not bad, as most of the others here mentioned as appertaining to the *bourgeois* class; but, good or bad, I can't but own that I like to see these honest hearty representations, which work upon good simple feeling in a good downright way; and if not works of art, are certainly works that can do a great deal of good, and make honest people happy. Who is the man that despises melodramas? I swear that T. P. Cooke is a benefactor to mankind. Away with him who has no stomach for such kind of entertainments, where vice is always punished, where virtue always meets its reward; where Mrs. James Vining is always sure to be made comfortable somewhere at the end of the third act; and if O. Smith is lying in agonies of death, in red breeches, on the front of the stage, or has just gone off in a flash of fire down one of the traps, I know it is only make-believe on his part, and believe him to be a good kind-hearted fellow, that would not do harm to mortal! So much for pictures of the serious melodramatic sort.

Monsieur Biard, whose picture of the "Slave-trade" made so much noise in London last year—and indeed it is as fine as Hogarth —has this year many comic pieces, and a series representing the present Majesty of France when Duke of Orleans, undergoing various perils by land and by water. There is much good in these pieces; but I mean no disrespect in saying I like the comic ones best. There is one entitled "Une Distraction." A National Guard is amusing himself by catching flies. You can't fail to laugh when you see it. There is "Le Gros Péché," and the biggest of all sins, no less than a drum-major confessing. You can't see the monster's face, which the painter has wisely hidden behind the curtain, as beyond the reach of art; but you see the priest's, and, murder! what a sin it must be that the big tambour has just imparted to him! All the French critics sneer at Biard, as they do at Paul de Kock, for not being artistical enough; but I do not think these gentlemen need mind the sneer; they have the millions with them, as Feargus O'Connor says, and they are good judges, after all.

A great comfort it is to think that there is a reasonable prospect that, for the future, very few more battle-pieces will be painted. They have used up all the victories, and Versailles is almost full. So this year, much to my happiness, only a few yards of warlike canvas are exhibited in place of the furlongs which one was called upon to examine in former exhibitions. One retreat from Moscow is there, and one storming of El Gibbet, or El Arish, or some such place in Africa. In the latter picture, you see a thousand fellows, in loose red pantaloons, rushing up a hill with base heathen Turks on the top, who are firing off guns, carabines, and other pieces of ordnance, at them. All this is very well painted by Monsieur Bollangé, and the rush of red breeches has a queer and pleasing effect. In the Russian piece, you have frozen men and cattle; mothers embracing their offspring; grenadiers scowling at the enemy, and especially one fellow standing on a bank with his bayonet placed in the attitude for receiving the charge, and actually charged by a whole regiment of Cossacks,—a complete pulk, my dear madam, coming on in three lines, with their lances pointed against this undaunted warrior of France. I believe Monsieur Thiers sat for the portrait, or else the editor of the *Courrier Français*,— the two men in this belligerent nation who are the belligerentest. *A propos* of Thiers ; the *Nouvelles à la Main* has a good story of this little sham Napoleon. When the second son of the Duke of Orleans was born (I forget his Royal Highness's title), news was brought to Monsieur Thiers. He was told the Princess was well, and asked the courier who brought the news, "Comment se portait *le Roi de Rome ?*" It may be said, in confidence, that there is not a single word of truth in the story. But what of that ? Are not sham stories as good as real ones ? Ask Monsieur Leullier ; who, in spite of all that has been said and written upon a certain sea-fight, has actually this year come forward with his

1311. "Héroïsme de l'Equipage du Vaisseau le Vengeur, 4 Juin, 1794."

"Après avoir soutenu longtemps un combat acharné contre trois vaisseaux Anglais, le vaisseau le Vengeur avait perdu la moitié de son équipage, le reste était blessé pour la plupart : le second capitaine avait été coupé en deux par un boulet ; le vaisseau était rasé par le feu de l'ennemi, sa mâture abattue, ses flancs criblés par les boulets étaient ouverts de toutes parts : sa cale se remplissait à vu d'œil ; il s'enfonçait dans la mer. Les marins qui restent sur son bord servent la batterie basse jusqu'à ce qu'elle se trouve au niveau de la mer ; quand elle va disparaître, ils s'élancent dans la seconde, où ils répètent la même manœuvre ; celle-ci engloutie, ils montent sur le pont. Un tronçon de mât d'artimon restait encore debout ; leurs pavillons en lambeaux y sont cloués ; puis, réunissant instinctivement leurs volontés en une seule pensée, ils veulent périr avec le navire qui leur a été confié. Tous, combattants, blessés, mourants se raniment : un cri immense s'élève, répété sur toutes les parties du tillac : *Vive la République ! Vive la France ! . . . Le Vengeur* coule . . . les cris continuent ; tous les bras sont dressés au ciel, et ces braves, préférant la mort à la captivité, emportent triomphalement leur pavillon dans ce glorieux tombeau."—*France Maritime.*

I think Mr. Thomas Carlyle is in the occasional habit of calling lies wind-bags. *This* wind-bag, one would have thought, exploded last year ; but no such thing. You *can't* sink it, do what you will ; it always comes bouncing up to the surface again, where it swims and bobs about gaily for the admiration of all. This lie the Frenchman will believe ; all the papers talk gravely about the affair of *Vengeur* as if an established fact : and I heard the matter disposed of by some artists the other day in a very satis-factory manner. One has always the gratification, in all French societies where the matter is discussed, of telling the real story (or if the subject be not discussed, of bringing the conversation round to it, and then telling the real story) ; one has always this gratifica-tion, and a great, wicked, delightful one it is,—you make the whole company uncomfortable at once ; you narrate the history in a calm, good-humoured, dispassionate tone ; and as you proceed, you see the different personages of the audience looking uneasily at one another, and bursting out occasionally with a "Mais cependant ;" but you continue your tale with perfect suavity of manner, and have the satisfaction of knowing that you have stuck a dagger into the heart of every single person using it.

Telling, I say, this story to some artists who were examining Monsieur Leullier's picture, and I trust that many scores of persons besides were listening to the conversation, one of them replied to my assertion, that Captain Renaudin's letters were extant, and that the whole affair was a humbug, in the following way.

"Sir," said he, "the sinking of the *Vengeur* is an *established fact of history.* It is completely proved by the documents of the time ; and as for the letters of Captain Renaudin of which you speak, have we not had an example the other day of some pre-tended letters of Louis Philippe's which were published in a news-paper here ? And what, sir, were those letters ? *Forgeries !* "

Q. E. D. Everybody said sansculotte was right : and I have no doubt that, if all the *Vengeur's* crew could rise from the dead, and that English cox—or boat—swain, who was last *on board the ship*,* of which he and his comrades had possession, and had to swim for his life, could come forward, and swear to the real story, I make no doubt that the Frenchmen would not believe it. Only one I know, my friend Julius, who, ever since the tale has been told to him, has been crying it into all ears and in all societies, and vows he is perfectly hoarse with telling it.

As for Monsieur Leullier's picture, there is really a great deal of good in it. Fellows embracing each other, and holding up hands and eyes to heaven ; and in the distance an English ship, with the crew in *red coats*, firing away on the doomed vessel. Possibly, they are only marines whom we see ; but as I once beheld several English naval officers in a play habited in top-boots, perhaps the legend in France may be, that the navy, like the army, with us, is caparisoned in scarlet. A good subject for another historical picture would be Cambronne, saying, " La Garde meurt, mais ne se rend pas." I have bought a couple of engravings of the *Vengeur* and Cambronne, and shall be glad to make a little historical collection of facts similarly authenticated.

Accursed, I say, be all uniform coats of blue or of red ; all ye epaulets and sabertashes ; all ye guns, shrapnels, and musketoons ; all ye silken banners embroidered with bloody reminiscences of successful fights : down—down to the bottomless pit with you all, and let honest men live and love each other without you ! What business have I, forsooth, to plume myself because the Duke of Wellington beat the French in Spain and elsewhere ; and kindle as I read the tale, and fancy myself of a heroic stock, because my uncle Tom was at the battle of Waterloo, and because we beat Napoleon there ? Who are *we*, in the name of Beelzebub ? Did we ever fight in our lives ? Have we the slightest inclination for fighting and murdering one another ? Why are we to go on hating one another from generation to generation, swelling up our little bosoms with absurd national conceit, strutting and crowing over our neighbours, and longing to be at fisticuffs with them again ? As Aristotle remarks, in war there are always two parties ; and though it often happens that both declare themselves to be victorious, it still is generally the case that one party beats and the other is beaten. The conqueror is thus filled with national pride, and the conquered with national hatred and a desire to do better next time. If he has his revenge and beats his opponent as desired, these agreeable feelings are reversed, and so Pride and Hatred con-

---

* The writer heard of this man from an English captain in the navy, who had him on board his ship.

tinue *in sæcula sæculorum,* and ribands and orders are given away, and great men rise and flourish. "Remember you are Britons!" cries our general ; "there is the enemy, and d—— 'em, give 'em the bayonet!" Hurrah ! helter-skelter, load and fire, cut and thrust, down they go ! "Soldats ! dans ce moment terrible là France vous regarde! Vive l'Empereur ! " shouts Jacques Bonhomme, and his sword is through your ribs in a twinkling. " Children ! " roars Feld-marechal Sauerkraut, "men of Hohenzollernsigmaringen ! remember the eyes of Vaterland are upon you ! " and murder again is the consequence. Tomahee-tereboo leads on the Ashantees with the very same war-cry, and they eat all their prisoners with true patriotic cannibalism.

Thus the great truth is handed down from father to son, that

A Briton,
A Frenchman,
An Ashantee,
A Hohenzollernsigmaringenite, &c.

} is superior to all the world ;

and by this truth the dullards of the respective nations swear, and by it statesmen govern.

Let the reader say for himself, does he not believe himself to be superior to a man of any other country ? We can't help it— in spite of ourselves we do. But if, by changing the name, the fable applies to yourself, why do you laugh ?

Κυιδ ριδης ; μυτατω νωμινε δη τη
Φαβυλα ναρρατυρ,

as a certain poet says (in a quotation that is pretty well known in England, and therefore put down here in a new fashion). Why do you laugh, forsooth ? Why do you *not* laugh ? If donkeys' ears are a matter of laughter, surely we may laugh at them when growing on our own skulls.

Take a couple of instances from "actual life," as the fashion-able novel-puffers say.

A little fat silly woman, who in no country but this would ever have pretensions to beauty, has lately set up a circulating library in our street. She lends the five-franc editions of the English novels, as well as the romances of her own country, and I have had several of the former works of fiction from her store : Bulwer's " Night and Morning," very pleasant kind-hearted reading ; " Peter Priggins," an astonishing work of slang, that ought to be translated if but to give Europe an idea of what a gay young gentleman in England sometimes is ; and other novels—never mind what. But to revert to the fat woman.

She sits all day ogling and simpering behind her little counter ;

and from the slow, prim, precise way in which she lets her silly sentences slip through her mouth, you see at once that she is quite satisfied with them, and expects that every customer should give her an opportunity of uttering a few of them for his benefit. Going there for a book, I always find myself entangled in a quarter of an hour's conversation.

This is carried on in not very bad French on my part; at least I find that when I say something genteel to the library-woman, she is not at a loss to understand me, and we have passed already many minutes in this kind of intercourse. Two days since, returning "Night and Morning" to the library-lady and demanding the romance of "Peter Priggins," she offered me instead "Ida," par Monsieur le Vicomte Darlincourt, which I refused, having already experienced some of his Lordship's works; next she produced "Stella," "Valida," "Eloa," by various French ladies of literary celebrity; but again I declined, declaring respectfully that, however agreeable the society of ladies might be, I found their works a little insipid. The fact is, that after being accustomed to such potent mixtures as the French romancers offer you, the mild compositions of the French romanceresses pall on the palate.*

"Madame," says I, to cut the matter short, "je ne demande qu'un roman Anglais, ' Peter Priggins ': l'avez-vous? oui ou non?"

"Ah!" says the library-woman, "Monsieur ne comprend pas notre langue, c'est dommage."

Now one might, at first sight, fancy the above speech an epigram, and not a bad one, on an Englishman's blundering French grammar and pronunciation; but those who know the library-lady must be aware that she never was guilty of such a thing in her life. It was simply a French bull, resulting from the lady's dulness, and by no means a sarcasm. She uttered the words with a great air of superiority and a prim toss of the head, as much as to say, "How much cleverer I am than you, you silly foreigner! and what a fine thing it is in me to know the finest language in the world!" In this way I have heard donkeys of our two countries address foreigners in broken English or French, as if people who could not understand a language when properly spoken could comprehend it when spoken ill. Why the deuce do people give themselves these impertinent stupid airs of superiority, and pique themselves upon the great cleverness of speaking their own language?

* In our own country, of course, Mrs. Trollope, Miss Mitford, Miss Pardoe, Mrs. Charles Gore, Miss Edgeworth, Miss Ferrier, Miss Stickney, Miss Barrett, Lady Blessington, Miss Smith, Mrs. Austin, Miss Austen, &c., form exceptions to this rule; and glad am I to offer per favour of this note a humble tribute of admiration to those ladies.

Take another instance of this same egregious national conceit. At the English pastrycook's—(you can't readily find a prettier or more graceful woman than Madame Colombin, nor better plum-cake than she sells)—at Madame Colombin's, yesterday, a huge Briton, with sandy whiskers and a double chin, was swallowing patties and cherry-brandy, and all the while making remarks to a friend similarly employed. They were talking about English and French ships.

"Hang me, Higgins," says Sandy-whiskers, "if *I'd* ever go into one of their cursed French ships! I should be afraid of sinking at the very first puff of wind !"

What Higgins replied does not matter. But think what a number of Sandy-whiskerses there are in our nation,—fellows who are proud of this stupid mistrust,—who think it a mark of national spirit to despise French skill, bravery, cookery, seamanship, and what not. Swallow your beef and porter, you great fat-paunched man ; enjoy your language and your country, as you have been bred to do ; but don't fancy yourself, on account of these inheritances of yours, superior to other people of other ways and language. You have luck, perhaps, if you will, in having such a diet and dwelling-place, but no *merit*. . . . And with this little discursive essay upon national prejudices let us come back to the pictures, and finish our walk through the gallery.

In that agreeable branch of the art for which we have I believe no name, but which the French call *genre*, there are at Paris several eminent professors ; and as upon the French stage the costume-pieces are far better produced than with us, so also are French costume-pictures much more accurately and characteristically handled than are such subjects in our own country. You do not see Cimabue and Giotto in the costume of Francis I., as they appeared (depicted by Mr. Simpson, I think) in the Royal Academy Exhibition of last year ; but the artists go to some trouble in collecting their antiquarian stuff, and paint it pretty scrupulously.

Monsieur Jacquard has some pretty small pictures *de genre* · a very good one, indeed, of fat "Monks granting Absolution from Fasting ;" of which the details are finely and accurately painted, a task more easy for a French artist than an English one, for the former's studio (as may be seen by a picture in this exhibition) is generally a magnificent curiosity shop ; and for old carvings, screens, crockery, armour, draperies, &c., the painter here has but to look to his own walls and copy away at his ease. Accordingly Jacquard's monks, especially all the properties of the picture, are admirable.

Monsieur Baron has "The Youth of Ribera," a merry Spanish

beggar-boy, among a crowd of his like, drawing sketches of them under a garden wall. The figures are very prettily thought and grouped; there is a fine terrace, and palace, and statues in the background, very rich and luxurious; perhaps too pretty and gay in colours, and too strong in details.

But the king of the painters of small history subjects is Monsieur Robert Fleury; a great artist indeed, and I trust heartily he may be induced to send one or two of his pieces to London, to show our people what he can do. His mind, judging from his works, is rather of a gloomy turn; and he deals somewhat too much, to my taste, in the horrible. He has this year "A Scene in the Inquisition." A man is howling and writhing with his feet over a fire; grim inquisitors are watching over him; and a dreadful executioner, with fierce eyes peering from under a mysterious capuchin, is doggedly sitting over the coals. The picture is down right horror, but admirably and honestly drawn; and in effect rich sombre, and simple.

"Benvenuto Cellini" is better still; and the critics have lauded the piece as giving a good idea of the fierce fantastic Florentine sculptor; but I think Monsieur Fleury has taken him in too grim a mood, and made his ferocity too downright. There was always a dash of the ridiculous in the man, even in his most truculent moments; and I fancy that such simple rage as is here represented scarcely characterises him. The fellow never cut a throat without some sense of humour, and here we have him greatly too majestic to my taste.

"Old Michael Angelo watching over the Sick-bed of his servant Urbino" is a noble painting; as fine in feeling as in design and colour. One can't but admire in all these the *manliness* of the artist. The picture is painted in a large, rich, massive, vigorous manner; and it is gratifying to see that this great man, after resolute seeking for many years, has found the full use of his hand at last, and can express himself as he would. The picture is fit to hang in the very best gallery in the world; and a century hence will no doubt be worth five times as many crowns as the artist asks or has had for it.

Being on the subject of great pictures, let us here mention,

712. "Portrait of a Lady," by Hippolyte Flandrin.

Of this portrait all I can say is, that if you take the best portraits by the best masters—a head of Sebastian or Michael Angelo, a head of Raphael, or one of those rarer ones of Andrea del Sarto—not one of them, for lofty character and majestic nobleness and simplicity, can surpass this magnificent work.

This seems, doubtless, very exaggerated praise, and people reading it may possibly sneer at the critic who ventures to speak in
such a way. To all such I say, Come and see it. You who admire
Sir Thomas and the "Books of Beauty" will possibly not admire
it; you who give ten thousand guineas for a blowsy Murillo will
possibly not relish Monsieur Flandrin's manner; but you who love
simplicity and greatness come and see how an old lady, with a
black mantilla and dark eyes, and grey hair and a few red flowers
in her cap, has been painted by Monsieur Flandrin of Lyons. If
I were Louis Philippe, I would send a legion-of-honour cross, of the
biggest sort, to decorate the bosom of the painter who has executed
this noble piece.

As for portraits (with the exception of this one, which no man
in England can equal, not even Mr. Samuel Lawrence, who is trying to get to this point, but has not reached it yet) our English
painters keep the lead still, nor is there much remarkable among
the hundreds in the gallery. There are vast numbers of English
faces staring at you from the canvases; and among the miniatures
especially one can't help laughing at the continual recurrence of the
healthy, vacant, simpering, aristocratic English type. There are
black velvets and satins, ladies with birds of paradise, deputies
on sofas, and generals and marshals in the midst of smoke and
cannon-balls. Nothing can be less to my taste than a pot-bellied
swaggering Marshal Soult, who rests his bâton on his stomach, and
looks at you in the midst of a dim cloud of war. The Duchess
de Nemours is done by Monsieur Winterhalter, and has a place of
honour, as becomes a good portrait; and, above all, such a pretty
lady. She is a pretty, smiling, buxom blonde, with plenty of hair,
and rather too much hands, not to speak disrespectfully; and a
slice of lace which goes across the middle of her white satin gown
seems to cut the picture very disagreeably in two. There is a
beautiful head in a large portrait of a lad of eighteen, painted by
himself; and here may be mentioned two single figures in pastel
by an architect, remarkable for earnest *spirituel* beauty; likewise
two heads in chalk by De Rudder; most charming sketches, full of
delicacy, grace, and truth.

The only one of the acknowledged great who has exhibited this
year is Monsieur Delacroix, who has a large picture relative to the
siege of Constantinople, that looks very like a piece of crumpled
tapestry, but that has nevertheless its admirers and its merits, as
what work of his has not?

His two smaller pieces are charming. "A Jewish Wedding at
Tangiers" is brilliant with light and merriment; a particular sort
of merriment, that is, that makes you gloomy in the very midst of

2 F

the heyday: and his "Boat" is awful. A score of shipwrecked men are in this boat, on a great, wide, swollen, interminable sea— no hope, no speck of sail—and they are drawing lots which shall be killed and eaten. A burly seaman, with a red beard, has just put his hand into the hat and is touching his own to the officer. One fellow sits with his hands clasped, and gazing—gazing into the great void before him. By Jupiter, his eyes are unfathomable; he is looking at miles and miles of lead-coloured, bitter, pitiless brine! Indeed one can't bear to look at him long; nor at that poor woman, so sickly and so beautiful, whom they may as well kill at once, or she will save them the trouble of drawing straws and give up to their maws that poor, white, faded, delicate, shrivelled carcass. Ah, what a thing it is to be hungry! Oh, Eugenius Delacroix! how can you manage, with a few paint bladders, and a dirty brush, and a careless hand, to dash down such savage histories as these, and fill people's minds with thoughts so dreadful? Ay, there it is; whenever I go through that part of the gallery where Monsieur Delacroix's picture is, I always turn away now, and look at a fat woman with a parroquet opposite. For what's the use of being uncomfortable.

Another great picture is one of about four inches square—"The Chess-Players," by Monsieur Meissonier—truly an astonishing piece of workmanship. No silly tricks of effect, and abrupt startling shadow and light, but a picture painted with the minuteness and accuracy of a daguerréotype, and as near as possible perfect in its kind. Two men are playing at chess, and the chess-men are no bigger than pin-heads; every one of them an accurate portrait, with all the light, shadow, roundness, character, and colour belonging to it.

Of the landscapes it is very hard indeed to speak, for professors of landscapes almost all execute their art well; but few so well as to strike one with especial attention, or to produce much remark. Constable has been a great friend to the new landscape-school in France, who have laid aside the slimy weak manner formerly in vogue, and perhaps have adopted in its place a method equally reprehensible—that of plastering their pictures excessively. When you wish to represent a piece of old timber, or a crumbling wall, or the ruts and stones in a road, this impasting method is very successful; but here the skies are trowelled on; the light vapouring distances are as thick as plum-pudding, the cool clear shadows are mashed-down masses of sienna and indigo. But it is undeniable that, by these violent means, a certain power is had, and noonday effects of strong sunshine are often dashingly rendered.

How much pleasanter is it to see a little quiet grey waste of David Cox than the very best and smartest of such works ! Some men from Düsseldorf have sent very fine scientific faithful pictures, that are a little heavy, but still you see that they are portraits drawn respectfully from the great, beautiful, various, divine face of Nature.

In the statue-gallery there is nothing worth talking about ; and so let us make an end of the Louvre, and politely wish a good-morning to everybody.

JEROME PATUROT

WITH CONSIDERATIONS ON NOVELS IN GENERAL—IN A LETTER FROM M. A. TITMARSH

PARIS: *July 20th.*

IF I had been his Majesty Louis Philippe, and the caricaturist had made fun of me ever so, I would, for the sake of the country, have put up with the insult—ay, perhaps gone a little farther, and encouraged it. I would be a good king, and give a premium to any fellow who, for a certain number of hours, could make a certain number of my subjects laugh. I would take the Salle des Pas Perdus, and have an exhibition of caricature-cartoons, with a dozen of handsome prizes for the artists who should invent the dozen ugliest likenesses of me. But, wise as the French King proverbially is, he has not attained this degree of wisdom. Let a poor devil but draw the royal face like a pear now, or in the similitude of a *brioche*, and he, his printer, and publisher, are clapped into prison for months, severe fines are imposed upon them, their wives languish in their absence, their children are deprived of their bread, and, pressing round the female author of their days, say sadly, "Maman, où est notre père?"

It ought not to be so. Laughing never did harm to any one yet; or if laughing does harm, and king's majesties suffer from the exhibition of caricatures, let them suffer. Mon Dieu! it is the lesser evil of the two. Majesties are to be had any day; but many a day passes without a good joke. Let us cherish those that come.

Indeed, I am inclined to believe that the opinion commonly held about the *gaieté Française* is no more than a mystification, a vulgar practical joke of the sort which the benevolent mind abhors. For it is a shame to promise us something pleasant, and then disappoint us. Men and children feel in this matter alike. To give a child an egg-shell, under pretence that it is an egg, is a joke; but the child roars in reply, and from such joking the gentle spirit turns away abashed, disgusted.

So about the *gaieté Française.* We are told that it still

exists, and are invited by persons to sit down and make a meal of
it. But it is almost all gone. Somebody has scooped out all the
inside and swallowed it, and left only the shell behind. I declare,
for my part, I know few countries where there is less joking than
in France; it is of a piece with the boasted amenity and politeness
of the Gauls. Really and truly, there is more real and true politeness in Wapping than in the Champs Elysées. People whom the
stranger addresses give him civil answers, and they are leaving off
this in France. Men in Wapping do not jostle ladies off the street,
and this they do in France, where the charcoal-man, drinking at
the corner of the wine-shop, will let a lady's muslin slip into the
gutter rather than step aside an inch to allow her to pass.

In the matter of novels especially, the national jocularity has
certainly passed away. Paul de Kock writes now in such a way
as not to make you laugh, but to make you blush for the intolerable
vulgarity of the man. His last book is so little humorous, that
even the English must give him up—the English, whose island is
said after dinner to be "the home of the world," and who certainly
gave Monsieur Paul a very hearty welcome. In his own country
this prophet has never been much honoured. People sneer at his
simple tricks for exciting laughter, and detect a vulgarity of style
which the foreigner is not so ready to understand. And as one
has seen many a vulgar fellow who dropped his *h*'s, and came from
Hislington, received with respect by foreigners, and esteemed as a
person of fashion, so we are on our side slow in distinguishing the
real and sham foreign gentleman.

Besides Paul de Kock, there is another humorous writer of a
very different sort, and whose works have of late found a considerable popularity among us—Monsieur de Bernard. He was
first discovered by one Michael Angelo Titmarsh, who wrote a
critique on one of his works, and pilfered one of his stories. Mrs.
Gore followed him by "editing" Bernard's novel of "Gerfeuil,"
which was badly translated, and pronounced by the press to be
immoral. It may be so in certain details, but it is not immoral in
tendency. It is full of fine observation and gentle feeling; it has
a gallant sense of the absurd, and is written—rare quality for a
French romance—in a gentlemanlike style.

Few celebrated modern French romance-writers can say as
much for themselves. Monsieur Sue has tried almost always, and,
in "Mathilde," very nearly succeeded, in attaining a tone of *bonne
compagnie*. But his respect for lacqueys, furniture, carpets, titles,
bouquets, and such aristocratic appendages, is too great. He slips
quietly over the carpet, and peers at the silk hangings, and looks
at Lafleur handing about the tea-tray with too much awe for a

13

gentleman. He is in a flutter in the midst of his marquesses and
princes—happy, clever, smiling, but uneasy. As for De Balzac, he
is not fit for the *salon*. In point of gentility, Dumas is about as
genteel as a courier; and Frédéric Soulié as elegant as a *huissier*.

These are hard words. But a hundred years hence (when, of
course, the frequenters of the circulating library will be as eager to
read the works of Soulié, Dumas, and the rest, as now), a hundred
years hence, what a strange opinion the world will have of the
French society of to-day! Did all married people, we may imagine
they will ask, break a certain commandment?—They all do in the
novels. Was French society composed of murderers, of forgers, of
children without parents, of men consequently running the daily
risk of marrying their grandmothers by mistake; of disguised
princes, who lived in the friendship of amiable cut-throats and
spotless prostitutes; who gave up the sceptre for the *savate*, and
the stars and pigtails of the court for the chains and wooden
shoes of the galleys? All these characters are quite common in
French novels, and France in the nineteenth century was the
politest country in the world. What must the rest of the world
have been?

Indeed, in respect to the reading of novels of the present day, I
would be glad to suggest to the lovers of these instructive works
the simple plan of always looking at the end of a romance, to see
what becomes of the personages, before they venture upon the
whole work, and become interested in the characters described in it.
Why interest oneself in a personage who you know must, at the
end of the third volume, die a miserable death? What is the use
of making oneself unhappy needlessly, watching the consumptive
symptoms of Leonora as they manifest themselves, or tracing
Antonio to his inevitable assassination?

Formerly, whenever I came to one of these fatally virtuous
characters in a romance (ladies are very fond of inventing such
suffering angels in their novels, pale, pious, pulmonary, crossed in
love of course; hence I do not care to read ladies' novels, except
those of Mesdames Gore and Trollope)—whenever I came to one
of those predestined creatures, and saw from the complexion of the
story that the personage in question was about to occupy a good
deal of the reader's attention, I always closed the book at once,
and in disgust, for my feelings are much too precious to be agitated
at threepence per volume. Even then it was often too late. One
may have got through half a volume before the ultimate fate of
Miss Trevanion was made clear to one. In that half volume, one
may have grown to be exceedingly interested in Miss Trevanion; and
hence one has all the pangs of parting with her, which were not

worth incurring for the brief pleasure of her acquaintance. *Le jeu ne valait pas la chandelle.* It is well to say, I never loved a young gazelle to glad me with his dark blue eye, but when he came to know me well he was sure to die ; and to add, that I never loved a tree or flower but 'twas the first to fade away. Is it not better, instead of making yourself unhappy, as you inevitably must be, to spare yourself the trouble of this bootless affection ? Do not let us give up our affections rashly to young gazelles, or trees, or flowers ; and confine our tenderness to creatures that are more long-lived.

Therefore, I say, it is much better to look at the end of a novel ; and when I read, " There is a fresh green mound in Brentford churchyard, and a humble stone, on which is inscribed the name of ' Anna Maria ' ; " or " Le jour après on voyait sur les dalles humides de la terrible Morgue le corps virginal et ruisselant de Bathilde ; " or a sentence to that effect, I shut the book at once, declining to agitate my feelings needlessly ; for at that stage I do not care a fig for Anna Maria's consumption or Bathilde's suicide : I have not the honour of their acquaintance, nor will I make it. If you had the gift of prophecy, and people proposed to introduce you to a man who you knew would borrow money of you, or would be inevitably hanged, or would subject you to some other annoyance, would you not decline the proposed introduction ? So with novels. The Book of Fate of the heroes and heroines is to be found at the end of Vol. III. One has but to turn to it to know whether one shall make their acquaintance or not. For my part, I heartily pardon the man who brought Cordelia to life (was it Cibber, or Sternhold and Hopkins ?) I would have the stomach-pump brought for Romeo at the fifth act ; for Mrs. Macbeth I am not in the least sorry ; but, as for the general, I would have him destroy that swaggering Macduff (who always looks as if he had just slipped off a snuff-shop), or, if not, cut him in pieces, disarm him, pink him certainly ; and then I would have Mrs. Macduff and all her little ones come in from the slips, stating that the account of their murder was a shameful fabrication of the newspapers, and that they were all of them perfectly well and hearty. The entirely wicked you may massacre without pity ; and I have always admired the German Red Riding-Hood on this score, which is a thousand times more agreeable than the ferocious English tale, because, when the wolf has gobbled up Red Riding-Hood and her grandmother, in come two foresters, who cut open the wolf, and out step the old lady and the young one quite happy.

So I recommend all people to act with regard to lugubrious novels, and eschew them. I have never read the *Nelly* part of the

"Old Curiosity Shop" more than once; whereas, I have Dick Swiveller and the Marchioness by heart; and, in like manner, with regard to "Oliver Twist," it did very well to frighten one in numbers; but I am not going to look on at Nancy's murder, and to writhe and twist under the Jew's nightmare again. No! no! give me Sam Weller and Mr. Pickwick for a continuance. Which are read most—"The Pirate" and "The Bride of Lammermoor," or "Ivanhoe" and "Quentin Durward"?—The former may be preferred by scowling Frenchmen, who pretend to admire Lord Byron. But, if we get upon the subject of Lord Byron, Heaven knows how far we may go. Let us return to the Frenchmen, and ask pardon for the above digression.

The taste for horrors in France is so general, that one can really get scarcely any novels to read in the country (and so much the better, no doubt, say you; the less of their immoralities any man reads the better); hence (perfectly disregarding the interruption of the reader), when a good, cheerful, clever, kind-hearted, merry, smart, bitter, sparkling romance falls in the way, it is a great mercy; and of such a sort is the "Life of Jerome Paturot." It will give any reader who is familiar with Frenchmen a couple of long summer evenings' laughter, and any person who does not know the country a curious insight into some of the social and political humbugs of the great nation.

Like many an idle honest fellow who is good for nothing else, honest Paturot commences life as a literary man. And here, but that a man must not abuse his own trade, would be a fair opportunity for a tirade on the subject of literary characters—those doomed poor fellows of this world whose pockets Fate has ordained shall be perpetually empty. Pray, all parents and guardians, that your darlings may not be born with literary tastes! If so endowed, make up your minds that they will be idle at school, and useless at college; if they have a profession, they will be sure to neglect it; if they have a fortune, they will be sure to spend it. How much money has all the literature of England in the Three per Cents? That is the question; and any bank-clerk could calculate accurately the advantage of any other calling over that of the pen. Is there any professional penman who has laid by five thousand pounds of his own earnings? Lawyers, doctors, and all other learned persons, save money; tradesmen and warriors save money; the Jew-boy who sells oranges at the coach-door, the burnt-umber Malay who sweeps crossings, save money; there is but Yates in the world who does not seem to know the art of growing rich, and, as a rule, leaves the world with as little coin about him as he had when he entered it.

So, when it is said that honest Paturot begins life by publishing certain volumes of poems, the rest is understood. You are sure he will come to the parish at the end of the third volume; that he will fail in all he undertakes; that he will not be more honest than his neighbours, but more idle and weak; that he will be a thriftless, vain, kind-hearted, irresolute, devil-may-care fellow, whose place is marked in this world; whom bankers sneer at, and tradesmen hold in utter discredit.

Jerome spends his patrimony, then, first, in eating, drinking, and making merry; secondly, in publishing four volumes of poems, four copies of which were sold; and he wondered to this day who bought them: and so, having got to the end of his paternal inheritance, he has to cast about for means of making a livelihood. There is his uncle Paturot, the old hosier, who has sold flannel and cotton nightcaps with credit for this half-century past. " Come and be my heir, and sell flannels, Jerome," says this excellent uncle (alas! it is only in novels that these uncles are found,—living literary characters have no such lucky relationships). But Jerome's soul is above nightcaps. How can you expect a man of genius to be anything but an idiot?

The events of his remarkable history are supposed to take place just after the late glorious Revolution. In the days of his *bombance*, Jerome had formed a connection with one of those interesting young females with whom the romances of Paul de Kock have probably made some readers acquainted,—a connection sanctified by everything except the magistrate and the clergyman,—a marriage to all intents and purposes, the ceremony only being omitted.

The lovely Malvina, the typification of the grisette, as warm an admirer of Paul de Kock as any in the three kingdoms, comes to Jerome's aid, after he has spent his money and pawned his plate, and while (with the energy peculiar to the character of persons who publish poems in four volumes) he sits with his hands in his pockets bemoaning his fate, Malvina has bethought herself of a means of livelihood, and says, " My Jerome, let us turn Saint-Simonians."

So Saint-Simonians they become. For some time, strange as it may seem, Saint-Simonianism was long a flourishing trade in this strange country; and the two new disciples were admitted into the community *chacun selon sa capacité*.

[A long extract from the book relating their experiences among the Saint-Simonians is omitted.]

The funds of the religion, as history has informed us, soon began to fail; and the high-priestess, little relishing the meagre diet on which the society was now forced to subsist, and likewise not at all approving of the extreme devotion which some of the priests manifested for her, quitted the Saint-Simonians, and established herself once more very contentedly in her garret, and resumed her flower-making. As for Paturot, he supported the falling cause as long as strength was left him, and for a while blacked the boots of the fraternity very meekly. But he was put upon a diet of sour grapes, which by no means strengthened his constitution, and at last, by the solicitations of his Malvina, was induced to recant, and come back again into common life.

Now begin new plans of advancement. Malvina makes him the treasurer of the Imperial Morocco Bitumen Company, which ends in the disappearance of the treasury with its manager, the despair and illness of the luckless treasurer. He is thrown on the world yet again, and resumes his literary labours. He becomes editor of that famous journal the *Aspick;* which, in order to gather customers round it, proposes to subscribers a journal and a pair of boots, a journal and a greatcoat, a journal and a leg of mutton, according to the taste of the individual. Then we have him as a dramatic critic, then a writer of romances, then the editor of a Government paper ; and all these numerous adventures of his are told with capital satire and hearty fun. The book is, in fact, a course of French humbug, commercial, legal, literary, political ; and if there be any writer in England who has knowledge and wit sufficient, he would do well to borrow the Frenchman's idea, and give a similar satire in our own country.

The novel in numbers is known with us, but the daily *Feuilleton* has not yet been tried by our newspapers, the proprietors of some of which would, perhaps, do well to consider the matter. Here is Jerome's theory on the subject, offered for the consideration of all falling journals, as a means whereby they may rise once more into estimation :—

"You must recollect, sir, that the newspaper, and, in consequence, the *Feuilleton,* is a family affair. The father and mother read the story first, from their hands it passes to the children, from the children to the servants, from the servants to the house porter, and becomes at once a part of the family. They cannot do without the story, sir, and, in consequence, must have the journal which contains it. Suppose, out of economy, the father stops the journal ; mamma is sulky, the children angry, the whole house is in a rage ; in order to restore peace to his family, the father must take in the newspaper again. It becomes as necessary as their coffee in a morning or as their soup for dinner.

"Well, granting that the *Feuilleton* is a necessity nowadays, what sort of a *Feuilleton* must one write in order to please all these various people?

"My dear sir, nothing easier. After you have written a number or two, you will see that you can write seventy or a hundred at your will. For example, you take a young woman, beautiful, persecuted, and unhappy. You add, of course, a brutal tyrant of a husband or father; you give the lady a perfidious friend, and introduce a lover, the pink of virtue, valour, and manly beauty. What is more simple? You mix up your characters well, and can serve them out hot in a dozen or fourscore numbers as you please.

"And it is the manner of cutting your story into portions to which you must look especially. One portion must be bound to the other, as one of the Siamese twins to his brother, and at the end of each number there must be a mysterious word, or an awful situation, and the hero perpetually the hero before your public. They never tire of the hero, sir, they get acquainted with him, and the more they do so the more they like him, and you may keep up the interest for years. For instance, I will show you a specimen of the interesting in number writing, made by a young man, whom I educated and formed myself, and whose success has been prodigious. It is a story of a mysterious castle.

　　　·　　　　·　　　·　　　·　　　·

"'Ethelgida was undressed for the night. Her attendant had retired, and the maiden was left in her vast chamber alone. She sat before the dressing-glass, revolving the events of the day, and particularly thinking over the strange and mysterious words which Alfred had uttered to her in the shrubbery. Other thoughts succeeded and chased through her agitated brain. The darkness of the apartment filled with tremor the sensitive and romantic soul of the young girl. Dusky old tapestries waved on the wall, against which a huge crucifix of ivory and ebony presented its image of woe and gloom. It seemed to her as if, in the night-silence, groans passed through the chamber, and a noise, as of chains clanking in the distance, jarred on her frightened ear. The tapers flickered, and seemed to burn blue. Ethelgida retired to bed with a shudder, and, drawing the curtains round her, sought to shut out the ghostly scene. But what was the maiden's terror when, from the wall at her bedside, she saw thrust forward a naked hand and arm, the hand was clasping by its clotted hair a living, bloody head! What was that hand!!!!—what was that head!!!!!!

'(*To be continued in our next.*)'"

This delightful passage has been translated for the benefit of literary men in England, who may learn from it a profitable lesson. The terrible and mysterious style has been much neglected with us of late, and if, in the recess of parliament, some of our newspapers are at a loss to fill their double sheets, or inclined to treat for a story in this *genre*, an eminent English hand, with the aid of Dumas, or Frédéric Soulié, might be got to transcribe such a story as would put even Mr. O'Connell's Irish romances out of countenance.

Having gone through all the phases of literary quackery, and succeeded in none, honest Jerome, driven to despair, has nothing for it, at the end of the first volume of his adventures, but to try the last quackery of all, the charcoal-pan and suicide. But in this juncture the providential uncle (by means of Malvina, who is by no means disposed to quit this world, unsatisfactory as it is), the uncle of the cotton nightcap steps in, and saves the unlucky youth, who, cured henceforth of his literary turn, submits to take his place behind the counter, performs all the ceremonies which were necessary for making his union with Malvina perfectly legal, and settles down into the light of common day.

May, one cannot help repeating, may all literary characters, at the end of the first volume of their lives, find such an uncle! but, alas! this is the only improbable part of the book. There is no such blessed resource for the penny-a-liner in distress. All he has to do is to write more lines, and get more pence, and wait for grim Death, who will carry him off in the midst of a penny, and, lo! where is he? You read in the papers that yesterday, at his lodgings in Grub Street, "died Thomas Smith, Esq., the ingenious and delightful author, whose novels have amused us all so much. This eccentric and kind-hearted writer has left a wife and ten children, who, we understand, are totally unprovided for, but we are sure that the country will never allow them to want." Smith is only heard of once or twice again. A publisher discovers a novel left by that lamented and talented author; on which another publisher discovers another novel by the same hand: and "Smith's last work," and "the last work of Smith," serve the bibliopolists' turn for a week, and then are found entirely stupid by the public; and so Smith, and his genius, and his wants, and his works, pass away out of this world for ever. The paragraph in the paper next to that which records Smith's death announces the excitement created by the forthcoming work of the admirable Jones; and so to the end of time. But these considerations are too profoundly melancholic, and we had better pass on to the second tome of Jerome Paturot's existence.

One might fancy that, after Monsieur Paturot had settled down in his nightcap and hosiery shop, he would have calmly enveloped himself in lambswool stockings and yards of flannel, and, so protected, that Fortune would have had no more changes for him. Such, probably, is the existence of an English hosier : but in "the empire of the middle classes" matters are very differently arranged, and the *bonnetier de France peut aspirer à tout.* The defunct Paturot whispered that secret to Jerome before he departed this world, and our honest tradesman begins presently to be touched by ambition, and to push forward towards the attainment of those dignities which the Revolution of July has put in his reach.

The first opportunity for elevation is offered him in the ranks of that cheap defence of nations, the National Guard. He is a warm man, as the saying is ; he is looked up to in his quarter, he is a member of a company ; why should he not be its captain too ? A certain Oscar, painter in ordinary to his Majesty, who paints spinach-coloured landscapes, and has an orange-coloured beard, has become the bosom friend of the race of Paturot, and is the chief agent of the gallant hosier in his attempts at acquiring the captain's epaulettes.

[An extract from the novel relates his election to the National Guard.]

Thus happily elected, the mighty Paturot determines that the eyes of France are on his corps of voltigeurs, and that they shall be the model of all National Guardsmen. He becomes more and more like Napoleon. He pinches the sentinels with whom "he is content" by the ear ; he swears every now and then with much energy ; he invents a costume (it was in the early days when the fancy of the National Guardsman was allowed to luxuriate over his facings and pantaloons at will) ; and in a grand review before Marshal Soban the Paturot company turns out in its splendid new uniform, yellow facings, yellow-striped trousers, brass buckles and gorgets—the most brilliant company ever seen. But, though these clothes were strictly military and unanimously splendid, the wearers had not been bred up in those soldatesque habits which render much inferior men more effective on parade. They failed in some manoeuvre which the old soldier of the Empire ordered them to perform—the front and rear ranks were mingled in hopeless confusion. "Ho, porter !" shouted the old general to the guard of the Carrousel gate, "shut the gates, porter ! these canaries will fly off if you don't."

Undismayed by this little check, and determined, like all noble spirits, to repair it, Captain Paturot now laboured incessantly to bring his company into discipline, and brought them not only to march and to countermarch, but to fire with great precision, until on an un lucky day, the lieutenant, being in advance of his men, a certain voltigeur, who had forgotten to withdraw his ramrod from his gun, discharged the rod into the fleshy part of the lieutenant's back, which accident caused the firing to abate somewhat afterwards.

Ambition, meanwhile, had seized upon the captain's wife, who too was determined to play her part in the world, and had chosen the world of fashion for her sphere of action. A certain Russian Princess, of undoubted grandeur, had taken a great fancy to Madame Paturot, and, under the auspices of that illustrious hyperborean chaperon, she entered into the genteel world.

Among the fashionable public of Paris, we are led by Monsieur Paturot's memoirs to suppose that they mingle virtue with their pleasure, and, so that they can aid in a charitable work, are ready to sacrifice themselves and dance to any extent. It happened that a part of the Borysthenes in the neighbourhood of the Princess Flibustikopfkoi's estate overflowed, and the Parisian public came forward as sympathisers, as they did for suffering Ireland and Prince O'Connell the other day. A great *fête* was resolved on, and Madame de Paturot became one of the ladies patronesses.

And at this *fête* we are presented to a great character, in whom the *habitué* of Paris will perhaps recognise a certain likeness to a certain celebrity of the present day, by name Monsieur Hector Berlioz, the musician and critic.

" The great artist promised his assistance. All the wind instruments in Paris were engaged in advance, and all the brass bands, and all the fiddles possible.

" ' Princess,' said the artist, agitating his locks, ' for your sake I would find the hymn of the creation that has been lost since the days of the deluge.'

" The day of the festival arrived. The artist would allow none but himself to conduct his own *chef-d'œuvre ;* he took his place at a desk five metres above the level of the waves of the orchestra, and around him were placed the most hairy and romantic musicians of the day, who were judged worthy of applauding at the proper place. The artist himself, the utterer of the musical apocalypse, cast his eyes over the assembly, seeking to dominate the multitude by that glance, and also to keep in order a refractory lock of hair which would insist upon interrupting it. I had more than once heard of the plan of this great genius, which consists in set- ting public and private life to music. A thousand extraordinary anecdotes are recorded of the extraordinary power which he possessed for so doing; among others is the story of the circumstance which occurred to him in a tavern. Having a wish for a dish of fricandeau and sorrel, the genius took a flageolet out of his pocket, and modulated a few notes.

' Tum-tiddle-di-tum-tiddle-de,' &c.

The waiter knew at once what was meant, and brought the fricandeau and the sauce required. Genius always overcomes its detractors in this way.

"I am not able to give a description of the wonderful *morceau* of music now performed. With it the festival terminated. The hero of the evening sat alone at his desk, vanquished by his emotions, and half-drowned in a lock of hair, which has previously been described. The music done, the hairy musicians round about rushed towards the maestro with the idea of carrying him in triumph to his coach, and of dragging him home in the same. But he, modestly retiring by a back-door, called for his cloak and his clogs, and walked home, where he wrote a critique for the newspapers of the music which he had composed and directed previously. It is thus that modern genius is made ; it is sufficient for all duties, and can swallow any glory you please."

Whether this little picture is a likeness or not, who shall say ? but it is a good caricature of a race in France, where geniuses *poussent* as they do nowhere else ; where poets are prophets, where romances have revelations. It was but yesterday I was reading in a Paris newspaper some account of the present state of things in Spain. "Battles in Spain are mighty well," says the genius ; "but what does Europe care for them ? *A single word* spoken in France has more influence than a pitched battle in Spain." So stupendous a genius is that of the country !

The nation considers, then, its beer the strongest that ever was brewed in the world ; and so with individuals. This has his artistical, that his musical, that his poetical beer, which frothy liquor is preferred before that of all other taps ; and the musician above has a number of brethren in other callings.

Jerome's high fortunes are yet to come. From being captain of his company he is raised to be lieutenant-colonel of his regiment, and as such has the honour to be invited to the palace of the Tuileries with Madame Paturot. This great event is described in the following eloquent manner :—

[Here follows a description of a ball at the Tuileries.]

If the respected reader, like the writer of this, has never had the honour of figuring at a ball at the Tuileries (at home, of course, we are as regular at Pimlico as Lord Melbourne used to be), here is surely in a couple of pages a description of the affair so accurate, that, after translating it, I for my part feel as if I were quite familiar with the palace of the French king. I can see Louis Philippe grinning endlessly, ceaselessly bobbing his august head up and down. I can see the footmen in red, the *officiers d'ordonnance* in stays, the spindle-shanked young princes frisking round to the sound of the brass bands. The chandeliers, the ambassadors, the flaccid Germans with their finger-rings, the Spaniards looking like gilded old clothesmen ; here and there a deputy lieutenant, of course, and one or two hapless Britons in their national court suits, that make the French mob, as the Briton descends from his carriage, exclaim, " Oh, ce marquis ! " Fancy besides fifteen hundred women, of whom fourteen hundred and fifty are ugly—it is the proportion in France. And how much easier is it to enjoy this Barmecide dance in the description of honest Paturot than to dress at midnight, and pay a guinea for a carriage, and keep out of one's wholesome bed, in order to look at King Louis Philippe smiling ! What a mercy it is not to be a gentleman ! What a blessing it is not to be obliged to drive a cab in white kid gloves, nor to sit behind a great floundering racing-tailed horse of Rotten Row, expecting momentarily that he will jump you into the barouche full of ladies just ahead ! What a mercy it is not to be obliged to wear tight lacquered boots, nor to dress for dinner, nor to go to balls at midnight, nor even to be a member of the House of Commons, nor to be prevented from smoking a cigar if you are so minded ! All which privileges of poverty may Fortune long keep to us ! Men do not know half their luck, that is the fact. If the real truth were known about things, we should have their Graces of Sutherland and Devonshire giving up their incomes to the national debt, and saying to the country, " Give me a mutton chop and a thousand a year ! "

In the fortunes of honest Paturot this wholesome moral is indicated with much philosophic acumen, as those will allow who are inclined from the above specimen of their quality to make themselves acquainted with the further history of his fortunes. Such persons may read how Jerome, having become a colonel of the National Guards, becomes, of course, a member of the Legion of Honour, how he is tempted to aspire to still further dignities, how he becomes a deputy, and how his constituents are served by him ; how, being deputy, he has perhaps an inclination to become minister, but that one fine day he finds that his house cannot meet certain bills which are presented for payment, and so the poor fellow becomes a bankrupt.

He gets a little place, he retires with Malvina into a country town ; she is exceedingly fond of canaries and dominoes, and Jerome cultivates cabbages and pinks with great energy and perfect contentment. He says he is quite happy. Ought he not to be so who has made a thousand readers happy, and perhaps a little wiser ?

I have just heard that "Jerome Paturot" is a political novel : one of the Reviews despatches this masterpiece in a few growling lines, and pronounces it to be a failure. Perhaps it *is* a political novel, perhaps there is a great deal of sound thinking in this careless, familiar, sparkling narrative, and a vast deal of reflection hidden under Jerome's ordinary cotton nightcap ; certainly it is a most witty and entertaining story, and as such is humbly recommended by the undersigned to all lovers of the Pantagruelian philosophy. It is a great thing nowadays to get a funny book which makes you laugh, to read three volumes of satire in which there is not a particle of bad blood, and to add to one's knowledge of the world, too, as one can't help doing by the aid of this keen and good-humoured wit. The author of "Jerome Paturot" is Monsieur Reybaud, understood to be a grave man, dealing in political economy, in Fourierism, and other severe sciences. There is a valuable work by the late Mr. Henry Fielding, the police-magistrate, upon the prevention of thieving in the metropolis, and some political pamphlets of merit by the same author ; but it hath been generally allowed that the history of Mr. THOMAS JONES by the same Mr. Fielding is amongst the most valuable of the scientific works of this author. And in like manner, whatever may be the graver works of Monsieur Reybaud, I heartily trust that he has some more of the Paturot kind in his brain or his portfolio, for the benefit of the lazy, novel-reading, unscientific world.

M. A. TITMARSH.

A BOX OF NOVELS

THE Argument.—Mr. Yorke having despatched to Mr. Titmarsh, in Switzerland, a box of novels (carriage paid), the latter returns to Oliver an essay upon the same, into which he introduces a variety of other interesting discourse. He treats of the severity of critics ; of his resolution to reform in that matter, and of the nature of poets; of Irishmen; of Harry Lorrequer, and that Harry is a sentimental writer ; of Harry's critics ; of Tom Burke ; of Rory O'More ; of the Young Pretender and the Duke of Bordeaux; of Irish Repeal and Repeal songs ; concerning one of which he addresseth to Rory O'More words of tender reproach. He mentioneth other novels found in the box, viz. "The Miser's Son," and "The Burgomaster of Berlin." He bestoweth a parting benediction on Boz.

SOME few—very few years since, dear sir, in our hot youth, when Will the Fourth was king, it was the fashion of many young and ardent geniuses who contributed their share of high spirits to the columns of this Magazine,* to belabour with unmerciful ridicule almost all the writers of this country of England, to sneer at their scholarship, to question their talents, to shout with fierce laughter over their faults historical, poetical, grammatical, and sentimental ; and thence to leave the reader to deduce our (the critic's) own immense superiority in all the points which we questioned in all the world beside. I say *our*, because the undersigned Michael Angelo has handled the tomahawk as well as another, and has a scalp or two drying in his lodge.

Those times, dear Yorke, are past. I found you, on visiting London last year, grown fat (pardon me for saying so)—fat and peaceful. Your children clambered smiling about your knee. You did not disdain to cut bread and butter for them ; and, as you poured out their milk and water at supper, I could not but see that you, too, had imbibed much of that sweet and wholesome milk of human kindness, at which in youth we are ready to sneer as a vapid and unprofitable potion ; but whereof as manhood advances we are

* *Fraser's Magazine.*

daily more apt to recognise the healthful qualities. For of all diets good-humour is the most easy of digestion ; if it does not create that mad boisterous flow of spirits which greater excitement causes, it has yet a mirth of its own, pleasanter, truer, and more lasting than the intoxication of sparkling satire ; above all, one rises the next morning without fever or headache, and without the dim and frightful consciousness of having broken somebody's undeserving bones in a frolic, while under the satirical frenzy. You are grown mild—we are all grown mild. I saw Morgan Rattler going home with a wooden horse for his little son. Men and fathers, we can assault men and fathers no more.

Besides, a truth dawns upon the mature mind, which may thus be put by interrogation Because a critic, deeming A and B to be blockheads for whom utter destruction is requisite, forthwith sets to work to destroy them is it clear that the public are interested in that work of demolition, and that they admire the critic hugely for his pains ? At my present mature age, I am inclined to think that the nation does not much care for this sort of executiveness ; and that it looks upon the press-Mohawks (this is not the least personal) as it did upon the gallant young noblemen who used a few years since to break the heads of policemen, and paint apothecaries' shops pea-green,—with amusement, perhaps, but with anything but respect and liking. And as those young noblemen, recognising the justice of public opinion, have retired to their estates, which they are now occupied peacefully in administering and improving, so have the young earls and marquesses of the court of REGINA of Regent Street calmly subsided into the tillage of the pleasant fields of literature, and the cultivation of the fresh green crops of good-humoured thought. *My* little work on the differential calculus, for instance, is in a most advanced state ; and you will correct me if I break a confidence in saying, that your translation of the first hundred and ninety-six chapters of the Mahabharata will throw some extraordinary light upon a subject most intensely interesting to England, viz. the Sanscrit theosophy.

This introduction, then, will have prepared you for an exceedingly humane and laudatory notice of the packet of works which you were good enough to send me, and which, though they doubtless contain a great deal that the critic would not write (from the extreme delicacy of his taste and the vast range of his learning), also contain, between ourselves, a great deal that the critic *could* not write if he would ever so : and this is a truth which critics are sometimes apt to forget in their judgments of works of fiction. As a rustical boy, hired at twopence per week, may fling stones at the blackbirds and drive them off and possibly hit one or two, yet if he get into the hedge and begin to sing, he will make a wretched business of the music, and Lubin and Colin and the dullest swains of the village will laugh egregiously at his folly ; so the critic employed to assault the poet—— But the rest of the simile is obvious, and will be apprehended at once by a person of your experience.

The fact is, that the blackbirds of letters—the harmless, kind singing creatures who line the hedgesides and chirp and twitter as nature bade them (they can no more help singing, these poets, than a flower can help smelling sweet), have been treated much too ruthlessly by the watch-boys of the press, who have a love for flinging stones at the little innocents, and pretend that it is their duty, and that every wren or sparrow is likely to destroy a whole field of wheat, or to turn out a monstrous bird of prey. Leave we these vain sports and savage pastimes of youth, and turn we to the benevolent philosophy of maturer age.

A characteristic of the Irish writers and people, which has not been at all appreciated by the English, is, I think, that of extreme melancholy. All Irish stories are sad, all humorous Irish songs are sad ; there is never a burst of laughter excited by them but, as I fancy, tears are near at hand ; and from " Castle Rackrent " downwards, every Hibernian tale that I have read is sure to leave a sort of woeful tender impression. Mr. Carleton's books—and he is by far the greatest *genius* who has written of Irish life—are preeminently melancholy. Griffin's best novel, " The Collegians," has the same painful character ; and I have always been surprised, while the universal English critic has been laughing over the stirring stories of " Harry Lorrequer," that he has not recognised the fund of sadness beneath. The most jovial song that I know of in the Irish language is " The Night before Larry was stretched ; " but, along with the joviality, you always carry the impression of the hanging the next morning. " The Groves of Blarney " is the richest nonsense that the world has known since the days of Rabelais ; but is it not very pathetic nonsense ? The folly is uttered with a sad look, and to the most lamentable wailing music : it affects you like the jokes of Lear's fool. An Irish landscape conveys the same impression. You may walk all Ireland through, and hardly see a cheerful one ; and whereas at five miles from the spot where this is published or read in England, you may be sure to light upon some prospect of English nature smiling in plenty, rich in comfort, and delightfully cheerful, however simple and homely, the finest and richest landscape in Ireland always appeared to me to be sad, and the people corresponded with the place. But we in England have adopted our idea of the Irishman, and, like the pig-imitator's audience in the fable (which simile is not to be construed into an opinion on the writer's part that the Irish resemble pigs, but simply that the Saxon is dull of comprehension), we *will* have the sham Irishman in preference to the real one, and will laugh at the poor wag, whatever his mood may be. The romance-writers and dramatists have wronged the Irish cruelly (and so has every Saxon among them, the O'Connellites will say) in misrepresenting them as they have done. What a number of false accounts, for instance, did poor Power give to English playgoers, about Ireland ! He led Cockneys to suppose that all that Irish gaiety was natural and constant; that Paddy was in a perpetual whirl of high spirits and whisky; for ever screeching and whooping mad songs and wild jokes ; a being entirely devoid of artifice and calculation : it is only after an Englishman has seen the country that he learns how false these jokes are ; how sad these high spirits, and how cunning and fitful that exuberant joviality, which we have been made to fancy are the Irishman's everyday state of mind. There is, for example, the famous Sir Lucius O'Trigger of Sheridan, at whose humours we all laugh delightfully. He is the most real character, in all that strange company of profligates and swindlers who people Sheridan's plays, and I think the most profoundly dismal of all. The poor Irish knight's jokes are only on the surface. He is a hypocrite all through the comedy, and his fun no more real than his Irish estate. He makes others laugh, but he does not laugh himself, as Falstaff does, and Sydney Smith, and a few other hearty humorists of the British sort.

So when he reads in the "Opinions of the Press" how the provincial journalists are affected with Mr. Lever's books; how the *Doncaster Argus* declares, "We have literally roared with laughter over the last number of 'Our Mess';" or the *Manx Mercury* vows it has "absolutely burst with cachinnation" over the *facetiæ* of friend Harry Lorrequer ; or the *Bungay Beacon* has been obliged to call in two printer's devils to hold the editorial sides while perusing "Charles O'Malley's" funny stories; let the reader be assured that he has fallen upon critical opinions not worth the having. It is impossible to yell with laughter through thirty-two pages. Laughter, to be worth having, can only come by fits and now and then. The main body of your laughter-inspiring book must be calm ; and if we may be allowed to give an opinion about Lorrequer after all that has been said for and against him, after the characteristics of boundless merriment which the English critic has found in him, and the abuse which the Irish writers have hurled at him for presenting degrading pictures of the national character, it would be to enter a calm protest against both opinions, and say that the author's characteristic is *not* humour, but sentiment,—neither more nor less than sentiment, in spite of all the rollicking and bawling, and the songs of Micky Free, and the horse-racing, and punch-making, and charging, and steeplechasing— the quality of the Lorrequer stories seems to me to be extreme delicacy, sweetness, and kindliness of heart. The *spirits* are for the most part artificial, the *fond* is sadness, as appears to me to be that of most Irish writing and people.

Certain Irish critics will rise up in arms against this dictum, and will fall foul of the author of the paradox and of the subject of these present remarks too. For while we have been almost universal in our praise of Lorrequer in England, no man has been more fiercely buffeted in his own country, Mr. O'Connell himself taking the lead to attack this kindly and gentle writer, and thundering out abuse at him from his *cathedra* in the Corn Exchange. A strange occupation this for a statesman! Fancy Sir Robert Peel taking occasion to bring "Martin Chuzzlewit" before the House of Commons; or the American President rapping "Sam Slick" over the knuckles in the thirty-fourth column of his speech; or Lord Brougham attacking Mr. Albert Smith in the Privy Council!

The great Corn Exchange critic says that Lorrequer has sent abroad an unjust opinion of the Irish character, which he (the Corn Exchange critic) is upholding by words and example. On this signal the Irish Liberal journals fall foul of poor Harry with a ferocity which few can appreciate in this country, where the labours of our Hibernian brethren of the press are little read. But you would fancy from the *Nation* that the man is a stark traitor and incendiary; that he has written a libel against Ireland such as merits cord and fire! O patriotic critic! what Brutus-like sacrifices will the literary man not commit! what a noble professional independence he has! how free from envy he is! how pleased with his neighbour's success! and yet how ready (on public grounds—of course, only on public grounds) to attack his nearest friend and closest acquaintance! Although he knows that the success of one man of letters is the success of all, that with every man who rises a score of others rise too, that to make what has hitherto been a struggling and uncertain calling an assured and respectable one, it is necessary that some should succeed greatly, and that every man who lives by his pen should, therefore, back the efforts and applaud the advancement of his brother; yet the virtues of professional literature are so obstinately republican, that it will acknowledge no honours, help no friend, have all on a level; and so the Irish press is at present martyrising the most successful member of its body. His books appeared; they were very pleasant; Tory and Liberal applauded alike the good-humoured and kindhearted writer, who quarrelled with none, and amused all. But his publishers sold twenty thousand of his books. He was a monster from that moment, a doomed man; if a man can die of articles, Harry Lorrequer ought to have yielded up the ghost long ago.

Lorrequer's military propensities have been objected to strongly by his squeamish Hibernian brethren. I freely confess, for my part, that there is a great deal too much fighting in the Lorrequerian romances for my taste, an endless clashing of sabres, unbounded alarums, "chambers" let off (as in the old Shakspeare stage-directions), the warriors drive one another on and off the stage until the quiet citizen is puzzled by their interminable evolutions, and gets a headache with the smell of the powder. But is Lorrequer the only man in Ireland who is fond of military spectacles? Why do ten thousand people go to the Phaynix Park twice a week? Why does the *Nation* newspaper publish those edifying and Christian war songs? And who is it that prates about the Irish at Waterloo, and the Irish at Fontenoy, and the Irish at Seringa-patam, and the Irish at Timbuctoo? If Mr. O'Connell, like a wise rhetorician, chooses, and very properly, to flatter the national military passion, why should not Harry Lorrequer? There is bad blood, bitter, brutal, unchristian hatred in every line of every single ballad of the *Nation*; there is none in the harmless war-pageants of honest Harry Lorrequer. And as for the Irish brigade, has not Mr. O'Connell bragged more about that than any other author of fiction in or out of his country?

The persons who take exception to numerous hunting and steeplechasing descriptions which abound in these volumes have, perhaps, some reason on their side. Those quiet people who have never leaped across anything wider than a gutter in Pall Mall, or have learned the chivalric art in Mr. Fozard's riding-school, are not apt to be extremely interested in hunting stories, and may find themselves morally thrown out in the midst of a long fox-chase, which gallops through ever so many pages of close type. But these descriptions are not written for such. Go and ask a "fast man" at college what he thinks of them. Go dine at Lord Cardigan's mess-table, and as the black bottle passes round ask the young cornets and captains whether they have read the last number of "Tom Burke," and you will see what the answer will be. At this minute those pink-bound volumes are to be found in every garrison, in every one of the towns, colonies, islands, continents, isthmuses, and promontories, where her Majesty's flag floats; they are the pleasure of country folk, high and low; they are not scientific treatises, certainly, but are they intended as such? They are not, perhaps, taken in by Dissenting clergymen and doctors of divinity (though for my part I have seen, in the hall of a certain college of

Dublin, a score of the latter, in gowns and bands, crowding round Harry Lorrequer and listening to his talk with all their might); but does the author aim especially at instructing their reverences? No. Though this is a favourite method with many critics—viz. to find fault with a book for what it does not give, as thus :— "Lady Smigsmag's new novel is amusing, but lamentably deficient in geological information." "Dr. Swishtail's 'Elucidations of the Digamma' show much sound scholarship, but infer a total absence of humour." And "Mr. Lever's tales are trashy and worthless, for his facts are not borne out by any authority, and he gives us no information upon the political state of Ireland. Oh! our country; our green and beloved, our beautiful and oppressed! accursed be the tongue that should now speak of aught but thy wrong; withered the dastard hand that should strike upon thy desolate harp another string!" &c. &c. &c.

And now, having taken exception to the pugnacious and horse-racious parts of the Lorrequer novels (whereof an admirable parody appeared some months since in *Tait's Magazine*), let us proceed to state further characteristics of Lorrequer. His stories show no art of construction; it is the good old plan of virtue triumphant at the end of the chapter, vice being woefully demolished some few pages previously. As Scott's heroes were, for the most part, canny, gallant, prudent, modest young North Britons, Lorrequer's are gallant young Irishmen, a little more dandified and dashing, per-haps, than such heroes as novelists create on this side of the water; wonderfully like each other in personal qualities and beauty; but, withal, modest and scrupulously pure-minded. And there is no reader of Mr. Lever's tales but must admire the extreme, almost womanlike, delicacy of the author, who, amidst all the wild scenes through which he carries his characters and with all his outbreaks of spirits and fun, never writes a sentence that is not entirely pure. Nor is he singular in this excellent chastity of thought and expres-sion; it is almost a national virtue with the Irish, as any person will acknowledge who has lived any time in their country or society.

The present hero of the Lorrequerian cyclus of romances re-sembles the other young gentlemen whose history they record in his great admiration for the military profession, in the which, after some adventurous half-dozen numbers of civil life, we find him launched. Drums, trumpets, blunderbusses, guns, and thunder form the subject of the whole set, and are emblazoned on the backs of every one of the volumes. The present volume is bound in a rich blood-coloured calico, and has a most truculent and ferocious look. The illustrations, from the hand of the famous Phiz, show to great advantage the merits of that dashing designer. He draws a horse admirably, a landscape beautifully, a female figure with extreme grace and tenderness; but as for his humour, it is stark naught; ay, worse! the humorous faces are bad caricatures, without, as I fancy, the slightest provocation to laughter. If one were to meet these monsters expanded from two inches to six feet, people would be frightened by them, not amused, so cruel are their grimaces and unearthly their ugliness. And a study of the admirable sketches of Raffet and Charlet would have given the designer a better notion of the costume of the soldiery of the Consulate than that which he has adopted. Indeed, one could point out sundry errors in costume which the author himself has committed, were the critic inclined to be severely accurate, and not actuated by that overflowing benevolence which is so delightful to feel.

"Tom Burke of Ours"[*] is so called because he enters the French service at an early age; but his opening adventures occur at the close of the rebellion, before the union of Ireland and England, and before the empire of Napoleon. The opening chapters are the best because they are the most real. The author is more at home in Ireland than in the French camp or capital, the scenes and landscapes he describes there are much more naturally depicted, and the characters to whom he introduces us more striking and lifelike. The novel opens gloomily and picturesquely. Old Burke is dying, alone in his dismal old tumble-down house, somewhere near the famous town of Athlone (who can describe with sufficient desolation the ride from that city to Ballinasloe?). Old Burke is dying, and this is young Tom's description of the appearance of an old house at home.

[A long extract is omitted.]

How Tom Burke further fared—how he escaped the dragoon's sabre and the executioner's rope—how he became the *protégé* of the facetious Bubbleton (a most unnatural character certainly, but who is drawn exactly from a great living model)—how Captain de Meudon, the French cuirassier, took a liking to the lad, and died in a uniform sparkling with crosses (which crosses were not yet invented in France), leaving Tom a sum of money, and a recommendation to the Ecole Polytechnique (where, by the way, students are not admitted with any such recommendations)—how Tom escaped to France, and beheld the great First Consul, and was tried for the infernal machine affair, and was present at the glorious field of Austerlitz, and made war, and blunders, and love—are not all

[*] "Our Mess." Edited by Charles Lever (Harry Lorrequer). Vol. ii. "Tom Burke of Ours," vol. i. Dublin: Curry, jun. & Co. London: Orr. Edinburgh: Fraser & Co. 1844.

these things written in the blood-coloured volume embroidered with blunderbusses aforesaid, and can the reader do better than recreate himself therewith? Indeed, as the critic lays down the lively, sparkling, stirring volume, and thinks of its tens of thousands of readers; and that it is lying in the little huckster's window at Dunleary, and upon the artillery mess-table at Damchun; and that it is, beyond the shadow of a doubt, taken in at Hong-kong, where poor dear Commissioner Lin has gazed, delighted, at the picture of " Peeping Tom "; or that it is to be had at the Library, Cape Town, where the Dutch boors and the Hottentot princes are long-ing for the reading of it—the critic, I say, considering the matter merely in a geographical point of view, finds himself overcome by an amazing and blushing modesty, timidly apologises to the reader for discoursing to him about a book which the universal public peruses, and politely takes his leave of the writer by wishing him all health and prosperity.

By the way, one solemn protest ought to be made regarding the volume. The monster of the latter part is a certain truculent captain (who is very properly done for), and who goes by the name of *Amédée Pichot*. Why this name above all others? Why not Jules Janin, or Alexandre Dumas, or Eugène Sue? Amédée Pichot is a friend to England in a country where friends to England are rare, and worth having. Amédée Pichot is the author of the excellent life of Charles Edward, the friend of Scott, and the editor of the *Revue Britannique*, in which he inserts more translations from *Fraser's Magazine* than from any other periodical produced in this empire. His translations of the works of a certain gentle-man with a remarkably good memory have been quoted by scores of French newspapers; his version of other articles (which, perhaps, modesty forbids the present writer to name) has given the French people a most exalted idea of English lighter literature; he is such a friend to English literature, that he will not review a late work called " Paris and the Parisians," lest France should have a con-temptible opinion of our tourists; it is a sin and a shame that Harry Lorrequer should have slaughtered Amédée Pichot in this wanton and cruel manner.

And now, having said our little say regarding " Tom Burke," we come to the work of an equally famous Irish novelist, the ingenious, the various author of " *£*. S. D.," * latterly called, though we know not for what very good reason, " Treasure Trove." †

* " *£*. S. D. ; or, Accounts of Irish Heirs furnished to the Public monthly." By Samuel Lover. London : Lover, and Groombridge. 1843.

† If the respected critic had read the preface of Mr. Lover's work, he would have perceived that " *£*. S. D." is the general name of a series of works, of

It is true that something concerning a treasure is to be discovered at the latter end of the novel, but "£. S. D.," or D.C.L., or what you will, is quite as good a title as another. It is the rose smells sweet, and not the name of it,—at least I take it is only a publisher who would assert the contrary. For instance, everybody quarrels with the title of "Martin Chuzzlewit," and all that incomprehensible manifesto about the silver spoons and the family plate which followed; but did we read it the less? No. The British public is of that order of gormandisers which would like a cabinet pudding, even though you called it hard-dumpling, and is not to be taken in by titles in the main. "£. S. D." is a good name; may all persons concerned have plenty of it!

The present tale of Mr. Lover's contains more action and incident than are to be found in his former works. It is an historical romance in due form,—a romance of war, and love, and fun, and sentiment, and intrigue, and escape, and rebellion. I have but the dozen first numbers, and the thirteenth of the series is to complete the tale; but the question is, how on earth is it to be finished? It is true the wicked rival has been done for—that circumstances look prosperously enough for the hero—that he has saved the heroine from a proper number of dangers, and made himself agreeable to her father; all this is very well. But the hero's name is *Corkery*. *Bon Dieu!* can the lovely Ellen Lynch of Galway, the admired of a Brady, a Bodkin, a Marshal Saxe, the affianced of a Kirwan (name equally illustrious, as Hardeman's "Galway" relates) —can Ellen Lynch marry a fellow by the name of Corkery? I won't believe it. It is against all the rules of romance. They must both die miserably in No. XIII., or young Ned Corkery must be found to be somebody else's son than his father's, the old grocer of Galway. But this matter has been settled long ere this; and if Ellen and Edward are married and happy (though, indeed, some people are married and unhappy, and some happy and unmarried, for the matter of that), if they have taken the matrimonial line, Ellen, I would lay a wager, is not Mrs. Corkery.*

The novel carries us back to the year 1745, when the respected Mr. Edward Waverley distinguished himself in the service of his late Royal Highness the Pretender, and when men, instead of bandying compliments and congees in Belgrave Square, flying thither

which "Treasure Trove" is only the first. Those who know Ireland must be aware that the title "£. S. D." is singularly applicable to that country, the quantity of specie there being immense—only a good deal of it is yet undiscovered.—O. Y.

* Private to the Editor.—Please to add here in a short note the catastrophe of the novel, which I don't know.

in hack-cabs, with white kid gloves on, and comfortable passports in their pockets, turned out on the hillside sword in hand, and faced Cumberland's thundering dragoons, and saw the backs of Johnny Cope's grenadiers. The contrast between the times is not a bad one, in the warriors of Perth and Falkirk yonder, with tartan and claymore, and the young French dandies, with oiled beards, and huge gold-topped canes, grinning over a *fricandeau* at Véry's! We have seen them, these warriors of the latter days— we have seen Belgrave Square—we have seen the chivalry of France (in cabs) collected round the Royal door, and battling about eightpenny fares at the sacred threshold—we have seen the cads shouting, "This way, my Lord! this way, Mounseer!"—we have seen Gunter's cart driving up with *orgeat* and *limonade* for the faithful warriors of HENRI! He was there—there, in the one-pair front, smiling royally upon them as they came; and there was *eau sucrée* in the dining-room if the stalwart descendants of Du Guesclin were athirst. *O vanitas!* O woeful change of times! The play is played up. Who dies for kings now? If Henri was to say to one of those martyrs in white paletots and lacquered boots, "Seigneur comte, coupez moi cette barbe, que vous paraissez tant chérir," would the count do it? Ah! do not ask! do not let us cut too deep into this dubious fidelity! let us have our opinions, but not speak them too loudly. At any rate, it was better for Mr. Lover to choose 1740 for a romance in place of 1840, which is the sole moral of the above sentence.

The book is written with ability, and inspires great interest. The incidents are almost too many. The scene varies too often. We go from Galway to Hamburg—from Hamburg to Bruges— from Bruges, *viâ* London, to Paris—from Paris to Scotland, and thence to Ireland, with war's alarms ringing in the ear the whole way, and are plunged into sea-fights, and land-fights, and shipwrecks, and chases, and conspiracies, without end. Our first battle is no less than the battle of Fontenoy, and it is described in a lively and a brilliant manner. Voltaire, out of that defeat, has managed to make such a compliment to the English nation, that a thrashing really becomes a pleasure, and Mr. Lover does not neglect a certain little opportunity:—

"'Dillon!' said Marshal Saxe, 'let the whole Irish brigade charge! to you I commend its conduct. Where Dillon's regiment leads the rest will follow. The cavalry has made no impression yet; let the Irish brigade show an example!'

"'It shall be done, Marshal!' said Dillon, touching his hat, and turning his horse.

" 'To victory !' cried Saxe emphatically.

" 'Or Death !' cried Dillon solemnly, kissing the cross of his sword, and plunging the rowels in his horse's side, that swiftly he might do his bidding, and that the Irish brigade might first have the honour of changing the fortune of the day.

" Galloping along the front of their line, where the brigade stood impatient of the order to advance, Dillon gave a word that made every man clench his teeth, firmly plunge his foot deep in the stirrup, and grip his sword for vengeance ; for the word that Dillon gave was talismanic as others that have been memorable ; he shouted, as he rode along, ' *Remember Limerick !*' and then, wheeling round, and placing himself at the head of his own regiment, to whom the honour of leading was given, he gave the word to charge ; and down swept the whole brigade, terrible as a thunderbolt, for the hitherto unbroken column of Cumberland was crushed under the fearful charge, the very earth trembled beneath that horrible rush of horse. Dillon was amongst the first to fall ; he received a mortal wound from the steady and well-directed fire of the English column, and, as he was struck, he knew his presentiment was fulfilled ; but he lived long enough to know also he completed his prophecy of a glorious charge ; plunging his spurs into his fiery horse, he jumped into the forest of bayonets, and, laying about him gallantly, he saw the English column broken, and fell, fighting, amidst a heap of slain. The day was won ; the column could no longer resist ; but, with the indomitable spirit of Englishmen, they still turned their faces to the foe, and retired without confusion ; *they lost the field with honour*, and, in the midst of defeat, it was some satisfaction to know it was the bold islanders of their own seas who carried the victory against them. It was no *foreigner* before whom they yielded. The thought *was* bitter that they themselves had disbanded a strength so mighty ; but they took consolation in a strange land in the thought that it was only their *own right arm* could deal a blow so heavy. Thanks be to God, these unnatural days are past, and the unholy laws that made them so are expunged. In little more than sixty years after, and not fifty miles from that very spot, Irish valour helped to win victory on the side of England ; for, at Waterloo, Erin gave to Albion, not only her fiery columns, but her unconquered chieftain."

That Irish brigade is the deuce, certainly. When once it appears, the consequences are obvious. No mortal can stand against it. Why does not some military Liberal write the history of this redoubtable legion ?

There is something touching in these legends of the prowess of the exile in his banishment, and no doubt it could be shown that where the French did not happen to have the uppermost in their contest with the Saxon, it was because their allies were engaged elsewhere, and not present in the field to ffag an Bealach, as Mr. Lover writes it, to "clear the way"; on which subject he writes a song, which, he says, "at least all Ireland will heartily digest."

"Fāg an Bealach.

" FILL the cup, my brothers,
  To pledge a toast,
Which, beyond all others,
  We prize the most:
As yet 'tis but a notion
  We dare not name;
But soon o'er land or ocean
  'Twill fly with fame!
Then give the game before us
  One view holla,
Hip! hurra! in chorus.
  Fāg an Bealach!

We our hearts can fling, boys,
  O'er this notion,
As the sea-bird's wing, boys,
  Dips the ocean.
'Tis too deep for words, boys,
  The thought we know—
So, like the ocean bird, boys,
  We touch and go:
For dangers deep surrounding,
  Our hopes might swallow;
So through the tempest bounding,
  Fāg an Bealach!

This thought with glory rife, boys,
  Did brooding dwell,
Till time did give it life, boys,
  To break the shell:
'Tis in our hearts yet lying,
  An unfledged thing;
But soon, an eaglet flying,
  'Twill take the wing!
For 'tis no timeling frail, boys—
  No summer swallow—
'Twill live through winter's gale, boys,
  Fāg an Bealach!

Lawyers may indict us
By crooked laws,
Soldiers strive to fright us
From country's cause ;
But we will sustain it
Living—dying—
Point of law or bay'net
Still defying !
Let their parchment rattle—
Drums are hollow,
So is lawyer's prattle—
Fāg an Bealach !

Better early graves, boys,
Dark locks gory,
Than bow the head as slaves, boys,
When they're hoary.
Fight it out we must, boys,
Hit or miss it ;
Better *bite* the dust, boys,
Than to *kiss* it !
For dust to dust at last, boys,
Death *will* swallow—
Hark ! the trumpet's blast, boys,
Fāg an Bealach ! "

Hurra ! clear the course ! Here comes Rory O'More thunder-ing down with his big alpeen ; his blood is up, and woe to the Saxon skull that comes in contact with the terrible fellow's oak-tick. He is in a mortal fury, that's a fact. He talks of dying s easy as of supping buttermilk ; he rattles out rhymes for bayonet ind cartouche-box as if they were his ordinary weapons ; he is a ea-bird, and then an eagle breaking his shell, and previously a untsman—anything for his country ! "Your sowl !" how I see he Saxons flying before Rory and his wild huntsmen, as the other oul animals did before St. Patrick !

It is a good rattling lyric, to be sure. But is it well sung by *ou*, O Samuel Lover ? Are *you*, too, turning rebel, and shouting ut songs of hatred against the Saxon ? You, whose gentle and indly muse never breathed anything but peace and goodwill as et : you whose name did seem to indicate your nature ; the happy iscoverer of the four-leaved shamrock, and of that blessed island where not a tear or aching heart should be found !" Leave the rawling to the politicians and the newspaper ballad-mongers. hey live by it. *You* need not. The lies which they tell, and he foul hatred which they excite, and the fierce lust of blood which hey preach,—leave to them. Don't let poets and men of genius oin in the brutal chorus, and lead on starving savages to murder.

Or do you, after maturely deliberating the matter, mean to say, you think a rebellion a just, feasible, and useful thing for your country—the *only* feasible thing, the inevitable slaughter which it would occasion, excusable on account of the good it would do? " A song," say you, ushering this incendiary lyric into print, " is the spawn of a poet, and, when healthy, a thing of life and feeling that should increase and multiply, and become food for the world." And so, with this conviction of the greatness of your calling, and this knowledge of the fact that every line you write is food for mankind to profit by, you sit down calmly and laboriously in your study in London, and string together rhymes for Faug a Bolla, and reasons for treason ! " All Ireland," forsooth, is " heartily to digest " the song ! A pretty morsel, truly, for all Ireland—a comfortable dinner ! Blood, arsenic, blue-vitriol, Prussic acid, to wash down pikes, cannon-balls, and red-hot shot !

Murder is the meaning of this song, or what is it? Let a Saxon beseech you to hold your hand before you begin this terrible sport. Can you say, on your honour and conscience, and after living in England, that you ever met an Englishman with a heart in his Saxony-cloth surtout that was not touched by the wrongs and miseries of your country ? How are these frantic denunciations of defiance and hatred, these boasts of strength and hints of murder, received in England ? Do the English answer you with a hundredth part of the ferocity with which you appeal to them ? Do they fling back hatred for your hatred ? Do they not forget your anger in regard for your misery, and receive your mad curses and outcries with an almost curious pitying forbearance ? *Now*, at least, the wrong is not on our side, whatever in former days it may have been. And I think a poet shames his great calling, and has no more right to preach this wicked, foolish, worn-out, unchristian doctrine from *his* altar than a priest from his pulpit. No good ever came of it. *This* will never " be food for the world," be sure of that. Loving, honest men and women were never made to live upon such accursed meat. Poets least of all should recommend it, for are they not priests, too, in their way ? do they not occupy a happy neutral ground, apart from the quarrels and hatred of the world,—a ground to which they should make all welcome, and where there should only be kindness and peace ? . . . I see Rory O'More relents. He drops his terrific club of battle ; he will spare the Sassenach this time, and leave him whole bones. Betty, take down the gentleman's stick, and make a fire with it in the kitchen, and we'll have a roaring pot of twankay.

While discussing the feast, in perfect good-humour and benevolence, let us say that the novel of " Treasure Trove " is exceedingly pleasant and lively. It has not been written without care, and a great deal of historical reading. Bating the abominable Faug a Bolla, it contains a number of pleasant, kindly, and sweet lyrics, such as the author has the secret of inventing, and of singing, and of setting to the most beautiful music; and is illustrated by a number of delicate and graceful etchings, far better than any before designed by the author.

Let us give another of his songs, which, albeit of the military sort, has the real, natural, *Lover*-like feeling about it :—

" *The Soldier.*

" 'Twas glorious day, worth a warrior's telling,
　　Two kings had fought, and the fight was done,
When midst the shout of victory swelling,
　　A soldier fell on the field he won.
He thought of kings and of royal quarrels,
　　And thought of glory without a smile ;
For what had he to do with laurels ?
　　He was only one of the rank and file.
But he pulled out his little *cruiskeen*,
　　And drank to his pretty *colleen :*
' Oh ! darling ! ' says he, ' when I die
　　You won't be a widow—for why ?—
Ah ! you never would have me, *vourneen.*'

A raven tress from his bosom taking,
　　That now was stained with his life-stream shed ;
A fervent prayer o'er that ringlet making,
　　He blessings sought on the loved one's head.
And visions fair of his native mountains
　　Arose, enchanting his fading sight ;
Their emerald valleys and crystal fountains
　　Were never shining more green and bright ;
And grasping his little *cruiskeen*,
　　He pledged the dear Island of green ;—
' Though far from thy valleys I die,
　　Dearest isle, to my heart thou art nigh,
As though absent I never had been.'

A tear now fell—for as life was sinking,
　　The pride that guarded his manly eye
Was weaker grown, and his last fond thinking
　　Brought heaven and home, and his true love nigh.
But, with the fire of his gallant nation,
　　He scorn'd surrender without a blow !
He made with death capitulation,
　　And with warlike honours he still would go ;

? H

> For draining his little *cruiskeen*,
> He drank to his cruel *colleen*,
>   To the emerald land of his birth—
>   And lifeless he sank to the earth,
> Brave a soldier as ever was seen !"

Here is the commencement of another lyric :—

> O rémember this life is but dark and brief ;
>   There are sorrows, and tears, and despair for all,
>   And hope and joy are as leaves that fall.
> Then pluck the beauteous and fragrant leaf
> Before the autumn of pain and grief !
>
> There are hopes and smiles with their starry rays,—
>   O press them tenderly to thy heart !
>   They will not return when they once depart !
> Rejoice in the radiant and joyous days
> Though the light, though the glee but a moment stays !"

But these pretty, wild, fantastical lines are not from "Treasure Trove." They come from another volume bound in yellow ; another monthly tale, from another bard who "lisps in numbers," and has produced a story called the "Miser's Son." *

The "Miser's Son" (no relation to the "Miser's Daughter") is evidently the work of a very young hand. It, too, is a stirring story of love and war ; and the Pretender is once more in the field of fiction. The writer aims, too, at sentiment and thoughtfulness, and writes sometimes wisely, sometimes poetically, and often (must it be said ?) bombastically and absurdly. But it is good to find a writer nowadays (whether it be profitable for himself is another question) who takes the trouble to think at all. Reflection is not the ordinary quality of novels, whereof it seems to be the writer's maxim to give the reader and himself no trouble of thinking at all, but rather to lull the mind into a genial doze and forgetfulness. For this wholesome and complete vacuity I would recommend——†

And now we come to the "Burgomaster of Berlin," ‡ from the German of Willebald Alexis, which has been admirably translated by W. A. G. It is a somewhat hard matter to peruse these three great volumes ; above all, the commencement is difficult. The type

---

* "The Miser's Son : a Tale." London : Thompson, James Street, Gray's Inn Lane.

† Here our correspondent's manuscript is quite illegible.

‡ "The Burgomaster of Berlin." From the German of Willebald Alexis. 3 vols. London : Saunders & Otley.

s close ; the German names very outlandish and hard to pronounce ;
he action of the novel rather confused and dilatory. But as soon
is the reader grows accustomed to the names and the style, he will
ind much to interest him in the volumes, and a most curious and
areful picture of German life in the fifteenth century exhibited to
im. German burghers, with their quarrels and carouses ; German
rinces, for whom the author has a very German respect ; German
unkers and knights gallantly robbing on the highway. The
vhole of that strange, wild, forgotten German life of the middle
ges is here resuscitated for him with true German industry,
nd no small share of humour. There are proverbs enough in the
ook to stock a dozen High-Dutch Sanchos with wisdom ; and
ou feel, after reading through the volumes, glad to have perused
hem, and not a little glad that the work is done. It is like
, heavy book of travels ; but it carries the reader into quite
new country, and familiarises him with new images, person-
ges, ideas.

And now there is but one book left in the box, the smallest
ne, but oh ! how much the best of all. It is the work of the
aster of all the English humorists now alive ; the young man who
ame and took his place calmly at the head of the whole tribe, and
vho has kept it. Think of all we owe Mr. Dickens since those half-
ozen years, the store of happy hours that he has made us pass,
he kindly and pleasant companions whom he has introduced to us ;
he harmless laughter, the generous wit, the frank, manly, human
ve which he has taught us to feel ! Every month of those years
as brought us some kind token from this delightful genius. His
ooks may have lost in art, perhaps, but could we afford to wait ?
ince the days when the *Spectator* was produced by a man of
indred mind and temper, what books have appeared that have
ken so affectionate a hold of the English public as these ? They
ive made millions of rich and poor happy ; they might have been
cked up for nine years, doubtless, and pruned here and there and
proved (which I doubt), but where would have been the reader's
enefit all this time, while the author was elaborating his per-
rmance ? Would the communion between the writer and the
ublic have been what it is now—something continual, confidential,
mething like personal affection ? I do not know whether these
ories are written for future ages : many sage critics doubt on this
ad. There are always such conjurers to tell literary fortunes ;
d, to my certain knowledge, Boz, according to them, has been
nking regularly these six years. I doubt about that mysterious
riting for futurity which certain big-wigs prescribe. Snarl has a
ance, certainly. His works, which have not been read in this

age, *may* be read in future ; but the receipt for that sort of writi
has never as yet been clearly ascertained. Shakspeare did n
write for futurity ; he wrote his plays for the same purpose whi
inspires the pen of Alfred Bunn, Esquire, viz. to fill his Theat
Royal. And yet we read Shakspeare now. Le Sage and Fieldi
wrote for their public ; and though the great Doctor Johnson p
his peevish protest against the fame of the latter, and voted hi
" a dull dog, sir,—a low fellow," yet somehow Harry Fielding h
survived in spite of the critic, and Parson Adams is at this minu
as real a character, as much loved by us as the old Doctor himse
What a noble divine power this of genius is, which, passing fro
the poet into his reader's soul, mingles with it, and there engende
as it were, real creatures, which is as strong as history, whi
creates beings that take their place by nature's own. All that ×
know of Don Quixote or Louis XIV. we got to know in the sa
way—out of a book. I declare I love Sir Roger de Coverley qui
as much as Izaak Walton, and have just as clear a consciousne
of the looks, voice, habit, and manner of being of the one as
the other.

And so with regard to this question of futurity ; if any bene
lent being of the present age is imbued with a yearning desire
know what his great-great-grandchild will think of this or th
author—of Mr. Dickens especially, whose claims to fame ha
raised the question—the only way to settle it is by the ordina
historic method. Did not your great-great-grandfather love a
delight in Don Quixote and Sancho Panza ? Have they l
their vitality by their age ? Don't they move laughter and awak
affection now as three hundred years ago ? And so with D
Pickwick and Sancho Weller, if their gentle humours, and kin
wit, and hearty benevolent natures, touch us and convince
as it were, now, why should they not exist for our children
well as for us, and make the twenty-fifth century happy, as th
have the nineteenth ? Let Snarl console himself, then, as to t
future.

As for the " Christmas Carol," * or any other book of a li
nature which the public takes upon itself to criticise, the individ
critic had quite best hold his peace. One remembers what Bo
parte replied to some Austrian critics, of much correctness a
acumen, who doubted about acknowledging the French Repub.
I do not mean that the " Christmas Carol " is quite as brilliant
self-evident as the sun at noonday ; but it is so spread over Engla

* " A Christmas Carol in Prose ; being a Ghost Story of Christmas."
Charles Dickens. With Illustrations by John Leech. London: Chapman & H
1843.

y this time, that no sceptic, no *Fraser's Magazine,*—no, not even he godlike and ancient *Quarterly* itself (venerable, Saturnian, ig wigged dynasty!) could review it down. "Unhappy people! eluded race!" one hears the cauliflowered god exclaim, mournfully haking the powder out of his ambrosial curls. "What strange new olly is this? What new deity do ye worship? Know ye what ye o? Know ye that your new idol hath little Latin and less Greek? Know ye that he has never tasted the birch of Eton, nor trodden he flags of Carfax, nor paced the academic flats of Trumpington? Know ye that in mathematics, or logics, this wretched ignoramus is ot fit to hold a candle to a wooden spoon? See ye not how, from escribing low humours, he now, forsooth, will attempt the sublime? Discern ye not his faults of taste, his deplorable propensity to write lank verse? Come back to your ancient, venerable, and natural nstructors. Leave this new, low, and intoxicating draught at which e rush, and let us lead you back to the old wells of classic lore. ome and repose with us there. We are your gods; we are the ncient oracles, and no mistake. Come listen to us once more, and ve will sing to you the mystic numbers of *as in presenti* under the rches of the Pons Asinorum." But the children of the present eneration hear not; for they reply, "Rush to the Strand! and urchase five thousand more copies of the 'Christmas Carol.'"

In fact, one might as well detail the plot of the "Merry Wives f Windsor," or "Robinson Crusoe," as recapitulate here the adven- ures of Scrooge the miser, and his Christmas conversion. I am ot sure that the allegory is a very complete one, and protest, with he classics, against the use of blank verse in prose; but here all bjections stop. Who can listen to objections regarding such a ook as this? It seems to me a national benefit, and to every man r woman who reads it a personal kindness. The last two people I heard speak of it were women; neither knew the other, or the uthor, and both said, by way of criticism, "God bless him!" A Scotch philosopher, who nationally does not keep Christmas Day, n reading the book, sent out for a turkey, and asked two friends o dine—this is a fact! Many men were known to sit down after erusing it, and write off letters to their friends, not about business, ut out of their fulness of heart, and to wish old acquaintances a appy Christmas. Had the book appeared a fortnight earlier, all he prize cattle would have been gobbled up in pure love and friend- ship, Epping denuded of sausages, and not a turkey left in Norfolk. His Royal Highness's fat stock would have fetched unheard-of rices, and Alderman Bannister would have been tired of slaying. But there is a Christmas for 1844, too; the book will be as early hen as now, and so let speculators look out.

13

As for TINY TIM, there is a certain passage in the book regarding that young gentleman, about which a man should hardly venture to speak in print or in public, any more than he would of any other affections of his private heart. There is not a reader in England but that little creature will be a bond of union between the author and him ; and he will say of Charles Dickens, as the woman just now, " GOD BLESS HIM ! " What a feeling is this for a writer to be able to inspire, and what a reward to reap !

MAY GAMBOLS; OR, TITMARSH IN THE PICTURE GALLERIES

THE readers of this miscellany * may, perhaps, have remarked that always, at the May season and the period of the exhibitions, our eccentric correspondent Titmarsh seems to be seized with a double fit of eccentricity, and to break out into such violent fantastical gambols as might cause us to be alarmed did we not know him to be harmless, and induce us to doubt of his reason but that the fit is generally brief, and passes off after the first excitement occasioned by visiting the picture galleries. It was in one of these fits, some years since, that he announced in this Magazine his own suicide, which we know to be absurd, for he has drawn many hundred guineas from us since :—on the same occasion he described his debts and sojourn at a respectable hotel, in which it seems he has never set his foot. But these hallucinations pass away with May, and next month he will, no doubt, be calmer, or, at least, not more absurd than usual. Some disappointments occurring to himself, and the refusal of his great picture of "Heliogabalus" in the year 1803 (which caused his retirement from practice as a painter), may account for his extreme bitterness against some of the chief artists in this or any other school or country. Thus we have him in these pages abusing Raphael; in the very last month he fell foul of Rubens, and in the present paper he actually pooh-poohs Sir Martin Shee and some of the Royal Academy. This is too much. "Cælum ipsum," as Horace says, "petimus stul-titiâ." But we will quote no more the well-known words of the Epicurean bard.

We only add that we do not feel in the least bound by any one of the opinions here brought forward, from most of which, except where the writer contradicts himself and so saves us the trouble, we cordially dissent ; and perhaps the reader had best pass on to the next article, omitting all perusal of this, excepting, of course, the editorial notice of—O. Y.

* *Fraser's Magazine.*

JACK STRAW'S CASTLE, HAMPSTEAD : *May* 25.

THIS is written in the midst of a general desolation and discouragement of the honest practitioners who dwell in the dingy first-floors about Middlesex Hospital and Soho. The long-haired ones are tearing their lanky locks : the velvet-coated sons of genius are plunged in despair ; the law has ordered the suppression of Art-Unions, and the wheel of Fortune has suddenly and cruelly been made to stand still. When the dreadful news came that the kindly harmless Art-lottery was to be put an end to, although Derby-lotteries are advertised in every gin-shop in London, and every ruffian in the City may gamble at his leisure, the men of the brush and palette convoked a tumultuous meeting, where, amidst tears, shrieks, and wrath, the cruelty of their case was debated. Wyse of Waterford calmly presided over the stormy bladder-squeezers, the insulted wielders of the knife and maulstick. Wyse soothed their angry spirits with words of wisdom and hope. He stood up in the assembly of the legislators of the land and pointed out their wrongs. The painters' friend, the kind old Lansdowne, lifted up his cordial voice among the peers of England, and asked for protection for the children of Raphael and Apelles. No one said nay. All pitied the misfortune of the painters ; even Lord Brougham was stilled into compassion, and the voice of Vaux was only heard in sobs.

These are days of darkness, but there is hope in the vista ; the lottery-subscription lies in limbo, but it shall be released therefrom and flourish, exuberantly revivified, in future years. Had the ruin been consummated, this hand should have withered rather than have attempted to inscribe jokes concerning it. No, *Fraser* is the artists' friend, their mild parent. While his Royal Highness Prince Albert dines with the Academicians, the rest of painters, less fortunate, are patronised by her Majesty REGINA.

Yes, in spite of the Art-Union accident, there is hope for the painters. Sir Martin Archer Shee thinks that the Prince's condescension in dining with the Academy will do incalculable benefit to the art. Henceforth its position is assured in the world. This august patronage, the President says, evincing the sympathy of the higher classes, must awaken the interest of the low: and the public (the ignorant rogues !) will thus learn to appreciate what they have not cared for hitherto. Interested ! Of course they will be. O Academicians ! ask the public to dinner, and you will see how much interested they will be. We are authorised to state that next year any person who will send in his name will have a cover provided ; Trafalgar Square is to be awned in, plates are to be laid for 250,000, one of the new basins is to be filled with turtle and the other with cold punch. The President and the *élite* are to sit upon Nelson's pillar, while rows of benches, stretching as far as the Union Club, Northumberland House, and Saint Martin's Church, will accommodate the vulgar. Mr. Toole is to have a speaking-trumpet; and a twenty-four-pounder to be discharged at each toast.

There are other symptoms of awakening interest in the public mind. The readers of newspapers will remark this year that the leaders of public opinion have devoted an unusually large space and print to reviews of the fine arts. They have been employing critics who, though they contradict each other a good deal, are yet evidently better acquainted with the subject than critics of old used to be, when gentlemen of the profession were instructed to report on a fire, or an Old Bailey trial, or a Greek play, or an opera, or a boxing-match, or a picture gallery, as their turn came. Read now the *Times*, the *Chronicle*, the *Post* (especially the *Post*, of which the painting critiques have been very good), and it will be seen that the critic knows his business, and from the length of his articles it may be conjectured that the public is interested in knowing what he has to say. This is all, probably, from the Prince having dined at the Academy. The nation did not care for pictures until then,—until the nobility taught us; gracious nobility! Above all, what a compliment to the public!

As one looks round the rooms of the Royal Academy, one cannot but deplore the fate of the poor fellows who have been speculating upon the Art-Unions; and yet in the act of grief there is a lurking satisfaction. The poor fellows can't sell their pieces; that is a pity. But why did the poor fellows paint such fiddle-faddle pictures? They catered for the *bourgeois*, the sly rogues! They know honest John Bull's taste, and simple admiration of namby-pamby, and so they supplied him with an article that was just likely to suit him. In like manner savages are supplied with glass beads; children are accommodated with toys and trash, by dexterous speculators who know their market. Well, I am sorry that the painting speculators have had a stop put to their little venture, and that the ugly law against lotteries has stepped in and seized upon the twelve thousand pounds, which was to furnish many a hungry British Raphael with a coat and a beefsteak. Many a Mrs. Raphael, who was looking out for a new dress, or a trip to Margate or Boulogne for the summer, must forego the pleasure, and remain in dingy Newman Street. Many little ones will go back to Turnham Green academies and not carry the amount of last half-year's bill in the trunk; many a landlord will bully about the non-payment of the rent; and a vast number of frame-makers will look wistfully at their carving and gilding as it returns after the exhibition to Mr. Tinto, Charlotte Street, along with poor Tinto's picture from the "Vicar of Wakefield" that he made sure of selling to an Art-Union prizeman. This is the pathetic side of the question. My heart is tender, and I weep for the honest painters peering dismally at the twelve thousand pounds like hungry boys do at a tart-shop.

But—here stern justice interposes, and the MAN having relented the CRITIC raises his inexorable voice—but, I say, the enemies of Art-Unions have had some reason for their complaints, and I fear it is too true that the effect of those institutions, as far as they have gone hitherto, has not been mightily favourable to the cause of art. One day, by custom, no doubt, the public taste will grow better, and as the man who begins by intoxicating himself with a glass of gin finishes sometimes by easily absorbing a bottle; as the law student, who at first is tired with a chapter of Blackstone, will presently swallow you down with pleasure a whole volume of Chitty; as EDUCATION, in a word, advances, it is humbly to be hoped that the great and generous British public will not be so easily satisfied as at present, and will ask for a better article for its money.

Meanwhile, their taste being pitiable, the artists supply them with poor stuff—pretty cheap tawdry toys and gimcracks in place of august and beautiful objects of art. It is always the case. I do not mean to say that the literary men are a bit better. Poor fellows of the pen and pencil! we must live. The public likes light literature and we write it. Here am I writing magazine jokes and follies, and why? Because the public like such, will purchase no other. Otherwise, as Mr. Nickisson, and all who are acquainted with M. A. Titmarsh in private, know, my real inclinations would lead me to write works upon mathematics, geology, and chemistry, varying them in my lighter hours with little playful treatises on questions of political economy, epic poems, and essays on the Æolic digamma. So, in fact, these severe rebukes with which I am about to belabour my neighbour must be taken, as they are given, in a humble and friendly spirit; they are not actuated by pride, but by deep sympathy. Just as we read in holy Mr. Newman's life of Saint Stephen Harding, that it was the custom among the godly Cistercian monks (in the good old times, which holy Newman would restore) to assemble every morning in full chapter; and there, after each monk had made his confession, it was free to— nay, it was strictly enjoined on—any other brother to rise and say, "Brother So-and-so hath not told all his sins; our dear brother has forgotten that yesterday he ate his split-peas with too much gormandise;" or, "This morning he did indecently rejoice over his water-gruel," or what not—these real Christians were called upon to inform, not only of themselves, but to be informers over each other; and, the information being given, the brother informed against thanked his brother the informer, and laid himself down on the desk, and was flagellated with gratitude. Sweet friends! be you like the Cistercians! Brother Michael Angelo is going to inform against you. Get ready your garments and prepare for flagellation. Brother Michael Angelo is about to lay on and spare not.

Brother Michael lifts up his voice against the young painters collectively in the first place, afterwards individually, when he will also take leave to tickle them with the wholesome stripes of the flagellum. In the first place, then (and my heart is so tender that, rather than begin the operation, I have been beating about the bush for more than a page, of which page the reader is cordially requested to omit the perusal, as it is not the least to the purpose), I say that the young painters of England, whose uprise this Magazine and this critic were the first to hail, asserting loudly their superiority over the pompous old sham classical big-wigs of the Academy—the young painters of England *are not doing their duty.* They are going backwards, or rather, they are flinging themselves under the wheels of that great golden Juggernaut of an Art-Union. The thought of the money is leading them astray; they are poets no longer, but money-hunters. They paint down to the level of the public intelligence, rather than seek to elevate the public to them. Why do these great geniuses fail in their duty of instruc- tion? Why, knowing better things, do they serve out such awful twaddle as we have from them? Alas! it is not for art they paint, but for the Art-Union.

The first dear brother I shall take the liberty to request to get ready for operation is brother Charles Landseer. Brother Charles has sinned. He has grievously sinned. And we will begin with this miserable sinner, and administer to him admonition in a friendly, though most fierce and cutting, manner.

The subject of brother Charles Landseer's crime is this. The sinner has said to himself, "The British public likes domestic pieces. They will have nothing but domestic pieces. I will give them one, and of a new sort. Suppose I paint a picture that must make a hit. My picture will have every sort of interest. It shall interest the religious public; it shall interest the domestic public; it shall interest the amateur for the clever- ness of its painting; it shall interest little boys and girls, for I will introduce no end of animals, camels, monkeys, elephants, and cockatoos; it shall interest sentimental young ladies, for I will take care to have a pretty little episode for them. I will take the town by storm, in a word." This is what I conceive was passing in brother Charles Landseer's sinful soul when he conceived and executed his NOAH'S ARK IN A DOMESTIC POINT OF VIEW.

Noah and his family (with some supplemental young children, very sweetly painted) are seated in the ark, and a port-hole is opened, out of which one of the sons is looking at the now peaceful waters. The sunshine enters the huge repository of the life of the world, and the dove has just flown in with an olive-branch and nestles in the bosom of one of the daughters of Noah; the patriarch and his aged partner are lifting up their venerable eyes in thankfulness; the children stand around, the peaceful labourer and the brown huntsman each testifying his devotion after his fashion. The animals round about participate in the joyful nature of the scene, their instinct seems to tell them that the hour of their deliverance is near.

There, the picture is described romantically and in the best of language. Now let us proceed to examine the poetry critically and to see what its claims are. Well, the ark is a great subject. The history from which we have our account of it, from a poet surely demands a reverent treatment; a blacksmith roaring from the desk of a conventicle may treat it familiarly, but an educated artist ought surely to approach such a theme with respect. The point here is only urged æsthetically. As a matter of *taste*, then (and the present humble writer has no business to speak on any other), such a manner of treating the subject is certainly reprehensible. The ark is vulgarised here and reduced to the proportions of a Calais steamer. The passengers are rejoicing: they are glad to get away. Their live animals are about them no more nor less sublime than so many cattle or horses in loose boxes. The parrots perched on the hoop yonder have as little signification as a set of birds in a cage at the Zoological Gardens; the very dove becomes neither more nor less than the *pet* of the pretty girl represented in the centre of the picture. All the greatness of the subject is lost; and, putting the historical nature of the personages out of the question, they have little more interest than a group of any emigrants in the hold of a ship, who rouse and rally at the sound of " Land ho !"

Why, if all great themes of poetry are to be treated in this way, the art would be easy. We might have Hector shaving himself before going out to fight Achilles, as, undoubtedly, the Trojan hero did; Priam in a cotton nightcap asleep in a four-poster on the night of the sack of Troy, Hecuba, of course, by his side, with curl-papers, and her *tour de téte* on the toilet-glass. We might have Dido's maid coming after her mistress in the shower with pattens and an umbrella; or Cleopatra's page guttling the figs in the basket which had brought the asp that killed the mistress of Antony. Absurd trivialities, or pretty trivialities, are nothing to the question; those I have adduced here are absurd, but they are just as poetical as prettiness, not a whit less degrading and commonplace. No painter has a right to treat great historical subjects in such a .fashion; and though the public are sure to admire, and young ladies, in raptures, look on at the darling of a dove, and little boys in delight cry, "Look, papa, at the parroquets!"—"Law, ma, what big trunks the elephants have!" it yet behoves the critic to say this is an unpoetical piece, and severely to reprehend the unhappy perpetrator thereof.

I know brother Charles will appeal. I know it will be pleaded in his favour that the picture is capitally painted, some of the figures very pretty; two, that of the old woman and the boy looking out, quite grand in drawing and colour; the picture charming for its silvery tone and agreeable pleasantry of colour. All this is true. But he has sinned, he has greatly sinned; let him acknowledge his fault in the presence of the chapter, and receive the customary and wholesome reward thereof.

Frater Redgrave is the next malefactor whose sins deserve a reprobation. In the namby-pamby line his errors are very sad. Has he not been already warned in this very miscellany of his propensity to small sentiment? Has he corrected himself of that grievous tendency? No: his weakness grows more and more upon him, and he is now more sinful than ever. One of his pictures is taken from the most startling lyric in our language, the "Song of the Shirt," a song as bitter and manly as it is exquisitely soft and tender, a song of which the humour draws tears.*

Mr. Redgrave has illustrated everything except the humour, the manliness, and the bitterness of the song. He has only depicted the tender good-natured part of it. It is impossible to quarrel with the philanthropy of the painter. His shirt-maker sits by her little neat bed, work, working away. You may see how late it is, for the candle is nearly burnt out, the clock (capital poetic notion!) says what o'clock it is, the grey-streaked dawn is rising over the opposite house seen through the cheerless casement, and where (from a light which it has in its window) you may imagine that another poor shirt maker is toiling too. The one before us is pretty,

---

* How is it that none of the papers have noticed the astonishing poem by Mr. Hood in the May number of his magazine, to which our language contains no parallel?—M. A. T.

pale, and wan ; she turns up the whites of her fine fatigued eyes to the little ceiling. She is ill, as the artist has shown us by a fine stroke of genius—a parcel of medicine-bottles on the mantelpiece ! The picture is carefully and cleverly painted—extremely popular— gazed at with vast interest by most spectators. Is it, however, a poetical subject? Yes, Hood has shown that it can be made one, but by surprising turns of thought brought to bear upon it, strange, terrible, unexpected lights of humour which he has flung upon it. And, to " trump" this tremendous card, Mr. Redgrave gives us this picture ; his points being the clock, which tells the time of day, the vials which show the poor girl takes physic, and such other vast labours of intellect !

Mr. Redgrave's other picture, the " Marriage Morning," is also inspired by that milk-and-water of human kindness, the flavour of which is so insipid to the roast-beef intellect. This is a scene of a marriage morning ; the bride is taking leave of her mamma after the ceremony, and that amiable lady, reclining in an easy-chair, is invoking benedictions upon the parting couple, and has a hand of her daughter and her son-in-law clasped in each of hers. She is smiling sadly, restraining her natural sorrow, which will break out so soon as the post-chaise you see through the window, and on which the footman is piling the nuptial luggage, shall have driven off to Salt Hill, or Rose Cottage, Richmond, which I recom- mend. The bride's father, a venerable bald-headed gentleman, with a most benignant, though slow-coachish look, is trying to console poor Anna Maria, the unmarried sister, who is losing the companion of her youth. Never mind, Anna Maria, my dear, your turn will come too ; there is a young gentleman making a speech in the parlour to the health of the new-married pair, who, I lay a wager, will be struck by your fine eyes, and be for serving you as your sister has been treated. This small fable is worked out with great care in a picture in which there is much clever and conscientious painting, from which, however, I must confess I derive little pleasure. The sentiment and colour of the picture somehow coincide ; the eye rests upon a variety of neat tints of pale drab, pale green, pale brown, pale puce colour, of a sickly warmth, not pleasant to the eye. The drawing is feeble, the expression of the faces pretty, but lackadaisical. The penance I would order Mr. Redgrave should be a pint of port-wine to be taken daily, and a devilled kidney every morning for breakfast before beginning to paint.

A little of the devil, too, would do Mr. Frank Stone no harm. He, too, is growing dangerously sentimental. His picture, with a quotation from Horace, " Mæcenas atavis edite regibus," represents a sort of game of tender cross-purposes, very difficult to describe in print. Suppose two lads, Jocky and Tommy, and two lasses, Jenny and Jessamy. They are placed thus :—

		Tommy.
Jessamy.	Jenny.	Jocky.
	A dog.	

Now Jocky is making love to Jenny in an easy off-hand sort of way, and though, or, perhaps, *because* he doesn't care for her much, is evidently delighting the young woman. She looks round, with a pleased smile on her fresh plump cheeks, and turns slightly towards heaven a sweet little *retroussé* nose, and twiddles her fingers (most exquisitely these hands are drawn and painted, by the way) in the most contented way. But, ah! how little does she heed Tommy, who, standing behind Jocky, reclining against a porch, is looking and longing for this light hearted Jenny! And, oh! why does Tommy cast such sheep's eyes upon Jenny, when by her side sits *Jessamy*, the tender and romantic, the dark-eyed and raven-haired being, whose treasures of affection are flung at heedless Tommy's feet? All the world is interested in Jessamy; her face is beautiful, her look of despairing love is so exquisitely tender, that it touches every spectator; and the ladies are unanimous in wondering how Tommy can throw himself away upon that simpering Jenny, when such a superior creature as Jessamy is to be had for the asking. But such is the way of the world, and Tommy will marry, simply because everybody tells him not.

Thus far for the sentiment of the picture. The details are very good; there is too much stippling and show of finish, perhaps, in the handling, and the painting might have been more substantial and lost nothing. But the colour is good, the group very well composed, and the variety of expression excellent. There is great passion, as well as charming delicacy, in the disappointed maiden's face; much fine appreciation of character in the easy smiling triumph of the rival; and, although this sentence was commenced with the express determination of rating Mr. Stone soundly, lo! it is finished without a word of blame. Well, let's vent our anger on the dog. That *is* very bad, and seems to have no more bones than an apple-dumpling. It is only because the artist has been painting disappointed lovers a great deal of late, that one is disposed to grumble, not at the work, but at the want of variety of subject.

As a sentimental picture, the best and truest, to my taste, is that by Mr. Webster, the "Portraits of Mr. and Mrs. Webster," painted to celebrate their fiftieth wedding-day. Such a charming old couple were never seen. There is delightful grace, sentiment, and purity in these two gentle kindly heads; much more sentiment and grace than even in Mr. Eastlake's "Heloïse," a face which the artist has painted over and over again; a beautiful woman, but tiresome, unearthly, unsubstantial, and no more like Heloïse than like the Duke of Wellington. If the late Mr. Pope's epistle be correct, Eloisa was a most unmistakable woman; this is a substanceless, passionless, solemn, mystical apparition; but I doubt if a woman be not the more poetical being of the two.

Being on the subject of sentimental pictures, Monsieur Delaroche's great "Holy Family" must be mentioned here; and, if there is reason to quarrel with the unsatisfactory nature of English sentiment, in truth it appears that the French are not much better provided with the high poetical quality. This picture has all the outside of poetry, all the costume of religion, all the prettiness and primness of the new German dandy-pietistical school. It is an agreeable compound of Correggio and Raphael, with a strong dash of Overbeck; it is painted as clean and pretty as a tulip on a dessert-plate, the lines made out so neatly that none can mistake them; the drawing good, the female face as pretty and demure as can be, her drapery of spotless blue, and the man's of approved red, the infant as pink as strawberries and cream, every leaf of the tree sweetly drawn, and the trunk of the most delicate dove-coloured grey. All these merits the picture has; it is a well-appointed picture. But is that all? Is that enough to make a poet? There are lines in the Oxford prize poems that are smooth as Pope's; and it is notorious that, for colouring, there is no painting like the Chinese. But I hope the French artists have better men springing up among them than the President of the French Academy at Rome.

Biard, the Hogarthian painter, whose slave-trade picture was so noble, has sent us a couple of pieces, which both, in their way, deserve merit. The one is an Arabian caravan moving over a brickdust-coloured desert, under a red arid sky. The picture is lifelike, and so far poetical that it seems to tell the truth. Then there is a steamboat disaster, with every variety of sea-sickness, laughably painted. Shuddering soldiery, sprawling dandies, Englishmen, Savoyards, guitars, lovers, monkeys,—a dreadful confusion of qualmish people, whose agonies will put the most misanthropic observer into good-humour. Biard's "Havre Packet" is much more praiseworthy in my mind than Delaroche's "Holy Family"; for I deny the merit of failing greatly in pictures—the great merit is to succeed. There is no greater error, surely, than that received dictum of the ambitious, to aim at high things; it is best to do what you mean to do; better to kill a crow than to miss an eagle.

As the French artists are sending in their works from across the water, why, for the honour of England, will not some of our painters let the Parisians know that here, too, are men whose genius is worthy of appreciation? They may be the best draughts-men in the world, but they have no draughtsman like Maclise, they have no colourist like Etty, they have no painter like MULREADY, above all, whose name I beg the printer to place in the largest capitals, and to surround with a wreath of laurels. Mr. Mulready was crowned in this Magazine once before. Here again he is pro-claimed. It looks like extravagance, or flattery, for the blushing critic to tell his real mind about the "Whistonian Controversy."

And yet, as the truth must be told, why not say it now at once? I believe this to be one of the finest cabinet pictures in the world. It seems to me to possess an assemblage of excellences so rare, to be in drawing so admirable, in expression so fine, in finish so exquisite, in composition so beautiful, in humour and beauty of expression so delightful, that I can't but ask where is a good picture if this be not one? And, in enumerating all the above perfections, I find I have forgotten the greatest of all, the colour; it is quite original this,—brilliant, rich, astonishingly luminous, and intense. The pictures of Van Eyck are not more brilliant in tone than this magnificent combination of blazing reds, browns, and purples. I know of no scheme of colour like it, and heartily trust that time will preserve it; when this little picture, and some of its fellows, will be purchased as eagerly as a Hemlinck or a Gerard Douw is bought nowadays. If Mr. Mulready has a mind to the Grand Cross of the Legion of Honour, he has but to send this picture to Paris next year, and, with the recommendation of *Fraser's Magazine*, the affair is settled. Meanwhile it is pleasant to know that the artist (although his work will fetch ten times as much money a hundred years hence) has not been ill rewarded, as times go, for his trouble and genius.

We have another great and original colourist among us, as luscious as Rubens, as rich almost as Titian, Mr. Etty; and every year the exhibition sparkles with magnificent little canvases, the works of this indefatigable strenuous admirer of rude Beauty. The form is not quite so sublime as the colour in this artist's paintings; the female figure is often rather too expansively treated, it swells here and there to the proportions of the Caffrarian, rather than the Medicean, Venus; but, in colour, little can be conceived that is more voluptuously beautiful. This year introduces to us one of the artist's noblest compositions, a classical and pictorial *orgy*, as it were,—a magnificent vision of rich colours and beautiful forms,—a grand feast of sensual poetry. The verses from " Comus," which the painter has taken to illustrate, have the same character :—

> " All amidst the gardens fair
> Of Hesperus and his daughters three,
> That sing about the golden tree,
> Along the crisped shades and bowers,
> Revels the spruce and jocund spring.
> Beds of hyacinths and roses,
> Where young Adonis oft reposes,
> Waxing well of his deep wound,
> In slumber soft and on the ground
> Sadly sits the Assyrian Queen ;
> But far above in spangled sheen,
> Celestial Cupid, her famed son, advanced,
> Holds his dear Psyche sweet entranced."

It is a dream rather than a reality, the words and images purposely indistinct and incoherent. In the same way the painter has made the beautiful figures sweep before us in a haze of golden sunshine. This picture is one of a series to be painted in fresco, and to decorate the walls of a summer-house in the gardens of Buckingham Palace, for which edifice Mr. Maclise and Mr. Leslie have also made paintings.

That of Mr. Leslie's is too homely. He is a prose painter. His kind buxom young lass has none of the look of Milton's lady, that charming compound of the saint and the fine lady—that sweet impersonation of the chivalric mythology—an angel, but with her sixteen quarterings—a countess descended from the skies. Leslie's lady has no such high breeding, the Comus above her looks as if he might revel on ale ; a rustic seducer, with an air of rude hob-nailed health. Nor are the demons and fantastic figures introduced imaginative enough ; they are fellows with masks from Covent Garden. Compare the two figures at the sides of the picture with the two Cupids of Mr. Etty. In the former there is no fancy. The latter are two flowers of poetry ; there are no words to characterise those two delicious little figures, no more than to describe a little air of Mozart, which, once heard, remains with you for ever ; or a new flower, or a phrase of Keats or Tennyson, which blooms out upon you suddenly, astonishing as much as it pleases. Well, in endeavouring to account for his admiration, the critic pumps for words in vain ; if he uses such as he finds, he runs the risk of being considered intolerably pert and affected ; silent pleasure, therefore, best beseems him ; but this I know, that were my humble recommendations attended to at Court, when the pictures are put in the pleasure-house, her sacred Majesty, giving a splendid banquet to welcome them and the painter, should touch Mr. Etty on the left shoulder and say, "Rise, my knight of the Bath, for painting the left-hand Cupid;" and the Emperor of Russia (being likewise present) should tap him on the right shoulder, exclaiming, "Rise, my knight of the Eagle, for the left-hand Cupid."

Mr. Maclise's "Comus" picture is wonderful for the variety of its design, and has, too, a high poetry of its own. All the figures are here still and solemn as in a tableau; the lady still on her unearthly snaky chair, Sabrina still stooping over her. On one side the brothers, and opposite the solemn attendant spirit; round these interminable groups and vistas of fairy beings, twining in a thousand attitudes of grace, and sparkling white and bloodless against a leaden blue sky. It is the most poetical of the artist's pictures, the most extraordinary exhibition of his proper skill. Is it true that the artists are only to receive three hundred guineas apiece for these noble compositions? Why, a print-seller would give more, and artists should not be allowed to paint simply for the honour of decorating a Royal summer-house.

Among the poetical pictures of the exhibition should be mentioned with especial praise Mr. Cope's delightful "Charity," than the female figures in which Raphael scarce painted anything more charmingly beautiful. And Mr. Cope has this merit, that his work is no prim imitation of the stiff old Cimabue and Giotto manner, no aping of the crisp draperies and hard outlines of the missal illuminations, without which the religious artist would have us believe religious expression is impossible. It is pleasant after seeing the wretched caricatures of old-world usages which stare us in the face in every quarter of London now—little dumpy Saxon chapels built in raw brick, spick and span *bandbox* churches of the pointed Norman style for Cockneys in zephyr coats to assemble in, new old painted windows of the twelfth century, tessellated pavements of the Byzantine school, gimcrack imitations of the Golden Legend printed with red letters, and crosses, and quaint figures stolen out of Norman missals—to find artists aiming at the Beautiful and Pure without thinking it necessary to resort to these paltry archæological quackeries, which have no Faith, no Truth, no Life in them; but which give us ceremony in lieu of reality, and insist on forms as if they were the conditions of belief.

Lest the reader should misunderstand the cause of this anger, we beg him to take the trouble to cross Pall Mall to Saint James's Street, where objects of art are likewise exhibited; he will see the reason of our wrath. Here are all the ornamental artists of

England sending in their works, and what are they?—All imitations. The Alhambra here; the Temple Church there; here a Gothic saint; yonder a Saxon altar-rail; farther on a sprawling rococo of Louis XV.; all worked neatly and cleverly enough, but with no originality, no honesty of thought. The twelfth century revived in Mr. Crockford's bazaar, forsooth! with examples of every century except our own. It would be worth while for some one to write an essay, showing how astonishingly Sir Walter Scott * has influenced the world; how he changed the character of novelists, then of historians, whom he brought from their philosophy to the study of pageantry and costume: how the artists then began to fall back into the middle ages and the architects to follow; until now behold we have Mr. Newman and his congregation of Littlemore marching out with taper and crosier, and falling down to worship Saint Willibald, and Saint Winnibald, and Saint Walberga the Saxon virgin. But Mr. Cope's picture is leading the reader rather farther than a critique about exhibitions has any right to divert him, and let us walk soberly back to Trafalgar Square.

Remark the beautiful figures of the children in Mr. Cope's picture (276), the fainting one, and the golden-haired infant at the gate. It is a noble and touching Scripture illustration. The artist's other picture, " Geneviève," is not so successful; the faces seem to have been painted from a dirty palette, the evening tints of the sky are as smoky as a sunset in Saint James's Park; the composition unpleasant, and not enough to fill the surface of canvas.

Mr. Herbert's picture of "The Trial of the Seven Bishops" is painted with better attention to costume than most English painters are disposed to pay. The characters in our artists' history-pieces, as indeed on our theatres, do not look commonly accustomed to the dresses which they assume; wear them awkwardly, take liberties of alteration and adjustment, and spoil thereby the truth of the delineation. The French artists, on the canvas or the boards, understand this branch of their art much better. Look at Monsieur Biard's "Mecca Pilgrims," how carefully and accurately they are attired; or go to the French play and see Cartigny in a Hogarthian dress. He wears it as though he had been born a hundred years back—looks the old marquess to perfection. In this attention to dress Mr. Herbert's picture is very praiseworthy; the men are quite at home in their quaint

---

* Or more properly Goethe. "Goetz von Berlichingen" was the father of the Scottish romances, and Scott remained constant to that mode, while the greater artist tried a thousand others.

coats and periwigs of James II.'s time ; the ladies at ease in their stiff long-waisted gowns, their fans, and their queer caps and patches. And the picture is pleasing from the extreme brightness and cleanliness of the painting. All looks as neat and fresh as Sam Pepys when he turned out in his new suit, his lady in her satin and brocade. But here the praise must stop. The great concourse of people delineated, the bishops and the jury, the judges and the sheriffs, the halberdiers and the fine ladies, seem very little interested in the transaction in which they are engaged, and look as if they were assembled rather for show than business. Nor, indeed, is the artist much in fault. Painters have not fair-play in these parade pictures. It is only with us that Reform-banquets, or views of the House of Lords at the passing of the Slopperton Railway Bill, or Coronation Processions, obtain favour ; in which vast numbers of public characters are grouped unreally together, and politics are made to give an interest to art.

Mr. Herbert's picture of " Sir Thomas More and his Daughter watching from the prisoner's room in the Tower four Monks led away to Execution," is not the most elaborate, perhaps, but the very best of this painter's works. It is full of grace, and sentiment, and religious unction. You see that the painter's heart is in the scenes which he represents. The countenances of the two figures are finely conceived : the sorrowful anxious beauty of the daughter's face, the resigned humility of the martyr at her side, and the accessories or properties of the pious little drama are cleverly and poetically introduced ; such as mystic sentences of hope and trust inscribed by former sufferers on the walls, the prisoner's rosary and book of prayers to the Virgin that lie on his bed. These types and emblems of the main story are not obtruded, but serve to increase the interest of the action ; just as you hear in a con-certed piece of music a single instrument playing its little plaintive part alone, and yet belonging to the whole.

If you want to see a picture where costume is *not* represented, behold Mr. Lauder's " Claverhouse ordering Morton to Execution." There sits Claverhouse in the centre in a Kean wig and ringlets, such as was never worn in any age of this world, except at the theatre in 1816, and he scowls with a true melodramatic ferocity ; and he lifts a signpost of a finger towards Morton, who forthwith begins to writhe and struggle into an attitude in the midst of a group of subordinate, cuirassed, buff-coated gentry. Morton is represented in tights, slippers, and a tunic ; something after the fashion of Retzsch's figures in " Faust " (which are refinements of costumes worn a century and a half before the days when Charles disported at Tillietudlem) ; and he, too, must proceed to scowl and frown "with a flashing eye and a distended nostril," as they say in the novels,—as Gomersal scowls at Widdicomb before the combat between those two chiefs begins; and while they are measuring each other according to the stage wont, from the toe of the yellow boot up to the tip of the stage-wig. There is a tragedy heroine in Mr. Lauder's picture, striking her attitude, too, to complete the scene. It is entirely unnatural, theatrical, of the Davidgian, nay, Richardsonian drama, and all such attempts at effect must be reprehended by the stern critic. When such a cool practitioner as Claverhouse ordered a gentleman to be shot, he would not put himself into an attitude: when such a quiet gentleman as Morton received the unpleasant communication in the midst of a company of grenadiers who must overpower him, and of ladies to whom his resistance would be unpleasant, he would act like a man and go out quietly, not stop to rant and fume like a fellow in a booth. I believe it is in Mr. Henningsen's book that there is a story of Zumalacarreguy, Don Carlos's Dundee, who, sitting at the table with a Christino prisoner, smoking cigars and playing picquet very quietly, received a communication which he handed over to the Christino. "Your people," says he, "have shot one of my officers, and I have promised reprisals; I am sorry to say, my dear general, that I must execute you in twenty minutes!" And so the two gentlemen finished their game at picquet, and parted company—the one to inspect his lines, the other for the courtyard hard by, where a file of grenadiers was waiting to receive his excellency —with mutual politeness and regret. It was the fortune of war. There was no help for it; no need of ranting and stamping, which would ill become any person of good breeding.

The Scotch artists have a tragic taste; and we should mention with especial praise Mr. Duncan's picture with the agreeable epigraph, "She set the bairn on the ground and tied up his head, and straighted his body, and covered him with her plaid, and laid down and wept over him." The extract is from Walker's "Life of Peden;" the martyrdom was done on the body of a boy by one of those bloody troopers whom we have seen in Mr. Lauder's picture carrying off poor shrieking Morton. Mr. Duncan's picture is very fine,—dark, rich, and deep in sentiment; the woman is painted with some of Rubens's swelling lines (such as may be seen in some of his best Magdalens), and with their rich tones of grey. If a certain extremely heavy Cupid poising in the air by a miracle be the other picture of Mr. Duncan's, it can be only said that his tragedy is better than his lightsome compositions—an arrow from yonder lad would bruise the recipient black and blue.

Another admirable picture of a Scotch artist is 427, "The

Highland Lament," by Alexander Johnston. It is a shame to put such a picture in such a place. It hangs on the ground almost invisible, while dozens of tawdry portraits are staring at you on the line. Could Mr. Johnston's picture be but seen properly, its great beauty and merit would not fail to strike hundreds of visitors who pass it over now. A Highland piper comes running forward, playing some wild lament on his dismal instrument; the women follow after, wailing and sad; the mournful procession winds over a dismal moor. The picture is as clever for its fine treatment and colour, for the grace and action of the figure, as it is curious as an illustration of national manners.

In speaking of the Scotch painters, the Wilkie-like pictures of Mr. Fraser, with their peculiar *smeary* manner, their richness of tone, and their pleasant effect and humour, should not be passed over; while those of Mr. Geddes and Sir William Allan may be omitted with perfect propriety. The latter presents her Majesty and Prince Albert perched on a rock; the former has a figure from Walter Scott, of very little interest to any but the parties concerned.

Among the Irish painters we remark two portraits by Mr. Crowley, representing Mrs. Aikenhead, superior*ess* of the Sisters of Charity in Ireland, who gives a very favourable picture of the Society—for it is impossible to conceive an abbess more comfortable, kind, and healthy-looking; and a portrait of Dr. Murray, Roman Catholic Archbishop of Dublin, not a good picture of a fine, benevolent, and venerable head. We do not know whether the painter of 149, "An Irish Peasant awaiting her Husband's Return," Mr. Anthony, is an Irishman; but it is a pretty sad picture, which well characterises the poverty, the affection, and the wretchedness of the poor Irish cabin, and tells sweetly and modestly a plaintive story. The largest work in the exhibition is from the pencil of an Irishman, Mr. Leahy, "Lady Jane Grey praying before Execution." One cannot but admire the courage of artists who paint great works upon these tragic subjects; great works quite unfitted for any private room, and scarcely suited to any public one. But, large as it is, it may be said (without any playing upon words) that the work grows upon estimation. The painting is hard and incomplete; but the principal figure excellent: the face especially is finely painted, and full of great beauty. Also, in the Irish pictures may be included Mr. Solomon Hart's Persian gentleman smoking a *calahan*,—a sly hit at the learned Serjeant member for Cork, who has often done the same thing.

Mr. Maclise's little scene from "Undine" does not seem to us German in character, as some of the critics call it, because it is clear and hard in line. What German artist is there who can draw with this astonishing vigour, precision, and variety of attitude? The picture is one of admirable and delightful fancy. The swarms of solemn little fairies crowding round Undine and her somewhat theatrical lover may keep a spectator for hours employed in pleasure and wonder. They look to be the real portraits of the little people, sketched by the painter in some visit to their country. There is, especially, on a branch in the top corner of the picture, a conversation going on between a fairy and a squirrel (who is a fairy too), which must have been taken from nature, or Mother Bunch's delightful super-nature. How awful their great glassy blue eyes are! How they peer out from under glass, and out of flowers, and from twigs and branches, and swing off over the tree-top, singing shrill little fairy choruses! We must have the Fairy Tales illustrated by this gentleman, that is clear; he is the only person, except Tieck, of Dresden, who knows anything about them.—Yes, there *is* some one else; and a word may be introduced here in welcome to the admirable young designer, whose hand has lately been employed to illustrate the columns of our facetious friend (and the friend of everybody) *Punch.* This young artist (who has avowed his name, a very well-known one, that of Doyle) has poured into *Punch's* columns a series of drawings quite extraordinary for their fancy, their variety, their beauty, and fun. It is the true genius of fairyland, of burlesque which never loses sight of beauty. Friend *Punch's* very wrapper is quite a marvel in this way, at which we can never look without discovering some new little quip of humour or pleasant frolic of grace.

And if we have had reason to complain of Mr. Leslie's "Comus" as deficient in poetry, what person is there that will not welcome "Sancho," although we have seen him before almost in the same attitude, employed in the same way, recounting his adventures to the kind smiling duchess, as she sits in state? There is only the sour old duenna, who refuses to be amused, and nothing has ever amused her these sixty years. But the ladies are all charmed, and tittering with one another; the black slave who leans against the pillar has gone off in an honest fit of downright laughter. Even the little dog, the wonderful little Blenheim, by the lady's side, would laugh if she could (but, alas! it is impossible), as the other little dog is said to have done on the singular occasion when "the cow jumped over the moon."* The glory of dulness is in Sancho's face. I don't believe there is a man in the world—no, not even in the House of Commons—so stupid as that. On the Whig side there

---

* " Qualia prospiciens Catulus ferit æthera risu
Ipsaque trans lunæ cornua Vacca salit."—LUCRETIUS.

is, certainly,—but no, it is best not to make comparisons which fall short of the mark. This is, indeed, the Sancho that Cervantes drew.

Although the editor of this Magazine had made a solemn condition with the writer of this notice that no pictures taken from the "Vicar of Wakefield" or "Gil Blas" should, by any favour or pretence, be noticed in the review ; yet, as the great picture of Mr. Mulready compelled the infraction of the rule, rushing through our resolve by the indomitable force of genius, we must, as the line is broken, present other Vicars, Thornhills, and Olivias, to walk in and promenade themselves in our columns, in spite of the vain placards at the entrance, "VICARS OF WAKEFIELD NOT ADMITTED." In the first place, let the Reverend Doctor Primrose and Miss Primrose walk up in Mr. Hollins's company. The Vicar is mildly expostulating with his daughter regarding the attentions of Squire Thornhill. He looks mild, too mild ; she looks ill-humoured, very sulky. Is it about the scolding, or the Squire ? The figures are very nicely painted ; but they do not look accustomed (the lady especially) to the dresses they wear. After them come Mrs. Primrose, the Misses and the young Masters Primrose, presented by Mr. Frith in his pretty picture (491). Squire Thornhill sits at his ease, and recounts his town adventures to the ladies ; the beautiful Olivia is quite lost in love with the slim red-coated dandy ; her sister is listening with respect ; but, above all, the old lady and children hearken with wonder. These latter are charming figures, as indeed are all in the picture. As for Gil Blas,—but we shall be resolute about *him*. Certain Gil Blas there are in the exhibition eating olla-podridas, and what not. Not a word, however, shall be said regarding any one of them.

Among the figure-pieces Mr. Ward's Lafleur must not be forgotten, which is pleasant, lively, and smartly drawn and painted ; nor Mr. Gilbert's " Pear-tree Well," which contains three graceful classical figures, which are rich in effect and colour ; nor Mr. MacInnes's good picture of Luther listening to the sacred ballad (the reformer is shut up in the octagon-room) ; nor a picture of Oliver Goldsmith on his rambles, playing the flute at a peasant's door, in which the colour is very pretty ; the character of the French peasants not French at all, and the poet's figure easy, correct, and well drawn.

Among more serious subjects may be mentioned with praise Mr. Dyce's two fierce figures, representing King Joash shooting the arrow of deliverance, which if the critic call " French," because they are well and carefully drawn, Mr. Dyce may be proud of being a Frenchman. Mr. Lauder's " Wise and Foolish Virgins " is a fine composition; the colour sombre and mysterious; some of the figures extremely graceful, and the sentiment of the picture excellent. This is a picture which would infallibly have had a chance of a prize, if the poor dear Art-Union were free to act.

Mr. Elmore's " Rienzi addressing the People " is one of the very best pictures in the Gallery. It is well and agreeably coloured, bright, pleasing, and airy. A group of people are gathered round the tribune, who addresses them among Roman ruins under a clear blue sky. The grouping is very good ; the figures rich and picturesque in attitude and costume. There is a group in front of a mother and child who are thinking of anything but Rienzi and liberty ; who, perhaps, ought not to be so prominent, as they take away from the purpose of the picture, but who are beautiful wherever they are. And the picture is further to be remarked for the clear, steady, and honest painting which distinguishes it.

What is to be said of Mr. Poole's " Moors beleaguered in Valencia " ? A clever hideous picture in the very worst taste ; disease and desperation characteristically illustrated. The Spaniards beleaguer the town, and everybody is starving. Mothers with dry breasts unable to nourish infants ; old men, with lean ribs and bloodshot eyes, moaning on the pavement ; brown young skeletons pacing up and down the rampart, some raving, all desperate. Such is the agreeable theme which the painter has taken up. It is worse than last year, when the artist only painted the plague of London. Some *did* recover from that. All these Moors will be dead before another day, and the vultures will fatten on their lean carcases, and pick out their red-hot eyeballs. Why do young men indulge in these horrors? Young poets and romancers often do so, and fancy they are exhibiting " power " ; whereas nothing is so easy. Any man with mere instinct can succeed in the brutal in art. The coarse fury of Zurbaran and Morales is as far below the sweet and beneficent calm of Murillo as a butcher is beneath a hero. Don't let us have any more of these hideous exhibitions—these ghoul festivals. It may be remembered that Amina in the " Arabian Nights," who liked churchyard suppers, could only eat a grain of rice when she came to natural food. There is a good deal of sly satire in the apologue which might be applied to many (especially French) literary and pictorial artists of the convulsionary school.

We must not take leave of the compositions without mentioning Mr. Landseer's wonderful " Shoeing " and " Stag " ; the latter the most poetical, the former the most dexterous, perhaps, of the works of this accomplished painter. The latter picture, at a little distance, expands almost into the size of nature. The enormous stag by the side of a great blue northern lake stalks over the snow down to the shore, whither his mate is coming through the water to join him. Snowy mountains bend round the lonely landscape, the stars are shining out keenly in the deep icy blue overhead; in a word, your teeth begin to chatter as you look at the picture, and it can't properly be seen without a greatcoat. The donkey and the horse in the shoeing picture are prodigious imitations of nature; the blacksmith only becomes impalpable. There is a charming portrait in the great room by the same artist in which the same defect may be remarked. A lady is represented with two dogs in her lap; the dogs look real; the lady a thin unsubstantial vision of a beautiful woman. You ought to see the landscape through her.

Amongst the landscape painters, Mr. Stanfield has really painted this year better than any former year—a difficult matter. The pictures are admirable, the drawing of the water wonderful, the look of freshness and breeze and motion conveyed with delightful skill. All Mr. Creswick's pictures will be seen with pleasure, especially the delicious "Summer Evening"; the most airy and clear, and also the most poetical of his landscapes. The fine "Evening Scene" of Danby also seems to have the extent and splendour, and to suggest the solemn feelings of a vast mountain-scene at sunset. The admirers of Sir Augustus Callcott's soft golden landscapes will here find some of his most delightful pieces. Mr. Roberts has painted his best in his Nile scene, and his French architectural pieces are of scarce inferior merit. Mr. Lee, Mr. Witherington, and Mr. Leitch have contributed works, showing all their well-known qualities and skill. And as for Mr. Turner, he has out-prodigied almost all former prodigies. He has made a picture with real rain, behind which is real sunshine, and you expect a rainbow every minute. Meanwhile, there comes a train down upon you, really moving at the rate of fifty miles an hour, and which the reader had best make haste to see, lest it should dash out of the picture, and be away up Charing Cross through the wall opposite. All these wonders are performed with means not less wonderful than the effects are. The rain, in the astounding picture called "Rain—Steam—Speed," is composed of dabs of dirty putty *slapped* on to the canvas with a trowel; the sunshine scintillates out of very thick smeary lumps of chrome yellow. The shadows are produced by cool tones of crimson lake, and quiet glazings of vermilion. Although the fire in the steam engine *looks* as if it were red, I am not prepared to say that it is not painted with cobalt and pea-green. And as for the manner in which the "*Speed*" is done, of that the less said the better,—only it is a positive fact that there is a steam-coach going fifty miles an hour. The world has never seen anything like this picture.

In respect of the portraits of the exhibition, if Royal Acade-micians will take the word of the *Morning Post*, the *Morning Chronicle*, the *Spectator*, and, far above all, of *Fraser's Magazine*, they will pause a little before they hang such a noble portrait as that of W. Conyngham, Esquire, by Samuel Lawrence, away out of sight, while some of their own paltry canvases meet the spectator nose to nose. The man with the glove of Titian in the Louvre has evidently inspired Mr. Lawrence, and his picture is so far an imitation ; but what then ? it is better to imitate great things well than to imitate a simpering barber's dummy, like No. 10000, let us say, or to perpetrate yonder horror,—weak, but, oh ! how heavy, smeared, flat, pink and red, grinning, ill-drawn portraits (such as Nos. 99999 and 99999ᵈ) which the old Academicians perpetrate ! You are right to keep the best picture in the room out of the way, to be sure ; it would sternly frown your simpering unfortunates out of countenance ; but let us have at least a chance of seeing the good pictures. Have one room, say, for the Academicians, and another for the clever artists. Diminish your number of exhibited pictures to six, if you like, but give the young men a chance. It is pitiful to see their works pushed out of sight, and to be offered what you give us in exchange.

This does not apply to all the esquires who paint portraits ; but, with regard to the names of the delinquents, it is best to be silent, lest a showing up of them should have a terrible effect on the otherwise worthy men, and drive them to an untimely despera-tion. So I shall say little about the portraits, mentioning merely that Mr. Grant has one or two, a small one especially, of great beauty and ladylike grace ; and one very bad one, such as that of Lord Forrester. Mr. Pickersgill has some good heads ; the little portrait of Mr. Ainsworth by Mr. Maclise is as clever and like as the artist knows how to make it. Mr. Middleton has some female heads especially beautiful. Mrs. Carpenter is one of the most manly painters in the exhibition ; and if you walk into the minia-ture-room, you may look at the delicious little gems from the pencil of Sir William Ross, those still more graceful and poetical by Mr. Thorburn, and the delightful coxcombries of Mr. Chalon. I have found out a proper task for that gentleman, and hereby propose that he should illustrate " Coningsby."

In the statue-room, Mr. Gibson's classic group attracts attention and deserves praise ; and the busts of Parker, Macdonald, Behnes, and other well-known portrait-sculptors, have all their usual finish, skill, and charm.

At the Water-Colour Gallery the pleased spectator lingers as usual delighted, surrounded by the pleasantest drawings and the most genteel company. It requires no small courage to walk through that avenue of plush breeches with which the lobby is lined, and to pass two files of whiskered men in canes and huge calves, who contemptuously regard us poor fellows with Bluchers and gingham umbrellas. But these passed, you are in the best society. Bishops, I have remarked, frequent this gallery in venerable numbers; likewise dignified clergymen with rosettes; Quakeresses, also, in dove-coloured silks meekly changing colour; squires and their families from the country; and it is a fact, that you never can enter the Gallery without seeing a wonderfully pretty girl. This fact merits to be generally known, and is alone worth the price of this article.

I suspect that there are some people from the country who admire Mr. Prout still; those fresh, honest, unalloyed country appetites! There are the Prout Nurembergs and Venices still; the awnings, the water-posts, and the red-capped bargemen drawn with a reed pen; but we *blasés* young *roués* about London get tired of these simple dishes, and must have more excitement. There, too, are Mr. Hill's stags with pink stomachs, his spinach pastures and mottled farmhouses; also innumerable windy downs and heaths by Mr. Copley Fielding:—in the which breezy flats I have so often wandered before with burnt-sienna ploughboys, that the walk is no longer tempting.

Not so, however, the marine pieces of Mr. Bentley. That gentleman, to our thinking, has never painted so well. Witness his "Indiaman towed up the Thames" (53), his "Signalling the Pilot" (161), and his admirable view of "Mont Saint Michel" (127), in which the vessel quite dances and falls on the water. He deserves to divide the prize with Mr. Stanfield at the Academy.

All the works of a clever young landscape-painter, Mr. G. A. Fripp, may be looked at with pleasure; they show great talent, no small dexterity, and genuine enthusiastic love of nature. Mr. Alfred Fripp, a figure-painter, merits likewise very much praise; his works are not complete as yet, but his style is thoughtful, dramatic, and original.

Mr. Hunt's dramas of one or two characters are as entertaining and curious as ever. His "Outcast" is amazingly fine, and tragic in character. His "Sick Cigar-boy," a wonderful delineation of nausea. Look at the picture of the toilette, in which, with the parlour-tongs, Betty, the housemaid, is curling little miss's hair: there is a dish of yellow soap in that drawing, and an old comb and brush, the fidelity of which make the delicate beholder shudder. On one of the screens there are some "bird's-nests," out of which I am surprised no spectator has yet stolen any of the eggs—you have but to stoop down and take them.

Mr. Taylor's delightful drawings are even more than ordinarily clever. His "Houseless Wanderers" is worthy of Hogarth in humour; most deliciously coloured and treated. "The Gleaner" is full of sunshine; the larder quite a curiosity, as showing the ease, truth, and dexterity with which the artist washes in his flowing delineations from nature. In his dogs, you don't know which most to admire, the fidelity with which the animals are painted, or the ease with which they are done.

This gift of facility Mr. Cattermole also possesses to an amazing extent. As pieces of effect, his "Porch" and "Rook-shooting" are as wonderful as they are pleasing. His large picture of "Monks in a Refectory" is very fine; rich, original, and sober in colour; excellent in sentiment and general grouping; in individual attitude and drawing not sufficiently correct. As the figures are much smaller than those in the refectory, these faults are less visible in the magnificent "Battle for the Bridge," a composition, perhaps, the most complete that the artist has yet produced. The landscape is painted as grandly as Salvator; the sky wonderfully airy, the sunshine shining through the glades of the wood, the huge trees rocking and swaying as the breeze rushes by them; the battling figures are full of hurry, fire, and tumult. All these things are rather indicated by the painter than defined by him; but such hints are enough from such a genius. The charmed and captivated imagination is quite ready to supply what else is wanting.

Mr. Frederick Nash has some unpretending, homely, exquisitely faithful scenes in the Rhine country, "Boppart," "Bacharach," &c., of which a sojourner in those charming districts will always be glad to have a reminiscence. Mr. Joseph Nash has not some of the cleverest of his mannerisms, nor Mr. Lake Price the best of his smart, dandified, utterly unnatural exteriors. By far the best designs of this kind are the Windsor and Buckingham Palace sketches of Mr. Douglas Morison, executed with curious fidelity and skill. There is the dining-hall in Buckingham Palace, with all the portraits, all the candles in all the chandeliers; the China gimcracks over the mantelpiece, the dinner-table set out, the napkins folded mitrewise, the round water-glasses, the sherry-glasses, the champagne ditto, and all in a space not so big as two pages of this Magazine. There is the Queen's own chamber at Windsor, her Majesty's piano, her Royal writing-table, an escritoire with pigeon-holes, where the august papers are probably kept; and very curious,

clever, and ugly all these pictures of furniture are too, and will be
a model for the avoidance of upholsterers in coming ages.

Mr. John William Wright's sweet female figures must not be
passed over; nor the pleasant Stothard-like drawings of his veteran
namesake. The "Gipsies" of Mr. Oakley will also be looked at
with pleasure; and this gentleman may be complimented as likely
to rival the Richmonds and the Chalons "in another place," where
may be seen a very good full-length portrait drawn by him.

The exhibition of the New Society of Water-Colour Painters
has grown to be quite as handsome and agreeable as that of its
mamma, the old Society in Pall Mall East. Those who remember
this little band of painters, to whom the gates of the elder Gallery
were hopelessly shut, must be glad to see the progress the younger
branch has made; and we have every reason to congratulate ourselves that, instead of one pleasant exhibition annually, the amateur
can recreate himself now with two. Many of the pictures here are
of very great merit.

Mr. Warren's Egyptian pictures are clever, and only need to
be agreeable where he takes a pretty subject, such as that of the
"Egyptian Lady" (150); his work is pretty sure to be followed
by that welcome little ticket of emerald green in the corner, which
announces that a purchaser has made his appearance. But the eye
is little interested by views of yellow deserts and sheikhs, and
woolly-headed warriors with ugly wooden swords.

And yet mere taste, grace, and beauty won't always succeed;
witness Mr. Absolon's drawings, of which few—far too few—boast
the green seal and which are one and all of them charming. There
is one in the first room from the "V–c–r of W–kef—ld" (we are
determined not to write that name again), which is delightfully
composed, and a fresh, happy picture of a country fête. "The
Dartmoor Turf-gatherers" (87) is still better; the picture is full
of air, grace, pretty drawing, and brilliant colour, and yet no green
seal. "A Little Sulky"; "The Devonshire Cottage-door"; "The
Widow on the Stile"; "The Stocking-knitter"; are all, too,
excellent in their way, and bear the artist's *cachet* of gentle and
amiable grace. But the drawings, in point of execution, do not go
far enough; they are not sufficiently bright to attract the eyes of
that great and respectable body of amateurs who love no end
of cobalt, carmine, stippling, and plenty of emerald green and
vermilion; they are not made out sufficiently in line to rank as
pictures.

Behold how Mr. Corbould can work when he likes—how *he* can
work you off the carmine stippling! In his large piece, "The

Britons deploring the Departure of the Romans," there is much very fine and extraordinary cleverness of pencil. Witness the draperies of the two women, which are painted with so much cleverness and beauty, that, indeed, one regrets that one of them has not got a little drapery more. The same tender regard pervades the bosom while looking at that of Joan of Arc, "While engaged in the servile offices of her situation as a menial at an inn, ruminating upon the distressing state of France." Her "servile situation" seems to be that of an ostler at the establishment in question, for she is leading down a couple of animals to drink; and as for the "distressing state of France," it ought not, surely, to affect such a fat little comfortable simple-looking undressed body. Bating the figure of Joan, who looks as pretty as a young lady out of the last novel, bating, I say, baiting Joan, who never rode horses, depend on't, in that genteel way, the picture is exceedingly skilful, and much better in colour than Mr. Corbould's former works.

Mr. Wehnert's great drawing is a failure, but an honourable defeat. It shows great power and mastery over the material with which he works. He has two pretty German figures in the fore-room : "The Innkeeper's Daughter" (38); and "Perdita and Florizel" (316). Perhaps he is the author of the pretty arabesques with which the Society have this year ornamented their list of pictures ; he has a German name, and *English* artists can have no need to be copying from Düsseldorf's embellishments to decorate the catalogues.

Mr. Haghe's great drawing of the "Death of Zurbaran" is not interesting from any peculiar fineness of expression in the faces of the actors who figure in this gloomy scene ; but it is largely and boldly painted, in deep sombre washes of colours, with none of the niggling prettinesses to which artists in water-colours seem forced to resort in order to bring their pictures to a high state of finish. Here the figures and the draperies look as if they were laid down at once with a bold yet careful certainty of hand. The effect of the piece is very fine, the figures grandly grouped. Among all the water-colour painters we know of none who can wield the brush like Mr. Haghe, with his skill, his breadth, and his certainty.

Mr. Jenkins's beautiful female figure in the drawing called "Love" (123) must be mentioned with especial praise ; it is charming in design, colour, and sentiment. Another female figure, "The Girl at the Stile," by the same artist, has not equal finish, roundness, and completeness, but the same sentiment of tender grace and beauty.

Mr. Bright's landscape-drawings are exceedingly clever, but there is too much of the drawing-master in the handling, too much dash, skurry, sharp cleverness of execution. Him Mr. Jutsum follows with cleverness not quite equal, and mannerism still greater. After the performance of which the eye reposes gratefully upon some pleasant evening scenes by Mr. Duncan (3, 10); and the delightful "Shady Land" of Mr. Youngman. Mr. Boys's pictures will be always looked at and admired for the skill and correctness of a hand which, in drawing, is not inferior to that of Canaletto.

As for Suffolk Street, that delicious retreat may or may not be still open. I have been there, but was frightened from the place by the sight of Haydon's Napoleon, with his vast head, his large body, and his little legs, staring out upon the Indigo sea, in a grass-green coat. Nervous people avoid that sight, and the Emperor remains in Suffolk Street as lonely as at Saint Helena.

PICTURE GOSSIP: IN A LETTER FROM MICHAEL ANGELO TITMARSH

ALL' ILLUSTRISSIMO SIGNOR, IL MIO SIGNOR COLENDISSIMO, AUGUSTO HA ARVÉ, PITTORE IN ROMA

I AM going to fulfil the promise, my dear Augusto, which I uttered, with a faltering voice and streaming eyes, before I stepped into the jingling old courier's vehicle, which was to bear me from Rome to Florence. Can I forget that night—that parting? Gaunter stood by so affected, that for the last quarter of an hour he did not swear once; Flake's emotion exhibited itself in audible sobs; Jellyson said nought, but thrust a bundle of Torlonia's four-baiocchi cigars into the hand of the departing friend; and you yourself were so deeply agitated by the event, that you took four glasses of absinthe to string up your nerves for the fatal moment. Strange vision of past days!—for vision it seems to me now. And have I been in Rome really and truly? Have I seen the great works of my Christian namesake of the Buonarroti family, and the light arcades of the Vatican? Have I seen the glorious Apollo, and that other divine fiddle-player whom Raphael painted? Yes— and the English dandies swaggering on the Pincian Hill! Yes— and have eaten woodcocks and drank Orvieto hard by the huge broad-shouldered Pantheon Portico, in the comfortable parlours of the "Falcone." Do you recollect that speech I made at Bertini's in proposing the health of the Pope of Rome on Christmas-day?— do you remember it? *I* don't. But his Holiness, no doubt, heard of the oration, and was flattered by the compliment of the illustrious English traveller.

I went to the exhibition of the Royal Academy lately, and all these reminiscences rushed back on a sudden with affecting volubility; not that there was anything in or out of the gallery which put me specially in mind of sumptuous and liberal Rome; but in the great room was a picture of a fellow in a broad Roman hat, in a velvet Roman coat, and large yellow mustachios, and that prodigious scowl which young artists assume when sitting for their portraits—he was one of our set at Rome; and the scenes of the winter came back pathetically to my mind, and all the friends, of that season,—Orifice and his sentimental songs; Father Giraldo and his poodle, and MacBrick, the trump of bankers. Hence the determination to write this letter; but the hand is crabbed, and the postage is dear, and instead of despatching it by the mail, I shall send it to you by means of the printer, knowing well that *Fraser's Magazine* is eagerly read at Rome, and not (on account of its morality) excluded in the *Index Expurgatorius.*

And it will be doubly agreeable to me to write to you regarding the fine arts in England, because I know, my dear Augusto, that you have a thorough contempt for my opinion—indeed, for that of all persons, excepting, of course, one whose name is already written in this sentence. Such, however, is not the feeling respecting my critical powers in this country; *here* they know the merit of Michael Angelo Titmarsh better, and they say, "He paints so badly, that, hang it! he *must* be a good judge;" in the latter part of which opinion, of course, I agree.

You should have seen the consternation of the fellows at my arrival!—of our dear brethren who thought I was safe at Rome for the season, and that their works, exhibited in May, would be spared the dreadful ordeal of my ferocious eye. When I entered the club-room in Saint Martin's Lane, and called for a glass of brandy-and-water like a bombshell, you should have seen the terror of some of the artists assembled! They knew that the frightful projectile just launched into their club-room must *burst* in the natural course of things. Who would be struck down by the explosion? was the thought of every one. Some of the hypocrites welcomed me meanly back, some of the timid trembled, some of the savage and guilty muttered curses at my arrival. You should have seen the ferocious looks of Daggerly, for example, as he scowled at me from the upper-table, and clutched the trenchant weapon with which he was dissevering his toasted cheese.

From the period of my arrival until that of the opening of the various galleries, I maintained with the artists every proper affability, but still was not too familiar. It is the custom of their friends before their pictures are sent in to the exhibitions, to visit the painters' works at their private studios, and there encourage them by saying, "Bravo, Jones!" (I don't mean Jones, R.A., for I defy any man to say bravo to *him*, but Jones in general). "Tomkins, this is your greatest work!" "Smith, my boy, they must elect you an Associate for this!"—and so forth. These harmless banalities of compliment pass between the painters and their friends on such occasions. I, myself, have uttered many such

civil phrases in former years under like circumstances. But it i
different now. Fame has its privations as well as its pleasures
The friend may see his companions in private, but the JUDG
must not pay visits to his clients. I stayed away from th
ateliers of all the artists (at least, I only visited one, kindly tellin
him that he didn't count as an artist at all), and would only se
their pictures in the public galleries, and judge them in the fai
race with their neighbours. This announcement and conduc
of mine filled all the Berners Street and Fitzroy Square distric
with terror.

As I am writing this after having had my fill of their work
so publicly exhibited in the country, at a distance from catalogues
my only book of reference being an orchard whereof the trees ar
now bursting into full blossom,—it is probable that my remark
will be rather general than particular, that I shall only discours
about those pictures which I especially remember, or, indeed, upo
any other point suitable to my honour and your delectation.

I went round the galleries with a young friend of mine, who
like yourself at present, has been a student of "High Art" a
Rome. He had been a pupil of Monsieur Ingres, at Paris. H
could draw rude figures of eight feet high to a nicety, and ha
produced many heroic compositions of that pleasing class and size
to the great profit of the paper-stretchers both in Paris and Rome
He came back from the latter place a year since, with his bear
and mustachios of course. He could find no room in all Newma
Street and Soho big enough to hold him and his genius, and wa
turned out of a decent house because, for the purposes of art, h
wished to batter down the partition-wall between the two drawing
rooms he had. His great cartoon last year (whether it wa
"Caractacus before Claudius," or a scene from the "Vicar o
Wakefield," I won't say) failed somehow. He was a good dea
cut up by the defeat, and went into the country to his relations
from whom he returned after awhile, with his mustachios shave
clean linen, and other signs of depression. He said (with a hollo
laugh) he should not commence on his great canvas this yea
and so gave up the completion of his composition of "Boadice
addressing the Iceni": quite a novel subject, which, with tha
ingenuity and profound reading which distinguish his brethren, l
had determined to take up.

Well, sir, this youth and I went to the exhibitions togethe
and I watched his behaviour before the pictures. At the tragi
swaggering, theatrical-historical pictures, he yawned; before son
of the grand flashy landscapes, he stood without the least emotio
but before some quiet scenes of humour or pathos, or some eas

little copy of nature, the youth stood in pleased contemplation, the nails of his highlows seemed to be screwed into the floor there, and his face dimpled over with grins.

"These little pictures," said he, on being questioned, "are worth a hundred times more than the big ones. In the latter you see signs of ignorance of every kind, weakness of hand, poverty of invention, carelessness of drawing, lamentable imbecility of thought. Their heroism is borrowed from the theatre, their sentiment is so maudlin that it makes you sick. I see no symptoms of thought or of minds strong and genuine enough to cope with elevated subjects. No individuality, no novelty, the decencies of costume" (my friend did not mean that the figures we were looking at were naked, like Mr. Etty's, but that they were dressed out of all historical propriety) "are disregarded ; the people are striking attitudes, as at the Coburg. There is something painful to me in this *naïve* exhibition of incompetency, this imbecility that is so unconscious of its own failure. If, however, the aspiring men don't succeed, the modest do ; and what they have really seen or experienced, our artists can depict with successful accuracy and delightful skill. Hence," says he, "I would sooner have So-and-so's little sketch, ('A Donkey on a Common') than What-d'ye-call-'em's enormous picture ('Sir Walter Manny and the Crusaders discovering Nova Scotia'), and prefer yonder unpretending sketch, 'Shrimp Catchers, Morning' (how exquisitely the long and level sands are touched off ! how beautifully the morning light touches the countenances of the fishermen, and illumines the rosy features of the shrimps !), to yonder pretentious illustration from Spencer, 'Sir Botibol rescues Una from Sir Uglimore in the Cave of the Enchantress Ichthyosaura.'"

I am only mentioning another's opinion of these pictures, and would not of course, for my own part, wish to give pain by provoking comparisons that must be disagreeable to some persons. But I could not help agreeing with my young friend and saying, "Well, then, in the name of goodness, my dear fellow, if you only like what is real, and natural, and unaffected—if upon such works you gaze with delight, while from more pretentious performances you turn away with weariness, why the deuce must *you* be in the heroic vein ? Why don't you *do* what you like ?" The young man turned round on the iron heel of his highlows, and walked downstairs clinking them sulkily.

There are a variety of classes and divisions into which the works of our geniuses may be separated. There are the heroic pictures, the theatrical-heroic, the religious, the historical sentimental, the historical-familiar, the namby-pamby, and so forth.

13

Among the heroic pictures of course Mr. Haydon's ranks the first, its size and pretensions call for that place. It roars out to you as it were with a Titanic voice from among all the competitors to public favour, " Come and look at me." A broad-shouldered, swaggering, hulking archangel, with those rolling eyes and distending nostrils which belong to the species of sublime caricature, stands scowling on a sphere from which the devil is just descending bound earth-wards. Planets, comets, and other astronomical phenomena, roll and blaze round the pair and flame in the new blue sky. There is something burly and bold in this resolute genius which will attack only enormous subjects, which will deal with nothing but the epic, something respectable even in the defeats of such characters. I was looking the other day at Southampton at a stout gentleman in a green coat and white hat, who a year or two since fully believed that he could walk upon the water, and set off in the presence of a great concourse of people upon his supermarine journey. There is no need to tell you that the poor fellow got a wetting and sank amidst the jeers of all his beholders. I think somehow they should not have laughed at that honest ducked gentleman, they should have respected the faith and simplicity which led him unhesitatingly to venture upon that watery experiment; and so, instead of laugh-ing at Haydon, which you and I were just about to do, let us check our jocularity, and give him credit for his great earnestness of purpose. I begin to find the world growing more pathetic daily, and laugh less every year of my life. Why laugh at idle hopes, or vain purposes, or utter blundering self-confidence? Let us be gentle with them henceforth; who knows whether there may not be something of the sort *chez nous?* But I am wandering from Haydon and his big picture. Let us hope somebody will buy. Who, I cannot tell; it will not do for a chapel; it is too big for a house; I have it—it might answer to hang up over a caravan at a fair, if a travelling orrery were exhibited inside.

This may be sheer impertinence and error, the picture may suit some tastes—it does the *Times* for instance, which pronounces it to be a noble work of the highest art; whereas the *Post* won't believe a bit, and passes it by with scorn. What a comfort it is that there are different tastes then, and that almost all artists have thus a chance of getting a livelihood somehow! There is Martin, for another instance, with his brace of pictures about Adam and Eve, which I would venture to place in the theatrical-heroic class. One looks at those strange pieces and wonders how people can be found to admire, and yet they do. Grave old people, with chains and seals, look dumbfoundered into those vast per-spectives, and think the apex of the sublime is reached there. In

one of Sir Bulwer Lytton's novels there is a passage to that effect.
I forget where, but there is a new edition of them coming out in
single volumes, and I am positive you will find the sentiment somewhere; they come up to his conceptions of the sublime, they answer
to his ideas of beauty, or the Beautiful as he writes it with a large B.
He is himself an artist and a man of genius. What right have we
poor devils to question such an authority? Do you recollect how
we used to laugh in the Capitol at the Domenichino Sibyl which
this same author praises so enthusiastically? a wooden, pink-faced,
goggle-eyed, ogling creature, we said it was, with no more beauty
or sentiment than a wax doll. But this was our conceit, dear
Augusto. On subjects of art, perhaps, there is no reasoning after
all: or who can tell why children have a passion for lollipops, and
this man worships beef while t'other adores mutton? To the child
lollipops may be the truthful and beautiful, and why should not
some men find Martin's pictures as much to their taste as Milton?

Another instance of the blessed variety of tastes may be mentioned here advantageously; while, as you have seen, the *Times*
awards the palm to Haydon, and Sir Lytton exalts Martin as the
greatest painter of the English school, the *Chronicle*, quite as well
informed, no doubt, says that Mr. Eddis is the great genius of the
present season, and that his picture of Moses's mother parting
with him before leaving him in the bulrushes is a great and noble
composition.

This critic must have a taste for the neat and agreeable, that is
clear. Mr. Eddis's picture is nicely coloured; the figures in fine
clean draperies, the sky a bright clean colour; Moses's mother is a
handsome woman: and as she holds her child to her breast for the
last time, and lifts up her fine eyes to heaven, the beholder may be
reasonably moved by a decent *bourgeois* compassion; a handsome
woman parting from her child is always an object of proper sympathy; but as for the greatness of the picture as a work of art,
that is another question of tastes again. This picture seemed to
me to be essentially a prose composition, not a poetical one. It tells
you no more than you can see. It has no more wonder or poetry
about it than a police-report or a newspaper paragraph, and should
be placed, as I take it, in the historic-sentimental school, which is
pretty much followed in England—nay, as close as possible to the
namby-pamby quarter.

Of the latter sort there are some illustrious examples; and as
it is the fashion for critics to award prizes, I would for my part
cheerfully award the prize of a new silver teaspoon to Mr. Redgrave,
the champion of suffering female innocence, for his "Governess."
That picture is more decidedly *spoony* than, perhaps, any other of

this present season : and the subject seems to be a favourite with the artist. We have had the " Governess " one year before, or a variation of her under the name of the " Teacher," or *vice versâ*. The Teacher's young pupils are at play in the garden, she sits sadly in the schoolroom ; there she sits, poor dear !—the piano is open beside her, and (oh, harrowing thought ! " Home, sweet home ! " is open in the music-book. She sits and thinks of that dear place, with a sheet of black-edged note-paper in her hand. They have brought her her tea and bread and butter on a tray. She has drunk the tea, *she has not tasted the bread and butter*. There is pathos for you ! there is art ! This is, indeed, a love for lollipops with a vengeance, a regular babyhood of taste, about which a man with a manly stomach may be allowed to protest a little peevishly, and implore the public to give up such puling food.

There is a gentleman in the Octagon Room who, to be sure, runs Mr. Redgrave rather hard, and should have a silver papspoon at any rate, if the teaspoon is irrevocably awarded to his rival. The Octagon Room prize is a picture called the " Arrival of the Overland Mail." A lady is in her bedchamber, a portrait of her husband, Major Jones (cherished lord of that bridal apartment, with its drab-curtained bed), hangs on the wainscot in the distance, and you see his red coat and mustachios gleaming there between the wardrobe and the washhand-stand. But where is his lady ? She is on her knees by the bedside, her face has sunk into the feather-bed ; her hands are clasped agonisingly together ; a most tremendous black-edged letter has just arrived by the overland mail. It is all up with Jones. Well, let us hope she will marry again, and get over her grief for poor J.

Is not there something *naïve* and simple in this downright way of exciting compassion ? I saw people looking at this pair of pictures evidently with yearning hearts. The great geniuses who invented them have not, you see, toiled in vain. They can command the sympathies of the public, they have gained Art-Union prizes let us hope, as well as those humble imaginary ones which I have just awarded, and yet my heart is not naturally hard, though it refuses to be moved by such means as are here employed.

If the simple statement of a death is to harrow up the feelings, or to claim the tributary tear, *mon Dieu !* a man ought to howl every morning over the newspaper obituary. If we are to cry for every governess who leaves home, what a fund of pathos the *Times* advertisements would afford daily ; we might weep down whole columns of close type. I have said before I am growing more inclined to the pathetic daily, but let us in the name of goodness make a stand somewhere, or the namby-pamby of the world will become unendurable; and we shall melt away in a deluge of blubber. This drivelling hysterical sentimentality, it is surely the critic's duty to grin down, to shake any man roughly by the shoulder who seems dangerously affected by it, and, not sparing his feelings in the least, tell him he is a fool for his pains, to have no more respect for those who invent it, but expose their error with all the downrightness that is necessary.

By far the prettiest of the maudlin pictures is Mr. Stone's "Premier Pas." It is that old, pretty, rococo, fantastic Jenny and Jessamy couple, whose loves the painter has been chronicling any time these five years, and whom he has spied out at various wells, porches, &c. The lad is making love with all his might, and the maiden is in a pretty confusion—her heart flutters, and she only seems to spin. She drinks in the warm words of the young fellow with a pleasant conviction of the invincibility of her charms. He appeals nervously, and tugs at a pink which is growing up the porch-side. It is that pink, somehow, which has saved the picture from being decidedly namby-pamby. There is something new, fresh, and delicate about the little incident of the flower. It redeems Jenny, and renders that young prig Jessamy bearable. The picture is very nicely painted, according to the careful artist's wont. The neck and hands of the girl are especially pretty. The lad's face is effeminate and imbecile, but his velveteen breeches are painted with great vigour and strength.

This artist's picture of the "Queen and Ophelia" is in a much higher walk of art. There may be doubts about Ophelia. She is too pretty to my taste. Her dress (especially the black bands round her arms) too elaborately conspicuous and coquettish. The Queen is a noble dramatic head and attitude. Ophelia seems to be looking at us, the audience, and in a pretty attitude expressly to captivate us. The Queen is only thinking about the crazed girl, and Hamlet, and her own gloomy affairs, and has quite forgotten her own noble beauty and superb presence. The colour of the picture struck me as quite new, sedate, but bright and very agreeable; the chequered light and shadow is made cleverly to aid in forming the composition; it is very picturesque and good. It is by far the best of Mr. Stone's works, and in the best line. Good bye, Jenny and Jessamy; we hope never to see you again—no more rococo rustics, no more namby-pamby : the man who can paint the Queen of "Hamlet" must forsake henceforth such fiddle-faddle company.

By the way, has any Shakspearian commentator ever remarked how fond the Queen really was of her second husband, the excellent Claudius? How courteous and kind the latter was always towards her? So excellent a family-man ought to be pardoned a few errors in consideration of his admirable behaviour to his wife. He *did* go a little far, certainly, but then it was to possess a jewel of a woman.

More pictures indicating a fine appreciation of the tragic sentiment are to be found in the exhibition. Among them may be mentioned specially Mr. Johnson's picture of "Lord Russell taking the Communion in Prison before Execution." The story is finely told here, the group large and noble. The figure of the kneeling wife, who looks at her husband meekly engaged in the last sacred office, is very good indeed; and the little episode of the gaoler, who looks out into the yard indifferent, seems to me to give evidence of a true dramatic genius. In "Hamlet," how those indifferent remarks of Guildenstern and Rosencrantz, at the end, bring out the main figures and deepen the surrounding gloom of the tragedy!

In Mr. Frith's admirable picture of the "Good Pastor," from Goldsmith, there is some sentiment of a very quiet, refined, Sir-Roger-de-Coverley-like sort—not too much of it—it is indicated rather than expressed. "Sentiment, sir," Walker of the "Original" used to say—"sentiment, sir, is like garlic in made dishes: it should be felt everywhere and seen nowhere."

Now, I won't say that Mr. Frith's sentiment is like garlic, or provoke any other savoury comparison regarding it; but say, in a word, this is one of the pictures I would like to have sent abroad to be exhibited at a European congress of painters, to show what an English artist can do. The young painter seems to me to have had a thorough comprehension of his subject and his own abilities. And what a rare quality is this, to know what you can do! An ass will go and take the grand historic walk, while, with lowly wisdom, Mr. Frith prefers the lowly path where there are plenty of flowers growing, and children prattling along the walks. This is the sort of picture that is good to paint nowadays—kindly, beautiful, inspiring delicate sympathies, and awakening tender good-humour. It is a comfort to have such a companion as that in a study to look up at when your eyes are tired with work, and to refresh you with its gentle quiet good-fellowship. I can see it now, as I shut my own eyes, displayed faithfully on the camera obscura of the brain—the dear old parson with his congregation of old and young clustered round him; the little ones plucking him by the gown, with wondering eyes, half-roguery, half-terror; the smoke is curling up from the cottage chimneys in a peaceful Sabbath-sort of way; the three village quidnuncs are chattering together at the churchyard stile; there's a poor girl seated there on a stone, who has been crossed in love evidently, and looks anxiously to the parson for a little doubtful consolation. That's the real sort of sentiment—there's no need of a great, clumsy, black-edged letter to placard her misery, as it were, after Mr. Redgrave's fashion; the sentiment is only the more sincere for being unobtrusive, and the spectator gives his compassion the more readily because the unfortunate object makes no coarse demands upon his pity.

The painting of this picture is exceedingly clever and dexterous. One or two of the foremost figures are painted with the breadth and pearly delicacy of Greuze. The three village politicians, in the background, might have been touched by Teniers, so neat, brisk, and sharp is the execution of the artist's facile brush.

Mr. Frost (a new name, I think, in the catalogue) has given us a picture of "Sabrina," which is so pretty that I heartily hope it has not been purchased for the collection from "Comus," which adorns the Buckingham Palace summer-house. It is worthy of a better place and price than our Royal patrons appear to be disposed to give for the works of English artists. What victims have those poor fellows been of this awful patronage. Great has been the commotion in the pictorial world, dear Augusto, regarding the fate of those frescoes which Royalty was pleased to order, which it con-descended to purchase at a price that no poor amateur would have the face to offer. Think of the greatest patronage in the world giving forty pounds for pictures worth four hundred—condescending to buy works from humble men who could not refuse, and paying for them below their value ! Think of august powers and princi-palities ordering the works of such a great man as Etty to be hacked out of the palace wall—that was a slap in the face to every artist in England ; and I can agree with the conclusion come to by an indignant poet of *Punch's* band, who says, for his part—

> " I will not toil for Queen and crown,
>   If princely patrons spurn me down ;
>   I will not ask for Royal job—
>   Let my Mæcenas be A SNOB ! "

This is, however, a delicate, an awful subject, over which loyal subjects like you and I had best mourn in silence ; but the fate of Etty's noble picture of last year made me tremble lest Frost should be similarly nipped : and I hope more genuine patronage for this promising young painter. His picture is like a mixture of very good Hilton and Howard raised to a state of genius. There is sameness in the heads, but great grace and beauty—a fine sweeping movement in the composition of the beautiful fairy figures, undu-lating gracefully through the stream, while the lilies lie gracefully overhead. There is another submarine picture of "Nymphs cajoling Young Hylas," which contains a great deal of very clever imitations of Boucher.

That youthful Goodall, whose early attempts promised so much, is not quite realising those promises I think, and is cajoled, like Hylas before mentioned, by dangerous beauty. His "Connemara Girls going to Market" are a vast deal too clean and pretty for such females. They laugh and simper in much too genteel a manner; they are washing such pretty white feet as I don't think are common about Leenane or Ballynahinch, and would be better at ease in white satin slippers than trudging up Croaghpatrick. There is a luxury of geographical knowledge for you! I have not done with it yet. Stop till we come to Roberts's "View of Jerusalem," and Müller's pictures of "Rhodes," and "Xanthus," and "Telmessus." This artist's sketches are excellent; like nature, and like Decamps, that best of painters of Oriental life and colours. In the pictures the artist forgets the brilliancy of colour which is so conspicuous in his sketches, and "Telmessus" looks as grey and heavy as Dover in March.

Mr. Pickersgill (not the Academician, by any means) deserves great praise for two very poetical pieces; one from Spenser, I think (Sir Botibol let us say, as before, with somebody in some hag's cave); another called the "Four Ages," which has still better grace and sentiment. This artist, too, is evidently one of the disciples of Hilton; and another, who has also, as it seems to me, studied with advantage that graceful and agreeable English painter, Mr. Hook, whose "Song of the Olden Time" is hung up in the Octagon Closet, and makes a sunshine in that exceedingly shady place. The female figure is faulty, but charming (many charmers have their little faults, it is said); the old bard who is singing the song of the olden time a most venerable, agreeable, and handsome old minstrel. In Alnaschar-like moods a man fancies himself a noble patron, and munificent rewarder of artists; in which case I should like to possess myself of the works of these two young men, and give them four times as large a price as the —— gave for pictures five times as good as theirs.

I suppose Mr. Eastlake's composition from "Comus" is the contribution in which *he* has been mulcted, in company with his celebrated brother artists, for the famous Buckingham Palace pavilion. Working for nothing is very well: but to work for a good, honest, remunerating price is, perhaps, the best way, after all. I can't help thinking that the artist's courage has failed him over his "Comus" picture. Time and pains he has given, that is quite evident. The picture is prodigiously laboured, and hatched, and tickled up with a Chinese minuteness ; but there is a woeful lack of *vis* in the work. That poor labourer has kept his promise, has worked the given number of hours ; but he has had no food all the while, and has executed his job in a somewhat faint manner. This face of the lady is pure and beautiful ; but we have seen it at any time these ten years, with its red transparent shadows, its mouth in which butter wouldn't melt, and its beautiful brown-madder hair. She is getting rather tedious, that sweet irreproachable creature, that is the fact. She may be an angel ; but sky-blue, my wicked senses tell me, is a feeble sort of drink, and men require stronger nourishment.

Mr. Eastlake's picture is a prim, mystic, cruciform composition. The lady languishes in the middle ; an angel is consoling her, and embracing her with an arm out of joint ; little rows of cherubs stand on each side the angels and the lady,— wonderful little children, with blue or brown beady eyes, and sweet little flossy curly hair, and no muscles or bones, as becomes such supernatural beings, no doubt. I have seen similar little darlings in the toy-shops in the Lowther Arcade for a shilling, with just such pink cheeks and round eyes, their bodies formed out of cotton-wool, and their extremities veiled in silver paper. Well ; it is as well, perhaps, that Etty's jovial nymphs should not come into such a company. Good Lord ! how they would astonish the weak nerves of Mr. Eastlake's *précieuse* young lady !

Quite unabashed by the squeamishness exhibited in the highest quarter (as the newspapers call it), Mr. Etty goes on rejoicing in his old fashion. Perhaps he is worse than ever this year, and despises *nec dulces amores nec choreas*, because certain great personages are offended. Perhaps, this year, his ladies and Cupids are a little *hasardés ;* his Venuses expand more than ever in the line of Hottentot beauty ; his drawing and colouring are still more audacious than they were ; patches of red shine on the cheeks of his blowsy nymphs ; his idea of form goes to the verge of monstrosity. If you look at the pictures closely (and, considering all things, it requires some courage to do so), the forms disappear ; feet and hands are scumbled away, and distances appear to be dabs and blotches of lakes, and brown and ultramarine. It must be con fessed that some of these pictures would *not* be suitable to hang up everywhere—in a young ladies' school, for instance. But, how rich and superb is the colour ! Did Titian paint better, or Rubens as well ? There is a nymph and child in the left corner of the Great Room, sitting, without the slightest fear of catching cold, in a sort of moonlight, of which the colour appears to me to be as rich and wonderful as Titian's best—" Bacchus and Ariadne," for instance—

and better than Rubens's. There is a little head of a boy in a blue dress (for once in a way) which kills every picture in the room, out-stares all the red-coated generals, out-blazes Mrs. Thwaites and her diamonds (who has the place of honour) ; and has that unmistak-able, inestimable, indescribable mark of the GREAT painter about it, which makes the soul of a man kindle up as he sees it and owns that there is Genius. How delightful it is to feel that shock, and how few are the works of art that can give it !

The author of that sibylline book of mystic rhymes, the un revealed bard of the " Fallacies of Hope," is as great as usual, vibrating between the absurd and the sublime, until the eye grows dazzled in watching him, and can't really tell in what region he is. If Etty's colour is wild and mysterious, looking here as if smeared with the finger, and there with the palette knife, what can be said about Turner ? Go up and look at one of his pictures, and you laugh at yourself and at him, and at the picture, and that wonder-ful amateur who is invariably found to give a thousand pounds for it, or more—some sum wild, prodigious, unheard-of, monstrous, like the picture itself. All about the author of the " Fallacies of Hope " is a mysterious extravaganza ; price, poem, purchaser, picture. Look at the latter for a little time, and it begins to affect you too, —to mesmerise you. It is revealed to you ; and, as it is said in the East, the magicians make children see the sultauns, carpet-bearers, tents, &c., in a spot of ink in their hands ; so the magician, Joseph Mallord, makes you see what he likes on a board, that to the first view is merely dabbed over with occasional streaks of yellow, and flicked here and there with vermilion. The vermilion blotches become little boats full of harpooners and gondolas with a deal of music going on on board. That is not a smear of purple you see yonder, but a beautiful whale, whose tail has just slapped a half-dozen whale-boats into perdition ; and as for what you fancied to be a few zig-zag lines spattered on the canvas at haphazard, look ! they turn out to be a ship with all her sails ; the captain and his crew are clearly visible in the ship's bows : and you may distinctly see the oil-casks getting ready under the superintendence of that man with the red whiskers and the cast in his eye ; who is, of course, the chief mate. In a word, I say that Turner is a great and awful mystery to me. I don't like to contemplate him too much, lest I should actually begin to believe in his poetry as well as his paintings, and fancy the " Fallacies of Hope " to be one of the finest poems in the world.

Now Stanfield has no mysticism or oracularity about him. You can see what he means at once. His style is as simple and manly as a seaman's song. One of the most dexterous, he is also one of the most careful of painters. Every year his works are more elaborated, and you are surprised to find a progress in an artist who had seemed to reach his acme before. His battle of frigates this year is a brilliant sparkling pageant of naval war ; his great picture of the " Mole of Ancona," fresh, healthy, and bright as breeze and sea can make it. There are better pieces still by this painter, to my mind ; one in the first room, especially,—a Dutch landscape, with a warm sunny tone upon it, worthy of Cuyp and Callcott. Who is G. Stanfield, an exhibitor and evidently a pupil of, the Royal Academician ? Can it be a son of that gent ? If so, the father has a worthy heir to his name and honours. G. Stanfield's Dutch picture may be looked at by the side of his father's.

Roberts has also distinguished himself and advanced in skill, great as his care had been and powerful his effects before. " The Ruins of Karnac " is the most poetical of this painter's works, I think. A vast and awful scene of gloomy Egyptian ruin ! the sun lights up tremendous lines of edifices, which were only parts formerly of the enormous city of the hundred gates ; long lines of camels come over the reddening desert, and camps are set by the side of the glowing pools. This is a good picture to gaze at, and to fill your eyes and thoughts with grandiose ideas of Eastern life.

This gentleman's large picture of " Jerusalem " did not satisfy me so much. It is yet very faithful ; anybody who has visited this place must see the careful fidelity with which the artist has mapped the rocks and valleys, and laid down the lines of the buildings ; but the picture has, to my eyes, too green and trim a look ; the mosques and houses look fresh and new, instead of being mouldering, old, sun-baked edifices of glaring stone rising amidst wretchedness and ruin. There is not, to my mind, that sad fatal aspect, which the city presents from whatever quarter you view it, and which haunts a man who has seen it ever after with an impression of terror. Perhaps in the spring for a little while, at which season the sketch for this picture was painted, the country round about may look very cheerful. When we saw it in autumn, the mountains that stand round about Jerusalem were not green, but ghastly piles of hot rock, patched here and there with yellow weedy herbage. A cactus or a few bleak olive-trees made up the vegetation of the wretched gloomy landscape ; whereas in Mr. Roberts's picture the valley of Jehoshaphat looks like a glade in a park, and the hills, up to the gates, are carpeted with verdure.

Being on the subject of Jerusalem, here may be mentioned with praise Mr. Hart's picture of a Jewish ceremony, with a Hebrew name I have forgotten. This piece is exceedingly bright and pleas- ing in colour, odd and novel as a representation of manners and costume, a striking and agreeable picture. I don't think as much can be said for the same artist's "Sir Thomas More going to Execution." Miss More is crying on papa's neck, pa looks up to heaven, halberdiers look fierce, &c. : all the regular adjuncts and property of pictorial tragedy are here brought into play. But nobody cares, that is the fact ; and one fancies the designer himself cannot have cared much for the orthodox historical group whose misfortunes he was depicting.

These pictures are like boys' hexameters at school. Every lad of decent parts in the sixth form has a knack of turning out great quantities of respectable verse, without blunders, and with scarce any mental labour ; but these verses are not the least like poetry, any more. than the great Academical paintings of the artists are like great painting. You want something more than a composition, and a set of costumes and figures decently posed and studied. If these were all, for instance, Mr. Charles Landseer's picture of "Charles I. before the Battle of Edge Hill" would be a good work of art. Charles stands at a tree before the inn-door, officers are round about, the little princes are playing with a little dog, as becomes their youth and innocence, rows of soldiers appear in red coats, nobody seems to have anything particular to do, except the Royal martyr, who is looking at a bone of ham that a girl out of the inn has hold of.

Now this is all very well, but you want something more than this in an historic picture, which should have its parts, characters, varieties, and climax like a drama. You don't want the *Deus intersit* for no other purpose than to look at a knuckle of ham ; and here is a piece well composed and (bating a little want of life in the figures) well drawn, brightly and pleasantly painted, as all this artist's works are, all the parts and accessories studied and executed with care and skill, and yet meaning nothing—the part of Hamlet omitted. The King in this attitude (with the bâton in his hand, simpering at the bacon aforesaid) has no more of the heroic in him than the pork he contemplates, and he deserves to lose every battle he fights. I prefer the artist's other still-life pictures to this. He has a couple more, professedly so called, very cleverly executed and capital cabinet pieces.

Strange to say, I have not one picture to remark upon taken from the "Vicar of Wakefield." Mr. Ward has a very good Hogarthian work, with some little extravagance and caricature, representing Johnson waiting in Lord Chesterfield's ante-chamber, among a crowd of hangers-on and petitioners, who are sulky, or yawning, or neglected, while a pretty Italian singer comes out, having evidently had a very satisfactory interview with his Lordship, and who (to lose no time) is arranging another rendezvous with another admirer. This story is very well, coarsely, and humorously told, and is as racy as a chapter out of Smollett. There is a yawning chaplain, whose head is full of humour ; and a pathetic episode of a widow and pretty child, in which the artist has not succeeded so well.

There is great delicacy and beauty in Mr. Herbert's picture of " Pope Gregory teaching Children to Sing." His Holiness lies on his sofa languidly beating time over his book. He does not look strong enough to use the scourge in his hands, and with which the painter says he used to correct his little choristers. Two ghostly aides-de-camp in the shape of worn, handsome, shaven ascetic friars, stand behind the pontiff demurely ; and all the choristers are in full song, with their mouths as wide open as a nest of young birds when the mother comes. The painter seems to me to have acquired the true spirit of the middle-age devotion. All his works have unction ; and the prim, subdued, ascetic face, which forms the charm and mystery of the missal-illuminations, and which has operated to convert some imaginative minds from the new to the old faith.

And, by way of a wonder, behold a devotional picture from Mr. Edwin Landseer, " A Shepherd Praying at a Cross in the Fields." I suppose the Sabbath church-bells are ringing from the city far away in the plain. Do you remember the beautiful lines of Uhland ?—

> " Es ist der Tag des Herrn :
> Ich bin allein auf weitern Flur,
> Noch eine Morgenglocke nur,
> Und Stille nah und fern.
>
> Anbetend knie ich hier.
> O süsses Graun, geheimes Wehn,
> Als knieeten Viele ungesehn
> Und beteten mit mir."

Here is a noble and touching pictorial illustration of them—of Sabbath repose and *recueillement*—an almost endless flock of sheep lies around the pious pastor : the sun shines peacefully over the vast fertile plain ; blue mountains keep watch in the distance ; and the sky above is serenely clear. I think this is the highest flight of poetry the painter has dared to take yet. The numbers and variety of attitude and expression in that flock of sheep quite startle the spectator as he examines them. The picture is a wonder of skill.

How richly the good pictures cluster at this end of the room !

There is a little Mulready, of which the colour blazes out like sapphires and rubies ; a pair of Leslies—one called the "Heiress" —one a scene from Molière—both delightful :—these are flanked by the magnificent nymphs of Etty, before mentioned. What school of art in Europe, or what age, can show better painters than these in their various lines ? The young men do well, but the eldest do best still. No wonder the English pictures are fetching their thousands of guineas at the sales. They deserve these great prices as well as the best works of the Hollanders.

I am sure that three such pictures as Mr. Webster's "Dame's School" ought to entitle the proprietor to pay the income-tax. There is a little caricature in some of the children's faces ; but the schoolmistress is a perfect figure, most admirably natural, humorous, and sentimental. The picture is beautifully painted, full of air, of delightful harmony and tone.

There are works by Creswick that can hardly be praised too much. One particularly, called "A Place to be Remembered," which no lover of pictures can see and forget. Danby's great "Evening Scene" has portions which are not surpassed by Cuyp or Claude ; and a noble landscape of Lee's, among several others—a height with some trees and a great expanse of country beneath.

From the fine pictures you come to the class which are very nearly being fine pictures. In this I would enumerate a landscape or two by Collins ; Mr. Leigh's "Polyphemus," of which the landscape part is very good, and only the figure questionable ; and let us say Mr. Elmore's "Origin of the Guelf and Ghibelline Factions," which contains excellent passages, and admirable drawing and dexterity, but fails to strike as a whole somehow. There is not sufficient purpose in it, or the story is not enough to interest, or, though the parts are excellent, the whole is somewhere deficient.

There is very little comedy in the exhibition, most of the young artists tending to the sentimental rather than the ludicrous. Leslie's scene from Molière is the best comedy. Collins's "Fetching the Doctor" is also delightful fun. The greatest farce, however, is Chalon's picture with an Italian title, "B. Virgine col," &c. Impudence never went beyond this. The infant's hair has been curled into ringlets, the mother sits on her chair with painted cheeks and a Haymarket leer. The picture might serve for the oratory of an opera-girl.

Among the portraits, Knight's and Watson Gordon's are the best. A "Mr. Pigeon" by the former hangs in the place of honour usually devoted to our gracious Prince, and is a fine rich state picture. Even better are those by Mr. Watson Gordon : one representing a gentleman in black silk stockings whose name has

escaped the memory of your humble servant; another, a fine
portrait of Mr. De Quincey, the opium-eater. Mr. Lawrence's
heads, solemn and solidly painted, look out at you from their
frames, though they be ever so high placed, and push out of sight
the works of more flimsy but successful practitioners. A portrait
of great power and richness of colour is that of Mr. Lopez by
Linnell. Mr. Grant is a favourite; but a very unsound painter
to my mind, painting like a brilliant and graceful amateur rather
than a serious artist. But there is a quiet refinement and beauty
about his female heads, which no other painter can perhaps give,
and charms in spite of many errors. Is it Count d'Orsay, or is it
Mr. Ainsworth, that the former has painted? Two peas are not
more alike than these two illustrious characters.

In the miniature-room, Mr. Richmond's drawings are of so
grand and noble a character, that they fill the eye as much as full-
length canvases. Nothing can be finer than Mrs. Fry and the
grey-haired lady in black velvet. There is a certain severe, respectable, Exeter-Hall look about most of this artist's pictures,
that the observer may compare with the Catholic physiognomies of
Mr. Herbert: see his picture of Mr. Pugin, for instance; it tells
of chants and cathedrals, as Mr. Richmond's work somehow does
of Clapham Common and the May Meetings. The genius of
Mayfair fires the bosom of Chalon, the tea-party, the quadrille,
the hairdresser, the tailor, and the flunkey. All Ross's miniatures
sparkle with his wonderful and minute skill; Carrick's are excellent;
Thorburn's almost take the rank of historical pictures. In his
picture of two sisters, one has almost the most beautiful head in the
world; and his picture of Prince Albert, clothed in red and leaning
on a turquoise sabre, has ennobled that fine head, and given His
Royal Highness's pale features an air of sunburnt and warlike
vigour. Miss Corbaux, too, has painted one of the loveliest heads
ever seen. Perhaps this is the pleasantest room of the whole, for
you are sure to meet your friends here; kind faces smile at you
from the ivory; and features of fair creatures, oh! how——

.   .   .   .

Here the eccentric author breaks into a rhapsody of thirteen
pages regarding No. 2576, Mrs. Major Blogg, who was formerly
Miss Poddy of Cheltenham, whom it appears that Michael Angelo
knew and admired. The feelings of the Poddy family might be
hurt, and the jealousy of Major Blogg aroused, were we to print
Titmarsh's rapturous description of that lady; nor, indeed, can we
give him any further space, seeing that this is nearly the last page
of the Magazine.* He concludes by a withering denunciation of

* *Fraser's Magazine.*

most of the statues in the vault where they are buried ; praising however, the children, Paul and Virginia, the head of Bayly's nymph, and M'Dowall's boy. He remarks the honest character of the English countenance as exhibited in the busts, and contrasts it with Louis Philippe's head by Jones, on whom, both as a sculptor and a singer, he bestows great praise. He indignantly remonstrates with the committee for putting by far the finest female bust in the room, No. 1434, by Powers of Florence, in a situation where it cannot be seen ; and, quitting the gallery finally, says he must go before he leaves town and give one more look at Hunt's " Boy at Prayers," in the Water-Colour Exhibition which he pronounces to be the finest serious work of the year.

A BROTHER OF THE PRESS ON THE HISTORY OF A LITERARY MAN, LAMAN BLANCHARD, AND THE CHANCES OF THE LITERARY PROFESSION

IN A LETTER TO THE REVEREND FRANCIS SYLVESTER AT ROME, FROM MICHAEL ANGELO TITMARSH, ESQUIRE

LONDON: *Feb.* 20, 1846.

MY DEAR SIR,—Our good friend and patron, the publisher of this Magazine,* has brought me your message from Rome, and your demand to hear news from the *other* great city of the world. As the forty columns of the *Times* cannot satisfy your reverence's craving, and the details of the real great revolution of England which is actually going on do not sufficiently interest you, I send you a page or two of random speculations upon matters connected with the literary profession : they were suggested by reading the works and the biography of a literary friend of ours, lately deceased, and for whom every person who knew him had the warmest and sincerest regard. And no wonder. It was impossible to help trusting a man so thoroughly generous and honest, and loving one who was so perfectly gay, gentle, and amiable.

A man can't enjoy everything in the world ; but what delightful gifts and qualities are these to have ! Not having known Blanchard as intimately as some others did, yet, I take it, he had in his life as much pleasure as falls to most men ; the kindest friends, the most affectionate family, a heart to enjoy both ; and a career not undistinguished, which I hold to be the smallest matter of all. But we have a cowardly dislike, or compassion for, the fact of a man dying poor. Such a one is rich, bilious, and a curmudgeon, without heart or stomach to enjoy his money, and we set him down as respectable : another is morose or passionate, his whole view of life seen blood-shot through passion, or jaundiced through moroseness : or he is a fool who can't see, or feel, or enjoy anything at all, with no ear for music, no eye for beauty, no heart for love, with nothing

* *Fraser's Magazine.*

except money : we meet such people every day, and respect them somehow. That donkey browses over five thousand acres; that madman's bankers come bowing him out to his carriage. You feel secretly pleased at shooting over the acres, or driving in the carriage. At any rate, nobody thinks of compassionating their owners. We are a race of flunkeys, and keep our pity for the poor.

The kind and distinguished gentleman who has written Blanchard's Memoir has, it seems to me, couched it in much too despondent a strain. The lot of the hero of the little story was by no means deplorable; and there is not the least call at present to be holding up literary men as martyrs. Even that prevailing sentiment which regrets that means should not be provided for giving them leisure, for enabling them to perfect great works in retirement, that they should waste away their strength with fugitive literature, &c., I hold to be often uncalled for and dangerous. I believe, if most men of letters were to be pensioned, I am sorry to say I believe they wouldn't work 'at all; and of others, that the labour which is to answer the calls of the day is the one quite best suited to their genius. Suppose Sir Robert Peel were to write to you, and enclosing a cheque for £20,000, instruct you to pension any fifty deserving authors, so that they might have leisure to retire and write "great" works, on whom would you fix?

People in the big-book interest, too, cry out against the fashion of fugitive literature, and no wonder. For instance—

The *Times* gave an extract the other day from a work by one Doctor Carus, physician to the King of Saxony, who attended his Royal master on his recent visit to England, and has written a book concerning the journey. Among other London lions, the illustrious traveller condescended to visit one of the largest and most remarkable, certainly, of metropolitan roarers—the *Times* printing-office; of which the Doctor, in his capacity of a man of science, gives an exceedingly bad, stupid, and blundering account.

Carus was struck with "disgust," he says, at the prodigious size of the paper, and at the thought which suggested itself to his mind from this enormity. There was as much printed every day as would fill a thick volume. It required ten years of life to a philosopher to write a volume. The issuing of these daily tomes was unfair upon philosophers, who were put out of the market; and unfair on the public, who were made to receive (and, worse still, to get a relish for) crude daily speculations, and frivolous ephemeral news, when they ought to be fed and educated upon stronger and simpler diet.

We have heard this outcry a hundred times from the bigwig body. The world gives up a lamentable portion of its time to fleeting literature; authors who might be occupied upon great works fritter away their lives in producing endless hasty sketches. Kind, wise, and good Doctor Arnold deplored the fatal sympathy which the "Pickwick Papers" had created among the boys of his school; and it is a fact that *Punch* is as regularly read among the boys at Eton as the Latin Grammar.

Arguing for liberty of conscience against any authority, however great—against Doctor Arnold himself, who seems to me to be the greatest, wisest, and best of men, that has appeared for eighteen hundred years; let us take a stand at once, and ask, why should not the day have its literature? Why should not authors make light sketches? Why should not the public be amused daily or frequently by kindly fictions? It is well and just for Arnold to object. Light stories of Jingle and Tupman, and Sam Weller quips and cranks, must have come with but a bad grace before that pure and lofty soul. The trivial and familiar are out of place there; the harmless joker must walk away abashed from such a presence, as he would be silent and hushed in a cathedral. But all the world is not made of that angelic stuff. From his very height and sublimity of virtue he could but look down and deplore the ways of small men beneath him. I mean, seriously, that I think the man was of so august and sublime a nature, that he was not a fair judge of us, or of the ways of the generality of mankind. One has seen a delicate person sicken and faint at the smell of a flower; it does not follow that the flower was not sweet and wholesome in consequence; and I hold that laughing and honest story-books are good, against all the doctors.

Laughing is not the highest occupation of a man, very certainly; or the power of creating it the height of genius. I am not going to argue for that. No more is the blacking of boots the greatest occupation. But it is done, and well and honestly, by persons ordained to that calling in life, who arrogate to themselves (if they are straightforward and worthy shoeblacks) no especial rank or privilege on account of their calling; and not considering boot-brushing the greatest effort of earthly genius, nevertheless select their Day and Martin, or Warren, to the best of their judgment; polish their upper-leathers as well as they can; satisfy their patrons; and earn their fair wage.

I have chosen the unpolite shoeblack comparison, not out of disrespect to the trade of literature; but it is as good a craft as any other to select. In some way or other, for daily bread and hire, almost all men are labouring daily. Without necessity they would not work at all, or very little, probably. In some instances you reap Reputation along with Profit from your labour, but Bread, in the main, is the incentive. Do not let us try to blink this fact, or imagine that the men of the press are working for their honour and glory, or go onward impelled by an irresistible afflatus of genius. If only men of genius were to write, Lord help us ! how many books would there be ? How many people are there even capable of appreciating genius ? Is Mr. Wakley's or Mr. Hume's opinion about poetry worth much ? As much. as that of millions of people in this honest stupid empire ; and they have a right to have books supplied for them as well as the most polished and accomplished critics have. The literary man gets his bread by providing goods suited to the consumption of these. This man of letters contributes a police-report ; that, an article containing some downright information ; this one, as an editor, abuses Sir Robert Peel, or lauds Lord John Russell, or *vice versâ ;* writing to a certain class who coincide in his views, or are interested by the question which he moots. The literary character, let us hope or admit, writes quite honestly ; but no man supposes he would work perpetually but for money. And as for immortality, it is quite beside the bargain. Is it reasonable to look for it, or to pretend that you are actuated by a desire to attain it ? Of all the quill-drivers, how many have ever drawn that prodigious prize ? Is it fair even to ask that many should ? Out of a regard for poor dear posterity and men of letters to come, let us be glad that the great immortality number comes up so rarely. Mankind would have no time otherwise, and would be so gorged with old masterpieces, that they could not occupy themselves with new, and future literary men would have no chance of a livelihood.

To do your work honestly, to amuse and instruct your reader of to-day, to die when your time comes, and go hence with as clean a breast as may be ; may these be all yours and ours, by God's will. Let us be content with our *status* as literary craftsmen, telling the truth as far as may be, hitting no foul blow, condescending to no servile puffery, filling not a very lofty, but a manly and honourable part. Nobody says that Doctor Locock is wasting his time because he rolls about daily in his carriage, and passes hours with the nobility and gentry, his patients, instead of being in his study wrapt up in transcendental medical meditation. Nobody accuses Sir Fitzroy Kelly of neglecting his genius because he will take anybody's brief, and argue it in court for money, when he might sit in chambers with his oak sported, and give up his soul to investigations of the nature, history, and improvement of law. There is no question but that either of these eminent persons, by profound study, might increase their knowledge in certain branches of their profession ; but in the meanwhile the practical part must go on—causes come on for hearing, and ladies lie in, and some one must be there. The commodities in which the lawyer and the doctor deal are absolutely required by the public, and liberally paid for; every day, too, the public requires more literary handicraft done; the practitioner in that trade gets a better pay and place. In another century, very likely, his work will be so necessary to the people, and his market so good, that his prices will double and treble; his social rank rise; he will be getting what they call "honours," and dying in the bosom of the genteel. Our calling is only sneered at because it is not well paid. The world has no other criterion for respectability. In heaven's name, what made people talk of setting up a statue to Sir William Follett? What had he done? He had made £300,000. What has George IV. done that he, too, is to have a brazen image? He was an exemplar of no greatness, no good quality, no duty in life; but a type of magnificence, of beautiful coats, carpets, and gigs, turtle-soup, chandeliers, cream-coloured horses, and delicious Maraschino,—all these good things he expressed and represented: and the world, respecting them beyond all others, raised statues to "the first gentleman in Europe." Directly the men of letters get rich, they will come in for their share of honour too; and a future writer in this miscellany may be getting ten guineas where we get one, and dancing at Buckingham Palace while you and your humble servant, dear Padre Francesco, are glad to smoke our pipes in quiet over the sanded floor of the little D——.

But the happy _homme de lettres_, whom I imagine in futurity kicking his heels _vis-à-vis_ to a duchess in some fandango at the Court of her Majesty's grandchildren, will be in reality no better or honester, or more really near fame, than the quill-driver of the present day, with his doubtful position and small gains. Fame, that guerdon of high genius, comes quite independent of Berkeley Square, and is a republican institution. Look around in our own day among the holders of the pen: begin (without naming names, for that is odious) and count on your fingers those whom you will back in the race for immortality. How many fingers have you that are left untold? It is an invidious question. Alas! dear ——, and dear * *, and dear † †, you who think you are safe, there is futurity, and limbo, and blackness for you, beloved friends! _Cras ingens iterabimus æquor:_ there's no use denying it, or shirking the fact; in we must go, and disappear for ever and ever.

And after all, what is this Reputation, the cant of our trade, the goal that every scribbling penny-a-liner demurely pretends that he is hunting after? Why should we get it? Why can't we do without it? We only fancy we want it. When people say of such and such a man who is dead, "He neglected his talents; he frittered away in fugitive publications time and genius, which might have led to the production of a great work;" this is the gist of Sir Bulwer Lytton's kind and affecting biographical notice of our dear friend and comrade Laman Blanchard, who passed away so melancholily last year.

I don't know anything more dissatisfactory and absurd than that insane test of friendship which has been set up by some literary men—viz., admiration of their works. Say that this picture is bad, or that poem poor, or that article stupid, and there are certain authors and artists among us who set you down as an enemy forthwith, or look upon you as a *faux-frère*. What is there in common with the friend and his work of art? The picture or article once done and handed over to the public is the latter's property, not the author's, and to be estimated according to its honest value; and so, and without malice, I question Sir Bulwer Lytton's statement about Blanchard—viz., that he would have been likely to produce with leisure, and under favourable circumstances, a work of the highest class. I think his education and habits, his quick easy manner, his sparkling hidden fun, constant tenderness, and brilliant good-humour were best employed as they were. At any rate he had a duty, much more imperative upon him than the preparation of questionable great works,—to get his family their dinner. A man must be a very Great man, indeed, before he can neglect this precaution.

His three volumes of essays, pleasant and often brilliant as they are, give no idea of the powers of the author, or even of his natural manner, which, as I think, was a thousand times more agreeable. He was like the good little child in the fairy tale, his mouth dropped out all sorts of diamonds and rubies. His wit, which was always playing and frisking about the company, had the wonderful knack of never hurting anybody. He had the most singular art of discovering good qualities in people; in discoursing of which the kindly little fellow used to glow and kindle up, and emphasise with the most charming energy. Good-natured actions of others, good jokes, favourite verses of friends, he would bring out fondly, whenever they met, or there was question of them; and he used to toss and dandle their sayings or doings about, and hand them round to the company, as the delightful Miss Slowboy does the baby in the last Christmas Book. What was better than wit in his talk was, that it was so genial. He *enjoyed* thoroughly, and chirped over his wine with a good-humour that could not fail to be infectious. His own hospitality was delightful: there was something about it charmingly brisk, simple, and kindly. How he used to laugh!

As I write this, what a number of pleasant hearty scenes come back! One can hear his jolly, clear laughter; and see his keen, kind, beaming Jew face,—a mixture of Mendelssohn and Voltaire.

Sir Bulwer Lytton's account of him will be read by all his friends with pleasure, and by the world as a not uncurious specimen of the biography of a literary man. The memoir savours a little too much of the funeral oration. It might have been a little more particular and familiar, so as to give the public a more intimate acquaintance with one of the honestest and kindest of men who ever lived by pen; and yet, after a long and friendly intercourse with Blanchard, I believe the praises Sir Lytton bestows on his character are by no means exaggerated: it is only the style in which they are given, which is a little too funereally encomiastic. The memoir begins in this way, a pretty and touching design of Mr. Kenny Meadows heading the biography :—

"To most of those who have mixed generally with the men who, in our day, have chosen literature as their profession, the name of Laman Blanchard brings recollections of peculiar tenderness and regret. Amidst a career which the keenness of anxious rivalry renders a sharp probation to the temper and the affections, often yet more embittered by that strife of party, of which, in a Representative Constitution, few men of letters escape the eager passions and the angry prejudice—they recall the memory of a competitor, without envy; a partisan, without gall; firm as the firmest in the maintenance of his own opinions; but gentle as the gentlest in the judgment he passed on others.

"Who, among our London brotherhood of letters, does not miss that simple cheerfulness—that inborn and exquisite urbanity—that childlike readiness to be pleased with all—that happy tendency to panegyrise every merit, and to be lenient to every fault? Who does not recall that acute and delicate sensibility — so easily wounded, and therefore so careful not to wound—which seemed to infuse a certain intellectual fine breeding, of forbearance and sympathy, into every society where it insinuated its gentle way? Who, in convivial meetings, does not miss, and will not miss for ever, the sweetness of those unpretending talents—the earnestness of that honesty which seemed unconscious it was worn so lightly— the mild influence of that exuberant kindness which softened the acrimony of young disputants, and reconciled the secret animosities of jealous rivals? Yet few men had experienced more to sour them than Laman Blanchard, or had gone more resolutely through the author's hardening ordeal of narrow circumstance, of daily labour, and of that disappointment in the higher aims of ambition, which must almost inevitably befall those who retain ideal standards of excellence, to be reached but by time and leisure, and who are yet condemned to draw hourly upon unmatured resources for the practical wants of life. To have been engaged from boyhood in such struggles, and to have preserved, undiminished, generous admiration for those more fortunate, and untiring love for his own noble yet thankless calling; and this with a constitution singularly finely strung, and with all the nervous irritability which usually accompanies the indulgence of the imagination; is a proof of the rarest kind of strength, depending less upon a power purely intellectual, than upon the higher and more beautiful heroism which woman, and such men alone as have the best feelings of a woman's nature, take from instinctive enthusiasm for what is great, and uncalculating faith in what is good.

"It is, regarded thus, that the character of Laman Blanchard assumes an interest of a very elevated order. He was a choice and worthy example of the professional English men of letters, in our day. He is not to be considered in the light of the man of daring and turbulent genius, living on the false excitement of vehement calumny and uproarious praise. His was a career not indeed obscure, but sufficiently quiet and unnoticed to be solaced with little of the pleasure with which, in aspirants of a noisier fame, gratified and not ignoble vanity rewards the labour and stimulates the hope. For more than twenty years he toiled on through the most fatiguing paths of literary composition, mostly in periodicals, often anonymously; pleasing and lightly instructing thousands, but gaining none of the prizes, whether of weighty reputation or popular renown, which more fortunate chances, or more pretending modes of investing talent, have given in our day to men of half his merits."

Not a feature in this charming character is flattered, as far as I know. Did the subject of the memoir feel disappointment in the higher aims of ambition? Was his career not solaced with pleasure? Was his noble calling a thankless one? I have said before, his calling was not thankless; his career, in the main, pleasant; his disappointment, if he had one of the higher aims of ambition, one that might not uneasily be borne. If every man is disappointed because he cannot reach supreme excellence, what a mad misanthropical world ours would be! Why should men of letters aim higher than they can hit, or be "disappointed" with the share of brains God has given them? Nor can you say a man's career is unpleasant who was so heartily liked and appreciated as Blanchard was, by all persons of high intellect, or low, with whom he came in contact. He had to bear with some, but not unbearable poverty.

At home he had everything to satisfy his affection : abroad, every sympathy and consideration met this universally esteemed, good man. Such a calling as his is *not* thankless, surely. Away with this discontent and morbid craving for renown ! A man who writes (Tennyson's) " Ulysses," or " Comus," *may* put in his claim for fame if you will, and demand and deserve it : but it requires no vast power of intellect to write most sets of words, and have them printed in a book :—To write this article, for instance, or the last novel, pamphlet, book of travels. Most men with a decent education and practice of the pen, could go and do the like, were they so professionally urged. Let such fall into the rank and file, and shoulder their weapons, and load, and fire cheerfully. An every-day writer has no more right to repine because he loses the great prizes, and can't write like Shakspeare, than he has to be envious of Sir Robert Peel, or Wellington, or King Hudson, or Taglioni. Because the sun shines above, is a man to warm himself and admire ; or to despond because he can't in his person flare up like the sun ? I don't believe that Blanchard was by any means an amateur martyr, but was, generally speaking, very decently satisfied with his condition.

Here is the account of his early history—a curious and interest ing one :—

" Samuel Laman Blanchard was born of respectable parents in the middle class at Great Yarmouth, on the 15th of May, 1803. His mother's maiden name was Mary Laman. She married first Mr. Cowell, at Saint John's Church, Bermondsey, about the year 1796 ; he died in the following year. In 1799, she was married again to Samuel Blanchard, by whom she had seven children, but only one son, the third child, christened Samuel Laman.

" In 1805 Mr. Blanchard (the father) appears to have removed to the metropolis, and to have settled in Southwark as a painter and glazier. He was enabled to give his boy a good education—an education, indeed, of that kind which could not but unfit young Laman for the calling of his father ; for it developed the abilities and bestowed the learning, which may be said to lift a youth morally out of trade, and to refine him at once into a gentleman. At six years old he was entered a scholar of Saint Olave's School, then under the direction of the Reverend Doctor Blenkorm. He became the head Latin scholar, and gained the chief prize in each of the last three years he remained at the academy. When he left, it was the wish of the master and trustees that he should be sent to College, one boy being annually selected from the pupils, to be maintained at the University, for the freshman's year, free of expense ; for the charges of the two remaining years the parents were to provide. So strong, however, were the hopes of the master for his promising pupil, that the trustees of the school consented to depart from their ordinary practice, and offered to defray the collegiate expenses for two years. Unfortunately, the offer was not accepted. No wonder that poor Laman regretted in after life the loss of this golden opportunity. The advantages of a University career to a young man in his position, with talents and application, but without interest, birth, and fortune, are incalculable. The pecuniary independence afforded by the scholarship and the fellowship is in itself no despicable prospect ; but the benefits which distinction, fairly won at those noble and unrivalled institutions, confers, are the greatest where least obvious : they tend usually to bind the vagueness of youthful ambition to the secure reliance on some professional career, in which they smooth the difficulties and abridge the novitiate. Even in literature a College education not only tends to refine the taste, but to propitiate the public. And in all the many walks of practical and public life, the honours gained at the University never fail to find well-wishers amongst powerful contemporaries, and to create generous interest in the fortunes of the aspirant.

"But my poor friend was not destined to have one obstacle smoothed away from his weary path.* With the natural refinement of his disposition, and the fatal cultivation of his intellectual susceptibilities, he was placed at once in a situation which it was impossible that he could fill with steadiness and zeal. Fresh from classical studies, and his emulation warmed by early praise and schoolboy triumph, he was transferred to the drudgery of a desk in the office of Mr. Charles Pearson, a proctor in Doctors Commons. The result was inevitable ; his mind, by a natural reaction, betook itself to the pursuits most hostile to such a career. Before this, even from the age of thirteen, he had trifled with the Muses ; he now conceived in good earnest the more perilous passion for the stage.

"Barry Cornwall's 'Dramatic Scenes' were published about this time—they exercised considerable influence over the taste and aspirations of young Blanchard—and many dramatic sketches of brilliant promise, bearing his initials, S. L. B., appeared in a

---

* "The elder Blanchard is not to be blamed for voluntarily depriving his son of the advantages proffered by the liberal trustees of Saint Olave's ; it appears from a communication by Mr. Keymer (brother-in-law to Laman Blanchard)—that the circumstances of the family at that time were not such as to meet the necessary expenses of a student—even for the *last* year of his residence at the University."

periodical work existing at that period called *The Drama*. In them, though the conception and general treatment are borrowed from Barry Cornwall, the style and rhythm are rather modelled on the peculiarities of Byron. Their promise is not the less for the imitation they betray. The very characteristic of genius is to be imitative—first of authors, then of nature. Books lead us to fancy feelings that are not yet genuine. Experience is necessary to record those which colour our own existence : and the style only becomes original in proportion as the sentiment it expresses is sincere. More touching, therefore, than these 'Dramatic Sketches,' was a lyrical effusion on the death of Sidney Ireland, a young friend to whom he was warmly attached, and over whose memory, for years afterwards, he often shed tears. He named his eldest son after that early friend. At this period, Mr. Douglas Jerrold had written three volumes of Moral Philosophy, and Mr. Buckstone, the cele- brated comedian, volunteered to copy the work for the juvenile moralist. On arriving at any passage that struck his fancy, Mr. Buckstone communicated his delight to his friend Blanchard, and the emulation thus excited tended more and more to sharpen the poet's distaste to all avocations incompatible with literature. Anxious, in the first instance, to escape from dependence on his father (who was now urgent that he should leave the proctor's desk for the still more ungenial mechanism of the paternal trade), he meditated the best of all preparatives to dramatic excellence ; viz., a practical acquaintance with the stage itself : he resolved to become an actor. Few indeed are they in this country who have ever suc- ceeded eminently in the literature of the stage, who have not either trod its boards, or lived habitually in its atmosphere. Blanchard obtained an interview with Mr. Henry Johnston, the actor, and recited, in his presence, passages from Glover's 'Leonidas.' He read admirably—his elocution was faultless—his feeling exquisite ; Mr. Johnston was delighted with his powers, but he had experience and wisdom to cool his professional enthusiasm, and he earnestly advised the aspirant not to think of the stage. He drew such a picture of the hazards of success—the obstacles to a position—the precariousness even of a subsistence, that the poor boy's heart sunk within him. He was about to resign himself to obscurity and trade, when he suddenly fell in with the manager of the Margate Theatre ; this gentleman proposed to enrol him in his own troop, and the proposal was eagerly accepted, in spite of the warnings of Mr. Henry Johnston. 'A week,' says Mr. Buckstone (to whom I am indebted for these particulars, and whose words I now quote), 'was sufficient to disgust him with the beggary and drudgery of the country player's life ; and as there were no "Harlequins" steaming it from Margate to London Bridge at that day, he performed his journey back on foot, having, on reaching Rochester, but his last shilling—the poet's veritable last shilling—in his pocket.

"'At that time a circumstance occurred, which my poor friend's fate has naturally brought to my recollection. He came to me late one evening, in a state of great excitement; informed me that his father had turned him out of doors; that he was utterly hopeless and wretched, and was resolved to destroy himself. I used my best endeavours to console him, to lead his thoughts to the future, and hope in what chance and perseverance might effect for him. Our discourse took a livelier turn; and after making up a bed on a sofa in my own room, I retired to rest. I soon slept soundly, but was awakened by hearing a footstep descending the stairs. I looked towards the sofa, and discovered he had left it; I heard the street door close; I instantly hurried on my clothes, and followed him; I called to him, but received no answer; I ran till I saw him in the distance also running; I again called his name; I implored him to stop, but he would not answer me. Still continuing his pace, I became alarmed, and doubled my speed. I came up with him near to Westminster Bridge; he was hurrying to the steps leading to the river; I seized him; he threatened to strike me if I did not release him; I called for the watch; I entreated him to return; he became more pacified, but still seemed anxious to escape from me. By entreaties; by every means of persuasion I could think of; by threats to call for help; I succeeded in taking him back. The next day he was more composed, but I believe rarely resided with his father after that time. Necessity compelled him to do something for a livelihood, and in time he became a reader in the office of the Messrs. Bayliss, in Fleet Street. By that employ joined to frequent contributions to the *Monthly Magazine*, at that time published by them, he obtained a tolerable competence.

"'Blanchard and Jerrold had serious thoughts of joining Lord Byron in Greece; they were to become warriors, and assist the poet in the liberation of the classic land. Many a nightly wandering found them discussing their project. In the midst of one of these discussions they were caught in a shower of rain, and sought shelter under a gateway. The rain continued; when their patience becoming exhausted, Blanchard, buttoning up his coat, exclaimed "Come on, Jerrold! what use shall we be to the Greeks if we stand up for a shower of rain?" So they walked home and were heroically wet through.'"

It would have been worth while to tell this tale more fully not to envelop the chief personage in fine words, as statuaries d their sitters in Roman togas, and, making them assume the heroic-conventional look, take away from them that infinitely more in-teresting one which Nature gave them. It would have been well if we could have had this stirring little story in detail. The young fellow, forced to the proctor's desk, quite angry with the drudgery, theatre-stricken, poetry-stricken, writing dramatic sketches in Barry Cornwall's manner, spouting "Leonidas" before a manager, driven away starving from home, and, penniless and full of romance, court-ing his beautiful young wife. "*Come on, Jerrold! what use shall we be to the Greeks if we stand up for a shower of rain?*" How the native humour breaks out of the man! Those who knew them can fancy the effect of such a pair of warriors steering the Greek fire-ships, or manning the breach at Missolonghi. Then there comes that pathetic little outbreak of despair, when the poor young fellow is nearly giving up; his father banishes him, no one will buy his poetry, he has no chance on his darling theatre, no chance of the wife that he is longing for. Why not finish with life at once? He has read "Werter," and can understand suicide. "None," he says, in a sonnet—

> "None, not the hoariest sage, may tell of all
> The strong heart struggles with before it fall."

If Respectability wanted to point a moral, isn't there one here? Eschew poetry, avoid the theatre, stick to your business, do not read German novels, do not marry at twenty. All these injunctions seem to hang naturally on the story.

And yet the young poet marries at twenty, in the teeth of poverty and experience; labours away, not unsuccessfully, puts Pegasus into harness, rises in social rank and public estimation, brings up happily round him an affectionate family, gets for himself a circle of the warmest friends, and thus carries on for twenty years, when a providential calamity visits him and the poor wife almost together, and removes them both.

In the beginning of 1844, Mrs. Blanchard, his affectionate wife and the excellent mother of his children, was attacked with paralysis, which impaired her mind and terminated fatally at the end of the year. Her husband was constantly with her, occupied by her side, whilst watching her distressing malady, in his daily task of literary business. Her illness had the severest effect upon him. He, too, was attacked with partial paralysis and congestion of the brain, during which first seizure his wife died. The rest of the story was told in all the newspapers of the beginning of last year. Rallying partially from his fever at times, a sudden catas-trophe overwhelmed him. On the night of the 14th February, in

2 M

a gust of delirium, having his little boy in bed by his side, and having said the Lord's Prayer but a short time before, he sprang out of bed in the absence of his nurse (whom he had besought not to leave him), and made away with himself with a razor. He was no more guilty in his death than a man who is murdered by a madman, or who dies of the rupture of a blood-vessel. In his last prayer he asked to be forgiven, as he in his whole heart forgave others ; and not to be led into that irresistible temptation under which it pleased Heaven that the poor wandering spirit should succumb.

At the very moment of his death his friends were making the kindest and most generous exertions in his behalf. Such a noble, loving, and generous creature is never without such. The world, it is pleasant to think, is always a good and gentle world to the gentle and good, and reflects the benevolence with which they regard it. This memoir contains an affecting letter from the poor fellow himself, which indicates Sir Edward Bulwer's admirable and delicate generosity towards him. " I bless and thank you always," writes the kindly and affectionate soul, to another excellent friend, Mr. Forster. There were other friends, such as Mr. Fonblanque, Mr. Ainsworth, with whom he was connected in literary labour, who were not less eager to serve and befriend him.

As soon as he was dead, a number of other persons came forward to provide means for the maintenance of his orphan family. Messrs. Chapman & Hall took one son into their publishing-house, another was provided in a merchant's house in the city, the other is of an age and has the talents to follow and succeed in his father's profession. Mr. Colburn and Mr. Ainsworth gave up their copyrights of his Essays, which are now printed in three handsome volumes, for the benefit of his children.

Out of Blanchard's life (except from the melancholy end, which is quite apart from it) there is surely no ground for drawing charges against the public of neglecting literature. His career, untimely concluded, is in the main a successful one. In truth, I don't see how the aid or interposition of Government could in any way have greatly benefited him, or how it was even called upon to do so. It does not follow that a man would produce a great work even if he had leisure. Squire Shakspeare of Stratford, with his lands and rents, and his arms over his porch, was not the working Shakspeare ; and indolence (or contemplation, if you like) is no unusual quality in the literary man. Of all the squires who have had acres and rents, all the holders of lucky easy Government places, how many have written books, and of what worth are they ? There are some persons whom Government, having a want of, employs and pays—

barristers, diplomatists, soldiers, and the like; but it doesn't want poetry, and can do without tragedies. Let men of letters stand for themselves. Every day enlarges their market, and multiplies their clients. The most skilful and successful among the cultivators of light literature have such a hold upon the public feelings, and awaken such a sympathy, as men of the class never enjoyed until now : men of science and learning, who aim at other distinction, get it; and in spite of Dr. Carus's disgust, I believe there was never a time when so much of the practically useful was written and read, and every branch of book-making pursued, with an interest so eager.

But I must conclude. My letter has swelled beyond the proper size of letters, and you are craving for news : have you not to-day's *Times'* battle of Ferozeshah ? Farewell. M. A. T.

JOHN LEECH'S PICTURES OF LIFE
AND CHARACTER*

W E, who can recall the consulship of Plancus, and quite respectable old fogeyfied times, remember amongst other amusements which we had as children the pictures at which we were permitted to look. There was Boydell's Shakspeare, black and ghastly gallery of murky Opies, glum Northcotes, straddling Fuselis! there were Lear, Oberon, Hamlet, with starting muscles, rolling eyeballs, and long pointing quivering fingers; there was little Prince Arthur (Northcote) crying, in white satin, and bidding good Hubert not put out his eyes; there was Hubert crying; there was little Rutland being run through the poor little body by bloody Clifford; there was Cardinal Beaufort (Reynolds) gnashing his teeth, and grinning and howling demoniacally on his deathbed (a picture frightful to the present day); there was Lady Hamilton (Romney) waving a torch, and dancing before a black background,—a melancholy museum indeed. Smirke's delightful "Seven Ages" only fitfully relieved its general gloom. We did not like to inspect it unless the elders were present, and plenty of lights and company were in the room.

Cheerful relatives used to treat us to Miss Linwood's. Let the children of the present generation thank their stars *that* tragedy is put out of their way. Miss Linwood's was worsted-work. Your grandmother or grandaunts took you there, and said the pictures were admirable. You saw "The Woodman" in worsted, with his axe and dog, trampling through the snow; the snow bitter cold to look at, the woodman's pipe wonderful: a gloomy piece, that made you shudder. There were large dingy pictures of woollen martyrs, and scowling warriors with limbs strongly knitted; there was especially, at the end of a black passage, a den of lions, that would frighten any boy not born in Africa, or Exeter 'Change, and accustomed to them.

Another exhibition used to be West's Gallery, where the pleasing

* Reprinted from the *Quarterly Review*, No. 191, Dec. 1854, by permission of Mr. John Murray.

figures of Lazarus in his grave-clothes, and Death on the pale horse, used to impress us children. The tombs of Westminster Abbey, the vaults at St. Paul's, the men in armour at the Tower, frowning ferociously out of their helmets, and wielding their dreadful swords; that superhuman Queen Elizabeth at the end of the room, a livid sovereign with glass eyes, a ruff, and a dirty satin petticoat, riding a horse covered with steel: who does not remember these sights in London in the consulship of Plancus? and the waxwork in Fleet Street, not like that of Madame Tussaud's, whose chamber of death is gay and brilliant; but a nice old gloomy waxwork, full of murderers; and as a chief attraction, the Dead Baby and the Princess Charlotte lying in state?

Our story-books had no pictures in them for the most part. "Frank" (dear old Frank!) had none; nor the "Parent's Assistant"; nor the "Evenings at Home"; nor our copy of the "Ami des Enfans": there were a few just at the end of the Spelling-Book; besides the allegory at the beginning, of Education leading up Youth to the temple of Industry, where Dr. Dilworth and Professor Walkinghame stood with crowns of laurel. There were, we say, just a few pictures at the end of the Spelling-Book, little oval grey woodcuts of Bewick's, mostly of the Wolf and the Lamb, the Dog and the Shadow, and Brown, Jones, and Robinson with long ringlets and little tights; but for pictures, so to speak, what had we? The rough old woodblocks in the old harlequin-backed fairy-books had served hundreds of years; before *our* Plancus, in the time of Priscus Plancus—in Queen Anne's time, who knows? We were flogged at school; we were fifty boys in our boarding-house, and had to wash in a leaden trough, under a cistern, with lumps of fat yellow soap floating about in the ice and water. Are *our* sons ever flogged? Have they not dressing-rooms, hair-oil, hip-baths, and Baden towels? And what picture-books the young villains have! What have these children done that they should be so much happier than we were?

We had the "Arabian Nights" and Walter Scott, to be sure. Smirke's illustrations to the former are very fine. We did not know how good they were then; but we doubt whether we did not prefer the little old "Miniature Library Nights" with frontispieces by Uwins; for *these* books the pictures don't count. Every boy of imagination does his own pictures to Scott and the "Arabian Nights" best.

Of funny pictures there were none especially intended for us children. There was Rowlandson's "Doctor Syntax": Doctor Syntax, in a fuzz-wig, on a horse with legs like sausages, riding races, making love, frolicking with rosy exuberant damsels. Those

13

pictures were very funny, and that aquatinting and the gay-coloured plates very pleasant to witness; but if we could not read the poem in those days, could we digest it in this? Nevertheless, apart from the text which we could not master, we remember Doctor Syntax pleasantly, like those cheerful painted hieroglyphics in the Nineveh Court at Sydenham. What matter for the arrow-head, illegible stuff? give us the placid grinning kings, twanging their jolly bows over their rident horses, wounding those good-humoured enemies, who tumble gaily off the towers, or drown, smiling, in the dimpling waters, amidst the anerithmon gelasma of the fish.

After Doctor Syntax, the apparition of Corinthian Tom, Jerry Hawthorn, and the facetious Bob Logic must be recorded—a wondrous history indeed theirs was! When the future student of our manners comes to look over the pictures and the writing of these queer volumes, what will he think of our society, customs, and language in the consulship of Plancus? "Corinthian," it appears, was the phrase applied to men of fashion and *ton* in Plancus's time: they were the brilliant predecessors of the "swell" of the present period—brilliant, but somewhat barbarous, it must be confessed. The Corinthians were in the habit of drinking a great deal too much in Tom Cribb's parlour: they used to go and see "life" in the gin-shops; of nights, walking home (as well as they could), they used to knock down "Charleys," poor harmless old watchmen with lanterns, guardians of the streets of Rome, Planco Consule. They perpetrated a vast deal of boxing; they put on the "mufflers" in Jackson's rooms; they "sported their prads" in the Ring in the Park; they attended cock-fights, and were enlightened patrons of dogs and destroyers of rats. Besides these sports, the *délassemens* of gentlemen mixing with the people, our patricians, of course, occasionally enjoyed the society of their own class. What a wonderful picture that used to be of Corinthian Tom dancing with Corinthian Kate at Almack's! What a prodigious dress Kate wore! With what graceful *abandon* the pair flung their arms about as they swept through the mazy quadrille, with all the noblemen standing round in their stars and uniforms! You may still, doubtless, see the pictures at the British Museum, or find the volumes in the corner of some old country-house library. You are led to suppose that the English aristocracy of 1820 *did* dance and caper in that way, and box and drink at Tom Cribb's, and knock down watchmen; and the children of to-day, turning to their elders, may say, "Grandmamma, did you wear such a dress as that when you danced at Almack's? There was very little of it, Grandmamma. Did Grandpapa kill many watchmen when he was a young man, and frequent thieves' gin-shops, cock-fights, and the ring, before you married him? Did he use to talk the extraordinary slang and jargon which is printed in this book? He is very much changed. He seems a gentlemanly old boy enough now."

In the above-named consulate, when *we* had grandfathers alive, there would be in the old gentleman's library in the country two or three old mottled portfolios, or great swollen scrap-books of blue paper, full of the comic prints of grandpapa's time, ere Plancus ever had the fasces borne before him. These prints were signed Gilray, Bunbury, Rowlandson, Woodward, and some actually George Cruikshank—for George is a veteran now, and he took the etching needle in hand as a child. He caricatured "Boney," borrowing not a little from Gilray in his first puerile efforts. He drew Louis XVIII. trying on Boney's boots. Before the century was actually in its teens we believe that George Cruikshank was amusing the public.

In those great coloured prints in our grandfathers' portfolios in the library, and in some other apartments of the house, where the caricatures used to be pasted in those days, we found things quite beyond our comprehension. Boney was represented as a fierce dwarf, with goggle eyes, a huge laced hat and tricoloured plume, a crooked sabre reeking with blood: a little demon revelling in lust, murder, massacre. John Bull was shown kicking him a good deal: indeed he was prodigiously kicked all through that series of pictures; by Sidney Smith and our brave allies the gallant Turks: by the excellent and patriotic Spaniards; by the amiable and indignant Russians,—all nations had boots at the service of poor Master Boney. How Pitt used to defy him! How good old George, King of Brobdingnag, laughed at Gulliver-Boney, sailing about in his tank to make sport for their Majesties! This little fiend, this beggar's brat, cowardly, murderous, and atheistic as he was (we remember, in those old portfolios, pictures representing Boney and his family in rags, gnawing raw bones in a Corsican hut; Boney murdering the sick at Jaffa; Boney with a hookah and a large turban, having adopted the Turkish religion, &c.)—this Corsican monster, nevertheless, had some devoted friends in England, according to the Gilray chronicle,—a set of villains who loved atheism, tyranny, plunder, and wickedness in general, like their French friend. In the pictures these men were all represented as dwarfs, like their ally. The miscreants got into power at one time, and, if we remember right, were called the Broad-backed Administration. One with shaggy eyebrows and a bristly beard, the hirsute ringleader of the rascals, was, it appears, called Charles

James Fox; another miscreant, with a blotched countenance, was a certain Sheridan; other imps were hight Erskine, Norfolk (Jockey of), Moira, Henry Petty. As in our childish innocence we used to look at these demons, now sprawling and tipsy in their cups; now scaling heaven, from which the angelic Pitt hurled them down; now cursing the light (their atrocious ringleader Fox was represented with hairy cloven feet, and a tail and horns); now kissing Boney's boot, but inevitably discomfited by Pitt and the other good angels: we hated these vicious wretches, as good children should: we were on the side of Virtue and Pitt and Grandpapa. But if our sisters wanted to look at the portfolios, the good old grandfather used to hesitate. There were some prints among them very odd indeed; some that girls could not understand; some that boys, indeed, had best not see. We swiftly turn over those prohibited pages. How many of them there were in the wild, coarse, reckless, ribald, generous book of old English humour!

How savage the satire was—how fierce the assault—what garbage hurled at opponents—what foul blows were hit—what language of Billingsgate flung! Fancy a party in a country-house now looking over Woodward's facetiæ or some of the Gilray comicalities, or the slatternly Saturnalia of Rowlandson! Whilst we live we must laugh, and have folks to make us laugh. We cannot afford to lose Satyr with his pipe and dances and gambols. But we have washed, combed, clothed, and taught the rogue good manners: or rather, let us say, he has learned them himself; for he is of nature soft and kindly, and he has put aside his mad pranks and tipsy habits; and, frolicksome always, has become gentle and harmless, smitten into shame by the pure presence of our women and the sweet confiding smiles of our children. Among the veterans, the old pictorial satirists, we have mentioned the famous name of one humorous designer who is still alive and at work. Did we not see, by his own hand, his own portrait of his own famous face, and whiskers, in the *Illustrated London News* the other day? There was a print in that paper of an assemblage of Teetotallers in "Sadler's Wells Theatre," and we straightway recognised the old Roman hand—the old Roman's of the time of Plancus—George Cruikshank's. There were the old bonnets and droll faces and shoes, and short trousers, and figures of 1820 sure enough. And there was George (who has taken to the water-doctrine, as all the world knows) handing some teetotalleresses over a plank to the table where the pledge was being administered. How often has George drawn that picture of Cruikshank! Where haven't we seen it? How fine it was, facing the effigy of Mr. Ainsworth in *Ainsworth's Magazine* when George illustrated that periodical!

How grand and severe he stands in that design in G. C.'s " Omnibus,"
where he represents himself tonged like St. Dunstan, and tweaking
a wretch of a publisher by the nose ! The collectors of George's
etchings—oh the charming etchings !—oh the dear old " German
Popular Tales " !—the capital " Points of Humour "—the delightful
" Phrenology " and " Scrap-books," of the good time, *our* time—
Plancus's in fact !—the collectors of the Georgian etchings, we say,
have at least a hundred pictures of the artist. Why, we remember
him in his favourite Hessian boots in " Tom and Jerry " itself ; and
in woodcuts as far back as the Queen's trial. He has rather
deserted satire and comedy of late years, having turned his attention
to the serious, and warlike, and sublime. Having confessed our age
and prejudices, we prefer the comic and fanciful to the historic,
romantic, and at present didactic George. May respect, and length
of days, and comfortable repose attend the brave, honest, kindly,
pure-minded artist, humorist, moralist ! It was he first who
brought English pictorial humour and children acquainted. Our
young people and their fathers and mothers owe him many a
pleasant hour and harmless laugh. Is there no way in which the
country could acknowledge the long services and brave career of
such a friend and benefactor ?

Since George's time humour has been converted. Comus and
his wicked satyrs and leering fauns have disappeared, and fled into
the lowest haunts ; and Comus's lady (if she had a taste for humour,
which may be doubted) might take up our funny picture-books
without the slightest precautionary squeamishness. What can be
purer than the charming fancies of Richard Doyle ? In all Mr.
Punch's huge galleries can't we walk. as safely as through Miss
Pinkerton's schoolrooms ? And as we look at Mr. Punch's pictures,
at the *Illustrated News* pictures, at all the pictures in the book-
shop windows at this Christmas season, as oldsters, we feel a certain
pang of envy against the youngsters—they are too well off. Why
hadn't *we* picture-books ? Why were we flogged so ? A plague on
the lictors and their rods in the time of Plancus !

And now, after this rambling preface, we are arrived at the
subject in hand—Mr. John Leech and his " Pictures of Life and
Character," in the collection of Mr. Punch. This book is better
than plum-cake at Christmas. It is an enduring plum-cake, which
you may eat and which you may slice and deliver to your friends ;
and to which, having cut it, you may come again and welcome, from
year's end to year's end. In the frontispiece you see Mr. Punch
examining the pictures in his gallery— a portly, well-dressed, middle-
aged, respectable gentleman, in a white neckcloth, and a polite
evening costume—smiling in a very bland and agreeable manner

upon one of his pleasant drawings, taken out of one of his handsome portfolios. Mr. Punch has very good reason to smile at the work and be satisfied with the artist. Mr. Leech, his chief contributor, and some kindred humorists, with pencil and pen have served Mr. Punch admirably. Time was, if we remember Mr. P.'s history rightly, that he did not wear silk stockings nor well-made clothes (the little dorsal irregularity in his figure is almost an ornament now, so excellent a tailor has he). He was of humble beginnings. It is said he kept a ragged little booth, which he put up at corners of streets; associated with beadles, policemen, his own ugly wife (whom he treated most scandalously), and persons in a low station of life; earning a precarious livelihood by the cracking of wild jokes, the singing of ribald songs, and half-pence extorted from passers-by. He is the Satyric genius we spoke of anon: he cracks his jokes still, for satire must live; but he is combed, washed, neatly clothed, and perfectly presentable. He goes into the very best company; he keeps a stud at Melton; he has a moor in Scotland; he rides in the Park; has his stall at the Opera; is constantly dining out at clubs and in private society; and goes every night in the season to balls and parties, where you see the most beautiful women possible. He is welcomed amongst his new friends the great; though, like the good old English gentleman of the song, he does not forget the small. He pats the heads of street boys and girls; relishes the jokes of Jack the costermonger and Bob the dustman; good-naturedly spies out Molly the cook flirting with policeman X, or Mary the nursemaid as she listens to the fascinating guardsman. He used rather to laugh at guardsmen, "plungers," and other military men; and was until latter days very contemptuous in his behaviour towards Frenchmen. He has a natural antipathy to pomp, and swagger, and fierce demeanour. But now that the guardsmen are gone to war, and the dandies of "The Rag" —dandies no more—are battling like heroes at Balaklava and Inkermann * by the side of their heroic allies, Mr. Punch's laughter is changed to hearty respect and enthusiasm. It is not against courage and honour he wars: but this great moralist—must it be owned?—has some popular British prejudices, and these led him in peace time to laugh at soldiers and Frenchmen. If those hulking footmen who accompanied the carriages to the opening of Parliament the other day, would form a plush brigade, wear only gunpowder in their hair, and strike with their great canes on the enemy, Mr. Punch would leave off laughing at Jeames, who meanwhile remains among us, to all outward appearance regardless of satire, and calmly consuming his five meals per diem. Against lawyers,

* This was written in 1854.

beadles, bishops and clergy, and authorities, Mr. Punch is still rather
bitter. At the time of the Papal aggression he was prodigiously
angry; and one of the chief misfortunes which happened to him at
that period was that, through the violent opinions which he expressed
regarding the Roman Catholic hierarchy, he lost the invaluable
services, the graceful pencil, the harmless wit, the charming fancy
of Mr. Doyle. Another member of Mr. Punch's cabinet, the
biographer of Jeames, the author of the "Snob Papers," resigned
his functions on account of Mr. Punch's assaults upon the present
Emperor of the French nation, whose anger Jeames thought it was
unpatriotic to arouse. Mr. Punch parted with these contributors :
he filled their places with others as good. The boys at the railroad
stations cried *Punch* just as cheerily, and sold just as many numbers,
after these events as before.

There is no blinking the fact that in Mr. Punch's cabinet John
Leech is the right-hand man. Fancy a number of *Punch* without Leech's pictures! What would you give for it? The learned
gentlemen who write the work must feel that, without him, it
were as well left alone. Look at the rivals whom the popularity
of *Punch* has brought into the field; the direct imitators of Mr.
Leech's manner—the artists with a manner of their own—how
inferior their pencils are to his in humour, in depicting the public
manners, in arresting, amusing the nation. The truth, the strength,
the free vigour, the kind humour, the John Bull pluck and spirit
of that hand are approached by no competitor. With what
dexterity he draws a horse, a woman, a child! He feels them all,
so to speak, like a man. What plump young beauties those are
with which Mr. Punch's chief contributor supplies the old gentleman's pictorial harem! What famous thews and sinews Mr.
Punch's horses have, and how Briggs, on the back of them,
scampers across country! You see youth, strength, enjoyment,
manliness in those drawings, and in none more so, to our thinking,
than in the hundred pictures of children which this artist loves to
design. Like a brave, hearty, good-natured Briton, he becomes
quite soft and tender with the little creatures, pats gently their
little golden heads, and watches with unfailing pleasure their ways,
their sports, their jokes, laughter, caresses. *Enfans terribles* come
home from Eton; young Miss practising her first flirtation; poor
little ragged Polly making dirt-pies in the gutter, or staggering
under the weight of Jacky, her nurse-child, who is as big as herself
—all these little ones, patrician and plebeian, meet with kindness
from this kind heart, and are watched with curious nicety by this
amiable observer.

We remember, in one of those ancient Gilray portfolios, a print which used to cause a sort of terror in us youthful spectators, and in which the Prince of Wales (his Royal Highness was a Foxite then) was represented as sitting alone in a magnificent hall after a voluptuous meal, and using a great steel fork in the guise of a tooth-pick. Fancy the first young gentleman living employing such a weapon in such a way! The most elegant Prince of Europe engaged with a two-pronged iron fork—the heir of Britannia with a *bident!* The man of genius who drew that picture saw little of the society which he satirised and amused. Gilray watched public characters as they walked by the shop in St. James's Street, or passed through the lobby of the House of Commons. His studio was a garret, or little better; his place of amusement a tavern-parlour, where his club held its nightly sittings over their pipes and sanded floor. You could not have society represented by men to whom it was not familiar. When Gavarni came to England a few years since—one of the wittiest of men, one of the most brilliant and dexterous of draughtsmen—he published a book of "Les Anglais," and his *Anglais* were all Frenchmen. The eye, so keen and so long prac-tised to observe Parisian life, could not perceive English character. A social painter must be of the world which he depicts, and native to the manners which he portrays.

Now, any one who looks over Mr. Leech's portfolio must see that the social pictures which he gives us are authentic. What comfortable little drawing-rooms and dining-rooms, what snug libraries we enter; what fine young-gentlemanly wags they are, those beautiful little dandies who wake up gouty old grandpapa to ring the bell; who decline aunt's pudding and custards, saying that they will reserve themselves for an anchovy toast with the claret; who talk together in ball-room doors, where Fred whispers Charley —pointing to a dear little partner seven years old—"My dear Charley, she has very much gone off; you should have seen that girl last season!" Look well at everything appertaining to the economy of the famous Mr. Briggs: how snug, quiet, appropriate all the appointments are! What a comfortable, neat, clean, middle-class house Briggs's is (in the Bayswater suburb of London, we should guess from the sketches of the surrounding scenery)! What a good stable he has, with a loose-box for those celebrated hunters which he rides! How pleasant, clean, and warm his breakfast-table looks! What a trim little maid brings in the top-boots which horrify Mrs. B.! What a snug dressing-room he has, complete in all its appointments, and in which he appears trying on the delightful hunting-cap which Mrs. Briggs flings into the fire! How cosy all the Briggs party seem in their dining-room: Briggs reading a Treatise on Dog-breaking by a lamp; Mamma and Grannie with their respective needleworks ; the children clustering round a great book of prints—a great book of prints such as this before us, which at this season must make thousands of children happy by as many firesides ! The inner life of all these people is represented : Leech draws them as naturally as Teniers depicts Dutch boors, or Morland pigs and stables. It is your house and mine : we are looking at everybody's family circle. Our boys coming from school give themselves such airs, the young scapegraces ! our girls, going to parties, are so tricked out by fond mammas—a social history of London in the middle of the nineteenth century. As such, future students— lucky they to have a book so pleasant—will regard these pages : even the mutations of fashion they may follow here if they be so inclined. Mr. Leech has as fine an eye for tailory and millinery as for horse-flesh. How they change those cloaks and bonnets. How we have to pay milliners' bills from year to year ! Where are those prodigious châtelaines of 1850 which no lady could be without ? Where those charming waistcoats, those " stunning " waistcoats, which our young girls used to wear a few brief seasons back, and which cause 'Gus, in the sweet little sketch of " La Mode," to ask Ellen for her tailor's address ? 'Gus is a young warrior by this time, very likely facing the enemy at Inkermann ; and pretty Ellen, and that love of a sister of hers, are married and happy, let us hope, superintending one of those delightful nursery scenes which our artist depicts with such tender humour. Fortunate artist, indeed ! You see he must have been bred at a good public school ; that he has ridden many a good horse in his day ; paid, no doubt, out of his own purse for the originals of some of those lovely caps and bonnets ; and watched paternally the ways, smiles, frolics, and slumbers of his favourite little people.

As you look at the drawings, secrets come out of them,— private jokes, as it were, imparted to you by the author for your special delectation. How remarkably, for instance, has Mr. Leech observed the hair-dressers of the present age ! Look at " Mr. Tongs," whom that hideous old bald woman, who ties on her bonnet at the glass, informs that " she has used the whole bottle of Balm of California, but her hair comes off yet." You can see the bear's-grease not only on Tongs' head but on his hands, which he is clapping clammily together. Remark him who is telling his client " there is cholera in the hair " ; and that lucky rogue whom the young lady bids to cut off " a long thick piece "— for somebody, doubtless. All these men are different, and delightfully natural and absurd. Why should hair-dressing be an absurd profession ?

The amateur will remark what an excellent part hands play in

Mr. Leech's pieces; his admirable actors use them with perfect naturalness. Look at Betty, putting the urn down; at cook, laying her hands on the kitchen table, whilst her policeman grumbles at the cold meat. They are cook's and housemaid's hands without mistake, and not without a certain beauty too. The bald old lady, who is tying her bonnet at Tongs', has hands which you see are trembling. Watch the fingers of the two old harridans who are talking scandal: for what long years past they have pointed out holes in their neighbours' dresses and mud on their flounces. "Here's a go! I've lost my diamond ring." As the dustman utters this pathetic cry, and looks at his hand, you burst out laughing. These are among the little points of humour. One could indicate hundreds of such as one turns over the pleasant pages.

There is a little snob or gent, whom we all of us know, who wears little tufts on his little chin, outrageous pins and panta-loons, smokes cigars on tobacconists' counters, sucks his cane in the streets, struts about with Mrs. Snob and the baby (Mrs. S. an immense woman, whom Snob nevertheless bullies), who is a favourite abomination of Leech, and pursued by that savage humorist into a thousand of his haunts. There he is, choosing waistcoats at the tailor's—such waistcoats! Yonder he is giving a shilling to the sweeper who calls him "Capting"; now he is offering a paletot to a huge giant who is going out in the rain. They don't know their own pictures, very likely; if they did, they would have a meeting, and thirty or forty of them would be deputed to thrash Mr. Leech. One feels a pity for the poor little bucks. In a minute or two, when we close this discourse and walk the streets, we shall see a dozen such.

Ere we shut the desk up, just one word to point out to the unwary specially to note the backgrounds of landscapes in Leech's drawings—homely drawings of moor and wood, and seashore and London street—the scenes of his little dramas. They are as excellently true to nature as the actors themselves; our respect for the genius and humour which invented both increases as we look and look again at the designs. May we have more of them; more pleasant Christmas volumes, over which we and our children can laugh together. Can we have too much of truth, and fun, and beauty, and kindness?

TALES

TALES

THE PROFESSOR

A TALE OF SENTIMENT

" Why, then, the World's mine oyster."

CHAPTER I

I HAVE often remarked that, among other ornaments and curiosities, Hackney contains more ladies' schools than are to be found in almost any other village, or indeed city, in Europe. In every green rustic lane, to every tall old-fashioned house there is an iron gate, an ensign of blue and gold, and a large brass plate, proclaiming that a ladies' seminary is established upon the premises. On one of these plates is written—(or rather was,—for the pathetic occurrence which I have to relate took place many years ago)—on one of these plates, I say, was engraven the following inscription :—

" BULGARIA HOUSE.

Seminary for Young Ladies from three to twenty.

BY THE MISSES PIDGE.

(Please wipe your shoes.) "

The Misses Pidge took a limited number of young ladies (as limited, in fact, or as large as the public chose), and instructed them in those branches of elegant and useful learning which make the British female so superior to all other shes. The younger ones learned the principles of back-stitch, cross-stitch, bob-stitch, Doctor Watts's Hymns, and " In my Cottage near a Wood." The elder pupils diverged at once from stitching and samplers : they played like Thalberg, and pirouetted like Taglioni ; they learned geography, geology, mythology, entomology, modern history, and simple equations (Miss Z. Pidge); they obtained a complete knowledge of the French, German, and Italian tongues, not including English, taught by Miss Pidge; Poonah painting and tambour (Miss E. Pidge); Brice's questions and elocution (Miss F. Pidge); and, to crown all, dancing and gymnastics (which had a very flourishing look in the Pidge prospectus, and were printed in German text), DANCING and GYMNASTICS, we say, by Professor DANDOLO. The names of other professors and assistants followed in modester type.

Although the Signor's name was decidedly foreign, so English was his appearance, and so entirely did he disguise his accent, that it was impossible to tell of what place he was a native, if not of London, and of the very heart of it; for he had caught completely the peculiarities which distinguish the so-called cockney part of the City, and obliterated his h's and doubled his v's, as if he had been for all his life in the neighbourhood of Bow bells. Signor Dandolo was a stout gentleman of five feet nine, with amazing expanse of mouth, chest, and whiskers, which latter were of a red hue.

I cannot tell how this individual first received an introduction to the academy of the Misses Pidge, and established himself there. Rumours say that Miss Zela Pidge at a Hackney ball first met him, and thus the intimacy arose : but, since the circumstances took place which I am about to relate, that young lady declares that *she* was not the person who brought him to Bulgaria House,—nothing but the infatuation and entreaties of Mrs. Alderman Grampus could ever have induced her to receive him. The reader will gather from this, that Dandolo's after-conduct at Miss Pidge's was not satisfactory, nor was it; and may every mistress of such an establishment remember that confidence can be sometimes misplaced; that friendship is frequently but another name for villainy.

But to our story. The stalwart and active Dandolo delighted for some time the young ladies at Miss Pidge's by the agility which he displayed in the dance, as well as the strength and manliness of his form, as exhibited in the new amusement which he taught. In a very short time, Miss Binx, a stout young lady of seventeen, who had never until his appearance walked half a mile without puffing like an apoplectic Lord Mayor, could dance the cachuca, swarm up a pole with the agility of a cat, and hold out a chair for three minutes without winking. Miss Jacobs could very nearly climb through a ladder (Jacob's ladder, he profanely called it); and Miss Bole ring such changes upon the dumb-bells as might have been heard at Edmonton, if the bells could have spoken. But the most promising pupil of Professor Dandolo, as indeed the fairest young creature in the establishment of Bulgaria House, was Miss Adeliza

Grampus, daughter of the alderman whose name we have mentioned. The pride of her mother, the idol of her opulent father, Adeliza Grampus was in her nineteenth year. Eyes have often been described; but it would require bluer ink than ours to depict the orbs of Adeliza. The snow when it first falls in Cheapside is not whiter than her neck,—when it has been for some days upon the ground, trampled by dustmen and jarvies, trodden down by sweeps and gentlemen going to business, not blacker than her hair. Slim as the Monument on Fish Street Hill, her form was slender and tall: but it is needless to recapitulate her charms, and difficult indeed to describe them. Let the reader think of his first love, and fancy Adeliza. Dandolo, who was employed to instruct her, saw her, and fancied her too, as many a fellow of his inflammable temperament would have done in his place.

There are few situations in life which can be so improved by an enterprising mind as that of a dancing-master,—I mean in a tender or amatory point of view. The dancing-master has over the back, the hands, the feet and shoulders of his pupils an absolute command; and, being by nature endowed with so much authority, can speedily spread his way from the limbs to the rest of the body, and to the mind inclusive. " *Toes a little more out, Miss Adeliza,*" cries he, with the tenderest air in the world : " back a *little* more straight," and he gently seizes her hand, he raises it considerably above the level of her ear, he places the tips of his left-hand fingers gently upon the young lady's spine, and in this seducing attitude gazes tenderly into her eyes ! I say that no woman at any age can stand this attitude and this look, especially when darted from such eyes as those of Dandolo. On the two first occasions when the adventurer attempted this audacious manœuvre, his victim blushed only, and trembled ; on the third, she dropped her full eyelids and turned ghastly pale. " A glass of water," cried Adeliza, " or I faint." The dancing-master hastened eagerly away to pro- cure the desired beverage, and, as he put it to her lips, whispered thrillingly in her ear, " Thine, thine for ever, Adeliza ! "

Miss Grampus sank back in the arms of Miss Binx, but not before her raptured lover saw her eyes turning towards the ceiling, and her clammy lips whispering the name of " Dandolo."

When Madame Schroeder, in the opera of " Fidelio," cries, " Nichts, nichts, mein Florestan," it is as nothing compared to the tenderness with which Miss Grampus uttered that soft name.

" Dandolo ! " would she repeat to her confidante, Miss Binx ; " the name was beautiful and glorious in the olden days ; five hundred years since, a myriad of voices shouted it in Venice, when one who bore it came forward to wed the sea—the doge's bride !

the blue Adriatic! the boundless and eternal main! The frightened Turk shrank palsied at the sound; it was louder than the loudest of the cannon, or the stormy screaming of the tempest! Dandolo! How many brave hearts beat to hear that name! how many bright swords flashed forth at that resistless war-cry! Oh, Binx!" would Adeliza continue, fondly pressing the arm of that young lady, "is it not passing strange that one of that mighty ducal race should have lived to this day, and lived to love *me?* But I, too," Adeliza would add archly, "am, as you know, a daughter of the sea."

The fact was, that the father of Miss Adeliza Grampus was a shell-fishmonger, which induced the young lady to describe herself as a daughter of Ocean. She received her romantic name from her mother, after reading Miss Swipes's celebrated novel of " Toby of Warsaw "; and had been fed from her youth upwards with so much similar literary ware, that her little mind had gone distracted. Her father had sent her from home at fifteen, because she had fallen in love with the young man who opened natives in the shop, and had vowed to slay herself with the oyster-knife; at Miss Pidge's her sentiment had not deserted her; she knew all Miss Landon by heart, had a lock of Mr. Thomas Moore's hair or wig, and read more novels and poetry than ever. And thus the red-haired dancing-master became in her eyes a Venetian nobleman, with whom it was her pride and pleasure to fall in love.

Being a parlour-boarder at Miss Pidge's seminary (a privilege which was acquired by paying five annual guineas extra), Miss Grampus was permitted certain liberties which were not accorded to scholars of the ordinary description. She and Miss Binx occasionally strolled into the village by themselves; they visited the library unattended; they went upon little messages for the Misses Pidge; they walked to church alone, either before or after the long row of young virgins who streamed out on every Sabbath day from between the filigree iron railings of Bulgaria House. It is my painful duty to state, that on several of these exclusive walks they were followed, or met, by the insidious and attentive teacher of gymnastics.

Soon Miss Binx would lag behind, and—shall I own it?—would make up for the lost society of her female friend by the company of a man, a friend of the Professor, mysterious and agreeable as himself. May the mistresses of all the establishments for young ladies in this kingdom, or queendom rather, peruse this, and reflect how dangerous it is for young ladies of any age—ay, even for parlour boarders—to go out alone! In the present instance Miss Grampus enjoyed a more than ordinary liberty, it is true: when the elder Miss Pidge would remonstrate, Miss Zela would anxiously yield to her request; and why?—the reason may be gathered from the following conversation which passed between the infatuated girl and the wily *maître-de-danse*.

"How, Roderick," would Adeliza say, "how, in the days of our first acquaintance, did it chance that you always addressed yourself to that odious Zela Pidge, and never deigned to breathe a syllable to me?"

"My lips didn't speak to you, Addly" (for to such a pitch of familiarity had they arrived), "but my heyes did."

Adeliza was not astonished by the peculiarity of his pronunciation, for, to say truth, it was that commonly adopted in her native home and circle. "And mine," said she tenderly, "they followed when yours were not fixed upon them, for *then* I dared not look upwards. And though all on account of Miss Pidge you could not hear the accents of my voice, you might have heard the beatings of my heart!"

"I did, I did," gasped Roderick; "I 'eard them haudibly. I never spoke to you then, for I feared to waken that foul fiend sispicion. I wished to henter your seminary, to be continually near you, to make you love me; therefore I wooed the easy and foolish Miss Pidge, therefore I took upon me the disguise of—ha! ha!—of a dancing-master." (And the young man's countenance assumed a grim and demoniac smile.) "Yes; I degraded my name and my birthright—I wore these ignoble trappings, and all for the love of thee, my Adeliza!" Here Signor Dandolo would have knelt down, but the road was muddy; and, his trousers being of nankeen, his gallant purpose was frustrated.

But the story must out, for the conversation above narrated has betrayed to the intelligent reader a considerable part of it. The fact is, as we have said, that Miss Zela Pidge, dancing at the Hackney assembly, was introduced to this man; that he had no profession—no means even of subsistence; that he saw enough of this lady to be aware that he could make her useful to his purpose; and he who had been, we believe it in our conscience, no better than a travelling mountebank or harlequin, appeared at Bulgaria House in the character of a professor of gymnastics. The governess, in the first instance, entertained for him just such a *penchant* as the pupil afterwards felt: the latter discovered the weakness of her mistress, and hence arose Miss Pidge's indulgence, and Miss Grampus's fatal passion.

"Mysterious being!" continued Adeliza, resuming the conversation which has been broken by the above explanatory hints, "how did I learn to love thee? Who art thou?—what dire fate has brought thee hither in this lowly guise to win the heart of Adeliza?"

"Hadeliza," cried he, "you say well; *I am not what I seem.* I cannot tell thee what I am; a tale of horror, of crime, forbids the dreadful confession! But dark as I am, and wretched, nay, wicked and desperate, I love thee, Hadeliza—love thee with the rapturous devotion of purer days—the tenderness of happier times! I am sad now, and fallen, lady; suffice it that I once was happy, ay, respectable."

Adeliza's cheek grew deadly pale, her step faltered, and she would have fallen to the ground, had she not been restrained by the strong arm of her lover. "I know not," said she, as she clung timidly to his neck,—

> " I know not, I hask not, if guilt's in that art,
> I know that I love thee, whatever thou hart."

"*Gilt* in my heart," said Dandola, "gilt in the heart of Roderick? No, never!" and he drew her towards him, and on her bonnet, her veil, her gloves, nay, on her very cheeks, he imprinted a thousand maddening kisses. "But say, my sweet one," continued he, "who art *thou?* I know you as yet only by your lovely baptismal name, and your other name of Grampus."

Adeliza looked down and blushed. "My parents are lowly," she said.

"But how, then, came you at such a seminary?" said he; "twenty pound a quarter, extras and washing not included."

"They are humble, but wealthy."

"Ha! who is your father?"

"An alderman of yon metropolis."

"An alderman! and what is his profession?"

"I blush to tell: he is—*an oystermonger.*"

"AN OYSTERMONGER!" screamed Roderick, in the largest capitals. "Ha! ha! ha! this is too much!" and he dropped Adeliza's hand, and never spoke to her during the rest of her walk. They moved moodily on for some time, Miss Binx and the other young man marching astonished in the rear. At length they came within sight of the seminary. "Here is Bulgaria House," cried the maiden steadily; "Roderick, we must part!" The effort was too much for her; she flung herself hysterically into his arms.

But, oh, horror! a scream was heard from Miss Binx, who was seen scuttling at double-quick time towards the schoolhouse. Her young man had bolted completely; and close at the side of the lovely, though imprudent couple, stood the angry—and justly angry—Miss Zela Pidge!

"Oh, Ferdinand," said she, "is it thus you deceive me? Did I bring you to Bulgaria House for this?—did I give you money to buy clothes for this, that you should go by false names, and make love to that saucy, slammerkin, sentimental Miss Grampus! Ferdinand, Ferdinand," cried she, "is this true? can I credit my eyes?"

"D—— your eyes!" said the Signor angrily, as he darted at her a withering look, and retired down the street. His curses might be heard long after he had passed. He never appeared more at Bulgaria House, for he received his dismissal the next day.

That night all the front windows of the Miss Pidges' seminary were smashed to shivers.

．　　．　　．　　．　　．　　．　　．

On the following Thursday, *two* places were taken in the coach to town. On the back seat sate the usher; on the front, the wasted and miserable Adeliza Grampus.

．　　．　　．　　．　　．　　．　　．

CHAPTER II

BUT the matter did not end here. Miss Grampus's departure elicited from her a disclosure of several circumstances which, we must say, in no degree increased the reputation of Miss Zela Pidge. The discoveries which she made were so awkward, the tale of crime and licentiousness revealed by her so deeply injurious to the character of the establishment, that the pupils emigrated from it in scores. Miss Binx retired to her friends at Wandsworth, Miss Jacobs to her relations in Houndsditch, and other young ladies, not mentioned in this history, to other and more moral schools; so that absolutely, at the end of a single half-year, such had been the scandal of the story, the Misses Pidge were left with only two pupils—Miss Dibble, the articled young lady, and Miss Bole, the grocer's daughter, who came in exchange for tea, candles, and other requisites supplied to the establishment by her father.

"I knew it! I knew it!" cried Zela passionately, as she trod the echoing and melancholy schoolroom; "he told me that none ever prospered who loved him—that every flower was blighted upon which he shone! Ferdinand! Ferdinand, you have caused ruin there!" (pointing to the empty cupboards and forms); "but what is that to the blacker ruin *here?*" and the poor creature slapped her heart, and the big tears rolled down her chin, and so into her tucker.

A very very few weeks after this, the plate on Bulgaria House was removed for ever. That mansion is now designated "Moscow Hall, by Mr. Swishtail and assistants : "—the bankrupt and fugitive Misses Pidge have fled, Heaven knows whither ! for the steamers to Boulogne cost more than five shillings in those days.

Alderman Grampus, as may be imagined, did not receive his daughter with any extraordinary degree of courtesy. "He was as grumpy," Mrs. G. remarked, "on the occasion as a sow with the measles." But had he not reason ? A lovely daughter who had neglected her education, forgotten her morals for the second time, and fallen almost a prey to villains ! Miss Grampus for some months was kept in close confinement, nor ever suffered to stir, except occasionally to Bunhill Row for air, and to church for devotion. Still, though she knew him to be false,—though she knew that under a different, perhaps a prettier name, he had offered the same vows to another—she could not but think of Roderick.

That *Professor* (as well—too well—he may be called !) knew too well her father's name and reputation to experience any difficulty in finding his abode. It was, as every City man knows, in Cheapside ; and thither Dandolo constantly bent his steps : but though he marched unceasingly about the mansion, he never (mysteriously) would pass it. He watched Adeliza walking, he followed her to church ; and many and many a time as she jostled out at the gate of the Artillery-ground or the beadle-flanked portal of Bow, a tender hand would meet hers, an active foot would press upon hers, a billet discreetly delivered was as adroitly seized, to hide in the recesses of her pocket-handkerchief, or to nestle in the fragrance of her bosom ! Love ! Love ! how ingenious thou art ! thou canst make a ladder of a silken thread, or a weapon of a straw ; thou peerest like sunlight into a dungeon ; thou scalest, like forlorn hope, a castle wall ; the keep is taken !—the foeman has fled !—the banner of love floats triumphantly over the corpses of the slain ! *

Thus, though denied the comfort of personal intercourse, Adeliza and her lover maintained a frequent and tender correspondence. Nine times at least in a week, she, by bribing her maid-servant, managed to convey letters to the Professor, to which he at rarer intervals, though with equal warmth, replied.

"Why," said the young lady in the course of this correspondence, "why when I cast my eyes upon my Roderick, do I see

---

* We cannot explain this last passage ; but it is so beautiful that the reader will pardon the omission of sense, which the author certainly could have put in if he liked.

him so woefully changed in outward guise? He wears not the dress which formerly adorned him. Is he poor?—is he in disguise? —do debts oppress him, or traitors track him for his blood? Oh that my arms might shield him!—Oh that my purse might aid him! It is the fondest wish of   ADELIZA G.

"*P.S.*—Aware of your fondness for shell-fish, Susan will leave a barrel of oysters at the Swan with Two Necks, directed to you, as per desire.   AD. G.

"*P.S.*—Are you partial to kippered salmon? The girl brings three pounds of it wrapped in a silken handkerchief. 'Tis marked with the hair of   ADELIZA.

"*P.S.*—I break open my note to say that you will find in it a small pot of anchovy paste: may it prove acceptable. Heigho! I would that I could accompany it.   A. G."

It may be imagined, from the text of this note, that Adeliza had profited not a little by the perusal of Miss Swipes's novels; and it also gives a pretty clear notion of the condition of her lover. When that gentleman was a professor at Bulgaria House, his costume had strictly accorded with his pretensions. He wore a black German coat loaded with frogs and silk trimming, a white broad-brimmed beaver, hessians, and nankeen tights. His costume at present was singularly changed for the worse; a rough brown frock-coat dangled down to the calves of his brawny legs, where likewise ended a pair of greasy shepherd's-plaid trousers; a dubious red waistcoat, a blue or bird's-eye neckerchief, and bluchers (or half-boots), remarkable for thickness and for mud, completed his attire. But he looked superior to his fortune; he wore his grey hat very much on one ear; he incessantly tugged at his smoky shirt-collar, and walked jingling the halfpence (when he had any) in his pocket. He was, in fact, no better than an adventurer, and the innocent Adeliza was his prey.

Though the Professor read the first part of this letter with hope and pleasure, it may be supposed that the three postscripts were still more welcome to him—in fact, he literally did what is often done in novels, he *devoured* them; and Adeliza, on receiving a note from him the next day, after she had eagerly broken the seal, and with panting bosom and flashing eye glanced over the contents—Adeliza, we say, was not altogether pleased when she read the following :—

"Your goodness, dearest, passes belief; but never did poor fellow need it more than your miserable faithful Roderick. Yes! I *am* poor—I *am* tracked by hell-hounds—I *am* changed in looks, and dress, and happiness—in all but love for thee!

"Hear my tale! I come of a noble Italian family—the noblest, ay, in Venice. We were free once, and rich, and happy; but the Prussian autograph has planted his banner on our towers—the talents of his haughty heagle have seized our wealth, and consigned most of our race to dungeons. I am not a prisoner, only an exile. A mother, a bed-ridden grandmother, and five darling sisters escaped with me from Venice, and now share my poverty and my home. But I have wrestled with misfortune in vain; I have struggled with want, till want has overcome me. Adeliza, I WANT BREAD!

"The kippered salmon was very good, the anchovies admirable. But, oh, my love! how thirsty they make those who have no means of slaking thirst! My poor grandmother lies delirious in her bed, and cries in vain for drink. Alas! our water is cut off; I have none to give her. The oysters was capital. Bless thee, bless thee! angel of bounty! Have you any more sich, and a few srimps? My sisters are *very* fond of them.

"Half-a-crown would oblige. But thou art too good to me already, and I blush to ask thee for more. Adieu, Adeliza.—The wretched but faithful, RODERICK FERDINAND

(38th Count of Dandolo).

"BELL YARD: *June* —."

A shade of dissatisfaction, we say, clouded Adeliza's fair features as she perused this note; and yet there was nothing in it which the tenderest lover might not write. But the shrimps, the half-crown, the horrid picture of squalid poverty presented by the Count, sickened her young heart; the innate delicacy of the woman revolted at the thought of all this misery.

But better thoughts succeeded: her breast heaved as she read and re-read the singular passage concerning the Prussian autograph, who had planted his standard at Venice. "I knew it!" she cried, "I knew it!—he is of noble race! Oh Roderick, I will perish, but I will help thee!"

Alas! she was not well enough acquainted with history to perceive that the Prussian autograph had nothing to do with Venice, and had forgotten altogether that she herself had coined the story which this adventurer returned to her.

But a difficulty presented itself to Adeliza's mind. Her lover asked for money—where was she to find it? The next day the till of the shop was empty, and a weeping apprentice dragged before the Lord Mayor. It is true that no signs of the money were found upon him ; it is true that he protested his innocence ; but he was dismissed the alderman's service, and passed a month at Bridewell because Adeliza Grampus had a needy lover.

"Dearest," she wrote, "will three-and-twenty and sevenpence suffice ? 'Tis all I have : take it, and with it the fondest wishes of your Adeliza.

"A sudden thought ! Our apprentice is dismissed. My father dines abroad ; I shall be in the retail establishment all the night, *alone*.   A. G."

No sooner had the Professor received this note than his mind was made up. "I will see her," he said ; "I will enter that accursed shop." He did, and *to his ruin*.

. . . .

That night Mrs. Grampus and her daughter took possession of the bar or counter, in the place which Adeliza called the retail establishment, and which is commonly denominated the shop. Mrs. Grampus herself operated with the oyster-knife, and served the Milton morsels to the customers. Age had not diminished her skill, nor had wealth rendered her too proud to resume at need a profession which she had followed in early days. Adeliza flew gracefully to and fro with the rolls, the vinegar-bottle with perforated cork, and the little pats of butter. A little boy ran backwards and forwards to the "Blue Lion" over the way, for the pots of porter, or for the brandy and water, which some gentlemen take after the play.

Midnight arrived. Miss Grampus was looking through the window, and contrasting the gleaming gas which shone upon the ruby lobsters with the calm moon which lightened up the Poultry, and threw a halo round the Royal Exchange. She was lost in maiden meditation, when her eye fell upon a pane of glass in her own window : squeezed against this, flat and white, was the nose of a man !—that man was Roderick Dandolo ! He seemed to be gazing at the lobsters more intensely than at Adeliza ; he had his hands in his pockets, and was whistling "Jim Crow." *

Miss Grampus felt sick with joy : she staggered to the counter, and almost fainted. The Professor concluded his melody, and entered at once into the shop. He pretended to have no knowledge of Miss Grampus, but *aborded* the two ladies with easy elegance and irresistible good-humour.

"Good evening, ma'am," said he, bowing profoundly to the

* I know this is an anachronism ; but I only mean that he was performing one of the popular melodies of the time.—M. A. T.

elder lady. "What a precious hot evening *to* be sure!—hot, ma'am, and hungry, as they say. I could not resist them lobsters, 'specially when I saw the lady behind 'em."

At this gallant speech Mrs. Grampus blushed, or looked as if she would blush, and said—

"Law, sir!"

"Law, indeed, ma'am," playfully continued the Professor: "you're a precious deal better than law—you're *divinity*, ma'am; and this, I presume, is your sister?"

He pointed to Adeliza as he spoke, who, pale and mute, stood fainting against a heap of ginger-beer bottles. The old lady was quite won by this stale compliment.

"My daughter, sir," she said. "Addly, lay a cloth for the gentleman. Do you take hoysters, sir, hor lobsters? Both is very fine."

"Why, ma'am," said he, "to say truth, I have come forty miles since dinner, and don't care if I have a little of both. I'll begin, if you please, with that there (Lord bless its claws, they're as red as your lips!), and we'll astonish a few of the natives afterwards, *by* your leave."

Mrs. Grampus was delighted with the manners and the appetite of the stranger. She proceeded forthwith to bisect the lobster, while the Professor, in a *dégagé* manner, his cane over his shoulder, and a cheerful whistle upon his lips, entered the little parlour, and took possession of a box and a table.

He was no sooner seated than, from a scuffle, a giggle, and a smack, Mrs. Grampus was induced to suspect that something went wrong in the oyster-room.

"Hadeliza!" cried she: and that young woman returned blushing now like a rose, who had been as pale before as a lily.

Mrs. G. herself took in the lobster, bidding her daughter sternly to stay in the shop. She approached the stranger with an angry air, and laid the lobster before him.

"For shame, sir!" said she solemnly; but all of a sudden she began to giggle like her daughter, and her speech ended with an "*Have done now!*"

We were not behind the curtain, and cannot of course say what took place; but it is evident that the Professor was a general lover of the sex.

Mrs. Grampus returned to the shop, rubbing her lips with her fat arms, and restored to perfect good-humour. The little errand-boy was despatched over the way for a bottle of Guinness and a glass of brandy and water.

"HOT WITH!" shouted a manly voice from the eating-room,

and Adeliza was pained to think that in her presence her lover could eat so well.

He ate indeed as if he had never eaten before : here is the bill as written by Mrs. Grampus herself :—

	£.	s.	d.
" Two lobsters at 3s. 6d.		7	0
Salit		1	3
2 Bottils Doubling Stott		2	4
11 Doz. Best natifs		7	4
14 Pads of Botter		1	2
4 Glasses B. & W.		4	0
Bredd (love & ½)		1	2
Brakitch of tumler		1	6
	1	5	9

" *To Samuel Grampus,*
" *At the Mermaid in Cheapside.*

" Shell-fish in all varieties. N.B.—A great saving in taking a quantity."

" A saving in *taking a quantity*," said the stranger archly. " Why, ma'am, you ought to let me off *very cheap ;* " and the Professor, the potboy, Adeliza, and her mamma, grinned equally at this pleasantry.

" However, never mind the pay, missis," continued he ; " we an't a-going to quarrel about *that.* Hadd another glass of brandy and water to the bill, and bring it me, when it shall be as I am now."

" Law, sir," simpered Mrs. Grampus, " how's that ? "

" *Reseated,* ma'am, to be sure," replied he, as he sank back upon the table. The old lady went laughing away, pleased with her merry and facetious customer ; the little boy picked up the oyster-shells, of which a mighty pyramid was formed at the Professor's feet.

" Here, Sammy," cried out shrill Mrs. Grampus from the shop, " go over to the ' Blue Lion ' and get the gentleman his glass : but no, you are better where you are, pickin' up them shells. Go you, Hadeliza ; it is but across the way."

Adeliza went with a very bad grace ; she had hoped to exchange at least a few words with him her soul adored ; and her mother's jealousy prevented the completion of her wish.

She had scarcely gone when Mr. Grampus entered from his dinner-party. But, though fond of pleasure, he was equally faithful to business: without a word he hung up his brass-buttoned coat, put on his hairy cap, and stuck his sleeves through his apron.

As Mrs. Grampus was tying it (an office which this faithful lady regularly performed), he asked her what business had occurred during his absence.

"Not so bad," said she; "two pound ten to-night, besides one pound eight to receive," and she handed Mr. Grampus the bill.

"How many are there on 'em?" said that gentleman, smiling, as his eye gladly glanced over the items of the account.

"Why, that's the best of all: how many do you think?"

"If four did it," said Mr. Grampus, "they wouldn't have done badly neither."

"What do you think of one?" cried Mrs. G., laughing, "and he an't done yet. Haddy is gone to fetch him another glass of brandy and water."

Mr. Grampus looked very much alarmed. "Only one, and you say he an't paid?"

"No," said the lady.

Mr. Grampus seized the bill, and rushed wildly into the dining-room: the little boy was picking up the oyster-shells still, there were so many of them; the Professor was seated on the table, laughing as if drunk, and picking his teeth with his fork.

Grampus, shaking in every joint, held out the bill: a horrid thought crossed him; he had seen that face before!

The Professor kicked sneeringly into the air the idle piece of paper, and swung his legs recklessly to and fro.

"What a flat you are," shouted he, in a voice of thunder, "to think I'm a-goin' to pay! Pay! I never pay—I'M DANDO!"

The people in the other boxes crowded forward to see the celebrated stranger; the little boy grinned as he dropped two hundred and forty-four oyster-shells, and Mr. Grampus rushed madly into his front shop, shrieking for a watchman.

As he ran, he stumbled over something on the floor—a woman and a glass of brandy and water lay there extended. Like Tarquinia reversed, Elijah Grampus was trampling over the lifeless body of Adeliza.

Why enlarge upon the miserable theme? The confiding girl, in returning with the grog from the "Blue Lion," had arrived at the shop only in time to hear the fatal name of DANDO. She saw him, tipsy and triumphant, bestriding the festal table, and yelling with horrid laughter! The truth flashed upon her—she fell!

Lost to worldly cares in contemplating the sorrows of their idolised child, her parents forgot all else beside. Mrs. G. held the vinegar-cruet to her nostrils; her husband brought the soda water fountain to play upon her; it restored her to life, but not to sense. When Adeliza Grampus rose from that trance, she was a MANIAC!

But what became of *the deceiver?* The gormandising ruffian, the lying renegade, the fiend in human shape, escaped in the midst of this scene of desolation. He walked unconcerned through the shop, his hat cocked on one side as before, swaggering as before, whistling as before: far in the moonlight might you see his figure; long, long in the night-silence rang his demoniac melody of "Jim Crow"!

. . . .

When Samuel the boy cleaned out the shop in the morning, and made the inventory of the goods, a silver fork, a plated ditto, a dish, and a pewter-pot were found to be wanting. Ingenuity will not be long in guessing the name of *the thief.*

Gentles, my tale is told. If it may have deterred one soul from vice, my end is fully answered: if it may have taught to schoolmistresses carefulness, to pupils circumspection, to youth the folly of sickly sentiment, the pain of bitter deception; to manhood the crime, the *meanness* of gluttony, the vice which it occasions, and the wicked passions it fosters; if these, or any of these, have been taught by the above tale, the writer seeks for no other reward.

NOTE.—Please send the proceeds as requested per letter; the bearer being directed not to give up the manuscript without.

BLUEBEARD'S GHOST

FOR some time after the fatal accident which deprived her of her husband, Mrs. Bluebeard was, as may be imagined, in a state of profound grief.

There was not a widow in all the country who went to such an expense for black bombazeen. She had her beautiful hair confined in crimped caps, and her weepers came over her elbows. Of course she saw no company except her sister Anne (whose company was anything but pleasant to the widow); as for her brothers, their odious mess-table manners had always been disagreeable to her. What did she care for jokes about the major, or scandal concerning the Scotch surgeon of the regiment? If they drank their wine out of black bottles or crystal, what did it matter to her? Their stories of the stable, the parade, and the last run with the hounds, were perfectly odious to her; besides, she could not bear their impertinent mustachios and filthy habit of smoking cigars.

They were always wild vulgar young men at the best; but *now*, oh! their presence to her delicate soul was horror! How could she bear to look on them after what had occurred? She thought of the best of husbands ruthlessly cut down by their cruel heavy cavalry sabres; the kind friend, the generous landlord, the spotless justice of peace, in whose family differences these rude cornets of dragoons had dared to interfere, whose venerable blue hairs they had dragged down with sorrow to the grave!

She put up a most splendid monument to her departed lord over the family vault of the Bluebeards. The rector, Doctor Sly, who had been Mr. Bluebeard's tutor at college, wrote an epitaph in the most pompous yet pathetic Latin:—"Siste, viator! mœrens conjux heu! quanto minus est cum reliquis versari quam tui meminisse; in a word, everything that is usually said in epitaphs. A bust of the departed saint, with Virtue mourning over it, stood over the epitaph, surrounded by medallions of his wives, and one of these medallions had as yet no name in it, nor (the epitaph said) could the widow ever be consoled until her own name was inscribed there "For then I shall be with him. In cœlo quies," she would say throwing up her fine eyes to heaven, and quoting the enormous words of the hatchment which was put up in the church and over Bluebeard's hall, where the butler, the housekeeper, the footman, the housemaid, and scullions were all in the profoundest mourning. The keeper went out to shoot birds in a crape band; nay, the very scarecrows in the orchard and fruit-garden were ordered to be dressed in black.

Sister Anne was the only person who refused to wear black. Mrs. Bluebeard would have parted with her, but she had no other female relative. Her father, it may be remembered by readers of the former part of her Memoirs, had married again; and the mother in-law and Mrs. Bluebeard, as usual, hated each other furiously. Mrs. Shacabac had come to the hall on a visit of condolence; but the widow was so rude to her on the second day of the visit that the stepmother quitted the house in a fury. As for the Bluebeards, of course *they* hated the widow. Had not Mr. Bluebeard settled every shilling upon her? and, having no children by his former marriage, her property, as I leave you to fancy, was pretty handsome. So sister Anne was the only female relative whom Mrs. Bluebeard would keep near her, and, as we all know, a woman *must* have a female relative under any circumstances of pain, or pleasure, or profit—when she is married, or when she is in a delicate situation. But let us continue our story.

"I will never wear mourning for that odious wretch, sister!" Anne would cry.

"I will trouble you, Miss Anne, not to use such words in my presence regarding the best of husbands, or to quit the room at once!" the widow would answer.

"I'm sure it's no great pleasure to sit in it. I wonder you don't make use of the closet, sister, where the *other* Mrs. Bluebeards are."

"Impertinence! they were all embalmed by Monsieur Gannal. How dare you report the monstrous calumnies regarding the best of men? Take down the family Bible and read what my blessed saint says of his wives—read it written in his own hand :—

"'*Friday, June* 20.—Married my beloved wife, Anna Maria Scrogginsia.

"'*Saturday, August* 1.—A bereaved husband has scarcely strength to write down in this chronicle that the dearest of wives, Anna Maria Scrogginsia, expired this day of sore throat.'

"There! can anything be more convincing than that? Read again :—

"'*Tuesday, Sept.* 1.—This day I led to the hymeneal altar
2 o

my soul's blessing, Louisa Matilda Hopkinson. May this angel supply the place of her I have lost!

"'*Wednesday, October* 5.—Oh, heavens! pity the distraction of a wretch who is obliged to record the ruin of his dearest hopes and affections! This day my adored Louisa Matilda Hopkinson gave up the ghost! A complaint of the head and shoulders was the sudden cause of the event which has rendered the unhappy subscriber the most miserable of men.   BLUEBEARD.'

"Every one of the women are calendared in this delightful, this pathetic, this truly virtuous and tender way; and can you suppose that a man who wrote such sentiments could be a *murderer*, miss?"

"Do you mean to say that he did not *kill* them, then?" said Anne.

"Gracious goodness, Anne, kill them! they died all as naturally as I hope you will. My blessed husband was an angel of goodness and kindness to them. Was it *his* fault that the doctors could not cure their maladies? No, that it wasn't! and when they died the inconsolable husband had their bodies embalmed, in order that on this side of the grave he might never part from them."

"And why did he take you up in the tower, pray? and why did you send me in such a hurry to the leads? and why did he sharpen his long knife, and roar out to you to COME DOWN?"

"Merely to punish me for my curiosity—the dear, good, kind, excellent creature!" sobbed the widow, overpowered with affectionate recollections of her lord's attentions to her.

"I wish," said sister Anne sulkily, "that I had not been in such a hurry in summoning my brothers."

"Ah!" screamed Mrs. Bluebeard, with a harrowing scream, "don't—don't recall that horrid fatal day, miss! If you had not misled your brothers, my poor dear darling Bluebeard would still be in life, still—still the soul's joy of his bereaved Fatima!"

Whether it is that all wives adore husbands when the latter are no more, or whether it is that Fatima's version of the story is really the correct one, and that the common impression against Bluebeard is an odious prejudice, and that he no more murdered his wives than you and I have, remains yet to be proved, and, indeed, does not much matter for the understanding of the rest of Mrs. B.'s adventures. And though people will say that Bluebeard's settlement of his whole fortune on his wife, in event of survivorship, was a mere act of absurd mystification, seeing that he was fully determined to cut her head off after the honeymoon, yet the best

:est of his real intentions is the profound grief which the widow manifested for his death, and the fact that he left her mighty well o do in the world.

If any one were to leave you or me a fortune, my dear friend, would we be too anxious to rake up the how and the why? Pooh! pooh! we would take it and make no bones about it, and Mrs. Bluebeard did likewise. Her husband's family, it is true, argued the point with her, and said, "Madam, you must perceive hat Mr. Bluebeard never intended the fortune for you, as it was is fixed intention to chop off your head! it is clear that he meant o leave his money to his blood relations, therefore you ought in quity to hand it over." But she sent them all off with a flea in heir ears, as the saying is, and said, "Your argument may be a very good one, but I will, if you please, keep the money." And he ordered the mourning as we have before shown, and indulged n grief, and exalted everywhere the character of the deceased. If ny one would but leave me a fortune, what a funeral and what a haracter I would give him!

Bluebeard Hall is situated, as we all very well know, in a emote country district, and, although a fine residence, is remark-bly gloomy and lonely. To the widow's susceptible mind, after he death of her darling husband, the place became intolerable. 'he walk, the lawn, the fountain, the green glades of park over which frisked the dappled deer, all—all recalled the memory of er beloved. It was but yesterday that, as they roamed through he park in the calm summer evening, her Bluebeard pointed out ɔ the keeper the fat buck he was to kill. "Ah!" said the widow, ith tears in her fine eyes, "the artless stag was shot down, the aunch was cut and roasted, the jelly had been prepared from the irrant-bushes in the garden that he loved, but my Bluebeard ever ate of the venison! Look, Anna sweet, pass we the old oak all; 'tis hung with trophies won by him in the chase, with pictures f the noble race of Bluebeard! Look! by the fireplace there is e gig-whip, his riding-whip, the spud with which you know he sed to dig the weeds out of the terrace-walk; in that drawer are his ɔurs, his whistle, his visiting-cards, with his dear dear name engraven ɔon them! There are the bits of string that he used to cut off the ircels and keep because string was always useful; his button-hook, id there is the peg on which he used to hang his h—h—*hat!*"

Uncontrollable emotions, bursts of passionate tears, would llow these tender reminiscences of the widow; and the long and ort of the matter was, that she was determined to give up Blue-ard Hall and live elsewhere; her love for the memory of the ceased, she said, rendered the place too wretched.

Of course an envious and sneering world said that she wa
tired of the country and wanted to marry again ; but she littl
heeded its taunts, and Anne, who hated her stepmother and coul
not live at home, was fain to accompany her sister to the tow
where the Bluebeards have had for many years a very large, gentee
old-fashioned house. So she went to the town-house, where the
lived and quarrelled pretty much as usual ; and though Anne ofte
threatened to leave her and go to a boarding-house, of which ther
were plenty in the place, yet after all to live with her sister, an
drive out in the carriage with the footman and coachman in mourn
ing, and the lozenge on the panels, with the Bluebeard and Shacaba
arms quartered on it, was far more respectable, and so the lovel
sisters continued to dwell together.

For a lady under Mrs. Bluebeard's circumstances, the tow
house had other and peculiar advantages. Besides being an ex
ceedingly spacious and dismal brick building, with a dismal iro
railing in front, and long dismal thin windows with little panes c
glass, it looked out into the churchyard where, time out of mind
between two yew-trees, one of which is cut into the form of
peacock, while the other represents a dumb-waiter—it looked int
the churchyard where the monument of the late Bluebeard wa
placed over the family vault. It was the first thing the wido
saw from her bedroom window in the morning, and 'twas sweet t
watch at night from the parlour the pallid moonlight lighting u
the bust of the departed, and Virtue throwing great black shadow
athwart it. Polyanthuses, rhododendra, ranunculuses, and othe
flowers with the largest names and of the most delightful odour
were planted within the little iron railing that enclosed the la
resting-place of the Bluebeards ; and the beadle was instructed
half-kill any little boys who might be caught plucking these swee
testimonies of a wife's affection.

Over the sideboard in the dining-room hung a full-length of M
Bluebeard, by Ticklegill, R.A., in a militia uniform, frowning dow
upon the knives and forks and silver trays. Over the mantelpie
he was represented in a hunting costume on his favourite hors
there was a sticking-plaster silhouette of him in the widow's be
room, and a miniature in the drawing-room, where he was drawn in
gown of black and gold, holding a gold-tasselled trencher-cap wit
one hand, and with the other pointing to a diagram of Pons Asinoru
This likeness was taken when he was a fellow-commoner
Saint John's College, Cambridge, and before the growth of th
blue beard which was the ornament of his manhood, and a part
which now formed a beautiful blue neck-chain for his bereaved wi

Sister Anne said the town house was even more dismal than the country-house, for there was pure air at the Hall, and it was pleasanter to look out on a park than on a churchyard, however fine the monuments might be. But the widow said she was a light-minded hussy, and persisted as usual in her lamentations and mourning. The only male whom she would admit within her doors was the parson of the parish, who read sermons to her; and, as his reverence was at least seventy years old, Anne, though she might be ever so much minded to fall in love, had no opportunity to indulge her inclination; and the townspeople, scandalous as they might be, could not find a word to say against the *liaison* of the venerable man and the heart-stricken widow.

All other company she resolutely refused. When the players were in the town, the poor manager, who came to beg her to bespeak a comedy, was thrust out of the gates by the big butler. Though there were balls, card-parties, and assemblies, Widow Bluebeard would never subscribe to one of them; and even the officers, those all-conquering heroes who make such ravages in ladies' hearts, and to whom all ladies' doors are commonly open, could never get an entry into the widow's house. Captain Whiskerfield strutted for three weeks up and down before her house, and had not the least effect upon her. Captain O'Grady (of an Irish regiment) attempted to bribe the servants, and one night actually scaled the garden wall; but all that he got was his foot in a man-trap, not to mention being dreadfully scarified by the broken glass; and so *he* never made love any more. Finally, Captain Blackbeard, whose whiskers vied in magnitude with those of the deceased Bluebeard himself, although he attended church regularly every week—he who had not darkened the doors of a church for ten years before—even Captain Blackbeard got nothing by his piety; and the widow never once took her eyes off her book to look at him. The barracks were in despair; and Captain Whiskerfield's tailor, who had supplied him with new clothes in order to win the widow's heart, ended by clapping the Captain into gaol.

His reverence the parson highly applauded the widow's conduct to the officers; but, being himself rather of a social turn, and fond of a good dinner and a bottle, he represented to the lovely mourner that she should endeavour to divert her grief by a little respectable society, and recommended that she should from time to time entertain a few grave and sober persons whom he would present to her. As Doctor Sly had an unbounded influence over the fair mourner, she acceded to his desires; and accordingly he introduced to her house some of the most venerable and worthy of his acquaintance,—all married people, however, so that the widow should not take the least alarm.

13

It happened that the Doctor had a nephew, who was a lawyer in London, and this gentleman came dutifully in the long vacation to pay a visit to his reverend uncle. "He is none of your roystering dashing young fellows," said his reverence; "he is the delight of his mamma and sisters; he never drinks anything stronger than tea; he never missed church thrice a Sunday for these twenty years; and I hope, my dear and amiable madam, that you will not object to receive this pattern of young men for the sake of your most devoted friend, his uncle."

The widow consented to receive Mr. Sly. He was not a handsome man certainly. "But what does that matter?" said the Doctor; "he is *good*, and virtue is better than all the beauty of all the dragoons in the Queen's service."

Mr. Sly came there to dinner, and he came to tea; and he drove out with the widow in the carriage with the lozenge on it; and at church he handed the psalm-book; and, in short, he paid her every attention which could be expected from so polite a young gentleman.

At this the town began to talk, as people in towns will. "The Doctor kept all bachelors out of the widow's house," said they, "in order that that ugly nephew of his may have the field entirely to himself." These speeches were of course heard by sister Anne, and the little minx was not a little glad to take advantage of them, in order to induce her sister to see some more cheerful company. The fact is, the young hussy loved a dance or a game at cards much more than a humdrum conversation over a tea-table; and so she plied her sister day and night with hints as to the propriety of opening her house, receiving the gentry of the county, and spending her fortune.

To this point the widow at length, though with many sighs and vast unwillingness, acceded; and she went so far as to order a very becoming half-mourning, in which all the world declared she looked charming. "I carry," said she, "my blessed Bluebeard in my heart,—*that* is in the deepest mourning for him, and when the heart grieves there is no need of outward show."

So she issued cards for a little quiet tea and supper, and several of the best families in the town and neighbourhood attended her entertainment. It was followed by another and another; and at last Captain Blackbeard was actually introduced, though, of course, he came in plain clothes.

Doctor Sly and his nephew never could abide the Captain. "They had heard some queer stories," they said, "about proceedings in barracks. Who was it that drank three bottles at a sitting? who had a mare that ran for the plate? and why was it that Dolly

Coddlins left the town so suddenly?" Mr. Sly turned up the whites of his eyes as his uncle asked these questions, and sighed for the wickedness of the world. But for all that he was delighted, especially at the anger which the widow manifested when the Dolly Coddlins affair was hinted at. She was furious, and vowed she would never see the wretch again. The lawyer and his uncle were charmed. O short-sighted lawyer and parson, do you think Mrs. Bluebeard would have been so angry if she had not been jealous?— do you think she would have been jealous if she had not——had not what? She protested that she no more cared for the Captain than she did for one of her footmen; but the next time he called she would not condescend to say a word to him.

"My dearest Miss Anne," said the Captain, as he met her in Sir Roger de Coverley (she was herself dancing with Ensign Trippet), "what is the matter with your lovely sister?"

"Dolly Coddlins is the matter," said Miss Anne. "Mr. Sly has told all;" and she was down the middle in a twinkling.

The Captain blushed so at this monstrous insinuation that any one could see how incorrect it was. He made innumerable blunders in the dance, and was all the time casting such ferocious glances at Mr. Sly (who did not dance, but sate by the widow and ate ices), that his partner thought he was mad, and that Mr. Sly became very uneasy.

When the dance was over, he came to pay his respects to the widow, and, in so doing, somehow trod so violently on Mr. Sly's foot that that gentleman screamed with pain, and presently went home. But though he was gone the widow was not a whit more gracious to Captain Blackbeard. She requested Mr. Trippet to order her carriage that night, and went home without uttering one single word to Captain Blackbeard.

The next morning, and with a face of preternatural longitude, the Reverend Doctor Sly paid a visit to the widow. "The wickedness and bloodthirstiness of the world," said he, "increase every day. O my dear madam, what monsters do we meet in it—what wretches, what assassins, are allowed to go abroad! Would you believe it, that this morning, as my nephew was taking his peaceful morning meal, one of the ruffians from the barracks presented himself with a challenge from Captain Blackbeard?"

"Is he hurt?" screamed the widow.

"No, my dear friend, my dear Frederick is not hurt. And oh, what a joy it will be to him to think you have that tender solicitude for his welfare!"

"You know I have always had the highest respect for him," said the widow; who, when she screamed, was in truth thinking of somebody else. But the Doctor did not choose to interpret her thoughts in that way, and gave all the benefit of them to his nephew.

"That anxiety, dearest madam, which you express for him emboldens me, encourages me, authorises me, to press a point on you which I am sure must have entered your thoughts ere now. The dear youth in whom you have shown such an interest lives but for you! Yes, fair lady, start not at hearing that his sole affections are yours; and with what pride shall I carry to him back the news that he is not indifferent to you!"

"Are they going to fight?" continued the lady, in a breathless state of alarm. "For Heaven's sake, dearest Doctor, prevent the horrid horrid meeting. Send for a magistrate's warrant; do anything; but do not suffer those misguided young men to cut each other's throats!"

"Fairest lady, I fly!" said the Doctor, and went back to lunch quite delighted with the evident partiality Mrs. Bluebeard showed for his nephew. And Mrs. Bluebeard, not content with exhorting him to prevent the duel, rushed to Mr. Pound, the magistrate, informed him of the facts, got out warrants against both Mr. Sly and the Captain, and would have put them into execution; but it was discovered that the former gentleman had abruptly left town, so that the constable could not lay hold of him.

It somehow, however, came to be generally known that the widow Bluebeard had declared herself in favour of Mr. Sly, the lawyer; that she had fainted when told her lover was about to fight a duel; finally, that she had accepted him, and would marry him as soon as the quarrel between him and the Captain was settled. Doctor Sly, when applied to, hummed and ha'd, and would give no direct answer; but he denied nothing, and looked so knowing, that all the world was certain of the fact; and the county paper next week stated :—

"We understand that the lovely and wealthy Mrs. Bl—b—rd is about once more to enter the bands of wedlock with our distinguished townsman, Frederick S—y, Esquire, of the Middle Temple, London. The learned gentleman left town in consequence of a dispute with a gallant son of Mars which was likely to have led to warlike results, had not a magistrate's warrant intervened, when the Captain was bound over to keep the peace."

In fact, as soon as the Captain was so bound over, Mr. Sly came back, stating that he had quitted the town not to avoid a duel,— far from it, but to keep out of the way of the magistrates, and give the Captain every facility. *He* had taken out no warrant; *he* had been perfectly ready to meet the Captain; if others had been more prudent, it was not his fault. So he held up his head, and cocked his hat with the most determined air; and all the lawyers' clerks in the place were quite proud of their hero.

As for Captain Blackbeard, his rage and indignation may be imagined; a wife robbed from him, his honour put in question by an odious, lanky, squinting lawyer! He fell ill of a fever incontinently; and the surgeon was obliged to take a quantity of blood from him, ten times the amount of which he swore he would have out of the veins of the atrocious Sly.

The announcement in the *Mercury*, however, filled the widow with almost equal indignation. "The widow of the gallant Bluebeard," she said, "marry an odious wretch who lives in dingy chambers in the Middle Temple! Send for Doctor Sly." The Doctor came; she rated him soundly, asked him how he dared set abroad such calumnies concerning her; ordered him to send his nephew back to London at once; and, as he valued her esteem, as he valued the next presentation to a fat living which lay in her gift, to contradict everywhere, and in the fullest terms, the wicked report concerning her.

"My dearest madam," said the Doctor, pulling his longest face, "you shall be obeyed. The poor lad shall be acquainted with the fatal change in your sentiments!"

"Change in my sentiments, Doctor Sly!"

"With the destruction of his hopes, rather let me say; and Heaven grant that the dear boy have strength to bear up against the misfortune which comes so suddenly upon him!"

The next day sister Anne came with a face full of care to Mrs. Bluebeard. "Oh that unhappy lover of yours!" said she.

"Is the Captain unwell?" exclaimed the widow.

"No, it is the other," answered sister Anne. "Poor, poor Mr. Sly! He made a will leaving you all, except five pounds a year to his laundress: he made his will, locked his door, took heartrending leave of his uncle at night, and this morning was found hanging at his bed-post when Sambo, the black servant, took him up his water to shave. 'Let me be buried,' he said, 'with the pincushion she gave me and the locket containing her hair.' *Did* you give him a pincushion, sister? *did* you give him a locket with your hair?"

"It was only silver-gilt!" sobbed the widow; "and now, oh heavens! I have killed him!" The heart-rending nature of her sobs may be imagined; but they were abruptly interrupted by her sister.

"Killed him ?—no such thing! Sambo cut him down when he was as black in the face as the honest negro himself. He came down to breakfast, and I leave you to fancy what a touching meeting took place between the nephew and uncle."

"So much love!" thought the widow. "What a pity he squints so! If he would but get his eyes put straight, I might perhaps——" She did not finish the sentence: ladies often leave this sort of sentence in a sweet confusion.

But hearing some news regarding Captain Blackbeard, whose illness and blood-letting were described to her most pathetically, as well as accurately, by the Scotch surgeon of the regiment, her feelings of compassion towards the lawyer cooled somewhat; and when Doctor Sly called to know if she would condescend to meet the unhappy youth, she said, in rather a *distrait* manner, that she wished him every happiness; that she had the highest regard and respect for him; that she besought him not to think any more of committing the dreadful crime which would have made her unhappy for ever; *but* that she thought, for the sake of both parties, they had better not meet until Mr. Sly's feelings had grown somewhat more calm.

"Poor fellow! poor fellow!" said the Doctor, "may he be enabled to bear his frightful calamity! I have taken away his razors from him, and Sambo, my man, never lets him out of his sight."

The next day Mrs. Bluebeard thought of sending a friendly message to Doctor Sly's, asking for news of the health of his nephew; but, as she was giving her orders on that subject to John Thomas, the footman, it happened that the Captain arrived, and so Thomas was sent downstairs again. And the Captain looked so delightfully interesting with his arm in a sling, and his beautiful black whiskers curling round a face which was paler than usual, that at the end of two hours the widow forgot the message altogether, and, indeed, I believe, asked the Captain whether he would not stop and dine. Ensign Trippet came, too, and the party was very pleasant; and the military gentlemen laughed hugely at the idea of the lawyer having been cut off the bed-post by the black servant, and were so witty on the subject, that the widow ended by half believing that the bed-post and hanging scheme on the part of Mr. Sly was only a feint—a trick to win her heart. Though this, to be sure, was not agreed to by the lady without a pang, for *entre nous*, to hang oneself for a lady is no small compliment to her attractions, and, perhaps, Mrs. Bluebeard was rather disappointed at the notion that the hanging was not a *bonâ fide* strangulation.

However, presently her nerves were excited again; and she was consoled or horrified, as the case may be (the reader must settle the point according to his ideas and knowledge of woman-kind)—she was at any rate dreadfully excited by the receipt of a billet in the well-known clerk-like hand of Mr. Sly. It ran thus :—

"I saw you through your dining-room windows. You were hobnobbing with Captain Blackbeard. You looked rosy and well. You smiled. You drank off the champagne at a single draught.

"I can bear it no more. Live on, smile on, and be happy. My ghost shall repine, perhaps, at your happiness with another—but in life I should go mad were I to witness it.

"It is best that I should be gone.

"When you receive this, tell my uncle to drag the fish-pond at the end of Bachelor's Acre. His black servant Sambo accompanies me, it is true. But Sambo shall perish with me should his obstinacy venture to restrain me from my purpose. I know the poor fellow's honesty well, but I also know my own despair.

"Sambo will leave a wife and seven children.   Be kind to those orphan mulattoes for the sake of   FREDERICK."

The widow gave a dreadful shriek, and interrupted the two Captains, who were each just in the act of swallowing a bumper of claret. "Fly—fly—save him," she screamed; "save him, monsters, ere it is too late! Drowned !—Frederick !—Bachelor's Wa——" Syncope took place, and the rest of the sentence was interrupted.

Deucedly disappointed at being obliged to give up their wine, the two heroes seized their cocked-hats, and went towards the spot which the widow in her wild exclamations of despair had sufficiently designated.

Trippet was for running to the fish-pond at the rate of ten miles an hour. "Take it easy, my good fellow," said Captain Blackbeard; "running is unwholesome after dinner. And if that squinting scoundrel of a lawyer *does* drown himself, I shan't sleep any the worse." So the two gentlemen walked very leisurely on towards the Bachelor's Walk; and, indeed, seeing on their way thither Major Macabaw looking out of the window at his quarters and smoking a cigar, they went upstairs to consult the Major, as also a bottle of Schiedam he had.

"They come not !" said the widow, when restored to herself. "Oh, heavens ! grant that Frederick is safe ! Sister Anne, go up to the leads and look if anybody is coming." And up, accordingly, to the garrets sister Anne mounted. "Do you see anybody coming, sister Anne ?"

"I see Doctor Drench's little boy," said sister Anne; "he is leaving a pill and draught at Miss Molly Grub's."

"Dearest sister Anne, don't you see any one coming?" shouted the widow once again.

"I see a flock of dust,—no! a cloud of sheep. Pshaw! I see the London coach coming in. There are three outsides, and the guard has flung a parcel to Mrs. Jenkins's maid."

"Distraction! Look once more, sister Anne."

"I see a crowd—a shutter—a shutter with a man on it—a beadle—forty little boys—Gracious goodness! what *can* it be?" and downstairs tumbled sister Anne, and was looking out of the parlour-window by her sister's side, when the crowd she had perceived from the garret passed close by them.

At the head walked the beadle, slashing about at the little boys.

Two scores of these followed and surrounded

A SHUTTER carried by four men.

On the shutter lay *Frederick!* He was ghastly pale; his hair was draggled over his face; his clothes stuck tight to him on account of the wet; streams of water gurgled down the shutter sides. But he was not dead! He turned one eye round towards the window where Mrs. Bluebeard sat, and gave her a look which she never could forget.

Sambo brought up the rear of the procession. He was quite wet through; and, if anything would have put his hair out of curl, his ducking would have done so. But, as he was not a gentleman, he was allowed to walk home on foot, and, as he passed the widow's window, he gave her one dreadful glance with his goggling black eyes, and moved on pointing with his hands to the shutter.

John Thomas, the footman, was instantly despatched to Doctor Sly's to have news of the patient. There was no shilly-shallying now. He came back in half-an-hour to say that Mr. Frederick flung himself into Bachelor's Acre fish-pond with Sambo, had been dragged out with difficulty, had been put to bed, and had a pint of white wine whey, and was pretty comfortable. "Thank Heaven!" said the widow, and gave John Thomas a seven-shilling piece, and sat down with a lightened heart to tea. "What a heart!" said she to sister Anne. "And, oh, what a pity it is that he squints!"

Here the two Captains arrived. They had not been to the Bachelor's Walk; they had remained at Major Macabaw's consulting the Schiedam. They had made up their minds what to say. "Hang the fellow! he will never have the pluck to drown himself," said Captain Blackbeard. "Let us argue on that, as we may safely."

"My sweet lady," said he, accordingly, "we have had the pond dragged. No Mr. Sly. And the fisherman who keeps the punt assures us that he has not been there all day."

"Audacious falsehood!" said the widow, her eyes flashing fire. "Go, heartless man! who dares to trifle thus with the feelings of a respectable and unprotected woman. Go, sir, you're only fit for the love of a—Dolly—Coddlins!" She pronounced the *Coddlins* with a withering sarcasm that struck the Captain aghast; and sailing out of the room, she left her tea untasted, and did not wish either of the military gentlemen good-night.

But, gentles, an ye know the delicate fibre of woman's heart, ye will not in very sooth believe that such events as those we have described—such tempests of passion—fierce winds of woe—blinding lightnings of tremendous joy and tremendous grief—could pass over one frail flower and leave it all unscathed. No! Grief kills as joy doth. Doth not the scorching sun nip the rose-bud as well as the bitter wind? As Mrs. Sigourney sweetly sings—

> " Ah! the heart is a soft and a delicate thing ;
> Ah! the heart is a lute with a thrilling string ;
> A spirit that floats on a gossamer's wing! "

Such was Fatima's heart. In a word, the preceding events had a powerful effect upon her nervous system, and she was ordered much quiet and sal-volatile by her skilful medical attendant, Doctor Glauber.

To be so ardently, passionately loved as she was, to know that Frederick had twice plunged into death from attachment to her, was to awaken in her bosom "a thrilling string" indeed! Could she witness such attachment, and not be touched by it? She *was* touched by it—she was influenced by the virtues, by the passion, by the misfortunes of Frederick; but then he was so abominably ugly that she could not—she could not consent to become his bride!

She told Doctor Sly so. "I respect and esteem your nephew," said she; "but my resolve is made. I will continue faithful to that blessed saint, whose monument is ever before my eyes" (she pointed to the churchyard as she spoke). "Leave this poor tortured heart in quiet. It has already suffered more than most hearts could bear. I will repose under the shadow of that tomb until I am called to rest within it—to rest by the side of my Bluebeard!"

The ranunculuses, rhododendra, and polyanthuses, which ornamented that mausoleum, had somehow been suffered to run greatly to seed during the last few months, and it was with no slight self-accusation that she acknowledged this fact on visiting the "garden of the grave," as she called it; and she scolded the beadle soundly for neglecting his duty towards it. He promised obedience for the future, dug out all the weeds that were creeping round the family vault, and (having charge of the key) entered that awful place, and swept and dusted the melancholy contents of the tomb.

Next morning the widow came down to breakfast looking very pale. She had passed a bad night ; she had had awful dreams ; she had heard a voice call her thrice at midnight. " Pooh ! my dear ; it's only nervousness," said sceptical sister Anne.

Here John Thomas the footman entered, and said the beadle was in the hall, looking in a very strange way. He had been about the house since daybreak, and insisted on seeing Mrs. Bluebeard. " Let him enter," said that lady, prepared for some great mystery. The beadle came ; he was pale as death ; his hair was dishevelled, and his cocked-hat out of order. " What have you to say ? " said the lady, trembling.

Before beginning, he fell down on his knees.

" Yesterday," said he, " according to your Ladyship's orders, I dug up the flower-beds of the family vault—dusted the vault and the—the coffins " (added he, trembling) " inside. Me and John Sexton did it together, and polished up the plate quite beautiful."

" For Heaven's sake, don't allude to it," cried the widow, turning pale.

" Well, my Lady, I locked the door, came away, and found in my hurry—for I wanted to beat two little boys what was playing at marbles on Alderman Paunch's monument—I found, my Lady, I'd forgot my cane. I couldn't get John Sexton to go back with me till this morning, and I didn't like to go alone, and so we went this morning, and what do you think I found ? I found his honour's coffin turned round, and the cane broke in two. Here's the cane ! "

" Ah ! " screamed the widow, " take it away—take it away ! "

" Well, what does this prove," said sister Anne, " but that somebody moved the coffin, and broke the cane ? "

" Somebody ! *who's somebody ?* " said the beadle, staring round about him. And all of a sudden he started back with a tremendous roar, that made the ladies scream, and all the glasses on the sideboard jingle, and cried, " *That's the man !* "

He pointed to the portrait of Bluebeard, which stood over the jingling glasses on the sideboard. " That's the man I saw last night walking round the vault, as I'm a living sinner. I saw him a-walking round and round, and, when I went up to speak to him, I'm blessed if he didn't go in at the iron gate, which opened afore him like—like winking, and then in at the vault door, which I'd double-locked, my Lady, and bolted inside, I'll take my oath on it!"

"Perhaps you had given him the key?" suggested sister Anne.

"It's never been out of my pocket. Here it is," cried the beadle, "I'll have no more to do with it;" and he flung down the ponderous key, amidst another scream from widow Bluebeard.

"At what hour did you see him?" gasped she.

"At twelve o'clock, of course."

"It must have been at that very hour," said she, "I heard the voice."

"What voice?" said Anne.

"A voice that called 'Fatima! Fatima! Fatima!' three times as plain as ever voice did."

"It didn't speak to me," said the beadle; "it only nodded its head and wagged its head and beard."

"W—w—was it a *bl—ue beard?*" said the widow.

"Powder-blue, ma'am, as I've a soul to save!"

Doctor Drench was of course instantly sent for. But what are the medicaments of the apothecary in a case where the grave gives up its dead? Doctor Sly arrived, and he offered ghostly—ah! too ghostly—consolation. He said he believed in them. His own grandmother had appeared to his grandfather several times before he married again. He could not doubt that supernatural agencies were possible, even frequent.

"Suppose he were to appear to me alone," ejaculated the widow, "I should die of fright."

The Doctor looked particularly arch. "The best way in these cases, my dear madam," said he—"the best way for unprotected ladies is to get a husband. I never heard of a first husband's ghost appearing to a woman and her second husband in my life. In all history there is no account of one."

"Ah! why should I be afraid of seeing my Bluebeard again?" said the widow; and the Doctor retired quite pleased, for the lady was evidently thinking of a second husband.

"The Captain would be a better protector for me certainly than Mr. Sly," thought the lady, with a sigh; "but Mr. Sly will certainly kill himself, and will the Captain be a match for two ghosts? Sly will kill himself; but ah! the Captain won't;" and the widow thought with pangs of bitter mortification of Dolly Coddlins. How, how should these distracting circumstances be brought to an end?

She retired to rest that night not without a tremor—to bed, but not to sleep. At midnight a voice was heard in her room crying "Fatima! Fatima! Fatima!" in awful accents. The doors

banged to and fro, the bells began to ring, the maids went up and
down stairs skurrying and screaming, and gave warning in a body.
John Thomas, as pale as death, declared that he found Bluebeard's
yeomanry sword, that hung in the hall, drawn and on the ground ;
and the sticking-plaster miniature in Mr. Bluebeard's bedroom was
found turned topsy-turvy !

"It is some trick," said the obstinate and incredulous sister
Anne. "To-night I will come and sleep with you, sister;" and
the night came, and the sisters retired together.

'Twas a wild night. The wind howling without went crashing through the old trees of the old rookery round about the old
church. The long bedroom windows went thump—thumping; the
moon could be seen through them lighting up the graves with their
ghastly shadows ; the yew-tree, cut into the shape of a bird, looked
particularly dreadful, and bent and swayed as if it would peck
something off that other yew-tree which was of the shape of a
dumb-waiter. The bells at midnight began to ring as usual, the
doors clapped, jingle—jingle down came a suit of armour in the
hall, and a voice came and cried, "Fatima! Fatima! Fatima! look,
look, look ; the tomb, the tomb, the tomb!"

She looked. The vault door was open; and there in the
moonlight stood Bluebeard, exactly as he was represented in the
picture in his yeomanry dress, his face frightfully pale and his
great blue beard curling over his chest, as awful as Mr. Muntz's.

Sister Anne saw the vision as well as Fatima. We shall
spare the account of their terrors and screams. Strange to say,
John Thomas, who slept in the attic above his mistress's bedroom,
declared he was on the watch all night and had seen nothing in
the churchyard, and heard no sort of voices in the house.

And now the question came, What could the ghost want by
appearing? "Is there anything," exclaimed the unhappy and
perplexed Fatima, "that he would have me do? It is well to say
'now, now, now,' and to show himself; but what is it that makes
my blessed husband so uneasy in his grave?" And all parties
consulted agreed that it was a very sensible question.

John Thomas, the footman, whose excessive terror at the
appearance of the ghost had procured him his mistress's confidence,
advised Mr. Screw, the butler, who communicated with Mrs.
Baggs, the housekeeper, who condescended to impart her observations to Mrs. Bustle, the lady's-maid—John Thomas, I say,
decidedly advised that my Lady should consult a cunning man.
There was such a man in town ; he had prophesied who should
marry his (John Thomas's) cousin ; he had cured Farmer Horn's
cattle, which were evidently bewitched ; he could raise ghosts, and

make them speak, and he therefore was the very person to be consulted in the present juncture.

"What nonsense is this you have been talking to the maids, John Thomas, about the conjurer who lives in—in——"

"In Hangman's Lane, ma'am, where the old gibbet used to stand," replied John, who was bringing in the muffins. "It's no nonsense, my Lady. Every word as that man says comes true, and he knows everything."

"I desire you will not frighten the girls in the servants' hall with any of those silly stories," said the widow; and the meaning of this speech may, of course, at once be guessed. It was that the widow meant to consult the conjurer that very night. Sister Anne said that she would never, under such circumstances, desert her dear Fatima. John Thomas was summoned to attend the ladies with a dark lantern, and forth they set on their perilous visit to the conjurer at his dreadful abode in Hangman's Lane.

. . . .

What took place at that frightful interview has never been entirely known. But there was no disturbance in the house on the night after. The bells slept quietly, the doors did not bang in the least, twelve o'clock struck and no ghost appeared in the churchyard, and the whole family had a quiet night. The widow attributed this to a sprig of rosemary which the wizard gave her, and a horseshoe which she flung into the garden round the family vault, and which would keep *any* ghost quiet.

It happened the next day that, going to her milliner's, sister Anne met a gentleman who has been before mentioned in this story, Ensign Trippet by name; and, indeed, if the truth must be known, it somehow happened that she met the Ensign somewhere every day of the week.

"What news of the ghost, my dearest Miss Shacabac?" said he (you may guess on what terms the two young people were by the manner in which Mr. Trippet addressed the lady); "has Bluebeard's ghost frightened your sister into any more fits, or set the bells a-ringing?"

Sister Anne, with a very grave air, told him that he must not joke on so awful a subject; that the ghost had been laid for awhile; that a cunning man had told her sister things so wonderful that *any* man must believe in them; that, among other things, he had shown to Fatima her future husband.

"Had," said the Ensign, "he black whiskers and a red coat?"

"No," answered Anne, with a sigh, "he had red whiskers and a black coat."

"It can't be that rascal Sly!" cried the Ensign. But Anne only sighed more deeply, and would not answer yes or no. "You may tell the poor Captain," she said, "there is no hope for him, and all he has left is to hang himself."

"He shall cut the throat of Sly first, though," replied Mr. Trippet fiercely. But Anne said things were not decided as yet. Fatima was exceedingly restive and unwilling to acquiesce in the idea of being married to Mr. Sly; she had asked for further authority. The wizard said he could bring her own husband from the grave to point out her second bridegroom, who shall be, can be, must be, no other than Frederick Sly.

"It's a trick," said the Ensign. But Anne was too much frightened by the preceding evening's occurrences to say so. "To-night," she said, "the grave will tell all." And she left Ensign Trippet in a very solemn and affecting way.

. . . .

At midnight three figures were seen to issue from widow Blue-beard's house and pass through the churchyard turnstile and so away among the graves.

"To call up a ghost is bad enough," said the wizard; "to make him speak is awful. I recommend you, ma'am, to beware, for such curiosity has been fatal to many. There was one Arabian necromancer of my acquaintance who tried to make a ghost speak, and was torn in pieces on the spot. There was another person who *did* hear a ghost speak certainly, but came away from the interview deaf and dumb. There was another——"

"Never mind," says Mrs. Bluebeard, all her old curiosity aroused, "see him and hear him I will. Haven't I seen him and heard him, too, already? When he's audible *and* visible, *then's* the time."

"But when you heard him," said the necromancer, "he was invisible, and when you saw him he was inaudible; so make up your mind what you will ask him, for ghosts will stand no shilly-shallying. I knew a stuttering man who was flung down by a ghost, and——"

"I *have* made up my mind," said Fatima, interrupting him.

"To ask him what husband you shall take," whispered Anne.

Fatima only turned red, and sister Anne squeezed her hand; they passed into the graveyard in silence.

There was no moon; the night was pitch-dark. They threaded their way through the graves, stumbling over them here and there. An owl was toowhooing from the church tower, a dog was howling somewhere, a cock began to crow, as they will sometimes at twelve o'clock at night.

"Make haste," said the wizard. "Decide whether you will go on or not."

"Let us go back, sister," said Anne.

"I *will* go on," said Fatima. "I should die if I gave it up, I feel I should."

"Here's the gate; kneel down," said the wizard. The women knelt down.

"Will you see your first husband or your second husband?"

"I will see Bluebeard first," said the widow; "I shall know then whether this be a mockery, or you have the power you pretend to."

At this the wizard uttered an incantation, so frightful and of such incomprehensible words, that it is impossible for any mortal to repeat them. And at the end of what seemed to be a versicle of his chant he called "Bluebeard!" There was no noise but the moaning of the wind in the trees, and toowhooing of the owl in the tower.

At the end of the second verse he paused again and called "Bluebeard!" The cock began to crow, the dog began to howl, a watchman in the town began to cry out the hour, and there came from the vault within a hollow groan, and a dreadful voice said, "Who wants me?"

Kneeling in front of the tomb, the necromancer began the third verse: as he spoke, the former phenomena were still to be remarked. As he continued, a number of ghosts rose from their graves and advanced round the kneeling figures in a circle. As he concluded, with a loud bang the door of the vault flew open, and there in blue light stood Bluebeard in his blue uniform, waving his blue sword and flashing his blue eyes round about!

"Speak now, or you are lost," said the necromancer to Fatima. But, for the first time in her life, she had not a word to say. Sister Anne, too, was dumb with terror. And, as the awful figure advanced towards them as they were kneeling, the sister thought all was over with them, and Fatima once more had occasion to repent her fatal curiosity.

The figure advanced, saying, in dreadful accents, "Fatima! Fatima! Fatima! wherefore am I called from my grave?" when all of a sudden down dropped his sword, down the ghost of Bluebeard went on his knees, and, clasping his hands together, roared out, "Mercy, mercy!" as loud as man could roar.

Six other ghosts stood round the kneeling group. "Why do you call me from the tomb?" said the first; "Who dares disturb my grave?" said the second; "Seize him and away with him!" cried the third. "Murder, mercy!" still roared the ghost of

Bluebeard, as the white-robed spirits advanced and caught hold of him.

"It's only Tom Trippet," said a voice at Anne's ear.

"And your very humble servant," said a voice well known to Mrs. Bluebeard ; and they helped the ladies to rise, while the other ghosts seized Bluebeard. The necromancer took to his heels and got off; he was found to be no other than Mr. Claptrap, the manager of the theatre.

It was some time before the ghost of Bluebeard could recover from the fainting fit into which he had been plunged when seized by the opposition ghosts in white ; and while they were ducking him at the pump his blue beard came off, and he was discovered to be—who do you think ? Why, Mr. Sly, to be sure ; and it appears that John Thomas, the footman, had lent him the uniform, and had clapped the doors, and rung the bells, and spoken down the chimney ; and it was Mr. Claptrap who gave Mr. Sly the blue fire and the theatre gong, and he went to London next morning by the coach ; and, as it was discovered that the story concerning Miss Coddlins was a shameful calumny, why, of course, the widow married Captain Blackbeard. Doctor Sly married them, and has always declared that he knew nothing of his nephew's doings, and wondered that he has not tried to commit suicide since his last disappointment.

Mr. and Mrs. Trippet are likewise living happily together, and this, I am given to understand, is the ultimate fate of a family in whom we were all very much interested in early life.

You will say that the story is not probable. Psha ! Isn't it written in a book ? and is it a whit less probable than the first part of the tale ?

VARIOUS ESSAYS, LETTERS,
SKETCHES. ETC.

VARIOUS ESSAYS, LETTERS,
SKETCHES, ETC.

TIMBUCTOO

To the Editor of "The Snob."

SIR,—Though your name be "Snob," I trust you will not refuse this tiny "Poem of a Gownsman," which was unluckily not finished on the day appointed for delivery of the several copies of verses on Timbuctoo. I thought, Sir, it would be a pity that such a poem should be lost to the world; and conceiving *The Snob* to be the most widely circulated periodical in Europe, I have taken the liberty of submitting it for insertion or approbation.—I am, Sir, yours, &c. &c. &c.   T.

TIMBUCTOO.*

The situation.   In Africa (a quarter of the world)
                  Men's skins are black, their hair is crisp and curl'd;
                  And somewhere there, unknown to public view,
                  A mighty city lies, called Timbuctoo.

Line 1 and 2.   See Guthrie's Geography.
The site of Timbuctoo is doubtful; the Author has neatly expressed this in the Poem, at the same time giving us some slight hints relative to its situation.

---

* This parody probably represents Mr. Thackeray's first appearance in print. In the year 1829, when only eighteen years of age, he was chiefly concerned in starting a short-lived Cambridge undergraduate magazine entitled *The Snob.* He is believed to have been responsible for a considerable proportion of the contents, which are not of any particular merit, but with the exception of this parody of a Cambridge Prize Poem (on the subject, as will be remembered, for which Tennyson gained the Chancellor's Medal), it is not possible to be certain which contributions were from his pen, though there are several epigrammatic verses and some letters full of misspelling and Malapropisms, from Dorothea Julia Ramsbottom, which are almost unmistakably his.

The natural
history.

There stalks the tiger, there the lion roars   5
Who sometimes eats the luckless blackamoors;
All that he leaves of them the monster throws
To jackals, vultures, dogs, cats, kites, and crows.
His hunger thus the forest monarch gluts,
And then lies down 'neath trees called cocoa nuts.   10

The lion hunt.

Quick issue out, with musket, torch, and brand,
The sturdy blackamoors, a dusky band!
The beast is found,—pop goes the musketoons,—
The lion falls, covered with horrid wounds.

Their lives
at home.

At home their lives in pleasure always flow,   15
But many have a different lot to know!

Abroad.

They're often caught, and sold as slaves, alas!

Reflections on
the foregoing.

Thus men from highest joy to sorrow pass.
Yet though thy monarchs and thy nobles boil
Rack and molasses in Jamaica's isle!   20
Desolate Afric! thou art lovely yet!!
One heart yet beats which ne'er shall thee forget.
What though thy maidens are a blackish brown,
Does virtue dwell in whiter breasts alone?

Line 5.   So Horace.—leonum arida nutrix.
Line 8.   Thus Apollo   ἐλώρια τεῦχε κύνεσσιν
                            Οἰωνοῖσί τε πᾶσι.
Line 5–10.   How skilfully introduced are the animal and vegetable
productions of Africa! It is worthy to remark the various garments
in which the Poet hath clothed the Lion. He is called 1st, the Lion;
2nd, the Monster (for he is very large); and 3rd, the Forest Monarch,
which he undoubtedly is.
Line 11–14.   The Author confesses himself under peculiar obligations
to Denham's and Clapperton's Travels, as they suggested to him the
spirited description contained in these lines.
Line 13.   "Pop goes the musketoons." A learned friend suggested
"Bang," as a stronger expression; but, as African gunpowder is notoriously bad, the Author thought "Pop" the better word.
Line 15–18.   A concise but affecting description is here given of the
domestic habits of the people,—the infamous manner in which they are
entrapped and sold as slaves is described,—and the whole ends with an
appropriate moral sentiment. The Poem might here finish, but the
spirit of the bard penetrates the veil of futurity, and from it cuts off
a bright piece for the hitherto unfortunate Africans, as the following
beautiful lines amply exemplify.
It may perhaps be remarked that the Author has here "changed his
hand;" he answers that it was his intention so to do. Before it was
his endeavour to be elegant and concise, it is now his wish to be
enthusiastic and magnificent. He trusts the Reader will perceive the
aptness with which he hath changed his style: when he narrated facts
he was calm, when he enters on prophecy he is fervid.

Oh no, oh no, oh no, oh no, oh no! 25
It shall not, must not, cannot, e'er be so.
The day shall come when Albion's self shall feel
Stern Afric's wrath, and writhe 'neath Afric's steel.
I see her tribes the hill of glory mount,
And sell their sugars on their own account; 30
While round her throne the prostrate nations come,
Sue for her rice, and barter for her rum. 32

The enthusiasm which he feels is beautifully expressed in lines 25, 26. He thinks he has very successfully imitated in the last six lines the best manner of Mr. Pope, and in lines 19–26 the pathetic elegance of the Author of Australasia and Athens.

The Author cannot conclude without declaring that his aim in writing this Poem will be fully accomplished, if he can infuse in the breasts of Englishmen a sense of the danger in which they lie. Yes— Africa! If he can awaken one particle of sympathy for thy sorrows, of love for thy land, of admiration for thy virtue, he shall sink into the grave with the proud consciousness that he has raised esteem, where before there was contempt, and has kindled the flame of hope, on the smouldering ashes of Despair!

READING A POEM

Part I.

LORD DAUDLEY, the Earl of Bagwig's eldest son, a worshipper of the Muses ; in a dressing-gown, with his shirt collars turned down.

MR. BOGLE, the celebrated Publisher ; in a publisher's costume of deep black.

MR. BLUDYER, an English gentleman of the press, editor of the *Weekly Bravo;* green coat, red velvet waistcoat, dirty blue satin cravat, dirty trousers, dirty boots.*

MR. DISHWASH, an English gentleman of the press, editor of the *Castalian Magazine;* very neat, in black, and a diamond pin.

MR. YELLOWPLUSH, my lord's body servant ; in an elegant livery.

Voices without. The door bell. Nicholas, my lord's tiger.

The scene is Lord Daudley's drawing-room in the Albany.

THE door bell (*timidly*). Ting, ting.

YELLOWPLUSH (*in an armchair before the fire, reading the "Morning Post"*).—" Yesterday, at St. George's, Hanover Square, by the Lord Bishop of Lawn, the Lord John Fitzwhiskers, to Amelia Frances Annabel, the lovely and accomplished daughter of Samuel Botts, Esq., of Portland Place. After an elegant *déjeuné* at Lord Tufton's mansion, in Cavendish Square, the happy pair set off——"

The door bell. Ring, ting, ting.

YELLOWPLUSH.—Where's that hidle Nicholas ? The bell's been going it these ten minutes, and distubbing me at my studies.— " The happy pair set off for a tour on the continent, and intend, we hear, to pass the carivan—no, the carnival at Naples." And a pretty junny they'll have of it ! Winter—iniondations at Lyons ; four mortial days on board the steamboat ! *I've* been the trip myself, and was half froze on the rumble. Luckily, Mademsell Léocadie, my lady's maid, was with me, and so we kep warm, but——

* This actor should smell very much of stale smoke, and need not shave for two or three days before performing the part.

The door bell. Ring-aring-ring-ring.

YELLOWPLUSH (*in a voice of thunder*).—NICHOLAS, you lazy young raggymuffian! do you hear the bell? Do you want to wake my lord?

NICHOLAS (*without*).—This way, sir, *if* you please.

DISHWASH (*entering*).—Thank you, Nicholas; I am afraid I disturbed you. Never mind, I've not been there long. Thank you. Just put my galoshes to the fire, will you, like a good lad? for it's bad wet weather.

YELLOWPLUSH.—O! it's only one of them lettery chaps; I wonder how my lord can have to do with such. Let us go on with the news.—" On Thursday, Mr. F. Hogawn, of Peckham Rye, to Mary Jane, daughter of John Rudge, Esq., of the same place." Why can they put such stuff in a genteel newspaper?—Is that you, Mr. Dishwash? Pray, do you come by appointment? My lord ain't up yet, but you may as well set down. There's yesterday's paper somewhere about.

DISHWASH.—Thank you, Yellowplush: and how goes it, my fine fellow; any more memoirs, ey? Send me the proofs, my boy, and you shan't want for a good word, you know.

YELLOWPLUSH (*pacified*).—Thank you, in return; and here's to-day's *Post.* I've quite done with it; indeed my lord has kep me here this half hour a poring over it. I took him his pens, ink, and chocklate at eleven; and I b'lieve he's cumposing something in his warm bath.

DISHWASH.—Up late, I suppose? There were three great parties, I know, last night.

YELLOWPLUSH (*aside*).—How the juice should *he* know?

DISHWASH.—Where was he, now? Come, tell me. Was it at Lord Doldrum's, or at the Duke's? Lady Smigsmag had a small conversazione, and very select, too, where I had the honour to pass the evening, and all the world was on the look-out for the famous Lord Daudley, who had promised to come and read us some of his poems.

YELLOWPLUSH. — His poems! — his gammin. Since Lord Byrom's time, cuss me if the whole aristoxy has not gone poetry-mad, and writes away like so many common press men. What the juice *do* they write for?—they can't do it half so well as the reglar hacks at the business.

DISHWASH.—O, you flatter us, Yellowplush, that you do.

YELLOWPLUSH.—I say they *can't* do it as well; and why do they go on? *They* don't want money, as you and I do, Mr. Whatsyourname—Mr. Dishwash. I suppose you only write for money, do you? If you were a gentleman, now—confess, would you ever put pen to paper ? I wouldn't, I know ;—but there's my lord's bell, and so you can just look over the junnel till I return. We made a pretty good speech in the House of Commins, last night, as you will see. ⌊*Exit.*

DISHWASH.—Vulgar, low-bred upstart ! That creature now has all the vices of the aristocracy, without their virtues. He has no idea of the merit, the dignity of a man of letters, and talks of our divine calling as a trade, and dares to treat me, a poet and a man of letters, on a footing of equality. Ah, for the time when men of our profession shall take their rank with the foremost in the land, and the great republic of genius shall be established. I feel it in my heart—the world demands a republic ;—genius will never prosper without it ! All men are equal,—and we, above all, ought to be the equals of the highest ; and here am I spoken to, familiarly, by a lacquey ! I, who am—

BLUDYER (*who has entered with his hat on during* DISHWASH'S *speech, and slaps the latter on the shoulder*).—You are very little better. Confess, now, old buck, wasn't your father a washerwoman, and your mother a linendraper's clerk ?

DISHWASH.—No ! It's a calumny, Bludyer,—a base falsehood.

BLUDYER.—Well, then, what are they ?

DISHWASH (*sulkily*).—What's that to you ?

BLUDYER.—There, now, you great noodle, you. You calumniate your own parents more than any one else does, by being ashamed of their calling, whatever it may be. Be a man, now, and don't affect this extra gentility, which all the world laughs at. Be a man, and act like me ! Do you suppose *I* care who knows my birth and parentage ? No, hang it ; anybody may have the history of Jack Bludyer. *He* doesn't go sneaking and cringing to tea-parties ;—*he's* no milksop. Jack Bludyer, I tell you, can drink seven bottles of claret at a setting, and twice as many glasses of whisky-and-water. I've no pride, and no humility, neither—I don't care to own it. I back myself, look you, Dishwash, and don't give the wall to the first man in Europe.

DISHWASH.—I wonder what brings you here, then, my good fellow ?

BLUDYER.—The same thing that brings you—interest, my fine fellow, and worthy Dishwash : not friendship. I don't care a straw for any man alive ; no more do you, although you are so sentimental. I think you a fool about many matters—don't think you such a fool as to admire Daudley's poems.

DISHWASH (*looking round timidly*).—He, he, he ! Why, between ourselves, they are not first-rate ; and *entre nous.* I know who wrote the best part of them. There's not a single passage in the " Death-knell; or, the Lay to Laura," that's worth reading; but, between ourselves, I wrote it. Don't peach, now;—don't betray me.

BLUDYER.—Betray *you?* " There's not a single passage in the 'Death-knell; or, the Lay to Laura,' that's worth twopence ;— but *I* wrote it." *You*—you've as much strength as milk-and-water, and. as much originality as a looking-glass. You. write poetry, indeed! You don't drink a bottle of wine in a year. Hang me if I believe you were ever drunk in your life !

DISHWASH.—I don't profess to believe, my good sir, that drunkenness is an essential poetic qualification, or that Helicon is gin-and-water—he, he ! and if you ever read my little book of " Violets," you might have found that out.

BLUDYER.—Violets be hanged ! I say juniper berries. Give me a good, vigorous style, and none of your namby-pamby milk-and-water. Do you ever read my paper? If you want to see what power is, look at that.

DISHWASH.—Indeed. The fact is, I never *do* read it.

BLUDYER.—Well, you're right, you're right. I never read anything but what I am forced to read, especially if it's written by my friends. I like to think well of them, Dishwash, and always considered you a clever fellow, till I read that absurd ode of yours about a heliotrope.

DISHWASH.—It's quite as good as your ballad in last Sunday's *Bravo;* and my poor article in the *Castalian* is, I am sure, as strong as yours.

BLUDYER.—Oh, you *have* read the *Bravo*, have you? What a fool I am, Dishwash,—a great, raw, silly fool. Upon my word and honour, I believed you what you said ; but it will be a lesson to me, and I won't, my boy, do so again.

DISHWASH.—Insufferable coarseness ! How goes the *Bravo*, Bludyer?

BLUDYER.—We're at 3500. I don't ask you to credit my word, but look at the stamps.

DISHWASH.—Your advertisements pretty good ?

BLUDYER.—For six months they made a conspiracy against us in the Row ; but we beat 'em. You of the *Castalian*, I know, go on the puffing plan : we are a new paper, and take the tomahawking line. I tell you, sir, we've beat the booksellers, and they are all flocking to us. Last week I attacked a new book of Fogle's so severely—a very good book, too, it was—very well and carefully done, by a scholar and a clever man. Well, sir, I belaboured the book so, that Fogle came down to our place with tears in his eyes, and a whole bundle of advertisements, and cried *"Peccavi."* The abuse of that book will be worth £300 a year to the *Bravo*. But what is gratitude? If I, who have done our proprietors that service, get a five-pound-note for my share, it is all I can look for. What rascals publishers are, hey, Dishwash? Are we to be kept here for ever? How long have you been waiting?

DISHWASH.—Why, a quarter of an hour, or may be longer.

BLUDYER.—That's the way with you all. You cringe to these aristocrats. Curse them; take them by the horns, and be a man. You have waited an hour: see, now, how Daudley will admit *me*. (MR. BLUDYER *kicks against the panels of* LORD DAUDLEY'S *bedroom, and shouts*)—Hallo! Daudley—Lord Daudley, don't keep me here all day! I've got some proofs of the *Bravo* to read to you, and can't wait.

YELLOWPLUSH (*putting his nose out*).—You can't come in, my lord's in his bath.

BLUDYER (*through the door*).—Well, I'm off, then; and by Jupiter, my lord, look to yourself.

YELLOWPLUSH.—My lord says that, if you don't mind seeing him in his dishybeel, you may come in to him, Mr. Bludyer.

BLUDYER (*to* DISHWASH).—There, spooney! didn't I tell you so?

DISHWASH.—Use a little more gentlemanly language, Mr. Bludyer, if you please.

BLUDYER.—Gentlemanly language? Hang it, sir, do you mean I'm no gentleman? Say so again, and I'll pull your nose.

YELLOWPLUSH.—My lord's waiting, Mr. Bludyer.

[*They go in.*

DISHWASH.—I wonder whether he *would* pull my nose, now—the great coarse, vulgar, gin-drinking monster! It is those men who are a disgrace to our profession; and, with all his affectation of independence and bluntness, I know that man to be as servile a sycophant as crawls. Oh, for a little honesty in this world; and oh that the man of letters would understand the dignity of his pro——

NICHOLAS (*without*).—Mr. Bogle!

Enter Mr. BOGLE.

BOGLE.—My appointment's at eleven, and tell his lordship I must see his lordship soon, if he can make it convenient. I've fourteen other calls to make on the tip-top people of the town. Ha! Dish., how are you? I've fourteen other calls—fourteen volumes of poems, by fourteen dukes, duchesses, and so on, down to baronets; but they're common, now, Dish., quite common. Why, sir, a few years ago I could sell an edition with a baronet's name to it; and now the public won't have anything under an earl. Fact, upon honour!—And how goes on the *Castilian*, hey, Dishwash?

DISHWASH.—*Castalian*, Mr. Bogle—he, he! You sell books, but you don't *read* them, I fancy?

BOGLE.—No more I do, my boy—no such fool; I keep a man to read them, one of your fellows.

DISHWASH (*sneeringly*).—O yes—Diddle; I know your man well enough.

BOGLE.—Well, sir! I pay Mr. Diddle three hundred a-year, and you don't fancy I would be such a flat as to read my books when I have a man of his experience in my establishment. Have you anything to say against Mr. Diddle, sir?

DISHWASH.—Not a syllable; he is not exactly a *genius*—he, he!—but I believe he is a very estimable man.

BOGLE.—Well, I tell you, then, that he has a great deal to say against *you*. Your magazine is not strong enough in its language, sir. Our books have not their fair chance, sir. You gave Fogle's house three columns last week, and us only two. I'll withdraw my advertisements if this kind of game continues, and carry them over to the *Aperian*.

DISHWASH.—The *Pierian !* why, our sale is double theirs.

BOGLE.—I don't care! I'll have my books properly reviewed; or else, I'll withdraw my ads. Four hundred a-year, Mr. Dishwash; take 'em or leave 'em, as you like, sir. But my house is not going to be sacrificed for Fogle's. No, no.

DISHWASH.—My dear good sir, what in conscience can you want now? I said that Lady Laura Lippet's "Gleanings of Fantasy" were gorgeous lucubrations of divine intellect, and that the young poetess had decked her brow with that immortal wreath which Sappho bore of yore. I said that no novelist since the days of Walter Scott had ever produced so divine a composition as Countess Swanquil's "Amarantha." I said that Lord Cutthrust's account of the military operations at Wormwood Scrubs was written with the iron pen of a Tacitus.

BOGLE.—I believe you, it *was* written well. Diddle himself wrote the whole book.

DISHWASH.—And because Fogle's house published a remarkable work, really now a remarkable history, that must have taken the author ten years of labour—

BOGLE.—Don't remarkable history me, sir. You praise *all* Fogle's books. Hark ye, Dishwash, you praise so much and so profusely, that no one cares a straw for your opinions. You must abuse, sir; look at Bludyer, now—the *Bravo's* the paper for my money. See what *he* says about that famous history that you talk of—(*takes out a paper and reads*).—" Senseless trash ; stupid donkey ; absurd ignoramus ; disgusting twaddle ! " and disposes of the whole in a few lines—that's the way to crush a book, sir.

DISHWASH.—Well, well, I will abuse some poor devil to please you. But you know if I am severe on one house, I must be so on another. I can't praise all your books and abuse all Fogle's.

BOGLE.—Of course not, of course not ; fair's the word, and I'll give you a list now of some of my books which you may attack to your heart's content. Here—here's a history, two poems, a volume of travels, and an Essay on Population.

DISHWASH.—He, he, he ! I suppose you publish these books *on the author's account*, hey ?

BOGLE.—Get along, you sly dog. What ! you know *that*, do you ? You don't suppose I am such a fool as to cry out against my own property. No, no, leave Tom Bogle alone.

DISHWASH.—Well, I suppose you are here about Lord Daudley's new volume.

BOGLE.—" Passion-Flowers ! " there's a title ! there's no man in England can invent a title like my friend Diddle. " Passion-Flowers, by the Lord Daudley, with twenty illustrations on steel ; " let my lord put his name to it, and I'd make my fortune, sir. It's nothing ; he can get anybody to do the book ; you could knock it off yourself, Mr. Dishwash, in a month, for I've heard Diddle say that you've a real talent that way.

DISHWASH. — Did he now, really ? that Diddle's a clever fellow.

BOGLE (*musing*).—Twenty plates—red velvet binding—four thousand. Yes, I could give my lord eight hundred pounds for that book. I'll give it him for his name ; I don't want him to write a word of it.

DISHWASH.—No, no, of course ; you and I know that it must be done by one of *us*. Well, now, suppose, under the rose, that I undertake the work ?

BOGLE.—Well, I have no objection ; I told you what Diddle said.

DISHWASH.—And about the terms, ay, Bogle ?

BOGLE.—Why, though there are half-a dozen men about my place who could turn out the work famously, yet I should like to employ you, as Diddle says you are a clever man. My terms shall be liberal. Yes—let me see, I'll give you, for seventy short poems, mere trifles, you know——

DISHWASH.—A short poem often requires a deal of labour, Mr. Bogle. Look at my " Violets " ; now, there's a sonnet in

that book dedicated to Lady Titterton, whom Sultan Mahmoud fell
in love with, which took me six weeks' time. You *must* remember
it; it runs so:—

> " As 'tis his usage in the summer daily,
>   Impelled by fifty Moslemitish oars,
>   With crescent banners floating at the mast,
>   And loyal cannon shouting from the shores,
>   The great Commander of the Faithful past
>   Towards his pleasure-house at Soujout Kalé.
>   Why turns the imperial cheek so ashy paly ? " . . .

BOGLE.—O, never mind your verses. You literary men are
always talking of your shop; nothing is so vulgar, my good fellow,
and so listen to me. Will you write the " Passion-Flowers," or
will you not? If you choose to do me seventy-two sets of verses
(the time is *your* look out, you know, not mine), I'll give you six-
and-thirty guineas.

DISHWASH.—Six-and-thirty guineas !

BOGLE.—In bills at one, two, and three years. There are my
terms,—take 'em or leave 'em.

YELLOWPLUSH (*entering*).—Gentlemen, MY LORD !

LORD DAUDLEY *and* BLUDYER *enter*.

DAUDLEY.—Charles, get some soda-water for Mr. Bludyer.

BLUDYER.—And some sherry, Charles. I was as drunk as a
lord last night.

DAUDLEY.—Bludyer, you compliment the aristocracy

DISHWASH.—Ha, ha, ha ! very good, isn't it, Bogle ?

BOGLE.—Is it ? O yes ! ha, ha, ha ! capital !

BLUDYER.—Not so bad, Daudley : for a lord you are really a
clever fellow. I don't say it to flatter you—no, hang me ! I flatter
nobody, and hate the aristocracy ; but you are a clever fellow.

DISHWASH.—It is a comfort to have Mr. Bludyer's word for it,
at any rate ; he, he !

BLUDYER.—Well, sir, are you going to doubt Mr. Bludyer's
word ? Give me leave to tell you, that your remark is confoundedly
impertinent !

YELLOWPLUSH (*going out*).—Oh, these lettery people? What
infurnal corseness and wulgarity !

DAUDLEY.—Come, come—no quarrelling. You fellows of the
what's-his-name, you know—what we used to say at Oxon, you
know, of the *genus irritabile*, hay ? Bludy, you must be a little
more placable ; and, Washy, your language was a little too strong.

2 Q

Hay, Bogle, you understand? I call these two fellows Bludy and Washy; and as for Dishwash, if I don't call him Washy, I'll call him Dishy, hay?

BOGLE.—Capital! capital! You'll kill me with laughing;— and I want to talk to your lordship about the "Passion-Flower" business.

DAUDLEY.—Your rival bookseller, Mr. Fogle, has been with me already about the book.

BOGLE.—What! with my title? The scoundrel! My lord, it's a felony. You are not going to lend yourself to such a transaction, I am sure. Fogle publish the "Passion-Flowers!" I'll prosecute the unprincipled ruffian; I will, as sure as my name's Bo——

DAUDLEY.—To a goose. Fogle is not going to publish a book called "Passion-Flowers"; but he has a project of a little work, bound in blue velvet, containing twenty-two illustrations on steel, written by the Lord D'Audley, and called "The Primavera."

BOGLE.—The what? It's a forgery all the same. I'll prosecute him—by all the gods, I will!

DAUDLEY.—Well, well, we have come to no bargains. *Entre nous*, you publishers are deuced stingy fellows.

DISHWASH.—He, he, he!

BLUDYER.—Haw, haw, haw! Had you there, old Bogle!

DAUDLEY.—And that rascal only offers me six hundred pounds.

BOGLE.—I'll give six-and-fifty.

DAUDLEY.—No go.

BOGLE.—Seven hundred, then?

DAUDLEY.—Won't do.

BOGLE.—Well, make it eight hundred, and ruin me at once.

DAUDLEY.—Mr. Bogle, my worthy man, my terms are a thousand pounds. A thousand pounds, look you, or curse me if you get a single "Passion-Flower" out of George Daudley.

YELLOWPLUSH (*entering*).—Mr. Fogle, my lord, the publisher.

BOGLE.—What?

YELLOWPLUSH.—Mr. Fogle, my lord, according to appointment he says. Shall I show him in?

DAUDLEY.—Yes, you may as well. Yes, certainly.—(*Aside.*)— Egad, he's come just at the proper moment!

BOGLE.—Stop, my lord; pray, stop one minute. That ruffian follows me like my shadow. Show him into the study. For heaven's sake, let me say a word.

DAUDLEY.—Show Mr. Fogle into the study, Charles. (*Exit* YELLOWPLUSH.) Well, now, my worthy man, what have you to say?

Bogle.—Well, then, my lord, just to keep your name upon my lists, I'll make the money nine hundred.

Daudley.—Sir, give me leave to tell you that your offer is impertinent.—Charles!

Bogle (*drawing out a paper*).—Very good, then; here's the agreement. Sign this: a thousand pounds; the MSS. to be delivered in three months; half the money on delivery; the rest in bills, at three and six months. Will that suit you?—No? Say two hundred pounds down. Here's the money.

Daudley.—Egad, this will do! Here, I'll sign it, and let our two friends here be witnesses.

Bogle.—But, my lord, a word with you—about—about the writing of the poems. Will you do them, or shall we? There is a capital hand in our house, who could knock them off in a month.

Daudley.—Upon my word, this surpasses everything I ever knew. Do you suppose I am an impostor, Mr. Bogle? Take your money, and your infernal agreement, and your impertinent self, out of the room.

Bogle.—A million pardons, my dear, dear, dear, *dear* lord; I wouldn't offend your lordship for the world. Come, come, let us sign. You will sign? Here, where the wafer is. I've made my clerk copy out the agreement; one copy for me and one for your lordship. There, there's my name—"Henry Bogle." And here are the notes, of which your lordship will just acknowledge the receipt. Please, gents, to witness this here understanding between his lordship and me.

Dishwash (*signs*).—"*Percy Dishwash.*" ⎫ Of course you give
Bludyer.—   "*John Bludyer.*" ⎭ us a dinner, Bogle?

Bogle.—Oh, certainly, some day. Bless my soul! twelve o'clock, and I an appointment with Lady Mantrap at half-past eleven! Good-bye, my lord, my *dear* lord.—Good-bye, Dish.— Bludyer, you owe me ten pounds, remember, and our magazine wants your article very much. Good-bye, good-bye, good-b—. (*Here the door shuts upon* Mr. Bogle.)

Dishwash.—Well, the bargain is not a bad one. Do you know, my lord, that Bogle had the conscience to offer me six-and-thirty guineas for the book, which will bring you a thousand?

Daudley.—Very possibly, my good fellow; but the name's everything. I have not the vanity to suppose that I can write much better than you, or Bludyer, here.

Dishwash.—Oh, my lord! my lord!

Daudley.—No, indeed; really, now, I don't think so. But if the public chooses to buy Lord Daudley's verses, and not to care—

DISHWASH.—For poor, humble Percy Dishwash, heigho ! you were in the right to make the best bargain you can, as I should be the last to deny.

(MR. YELLOWPLUSH *here enters with* MR. BLUDYER'S *soda water.*)

Soda water—P-f-f-f-f-f-f—op whizz.   (MR. BLUDYER *drinks.*)

DISHWASH.—But where is Fogle all this while ? you should have had him in and pitted him against his rival.

DAUDLEY (*archly*).—Ask Charles.—Charles, you rogue, why do you keep Mr. Fogle waiting ?

YELLOWPLUSH. — Mr. Fogle's *non inventus,* my lord. — He never was there at all, gentlemen ; it was only a *de ruse* of mine, which I hope your lordship will igscuse, but happening to be at the door—

BLUDYER.—And happening to be listening !

YELLOWPLUSH.—Well, sir ! I confess I *was* listening—in my lord's interest, in course ; and I am sure my stepping in at that moment caused Mr. Bogle to sign the agreement.   My lord won't forget it, I trust, and cumsider that, without that sackimstans, he mightn't have made near such a good barging.—

[*Exit* YELLOWPLUSH.

DAUDLEY.—No, I won't forget it, you may be sure, Master Charles.   And, egad ! as soon as I have paid the fellow his wages, I'll send him off.   He's a great deal too clever for me ; the rogue writes, gentlemen, would you believe it ? and has just had the impudence to republish his works.

DISHWASH.—Never mind him, my dear lord ; but do now let us hear some of yours.   What were you meditating this morning ?   Confess now—some delightful poem I am sure.

PART II.

D AUDLEY.—Well, then, if you must know the truth, I was scribbling a little something ; just a trifling thought that came into my brain this morning, as I was looking out at the mignonette-pot in my bedroom window.   You know it was Lady Blanche Bluenose that gave it me, and I promised her a little copy of verses in return.   " Well," says I, thinking over my bargain with that fellow Bogle, " as I have agreed to write something about flowers, my little poem for Lady Blanche's album will answer for my volume too, and so I shall kill two birds with one stone."   That's the very thing I said ; not bad, was it ?

BLUDYER.—Not bad ? devilish good, by the immortal Jove. Hang me, my lord, but you're a regular Joe Miller.

DISHWASH.—Really now, Lord Daudley, you should write a comic novel. Something in the Dickens style.

DAUDLEY.—I shouldn't wonder if I did; I've thought of it, Dishwash, often. The "New Novel of Low Life, by Lord Daudley," hay? forty illustrations by Whiz; it wouldn't sound badly. But, to return to the "Passion-Flowers."

DISHWASH.—We are all ear.

BLUDYER.—Not all ear, Dish.; a good deal of you is nose.

DAUDLEY.—Mr. Bludyer, for Heaven's sake, a truce to these personalities, if you have a mind to listen to me. I told you I was thinking in bed this morning about Lady Blanche's present, and the poem I had promised her. "Egad!" says I, starting up in bed, and flinging my green velvet night-cap very nearly out of window, "why should I not write about that flower-pot?"

BLUDYER.—And a dev'lish good idea, too.

DISHWASH.—(*Aside.*—Toad-eater.) O! leave Lord Daudley alone for ideas.

DAUDLEY.—Well, sir, I instantly rung my body-fellow, Charles, had my bath, ordered my chocolate, and, with the water exactly at ninety-two, began my poem.

BLUDYER.—O! you practise the hot-water stimulus, do you, my lord? And so do I; but I always have mine at Fahrenheit; boiling, my lord, as near as possible.

DAUDLEY.—Gad now! you don't say so?

BLUDYER.—Boiling, yes, with a glass of brandy in it—do you take? Once, when I wrote for the Whigs—you know I am Radical now—I wrote eight-and-thirty stanzas at a sitting. And how do you think I did it? By nineteen glasses of brandy-and-water. That's your true Castalian, ay, Dishwash? But, I beg pardon for interrupting you in your account of your brilliant idea; tell us more about the "Flower-pot," my lord.

DISHWASH.—The verses, the verses, my lord, by all means— positively now, I'm dying to know them.

DAUDLEY.—O, ah! the verses—yes—that is—why, egad, I've not written down any yet, but I have them here in my brain—all the ideas at least, and that's the chief thing.

BLUDYER.—Why, I don't know; I don't think it's of any use to have ideas, or too many of them, in a set of verses.

DAUDLEY.—You are satirical, you rogue Bludyer, you—dev'lish satirical, by Jove. But the fact is, I can't help having ideas, and a deuced many of them, too. My first idea was to say, that that

13

humble flower-pot of mignonette was more precious to me than, egad ! all the flowers in a conservatory.

BLUDYER.—Very good and ingenious.

DISHWASH.—Very pretty and pastoral ; and how, my lord, did you begin ?

DAUDLEY.—Why, I begin—quite modestly you know,—

" My little humble flower-pot "—

and there, egad ! I stuck fast—for my bell began a cursed ringing, and presently this monster of a Bludyer came and kicked down my dressing-room door almost, and drove poetry out of my head. So as you served me so, why, gentlemen, you must help me in my ode. I want to say how it looks out into Piccadilly, you know, and on St. James's Church, and all that.

BLUDYER.—Excuse me, that will never do ; say it looks out on your park in Yorkshire. Mrs. Grange, the pastry-cook's window, looks into Piccadilly just as well as your lordship's. You must have something more aristocratic.

DAUDLEY.—Egad ! yes, not bad. Well, it *shall* look into my park at Daudley. I thought so myself ; do you like the idea, ay, gentlemen ? You do like it, I thought you would. Well, then, my flower-pot stands in a window, and the window is in a tower, and the tower is in Daudley park, and I begin—

> *My little humble flower-pot,*
> *My little hum——*

DISHWASH.—*Upon my turret flaunting free,*—flaunting free ! there's an expression !—there's a kind of *laisser aller* about it.

BLUDYER.—

> My little humble flower-pot,
> Upon my turret flaunting free,
> Thou art more loved by me I wot,
> Than all the sweets of Araby.

DAUDLEY.—Stop, stop !—by Gad, the very thing I was going to say ; I thought of " I wot " and " Araby," at once, only Bludyer interrupted me. It wasn't a bad notion, was it ? (*Reads*) Hum, hum—" flower *pot*—flaunting *free*—by me, I *wot*—Ara*by*." Well, I've done for *that* idea, at any rate,—now let's see for another.

BLUDYER.—Done with that, already ? Good heavens, Daudley, you had need be a lord, and a rich one, to fling about your wealth in that careless kind of way,—a commoner can't afford to be so prodigal ; and, if you will take my advice in the making of poems

—whenever you get an idea, make a point of repeating it two or three times, thus :—

> . Not all the sweets of Eastern bower——

DAUDLEY.—Egad, the very words out of my own mouth—(*writes*) " Eastern bower "——

BLUDYER.—

> Are half so dearly prized by me,
> As is the little gentle flower——

DAUDLEY.-—

> " Pot, in my turret flaunting free."

That's the thing.

DISHWASH.—Why, no, my dear lord, if I might advise, it's well to repeat the same sentiment two or three times over, as Mr. Bludyer says. In one of Sir Edward's tragedies, I counted the same simile fourteen times, but at intervals of two or three pages, or so. Suppose, now, instead of your admirable line——

BLUDYER.—Which divides the pot from the flower, you see.

DISHWASH.—We say—

> As is the little gentle flower,
> The mignonette, that blooms in thee !

DAUDLEY.—Bravo !—eight lines already. Egad, gentlemen, I'm in the vein.

BLUDYER.—There's nothing like backing your luck in these cases, my lord, and so let us throw in another stanza—

> My little dewy moss-grown vase,
> Forth from its turret looks and sees,
> Wide stretched around the park and chase,
> The dappled deer beneath the trees.

Ha ! what do you say to that ? There's nothing like the use of venison in a poem—it has a liberal air ; now let's give them a little mutton. I presume you feed sheep in your park, Lord Daudley, as well as deer ?

DAUDLEY.—O yes, 'gad ! and cows too—hundreds of them.

BLUDYER.—

> Beside the river bask the kine,
> The sheep go browsing o'er the sward ;
> And kine, and sheep, and deer are mine,
> And all the park calls Daudley lord.

DAUDLEY.—It *doesn't*, my dear fellow—egad, I wish it did—but till my father's death, you know——

DISHWASH.—Bagwig is a sad unromantic name for a poem.

DAUDLEY.—Well, well—I'll yield to my friends, and sacrifice my own convictions. I'll say Daudley, then, and not Bagwig. And, Dishwash, you may say everywhere, that in my poem of the "Flower-pot," you suggested that alteration. (*Writes*)—"And all the park calls Daudley lord."

BLUDYER.——

> Safe sheltered in thy turret nook,
> My gentle flower-pot, 'tis thine
> Upon this peaceful scene to look,
> The lordship of my ancient line!
> Rich are my lands, and wide they range——

DAUDLEY (*who writes always as* BLUDYER *dictates*).—"Rich are my lands, and wide they range."—Egad! they're devilishly mortgaged though, Master Bludyer; but I won't say anything about *that*.

DISHWASH.—Bravo! Capital!

BLUDYER.——

> Rich are my lands, and wide they range,
> And yet do I esteem them not,
> And lightly would my lordships change
> Against my little flower-pot.

DISHWASH.—Whew!

DAUDLEY.—Come, come, Bludyer, that's *too* much.

BLUDYER.—Not a whit, as you shall see.——

> By wide estates I set no store,
> No store on sparkling coronet;
> The *poet's heart* can value more
> This fragrant plant of mignonette.
> And, as he fondly thinks of her
> Who once the little treasure owned,
> The lover may the gift prefer
> To mines of gold and diamond.

Isn't that, now, perfectly satisfactory? You are a lover, and your mistress's gift is more precious to you than Potosi; a poet (and that you know you are), and a little flower provokes in you——

DISHWASH.—Hopes, feelings, passionate aspirations, thoughts that do often lie too deep for tears. Holy memories of bygone times, pure as the innocent dew that twinkles on the cup of the flower; fragrant, mysterious, stealing on the senses as—as——

DAUDLEY.—Exactly so. You are perfectly right, egad ; though I never thought that I had those feelings before.

DISHWASH.—O, it's astonishing how the merest trifle serves to awaken the vastest thoughts : and, in such a way, my hint might aid your lordship. Suppose we continue : —

My mild and winsome flower-pot !

BLUDYER (*aside*).—Mild and winsome ! there's affectation ! but let the epithets pass, they're good enough for a lord.

DISHWASH (*continuing*)—

My mild and winsome flower-pot,
As—let me see—as on thy dewy buds I gaze,
I think how different is my lot,
Unto my sire's in ancient days.
Where softly droops my bonny flower,
My free and feathery mignonette,
Upon its lofty, ancient tower,
The banner of my race was set.

DAUDLEY.—"Race was set." Bravo ! we're getting on,—hay, Bludyer ? But you are no hand at an impromptu, like Dishwash and myself ; he's quite beaten, I declare, and has not another rhyme for the dear life.

BLUDYER.—Not another rhyme ! my dear lord, a dozen ; as thus :—

Where peaceful roam the kine and sheep,
Were men-at-arms with bow and bill ;
Where blooms my flower upon the keep,
. A warder blew his clarion shrill.

And now for the moral :—

Dark memories of blood and crime
Away ! the poet loves you not.
Ah me ! the chieftains of that time
Had never seen a flower-pot ! *

DAUDLEY.—Bravo, bravissimo ! six stanzas, by the immortal gods ! Upon my word, you were right, Bludyer, and I was in the vein. Why, this will fill a couple of pages, and we may get the " Passion-Flowers " out in a month. Come and see me often, my lads, hay ? and, egad ! yes, I'll read you some more poems.

DISHWASH.—Two o'clock, heaven bless me ! my lord, I really

* A poem very much of this sort, from which the writer confesses he has borrowed the idea and all the principal epithets, such as "free and feathery," "mild and winsome," &c., is to be found in the " Keepsake," nor is it by any means the worst ditty in the collection.

must be off to my office, for I have several columns of the *Castalian* to get ready before night. As I shall be very much pressed for time and copy, might I ask, as the greatest favour in the world, permission to insert into the paper a part of that charming little poem which you have just done us the favour to read to us?

DAUDLEY.—Well, I don't mind, my good fellow. You will say, of course, that it is from Lord Daudley's forthcoming volume of " Passion-Flowers "; and, I am sure, will add something, something good-natured, you know, in your way, about the projected book.

DISHWASH.—O, certainly, with the greatest pleasure. Farewell, my dear lord, I must tear myself away, though I could stay and listen to your poetry for hours ; there is nothing more delightful than to sit by a great artist, and watch the progress of his work. Good-bye, good-bye. Don't ring, I shall find the way easily myself, and I hope you will not be on any ceremony with me.

DAUDLEY.—Good-bye, Dishwash. And, I say, come in sometimes of a morning, like a worthy fellow as you are, and perhaps I may read to you some more of my compositions. (*Exit* DISHWASH, *bowing profusely.*)—A good useful creature that, ay, Bludyer? but no power, no readiness, no *vis.* The fellow scarcely helped us with a line or a rhyme in my poem.

BLUDYER.—A good-natured milksop of a creature, and very useful, as you say. He will give you a famous puff in the *Castalian*, be sure.

DAUDLEY.—As you will, I am certain, in the *Bravo.*

BLUDYER.—Perhaps, perhaps ; but we are, as you are aware, in the satirical vein, and I don't know whether our proprietors will allow me to be complimentary even to my own—I mean, to your works. However, between ourselves, there is a way of mollifying them.

DAUDLEY.—As how?

BLUDYER.—By a bribe, to be sure. To be plain with you, my lord, suppose you send through me a five pound note to be laid out in paragraphs in the *Bravo ;* I will take care to write them all myself, and that they shall be well worth the money.

DAUDLEY.—Nonsense ! you do not mean that your people at the *Bravo* are so unprincipled as that?

BLUDYER.—Unprincipled? the word is rather strong, my lord : but do exactly as you please. Nobody forces you to advertise with us ; only do not, for the future, ask me to assist at the reading of your poems any more, that's all.

DAUDLEY.—(*Aside.*—Unconscionable scoundrel !) Come, come, Bludyer, here's the five pound note ; you are very welcome to take it——

BLUDYER.—To my proprietors, of course. You do not fancy it is for *me* ?

DAUDLEY.—Not in the least degree; pray take it and lay it out for me.

BLUDYER.—*Entre nous*, I wish it *were* for me; for, between ourselves, I am sadly pressed for money; and if you could, out of our friend Bogle's heap, lend me five pounds for myself—indeed, now, you would be conferring a very great obligation upon me. I will pay you, you know, upon my honour as a gentleman.

DAUDLEY.—Not a word more ; here is the money, and pray pay me or not, as it suits you.

BLUDYER.—Thank you, Daudley ; the turn shall not be lost, depend upon it; and if ever you are in want of a friend in the press, count upon Jack Bludyer, and no mistake. (*Exit* BLUDYER, *with his hat very much on one side.*)

Enter YELLOWPLUSH.

DAUDLEY.—Well, Charles, you scoundrel, you are a literary man, and know the difficulty of composition.

CHARLES.—I b'leave you, my lord.

DAUDLEY.—Well, sir, what do you think of my having written a poem of fifty lines, while those fellows were here all the time chattering and talking to me ?

CHARLES.—Is it posbil ?

DAUDLEY.—Possible ? Egad, you shall hear it ;—just listen. (*Reads*)—

"THE SONG OF THE FLOWER-POT."

(*The 'Flower-pot' was presented to the writer by the
Lady Blanche Bluenose.*)

" My little gentle flower-pot,
    Upon my turret flaunting free——"

. . . .

[*As his lordship is reading his poem, the curtain drops.* The *Castalian Magazine* of the next week contains a flaming puff upon Lord Daudley's " Passion-Flowers " ; but the *Weekly Bravo* has a furious attack upon the work, because Lord Daudley refused to advance a third £5 note to the celebrated Bludyer. After the critique, his lordship advances the £5 note. And, at a great public dinner, where my Lord Daudley is called upon to speak to a toast, he discourses upon the well-known sentiment—THE INDEPENDENCE OF THE PRESS ! IT IS LIKE THE AIR WE BREATHE : WITHOUT IT WE DIE.]

A ST. PHILIP'S DAY AT PARIS

Part I

WHEN the Champs Elysées were last decorated, it was for that grand serio-comic melodramatic spectacle of December 15th, in the midst of which the bones of Napoleon were restored to us. Here is May, and the men are again busy with shows, and lamps, and trophies. To-day, we are hailing the birthday of the King; to-morrow, we rejoice at the christening of a young prince, whom three cardinals attended to the font, and for whom has been provided a certain quantity of fluid from the river of Jordan. Upon King Louis Philippe—upon St. Philippe, his patron (the elder branch have monopolised *St. Louis*)—upon the Count of Paris—upon the city of the same name, and the fools dwelling in it who have gratified the young papdevourer with the present of a fine sword that, pray Heaven, he may never use—upon the French custom of giving fêtes ; viz., upon the fête at the entry of the Queen of Louis XIV., whom he treated so well, upon the fêtes of Louis XV., upon the grand fêtes of Louis XVI., of the federation, of Robespierre and the Supreme Being, of Buonaparte, Napoleon, Louis XVIII., Napoleon again, and the Champ de Mai, then Louis XVIII. once more, of Charles's fêtes, of Louis Philippe's fêtes—of all these it would be pretty easy to make jokes, and speak wholesome moralities : but what is the use ? Come what will, these people will have their poles, their drums, their squibs and fireworks, and their other means of sunshiny recreation.

And quite right too. If men are to be amused, they may just as well take a bad reason for amusing themselves as a good one : nay, a bad one *is* a good one. If I say to you, " I feel myself excessively happy, because it is the King's birthday ; and, because I am happy, I intend to climb up a pole, to eat a certain quantity of gingerbread, to play at pitch-and-toss for macaroons, or at jack-in-the-box for a given period,"—you have no right to ask me either—

1. Why I am happy on account of the King ?

2. Or, why I am happier on his *pseudo* birthday than on any other day in the year ?

3. Or, why, because I am happy, it is necessary that fellow-creatures should get up greased poles ?

4. Or, why, as I can fill my belly with gingerbread every day of the week, it is necessary that, on this particular day, I should eat that condiment, play at pitch-and-toss, jack-in-the-box, &c. ?

All these are points wholly impertinent, and I should consider a man grossly flippant and conceited who proved them. If men are happy, why the deuce need we inquire why or how ? Nature has supplied them with a variety of mysterious ways for being happy ; they extract pleasure from substances where one would never have thought that it lurked—viz., some men from reading Parliamentary debates ; some from swinging on gates, or butterfly chasing ; some, on the contrary, from political economy, from the study of the law, from the leading articles of the *Times* newspaper ; or from many other things equally strange. Newton, lying under a tree, had his nose tickled by an apple—Bottom, sprawling on Titania's lap, had his deliciously excited by a straw ; and the spirit of each, inspired by the circumstance, went off straight to his own heaven, soaring into a height of blissful considerations, which it never could have reached but for the aid of the pippin or the straw. Give a man, then, his pleasure where he finds it. A million bushels of Ribstons might have tumbled from trees and smashed my nose to a jelly, without my discovering the doctrine of gravitation ; and the fairies have scratched and tickled me all Midsummer through, without causing the ravishing delight felt by the honest weaver. There are secrets in every man's pleasure : let us respect them even without knowing them. I saw a man to-day, in the Champs Elysées—a large, fat man, with ear-rings and immense shirt-collar—a grandfather at least—walking placidly in the sunshine, sucking a stick of barley-sugar. He had sucked it in a beautiful conical way, and was examining its amber apex, glistening between his eye and the orb of day. He was showing his loyalty, in a word, to his King, and manifesting his joy, his reverential joy, at the christening of the Count de Paris. And why not ?

That same day other men were showing their loyal hilariousness in other ways, viz. :—

All the dignitaries of the state, the church, law, &c., made speeches in their best clothes, according to their several degrees.

All the ambassadors put on their cordons, placques, crachats, and white breeches ; and one of their body, in the name of this sympathising society, made an oration. At night their hotels covered themselves over with pieces of cork and fat, in which wicks joyfully blazed.

Five hundred soldiers scaled the summit of the Arc of the Etoile, and fired a shot of squibs out of their guns. Artillerymen stood at the foot of the arch, and their pieces propelled many roaring rounds of gunpowder and wadding to hail the happy anniversary.

Perhaps I thought the fat, silent, sunshiny man, calmly sucking his sugar-stick, the most sincerely happy and loyal of them all; for as for the guns and the ambassadors, it is their business to shout, and they are loaded, wadded, greased, and polished for the purpose. But let us take things as we find them : let us, contented with effects, not be too squeamish and curious about the causes. Here is the sun shining, the heaven faultlessly blue, the leaves bright, the fountains playing, and five hundred thousand people happy. What can one want more ? If people had but the means, it would be a blessing to have eighteen-score-and-five kings' birthdays in the year.

I have always had an objection to guns in theatrical pieces, for they make a sad noise and roaring, cause the eyes to wink, and the head to ache, among men not nurtured in the uncomfortable lap of Bellona. And as at theatres, where the heroes are supposed to drink champagne, they are provided with a cool and wholesome bottle of soda-water, that all the pit takes to be real moët ; so it has long been my wish that some mild kind of gun should be invented, going off with a pop, just for ceremony's sake, but never roaring out a great fierce bang, as they will do in stage pieces, whether performed at St. Stephen's theatre, the Cobourg, or else-where.

Bang, bung, bom, boom ! there they go, and all the breakfast things begin to clatter. I don't care to own that I feel nervous at hearing them ; each roar gives one a slight epigastric thump ; one affects to be at his ease, but waits all the time most anxiously for the succeeding boom ; you play with your egg during the time, and make believe to read the newspaper, but in reality you enjoy neither. While the guns were at their work this morning, I pre-tended to read Sir Robert Peel's and Lord John's speeches, but declare, at the end of the time, I did not understand or remember a single word of them. There it is ! those two matchless pieces of eloquence lost to a man, because the guns must, forsooth, celebrate the birthday of Louis Philippe. *Inter arma silent*, &c. O, brazen-throated war ! shut those brazen yelling jaws of thine, and let honest politicians talk in quiet. But what is the use of wishing and ejaculating ? Wherever we go *Miles* takes the wall of us ; and, accordingly, the first thing we heard of the fête this morning was the guns ; and the first thing we saw of it, the great, stalwart, jackbooted, brazen-helmeted gendarme, trotting his heavy Mecklenbourg horse down the avenues of the Champs Elysées, and standing at every corner of every street leading thither.

Having passed the gendarmes (and may the time come when the Parisians, like ourselves, may find one in every street, not to watch their politicians, but their pockets !), we come immediately upon the Champs Elysées, where the fête is in the very act of going on. The trees are lined with beggars of various queer descriptions ; old men with wonderful beards, and looking old enough to have seen Louis XIV. pass down the road on his way to Versailles. A great wanderer about the town knows most of the beggars who exercise their trade in it ; but these mysterious men come from their dens and haunts in the provinces—perhaps from foreign lands, across Alp or Pyrenee, attracted hither by the news of the great festival. The tales of beggars in story-books are always marvellous and pleasant in the romances of chivalry. In the Spanish novels, in the old English comedies, what a jolly, easy life do they lead !—what good scraps of songs do they sing !—how full are they of bitter Diogenic jokes, and moral comparisons of their state and that of kings, great personages, &c. ! I saw the other day, a hump-back beggar boy lying in the sun, and counting his day's gains ; he had, for a certainty, forty penny-pieces in his hand—but, whenever any one passed, interrupted his arithmetic to ask, in a whining voice, for some more coppers. Yonder is an old, wooden-legged Orpheus, reclining against a tree and singing a most doleful ditty about a poor blind man who lost his dog. He sings so atrociously, that it is your bounden duty to give him a penny. He has at his feet, or foot, a little carpet, covered all over, *pardi*, with larger and smaller copper coins. Ah ! why are not princes christened every day ? That honest wooden-legged man would make a fortune in that case, and nobody be the poorer. Who is ever the poorer for giving away pence to beggars ?

Yonder is the very finest of the mendicant order I ever saw. His face is faultlessly beautiful ; he has old bland, blind venerable eyes ; a little green velvet skull-cap covers a part of his head, under which fall thick flakes of snow-white hair ; upon his old bosom reposes a beard—the wool of the Cashmere goat is not whiter or finer. He has a little bird-organ—a little old bird-organ, that pipes feeble tunes. That organ must be many, many centuries old ; mayhap invented in those very days when fair Cecilia took her patent out, and angels hushed the flutter of their wings, and listened to her piping. Say, old man—sightless old man ! thine eyes are calm and bright,—blue limpid lakes which do reflect the sun, and yet are cool ! O, ancient organ-man, when were thine

eyes lit up with natural fires? Perhaps the blazing sand of Damiet
—fire against fire, did scorch their lustre out, where good Saint
Louis led his red-cross knights, and being conquered, led them back
again. Perhaps fierce Bajazet, dread Ilderim (what time the rash
Burgundian Nevers, with Eu, de Bar, Trimouille, and de la Marche,
Coucy, and Boucicault, the pride of France, laid down their arms
before the conquering Turk, upon the meadows of Nicopolis), put
out the beacons of this old man's eyes. A gallant warrior then,
and blithe and young, with pennoned lance, shouting his battle-cry,
and ever foremost in the press of war.

This would make our old man, at least, five hundred and
seventy years old; perhaps he is not so much—perhaps he is only
Louis XIX. in disguise, come from Prague to visit his capital. We
have in history hundreds of such examples. In the "History of
Beggars Bush," who, I pray you, is the old bearded beggar Claus,
but a rightful Duke of Gueldres? In the still more authentic story
of "The Duchess Penelope and her Suitors," who was the beggar
that came and saw the knights carousing, but Duke Ulysses, forsooth? Psha!—a fig for such rambling nonsense; drop a penny
into the old man's tray, and pass on. Very likely, if he get enough
of them, he will fuddle himself to-night; and so he, too, will
rejoice, after his fashion, on the King's birthday.

A point that must strike an Englishman naturally, is this.
Under the trees there are many scores of comfortable booths—
barrels of wine advantageously placed, legs of mutton,* and
sausages gazing upon the passer-by with friendly eyes; and yet,
though it is three o'clock, nobody eats. The French are not a
gormandising nation; at this hour, and with such a sun over our
heads, in an English fair, many thousand dozens of bottled porter
would have frothed down British throats, and cart-loads of beef,
separated into the most attenuated slices, have disappeared for
ever! But here, nobody eats. I had the curiosity to count in a
dozen booths;—in one there was an elderly lady with three boys,
in a school uniform; in others, a few fellows in blouses—a few
couples of soldiers, with a little small beer before them. But it is,
evidently, sad work for the boothmen, and let us hope the Government gives the honest people some subvention, to make them amends
for the painful sobriety of the nation.

On the other hand, gambling goes on at a frightful rate. Look,
there is the celebrated Polish game, with the hooks;—there is a
table with fifty hooks, all numbered, and a ring, swinging by a
cord, at a short distance. It is a penny a throw. He who places
the ring on the hook marked 50, thrice running, wins a watch; but

* Everybody knows the eye of a leg of mutton.

this was never known since the memory of man. If you hit number 20, you have twenty macaroons ; if 3, three macaroons, and so on. Will it be believed, that sometimes one does not hit any hook at all ? I had six pennyworth of throws, and came off with nine macaroons—and very nasty macaroons too ! Now, if I had laid out a penny in the regular way of barter, I might have had twelve macaroons, with a good profit to the vendor, too. Such is chance ; —O, cursed lust of gain ! But if I lose, somebody wins ; let us console ourselves, therefore, and be happy, for is it not St. Philip's day ?

Besides the hooks, there was the old roulette table, in which skill goes for naught ; and here the high prizes were not merely macaroon cakes, but pictures, neatly framed ; representing "*le bonheur conjugal*," or " *la bonne mère*," or the Prince de Joinville, in jack-boots, superintending the exhumation of Napoleon, or other subjects connected with the life or burial of the great hero of the people. There is something affecting about these rude pictures. The people always have a kind, hearty taste. *They* don't care for ogling nudities, such as excite the eyes of their betters. Their simple faith is raised by homely parables ; and no doubt the reader remembers the time when, as a little child, he placed implicit reliance in all the pictures of his spelling-book. The picture of Doctor Dilworth in the beginning, and the allegory underneath ; the picture of Masters Smith, Brown, Jones, and Robinson ; that of the three tradesmen disputing about fortifying the city ; that of the dog going across the water with the beef in his mouth; of the envious brute in the manger,—and so on. In all the ways of children there is something sacred ;—and yonder wondering peasants in sabots and high caps, those grave, brown-faced simple soldiers taking shots with the pop-gun, are children in their way. There are many pop-gun establishments about the Champs Elysées : one has for target, a great Turk ; if you hit him straight in the middle, the monster fires off a pistol. Another is a Scotchman, who salutes you in a similar fashion. By the way, this is the only time in France that I have seen a Scotch Highlander represented in a grotesque fashion ; whether it is because their costume is becoming and bizarre, or because the Scots in old days were allied with our neighbours, or because the French love Walter Scott's novels, certain it is, they never make jokes at the expense of the Caledonians, but content themselves with hating and girding at us English. I saw a soldier as brown as a halfpenny take a vast number of shots at one of these targets ; and at last he hit the bull's eye ; down came Cupid, and crowned the fellow with calico roses, by which wreath he was made as happy as if he had knocked down Abd-el-Kader himself.

Numbers of people were riding with perfect contentment in the merry-go-rounds ; many an Englishman might like to do this, but for his stupid shame. Indeed, when I saw the man sucking the barley-sugar, I felt as if I should like a piece, but dared not get one. Ah, lollypops, hardbake, alicompaine, brandy-balls ! how good you were forty years ago ; though we don't meet or see each other now, yet we are attached, and I never never shall forget you. Turtle soup is good ; but is it as good as open tarts ? A cool glass of claret is not bad ; but is it as pleasant as a halfpenny-worth of liquorice, and brown sugar to the same amount, mixed with water in a twopenny vial, and kept hot in your pocket in the warm summer days ? When you take it, or give it to a friend, you give the liquor a shake to make it froth, and take out the cork with your teeth, and bid your friend drink only to a certain place which you mark with your finger.

I have not tasted a drop for forty-three years—but what then ? There are things *qui ne s'oublient pas.* "Fresh is the picture of one's prime, the later trace is dim." A few days ago I met a gentleman of sixty-five years old, who had been at Charterhouse-school, and who said he dreamed the night before of having been flogged by Doctor Beardmore. Five-and-fifty years, in a night, the spirit whisks backward ! Napoleon has risen and died in the meanwhile ; kingdoms have changed hands ; cares, gout, grand-children have seized upon the old man ; what a number of kind eyes have looked on him that are shut now ! how many kind hearts have beat for him, that have been loved and passionately deplored, and forgotten by him ! what insurmountable woes has he climbed over ! what treacheries and basenesses has he, by the slow discoveries of friendship, laid bare ! what a stir and turmoil of fifty years has he gone through ! one care pushing down another, one all-absorbing wish or interest giving place as another came on ;—and, see here, he falls asleep, and straightway, through the immense labyrinth of a life's recollection, his spirit finds its way back to the flogging-block, and he wistfully fumbles at his breeches, and looks up at great Beardmore with the rod ! Be gentle with the little ones, ye schoolmasters ! Love them, but strike them not. How are the cherubim represented ? They are the children of the skies, and so conformed that if you were to catch a stray one, you could not flog him if you would.

I always think the invention of toys and toy-shops a very beautiful and creditable part of human nature. And it is pleasant to see in all fairs and public fêtes, in all watering-places whither people flock for pleasure, how many simple inventions are gathered together for the mere amusements of children—innumerable varieties

of gingerbread, drums, go-carts, rocking-horses, by the sale of which
honest people make their livelihood ! The French are essentially a
child-loving race, much more kindly and simple in their domestic
ways than are we with our absurd, cold, dignified airs (the men,
I mean, for the mothers are the same all over God's world) ; and
it gives a man with the philoprogenitive bump great pleasure to
walk into the fête, and see the worthy fathers walking with their
children, or dragging them in little carriages, or holding them on
patient shoulders to see the shows of the place.

Round the open square of the Champs Elysées are a vast
number of booths and exhibitions ; all Napoleon's battles, of course ;
no less than four companies of strong men ; " Les Hercules des
Hercules ; " " the Indian strong men ; " " the strong men with the
fairy pony," &c. The drums and trumpets make an awful banging
and braying ; Socrisse stands in front, in his jacket and tow-wig,
and makes melancholy jokes. When the ladies with short petticoats
have done dancing on the ropes within, they come out solemnly, and
range their bandy legs, and dirty pink cotton pantaloons before the
eyes of the vulgar, to tempt them to go into the booth. But this
is a great mistake ; I, for my part, was just on the point of entering
the booth of the Indian athletes, upon the faith of a picture in
which these personages were represented—the men of swarthy hue,
in incredible postures of strength, the women of ravishing beauty—
when, on a sudden, a company of these Indians came forward to
the outer stage, and a homelier, uglier race of Frenchmen I never
saw. So it is with other shows. There is the fat Belgian woman,
only sixteen, and four-and-twenty stone ; though so young she
possesses, it is said, every ' accomplishment ; can talk a dozen
languages, play upon innumerable instruments, and dance with
grace and lightness. But the Indian jugglers made us incredulous,
and our party determined not to visit the fat young Belgian lady.

We had, however, an excellent view of the gentlemen climbing
the immense *mât de cocagne* for the prizes dangling at the top.
There was a gold watch, two silver ditto, silver mugs, forks and
spoons of the same precious metal to reward the enterprising men
who ascended to the summit of the pole. But even this institution,
simple and praiseworthy as it seems, is not altogether pure. It
appears that there is a society of climbers in Paris, fellows who can
walk up a greased pole as easily as common mortals up a staircase,
and these individuals come early round the mast, seize upon the
principal prizes, and, selling them, divide their profits among their
corporation. The age of maypoles is extinct when you see them
delivered over to this unhallowed commerce. For my part, too, I
very much doubt the sincerity of a person who accosted us, having

in his possession some gold rings, a pair of razors, and other articles, all of which he said he had *found*, and offered to sell at a great loss. In the first place, a man can't find so many gold rings in the course of the day; and as for the razors, who the deuce would bring his case into such a place as this?

We now saw a play at a very cheap rate, in one of the theatres erected in the square. There was a gentleman in a Spanish costume taken prisoner by some Turks; how his faithful squire wept at his own cowardice, which made him forsake his master at such a pass! But so it is, my good squire! men of your profession are always cowardly; read all the plays and novels ever written—always gluttonous, always talkative: here, however, you could not be, be cause the play was a pantomime, and so, luckily, you were freed from one of the vices inherent to your profession.

When the news of her lover's capture was brought to the Lady Ismena, far from being down-hearted and dismayed, as other ladies would, after the first burst of natural emotion, what did she do? Why, she dressed herself in a light blue velvet page's costume, to be sure, slung a guitar across her shoulders, summoned the squire and a battalion of Austrian grenadiers, and followed the captors of her lord.

When the scene changed, and showed us the Moorish castle in which that nobleman was to be confined, we saw a Turkish sentinel pacing the battlements.

"*Tiens, c'est le Turc en faction,*" said one of two soldiers behind us, who had just come from Africa. But the sentinel paced up and down without taking the least notice of anything but his duty.

In immediately came the captive nobleman with the Turkish soldiers; how he threatened and resisted, how he writhed and how he twisted! he thrust his fist in the captain's face, in the lieutenant's : strove to break away from his guard, though weighed down by immense chains; and though, for a short time, he became quiescent, yet when the governor of the fortress——

"*C'est Sidi Abdalla,*" said one soldier.

"*C'est Mahomet,*" cried another, "*le v'la qui sort de l'église.*"

"*Ca s'appelle une mosque,*" said the first soldier ; and a mosque it was, sure enough, with an immense crescent on the top.

When the governor of the fortress, a most venerable Mahometan, with a silver beard, came out, and all the officers and privates of the guard fell to salaaming him, the captive knight burst out into a fury again, shook his fist in the governor's face, kicked and plunged like a madman, and we all thought would escape. But no ; numbers prevailed—he was carried into the fort with the most horrible contortions, the portcullis was drawn up, and the silent sentinel resumed his walk.

At that instant the Lady Ismena arrived in her light blue dress, and we, knowing well enough that the grenadiers were behind her, expected that they would instantly fall to and fight. But no ; unslinging her guitar, she struck a few wild notes on it, and a number of Turkish peasants in the neighbourhood flocked in to dance.

Expecting a fight, as I said, I never was more grossly disappointed than at the sight of these ugly heathens dancing gracefully, and, having moved off immediately, can't tell what took place afterwards. But it is very probable that the castle *was* stormed finally, and the knight rescued, and poor old Sidi Mahomet put to an ignominious death by Ismena herself, with her natty little sword.

All persons who frequent these public spectacles should take the writer's advice, and have a cigar to smoke. It is much more efficacious than scent bottles of any sort.

As for the evening amusements, knowing that, however brilliant a man's style may be, it is quite impossible to describe rockets and Bengal lights properly, and having seen a number of these fireworks, viz., at Rome, at Easter—at the Feast of Lanterns, at Canton—at the peace, in Hyde Park, in 1814—our society determined to quit the town altogether for the evening, and to partake of a rustic dinner in the pretty village of Ville d'Avray. It is half-an-hour's walk from Saint Cloud, through the park, and you travel in the same time by the railroad from Paris.

Here, at the park-gates, is a pretty little restaurant, with a garden, where there are balls sometimes and dinner always, which latter we preferred. We had beefsteaks for four in a snug sort of hermitage, and very good wine, and quiet, and a calm sky, and numberless green trees round about. The waiter's name is Amelia. She whispered to us knowingly that, in the hermitage above ours a couple of couples were *en partie fine ;* and so, sure enough, after these ladies and gentlemen had taken their little sober modicum of wine, their hearts rose, and their tongues wagged, and they sang songs ; the men, in parts, very prettily, the ladies sang solos atrociously out of tune. Presently came a fellow with an organ, and our jovial neighbours instantly got up and danced, in the midst of a great shrieking and laughter.

When the organ-man had done with the *partie-fine*, he came down to us and struck up two beautiful melodies, viz., "Getting up Stairs," and "Jim Crow." He had never been in England, he said, but his organ had, and there, no doubt, learned that delicious music.

By this time the *partie-fine* had grown quite uproarious ; they were talking English to one another for our benefit—crying " Yase," " Godem," " How you do, mister," and so on. The clocks tolled eight, and Amelia's uncle, a *maréchal des logis gendarmes* at Saint Cloud, who had come down to see his niece, because the poor girl had cut her two thumbs the day before, conducted us through the silent grey park of Saint Cloud, across the palace, and so to the railroad station.

Of course, the train had just set off ; and there was no cuckoo or other vehicle, though there would be hundreds for the *grandes eaux* the next day ; wherefore Todd, Higgins, Blatherwick, and your humble servant, walked through the Bois de Boulogne, and so home.

Part II.

THERE was a second day of fêtes, and in respect of popular amusements, the morning and evening of the second day were like the morning and evening of the first. The may-poles were furnished with a second supply of watches and silver spoons. The Don was again taken prisoner, and rescued by his Elvira in her light blue dress ; the untiring strong men, and Herculeses of the booths, performed their prodigious labours, and the indefatigable female Falstaff of Belgium was quite as fat on Sunday as on Saturday. More squibs and crackers blazed in the evening, and many more hundreds of pounds of macaroons were gambled for and devoured by the happy population.

The second day was appropriated to the christening of the Count of Paris, as the first to the birthday of the king ; and the papers are filled with long accounts of the former ceremony ; how the cardinals attended ; how the young prince about to be chris-tened gave his own names in an audible voice to his Grandeur the Archbishop ; how his Grandeur made an harangue to the king, and was, after the ceremony, rewarded by a very handsome diamond cross and ring, on his Majesty's part, and complimented with a most elegant mitre from the Duke of Orleans.

Money was distributed largely to all the churches for the poor in Paris. The bounty of this royal family is untiring, extraordinary. No disaster occurs, but they come forward to soothe it ; wherever they move, they scatter presents and kindness ; to all sorts of poor and wretched the queen seems to act as the gentle protectress and mother. They say that the family loves to publish its acts of

charity; and the frequent appearance of their names in all subscription lists would indeed appear like ostentation, did one not
know that it is the duty of persons so high placed to make some
of their kindnesses public, to induce others to be generous who
might not be so but for their example. One reads in novels of
people who give pharisaically in public, that in private keep their
purse-strings close; but I am inclined not to believe that there are
many such. Men are ostentatious, but charitable, too. The very
fact of giving away large sums even for ostentation's sake, must
generate a feeling of kindness.

As for the Orleans family, some of their good deeds they publish,
and they are right. But how much do they do, of which the world
never hears, or only a small portion of it, from the grateful lips of
the persons obliged! I have heard of three instances myself lately,
of simple, judicious, delicate generosity on the part of the king and
his family. How many thousand more such must there be which
are never blazoned in newspapers! O glorious godlike privilege of
wealth to make the wretched happy!

There was a great concert and illumination to conclude the day's
festival; and if my dear Smith would know how much of them the
humblest of her servants personally witnessed, indeed he must confess that he only saw the heavens lighted up by the fire of the
rockets, and heard the banging of the guns, and such stray gusts
of the concert as the wind chose to bring to a certain balcony in
a street leading off the Rue Rivoli, where several personages were
seated, enjoying a calm and philosophical summer's evening conversation.

We heard the "Marseillaise" pretty distinctly; it was the
opening of the concert, and the audience of course encored their
fiery national anthem. It is a noble strain, indeed; but a war-
song, breathing blood and vengeance, is a bad subject for everyday
enthusiasm; and one had better, perhaps, for a continuance, recreate
oneself with some more peaceful musical diet. Even the fit of war
is bad enough; but war every day, murder and blood on week-days
as well as on Sundays—*Entendez vous dans nos campagnes mugir
ces féroces soldats ?—égorger vos fils, vos compagnes*—I forget how
the song runs. *Mon Dieu!* the ferocious soldiery is not in the
country; French women and children are perfectly safe from Cossack
or Prussian; the story is now fifty years old, and still Frenchmen
lash themselves in a fury of conceit and blood-thirstiness whenever
they hear it, and fancy their brutality patriotism. Napoleon established a Valhalla idea of a Frenchman's paradise—it was conquest
and murder all day.

Just before this bloody chorus was set up, the King showed

himself at the balcony of the palace, and was received, it is said, with a dead silence;—then he went out and fetched the little boy who had just been christened, but the audience received him, too, coldly, and so the royal pair went back again, and gave place to the more popular concert.

To such as are inclined to moralise, is there not here matter enough ? Think of this old man and his condition. He is the wisest, the greatest—the most miserable man in Europe. His bounty makes thousands happy,—it shines on all, like the sun; but the sun, they say, is cold itself, and in the midst of its splendours, lonely. Think of this man, how prudent and wise he is ; through what dangers and crooked paths he has managed to conduct the fiercest, most obstinate team that ever was reined by imperial hand. Napoleon let them run ahead at mad gallop—this man has been keeping them at a decent pace ; by what extraordinary exertion of wisdom and stratagem, coaxing and firmness, has he achieved this eleven years' miracle ? O, Polumetis ! I wonder whether you ever sleep ?—if you, with your staunch spirit, can bear to look at the sword hanging over you ? There is a poor woman at your side who has no such courage, and never sees the door shut upon you without shuddering—nor open, without receiving you as if you were come out of the jaws of death. Go where you will, calumny follows you like your shadow ;—do your best in the brightest lights, it only turns the blacker. Sullen conspiracy is always dogging at your heels, growling curses at you, until it can have its way, and make its spring. You have suffered much, but were always kind and simple in humour, and mercifully bent ;—you never signed away a man's life without feeling a pang : more than one wretch have you pardoned—only gently putting away his knife from your throat ! But what boots your benevolence ? A day does not pass without its conspiracy ; and men lust for your blood, and are ready to lie in God's face, and to call your murder virtue. See what it is to be so wise, O King ; not one single man trusts you. To be so great, no person loves you ; except, perhaps, a few women and children whom you have bred. There is scarcely a beggar or outcast in the country, but has as large a circle of friends who trust him, and whom he can trust : no thief that deems each bush an officer, but can take almost as quiet a sleep as you.

And when day comes, and you have your many labours to go through—you, who are so wise, know that not one single man you meet trusts you ;—you hear speeches from old peers and chancellors who have sworn and flattered for a dozen men who stood in your shoes :—you know that no man, be he ever so candid, can speak to you the whole truth ; and to public and private lies, you have to reply properly—lying gravely in your task. My Lord Archbishop stalks in and addresses you in a grave compliment, in which he includes yourself, Saint Louis, and God Almighty? My Lord Ambassador comes bowing, and congratulates you on your birthday. Sweet innocent!—what a touching testimonial of family love! It isn't your birthday; and the ambassador does not care one fig; but both of you pretend he does, and bow and cringe to each other gravely, and waggle your old wigs solemnly, and turn up to heaven the white of your old eyes . . .

But stop—it is time we withdraw the old King from the balcony. Ah! but it must be a sad life to stifle all day through, under this sickly mask of ceremony; to be lonely, and yet never alone; to labour, and never look for either rest or sympathy; to wear a crown, and have outlived royalty; to bear all the burthens of royalty, without any of the old magnificent privileges of it; to have toiled, and striven for, and won this wretched solitary eminence, and feel it crumbling; and to look down from it and see the great popular deluge rising which shall swallow it under its level.

While the bonfires and music were roaring in the terraces and garden hard by, we were rather amused to see a philosophical artist in his garret opposite, who was seated near his open window, and had lighted his lamp, and was smoking his pipe, and very calmly copying a portrait of Madame de la Vallière. Here was food for new moralities for those who were inclined for such meat.

SHROVE TUESDAY IN PARIS

THE particulars of the fête need not be described at present, as many hundred English writers have, no doubt, given an account of it, and everybody knows very well that on Sunday, Monday, and Tuesday, *des Cendres*, the annual fat ox of the Carnival is made to take sundry walks through Paris, a little chubby butcher's boy, seated behind his gilded horns, with pink breeches on, in the guise of a Cupid, and a number of grown up butchers and butcherlings habited as Spanish grandees, Turkish agas, Roman senators, and what not, following the animal, and causing the air to resound with a most infernal music of horns and instruments of brass. Triumphal cars, adorned with tinsel and filled with musicians—troops of actors from Franconi's, mounted on the steeds of that establishment, and decorated in its finest costumes, join in the august ceremonial, and crowds of masks which cover the faces of many idle, merry young people of both sexes, and of an infinite number of blackguards of the capital, wander up and down the Boulevards on foot, on horseback, in carriages, and jingling *cabriolets de place*, and have done so from time immemorial.

At three o'clock, as the papers say ominously, the ox's promenade is concluded ;—at about four, very likely, that enormous quadruped receives a blow from a hammer betwixt his gilded horns, and has been served out to-day in steaks and collops to the beef amateurs who frequent Mr. Roland's shop. And a curious thing it is that the wondrous animal has the faculty of indefinite multiplication ; there is not an eating-house in Paris but can give you a slice of him—a real authentic *bonâ fide* fillet or *entrecôte*. Half-a-dozen hecatombs of oxen must be slaughtered if the facts were known ; but each man is fain to believe that his particular portion is genuine—as they show you in convents five hundred undoubted skulls of St. This or St. That, and bits of the true cross, that added together, would be enough to furnish all the woodwork for Oxford Street.

For more than a month previous, the town has been running madly to masquerades at the theatres, and every young man and maiden (the latter word is used from pure politeness) who had a few franc pieces in their pockets, saved against the happy period, or a coat or a shawl which would produce a little money *chez ma tante*—"my uncle," is the affectionate term applied to the same personage in England—had been intriguing here, and dancing to his mad heart's content. You see a tolerable number of great raw young English lads joining clumsily in the festivities of the masquerades; but on this point I can only speak from hearsay, not having seen one of these balls for more than ten years, when I was so frightened and wonder stricken by the demoniacal frantic yells and antics of the frequenters of the place, as to slink home perfectly dumb and miserable, not without some misgivings lest some real demons from below, with real pitchforks and tails, should spring out of the trap-doors of the playhouse, as the sham-fiends do in Don Juan, and drive the dancers and musicians headlong down, sending the theatre itself down after them, and leaving only behind them a smoky warning smell of sulphur. However, the next day there was the theatre in its place, having a dismal, rakish appearance (with dead lamps over the doors, and pale, blear-eyed transparencies that looked as if they had been up all night); and it is probable that the three thousand mad people of the night before were pretty well restored to their sober senses and back to their counters and their work again.

The only acquaintance I had in the place upon the awful night of the masked-ball, was a lady who tapped me on my shoulder, saluted me by name, and was good enough to put her arm into mine quite uninvited, and to walk once or twice with me up and down the room. This lovely creature appeared to be about five-and-thirty years of age;—she was dressed like a man, in a blouse and pair of very dirty-white trousers—had an oilskin hat, orna-mented with a huge quantity of various-coloured ribbons, and under it an enormous wig with three tails, that dangled down the lady's back; it was of the fashion of the time of Louis XV., and so old and dirty that I have no doubt it had been worn at Carnivals any time since the death of that monarch.—"Don't you know me?" said she, after a moment, seeing my wonder, and as confessing my forgetfulness, she told me who she was.

Indeed, I recollect her a governess in a very sober, worthy family in England, where she brought up the daughters, and had been selected especially because she was a *Protestant*. I believe the woman did her duty perfectly well in her station, but, upon my word, she told me she had pawned her gown to get this disgusting old dress, and dance at this disgusting masquerade. She was not very young, as has been seen, and had never been pretty. Squalid poverty had not increased her charms; but here she was, as mad after the Carnival as the rest, and enjoying herself along with the other mad men and women. In her private capacity she was a workwoman; she lived in the Rue Neuve St. Augustin, and I found her a few days afterwards eating garlic soup in a foul porter's lodge, from which she conducted me up a damp, mouldy staircase to her own apartment, on the seventh floor, with the air and politeness of a duchess.

If a wicked world is anxious to know what took a married man into such a quarter, let it be honestly confessed that the visit arose upon the subject of a half-dozen of shirts which the lady made for me. She did not cheat her customer out of a sixpence-worth of cloth, and finished the collars and wristbands to admiration. An honest *lingère* of the Rue Vivienne asked double the sum for a similar article.

Madame or Mademoiselle Pauline must be now five-and-forty years old, and I wonder whether she still goes to the Carnival balls? If she is alive, and has a gown to pawn, or a shilling to buy a ticket, or a friend to give her one, or is not' in the hospital, no doubt she was dancing away last night to the sound of Monsieur Dufrêsne's trumpets, and finished the morning at the Courtille.

Que voulez-vous? it is her nature. Before she turned Protestant, and instructed that respectable English family in whose bosom she found a home, where she became acquainted with all the elegancies of life, and habituated to the luxuries of refinement, where she had a comfortable hot joint every day with the children, in the nursery, at one, and passed the evening deliciously in the drawing-room, listening to the conversation of the ladies, making tea, mayhap, for the gentlemen as they came up from their wine, or playing quadrilles and waltzes when her lady desired her to do so—before this period of her genteel existence, it is probable that Mademoiselle Pauline was a grisette. When she quitted Sir John's family, she had his recommendation, and an offer of another place equally eligible; more children to bring up, more walks in the park or the square, more legs of mutton at one. She might have laid by a competence if she had been thrifty, or have seized upon a promise of marriage from young Master Tom, at college, if she had been artful; or, better still, from a respectable governess have become a respectable step-mother, as many women with half her good looks have done. But no. A grisette she was, and a grisette she would be; and left the milords and miladies, and *cette triste ville de Londres, où l'on ne danse pas seulement le Dimanche*, for her old quarters, habits, and companions, and that dear old gutter in the Rue du Bac, which Madame de Staël has spoken of so fondly.

A fierce, honest moralist might, to be sure, find a good deal to blame in Madame Pauline's conduct and life; and I should probably offend the reader if I imparted to him secrets which the lady told me with the utmost simplicity, and without the slightest appearance of confusion. But to rightly judge the woman's character, we must take the good and the bad together. It would have been easy for us to coin a romantic, harrowing story of some monstrous seducer, in three volumes, who, by his superior blackness of character, should make Madame Pauline appear beside him as white as snow; but I want to make no heroine of her. Let us neither abuse her nor pity her too much, but look at the woman such as we find her, if we look at her at all. Her type is quite unknown in England; it tells a whole social history, and speaks of manners and morals widely different from those which obtain in our own country. There are a hundred thousand Pauline's in Paris, cheerful in poverty, careless and prodigal in good fortune, but dreadfully lax in some points of morals in which our own females are praiseworthily severe.

No more, however, of the grisette, the jovial devil-may-care patroness of the masked ball. Béranger has immortalised her and her companion; and the reader has but to examine his song of the *Bonne Vieille*, for instance, by the side of Burns's "John Anderson," to see the different feelings of the two countries upon the above point of morals. Thank God! the Scotchman's is a purer and heartier theory than that of the Frenchman; both express the habits of the people amongst whom they live.

In respect of the *griset*, if one may coin such a word, to denote the male companion of the grisette, almost all the youth of Paris (and youth extends to a very good old age in that city) may be ranked. What sets all these men so mad for dancing at a certain age? They lead a life of immorality so extraordinary that an Englishman cannot even comprehend, much more share it. And while we reproach them, and justly, for their immorality, they are, on their part, quite as justly indignant with ours. A Frenchman hardly ever commits an excess of the table;—what Englishman has not in his time? A French gentleman would be disgraced, were he deeply in debt to his tradesman;—is an Englishmen disgraced on any such account? Far from it. Debt is a staple joke to our young men, "Who suffers for your coat?" is, or used to be, a cant phrase; comedies upon comedies are written, where the creditor is the universal butt;—the butt of French comedy is the husband. The same personage and the complication of wrongs which, in his marital quality, he may suffer, forms almost the sole theme of graver French romance. With this means of exciting interest, the usages of our country forbid the English romancer to deal, and he is obliged to resort to murder, robbery, excessive low life, where-with to tickle his reader. I have never met a Frenchman who could relish the works of our two modern most popular writers, Mr. Dickens and Mr. Ainsworth ; Mr. Weller and Dick Turpin are to them immoral and indecent. The French writer whose works are best known in England is Monsieur Paul de Kock. Talk to a French educated gentleman about this author, and he shrugs his shoulders, and says it is "*pitoyable*."

This disquisition is a great deal more *apropos* of the Carnival than, perhaps, the reader thinks for. It does not seem to enter into our neighbours' heads that gallantry is immoral. When they grow old, perhaps, they leave off gallantry and carnivalising ; but then it is because they are tired of it ; or, because they have the rheumatism, and are better at home in bed ; or, because they prefer a quiet rubber of whist, and so they leave carnivalising to the *jeunesse ;* and the *jeunesse* of to-day will probably hand over the same principles and practice to their sons, thinking their *fredaines* as harmless matters of course, and on the score of morality quite easy. There was a time in our country when the process of what was called sowing a man's wild oats, was regarded by his elders with great good humour ; but with regard to certain wild oats, our society luckily is growing a great deal more rigid and sensible. There was a time, too, in France when *roueries* were the fashion, and it was permitted to young gentlemen of condition to intoxicate themselves *au cabaret,* and beat the watch, like my Lord W—— in England ; but such *roueries* are immoral now in France, and would cause a man to be degraded and scorned ; our public has not gone quite so far, and such conduct, as far as I can judge, is not supposed to affect a man's honour. Thus, on one side and the other, some vices we have abolished, and some we have compounded for.

Apropos of the Carnival ; I have just been to visit a man who has sinned most cruelly against one of the severest laws of French Society. He is only five-and-twenty, has not a shilling in the world but what he earns, and has actually committed the most unheard-of crime of *marrying.* Had he made a *ménage* with some young lady of Mademoiselle Pauline's stamp, nobody would have blamed him. His parents, sisters, and friends would have considered and spoken of the thing as a matter of course, and as one quite compatible with prudence and morality. Louis, however, has married, and is now paying the price of his crime.

He is an engraver and artist by trade ; and if he gains a hundred-and-fifty pounds a-year by his labour, it is all that he does. Out of this he has to support a wife, a child, and a *bonne* to cook for him ; and to lay by money, if he can, for a rainy day. He works twelve hours at least every day of his life. He can't go into society of evenings, but must toil over his steel-plates all night ; he is forced to breakfast off a lump of bread and cheese and a glass of water, in his *atelier ;* very often he cannot find time to dine with his family, but his little wife brings him his soup, and a morsel of beef, of which he snatches a bit as he best may, but can never hope for any-thing like decent comfort. Fancy how his worthy parents must be *désolés,* at this dreadful position of their son. *Régardez donc Louis,* say his friends, *et puis faites la bêtise de vous marier !*

Well, this monster, who has so outraged all the laws of decency, who does not even smoke his pipe at the café, and play his *partie* at dominoes, as every honest reputable man should, is somehow or the other, and in the teeth of all reason, the most outrageously absurdly happy man I ever saw. His wife works almost as hard at her needle as he does at his engraving. They live in a garret in the Rue Cadet, and have got a little child, forsooth (as if the pair of them were not enough!), a little rogue that is always trotting from her mother's room to her father's, and is disturbing one or the other with her nonsensical prattle. Their lodging is like a cage of canary-birds ; there is nothing but singing in it from morning till night. You hear Louis beginning in a bass voice, Tra-la-la-la, Tra-la-la-la, and as sure as fate from Madame Louis's room, comes Tra-la-la-la, Tra-la-la-la, in a treble. Little Louise, who is only two years old, must sing too, the absurd little wretch !—and half-a-dozen times in the day, Madame Louis peeps into the *atelier,* and looks over her husband's work, and 'calls him *lolo,* or *mon bon,* or *mon gros,* or some such coarse name, and once, in my presence, although I was a perfect stranger, actually kissed the man.

Did mortal ever hear of such horrid vulgarity ? What earthly right have these people to be happy, and if you would know what Monsieur Louis had to do *apropos* of the Carnival, all I can say is, that I went to see him on that day, and found him at work as usual, working and singing in his obtuse, unreasonable way, when every person else who had a shade of common sense was abroad on the Boulevards, seeing the *Bœuf Gras* make his usual promenade ! Louis, though he looks upon the matter now with great philosophy, told me, with a rakish air, that there *was* a time when he was mad after masked balls like the rest, and would not have lost his Carnival for the world.

And not only in Paris does the *Bœuf Gras* make his walk. Beeves, more or less fat, promenade in the villages, too, and, having occasion to go to a miserable, mouldy, deserted, straggling place in the environs of Paris, where there are two shops, and two wretched inns or taverns, with faded pictures of billiard-balls and dishes of poultry, painted on the damp walls, and a long, straggling street, with almost every tottering tenement in it to let, I saw that the two shops had their windows filled with cheap masks, and met one or two little blackguards of the place disguised, and making their Carnival. In one of the houses of this delectable place a sick friend was lying, and, from his room, we heard a great braying of horns coming from the market-place, where the village fat ox was promenading. A donkey was roaring in concert with the horns, and you heard one or two voices of yelling children that were taking their part in the fête.

. . . .

One other instance, *apropos* of the Carnival, may as well be mentioned. A young lad of fifteen, who is at a school in Paris, has just been giving an account of his share of the festivities. The three last days of the Carnival are holidays for all the schoolboys of the metropolis, and my young informer had his full share of the pleasure. "Ah! Monsieur Titmarsh," said he, "comme je me suis amusé! J'ai dansé toute la soirée de Dimanche chez Madame—(il y avoient des demoiselles charmantes!) et puis j'ai dansé Lundi, et puis Mardi. Dieu! comme c'etoit amusant!"

With this the little fellow went off perfectly contented to his school, to get up at five o'clock the next morning and continue his studies. And, if the reader wishes to know how the foregoing essay upon Carnivals and English and French usages of society came about, let him be informed that it arose from considering the way in which Monsieur Ernest said he had "amused" himself.

Was there ever an English boy of fifteen heard of who could amuse himself with dancing for three nights running? What could bring the inhabitants of London to troop like madmen after a fat ox? What power on earth could set a couple of hundred thousand of them dancing and tramping, merely because it is the last day before Lent?

To us, considering these things, and the wonderful difference that a score of miles of salt water can make in the ways and morals of people, it appeared that the little personages above drawn, though very common in France, would be to England perfectly strange, and might, therefore, be appropriately placed in the BRITANNIA. And if it be in writing, as in drawing, that a sketch taken from nature of a place never so humble or unpicturesque, has always a certain good in it that is not to be found in fanciful works of far greater pretension—in this manner poor Pauline's rude portrait may find a little favour in the eyes of the public. There are certain little features in the countenance which might, to be sure, be much prettier than they are; but it is best, after all, to take such things as we find them, nor, be they ever so ugly, has nature made them in vain.

MEMORIALS OF GORMANDISING

IN A LETTER TO OLIVER YORKE, ESQUIRE, BY M. A. TITMARSH

Paris : *May* 1841.

SIR,—The man who makes the best salads in London, and whom, therefore, we have facetiously called Sultan Saladin,— a man who is conspicuous for his love and practice of all the polite arts—music, to wit, architecture, painting, and cookery— once took the humble personage who writes this into his library, and laid before me two or three volumes of manuscript year-books, such as, since he began to travel and to observe, he has been in the habit of keeping.

Every night, in the course of his rambles, his highness the sultan (indeed, his port is sublime, as, for the matter of that, are all the wines in his cellar) sets down with an iron pen, and in the neatest handwriting in the world, the events and observations of the day; with the same iron pen he illuminates the leaf of his journal by the most faithful and delightful sketches of the scenery which he has witnessed in the course of the four-and-twenty hours; and if he has dined at an inn or restaurant, gasthaus, posada, albergo, or what not, invariably inserts into his log-book the bill of fare. The sultan leads a jolly life—a tall stalwart man, who every day about six o'clock in London and Paris, at two in Italy, in Germany and Belgium at an hour after noon, feels the noble calls of hunger agitating his lordly bosom (or its neighbourhood, that is), and replies to the call by a good dinner. Ah! it is wonderful to think how the healthy and philosophic mind can accommodate itself in all cases to the varying circumstances of the time—how, in its travels through the world, the liberal and cosmopolite stomach recognises the national dinner-hour! Depend upon it that, in all countries, nature has wisely ordained and suited to their exigencies THE DISHES OF A PEOPLE. I mean to say that olla podrida is good in Spain (though a plateful of it, eaten in Paris, once made me so dreadfully ill that it is a mercy I was spared ever to eat another dinner); I mean to say, and have proved it, that sauerkraut is good in Germany; and I make no doubt that whale's blubber is a

2 s

very tolerable dish in Kamtschatka, though I have never visited the country. Cannibalism in the South Seas, and sheepsheadism in Scotland, are the only practices that one cannot, perhaps, reconcile with this rule—at least, whatever a man's private opinions may be, the decencies of society oblige him to eschew the expression of them upon subjects which the national prejudice has precluded from free discussion.

Well, after looking through three or four of Saladin's volumes, I grew so charmed with them, that I used to come back every day and study them. I declare there are bills of fare in those books over which I have cried ; and the reading of them, especially about an hour before dinner, has made me so ferociously hungry, that, in the first place, the sultan (a kind-hearted generous man, as every man is who loves his meals) could not help inviting me to take potluck with him ; and, secondly, I could eat twice as much as upon common occasions, though my appetite is always good.

Lying awake, then, of nights, or wandering solitary abroad or wide commons, or by the side of silent rivers, or at church when Doctor Snufflem was preaching his favourite sermon, or stretched on the flat of my back smoking a cigar at the club when X was talking of the corn-laws, or Y was describing that famous run they had with the Z hounds—at all periods, I say, favourable to self examination, those bills of fare have come into my mind, and often and often I have thought them over. "Titmarsh," I have said to myself, "if ever you travel again, do as the sultan has done, and *keep your dinner-bills.* They are always pleasant to look over they always will recall happy hours and actions, be you ever so hard pushed for a dinner, and fain to put up with an onion and a crust: of the past fate cannot deprive you. Yesterday is the philosopher's property ; and by thinking of it, and using it to advantage, he may gaily go through to-morrow, doubtful and dismal though it be. Try this lamb stuffed with pistachio-nuts ; another handful of this pillau. Ho, you rascals ! bring round the sherbet there, and never spare the jars of wine—'tis true Persian, on the honour of a Barmecide !" Is not that dinner in the "Arabian Nights" a right good dinner ? Would you have had Bedreddin to refuse and turn sulky at the windy repast, or to sit down grinning in the face of his grave entertainer, and gaily take what came Remember what came of the honest fellow's philosophy. He slapped the grim old prince in the face ; and the grim old prince who had invited him but to laugh at him, did presently order a real and substantial repast to be set before him—great pyramid of smoking rice and pillau (a good pillau is one of the best dishes in the world), savoury kids, snow-cooled sherbets, luscious wine of

Schiraz; with an accompaniment of moon-faced beauties from the
harem, no doubt, dancing, singing, and smiling in the most ravishing
manner.   Thus should we, my dear friends, laugh at Fate's beard,
as we confront him—thus should we, if the old monster be insolent,
pull to and box his ears.   He has a spice of humour in his composition ; and be sure he will be tickled by such conduct.

Some months ago, when the expectation of war between England and France grew to be so strong, and there was such a talk
of mobilising national guards, and arming three or four hundred
thousand more French soldiers—when such ferocious yells of hatred
against perfidious Albion were uttered by the liberal French press,
that I did really believe the rupture between the two countries was
about immediately to take place; being seriously alarmed, I set off
or Paris at once.   My good sir, what could we do without our
Paris?   I came here first in 1815 (when the Duke and I were a
good deal remarked by the inhabitants); I proposed but to stay a
week; stopped three months, and have returned every year since.
There is something fatal in the place—a charm about it—a wicked
one very likely—but it acts on us all; and perpetually the old
Paris man comes hieing back to his quarters again, and is to be
found, as usual, sunning himself in the Rue de la Paix.   Painters,
princes, gourmands, officers on half-pay—serious old ladies even
acknowledge the attraction of the place—are more at ease here than
at any other place in Europe; and back they come, and are to be
found sooner or later occupying their old haunts.

My darling city improves, too, with each visit, and has some
new palace, or church, or statue, or other gimcrack, to greet your
eyes withal.   A few years since, and lo ! on the column of the
Place Vendôme, instead of the shabby tri-coloured rag, shone the
bronze statue of Napoleon.   Then came the famous triumphal
arch; a noble building indeed !—how stately and white, and
beautiful and strong, it seems to dominate over the whole city !
Next was the obelisk; a huge bustle and festival being made to
welcome it to the city.   Then came the fair asphaltum terraces
round about the obelisk ; then the fountains to decorate the terraces.
I have scarcely been twelve months absent, and behold they have
added all the Naiads and Tritons ; they have clapped a huge
fountain in the very midst of the Champs Elysées—a great,
glittering, frothing fountain, that to the poetic eye looks like an
enormous shaving-brush ; and all down the avenue they have placed
hundreds of gilded flaring gas-lamps, that make this gayest walk in
the world look gayer still than ever.   But a truce to such descriptions, which might carry one far, very far, from the object proposed
in this paper.

I simply wish to introduce to public notice a brief dinner-journal. It has been written with the utmost honesty and simplicity of purpose; and exhibits a picture or table of the development of the human mind under a series of gastronomic experiments, diversified in their nature, and diversified, consequently, in their effects. A man in London has not, for the most part, the opportunity to make these experiments. You are a family man, let us presume, and you live in that metropolis for half a century. You have on Sunday say, a leg of mutton and potatoes for dinner. On Monday you have cold mutton and potatoes. On Tuesday, hashed mutton and potatoes; the hashed mutton being flavoured with little damp triangular pieces of toast, which always surround that charming dish. Well, on Wednesday, the mutton ended, you have beef: the beef undergoes the same alternations of cookery, and disappears. Your life presents a succession of joints, varied every now and then by a bit of fish and some poultry. You drink three glasses of a brandyfied liquor called sherry at dinner; your excellent lady imbibes one. When she has had her glass of port after dinner, she goes upstairs with the children, and you fall asleep in your arm-chair. Some of the most pure and precious enjoyments of life are unknown to you. You eat and drink, but you do not know the *art* of eating and drinking; nay, most probably you despise those who do. "Give me a slice of meat," say you, very likely, "and a fig for your gourmands." You fancy it is very virtuous and manly all this. Nonsense, my good sir; you are indifferent because you are ignorant, because your life is passed in a narrow circle of ideas, and because you are bigotedly blind and pompously callous to the beauties and excellences beyond you.

Sir, RESPECT YOUR DINNER; idolise it, enjoy it properly. You will be by many hours in the week, many weeks in the year and many years in your life the happier if you do.

Don't tell us that it is not worthy of a man. All a man's senses are worthy of employment, and should be cultivated as a duty. The senses are the arts. What glorious feasts does Nature prepare for your eye in animal form, in landscape, and painting. Are you to put out your eyes and not see? What royal dishes of melody does her bounty provide for you in the shape of poetry, music, whether windy or wiry, notes of the human voice, or ravishing song of birds! Are you to stuff your ears with cotton, and vow that the sense of hearing is unmanly?—you obstinate dolt you. No, surely; nor must you be so absurd as to fancy that the art of eating is in any way less worthy than the other two. You like your dinner, man; never be ashamed to say so. If you don't like your victuals, pass on to the next article; but remember that every man who has been worth a fig in this world, as poet, painter, or musician, has had a good appetite and a good taste. Ah, what a poet Byron would have been had he taken his meals properly, and allowed himself to grow fat—if nature intended him to grow fat— and not have physicked his intellect with wretched opium pills and acrid vinegar, that sent his principles to sleep, and turned his feelings sour ! If that man had respected his dinner, he never would have written " Don Juan."

Allons donc ! enough sermonising; let us sit down and fall to at once.

I dined soon after my arrival at a very pleasant Paris club, where daily is provided a dinner for ten persons, that is universally reported to be excellent. Five men in England would have consumed the same amount of victuals, as you will see by the bills of fare :—

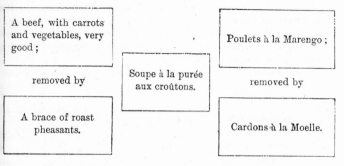

A beef, with carrots and vegetables, very good ;

removed by

A brace of roast pheasants.

Soupe à la purée aux croûtons.

Poulets à la Marengo ;

removed by

Cardons à la Moelle.

Desserts of cheese. Pears and Fontainebleau grapes.
Bordeaux red, and excellent Chablis at discretion.

This dinner was very nicely served. A venerable *maître d'hôtel* in black cutting up neatly the dishes on a trencher at the side-table, and several waiters attending in green coats, red plush tights, and their hair curled. There was a great quantity of light in the room ; some handsome pieces of plated ware ; the pheasants came in with their tails to their backs ; and the smart waiters, with their hair dressed and parted down the middle, gave a pleasant, lively, stylish appearance to the whole affair.

Now, I certainly dined (by the way, I must not forget to mention that we had with the beef some boiled kidney potatoes, very neatly dished up in a napkin)—I certainly dined, I say ; and
13

half-an-hour afterwards felt, perhaps, more at my ease than I should have done had I consulted my own inclinations, and devoured twice the quantity that on this occasion came to my share. But I would rather, as a man not caring for appearances, dine, as a general rule, off a beef-steak for two at the Café Foy, than sit down to take a tenth part of such a meal every day. There was only one man at the table besides your humble servant who did not put water into his wine; and he—I mean the other—was observed by his friends, who exclaimed, "Comment! vous buvez sec," as if to do so was a wonder. The consequence was, that half-a-dozen bottles of wine served for the whole ten of us; and the guests, having despatched their dinner in an hour, skipped lightly away from it, did not stay to ruminate, and to feel uneasy, and to fiddle about the last and penultimate waistcoat button, as we do after a house-dinner at an English club. What was it that made the charm of this dinner?—for pleasant it was. It was the neat and comfortable manner in which it was served; the pheasant-tails had a considerable effect; that snowy napkin coquettishly arranged round the kidneys gave them a *distingué* air; the light and glittering service gave an appearance of plenty and hospitality that sent everybody away contented.

I put down this dinner just to show English and Scotch housekeepers what may be done, and for what price. Say,

		s.	d.
Soup and fresh bread, Beef and carrots } prime cost	. .	2	6
Fowls and sauce	.	3	6
Pheasants (hens)	.	5	0
Grapes, pears, cheese, vegetables	. .	3	0
		14	0

For fifteenpence *par tête* a company of ten persons may have a dinner set before them,—nay, and be made to fancy that they dine well, provided the service is handsomely arranged, that you have a good stock of side-dishes, &c., in your plate-chest, and don't spare the spermaceti.

As for the wine, that depends on yourself. Always be crying out to your friends, "Mr. So-and-so, I don't drink myself, but pray pass the bottle. Tomkins, my boy, help your neighbour, and never mind me. What! Hopkins, are there two of us on the doctor's list? Pass the wine; *Smith* I'm sure won't refuse it;" and so on. A very good plan is to have the butler (or the fellow in the white waistcoat who "behaves as sich") pour out the wine when wanted (in half-glasses, of course), and to make a deuced great noise and shouting, "John, John, why the devil, sir, don't you help Mr. Simkins to another glass of wine?" If you point out Simkins once or twice in this way, depend upon it, *he* won't drink a great quantity of your liquor. You may thus keep your friends from being dangerous, by a thousand innocent manœuvres; and, as I have said before, you may very probably make them believe that they have had a famous dinner. There was only one man in our company of ten the other day who ever thought he had not dined; and what was he? a foreigner,—a man of a discontented inquiring spirit, always carping at things, and never satisfied.

Well, next day I dined *au cinquième* with a family (of Irish extraction, by the way), and what do you think was our dinner for six persons? Why, simply,

> Nine dozen Ostend oysters;
> Soup à la mulligatawny;
> Boiled turkey, with celery sauce;
> Saddle of mutton rôti.
> Removes. Plompouding; croûte de macaroni.
> Vin Beaune ordinaire, volnay, bordeaux, cham-
> pagne, eau chaude, cognac.

I forget the dessert. Alas! in moments of prosperity and plenty, one is often forgetful: I remember the dessert at the Cercle well enough.

A person whom they call in this country an *illustration littéraire*—the editor of a newspaper, in fact—with a very pretty wife, were of the party, and looked at the dinner with a great deal of good-humoured superiority. I declare, upon my honour, that I helped both the illustration and his lady twice to saddle of mutton; and as for the turkey and celery sauce, you should have seen how our host dispensed it to them! They ate the oysters, they ate the soup ("Diable! mais il est poivré!" said the illustration, with tears in his eyes), they ate the turkey, they ate the mutton, they ate the pudding; and what did our hostess say? Why, casting down her eyes gently, and with the modestest air in the world, she said—"There is such a beautiful piece of cold beef in the larder; lo somebody ask for a little slice of it."

Heaven bless her for that speech! I loved and respected her for it; it brought the tears to my eyes. A man who could sneer

at such a sentiment could have neither heart nor good-breeding
Don't you see that it shows

> Simplicity,
> Modesty,
> Hospitality ?

Put these against

> Waiters with their hair curled,
> Pheasants roasted with their tails on,
> A dozen spermaceti candles.

Add them up, I say, oh candid reader, and answer in the sum o
human happiness, which of the two accounts makes the better figure

I declare, I know few things more affecting than that littl
question about the cold beef; and considering calmly our nationa
characteristics, balancing in the scale of quiet thought our de
fects and our merits, am daily more inclined to believe that there
is something in the race of Britons which renders them usually
superior to the French family. This is but one of the traits of
English character that has been occasioned by the use of roast beef.

It is an immense question, that of diet. Look at the two bills
of fare just set down ; the relative consumption of ten animals and
six. What a profound physical and moral difference may we trace
here ! How distinct, from the cradle upwards, must have been
the thoughts, feelings, education of the parties who ordered those
two dinners ! It is a fact which does not admit of a question, that
the French are beginning, since so many English have come among
them, to use beef much more profusely. Everybody at the restaura
teur's orders beef-steak and pommes. Will the national character
slowly undergo a change under the influence of this dish ? Will
the French be more simple ? broader in the shoulders ? less inclined
to brag about military glory and such humbug ? All this in the
dark vista of futurity the spectator may fancy is visible to him, and
the philanthropist cannot but applaud the change. This brings me
naturally to the consideration of the manner of dressing beef-steaks
in this country, and of the merit of that manner.

I dined on a Saturday at the Café Foy, on the Boulevard, in a
private room, with a friend. We had

> Potage julienne, with a little purée in it ;
> Two entrecôtes aux épinards ;
> One perdreau truffé ;
> One fromage roquefort ;
> A bottle of nuits with the beef ;
> A bottle of Sauterne with the partridge.

And perhaps a glass of punch, with a cigar, afterwards: but that is neither here nor there. The insertion of the purée into the julienne was not of my recommending; and if this junction is effected at all, the operation should be performed with the greatest care. If you put too much purée, both soups are infallibly spoiled. A much better plan it is to have your julienne by itself, though I will not enlarge on this point, as the excellent friend with whom I dined may chance to see this notice, and may be hurt at the renewal in print of a dispute which caused a good deal of pain to both of us. By the way, we had half-a-dozen sardines while the dinner was getting ready, eating them with delicious bread and butter, for which this place is famous. Then followed the soup. Why the deuce *would* he have the pu——but never mind. After the soup, we had what I do not hesitate to call the very best beef-steak I ever ate in my life. By the shade of Heliogabalus! as I write about it now, a week after I have eaten it, the old, rich, sweet, piquant, juicy taste comes smacking on my lips again; and I feel something of that exquisite sensation I then had. I am ashamed of the delight which the eating of that piece of meat caused me. G—— and I had quarrelled about the soup (I said so, and don't wish to return to the subject); but when we began on the steak, we looked at each other, and loved each other. We did not speak,—our hearts were too full for that; but we took a bit, and laid down our forks, and looked at one another, and understood each other. There were no two individuals on this wide earth,—no two lovers billing in the shade,—no mother clasping baby to her heart, more supremely happy than we. Every now and then we had a glass of honest, firm, generous Burgundy, that nobly supported the meat. As you may fancy, we did not leave a single morsel of the steak; but when it was done, we put bits of bread into the silver dish, and wistfully sopped up the gravy. I suppose I shall never in this world taste anything so good again. But what then? What if I *did* like it excessively? Was my liking unjust or unmanly? Is my regret now puling or unworthy? No. "Laudo manentem!" as Titmouse says. When it is eaten, I resign myself, and can eat a two-franc dinner at Richard's without ill-humour and without a pang.

Any dispute about the relative excellence of the beef-steak cut from the fillet, as is usual in France, and of the *entrecôte*, must henceforth be idle and absurd. Whenever, my dear young friend, you go to Paris, call at once for the *entrecôte;* the fillet in comparison to it is a poor *fade* lady's meat. What folly, by the way, is that in England which induces us to attach an estimation to the part of the sirloin that is called the Sunday side,—poor, tender, stringy stuff, not comparable to the manly meat on the other side, handsomely garnished with crisp fat, and with a layer of horn! Give the Sunday side to misses and ladies'-maids, for men be the Monday's side, or, better still, a thousand times more succulent and full of flavour—the *ribs of beef*. This is the meat I would eat were I going to do battle with any mortal foe. Fancy a hundred thousand Englishmen, after a meal of stalwart beef ribs, encountering a hundred thousand Frenchmen who had partaken of a trifling collation of soup, turnips, carrots, onions, and Gruyère cheese. Would it be manly to engage at such odds? I say, no.

Passing by Véry's one day, I saw a cadaverous cook with a spatula, thumping a poor beef-steak with all his might. This is not only a horrible cruelty, but an error. They not only beat the beef, moreover, but they soak it in oil. Absurd, disgusting barbarity! Beef so beaten loses its natural spirit; it is too noble for corporal punishment. You may by these tortures and artifices make it soft and greasy, but tender and juicy never.

The landlord of the Café Foy (I have received no sort of consideration from him) knows this truth full well, and follows the simple honest plan; first, to have good meat, and next to hang it a long time. I have instructed him how to do the steaks to a turn, not raw, horribly livid and blue in the midst, as I have seen great flaps of meat (what a shame to think of our fine meat being so treated!), but *cooked* all the way through. Go to the Café Foy then, ask for a BEEF-STEAK À LA TITMARSH, and you will see what a dish will be set before you. I have dwelt upon this point at too much length, perhaps, for some of my readers; but it can't be helped. The truth is, beef is my weakness; and I do declare that I derive more positive enjoyment from the simple viand than from any concoction whatever in the whole cook's cyclopædia.

Always drink red wine with beef-steaks; port, if possible; if not, Burgundy, of not too high a flavour,—good Beaune, say. This fact, which is very likely not known to many persons who, forsooth, are too magnificent to care about their meat and drink,—this simple fact I take to be worth the whole price I shall get for this article.

But to return to dinner. We were left, I think, G—— and I, sopping up the gravy with bits of bread, and declaring that no power on earth could induce us to eat a morsel more that day. At one time, we thought of countermanding the perdreau aux truffes, that to my certain knowledge had been betruffed five days before.

Poor blind mortals that we were; ungrateful to our appetites, needlessly mistrustful and cowardly. A man may do what he dares; nor does he know, until he tries, what the honest appetite will bear. We were kept waiting between the steak and the partridge some ten minutes or so. For the first two or three minutes we lay back in our chairs quite exhausted indeed. Then we began to fiddle with a dish of toothpicks, for want of anything more savoury; then we looked out of the window; then G—— got in a rage, rang the bell violently, and asked, "Pourquoi diable nous fait-on attendre si longtemps?" The waiter grinned. He is a nice good-humoured fellow, Auguste; and I heartily trust that some reader of this may give him a five-franc piece for my sake. Auguste grinned and disappeared.

Presently, we were aware of an odour gradually coming towards us, something musky, fiery, savoury, mysterious,—a hot drowsy smell, that lulls the senses, and yet enflames them,—the *truffes* were coming! Yonder they lie, caverned under the full bosom of the red-legged bird. My hand trembled as, after a little pause, I cut the animal in two. G—— said I did not give him his share of the truffes; I don't believe I did. I spilled some salt into my plate, and a little cayenne pepper—very little: we began, as far as I can remember, the following conversation:—

Gustavus. Chop, chop, chop.

Michael Angelo. Globlobloblob.

G. Gobble.

M. A. Obble.

G. Here's a big one.

M. A. Hobgob. What wine shall we have? I should like some champagne.

G. It's bad here. Have some Sauterne.

M. A. Very well. Hobgobglobglob, &c.

Auguste (opening the Sauterne). Cloo-oo-oo-oop! The cork is out; he pours it into the glass, glock, glock, glock.

Nothing more took place in the way of talk. The poor little partridge was soon a heap of bones—a very little heap. A trufflesque odour was left in the room, but only an odour. Presently, the cheese was brought: the amber Sauterne flask has turned of a sickly green hue; nothing, save half a glass of sediment at the bottom, remained to tell of the light and social spirit that had but one half-hour before inhabited the flask. Darkness fell upon our little chamber; the men in the street began crying, "*Messager! Journal du Soir!*" The bright moon rose glittering over the tiles of the Rue Louis le Grand, opposite, illuminating two glasses of punch that two gentlemen in a small room of the Café Foy did ever and anon raise to their lips. Both were silent; both happy; both were smoking cigars,—for both knew that the soothing plant of Cuba is sweeter to the philosopher after dinner than the prattle of all the women in the world. Women—pshaw! The man who, after dinner—after a good dinner—can think about driving home, and shaving himself by candlelight, and enduing a damp shirt, and a pair of tight glazed pumps to show his cobweb stockings and set his feet in a flame; and, having undergone all this, can get into a cold cab, and drive off to No. 222 Harley Street, where Mrs. Mortimer Smith is at home; where you take off your cloak in a damp dark back parlour, called Mr. Smith's study, and containing, when you arrive, twenty-four ladies' cloaks and tippets, fourteen hats, two pairs of clogs (belonging to two gentlemen of the Middle Temple, who walk for economy, and think dancing at Mrs. Mortimer Smith's the height of enjoyment);—the man who can do all this, and walk, gracefully smiling, into Mrs. Smith's drawing-rooms, where the brown holland bags have been removed from the chandeliers; a man from Kirkman's is thumping on the piano, and Mrs. Smith is standing simpering in the middle of the room, dressed in red, with a bird of paradise in her turban, a tremulous fan in one hand, and the other clutching hold of her little fat gold watch and seals;—the man who, after making his bow to Mrs. Smith, can advance to Miss Jones, in blue crape, and lead her to a place among six other pairs of solemn-looking persons, and whisper *fadaises* to her (at which she cries, "Oh fie, you naughty man! how can you?"), and look at Miss Smith's red shoulders struggling out of her gown, and her mottled elbows that a pair of crumpled kid gloves leave in a state of delicious nature; and, after having gone through certain mysterious quadrille figures with her, lead her back to her mamma, who has just seized a third glass of muddy negus from the black footman;—the man who can do all this may do it, and go hang, for me! And many such men there be, my Gustavus, in yonder dusky London city. Be it ours, my dear friend, when the day's labour and repast are done, to lie and ruminate calmly; to watch the bland cigar smoke as it rises gently ceiling-wards; to be idle in body as well as mind; not to kick our heels madly in quadrilles, and puff and pant in senseless gallopades: let us appreciate the joys of idleness; let us give a loose to silence; and having enjoyed this, the best dessert after a goodly dinner, at close of eve, saunter slowly home.

As the dinner above described drew no less than three franc pieces out of my purse, I determined to economise for the next few days, and either to be invited out to dinner, or else to partake of some repast at a small charge, such as one may have here. I

had on the day succeeding the truffled partridge a dinner for a
shilling, viz. :—

> Bifsteck aux pommes (heu quantum mutatus ab illo !)
> Galantine de volaille,
> Fromage de Gruyère,
> Demi-bouteille du vin très-vieux de Mâcon ou Chablis,
> Pain à discrétion.

This dinner, my young friend, was taken about half-past two
o'clock in the day, and was, in fact, a breakfast,—a breakfast taken
at a two-franc house, in the Rue Haute Vivienne ; it was certainly a
sufficient dinner : I certainly was not hungry for all the rest of the
day. Nay, the wine was decently good, as almost all wine is in
the morning, if one had the courage or the power to drink it.
You see many honest English families marching into these two-franc
eating-houses, at five o'clock, and fancy they dine in great luxury.
Returning to England, however, they inform their friends that the
meat in France is not good ; that the fowls are very small, and
black ; the kidneys very tough ; the partridges and fruit have no
taste in them, and the soup is execrably thin. A dinner at
Williams's, in the Old Bailey, is better than the best of these ; and
therefore had the English Cockney better remain at Williams's
than judge the great nation so falsely.

The worst of these two-franc establishments is a horrid air of
shabby elegance which distinguishes them. At some of them, they
will go the length of changing your knife and fork with every dish ;
they have grand chimney-glasses, and a fine lady at the counter,
and fine arabesque paintings on the walls ; they give you your
soup in a battered dish of plated ware, which has served its best
time, most likely, in a first-rate establishment, and comes here to
étaler its second-hand splendour amongst amateurs of a lower grade.
I fancy the very meat that is served to you has undergone the
same degradation, and that some of the mouldy cutlets that are
offered to the two-franc epicures lay once plump and juicy in Véry's
larder. Much better is the sanded floor and the iron fork ! Homely
neatness is the charm of poverty : elegance should belong to wealth
alone. There is a very decent place where you dine for thirty-two
sous in the Passage Choiseul. You get your soup in china bowls ;
they don't change your knife and fork, but they give you very fit
portions of meat and potatoes, and mayhap a herring with mustard
sauce, a dish of apple fritters, a dessert of stewed prunes, and a
pint of drinkable wine, as I have proved only yesterday.

After two such banyan days, I allowed myself a little feasting ;

and as nobody persisted in asking me to dinner, I went off to the "Trois Frères" by myself, and dined in that excellent company.

I would recommend a man who is going to dine by himself here, to reflect well before he orders soup for dinner.

My notion is, that you eat as much after soup as without it, but you *don't eat with the same appetite.*

Especially if you are a healthy man, as I am—deuced hungry at five o'clock. My appetite runs away with me; and if I order soup (which is always enough for two), I invariably swallow the whole of it; and the greater portion of my *petit pain*, too, before my second dish arrives.

The best part of a pint of julienne, or purée à la Condé, is very well for a man who has only one dish besides to devour; but not for you and me, who like our fish and our *rôti* of game or meat as well.

Oysters you may eat. They do, for a fact, prepare one to go through the rest of a dinner properly. Lemon and cayenne pepper is the word, depend on it, and a glass of white wine braces you up for what is to follow.

French restaurateur dinners are intended, however, for two people, at least; still better for three; and require a good deal of thought before you can arrange them for one.

Here, for instance, is a recent *menu :—*

Trois Frères Provençaux.

	f.	c.
Pain	0	25
Beaune première	3	0
Purée à la Créci	0	75
Turbot aux capres	1	75
Quart poulet aux truffes	2	25
Champignons à la Provençale	1	25
Gelée aux pommes	1	25
Cognac	0	30
	10	80

A heavy bill for a single man; and a heavy dinner, too; for I have said before I have a great appetite, and when a thing is put before me I eat it. At Brussels I once ate fourteen dishes; and have seen a lady, with whom I was in love, at the table of a German grand-duke, eat seventeen dishes. This is a positive, though disgusting fact. Up to the first twelve dishes she had a very good chance of becoming Mrs. Titmarsh, but I have lost sight of her since.

Well, then, I say to you, if you have self-command enough to send away half your soup, order some ; but you are a poor creature if you do, after all. If you are a man, and have *not* that self-command, don't have any. The Frenchmen cannot live without it, but I say to you that you are better than a Frenchman. I would lay even money that you who are reading this are more than five feet seven in height, and weigh eleven stone ; while a Frenchman is five feet four, and does not weigh nine. The Frenchman has after his soup a dish of vegetables, where you have one of meat. You are a different and superior animal—a French-beating animal (the history of hundreds of years has shown you to be so) ; you must have, to keep up that superior weight and sinew, which is the secret of your superiority—as for public institutions, bah !—you must have, I say, simpler, stronger, more succulent food.

Eschew the soup, then, and have the fish up at once. It is the best to begin with fish, if you like it, as every epicure and honest man should, simply boiled or fried in the English fashion, and not tortured and bullied with oil, onions, wine, and herbs, as in Paris it is frequently done.

Turbot with lobster-sauce is too much ; turbot à la Hollandaise vulgar ; sliced potatoes swimming in melted butter are a mean concomitant for a noble, simple, liberal fish : turbot with capers is the thing. The brisk little capers relieve the dulness of the turbot ; the melted butter is rich, bland, and calm—it *should be*, that is to say ; not that vapid watery mixture that I see in London ; not oiled butter, as the Hollanders have it, but melted, with plenty of thickening matter : I don't know how to do it, but I know it when it is good.

They melt butter well at the " Rocher de Cancale," and at the " Frères."

Well, this turbot was very good ; not so well, of course, as one gets it in London, and dried rather in the boiling ; which can't be helped, unless you are a Lucullus or a Cambacérès of a man, and can afford to order one for yourself. This *grandeur d'âme* is very rare ; my friend Tom Willows is almost the only man I know who possessed it. Yes, * * * one of the wittiest men in London, I once knew to take the whole *intérieur* of a diligence (six places), because he was a little unwell. Ever since I have admired that man. He understands true economy ; a mean extravagant man would have contented himself with a single place, and been unwell in conse-quence. How I am rambling from my subject, however ! The fish was good, and I ate up every single scrap of it, sucking the bones and fins curiously. That is the deuce of an appetite, it *must* be satisfied ; and if you were to put a roast donkey before me, with the promise of a haunch of venison afterwards, I believe I should eat the greater part of the long-eared animal.

A pint of purée à la Créci, a pain de gruau, a slice of turbot— a man should think about ordering his bill, for he has had enough dinner ; but no, we are creatures of superstition and habit, and must have one regular course of meat. Here comes the poulet à la Marengo : I hope they've given me the wing.

No such thing. The poulet à la Marengo aux truffes is bad— too oily by far ; the truffles are not of this year, as they should be, for there are cartloads in town : they are poor in flavour, and have only been cast into the dish a minute before it was brought to table, and what is the consequence? They do not flavour the meat in the least ; some faint trufflesque savour you may get as you are crunching each individual root, but that is all, and that all not worth the having; for as nothing is finer than a good truffle, in like manner nothing is meaner than a bad one. It is merely pompous, windy, and pretentious, like those scraps of philosophy with which a certain eminent novelist decks out his meat.

A mushroom, thought I, is better a thousand times than these tough flavourless roots. I finished every one of them, however, and the fine fat capon's thigh which they surrounded. It was a disappointment not to get a wing, to be sure. They *always* give me legs ; but, after all, with a little good-humour and philosophy, a leg of a fine Mans capon may be found very acceptable. How plump and tender the rogue's thigh is ! his very drumstick is as fat as the calf of a London footman ; and the sinews, which puzzle one so over the lean black hen-legs in London, are miraculously whisked away from the limb before me. Look at it now ! Half-a-dozen cuts with the knife, and yonder lies the bone—white, large, stark naked, without a morsel of flesh left upon it, solitary in the midst of a pool of melted butter.

How good the Burgundy smacks after it ! I always drink Burgundy at this house, and that not of the best. It is my firm opinion that a third-rate Burgundy, and a third-rate claret— Beaune and Larose, for instance, are *better* than the best. The Bordeaux enlivens, the Burgundy invigorates ; stronger drink only inflames ; and where a bottle of good Beaune only causes a man to feel a certain manly warmth of benevolence—a glow something like that produced by sunshine and gentle exercise—a bottle of Chambertin will set all your frame in a fever, swell the extremities, and cause the pulses to throb. Chambertin should *never* be handed round more than twice ; and I recollect to this moment

the headache I had after drinking a bottle and a half of Romanée-
Gélée, for which this house is famous. Somebody else *paid* for
the—(no other than you, O Gustavus! with whom I hope to have
many a tall dinner on the same charges)—but 'twas in our hot
youth, ere experience had taught us that moderation was happiness, and had shown us that it is absurd to be guzzling wine at
fifteen francs a bottle.

By the way, I may here mention a story relating to some of
Blackwood's men, who dined at this very house. Fancy the fellows
trying claret, which they voted sour; then Burgundy, at which
they made wry faces, and finished the evening with brandy and
lunel ! This is what men call eating a French dinner. Willows
and I dined at the " Rocher," and an English family there feeding
ordered—mutton chops and potatoes. Why not, in these cases,
stay at home ? Chops are better chops in England (the best chops
in the world are to be had at the Reform Club) than in France.
What could literary men mean by ordering lunel ? I always
rather liked the descriptions of eating in the *Noctes*. They were
gross in all cases, absurdly erroneous in many ; but there was
manliness about them, and strong evidence of a great, though mis-
directed and uneducated, genius for victuals.

Mushrooms, thought I, are better than those tasteless truffles,
and so ordered a dish to try. You know what a *Provençale* sauce
is, I have no doubt ?—a rich savoury mixture of garlic and oil ;
which, with a little cayenne pepper and salt, impart a pleasant
taste to the plump little mushrooms, that can't be described but
may be thought of with pleasure.

The only point was, how will they agree with me to-morrow
morning ? for the fact is, I had eaten an immense quantity of
them, and began to be afraid ! Suppose we go and have a glass
of punch and a cigar ! Oh, glorious garden of the Palais Royal !
your trees are leafless now, but what matters ? Your alleys are
damp, but what of that ? All the windows are blazing with light
and merriment ; at least two thousand happy people are pacing
up and down the colonnades ; cheerful sounds of money chinking
are heard as you pass the changers' shops ; bustling shouts of
" Garçon ! " and " V'là, Monsieur ! " come from the swinging doors
of the restaurateurs. Look at that group of soldiers gaping at
Véfour's window, where lie lobsters, pineapples, fat truffle-stuffed
partridges, which make me almost hungry again. I wonder
whether those three fellows with mustachios and a toothpick
apiece have had a dinner, or only a toothpick. When the
" Trois Frères " used to be on the first-floor, and had a door
leading into the Rue de Valois, as well as one into the garden,

I recollect seeing three men with toothpicks mount the stair from the street, descend the stair into the garden, and give themselves as great airs as if they had dined for a napoleon a head. The rogues are lucky if they have had a sixteen-sous dinner; and the next time I dine abroad, I am resolved to have one myself. I never understood why Gil Blas grew so mighty squeamish in the affair of the cat and the hare. Hare is best, but why should not cat be good?

Being on the subject of bad dinners, I may as well ease my mind of one that occurred to me some few days back. When walking in the Boulevard, I met my friend, Captain Hopkinson, of the half-pay, looking very hungry, and indeed going to dine. In most cases one respects the dictum of a half-pay officer regarding a dining-house. He knows as a general rule where the fat of the land lies, and how to take his share of that fat in the most economical manner.

"I tell you what I do," says Hopkinson; "I allow myself fifteen francs a week for dinner (I count upon being asked out twice a week), and so have a three-franc dinner at Richard's, where, for the extra francs, they give me an excellent bottle of wine, and make me comfortable."

"Why shouldn't they?" I thought. "Here is a man who has served his country, and no doubt knows a thing when he sees it." We made a party of four, therefore, and went to the Captain's place to dine.

We had a private room *au second*; a very damp and dirty private room, with a faint odour of stale punch, and dingy glasses round the walls.

We had a soup of purée aux croûtons; a very dingy dubious soup, indeed, thickened, I fancy, with brown paper, and flavoured with the same.

At the end of the soup, Monsieur Landlord came upstairs very kindly, and gave us each a pinch of snuff out of a gold snuff-box.

We had four portions of anguille à la Tartare, very good and fresh (it is best in these places to eat freshwater fish). Each portion was half the length of a man's finger. Dish one was despatched in no time, and we began drinking the famous wine that our guide recommended. I have cut him ever since. It was four-sous wine,— weak, vapid, watery stuff, of the most unsatisfactory nature.

We had four portions of gigot aux haricots—four flaps of bleeding tough meat, cut unnaturally (that is, with the grain: the French gash the meat in parallel lines with the bone). We ate these up as we might, and the landlord was so good as to come up again and favour us with a pinch from his gold box.

With wonderful unanimity, as we were told the place was famous for civet de lièvre, we ordered civet de lièvre for four.

It came up, but we couldn't—really we couldn't. We were obliged to have extra dishes, and pay extra. Gustavus had a mayonnaise of crayfish, and half a fowl; I fell to work upon my cheese, as usual, and availed myself of the discretionary bread. We went away disgusted, wretched, unhappy. We had had for our three francs bad bread, bad meat, bad wine. And there stood the landlord at the door (and be hanged to him!) grinning and offering his box.

We don't speak to Hopkinson any more now when we meet him. How can you trust or be friendly with a man who deceives you in this miserable way?

What is the moral to be drawn from this dinner? It is evident. Avoid pretence; mistrust shabby elegance; cut your coat according to your cloth; if you have but a few shillings in your pocket, aim only at those humble and honest meats which your small store will purchase. At the Café Foy, for the same money, I might have had

	f.	s.
A delicious entrecôte and potatoes	1	5
A pint of excellent wine	0	10
A little bread (meaning a great deal)	0	5
A dish of stewed kidneys	1	0
	3	0

Or at Paolo's:

A bread (as before)	0	5
A heap of macaroni, or raviuoli	0	15
A Milanese cutlet	1	0
A pint of wine	0	10

And ten sous for any other luxury your imagination could suggest. The raviuoli and the cutlets are admirably dressed at Paolo's. Does any healthy man need more?

These dinners, I am perfectly aware, are by no means splendid ; and I might, with the most perfect ease, write you out a dozen bills of fare, each more splendid and piquant than the other, in which all the luxuries of the season should figure. But the remarks here set down are the result of experience, not fancy, and intended only for persons in the middling classes of life. Very few men can afford to pay more than five francs daily for dinner. Let us calmly, then, consider what enjoyment may be had for those five francs; how, by economy on one day, we may venture upon luxury the next; how, by a little forethought and care, we may be happy on all days. We knew and studied this cheap philosophy of life better than old Horace before quoted. . Sometimes (when in luck) he cherupped over cups that were fit for an archbishop's supper; sometimes he philosophised over his own *ordinaire* at his own farm. How affecting is the last ode of the first book :—

To his serving-boy.	*Ad ministram.*
Persicos odi,	Dear Lucy, you know what my wish is,—
Puer, apparatus;	I hate all your Frenchified fuss:
Displicent nexæ	Your silly entrées and made dishes
Philyrâ coronæ :	Were never intended for us.
Mitte sectari	No footman in lace and in ruffles
Rosa quo locorum	Need dangle behind my arm-chair ;
Sera moretur.	And never mind seeking for truffles,
	Although they be ever so rare.
Simplici myrto	But a plain leg of mutton, my Lucy,
Nihil allabores	I pr'ythee get ready at three :
Sedulus curæ :	Have it smoking, and tender, and juicy,
Neque te ministrum	And what better meat can there be ?
Dedecet myrtus,	And when it has feasted the master,
Neque me sub arctâ	'Twill amply suffice for the maid ;
Vite bibentem.	Meanwhile I will smoke my canaster,
	And tipple my ale in the shade.

Not that this is the truth entirely and for ever. Horatius Flaccus was too wise to dislike a good thing; but it is possible that the Persian apparatus was on that day beyond his means, and so he contented himself with humble fare.

A gentleman, by-the-bye, has just come to Paris to whom I am very kind ; and who will, in all human probability, between this and next month, ask me to a dinner at the " Rocher de Cancale." If so, something may occur worth writing about; or if you are anxious to hear more on the subject, send me over a sum to my address, to be laid out for you exclusively in eating. I give you my honour I will do you justice, and account for every farthing of it.

One of the most absurd customs at present in use is that of giving your friend—when some piece of good-luck happens to him, such as an appointment as Chief Judge of Owhyhee, or King's advocate to Timbuctoo—of giving your friend, because, forsooth, he may have been suddenly elevated from £200 a year to £2000, an enormous dinner of congratulation.

Last year, for instance, when our friend, Fred Jowling, got his place of Commissioner at Quashumaboo, it was considered absolutely necessary to give the man a dinner, and some score of us had to pay about fifty shillings apiece for the purpose. I had, so help me, Moses! but three guineas in the world at that period; and out of this sum the *bienséances* compelled me to sacrifice five-sixths, to feast myself in company of a man gorged with wealth, rattling sovereigns in his pocket as if they had been so much dross, and capable of treating us all without missing the sum he might expend on us.

Jow himself allowed, as I represented the case to him, that the arrangement *was* very hard; but represented fairly enough, that this was one of the sacrifices that a man of the world, from time to time, is called to make. '"You, my dear Titmarsh," said he, "know very well that I don't care for these grand entertainments" (the rogue, he is a five-bottle man, and just the most finished *gourmet* of my acquaintance!); "you know that I am perfectly convinced of your friendship for me, though you join in the dinner or not, but—it would look rather queer if you backed out,—*it would look rather queer.*" Jow said this in such an emphatic way, that I saw I must lay down my money; and accordingly Mr. Lovegrove of Blackwall, for a certain quantity of iced punch, champagne, cider cup, fish, flesh, and fowl, received the last of my sovereigns.

At the beginning of the year Bolter got a place too—Judge Advocate in the Topinambo Islands, of £3000 a year, which, he said, was a poor remuneration in consideration of *the practice* which he gave up in town. He may have practised on his laundress, but for anything else I believe the man never had a client in his life.

However, on his way to Topinambo—by Marseilles, Egypt, the Desert, the Persian Gulf, and so on—Bolter arrived in Paris; and I saw from his appearance, and his manner of shaking hands with me, and the peculiar way in which he talked about the "Rocher de Cancale," that he expected we were to give him a dinner, as we had to Jowling.

There were four friends of Bolter's in the capital besides myself, and among us the dinner question was mooted : we agreed that it should be a simple dinner of ten francs a head, and this was the bill of fare :—

1. Oysters (common), nice.
2. Oysters, green of Marennes (very good).
3. Potage, purée de gibier (very fair).

As we were English, they instantly then served us—

4. Sole en matelotte Normande (comme ça).
5. Turbot à la crème au gratin (excellent).

6. Jardinière cutlets (particularly seedy).

7. Poulet à la Marengo (very fair, but why the deuce is one always to be pestered by it ?).

8. }
9. } (Entrées of some kind, but a blank in my memory.)

10. A rôt of chevreuil.

11. Ditto of éperlans (very hot, crisp, and nice).

12. Ditto of partridges (quite good and plump).

13. Pointes d'asperges.

14. Champignons à la Provençale (the most delicious mushrooms I ever tasted).

15. Pineapple jelly.

16. Blanc, or red mange.

17. Pencacks. Let everybody who goes to the "Rocher" order these pancakes ; they are arranged with jelly inside, rolled up between various *couches* of vermicelli, flavoured with a *leetle* wine ; and, by everything sacred, the most delightful meat possible.

18. Timbale of macaroni.

The jellies and sucreries should have been mentioned in the dessert, and there were numberless plates of trifles, which made the table look very pretty, but need not be mentioned here.

The dinner was not a fine one, as you see. No rarities, no truffles even, no mets de primeur, though there were peas and asparagus in the market at a pretty fair price. But with rarities no man has any business except he have a colossal fortune. Hothouse strawberries, asparagus, &c., are, as far as my experience goes, most *fade*, mean, and tasteless meats. Much better to have a simple dinner of twenty dishes, and content therewith, than to look for impossible splendours and Apician morsels.

In respect of wine. Let those who go to the "Rocher" take my advice and order Madeira. They have here some pale old East India very good. How they got it is a secret, for the Parisians do not know good Madeira when they see it. Some very fair strong young wine may be had at the Hôtel des Américains, in the Rue Saint Honoré; as, indeed, all West India produce—pineapple rum, for instance. I may say, with confidence, that I never knew what rum was until I tasted this at Paris.

But to the "Rocher." The Madeira was the best wine served ; though some Burgundy, handed round in the course of dinner, and a bottle of Montrachet, similarly poured out to us, were very fair. The champagne was decidedly not good—poor, inflated, thin stuff. They say the drink we swallow in England is not genuine wine, but brandy loaded and otherwise doctored for the English market :

but, ah, what superior wine! *Au reste*, the French will not generally pay the money for the wine; and it therefore is carried from an ungrateful country to more generous climes, where it is better appreciated. We had claret and speeches after dinner; and very possibly some of the persons present made free with a jug of hot water, a few lumps of sugar, and the horrid addition of a glass of cognac. There can be no worse practice than this. After a dinner of eighteen dishes, in which you have drunk at least thirty-six glasses of wine—when the stomach is full, the brain heavy, the hands and feet inflamed—when the claret begins to pall—you, forsooth, must gorge yourself with brandy and water, and puff filthy cigars. For shame! Who ever does it? Does a gentleman drink brandy and water? Does a man who mixes in the society of the loveliest half of humanity befoul himself by tobacco-smoke? Fie, fie! avoid the practice. I indulge in it always myself; but that is no reason why you, a young man entering into the world, should degrade yourself in any such way. No, no, my dear lad, never refuse an evening party, and avoid tobacco as you would the upas plant.

By the way, not having my purse about me when the above dinner was given, I was constrained to borrow from Bolter, whom I knew more intimately than the rest; and nothing grieved me more than to find, on calling at his hotel four days afterwards, that he had set off by the mail post for Marseilles. Friend of my youth, dear dear Bolter! if haply this trifling page should come before thine eyes, weary of perusing the sacred rolls of Themis in thy far-off island in the Indian Sea, thou wilt recall our little dinner in the little room of the Cancalian Coffee-house, and think for a while of thy friend!

Let us now mention one or two places that the Briton, on his arrival here, should frequent or avoid. As a quiet dear house, where there are some of the best rooms in Paris—always the best meat, fowls, vegetables, &c.—we may specially recommend Monsieur Voisin's café, opposite the Church of the Assumption. A very decent and lively house of restauration is that at the corner of the Rue du Faubourg Montmartre, on the Boulevard. I never yet had a good dinner at Véfour's; *something* is always *manqué* at the place. The grand Vatel is worthy of note, as cheap, pretty, and quiet. All the English houses gentlemen may frequent who are so inclined; but though the writer of this has many times dined for sixteen sous at Catcomb's, cheek by jowl with a French chasseur or a labourer, he has, he confesses, an antipathy to enter into the confidence of a footman or groom of his own country.

A gentleman who purchases pictures in this town was lately

waited upon by a lady, who said she had in her possession one of the greatest rarities in the world,—a picture admirable, too, as a work of art,—no less than an original portrait of Shakspeare, by his comrade, the famous John Davis. The gentleman rushed off immediately to behold the wonder, and saw a head, rudely but vigorously painted on panel, about twice the size of life, with a couple of hooks drawn through the top part of the board, under which was written—

THE WILLIAM SHAKSPEARE,
BY JOHN DAVIS.

"Voyez-vous, Monsieur," said the lady; "il n'y a plus de doute. Le portrait de Shakspeare, du célèbre Davis, et signé même de lui!"

I remember it used to hang up in a silent little street in the Latin quarter, near an old convent, before a quaint old quiet tavern that I loved. It was pleasant to see the old name written up in a strange land, and the well-known friendly face greeting one. There was a quiet little garden at the back of the tavern, and famous good roast beef, clean rooms, and English beer. Where are you now, John Davis? Could not the image of thy august patron preserve thy house from ruin, or rally the faithful around it? Are you unfortunate, Davis? Are you a bankrupt? Let us hope not. I swear to thee, that when, one sunny afternoon, I saw the ensign of thy tavern, I loved thee for thy choice, and doused my cap on entering the porch, and looked around, and thought all friends were here.

In the queer old pleasant novel of the "Spiritual Quixote" honest Tugwell, the Sancho of the story, relates a Warwickshire legend, which at the time Graves wrote was not much more than a hundred years old: and by which it appears that the owner of New Place was a famous jesting gentleman, and used to sit at his gate of summer evenings, cutting the queerest merriest jokes with all the passers-by. I have heard from a Warwickshire clergyman that the legend still exists in the country; and Ward's "Diary" says that Master Shakspeare died of a surfeit, brought on by carousing with a literary friend who had come to visit him from London. And wherefore not? Better to die of good wine and good company than of slow disease and doctors' doses. Some geniuses live on sour misanthropy, and some on meek milk and water. Let us not deal too hardly with those that are of a jovial sort, and indulge in the decent practice of the cup and the platter.

A word or two, by way of conclusion, may be said about the

numerous pleasant villages in the neighbourhood of Paris, or rather
of the eating and drinking to be found in the taverns of those
suburban spots. At Versailles, Monsieur Duboux, at the Hôtel
des Reservoirs, has a good cook and cellars, and will gratify you
with a heavier bill than is paid at Véry's and the "Rocher." On
the beautiful terrace of Saint Germain, looking over miles of river
and vineyard, of fair villages basking in the meadows, and great
tall trees stretching wide round about, you may sit in the open air
of summer evenings, and see the white spires of Saint Denis rising
in the distance, and the grey arches of Marly to the right, and
before you the city of Paris with innumerable domes and towers.

Watching these objects, and the setting sun gorgeously illumin-
ing the heavens and them, you may have an excellent dinner served
to you by the *chef* of Messire Gallois, who at present owns the
pavilion where Louis XIV. was born. The *maître d'hotel* is from
the "Rocher," and told us that he came out to Saint Germain for
the sake of the air. The only drawback to the entertainment is,
that the charges are as atrociously high in price as the dishes provided are small in quantity ; and dining at this pavilion on the
15th of April, at a period when a *botte* of asparagus at Paris
cost only three francs, the writer of this and a chosen associate
had to pay seven francs for about the third part of a *botte* of
asparagus, served up to them by Messire Gallois.

Facts like these ought not to go unnoticed. Therefore let the
readers of *Fraser's Magazine* who propose a visit to Paris, take
warning by the unhappy fate of the person now addressing them,
and avoid the place or not, as they think fit. A bad dinner does
no harm to any human soul, and the philosopher partakes of such
with easy resignation ; but a bad and dear dinner is enough to
raise the anger of any man, however naturally sweet-tempered, and
he is bound to warn his acquaintance of it.

With one parting syllable in praise of the "Marroniers" at
Bercy, where you get capital eels, fried gudgeons fresh from the
Seine, and excellent wine of the ordinary kind, this discourse is
here closed. " En telle ou meilleure pensée, Beuueurs très illustres
(car à vous non à aultres sont dédiés cès escriptz), reconfortez vostre
malheur, et beuuez fraiz si faire se peult."

MEN AND COATS

THERE is some peculiar influence, which no doubt the reader has remarked in his own case, for it has been sung by ten thousand poets, or versifying persons, whose ideas you adopt, if perchance, as is barely possible, you have none of your own—there is, I say, a certain balmy influence in the spring-time, which brings a rush of fresh dancing blood into the veins of all nature, and causes it to wear a peculiarly festive and sporting look. Look at the old Sun,—how pale he was all the winter through! Some days he was so cold and wretched he would not come out at all,—he would not leave his bed till eight o'clock, and retired to rest, the old sluggard! at four; but lo! comes May, and he is up at five,—he feels, like the rest of us, the delicious vernal influence; he is always walking abroad in the fresh air, and his jolly face lights up anew! Remark the trees; they have dragged through the shivering winter-time without so much as a rag to cover them, but about May they feel obligated to follow the mode, and come out in a new suit of green. The meadows, in like manner, appear invested with a variety of pretty spring fashions, not only covering their backs with a bran-new glossy suit, but sporting a world of little coquettish ornamental gimcracks that are suited to the season. This one covers his robe with the most delicate twinkling white daisies; that tricks himself out with numberless golden cowslips, or decorates his bosom with a bunch of dusky violets. Birds sing and make love; bees wake and make honey; horses and men leave off their shaggy winter clothing and turn out in fresh coats. The only animal that does not feel the power of spring is that selfish, silent, and cold-blooded beast, the oyster, who shuts himself up for the best months of the year, and with whom the climate disagrees.

Some people have wondered how it is that what is called "the season" in London should not begin until spring. What an absurd subject for wondering at! How *could* the London season begin at any other time? How could the great, black, bilious, overgrown city, stifled by gas, and fogs, and politics, ever hope to have a season at all, unless nature with a violent effort came to its aid

about Easter-time, and infused into it a little spring blood? The
town of London feels then the influences of the spring, and salutes
it after its fashion. The parks are green for about a couple of
months. Lady Smigsmag, and other leaders of the *ton*, give their
series of grand parties; Gunter and Grange come forward with
iced-creams and champagnes; ducks and green-peas burst out;
the river Thames blossoms with whitebait; and Alderman Birch
announces the arrival of fresh lively turtle. If there are no birds
to sing and make love, as in country places, at least there are
coveys of opera-girls that frisk and hop about airily, and Rubini
and Lablache to act as a couple of nightingales. "A lady of
fashion remarked," says Dyson, in the *Morning Post*, "that for all
persons pretending to hold a position in genteel society,"—I forget
the exact words, but the sense of them remains indelibly engraven
upon my mind,—"for any one pretending to take a place in genteel
society two things are *indispensable*. And what are these?—a
BOUQUET AND AN EMBROIDERED POCKET-HANDKERCHIEF." This
is a self-evident truth. Dyson does not furnish the bouquets—he
is not a market-gardener—he is not the goddess Flora; but, a
townman, he knows what the season requires, and furnishes his
contribution to it. The lilies of the field are not more white and
graceful than his embroidered nose ornaments, and with a little
eau des cent milles fleurs, not more fragrant. Dyson knows that
pocket-handkerchiefs are necessary, and has "an express from
Longchamps" to bring them over.

Whether they are picked from ladies' pockets by Dyson's
couriers, who then hurry breathless across the Channel with them,
no one need ask. But the gist of Dyson's advertisement, and of all
the preceding remarks, is this great truth, which need not be carried
out further by any illustrations from geography or natural history,—
that in the spring-time all nature renews itself. There is not a
country newspaper published in England that does not proclaim
the same fact. Madame Hoggin informs the nobility and gentry
of Penzance that her new and gigantic stock of Parisian fashions
has just arrived from London. Mademoiselle M'Whirter begs to
announce to the *haut-ton* in the environs of John-o'-Groat's that
she has this instant returned from Paris, with her dazzling and
beautiful collection of spring fashions.

In common with the birds, the trees, the meadows,—in common
with the Sun, with Dyson, with all nature, in fact, I yielded to
the irresistible spring impulse—*homo sum, nihil humani a me
alienum*, &c.—I acknowledged the influence of the season, and
ordered a new coat, waistcoat, and tr—— in short, a new suit.
Now, having worn it for a few days, and studied the effect which

it has upon the wearer, I thought that perhaps an essay upon new clothes and their influence might be attended with some profit both to the public and the writer.

One thing is certain. A man does not have a new suit of clothes every day; and another general proposition may be advanced, that a man in sporting a coat for the first time is either

agreeably affected, or
disagreeably affected, or
not affected at all,—

which latter case I don't believe. There is no man, however accustomed to new clothes, but must feel some sentiment of pride in assuming them, — no philosopher, however calm, but must remark the change of raiment. Men consent to wear old clothes for ever,—nay, feel a pang at parting with them for new; but the first appearance of a new garment is always attended with exultation.

Even the feeling of shyness, which makes a man ashamed of his splendour, is a proof of his high sense of it. What causes an individual to sneak about in corners and shady places, to avoid going out in new clothes of a Sunday, lest he be mistaken for a snob? Sometimes even to go the length of ordering his servant to powder his new coat with sand, or to wear it for a couple of days, and remove the gloss thereof? Are not these manœuvres proofs of the effects of new coats upon mankind in general?

As this notice will occupy at least ten pages (for a reason that may be afterwards mentioned) I intend, like the great philosophers who have always sacrificed themselves for the public good, imbibing diseases, poisons, and medicines, submitting to operations, inhaling asphyxiations, &c., in order that they might note in themselves the particular phenomena of the case,—in like manner, I say, I intend to write this essay in five several coats, viz. :—

1. My old single-breasted black frock-coat, with patches at the elbows, made to go into mourning for William IV.

2. My double-breasted green ditto, made last year but one, and still very good, but rather queer about the lining, and snowy in the seams.

3. My grand black dress-coat, made by Messrs. Sparding and Spohrer, of Conduit Street, in 1836. A little scouring and renovating have given it a stylish look even now; and it was always a splendid cut.

4. My worsted-net jacket that my uncle Harry gave me on his departure for Italy. This jacket is wadded inside with a

wool like that one makes Welsh wigs of; and though not handsome, amazing comfortable, with pockets all over.

5. MY NEW FROCK-COAT.

Now, will the reader be able to perceive any difference in the style of writing of each chapter? I fancy I see it myself clearly; and am convinced that the new frock-coat chapter will be infinitely more genteel, spruce, and glossy than the woollen-jacket chapter; which, again, shall be more comfortable than the poor, seedy, patched William-the-Fourth's black frock chapter. The double-breasted green one will be dashing, manly, free-and-easy; and though not fashionable, yet with a well-bred look. The grand black-dress chapter will be solemn and grave, devilish tight about the waist, abounding in bows and shrugs, and small talk; it will have a great odour of bohea and pound-cake; perhaps there will be a faint whiff of negus; and the tails will whisk up in a quadrille at the end, or sink down, mayhap, on a supper-table bench before a quantity of trifles, lobster-salads, and champagnes; and near a lovely blushing white satin skirt, which is continually crying out, "O you ojous creature!" or, "O you naughty satirical man, you!" "And do you really believe Miss Moffat dyes her hair?" "And have you read that sweet thing in the 'Keepsake' by Lord Diddle?" "Well, only one *leetle* leetle drop, for Mamma will scold;" and "O you horrid Mr. Titmarsh, you have filled my glass, I declare!" Dear white satin skirt, what pretty shoulders and eyes you have! what a nice white neck, and bluish-mottled, round, innocent arms! how fresh you are and candid! and ah, my dear, what a fool you are!

.   .   .   .

I don't have so many coats nowadays as in the days of hot youth, when the figure was more elegant, and credit, mayhap, more plenty; and, perhaps, this accounts for the feeling of unusual exultation that comes over me as I assume this one. Look at the skirts how they are shining in the sun, with a delicate gloss upon them,— that evanescent gloss that passes away with the first freshness of the coat, as the bloom does from the peach. A friend meets you,—he salutes you cordially, but looks puzzled for a moment at the change in your appearance. "I have it!" says Jones. "Hobson, my boy, I congratulate you,—a new coat, and very neat cut,—puce-coloured frock, brown silk lining, brass buttons, and velvet collar,— quite novel, and quiet and genteel at the same time." You say, "Pooh, Jones! do you think so, though?" and at the same time turn round just to give him a view of the back, in which there is not a single wrinkle. You find suddenly that you must buy a new stock; that your old Berlin gloves will never do; and that a pair of three-and-sixpenny kids are absolutely necessary. You find your boots are cruelly thick, and fancy that the attention of the world is accurately divided between the new frock-coat and the patch on your great toe. It is very odd that that patch did not annoy you yesterday in the least degree,—that you looked with a good-natured grin at the old sausage-fingered Berlin gloves, bulging out at the end and concaved like spoons. But there *is* a change in the man, without any doubt. Notice Sir M—— O'D——; those who know that celebrated military man by sight are aware of one peculiarity in his appearance—his hat is never brushed. I met him one day with the beaver brushed quite primly; and looking hard at the baronet to ascertain the cause of this phenomenon, saw that he had a new coat. Even his great spirit was obliged to yield to the power of the coat,—he made a genteel effort,—he awoke up from his habitual Diogenic carelessness; and I have no doubt, had Alexander, before he visited the cynic, ordered some one to fling a new robe into his barrel, but that he would have found the fellow prating and boasting with all the airs of a man of fashion, and talking of tilburies, opera-girls, and the last ball at Devonshire House, as if the brute had been used all his life to no other company. Fie upon the swaggering vulgar bully! I have always wondered how the Prince of Macedon, a gentleman by birth, with an excellent tutor to educate him, could have been imposed upon by the, grovelling, obscene, envious tub-man, and could have uttered the speech we know of. It was a humbug, depend upon it, attributed to his Majesty by some maladroit *bon-mot* maker of the Court, and passed subsequently for genuine Alexandrine.

It is hardly necessary for the moralist earnestly to point out to persons moving in a modest station of life the necessity of not having coats of too fashionable and rakish a cut. Coats have been, and will be in the course of this disquisition, frequently compared to the flowers of the field; like them they bloom for a season, like them they grow seedy and they fade.

Can you afford always to renew your coat when this fatal hour arrives? Is your coat like the French monarchy, and does it never die? Have, then, clothes of the newest fashion, and pass on to the next article in the Magazine,*—unless, always, you prefer the style of this one.

But while a shabby coat, worn in a manly way, is a bearable, nay, sometimes a pleasing object, reminding one of "a good man struggling with the storms of fate," whom Mr. Joseph Addison has represented in his tragedy of "Cato,"—while a man of a certain character may look august and gentlemanlike in a coat of a certain

* *Fraser's Magazine.*

cut,—it is quite impossible for a person who sports an ultra-fashion-able costume to wear it with decency beyond a half-year say. *My* coats always last me two years, and any man who knows me knows how *I* look; but I defy Count d'Orsay thus publicly to wear a suit for seven hundred and thirty days consecutively, and look respectable at the end of that time. In like manner, I would defy, without any disrespect, the Marchioness of X——, or her Grace the Duchess of Z——, to sport a white satin gown constantly for six months and look decent. There is *propriety* in dress. Ah, my poor Noll Goldsmith, in your famous plum-coloured velvet! I can see thee strutting down Fleet Street, and stout old Sam rolling behind as Maister Boswell pours some Caledonian jokes into his ear, and grins at the poor vain poet. In what a pretty condition will Goldy's puce-coloured velvet be about two months hence, when it is covered with dust and grease, and he comes in his slatternly finery to borrow a guinea of his friend!

A friend of the writer's once made him a present of two very handsome gold pins; and what did the author of this notice do? Why, with his usual sagacity, he instantly sold the pins for five-and-twenty shillings, the cost of the gold, knowing full well that he could not afford to live up to such fancy articles. If you sport handsome gold pins, you must have everything about you to match. Nor do I in the least agree with my friend Bosk, who has a large amethyst brooch, and fancies that, because he sticks it in his shirt, his atrocious shabby stock and surtout may pass muster. No, no! let us be all peacock, if you please; but one peacock's feather in your tail is a very absurd ornament, and of course all moderate men will avoid it. I remember, when I travelled with Captain Cook in the South Sea Islands, to have seen Quashamaboo with nothing on him but a remarkably fine cocked-hat, his queen sported a red coat, and one of the princesses went frisking about in a pair of leather breeches, much to our astonishment.

This costume was not much more absurd than poor Goldsmith's, who might be very likely seen drawing forth from the gold-embroidered pocket of his plum-coloured velvet a pat of butter wrapped in a cabbage-leaf, a pair of farthing rushlights, an onion or two, and a bit of bacon.

I recollect meeting a great, clever, ruffianly boor of a man, who had made acquaintance with a certain set of very questionable aristocracy, and gave himself the air of a man of fashion. He had a coat made of the very pattern of Lord Toggery's,—a green frock, a green velvet collar, a green lining: a plate of spring cabbage is not of a brisker, brighter hue. This man, who had been a shop-keeper's apprentice originally, now declared that every man who was a gentleman wore white kid gloves, and for a certain period sported a fresh pair every day.

One hot, clear, sunshiny July day, walking down the Haymarket at two o'clock, I heard a great yelling and shouting of blackguard boys, and saw that they were hunting some object in their front.

The object approached us,—it was a green object,—a green coat, collar, and lining, and a pair of pseudo-white kid gloves. The gloves were dabbled with mud and blood, the man was bleeding at the nose, and slavering at the mouth, and yelling some unintelligible verses of a song, and swaying to and fro across the sunshiny street, with the blackguard boys in chase.

I turned round the corner of Vigo Lane with the velocity of a cannon-ball, and sprang panting into a baker's shop. It was Mr. Bludyer, our London Diogenes. Have a care, ye gay dashing Alexanders! how ye influence such men by too much praise, or debauch them by too much intimacy. How much of that man's extravagance, and absurd aristocratic airs, and subsequent *roueries*, and cutting of old acquaintance, is to be attributed to his imitation of Lord Toggery's coat!

Actors of the lower sort affect very much braiding and fur collars to their frock-coats ; and a very curious and instructive sight it is to behold these personages with pale lean faces, and hats cocked on one side, in a sort of pseudo-military trim. One sees many such sauntering under Drury Lane Colonnade, or about Bow Street, with sickly smiles on their faces. Poor fellows, poor fellows! how much of their character is embroidered in that seedy braiding of their coats! Near five o'clock, in the neighbourhood of Rupert Street and the Haymarket, you may still occasionally see the old, shabby, manly, gentlemanly, half-pay frock : but the braid is now growing scarce in London ; and your military man, with reason perhaps, dresses more like a civilian ; and understanding life better, and the means of making his half-crown go as far as five shillings in former days, has usually a club to dine at, and leaves Rupert Street eating-houses to persons of a different grade, —to some of those dubious dandies whom one sees swaggering in Regent Street in the afternoon, or to those gay spruce gentlemen whom you encounter in St. Paul's Churchyard at ten minutes after five, on their way westward from the City. Look at the same hour at the Temple, and issuing thence and from Essex Street, you behold many scores of neat barristers, who are walking to the joint and half a pint of Marsala at the Oxford and Cambridge Club. They are generally tall, slim, proper, well-dressed men, but their coats are too prim and professionally cut. Indeed, I have generally remarked that their clerks, who leave chambers about the same time, have a far more rakish and fashionable air; and if, my dear madam, you will condescend to take a beef-steak at the "Cock," or at some of the houses around Covent Garden, you will at once allow that this statement is perfectly correct.

I have always had rather a contempt for a man who, on arriving at home, deliberately takes his best coat from his back and adopts an old and shabby one. It is a mean precaution. Unless very low in the world indeed, one should be above a proceeding so petty. Once I knew a French lady very smartly dressed in a black velvet pelisse, a person whom I admired very much,—and indeed for the matter of that she was very fond of me, but that is neither here nor there,—I say I knew a French lady of some repute who used to wear a velvet pelisse, and how do you think the back of it was arranged?

Why, pelisses are worn, as you know, very full behind; and Madame de Tournuronval had actually a strip of black satin let into the hinder part of her dress, over which the velvet used to close with a spring when she walked or stood, so that the satin was invisible. But when she sat on a chair, especially one of the cane-bottomed species, Euphemia gave a loose to her spring, the velvet divided on each side, and she sat down on the satin.

Was it an authorised stratagem of millinery? Is a woman under any circumstances permitted to indulge in such a manœuvre? I say, No. A woman with such a gown is of a mean deceitful character. Of a woman who has a black satin patch behind her velvet gown, it is right that one should speak ill behind the back; and when I saw Euphemia Tournuronval spread out her wings (*non usitatæ pennæ*, but what else to call them?)—spread out her skirts and ensure them from injury by means of this dastardly *ruse*, I quitted the room in disgust, and never was intimate with her as before. A widow I know she was; I am certain she looked sweet upon me; and she said she had a fortune, but I don't believe it. Away with parsimonious ostentation! That woman, had I married her, would either have turned out a swindler, or we should have had *bouilli* five times a week for dinner,—*bouilli* off silver, and hungry lacqueys in lace looking on at the windy meal!

The old coat plan is not so base as the above female arrangement; but say what you will, it is not high-minded and honourable to go out in a good coat, to flaunt the streets in it with an easy *dégagé* air, as if you always wore such, and returning home assume another under pretext of dressing for dinner. There is no harm in putting on your old coat of a morning, or in wearing one always. Common reason points out the former precaution, which is at once modest and manly. If your coat pinches you, there is no harm in

2 U

changing it; if you are going out to dinner, there is no harm in changing it for a better. But I say the plan of habitual changing is a base one, and only fit for a man at last extremities; or for a clerk in the City, who hangs up his best garment on a peg, both at the office and at home; or for a man who smokes, and has to keep his coat for tea-parties,—a paltry precaution, however, this. If you like smoking, why shouldn't you? If you *do* smell a little of tobacco, where's the harm? The smell is not pleasant, but it does not kill anybody. If the lady of the house do not like it, she is quite at liberty not to invite you again. *Et puis?* Bah! Of what age are you and I? Have we lived? Have we seen men and cities? Have we their manners noted, and understood their idiosyncrasy? Without a doubt! And what is the truth at which we have arrived? This,—that a pipe of tobacco is many an hour in the day, and many a week in the month, a thousand times better and more agreeable society than the best Miss, the loveliest Mrs., the most beautiful Baroness, Countess, or what not. Go to tea-parties, those who will; talk fiddle-faddle, such as like; many men there are who do so, and are a little partial to music, and know how to twist the leaf of the song that Miss Jemima is singing exactly at the right moment. Very good. These are the enjoyments of dress-coats; but *men*,—are they to be put off with such fare for ever? No! One goes out to dinner, because one likes eating and drinking; because the very act of eating and drinking opens the heart, and causes the tongue to wag. But evening parties! O, milk and water, bread and butter! No, no, the age is wiser! The manly youth frequents his club for common society, has a small circle of amiable ladies for friendly intercourse, his book and his pipe always.

Do not be angry, ladies, that one of your most ardent and sincere admirers should seem to speak disparagingly of your merits, or recommend his fellows to shun the society in which you ordinarily assemble. No, miss, I am the man who respects you truly,—the man who respects and loves you when you are most lovely and respectable,—in your families, my dears. A wife, a mother, a daughter,—has God made anything more beautiful? A friend,—can one find a truer, kinder, a more generous and enthusiastic one, than a woman often will be? All that has to do with your hearts is beautiful, and in everything with which they meddle, a man must be a brute not to love and honour you.

But Miss Rudge in blue crape, squeaking romances at a harp, or Miss Tobin dancing in a quadrille, or Miss Blogg twisting round the room in the arms of a lumbering Life-guardsman;—what are these?—so many vanities. With the operations here described the heart has nothing to do. Has the intellect? O ye gods! think of Miss Rudge's intellect while singing—

> " Away, away to the mountain's brow,
> Where the trees are gently waving;
> Away, away to the fountain's flow,
> Where the streams are softly la-a-ving ! "

These are the words of a real song that I have heard many times, and rapturously applauded too. Such a song, such a poem,—such a songster !

No, madam, if I want to hear a song sung, I will pay eight-and-sixpence and listen to Tamburini and Persiani. I will not pay, gloves, three-and-six; cab, there and back, four shillings; silk stockings every now and then, say a shilling a time : I will not pay to hear Miss Rudge screech such disgusting twaddle as the above. If I want to see dancing, there is Taglioni for my money; or across the water, Mrs. Serle and her forty pupils; or at Covent Garden, Madame Vedy, beautiful as a houri, dark-eyed and agile as a gazelle. I can see all these in comfort, and they dance a great deal better than Miss Blogg and Captain Haggerty, the great red-whiskered monster, who always wears nankeens because he thinks his legs are fine. If I want conversation, what has Miss Flock to say to me, forsooth, between the figures of a cursed quadrille that we are all gravely dancing? By heavens, what an agony it is. Look at the he-dancers, they seem oppressed with dreadful care. Look at the cavalier seul ! if the operation lasted long the man's hair would turn white,—he would go mad ! And is it for this that men and women assemble in multitudes, for this sorry pastime ?

No ! dance as you will, Miss Smith, and swim through the quadrille like a swan, or flutter through the gallop like a sylphide, and have the most elegant fresh toilettes, the most brilliantly polished white shoulders, the blandest eyes, the reddest, simper-ingest mouth, the whitest neck, the—in fact, I say, be as charming as you will, *that* is not the place in which, if you are worth anything, you are most charming. You are beautiful; you are very much *décolletée;* your eyes are always glancing down at a pretty pearl necklace, round a pearly neck, or on a fresh fragrant bouquet, stuck—fiddlestick ! What is it that the men admire in you ?—the animal, miss,— the white, plump, external Smith, which men with their eye-glasses, standing at various parts of the room, are scanning pertly and curiously, and of which they are speaking brutally. A pretty admiration, truly ! But is it possible that these men can admire anything else in you who have so much that is really admirable ? Cracknell, in the course of the waltz, has

just time to pant into your ear, " Were you at Ascot Races?"
Kidwinter, who dances two sets of quadrilles with you, whispers
to you, " Do you pwefer thtwawbewy ithe aw wathbewy ithe?"
and asks the name of " that gweat enawmuth fat woman in wed
thatin and bird of pawadithe?" to which you reply, " Law, sir, it's
mamma!" The rest of the evening passes away in conversation
similarly edifying. What can any of the men admire in you, you
little silly creature, but the animal? There is your mother, now,
in red and a bird of paradise, as Kidwinter says. She has a large
fan which she flaps to and fro across a broad chest; and has one eye
directed to her Amelia, dancing with Kidwinter before mentioned;
another watching Jane, who is dancing *vis-à-vis* with Major Cutts;
and a third complacently cast upon Edward, who is figuring with
Miss Binx in the other quadrille. How the dear fellow has grown,
to be sure; and how like his papa at his age—heigho! There is
mamma, the best woman breathing; but fat, and even enormous,
as has been said of her. Does anybody gaze on *her ?* And yet she
was once as slim and as fair as you, O simple Amelia!

Does anybody care for her? Yes, one. Your father cares for
her; SMITH cares for her; and in his eyes she is still the finest
woman of the room; and he remembers when he danced down
seven-and-forty couples of a country dance with her, two years
before you were born or thought of. But it was all chance that
Miss Hopkins turned out to be the excellent creature she was.
Smith did not know any more than that she was gay, plump, good-
looking, and had five thousand pounds. Hit or miss, he took her,
and has had assuredly no cause to complain; but she might have
been a Borgia or Joan of Naples, and have had the same smiling
looks and red cheeks, and five thousand pounds, which won his
heart in the year 1814.

The system of evening parties, then, is a false and absurd one.
Ladies may frequent them professionally with an eye to a husband,
but a man is an ass who takes a wife out of such assemblies, having
no other means of judging of the object of his choice. You are
not the same person in your white crape and satin slip as you are
in your morning dress. A man is not the same in his tight coat
and feverish glazed pumps, and stiff white waistcoat, as he is in
his green double-breasted frock, his old black ditto, or his woollen
jacket. And a man is doubly an ass who is in the habit of fre-
quenting evening parties, unless he is forced thither in search of a
lady to whom he is attached, or unless he is compelled to go by
his wife. A man who loves dancing may be set down to be an
ass; and the fashion is greatly going out with the increasing good
sense of the age. Do not say that he who lives at home, or

frequents clubs in lieu of balls, is a brute, and has not a proper respect for the female sex ; on the contrary, he may respect it most sincerely. He feels that a woman appears to most advantage, not among those whom she cannot care about, but among those whom she loves. He thinks her beautiful when she is at home making tea for her old father. He believes her to be charming when she is singing a simple song at her piano, but not when she is screeching at an evening party. He thinks by far the most valuable part of her is her heart ; and a kind simple heart, my dear, shines in conversation better than the best of wit. He admires her best in her intercourse with her family and her friends, and detests the miserable twaddling slipslop that he is obliged to hear from and utter to her in the course of a ball ; and avoids and despises such meetings.

He keeps his evening coat, then, for *dinners*. And if this friendly address to all the mothers who read this miscellany may somewhat be acted upon by them ; if heads of families, instead of spending hundreds upon chalking floors, and Gunter, and cold suppers, and Weippert's band, will determine upon giving a series of plain, neat, nice dinners, of not too many courses, but well cooked, of not too many wines, but good of their sort, and according to the giver's degree, they will see that the young men will come to them fast enough ; that they will marry their daughters quite as fast, without injuring their health, and that they will make a saving at the year's end. I say that young men, young women, and heads of families should bless me for pointing out this obvious plan to them, so natural, so hearty, so hospitable, so different to the present artificial mode

A grand ball in a palace is splendid, generous, and noble,—a sort of procession in which people may figure properly. A family dance is a pretty and pleasant amusement ; and (especially after dinner) it does the philosopher's heart good to look upon merry young people who know each other, and are happy, natural, and familiar. But a Baker Street hop is a base invention, and as such let it be denounced and avoided.

A dressing-gown has great merits, certainly, but it is dangerous. A man who wears it of mornings generally takes the liberty of going without a neckcloth, or of not shaving, and is no better than a driveller. Sometimes, to be sure, it is necessary, in self-defence, not to shave, as a precaution against yourself that is to say ; and I know no better means of ensuring a man's remaining at home than neglecting the use of the lather and razor for a week, and encouraging a crop of bristles. When I wrote my tragedy, I shaved off for the last two acts my left eyebrow, and never stirred out of

13

doors until it had grown to be a great deal thicker than its right-hand neighbour. But this was an extreme precaution, and unless a man has very strong reasons indeed for stopping at home, and a very violent propensity to gadding, his best plan is to shave every morning neatly, to put on his regular coat, and go regularly to work, and to avoid a dressing-gown as the father of all evil. Painters are the only persons who can decently appear in dressing-gowns; but these are none of your easy morning-gowns; they are commonly of splendid stuff, and put on by the artist in order to render himself remarkable and splendid in the eyes of his sitter. Your loose-wadded German schlafrock, imported of late years into our country, is the laziest, filthiest invention; and I always augur as ill of a man whom I see appearing at breakfast in one, as of a woman who comes downstairs in curl-papers.

By the way, in the third act of "Macbeth," Mr. Macready makes his appearance in the courtyard of Glamis Castle in an affair of brocade that has always struck me as absurd and un-Macbethlike. Mac in a dressing-gown (I mean 'Beth, not 'Ready), —Mac in list slippers,—Mac in a cotton nightcap, with a tassel bobbing up and down,—I say the thought is unworthy, and am sure the worthy thane would have come out, if suddenly called from bed, by any circumstance, however painful, in a *good stout jacket*. It is a more manly, simple, and majestic wear than the lazy dressing-gown; it more becomes a man of Macbeth's mountainous habits; it leaves his legs quite free, to run whithersoever he pleases,—whether to the stables, to look at the animals,—to the farm, to see the pig that has been slaughtered that morning,—to the garden, to examine whether that scoundrel of a John Hoskins has dug up the potato-bed,—to the nursery, to have a romp with the little Macbeths that are spluttering and quarrelling over their porridge,—or whither you will. A man in a jacket is fit company for anybody; there is no shame about it as about being seen in a changed coat; it is simple, steady, and straightforward. It is as I have stated, all over pockets, which contain everything you want; in one, your buttons, hammer, small nails, thread, twine, and cloth-strips for the trees on the south wall; in another, your dog-whip and whistle, your knife, cigar-case, gingerbread for the children, paper of Epsom salts for John Hoskins's mother, who is mortal bad,—and so on: there is no end to the pockets, and to the things you put in them. Walk about in your jacket, and meet what person you will, you assume at once an independent air; and, thrusting your hands into the receptacle that flaps over each hip, look the visitor in the face, and talk to the ladies on a footing of perfect equality. Whereas, look at the sneaking way in which a man caught in a dressing-gown, in loose bagging trousers most likely (for the man who has a dressing-gown, has, two to one, no braces), and in shuffling slippers,—see how he whisks his dressing-gown over his legs, and looks ashamed and uneasy. His lanky hair hangs over his blowsy, fat, shining, unhealthy face; his bristly dumpling-shaped double-chin peers over a flaccid shirt-collar; the sleeves of his gown are in rags, and you see underneath a pair of black wrist-bands, and the rim of a dingy flannel waistcoat.

A man who is not strictly neat in his person is not an honest man. I shall not enter into this very ticklish subject of personal purification and neatness, because this essay will be read by hundreds of thousands of ladies as well as men; and for the former I would wish to provide nothing but pleasure. Men may listen to stern truths; but for ladies one should only speak verities that are sparkling, rosy, brisk, and agreeable. A man who wears a dressing-gown is not neat in his person; his moral character takes invariably some of the slatternliness and looseness of his costume; he becomes enervated, lazy, incapable of great actions; A man IN A JACKET is a man. All great men wore jackets. Walter Scott wore a jacket, as everybody knows; Byron wore a jacket (not that I count a man who turns down his collars for much); I have a picture of Napoleon in a jacket at Saint Helena; Thomas Carlyle wears a jacket; Lord John Russell always mounts a jacket on arriving at the Colonial Office; and if I have a single fault to find with that popular writer, the author of—— never mind what, you know his name as well as I,—it is that he is in the habit of composing his works in a large flowered damask dressing-gown, and morocco slippers; whereas, in a jacket he would write you off something, not so flowery, if you please, but of honest texture,—something, not so long, but terse, modest, and comfortable,—no great, long, strealing tails of periods,—no staring peonies and holly-hocks of illustrations,—no flaring cords and tassels of episodes,—no great, dirty, wadded sleeves of sentiment, ragged at the elbows and cuffs, and mopping up everything that comes in their way,—cigar-ashes, ink, candle-wax, cold brandy and water, coffee, or whatever aids to the brain he may employ as a literary man; not to mention the quantity of tooth-powder, whisker-dye, soapsuds, and pomatum that the same garment receives in the course of the toilets at which it assists. Let all literary men, then, get jackets. I prefer them without tails; but do not let this interfere with another man's pleasure: he may have tails if he likes, and I for one will never say him nay.

Like all things, however, jackets are subject to abuse; and the pertness and conceit of those jackets cannot be sufficiently reprehended which one sees on the backs of men at watering-places, with a telescope poking out of one pocket, and a yellow bandanna flaunting from the other. Nothing is more contemptible than Tims in a jacket, with a blue bird's-eye neck-handkerchief tied sailor-fashion, puffing smoke like a steamer, with his great broad orbicular stern shining in the sun. I always long to give the wretch a smart smack upon that part where his coat-tails ought to be, and advise him to get into a more decent costume. There is an age and a figure for jackets ; those who are of a certain build should not wear them in public. Witness fat officers of the dragoon-guards that one has seen bumping up and down the Steyne, at Brighton, on their great chargers, with a laced and embroidered coat, a cartridge-box, or whatever you call it, of the size of a twopenny loaf, placed on the small of their backs,—if their backs may be said to have a small,—and two little twinkling abortions of tails pointing downwards to the enormity jolting in the saddle. Officers should be occasionally measured, and after passing a certain width, should be drafted into other regiments, or allowed,—nay, ordered, to wear frock-coats.

The French tailors make frock-coats very well, but the people who wear them have the disgusting habit of wearing stays, than which nothing can be more unbecoming the dignity of man. Look what a waist the Apollo has, not above four inches less in the girth than the chest is. Look, ladies, at the waist of the Venus, and pray,—pray do not pinch in your dear little ribs in that odious and unseemly way. In a young man a slim waist is very well ; and if he looks like the Eddystone lighthouse, it is as nature intended him to look. A man of certain age may be built like a tower, stalwart and straight. Then a man's middle may expand from the pure cylindrical to the barrel shape ; well, let him be content. Nothing is so horrid as a fat man with a band ; an hour-glass is a most mean and ungracious figure. Daniel Lambert is ungracious, but not mean. One meets with some men who look in their frock-coats perfectly sordid, sneaking, and ungentlemanlike, who if you see them dressed for an evening have a slim, easy, almost fashionable, appearance. Set these persons down as fellows of poor spirit and milksops. Stiff white ties and waistcoats, prim straight tails, and a gold chain will give any man of moderate lankiness an air of fac-titious gentility ; but if you want to understand the individual, look at him in the daytime ; see him walking with his hat on. There is a great deal in the build and wearing of hats, a great deal more than at first meets the eye. I know a man who in a particular hat looked so extraordinarily like a man of property, that no tradesman on earth could refuse to give him credit. It was one of André's, and cost a guinea and a half ready money; but the person in question was frightened at the enormous charge, and afterwards purchased beavers in the City at the cost of seventeen-and-sixpence. And what was the consequence? He fell off in public estimation, and very soon after he came out in his City hat it began to be whispered abroad that he was a ruined man.

A blue coat is, after all, the best; but a gentleman of my acquaintance has made his fortune by an Oxford mixture, of all colours in the world, with a pair of white buckskin gloves. He looks as if he had just got off his horse, and as if he had three thousand a year in the country. There is a kind of proud humility in an Oxford mixture. Velvet collars, and all such gimcracks, had best be avoided by sober people. This paper is not written for drivelling dandies, but for honest men. There is a great deal of philosophy and forethought in Sir Robert Peel's dress; he does not wear those white waistcoats for nothing. I say that O'Connell's costume is likewise that of a profound rhetorician, slouching and careless as it seems. Lord Melbourne's air of reckless, good-humoured, don't-care-a-damn-ativeness is not obtained without an effort. Look at the Duke as he passes along in that stern little straight frock and plaid breeches; look at him, and off with your hat! How much is there in that little grey coat of Napoleon's! A spice of claptrap and dandyism, no doubt; but we must remember the country which he had to govern. I never see a picture of George III. in his old stout Windsor uniform without feeling a respect; or of George IV., breeches and silk stockings, a wig, a sham smile, a frogged frock-coat and a fur collar, without that proper degree of reverence which such a costume should inspire. The coat is the expression of the man,—οὕηπερ φύλλων, &c.; and as the peach-tree throws out peach-leaves, the pear-tree pear ditto, as old George appeared invested in the sober old garment of blue and red, so did young George in oiled wigs, fur collars, stays, and braided surtouts, according to his nature.

＊　　　＊　　　＊　　　＊　　　＊　　　＊

Enough,—enough; and may these thoughts, arising in the writer's mind from the possession of a new coat, which circumstance caused him to think not only of new coats but of old ones, and of coats neither old nor new,—and not of coats merely, but of men,— may these thoughts so inspired answer the purpose for which they have been set down on paper, and which is not a silly wish to instruct mankind,—no, no; but an honest desire to pay a deserving tradesman whose confidence supplied the garment in question.

PENTONVILLE: *April* 25, 1841.

GREENWICH—WHITEBAIT

I WAS recently talking in a very touching and poetical strain about the above delicate fish to my friend Foozle and some others at the Club, and expatiating upon the excellence of the dinner which our little friend Guttlebury had given us : when Foozle, looking round about him with an air of triumph and immense wisdom, said—

"I'll tell you what, Wagstaff, I'm a plain man, and despise all your gormandising and kickshaws. I don't know the difference between one of your absurd made dishes and another—give me a plain cut of mutton or beef. I'm a plain Englishman, I am, and no glutton."

Foozle, I say, thought this speech a terrible set-down for me— and indeed acted up to his principles—you may see him any day at six sitting down before a great reeking joint of meat ; his eyes quivering, his face red, and he cutting great smoking red collops out of the beef before .him, which he devours with corresponding quantities of cabbage and potatoes, and the other gratis luxuries of the club-table.

What I complain of is, not that the man should enjoy his great meal of steaming beef ; let him be happy over that as much as the beef he is devouring was in life happy over oil-cakes or mangel-wurzel : but I hate the fellow's brutal self-complacency, and his scorn of other people who have different tastes from his. A man who brags regarding himself, that whatever he swallows is the same to him, and that his coarse palate recognises no difference be-tween venison and turtle, pudding, or mutton-broth, as his indifferent jaws close over them, brags about a personal defect—the wretch— and not about a virtue. It is like a man boasting that he has no ear for music, or no eye for colour, or that his nose cannot scent the difference between a rose and a cabbage—I say, as a general rule, set that man down as a conceited fellow who swaggers about not caring for his dinner.

Why shouldn't we care about it? Was eating not made to be a pleasure to us? Yes, I say, a daily pleasure : a sweet solamen: a pleasure familiar, yet ever new, the same and yet how different! It is one of the causes of domesticity: the neat dinner makes the husband pleased, the housewife happy, the children consequently are well brought up and love their papa and mamma. A good dinner is the centre of the circle of the social sympathies —it warms acquaintanceship into friendship—it maintains that friendship comfortably unimpaired: enemies meet over it and are reconciled. How many of you, dear friends, has that late bottle of claret warmed into affectionate forgiveness, tender recollections of old times, and ardent glowing anticipations of new! The brain is a tremendous secret. I believe some chemist will arise anon, who will know how to doctor the brain as they do the body now, as Liebig doctors the ground. They will apply certain medicines, and produce crops of certain qualities that are lying dormant now for want of intellectual guano. But this is a subject for future speculation—a parenthesis growing out of another parenthesis. What I would urge especially here is a point which must be familiar with every person accustomed to eat good dinners—viz. the noble and friendly qualities that they elicit. How is it we cut such jokes over them? How is it we become so remarkably friendly? How is it that some of us, inspired by a good dinner, have sudden gusts of genius unknown in the quiet unfestive state? Some men make speeches, some shake their neighbour by the hand, and invite him or themselves to dine—some sing prodigiously— my friend, Saladin, for instance, goes home, he says, with the most beautiful harmonies ringing in his ears; and I, for my part, will take any given tune, and make variations upon it for any given period of hours, greatly, no doubt, to the delight of all hearers. These are only temporary inspirations given us by the jolly genius, but are they to be despised on that account? No. Good dinners have been the greatest vehicles of benevolence since man began to eat.

A taste for good living, then, is praiseworthy in moderation— like all the other qualities and endowments of man. If a man were to neglect his family or his business on account of his love for the fiddle or the fine arts—he would commit just the crime that the dinner-sensualist is guilty of: but to enjoy wisely is a maxim of which no man need be ashamed. But if you cannot eat a dinner of herbs as well as a stalled ox, then you are an unfortunate man—your love for good dinners has passed the wholesome boundary, and degenerated into gluttony.

Oh, shall I ever forget the sight of the only City dinner I ever attended in my life! at the hall of the Right Worshipful Company of Chimney-sweepers—it was in May, and a remarkably late pea-season. The hall was decorated with banners and escutcheons of deceased *chummies*—martial music resounded from the balconies as the Master of the Company and the great ones marched in. We sat down, grace was said, the tureen-covers removed, and instantly a silence in the hall—a breathless silence —and then a great gurgle!—grwlwlwlw it sounded like. The worshipful Company were sucking in the turtle! Then came the venison, and with it were two hundred quarts of peas, at five-and-twenty shillings a quart—oh, my heart sank within me, as we devoured the green ones! as the old waddling, trembling, winking citizens held out their plates quivering with anxiety, and, said Mr. Jones, " A little bit of the f-f-fat, another spoonful of the p-p-pe-as " —and they swallowed them down, the prematurely born children of the spring—and there were thousands in London that day without bread.

This is growing serious—and is a long grace before whitebait to be sure—but at a whitebait dinner, haven't you remarked that you take a number of dishes first? In the first place, water-souchy, soochy, or soojy—flounder-souchy is incomparably, exquisitely the best—perch is muddy, bony, and tough, compared to it, slips are coarse : and salmon—perhaps salmon is next to the flounder. You hear many people exclaim against flounder-souchy—I dined with Jorrocks, Sangsue, the Professor, and one or two more, only the other day, and they all voted it tasteless. Tasteless! It has an almost angelic delicacy of flavour : it is as fresh as the recollections of childhood—it wants a Correggio's pencil to describe it with sufficient tenderness.

" *If a flounder had two backs,*" Saladin said at the " Star and Garter " the other day, " it would be divine ! "

Foolish man, whither will your wild desires carry you? As he is, a flounder is a perfect being. And the best reply to those people who talk about its tastelessness, is to say " Yes," and draw over the tureen to yourself, and never leave it while a single slice of brown bread remains beside it, or a single silver-breasted fishlet floats in the yellow parsley-flavoured wave.

About eels, salmon, lobsters, either *au gratin* or in cutlets, and about the variety of sauces—Genevese sauce, Indian sauce (a strong but agreeable compound), &c., I don't think it is necessary to speak. The slimy eel is found elsewhere than in the stream of Thames (I have tasted him charmingly matelotted with mushrooms and onions, at the " Marroniers " at Passy), the lusty salmon flaps in other waters—by the fair tree-clad banks of Lismore—by the hospitable' margin of Ballynahinch—by the beauteous shores of Wye, and on the sandy flats of Scheveningen, I have eaten and loved him. I do not generally eat him at Greenwich. Not that he is not good. But he is not good in such a place. It is like Mrs. Siddons dancing a hornpipe, or a chapter of Burke in a novel —the salmon is too *vast* for Greenwich.

I would say the same, and more, regarding turtle. It has no business in such a feast as that fresh and simple one provided at the "Trafalgar" or the "Old Ship." It is indecorous somehow to serve it in that company. A fine large lively turtle, and a poor little whitebait by his side! Ah, it is wrong to place them by each other.

At last we come to the bait—the twelve dishes of preparatory fish are removed, the Indian sauced salmon has been attacked in spite of our prohibition, the stewed eels have been mauled, and the flounder soup-tureen is empty. All those receptacles of pleasure are removed—eyes turned eagerly to the door, and enter

Mr. Derbyshire (with a silver dish of whitebait).

John (brown bread and butter).

Samuel (lemons and cayenne).

Frederick (a dish of whitebait).

Gustavus (brown bread and butter).

Adolphus (whitebait).

A waiter with a napkin, which he flaps about the room in an easy *dégagé* manner.

"There's plenty more to follow, sir," says Mr. D., whisking off the cover. Frederick and Adolphus pass rapidly round with their dishes; John and Gustavus place their refreshments on the table, and Samuel obsequiously insinuates the condiments under his charge.

Ah! he must have had a fine mind who first invented brown bread and butter with whitebait! That man was a kind, modest, gentle benefactor to his kind. We don't recognise sufficiently the merits of those men who leave us such quiet benefactions. A statue ought to be put up to the philosopher who joined together this charming couple. Who was it? Perhaps it was done by the astronomer at Greenwich, who observed it when seeking for some other discovery. If it were the astronomer—why the next time we go to Greenwich we will go into the Park and ascend the hill, and pay our respects to the Observatory.

That, by the way, is another peculiarity about Greenwich. People leave town, and *say* they will walk in the Park before dinner. But we never do. We may suppose there is a Park from seeing trees; but we have never entered it. We walk wistfully up and down on the terrace before the Hospital, looking at the clock a great many times ; at the brown old seamen basking in the sun ; at the craft on the river ; at the nursery-maids mayhap, and the gambols of the shrill-voiced Jacks-ashore on the beach. But the truth is, one's thinking of something else all the time. Of the bait. Remark how silent fellows are on steamboats going down to Greenwich. They won't acknowledge it, but they are thinking of what I tell you.

Well, when the whitebait does come, what is it after all? Come now. Tell us, my dear sir, your real sentiments about this fish, this little little fish about which we all make such a noise! There it lies. Lemon it, pepper it : pop it into your mouth—and what then?—a crisp crunch, and it is gone. Does it realise your expectations—is it better than anything you ever tasted? Is it as good as raspberry open tarts used to be at school? Come, upon your honour and conscience now, is it better than a fresh dish of tittlebacks or gudgeons?

O fool, to pry with too curious eye into these secrets! O blunderer, to wish to dash down a fair image because it may be of plaster! O dull philosopher, not to know that pursuit is pleasure, and possession worthless without it! I, for my part, never will, as long as I live, put to myself that question about whitebait. Whitebait is a butterfly of the waters—and as the animal mentioned by Lord Byron invites the young pursuer near, and leads him through thy fields Cashmere—as it carries him in his chase through a thousand agreeable paths scented with violets, sparkling with sunshine, with beauty to feast his eyes, and health in the air—let the right-thinking man be content with the pursuit, nor inquire too curiously about the object. How many hunters get the brush of the fox, and what, when gotten, is the worth of that tawny wisp of hair?

Whitebait, then, is only a little means for acquiring a great deal of pleasure. Somehow it is always allied with sunshine : it is always accompanied by jolly friends and good-humour. You rush after that little fish, and leave the cares of London behind you—the row and struggle, the foggy darkness, the slippery pavement where every man jostles you, striding on his way, pre-occupied with care written on his brow. Look out of the window, the sky is tinted with a thousand glorious hues—the ships pass silent over the blue glittering waters—there is no object within sight that is not calm, and happy, and beautiful. Yes! turn your head a little, and there lie the towers of London in the dim smoky sunset. There lies Care, Labour, To-morrow. Friends, let us have another glass of claret, and thank our luck that we have still to-day.

On thinking over the various whitebait dinners which have fallen to our lot in the last month—somehow you are sure to find the remembrance of them all pleasant. I have seen some wretches taking whitebait and *tea*, which has always inspired me with a sort of terror, and a yearning to go up to the miserable objects so employed, and say, "My good friend, here is a crown-piece ; have a bottle of iced punch, or a tankard of delicious cider-cup—but not tea, dear sir ; no, no, not tea ; you can get that at home—there's no exhilaration in Congo. It was not made to be drunk on holidays. Those people are unworthy of the " Ship "—I don't wish to quarrel with the enjoyments of any man ; but fellows who take tea and whitebait should not be allowed to damp the festive feelings of persons better engaged. They should be consigned to the smiling damsels whom one meets on the walk to Mr. Derbyshire's, who issue from dingy tenements no bigger than houses in a pantomime, and who, whatever may be the rank of the individual, persist in saying, " Tea, sir—I can accommodate your party—tea, sir,— srimps ? "

About the frequenters of Greenwich and the various classes of ichthyophagi, many volumes might be written. All classes of English Christians, with the exception of her Majesty and Prince Albert (and the more is the pity that their exalted rank deprives them of an amusement so charming!) frequent the hospitable taverns —the most celebrated gormandiser and the very humble. There are the annual Ministerial Saturnalia, which, whenever I am called in by her Majesty, I shall have great pleasure in describing in these pages, and in which the lowest becomes the highest for the occasion, and Taper and Tadpole take just as high a rank as Lord Eskdale or Lord Monmouth. There are the private banquets in which Lord Monmouth diverts himself with his friends from the little French— but this subject has been already touched upon at much length. There are the lawyers' dinners, when Sir Frederick or Sir William is advanced to the honour of the bench or the attorney-generalship, and where much legal pleasantry is elicited. The last time I dined at the " Ship," hearing a dreadful Bacchanalian noise issuing from a private apartment, I was informed, " *It's the gentlemen of 'Punch,'* *sir*." What would I not have given to be present at such an assembly of choice spirits ! Even missionary societies and converters of the Quashimdoo Indians come hither for a little easy harmless pleasuring after their labours, and no doubt the whitebait slips down their reverend throats, and is relished by them as well as by the profane crowd.

Then in the coffee-room, let a man be by himself, and he is never lonely. Every table tells its little history. Yonder sit three City bucks, with all the elegant graces of the Custom-house and the Stock Exchange.

"That's a good glass of wine," says Wiggins.

"Ropy," says Figgins; "I'll put you in a pipe of that to stand you in three-and-twenty a dozen."

Once, in my presence, I heard a City "*gent*" speak so slightingly of a glass of very excellent brown sherry, that the landlord was moved almost to tears, and made a speech, of which the sorrow was only equalled by the indignation.

Sporting young fellows come down in great numbers, with cut-away coats and riding-whips, which must be very useful on the water. They discourse learnedly about Leander and Running Rein, and say, "I'll bet you three to two of that."

Likewise pink-faced lads from Oxford and Cambridge. Those from the former University wear lavender-coloured gloves, and drink much less wine than their jolly comrades from the banks of Cam. It would be a breach of confidence to report their conversation : but I lately heard some very interesting anecdotes about the Master of Trinity, and one Bumpkins, a gyp there.

Of course there are foreigners. I have remarked many " Mosaic Arabs " who dress and drink remarkably smartly ; honest pudding-faced Germans, who sit sentimentally over their punch ; and chattering little Frenchmen with stays, and whiskers, and canes, and little lacquered boots. These worthies drink ale, for the most part, saying, "Je ne bois que l'ale moi," or " Que la bière est bonne en Angleterre." " Et que le vin est mauvais," shrieks out the pigmy addressed, and so they club their sixpence, and remain faithful to the malt-and-hoppish liquor. It may be remarked that ladies and Frenchmen are not favourites with inn-waiters, coach-guards, cabmen, and such officials, doubtless for reasons entirely mercenary.

I could continue for many more pages, but the evening grey is tinging the river ; the packet-boat bells are ringing ; the sails of the ships look greyer and more ghostlike as they sweep silently by. It is time to be thinking of returning, and so let us call for the bill, and finish with a moral. My dear sir, it is this. The weather is beautiful. The whitebait singularly fine this season. You are sure to be happy if you go to Greenwich. Go then ; and, above all, TAKE YOUR AMIABLE LADY WITH YOU.

Ah ! if but ten readers will but follow this advice, Lancelot Wagstaff has not written in vain, and has made ten charming women happy !

AN EASTERN ADVENTURE OF THE FAT CONTRIBUTOR

WHEN our friend, the Fat Contributor, arrived from the East, he was the object of a good deal of curiosity, especially among the younger artists and writers connected with the facetious little periodical called *Punch ;* and his collection of Oriental curiosities, his beard (which, though originally red, he wore dyed of a rich purple), his pipes, narghilés, yataghans, and papooshes, made him a personage of no small importance. The crimson satin dressing-gown and red tarboosh, arrayed in which he used to lie on a sofa and smoke a long pipe all day, caused the greatest sensation in the neighbourhood of the New Cut, Lambeth, where the Contributor lived ; nor can a finer sight be imagined than our fat friend in this magnificent costume, ogling and smiling, and kissing his hand, to the six young ladies at Miss Runt's, the straw-bonnet makers over the way. Frank Delamere, the actor at the Victoria Theatre (his real name is Snoggin, by the way), got an old cotton robe covered with faded spangles, and used to attempt the same manœuvres out of his window; but he was voted an impostor, and our friend Bluebeard, as we used to call him, from the peculiar dye of his whiskers, was the Lion of Lambeth for 1845.

His stories about the East and his personal adventures were so outrageous that we all laughed at the fellow's gasconading, with the exception of young Speck, the artist, a credulous little creature, who swallowed all these legends with the most extraordinary good faith, smoked his long pipes, although tobacco disagreed wofully with his poor little chest, and absolutely began to grow *his* beard and moustachios forsooth ; just as if he had a beard to grow. Such are the foolish vanities indulged in by weak minds.

Over the Contributor's mantelpiece was an immense silver-mounted yataghan, of Damascus steel, in an embroidered filligree-case, with texts from the Koran engraved upon the hilt. Of this weapon the owner was excessively proud ; he read off the sentences of the handle with perfect ease (though he might have been reading gibberish for anything we knew to the contrary), and Speck came back from supping with him one night in a state of great consternation. "What do you think he told me?" Mr. Speck said. "We had a ham for supper (*we ad an am for supper*, S. pronounces it), and the knife being blunt, the Contributor took down his yataghan, and carved with it. He sliced off the meat as if he'd been bred to Woxall," Speck continued; "and as I took my last slice, 'Speck, my boy,' says he, 'what do you think I used that knife for last?'—'Well, mayhap to cut beef with,' Speck said. 'Beef? ha! ha! when I drew that knife last it was to cut off the head of Soliman Effendi!'

"I 'eard this," Speck said, "I laid down my knife and fork, and thought I should have fainted. I pressed him for further particulars; which he not only refused, but his countenance assumed an expression of intense agony, and he said circumstances had passed connected with that tragedy which he never, never could relate; and he made me solemnly promise never to reveal a single word even of that half-confidence which he had made."

Speck of course called upon every one of the Contributors to *Punch* the next day, and told them this terrific story, on which we rallied our fat friend remorselessly the next time we met.

Some fifteen days afterwards Messrs. Bradbury and Evans were greatly surprised by receiving a letter with the Alexandria postmark, and containing the following extraordinary document:—

"CAIRO, *the fourth day of the month Nishan, year* 1234 *of the Hegira. Sept.* 25, 1844.

"Three months after sight, please to pay the sum of one thousand tomauns on account of your obedient servant,

"THE FAT CONTRIBUTOR.

"Messrs. BRADBURY AND EVANS,
    "Whitefriars, London."

This extraordinary draft was crossed to the house of Ossum Hoosein and Company, Alexandria; and a note scrawled in pencil at the back of it, said, "*For Heaven's sake pay it: my life depends on it. F. C.*"

As the Contributor was back among us—as the draft came by the post, and was presented by nobody—of course Messrs. B. and E. did not pay the thousand tomauns, but sent over a printer's devil to the New Cut, requesting the Contributor to call in Whitefriars, and explain the meaning of this strange transaction.

He called. And now indeed we *did* begin to stare. "Gentle-men," said he, blushing and seeming very much agitated, "that paper was extracted from me by an Egyptian Bey, at the risk of my life. An unfortunate affair, which I can't particularise, put me into his power, and I only escaped by—*by killing him.* Don't ask me any more." Every one of our gents was amazed at this mystery, and our Contributor rose so much in importance that he instantly demanded an increase of his salary. He gave the law to our Society about all matters of fashion, about duelling, horse-flesh, &c. "That's a nice nag," he would say, while swaggering in the Park with us; "but you should see what horses I rode at the Etmeidan at Constantinople." "What do *you* know about the East?" he would exclaim, if any of us talked about our Eastern victories; and in fact became a perfect bully and nuisance to the Society.

One day, in Rotten Row, two very smart, though rather yellow-faced gentlemen, moustached and with a military look, came riding up, and seeing our fat friend, hailed him with loud voices and the utmost cordiality.

"The Contributor sprang over the railings to salute them, and shaking hands with the pair turned round with a beaming face to-wards us, as much as to say, "There, my boys, do *you* know any such swells as these, mounted on thoroughbred horses, who will shake hands with you in the full Park?"

"My friends, Bob Farcy and Frank Glanders, of the Bengal Cavalry," said he afterwards, tapping his boot with an easy air; "devilish good fellow, Bob; made that brilliant charge at Feroze-shah; met him in the East;"—and he swelled and swaggered about more pompously than ever.

That very day, some of us had made a little conspiracy to dine at Greenwich, and we were just sitting down to dinner at the "Trafalgar," when who should enter the coffee-room but the Con-tributor's Park friends? They singled him out in a moment. His countenance fell. "Can you and these gentlemen make room for us, Poddy, my boy?" they said. The tables were everywhere quite full; and, besides, these military gentlemen very likely were anxious to make the acquaintance of persons, I may say, *not* altogether disagreeable or unknown.

We congratulated these officers upon their achievements in the East, and they received our compliments with a great deal of manli-ness and modesty. The whole party speedily became very talkative and intimate. All the room was enlivened by our sallies, until, to tell the truth, we ordered in so many cool cups and tankards and bottles of claret, that at last we had the apartment to ourselves, and sat in great contentment looking out at the river and the shipping, and the moon rising as the sun sank away.

And now a history was revealed about our Fat Contributor, which was so terrible and instructive that we cannot do better than record it here.

It must be premised that the individual in question had in the early stage of the dinner been particularly loud and brilliant; that his loudness increased with the courses of the banquet; that somehow during the dessert he insisted upon making a speech, remarkable for its energetic incoherency; that then he proposed, without the least desire upon anybody else's part, to sing a song—a very sentimental one—which finished abruptly in a most melancholy falsetto; that he sate down affected to tears by something unknown, and was now sound asleep in his chair.

"Has he told you his adventures in the East?" Captain Glanders said, "and his famous night in the Harem?"

"La!" exclaimed Speck.

"In the Harem of Osman Effendi. We used to call him the Harem Scarum: a joke which, though old, we thought was pretty fair for a professional man."

"Do tell it us," we all exclaimed, and a snore from the poor Contributor seemed to encourage the Captain to go on.

"Gentlemen," he said, "Farcy here, and I, had the pleasure of making your friend's acquaintance on board the *Burrumpooter* steamer, which we found at Gibraltar on our way to our regiment in India. Your fat little friend got the name of Poddy, I don't know how; we found him christened when we came on board, and he was at that time in a great state of despondency, having just parted with a lady at Cadiz with whom he was violently smitten."

"Dolores!" we all exclaimed in chorus.

"The very same. Well, I am inclined to think that Poddy's heart was as fickle as it was inflammable; for during the course of our voyage to Alexandria he was in love with more than one person. He proposed to Miss Nokes, who was going to Bombay to be married to Livermore, of the Civil Service; had grown uncommonly sweet upon Colonel Hustler's daughter before we left Malta, and was ready to throw himself into the river when she refused him on the Nile. Tom Hustler, a young lad fresh from Addiscombe, was always the chief of the jokes against him, in which, indeed, every one of the passengers joined.

"When we arrived at Cairo I had the pleasure of accompanying your friend to the Pyramids, and saw him stick up the placard of *Punch* there, which I have no doubt may still be seen there; but all the way on the journey he was particularly anxious and reserved. At last he broke out to me in confidence :

"'Captain Glanders,' said he, 'do you know the language of flowers?' and of course, from my long residence in the East, I am acquainted with that elegant mode of orthography.

"'Look here,' says he, taking a bunch out of his bosom and thrusting it into my hand ; 'what do you think of *that?*'

"'Hallo ! this *is* a declaration indeed. A polyanthus, eternal constancy ; a rhododendron, my heart pines for you ; a magnolia, I am imprisoned by a wall ; a withered rose, I pine for my bulbul ; two tulips—upon my word you're a lucky fellow !'

"'The finest eyes you ever saw in the *world!*' Poddy exclaimed. 'The most extraordinary circumstance ! I was riding yesterday through the Frank Bazaar with young Hustler, when Soliman Effendi's harem passed—fourteen of them, mounted on donkeys, all covered over with hoods, like cab-heads, and black masks concealing everything but their eyes—but oh, such eyes ! Four hideous black slaves accompanied the procession, which was going to the Bath opposite the Mosque of Sultan Hassan ; and, seeing me gazing rather too eagerly, one brute rode up and actually handled his whip, when my servant Paolo dragged me away. The dear disguised creature rode on in the procession, throwing me back a glance—*one* glance of those delicious orbs.

"'Last night Paolo came to me with an air of mystery, and thrust that bouquet into my hand. "One old woman," he said, "bring me this—you see Egyptian lady—She love you—Soliman Effendi's daughter. Don't you go : he cut you head off." I was at a loss for the mystery. I showed the flowers to Farcy, and he read them *exactly as you do.*'

"'But, my dear fellow, recollect it's a dangerous matter entering a Turkish Harem—death threatens you.'

"'Death!' said Poddy : 'Ha, ha ! I'm *armed*, Glanders ;' and he showed me a pair of pistols and a knife that he had got. 'I'll run away with her, and take her to the Consul's and marry her. I'm told she has jewels to the amount of millions. I'm going to meet her to-night, I tell you, and (whispers) disguised as a woman.'

"You know what a figure your friend is ; and sure enough, on our return from the Pyramids, he dressed himself in a woman's dress and trousers, put a veil over his face, and one of those enormous hoods which the Egyptian ladies wear ; and though we could not help laughing at the absurdity of his appearance, yet, knowing the danger he was about to incur, we entreated him to give up his attempt. Go, however, he would.

"A black slave with a lantern, an old woman veiled, another slave holding a pair of donkeys, were in waiting at the door of the hotel, and on one of these beasts the undaunted Contributor mounted, taking rather a mournful farewell of half-a-dozen of us who were there to wish him good-bye. The streets of Cairo are quite dark at night. He and his people threaded through the lonely alleys environed by enormous masses of black houses, and were presently lost in the labyrinths of the city. But this is what, as we heard from him, afterwards took place.

"After winding and winding through the city for half-an-hour, the party came to a garden gate; and the guide knocking and uttering some words, the gate was cautiously unbarred. Poddy must have had good pluck, it must be owned, to pass that barrier alone.

"He was carried into a court, where he descended from his animal; then into another court, where there was a garden and a fountain; then into a gallery, where everything was dark; and at last—at last into the room, the harem itself, an ancient chamber ornamented with carved arabesques, and on a divan at the end of which, with a single faint lamp near her, sat—a lady.

"'Bring the lady to the divan,' said the veiled one, in the Egyptian language, 'and bring pipes and coffee.'

"Poddy shuffled up in his double yellow slippers and sate down opposite his charmer.

"Gudge mudge gurry bang hubaloo ?" says he, after the slaves who had brought the refreshment had retired. It is the Turkish for 'What is your elegant name, darling of my heart ? '

"The fair replied—'Emina.'

"'Chow row, wackyboss, coctaloo !' continued Poddy, repeating his lesson of the morning—meaning, 'angel of my soul, let me kiss your lily finger.' She gave him her hand, glittering with rings, and tinged with hennah.

"'I can speak English well,' said she, with ever so little foreign accent. 'I was born there. My poor mother was drowned in the Regent's Canal by my father, who was chief secretary to the Ottoman Embassy. I love your country, Christian. Emina pines here.'

"'Let us fly thither !' exclaimed the enraptured Contributor. 'My boat is on the sea, and my bark is on the shore. Pack up your jewels, and hasten with me to the Consul's. My palace at home awaits thee; thou shalt be the ornament of London Society; thou shalt share my heart and my fame.' And who knows how much farther the enraptured Contributor might have carried his

THE FAT CONTRIBUTOR

eloquence, when the black slave came rushing in, crying—'The Effendi! the Effendi!'

"'Gosh guroo!' cried Emina, 'my father!' Poddy let down his veil in a twinkling, crossed his legs, and puffed away at his pipe in the utmost trepidation, and a most ferocious Turk entered the room.

"'The English lady, my father,' Emina said, recovering from her perturbation. 'She came by the *Burrumpooter*. We—we met in the bazaar. Speak to her in her northern language, father of my heart!'

"'The English lady is welcome—the light of the sun is welcome—the Northern rose is beautiful in the Eastern garden. What a figure she has! as round as the full moon; and what eyes! as brilliant as carbuncles. Mashallah, the English lady is welcome. Will she not unveil?'

"'Before a stranger, my father!'

"'I have seen English ladies at Almack's unveiled before strangers—and shall not this one?' Soliman Effendi said; and, approaching the disguised lady, with a sudden jerk he tore off her veil, and the Contributor stood before him aghast.

"'Ha! by Mahomet,' roared the Effendi, 'have English ladies beards? Dog of an unbeliever! Disgrace of my house! Ho! Hassan, Muley, Hokey, Ibrahim, eunuchs of my guards!' and clapping his hands, a body of slaves ran in, just as, rushing upon Emina, he dashed a dagger into the poor girl's side, and she fell to the ground with a horrible hysteric scream!

"At the sight of this, Poddy, who had some courage, fell roaring on his knees, and cried out—'Amaun! amaun! Mercy! mercy! I'll write to the Consul. I'm enormously rich. I'll pay any ransom.'

"'Give me an order for a thousand tomauns!' said the Effendi gloomily; and, pointing to his daughter's body, 'Fling that piece of carrion into the Nile.' Poddy wrote a note for a thousand tomauns, which was prepared by the Effendi in the regular Oriental manner. 'And now,' said he, putting it into his waist-coat pocket,—'now, Christian, prepare to die! Bring the sack, mutes!' And they brought in a large one, in which they invited him to enter.

"'I'll turn Turk—I'll do anything,' screamed frantically the Fat Contributor."

. . . .

Here Captain Glander's story was interrupted by the subject of it, the Fat Contributor, bouncing up from his chair, and screaming out, "It is an infernal lie! I did *not* say I would turn Turk." And he rushed out of the room like a madman.

Captain Glanders then explained to us the whole circumstances of the hoax. Young Tom Hustler acted Emina. Glanders himself was Soliman Effendi; all that had been done was to lead the Contributor up and down the street for half-an-hour, and bring him in at the back part of the hotel, which was still a Turkish house

THE DIGNITY OF LITERATURE

TO THE EDITOR OF THE "MORNING CHRONICLE"

SIR,—In a leading article of your journal of Thursday, the 3rd instant, you commented upon literary pensions and the status of literary men in this country, and illustrated your arguments by extracts from the story of "Pendennis," at present in course of publication. You have received my writings with so much kindness, that, if you have occasion to disapprove of them or the author, I can't question your right to blame me, or doubt for a moment the friendliness and honesty of my critic; and however I might dispute the justice of your verdict in my case, I had proposed to submit to it in silence, being indeed very quiet in my conscience with regard to the charge made against me.

But another newspaper of high character and repute takes occasion to question the principles advocated in your article of Thursday, arguing in favour of pensions for literary persons as you argued against them; and the only point upon which the *Examiner* and the *Chronicle* appear to agree, unluckily regards myself, who am offered up to general reprehension in two leading articles by the two writers: by the latter for "fostering a baneful prejudice" against literary men; by the former for "stooping to flatter" this prejudice in the public mind, and "condescending to caricature (as is too often my habit) my literary fellow-labourers, in order to pay court to the non-literary class."

The charges of the *Examiner* against a man who has never, to his knowledge, been ashamed of his profession, or (except for its dulness) of any single line from his pen, grave as they are, are, I hope, not proven. "To stoop to flatter" any class is a novel accusation brought against my writings; and as for my scheme "to pay court to the non-literary class by disparaging my literary fellow-labourers," it is a design which would exhibit a degree not only of baseness but of folly upon my part of which, I trust, I am not capable. The editor of the *Examiner* may perhaps occasionally write, like other authors, in a hurry, and not be aware of the conclusions to which some of his sentences may lead. If I stoop to flatter anybody's prejudices for some interested motives of my own, I am no more nor less than a rogue and a cheat; which deductions from the *Examiner's* premisses I will not stoop to contradict, because the premisses themselves are simply absurd.

I deny that the considerable body of our countrymen described by the *Examiner* as " the non-literary class " has the least gratification in witnessing the degradation or disparagement of literary men. Why accuse " the non-literary class " of being so ungrateful? If the writings of an author give the reader pleasure or profit, surely the latter will have a favourable opinion of the person who benefits him. What intelligent man, of whatsoever political views, would not receive with respect and welcome that writer of the *Examiner* of whom your paper once said that " he made all England laugh and think "? Who would deny to that brilliant wit, that polished satirist, his just tribute of respect and admiration? Does any man who has written a book worth reading—any poet, historian, novelist, man of science —lose reputation by his character for genius or for learning? Does he not, on the contrary, get friends, sympathy, applause—money, perhaps?—all good and pleasant things in themselves, and not ungenerously awarded as they are honestly won. That generous faith in men of letters, that kindly regard in which the whole reading nation holds them, appear to me to be so clearly shown in our country every day, that to question them would be absurd, as, permit me to say for my part, it would be ungrateful. What is it that fills mechanics' institutes in the great provincial towns when literary men are invited to attend their festivals? Has not every literary man of mark his friends and his circle, his hundreds or his tens of thousands of readers? And has not every one had from these constant and affecting testimonials of the esteem in which they hold him? It is of course one writer's lot, from the nature of his subject or of his genius, to command the sympathies or awaken the curiosity of many more readers than shall choose to listen to another author; but surely all get their hearing. The literary profession is not held in disrepute; nobody wants to disparage it, no man loses his social rank, whatever it may be, by practising it. On the contrary; the pen gives a place in the world to men who had none before, a fair place, fairly achieved by their genius, as any other degree of eminence is by any other kind of merit. Literary men need not, as it seems to me, be in the least querulous about their position any more, or want the pity of anybody. The money-prizes which the chief among them get are not so high as those which fall to men of other callings—to bishops, or to judges, or to opera-singers and actors, nor have they received stars and garters as yet, or peerages and governorships of islands, such as fall to the lot of military officers. The rewards of the profession are not to be measured by the money standard, for one man may spend a life of learning and labour on a book which does not pay the printer's bill; and another gets a little fortune by a few light volumes. But putting the money out of the question, I believe that the social estimation of the man of letters is as good as it deserves to be, and as good as that of any other professional man.

With respect to the question in debate between you and the *Examiner*, as to the propriety of public rewards and honours to literary men, I don't see why men of letters should not cheerfully coincide with *Mr. Examiner*, in accepting all the honours, places, and prizes which they can get. The amount of such as will be awarded to them will not, we may be pretty sure, impoverish the country much; and if it is the custom of the State to reward by money, or titles of honour, or stars and garters of any sort, individuals who do the country service; and if individuals are grati-fied by having Sir, or my Lord, appended to their names, or stars and ribbons hooked on to their coats and waistcoats, as men most undoubtedly are, and as their wives, families, and relations are— there can be no reason why men of letters should not have the chance, as well as men of the robe or the sword; or why, if honour and money are good for one profession, they should not be good for another. No man in other callings thinks himself degraded by receiving a reward from his Government; nor surely need the literary man be more squeamish about pensions, and ribbons, and titles, than the ambassador, or general, or judge. Every European State but ours rewards its men of letters; the American Govern-ment gives them their full share of its small patronage; and if Americans, why not Englishmen? If Pitt Crawley is disappointed at not getting a ribbon on retiring from his diplomatic post at Pumpernickel; if General O'Dowd is pleased to be called Sir Hector O'Dowd, K.C.B., and his wife at being denominated my Lady O'Dowd—are literary men to be the only persons exempt from vanity, and is it to be a sin in them to covet honour?

And now with regard to the charge against myself of fostering baneful prejudices against our calling—to which I no more plead guilty than I should think Fielding would have done, if he had been accused of a design to bring the Church into contempt by describing Parson Trulliber—permit me to say, that before you deliver sentence it would be as well to have waited to hear the whole of the argument. Who knows what is coming in the future numbers of the work which has incurred your displeasure and the *Examiner's*, and whether you, in accusing me of prejudice, and the *Examiner* (alas!) of swindling and flattering the public, have not been premature? Time and the hour may solve this mystery, for which the candid reader is referred to "our next."

That I have a prejudice against running into debt, and drunkenness, and disorderly life, and against quackery and falsehood in my profession, I own; and that I like to have a laugh at those pretenders in it who write confidential news about fashion and politics for provincial *gobemouches*; but I am not aware of feeling any malice in describing this weakness, or of doing anything wrong in exposing the former vices. Have they never existed amongst literary men? Have their talents never been urged as a plea for improvidence, and their very faults adduced as a consequence of their genius? The only moral that I, as a writer, wished to hint in the descriptions against which you protest was, that it was the duty of a literary man, as well as any other, to practise regularity and sobriety, to love his family, and to pay his tradesmen. Nor is the picture I have drawn "a caricature which I condescend to," any more than it is a wilful and insidious design on my part to flatter "the non-literary class." If it be a caricature, it is the result of a natural perversity of vision, not of an artful desire to mislead; but my attempt was to tell the truth, and I meant to tell it not unkindly. I have seen the bookseller whom Bludyer robbed of his books; I have carried money, and from a noble brother man-of-letters, to some one not unlike Shandon in prison, and have watched the beautiful devotion of his wife in that place. Why are these things not to be described, if they illustrate, as they appear to me to do, that strange and awful struggle of good and wrong which takes place in our hearts and in the world? It may be that I work out my moral ill, or it may possibly be that the critic of the *Examiner* fails in apprehension. My effort as an artist came perfectly within his province as a censor; but when *Mr. Examiner* says of a gentleman that he is "stooping to flatter the public prejudice," which public prejudice does not exist, I submit that he makes a charge which is as absurd as it is unjust, and am thankful that it repels itself.

And instead of accusing the public of persecuting and disparaging us as a class, it seems to me that men of letters had best silently assume that they are as good as any other gentlemen; nor raise piteous controversies upon a question which all people of sense must take as settled. If I sit at your table, I suppose that I am my neighbour's equal, and that he is mine. If I begin straightway with a protest of "Sir, I am a literary man, but I would have you to know that I am as good as you," which of us is it that questions the dignity of the literary profession—my neighbour who would like to eat his soup in quiet, or the man of letters who commences the argument? And I hope that a comic writer, because he describes one author as improvident, and another as a parasite, may not only be guiltless of a desire to vilify his profession, but may really have its honour at heart. If there are no spendthrifts or parasites among us, the satire becomes unjust; but if such exist, or have existed, they are as good subjects for comedy as men of other callings. I never heard that the bar felt itself aggrieved because *Punch* chose to describe Mr. Dump's notorious state of insolvency, or that the picture of Stiggins, in " Pickwick," was intended as an insult to all Dissenters; or that all the attorneys in the empire were indignant at the famous history of the firm of " Quirk, Gammon, and Snap." Are we to be passed over because we are faultless, or because we cannot afford to be laughed at? And if every character in a story is to represent a class, not an individual—if every bad figure is to have its obliged contrast a good one, and a balance of vice and virtue is to be struck—novels, I think, would become impossible, as they would be intolerably stupid and unnatural; and there would be a lamentable end of writers and readers of such compositions. Believe me, Sir, to be your very faithful servant, W. M. THACKERAY.

REFORM CLUB: *Jan.* 8.

MR. THACKERAY IN THE UNITED STATES

TO THE EDITOR OF "FRASER'S MAGAZINE"

YOU may remember, my dear Sir, how I prognosticated a warm reception for your Mr. Michael Angelo Titmarsh in New York—how I advised that he should come by a Collins rather than a Cunard liner—how that he must land at New York rather than at Boston—or, at any rate, that he mustn't dare to begin lecturing at the latter city, and bring "cold joints" to the former one. In the last particular he has happily followed my suggestion, and has opened with a warm success in the chief city. The journals have been full of him. On the 19th of November, he commenced his lectures before the Mercantile Library Association (young ardent commercialists), in the spacious New York Church belonging to the flock presided over by the Reverend Mr. Chapin ; a strong row of ladies—the cream of the capital—and an "unusual number of the distinguished literary and professional celebrities." The critic of the *New York Tribune* is forward to commend his style of delivery as "that of a well-bred gentleman, reading with marked force and propriety to a large circle in the drawing-room." So far, excellent. This witness is a *gentleman* of the press, and is a credit to his order. But there are some others who have whetted the ordinary American appetite of inquisitiveness with astounding intelligence. Sydney Smith excused the national curiosity as not only venial, but laudable. In 1824, he wrote—"Where men live in woods and forests, as is the case, of course, in remote American settlements, it is the duty of every man to gratify the inhabitants by telling them his name, place, age, office, virtues, crimes, children, fortune, and remarks." It is not a matter of surprise, therefore, that this percontatorial foible has grown with the national growth.

You cannot help perceiving that the lion in America is public property and confiscate to the common weal. They trim the creature's nails, they cut the hair off his mane and tail (which is distributed or sold to his admirers), and they draw his teeth, which are frequently preserved with much the same care as you keep any memorable grinder whose presence has been agony and departure delight.

Bear-leading is not so much in vogue across the Atlantic as at your home in England ; but the lion-leading is infinitely more in fashion.

Some learned man is appointed Androcles to the new arrival. One of the familiars of the press is despatched to attend the latest attraction, and by this reflecting medium the lion is perpetually presented to the popular gaze. The guest's most secret self is exposed by his host. Every action—every word—every gesture is preserved and proclaimed—a sigh—a nod—a groan—a sneeze— a cough—or a wink—is each written down by this recording minister, who blots out nothing. No *tabula rasa* with him. The portrait is limned with the fidelity of Parrhasius, and filled up with the minuteness of the Daguerre process itself. No bloodhound or Bow-Street officer can be keener or more exact on the trail than this irresistible and unavoidable spy. 'Tis in Austria they calotype criminals : in the far West the public press prints the identity of each notorious visitor to its shores.

In turn, Mr. Dickens, Lord Carlisle, Jenny Lind, and now Mr. Thackeray, have been lionised in America.

" They go to see, themselves a greater sight than all."

In providing for a gaping audience, narrators are disposed rather to go beyond reality. Your famous Oriental lecturer at the British and Foreign Institute had a wallet of personal experience, from which Lemuel Gulliver might have helped himself. With such hyperbole one or two of "our own correspondents" of American journals tell Mr. Thackeray more about his habits than he himself was cognisant of. Specially I have selected from the *Sachem* and *Broadway Delineator* (the latter-named newspaper has quite a fabulous circulation) a pleasant history of certain of the peculiarities of your great humorist at which I believe he himself must smile.

Mr. Thackeray's person, height, breadth, hair, complexion, voice, gesticulation, and manner are, with a fair enough accuracy, described.

Anon, these recorders, upon which we play, softly whisper—

"One of his most singular habits is that of making rough sketches for caricatures on his finger-nails. The phosphoretic ink he originally used has destroyed the entire nails, so his fingers are now tipped with horn, on which he draws his portraits. The Duke of Marlboro' (under Queen Anne), General O'Gahagan (under Lord Lake), together with Ibrahim Pasha (at the Turkish Ambassador's), were thus taken. The celebrated engravings in the ' Paris Sketch Book,' ' Esmond,' &c., were made from these sketches. He has an insatiable passion for snuff, which he carries loose in his pockets.

2 Y

At a ball at the Duke of Northumberland's, he set a whole party sneezing, in a polka, in so convulsive a manner that they were obliged to break up in confusion. His pockets are all lined with tea-lead, after a fashion introduced by the late Lord Dartmouth.

"Mr. T. has a passion for daguerreotypes, of which he has a collection of many thousands. Most of these he took unobserved from the outer gallery of Saint Paul's. He generally carries his apparatus in one of Sangster's alpaca umbrellas, surmounted with a head of Doctor Syntax. (This umbrella, we believe, remained with the publishers of *Fraser's Magazine*, after the article on the London Exhibitions, in which it was alluded to.) He has been known to collar a beggar boy in the streets, drag him off to the nearest pastrycook's, and exercise his photographic art without ceremony. In London he had a tame laughing hyæna presented to him, on the breaking up of the Tower menagerie, which followed him like a dog, and was much attached to his master, though totally blind from confinement, deaf, and going on three legs and a wooden one. He was always surrounded by pets and domestic animals in his house; two owls live in the ivy-tod of the summer-house in the garden. His back sitting-room has an aviary. Monkeys, dogs, parrots, cats, and guinea-pigs swarm in the chambers. The correspondent of the *Buffalo Revolver*, who stayed three weeks with Mr. Thackeray during the Great Exhibition, gave us these particulars.

"His papers on the 'Greater Petty Chaps' or 'Garden Warbler (*Sylva hortensis*),' 'the Fauvette,' created an immense sensation when Madame Otto Goldschmidt was last in London. The study is at the end of the garden. The outside is richly covered with honeysuckle, jasmine, and Virginian creepers. Here Mr. T. sits in perfect solitude, 'chewing the cud of sweet and bitter fancy.' Being an early riser, he is generally to be found there in the morning, whence he can watch the birds. His daily costume is a hanging chlamys, or frock-coat, which he closely buttons, to avoid the encumbrance of a waistcoat. Hence the multiplicity of his coat-pockets, whose extreme utility to him during his lecture has been remarked elsewhere. He wears no braces, but his nether garments are sustained by a suspensory belt or bandage of hemp round his loins. Socks or stockings he despises as effeminate, and has been heard to sigh for the days of the *Solea* or σανδάλιον. A hair-shirt close to the skin, as Dejanira's robe, with a changeable linen front of the finest texture; a mortification, or penance, according to his cynical contempt and yet respect for human vanity, is a part of his ordinary apparel. A gibus hat and a pair of bluchers complete his attire. By a contrivance borrowed from the

disguises of pantomimists, he undresses himself in the twinkling of
a bedpost; and can slip into bed while an ordinary man is pulling
off his coat. He is awaked from his sleep (lying always on his
back in a sort of mesmeric trance) by a black servant (Joe's
domestic in 'Vanity Fair'), who enters the bedroom at four o'clock
precisely every morning, winter or summer, tears down the bed-
clothes, and literally saturates his master with a can of cold water
drawn from the nearest spring. As he has no whiskers, he never
needs to shave, and he is used to clean his teeth with the feather
end of the quill with which he writes in bed. (In this free and
enlightened country he will find he need not waste his time in
cleaning his teeth at all.) With all his excessive simplicity, he is
as elaborate in the arrangement of his dress as Count d'Orsay or
Mr. Brummel. His toilet occupies him after matin studies till
midday. He then sits down to a substantial 'bever,' or luncheon
of 'tea, coffee, bread, butter, salmon-shad, liver, black puddings,
and sausages.' At the top of this he deposits two glasses of ratafia
and three-fourths of a glass of rum-shrub. Immediately after the
meal his horses are brought to the door; he starts at once in a
mad gallop, or coolly commences a gentle amble, according to the
character of the work, fast or slow, that he is engaged upon.

"He pays no visits, and being a solitudinarian, frequents not
even a single club in London. He dresses punctiliously for dinner
every day. He is but a sorry eater, and avoids all vegetable diet,
as he thinks it dims the animal spirits. Only when engaged
on pathetic subjects does he make a hearty meal; for the body
macerated by long fasting, he says, cannot unaided contribute the
tears he would shed over what he writes. Wine he abhors, as a
true Mussulman. Mr. T.'s favourite drink is gin and toast and
water, or cider and bitters, cream and cayenne.

* * * * * * *

"In religion a Parsee (he was born in Calcutta), in morals a
Stagyrite, in philosophy an Epicurean; though nothing in his conversation or manners would lead one to surmise that he belonged to
either or any of these sects. In politics an unflinching Tory; fond
of the Throne, admiring the Court, attached to the peerage, proud
of the army and navy; a thick and thin upholder of Church and
State, he is for tithes and taxes as in Pitt's time. He wears hair
powdered to this day, from his entire reliance on the wisdom of his
forefathers. Besides his novels, he is the author of the 'Vestiges of
Creation,' the 'Errors of Numismatics,' 'Junius's Letters,' and
'Ivanhoe.' The sequel to this last he published three or four years
ago. He wrote all Louis Napoleon's works, and Madame H.'s

exquisite love letters ; and whilst secretary to that prince in confinement at Ham, assisted him in his escape, by knocking down
the sentry with a ruler with which he had been ruling accounts.
Mr. T. is very fond of boxing, and used to have an occasional set-to
with Ben Caunt, the Tipton Slasher, and young Sambo. He fences
admirably, and ran the celebrated Bertrand through the lungs twice,
at an *assaut d'armes* in Paris. He is an exquisite dancer, he
founded Laurent's Casino (was a pupil of Old Grimaldi, surnamed
Iron Legs), and played Harlequin in ' Mother Goose ' pantomime
once, when Ella, the regular performer, was taken ill and unable
to appear.

  " He has no voice, ear, or fancy even, for music, and the only
instruments he cares to listen to are the Jew's-harp, the bagpipes,
and the ' Indian drum.'

  " He is disputatious and loquacious to a degree in company ;
and at a dinner at the Bishop of Oxford's, the discussion with Mr.
Macaulay respecting the death of Mausolus, the husband of Zenobia,
occupied the disputants for thirteen hours ere either rose to retire.
Mr. Macaulay was found exhausted under the table. He has no
acquaintance with modern languages, and his French, which he
freely uses throughout his writings, is furnished by the Parisian
governess in the Baron de B.'s establishment. In the classics
he is superior to either Professor Sedgwick or Blackie (*vide* his
' Colloquies on Strabo,' and the ' Curtian Earthquake '). He was
twice senior opt. at Magdalen College, and three times running
carried off Barnes's prize for Greek Theses and Cantate," κ. τ. λ.

  Happily these delicate attentions have not ruffled Mr. Thackeray's
good temper and genial appreciation of the high position occupied
by literary men in the United States. Let me avow that this
position not only reflects credit on the country which awards it, but
helps to shed its lustre on the men of letters who become the guests
of its hospitality. Mr. Thackeray's last lecture of the series, on the
7th ult., gracefully conceded this in the following tribute :—

  " In England it was my custom, after the delivery of these
lectures, to point such a moral as seemed to befit the country I lived
in, and to protest against an outcry, which some brother authors
of mine most imprudently and unjustly raise, when they say that
our profession is neglected and its professors held in light esteem.
Speaking in this country, I would say that such a complaint could
not only not be advanced, but could not be even understood here,
where your men of letters take their manly share in public life ;

whence Everett goes as Minister to Washington, and Irving and Bancroft to represent the republic in the old country. And if to English authors the English public is, as I believe, kind and just in the main, can any of us say, will any who visit your country not proudly and gratefully own, with what a cordial and generous greeting you receive us? I look round on this great company. I think of my gallant young patrons of the Mercantile Library Association, as whose servant I appear before you, and of the kind hands stretched out to welcome me by men famous in letters, and honoured in our country as in their own, and I thank you and them for a most kindly greeting and a most generous hospitality. At home, and amongst his own people, it scarce becomes an English writer to speak of himself; his public estimation must depend upon his works; his private esteem on his character and his life. But here, among friends newly found, I ask leave to say that I am thankful; and I think with a grateful heart of those I leave behind me at home, who will be proud of the welcome you hold out to me, and will benefit, please God, when my days of work are over, by the kindness which you show to their father."

JOHN SMALL.

GOETHE IN HIS OLD AGE *

LONDON: *April* 28, 1855.

D EAR LEWES,—I wish I had more to tell you regarding
Weimar and Goethe. Five-and-twenty years ago, at least
a score of young English lads used to live at Weimar for
study, or sport, or society : all of which were to be had in the
friendly little Saxon capital. The Grand Duke and Duchess received us with the kindliest hospitality. The Court was splendid,
but yet most pleasant and homely. We were invited in our turns
to dinners, balls, and assemblies there. Such young men as had
a right appeared in uniforms, diplomatic and military. Some, I
remember, invented gorgeous clothing : the kind old Hof-Marschall
of those days, Monsieur de Spiegel (who had two of the most
lovely daughters eyes ever looked on), being in nowise difficult
as to the admission of these young Englanders. Of the winter
nights we used to charter sedan-chairs, in which we were carried
through the snow to those pleasant Court entertainments. I for
my part had the good luck to purchase Schiller's sword, which
formed a part of my Court costume, and still hangs in my study,
and puts me in mind of days of youth the most kindly and
delightful.

We knew the whole society of the little city, and but that the
young ladies, one and all, spoke admirable English, we surely might
have learned the very best German. The society met constantly.
The ladies of the Court had their evenings. The theatre was open
twice or thrice in the week, where we assembled, a large family
party. Goethe had retired from the direction, but the great traditions remained still. The theatre was admirably conducted ; and
besides the excellent Weimar company, famous actors and singers
from various parts of Germany performed " Gastrolle " † through
the winter. In that winter I remember we had Ludwig Devrient in

---

* This letter was written by Mr. Thackeray in answer to a request from
G. H. Lewes for some account of his recollections of Goethe. It is printed in
Lewes's "Life of Goethe," p. 560.

† What in England are called " starring engagements."

Shylock, " Hamlet," Falstaff, and the "Robbers " ; and the beautiful
Schröder in " Fidelio."

After three-and-twenty years' absence I passed a couple of
summer days in the well-remembered place, and was fortunate
enough to find some of the friends of my youth. Madame de
Goethe was there, and received me and my daughters with the
kindness of old days. We drank tea in the open air at the famous
cottage in the Park,* which still belongs to the family, and has
been so often inhabited by her illustrious father.

In 1831, though he had retired from the world, Goethe would
nevertheless very kindly receive strangers. His daughter-in-law's tea-
table was always spread for us. We passed hours after hours there,
and night after night, with the pleasantest talk and music. We
read over endless novels and poems in French, English, and German.
My delight in those days was to make caricatures for children. I
was touched to find that they were remembered, and some even
kept until the present time ; and very proud to be told, as a lad,
that the great Goethe had looked at some of them.

He remained in his private apartments, where only a very few
privileged persons were admitted ; but he liked to know all that
was happening, and interested himself about all strangers. Whenever a countenance struck his fancy, there was an artist settled in
Weimar who made a portrait of it. Goethe had quite a gallery of
heads, in black and white, taken by this painter. His house was
all over pictures, drawings, casts, statues, and medals.

Of course I remember very well the perturbation of spirit with
which, as a lad of nineteen, I received the long-expected intimation
that the Herr Geheimrath would see me on such a morning. This
notable audience took place in a little ante-chamber of his private
apartments, covered all round with antique casts and bas-reliefs.
He was habited in a long grey or drab redingote, with a white
neckcloth and a red ribbon in his button-hole. He kept his hands
behind his back, just as in Rauch's statuette. His complexion
was very bright, clear, and rosy. His eyes extraordinarily dark,†
piercing and brilliant. I felt quite afraid before them, and recollect
comparing them to the eyes of the hero of a certain romance called
"Melmoth the Wanderer," which used to alarm us boys thirty
years ago ; eyes of an individual who had made a bargain with a
Certain Person, and at an extreme old age retained these eyes in
all their awful splendour. I fancy Goethe must have been still
more handsome as an old man than even in the days of his youth.

* The *Gartenhaus*.

† This must have been the effect of the position in which he sat with regard
to the light. Goethe's eyes were dark brown, but not very dark.

His voice was very rich and sweet. He asked me questions about myself, which I answered as best I could. I recollect I was at first astonished, and then somewhat relieved, when I found he spoke French with not a good accent.

Vidi tantum. I saw him but three times. Once walking in the garden of his house in the *Frauenplan ;* once going to step into his chariot on a sunshiny day, wearing a cap and a cloak with a red collar. He was caressing at the time a beautiful little golden-aired granddaughter, over whose sweet fair face the earth has long since closed too.

Any of us who had books or magazines from England sent them to him, and he examined them eagerly. *Fraser's Magazine* had lately come out, and I remember he was interested in those admirable outline portraits which appeared for awhile in its pages. But there was one, a very ghastly caricature of Mr. Rogers, which, as Madame de Goethe told me, he shut up and put away from him angrily. "They would make me look like that," he said : though in truth I can fancy nothing more serene, majestic, and *healthy-*looking than the grand old Goethe.

Though his sun was setting, the sky round about was calm and bright, and that little Weimar illumined by it. In every one of those kind salons the talk was still of Art and Letters. The theatre, though possessing no very extraordinary actors, was still connected with a noble intelligence and order. The actors read books, and were men of letters and gentlemen, holding a not unkindly relationship with the *Adel.* At Court the conversation was exceedingly friendly, simple, and polished. The Grand Duchess (the present Grand Duchess Dowager), a lady of very remarkable endowments, would kindly borrow our books from us, lend us her own, and graciously talk to us young men about our literary taste and pursuits. In the respect paid by this Court to the Patriarch of letters, there was something ennobling, I think, alike to the subject and sovereign. With a five-and-twenty years' experience since those happy days of which I write, and an acquaintance with an immense variety of human kind, I think I have never seen a society more simple, charitable, courteous, gentleman-like, than that of the dear little Saxon city where the good Schiller and the great Goethe lived and lie buried.—Very sincerely yours,

W. M. THACKERAY.

A LEAF OUT OF A SKETCH-BOOK

I F you will take a leaf out of my sketch-book, you are welcome.
It is only a scrap, but I have nothing better to give. When
the fishing-boats come in at a watering-place, haven't you remarked that though these may be choking with great fish, you
can only get a few herrings or a whiting or two? The big fish
are all bespoken in London. As it is with fish, so it is with
authors, let us hope. Some Mr. Charles of Paternoster Row, some
Mr. Grove of Cornhill (or elsewhere), has agreed for your turbots
and your salmon, your soles and your lobsters. Take one of my
little fish—any leaf you like out of the little book—a battered
little book : through what a number of countries, to be sure, it has
travelled in this pocket !

The sketches are but poor performances, say you. I don't say
no ; and value them no higher than you do, except as recollections
of the past. The little scrawl helps to fetch back the scene which
was present and alive once, and is gone away now, and dead. The
past resurges out of its grave : comes up—a sad-eyed ghost sometimes—and gives a wan ghost-like look of recognition, ere it pops
down under cover again. Here's the Thames, an old graveyard,
an old church, and some old chestnuts standing behind it. Ah !
it was a very cheery place, that old graveyard ; but what a
dismal, cut-throat, cracked-windowed, disreputable residence was
that " charming villa on the banks of the Thames," which led me
on the day's excursion ! Why, the " capacious stabling " was a
ruinous wooden old barn, the garden was a mangy potato patch,
overlooked by the territories of a neighbouring washerwoman. The
housekeeper owned that the water was constantly in the cellars and
ground-floor rooms in winter. Had I gone to live in that place,
I should have perished like a flower in spring, or a young gazelle,
let us say, with dark blue eyes. I had spent a day and hired a
fly at ever so much charges, misled by an unveracious auctioneer,
against whom I have no remedy for publishing that abominable
work of fiction which led me to make a journey, lose a day, and
waste a guinea.

What is the next picture in the little show-book? It is a scene at Calais. The sketch is entitled "The Little Merchant." He was a dear pretty little rosy-cheeked merchant, four years old maybe. He had a little scarlet *képi ;* a little military frock-coat; a little pair of military red trousers and boots, which did not near touch the ground from the chair on which he sat sentinel. He was a little crockery merchant, and the wares over which he was keeping guard, sitting surrounded by walls and piles of them as in a little castle, were——well, I never saw such a queer little crockery merchant.

Him and his little chair, boots, *képi*, crockery, you can see in the sketch—but I see, nay, hear, a great deal more. At the end of the quiet little old old street, which has retired out of the world's business as it were, being quite too aged, feeble, and musty to take any part in life—there is a great braying and bellowing of serpents and bassoons, a nasal chant of clerical voices, and a pattering of multitudinous feet. We run towards the market. It is a Church fête day. Banners painted and gilt with images of saints are flaming in the sun. Candles are held aloft, feebly twinkling in the noontide shine. A great procession of children with white veils, white shoes, white roses, passes, and the whole town is standing with its hat off to see the religious show. When I look at my little merchant, then, I not only see him, but that procession passing over the place ; and as I see those people in their surplices, I can almost see Eustache de Saint Pierre and his comrades walking in their shirts to present themselves to Edward and Philippa of blessed memory. And they stand before the wrathful monarch,—poor fellows, meekly shuddering in their chemises, with ropes round their necks ; and good Philippa kneels before the royal conqueror, and says, "My King, my Edward, my *beau Sire !* Give these citizens their lives for our Lady's gramercy and the sake of thy Philippa !" And the Plantagenet growls, and scowls, and softens, and he lets those burgesses go. This novel and remarkable historical incident passes through my mind as I see the clergymen and clergy-boys pass in their little short white surplices on a mid-August day. The balconies are full, the bells are all in a jangle, and the blue noonday sky quivers overhead.

I suppose other pen and pencil sketchers have the same feeling. The sketch brings back, not only the scene, but the circumstances under which the scene was viewed. In taking up an old book, for instance, written in former days by your humble servant, he comes upon passages which are outwardly lively and facetious, but inspire their writer with the most dismal melancholy. I lose all cognisance of the text sometimes, which is hustled and elbowed out of sight by the crowd of thoughts which throng forward, and which were alive and active at the time that text was born. Ah, my good sir ! a man's books mayn't be interesting (and I could mention other authors' works besides this one's which set me to sleep), but if you knew *all* a writer's thoughts, how interesting his book would be ! Why, a grocer's day-book might be a wonderful history, if alongside of the entries of cheese, pickles, and figs, you could read the circumstances of the writer's life, and the griefs, hopes, joys, which caused the heart to beat, while the hand was writing and the ink flowing fresh. Ah memory ! ah the past ! ah the sad sad past ! Look under this waistcoat, my dear madam. There. Over the liver. Don't be frightened. You can't see it. But there, at this moment, I assure you, there is an enormous vulture gnawing, gnawing.

Turn over the page. You can't deny that this is a nice little sketch of a quaint old town, with city towers, and an embattled town gate, with a hundred peaked gables, and rickety balconies, and gardens sweeping down to the river wall, with its toppling ancient summer-houses under which the river rushes ; the rushing river, the talking river, that murmurs all day, and brawls all night over the stones. At early morning and evening under this terrace which you see in the sketch—it is the terrace of the Steinbock or Capricorn Hotel—the cows come ; and there, under the walnut-trees, before the tannery, is a fountain and pump where the maids come in the afternoon, and for some hours make a clatter as noisy as the river. Mountains gird it around, clad in dark green firs, with purple shadows gushing over their sides, and glorious changes and gradations of sunrise and setting. A more picturesque, quaint, kind, quiet little town than this of Coire, in the Grisons, I have seldom seen ; or a more comfortable little inn than this of the Steinbock or Capricorn, on the terrace of which we are standing. But quick, let us turn the page. To look at it makes one horribly melancholy. As we are on the inn-terrace, one of our party lies ill in the hotel within. When will that doctor come ? Can we trust to a Swiss doctor in a remote little town away at the confines of the railway world ? He is a good, sensible, complacent doctor, *laus Deo*,—the people of the hotel as kind, as attentive, as gentle, as eager to oblige. But oh, the gloom of those sunshiny days ; the sickening languor and doubt which fill the heart as the hand is making yonder sketch, and I think of the invalid suffering within !

Quick, turn the page. And what is here ? This picture, ladies and gentlemen, represents a steamer on the Alabama river, plying (or *which plied*) between Montgomery and Mobile. See, there is a black nurse with a cotton handkerchief round her head, dandling and tossing a white baby. Look in at the open door of that cabin, or "state-room" as they call the crib yonder. A mother is leaning by a bed-place; and see, kicking up in the air, are a little pair of white fat legs, over which that happy young mother is bending in such happy tender contemplation. That gentleman with a forked beard and a slouched hat, whose legs are sprawling here and there, and who is stabbing his mouth and teeth with his penknife, is quite good-natured, though he looks so fierce. A little time ago, as I was reading in the cabin, having one book in my hand and another at my elbow, he affably took the book at my elbow, read in it a little, and put it down by my side again. He meant no harm. I say he is quite good-natured and kind. His manners are not those of Mayfair, but is not Alabama a river as well as Thames? I wish that other little gentleman were in the cabin who asked me to liquor twice or thrice in the course of the morning, but whose hospitality I declined, preferring not to be made merry by wine or strong waters before dinner. After dinner, in return for his hospitality, I asked *him* if he would drink? "No, sir, I have dined," he answered, with very great dignity, and a tone of reproof. Very good. Manners differ. I have not a word to say.

Well, my little Mentor is not in my sketch, but he is in my mind as I look at it: and this sketch, ladies and gentlemen, is especially interesting and valuable, because *the steamer blew up on the very next journey:* blew up, I give you my honour,—burst her boilers close by my state-room, so that I might, had I but waited for a week, have witnessed a celebrated institution of the country, and had the full benefit of the boiling.

I turn a page, and who are these little men who appear on it? JIM and SADY are two young friends of mine at Savannah in Georgia. I made Sady's acquaintance on a first visit to America,—a pretty little brown boy with beautiful bright eyes,—and it appears that I presented him with a quarter of a dollar, which princely gift he remembered years afterwards, for never were eyes more bright and kind than the little man's when he saw me, and I dined with his kind masters on my second visit. Jim at my first visit had been a little toddling tadpole of a creature, but during the interval of the two journeys had developed into a full-blown beauty. On the day after my arrival these young persons paid me a visit, and here is an accurate account of a conversation which took place between us, as taken down on the spot by the elder of the interlocutors.

Jim is five years old : Sady is seben : only Jim is a great deal fatter. Jim and Sady have had sausage and hominy for breakfast. One sausage, Jim's, was the biggest. Jim can sing, but declines on being pressed, and looks at Sady and grins. They both work in de garden. Jim has been licked by Master, but Sady never. These are their best clothes. They go to church in these clothes. Heard a fine sermon yesterday, but don't know what it was about. Never heard of England, never heard of America. Like orangees best. Don't know any old woman who sells orangees. (*A pecuniary transaction takes place.*) Will give that quarter-dollar to Pa. That was Pa who waited at dinner. Are hungry, but dinner not cooked yet. Jim all the while is revolving on his axis, and when begged to stand still turns round in a fitful manner.

Exeunt Jim and Sady with a cake apiece which the house-keeper gives them. Jim tumbles downstairs.

In his little red jacket, his little—his little?—his immense red trousers, such a queer little laughing blackamoorkin I have never seen. Seen? I see him now, and Sady, and a half-dozen more of the good people, creeping on silent bare feet to the drawing-room door when the music begins, and listening with all their ears, with all their eyes. Good-night, kind warm-hearted little Sady and Jim! May peace soon be within your doors, and plenty within your walls! I have had so much kindness there, that I grieve to think of friends in arms, and brothers in anger.

DR. JOHNSON AND GOLDSMITH

THIS drawing was first published in the *North British Review* of February 1864, in the admirable article on Thackeray by Doctor John Brown. It had been sent to a friend with the following letter :—

"Behold a drawing instead of a letter. I've been thinking of writing you a beautiful one ever so long, but, etc., etc. And instead of doing my duty this morning, I began this here drawing, and will pay your debt some other day—no, *part* of your debt. I intend to owe the rest, and like to owe it, and think I'm sincerely grateful to you always, my dear good friends.   W. M. T."

The letter is not dated, but may probably be placed about the time of the "English Humorists." A slight sketch of the two principal figures has been published in the lecture on Sterne and Goldsmith, in which there are several allusions to the fine clothes which Filby the tailor made for Goldsmith, and often did not get paid for.

THE HISTORY

OF

DIONYSIUS DIDDLER

THE HISTORY OF DIONYSIUS DIDDLER*

LADIES AND GENTLEMEN,—Many thousand years ago, in the reign of Chrononhotonthologos, King of Brentford, there lived a young gentleman whose history is about to be laid before you.

He was sixty years of age, and his name was Dionysius Diddler; no relation of any other Dionysius, nor, indeed, a Brentfordian by birth; for (though the Diddlers are very numerous in Brentford) this was a young fellow from Patland, which country he quitted at a very early age.

He was by trade a philosopher,—an excellent profession in Brentford, where the people are more ignorant and more easily humbugged than any people on earth;—and no doubt he would have made a pretty fortune by his philosophy, but the rogue longed to be a man of fashion, and spent all his money in buying clothes and in giving treats to the ladies, of whom he was outrageously fond. Not that they were very partial to *him*, for he was not particularly handsome—especially without his wig and false teeth, both of which, I am sorry to say, this poor Diddler wore.

Well, the consequence of this extravagance was, that, although by his learning he had made himself famous (there was his Essay on the Tea-Kettle, his Remarks on Pumps, and his celebrated Closet Cyclopædia, that every one has heard of)—one day, after forty years of glory, Diddler found himself turned out of his lodging, without a penny, without his wig, which he had pawned without even his teeth, which he had pawned too, seeing he had no use for them.

And now befell a series of adventures that you shall all hear and so take warning, ye dashing blades of the town, by the awful fate of DIONYSIUS.

* First published in the *Autographic Mirror*, 1864. The drawings were made about 1838.

This is Dionysius Diddler! young, innocent, and with a fine head of hair,—when he was a student in the University of Ballybunion.—That is Ballybunion University, in the hedge.

Here he is, after forty years of fame, and he thinks upon dear Ballybunion.
"I'm femous," says he, "all the world over: but what's the use of riputetion?
Look at me with all me luggage at the end of me stick—all me money in me
left-hand breeches pocket—and it's oh! but I'd give all me celebrity for a bowl
of butther-milk and potaties."

He goes to call on Mr. Shortman, the publisher of the " Closet Cyclopædia,"
and, sure an ouns! Mr. Shortman gives him three sovereigns and three £5
notes.

The first thing he does is to take his wig out of pawn.

" And now," says he, " I'll go, take a sthroll to the Wist Ind, and call on
me frind, Sir Hinry Pelham."

He pays a visit to Sir Henry Pelham.

" Fait !" says Diddler, " the what-d'ye-call-'ems fit me like a glove. "

" And upon me honour and conshience, now I'm dthressed, but I look
intirely ginteel."

In Pelham's coat, hat, boots, and pantaloons,
Forth issues Diddler from the Baronet's house,
In famed Red Lion's fashionable square,
And was it strange that Hodge, Sir Henry's groom,

Said, reverently, " Master, will you mount?
This Dionysius did, and rode away,—
But fear then seized upon the soul of Hodge,
Says he, " *That gemman cannot be my master,*

THE ORPHAN OF PIMLICO

NOTE

M ISS WIGGLESWORTH'S Moral Tale was begun at Kensington one evening by lamplight. Her specimen-pages were put together vaguely at first; the Moral Preface was written afterwards, and the Title-page last of all. One page of the specimen is unfortunately missing, that upon which the Earl wrote the impassioned verses which Rigolette so basely gave up to the wicked Couleuvre. Perhaps the Countess destroyed them. Perhaps they were all the more impressive from the fact that they consisted of *tags* only. There was a picture of the unfortunate Earl in his dressing-gown, sitting at a desk in the agonies of composition. Upstairs, in an elegantly furnished drawing-room, the sarcastic Mordant was paying his deadly compliments to the frivolous Countess. A. I. R.

Specimen-Extracts from the New Novel.

The Orphan of

PIMLICO

a Moral Tale of Belgravian Life

by

Miss. M.T. Wigglesworth

many years Governess in the Nobilitys families, and authoress of
'Posies of Poesy' 'Thoughts on the Use of the Globes' &c

LONDON · 1851

PROLOGUE TO THE "HEIRESS OF PIMLICO"

THOSE who only view our nobility in their splendid equipages or gorgeous opera-boxes, who fancy that their life is a routine of pleasure, and that the rose-leaf of luxury *has no thorns*, are, alas, wofully mistaken!

Care oppresses the *coronetted brow*, and there is a skeleton in the most elegant houses of May Fair! The authoress has visited many of them and been on terms of familiarity (she is humbly proud to say) with more than one patrician family!

The knowledge of the above truths, and the idea that to disseminate them amongst my countrymen might be productive of *a deep and lasting benefit*, has determined me (with the advice of friends) to publish my tale of THE HEIRESS OF PIMLICO. The present is the mere prologue to that absorbing and harrowing story, wherein the consequences of crime and the beneficial effects of virtue, the manners of the nobility, the best Church principles, and the purest morality are pourtrayed.

I have engaged an artist at considerable expense to illustrate the first part of this momentous tale, and if I receive encouragement (which I do not doubt), shall hasten to deliver THE TALE to the public.

The Rev. Mr. Oriel, the Rev. Mr. Thurifer, and *other revered clergy* of the district, have kindly consented to give the testimony of their high names to the character of the reader's obliged servant,

MARIA THERESA WIGGLESWORTH.

For many years Governess in families of the highest distinction.

17 NORTH MOTCOMB STREET,
   BELGRAVE SQUARE.

IN the year 18—, a humble *but pious* governess of, as she trusts *satisfactory*, Church of England principles (being the daughter of the Rev. Clement Wigglesworth of Clapham Chapel of Ease), instructed two young ladies, by name Arabella and Emmeline.

The Lady Arabella Muggleton was daughter of the Earl of Trumpington; and her cousin Emmeline was only child of Admiral the Hon. Hugh Fitzmarlinspike, brother of the Earl of that name.

The Admiral commanded in the Mediterranean, whither his

Prologue to the
'Heiress of Pimlico.'

...hose who only view our nobility in their splendid equipages & opera boxes, who fancy that their life is a zenith of pleasure & that the rose leaf of luxury has no thorns, are, alas, woefully mistaken! Care oppresses the coroneted brow, and there is a skeleton in the most elegant houses of May Fair! The authoress had visited many of them and been on terms of familiarity (she is so humbly proud to say) with more than one patrician family!

The knowledge of the above truths, and the idea that to disseminate them amongst my countrymen might be productive of a deep and lasting benefit, has determined me (with the advice of friends) to publish my Tale of "The Heiress of Pimlico". The present is the mere prologue to that absorbing and harrowing story, wherein the consequences of crime and the beneficial effects of virtue, the manners of the nobility, the best Church principles, and the purest morality are portrayed.

I have engaged an Artist at considerable expense to illustrate the first part of this momentous tale, and if I receive encouragement (w?) I do not doubt I shall hasten to deliver THE TALE to the public.

The Rev? Mr Oriel, the Rev? Mr Thurifer and other revered clergy of the district have kindly consented to give their testimony of their high names to the character of the readers. obliged servant

Maria Theresa Wigglesworth

For many years Governess in families of the highest distinction of North Motcomb St. Belgrave Sq?

Miss Wigglesworth (from a sketch by herself)

In the year 18— a humble but pious governess of as she trusts satisfactory Church of England principles (being the daughter of the Rev? Clement Wigglesworth of Clapham Chapel of Ease) instructed two young ladies by name Arabella and Emmeline.

The lady Arabella Mugglestone was daughter of the Earl of Frumpington; and her cousin Emmeline was only child of Admiral the Hon?e Hugh Fitzmartin spite brother of the Earl of that name.

The Admiral commanded in the Mediterranean whither his charming but volatile daughter Emmeline went to join her Papa.

It was at Malta on board the Admirals flag ship "The Rumbustical" that Emmeline for the first time saw Henry 25th Earl of Lancelot, to whom she was united only 3 days before the news arrived at Valette of the death of the Admirals Elder brother the 2nd Earl of Fitz martinspike.

Our young couple passed several years abroad & it was not until their daughter Emmeline was more than two years old that they returned to London where his Lordship occupied a house no 76 Chesham Place Belgrave Square.

3

The cousins, my former pupils, hastened to each others arms; and Arabella now an orphan, came to dwell with her relative the amiable Countess of Lancelot.

Among the Earls acquaintances I grieve to state that there was a gentleman whom I shall call Mordant & who speedily became an assiduous frequenter of the mansion in Chesham place.

In vain I pointed out in my visits to my noble pupil, the danger likely to result from the society of this ill-regulated young man - It was not because in his vulgar insolence and odious contempt of the poor, old Mordant (as I heard through the keyhole) [open door] called me a "toothless old the dragon" and a "twaddling old catamaran" - that I disliked him, but from his general levity and daring licence of language. That my dislike was well founded this melancholy tale will too well show.

charming but volatile daughter Emmeline went to join her Papa.

It was at Malta, on board the Admiral's flagship, *The Rum-bustical*, that Emmeline for the first time saw Henry, 25th Earl of Lancelot, to whom she was united only three days before the news arrived at Valetta of the death of the Admiral's elder brother, the 2nd Earl of Fitzmarlinspike.

Our young couple passed several years abroad, and it was not until their daughter Emmeline was more than two years old that they returned to London, where his Lordship occupied a house, No. 76 Chesham Place, Belgrave Square.

The cousins, my former pupils, hastened to each other's arms; and Arabella, now an orphan, came to dwell with her relative the amiable Countess of Lancelot.

Among the Earl's acquaintances, I grieve to state that there was a gentleman whom I shall call Mordant, and who speedily became an assiduous frequenter of the mansion in Chesham Place.

In vain I pointed out, in my visits to my noble pupil, the danger likely to result from the society of this *ill-regulated young man.* It was not because, in his vulgar insolence and odious contempt of the poor, Mr. Mordant (as I heard through the open door) called me "a toothless old she-dragon," and "a twaddling old catamaran," that I disliked him, but from his general levity and daring licence of language. That my dislike was *well founded,* this melancholy tale *will too well show.*

Lady Arabella looked down at the little Lady Emmeline with a glance of unutterable affection.

"Is she not like me?" asked the lively but frivolous Countess.

Arabella thought with a sigh, "How like the cherub is to her father!" Poor Arabella!—*The Heiress of Pimlico,* vol. ii.

The good old Admiral, now Earl of Fitzmarlinspike, had "braved the battle and the breeze" for many years on every sea. He wore the collar and Grand Cross of our own and the French Orders, and came into the saloon shortly after ten o'clock.—*The Heiress of Pimlico.*

...dy Arabella looked down at the little Lady Emmeline with a glance of
unutterable affection.

She did like unmasked the lively but frivolous Countess
...abella thought with a sigh. How like the cherub is to her father!
or Arabella!

    The Heiress of Pimlico.
     Vol II.

The good old Admiral now Earl of Intermarlinspike
had "braved the battle and the breeze" for many years at every sea.
He wore the Collar and Grand Cross of his own order and the female
Orders & aunt came into the saloon shortly after ten o'clock

    The Heiress of Pimlico.

Mordant looked after the Countess with a glance in which rage, love, hatred, contempt, demoniac talent, and withering scorn were blended. "She has refused me," he said, "and she thinks she has escaped me! She has insulted me, and she imagines I will not be revenged!"

The young Earl rushed into the balcony, unable to control his emotions in the salon. "Cruel stars!" said he (apostrophising those luminaries, whose mild effulgence twinkled in the serene azure and lit up Chesham Place and Belgrave Square), "why, why did I marry the Countess so early, and know Lady Arabella so late?"

"A letter for Miladi Arabelle!" cried Rigolette, "and sealed with a couronne de Comte? Ah, mon Dieu, what would I not give to have such a distinguished correspondence!"

"I will give you a dinner at Richemont, a box at the French comedy, and the Cachemire shawl you admired so much, for that letter, Miss Rigolette," said Couleuvre, Mr. Mordant's man, who was taking tea in the housekeeper's room.

the Countess

Mordaunt looked after her with a glance in wh. rage love
hatred contempt demoniac talent and withering scorn were
blended: "She has refused me he said, and she thinks she has
escaped me! she has insulted me and she imagines I will not be
avenged!"

A letter for Miladi Arabelle! cried Rigolette and sealed with a couronne
de Comte! Ah mon
Dieu, what would
I not give to have
such a distinguished
Correspondence!"

The young Lord rushed into the balcony unable to
contain his emotions in the Salon. "Cruel Arra! As he
Capostrophizing those luminaries, whose mild effulgence
Twinkled in the serene azure and lit up Chesham Place
and Belgrave Square;) why why did I marry the Coun
tess so early, and know Lady Arabella so late?"

"I will give you a dinner at Richemont, a box at the French Comedy and the Castle
mine Shawl you admired so much for that letter Miss Rigolette, said Coulevure
Mr. Mordaunt's man,
who was taking tea
in the housekeeper's
room

"Lancelot a model man! haw, haw, haw, hah!" laughed Mordant, with a demoniacal sneer. "This will show you the morality of my Lord Lancelot." And with this Mordant handed to the Countess the Earl's impassioned and elegant verses to Arabella.

At the moment the unprincipled young man was speaking, Lord Lancelot entered at the portière. Having overheard their conversation, the agonised Earl retreated so silently that neither the heedless "Ladye" nor her false companion were aware that they had had a listener.

With all his vices Mordant was not a coward. And when the next morning Captain Ragg waited upon Mr. Mordant with a message from the Earl of Lancelot, Mordant's reply was, "Tell the Earl to make his will." A message which the Captain promised to convey to his Lordship.

It was five o'clock, and the Earl, who had passed the night in writing, stole on tiptoe to the chamber of his child. Emmeline was sleeping the rosy sleep of innocence—smiling in her sleep! "Bless thee, bless thee, my Emmeline!" exclaimed his Lordship, and printed a kiss on the cheek of his darling. Captain Ragg's brougham was heard at that instant to drive to the door.

5

"Lancelot a model man! ha! ha ha ha ha!" laughed
Mordaunt with a demoniacal sneer. "This will show you
the morality of my lord Lancelot." And with this
Mordaunt handed to the Countess
the Earl's impassioned & elegant
verses to Azubetta.

At the moment the unprincipled young man was
speaking Lord Lancelot entered at the postière
Having overheard their conversation
the agonized Earl retreated
so silently that neither the
heedless Ladye nor their
false companion were
aware that they had
had a listener

With all his vices Mordaunt was not a coward. And when the next
morning Captain Ragg waited upon Sir Mordaunt with a message
from the Earl of Lancelot, Mordaunt's reply was "Tell the Earl to make
his will": a message wh. the Captain promised to
convey to his Lordship.

It was five o'clock and the Earl who had passed the night in writing
note on billet to the Chamber of his child. Emmeline was sleeping
the rosy sleep of innocence - smiling in her sleep! "Bless
thee thee my Emmeline exclaimed his Lordship and printed
a kiss on the cheek of
his darling!"
Captain Raggs Brougham
was heard at that
instant to drive
to the door.

The Earl and his companion now drove to Wimbledon Common, where, faithful to his diabolical appointment, Mordant was already in waiting, accompanied by his friend Lieutenant Famish. The two broughams pulled up together. How often had they done so before at the parties of the nobility and gentry !

The gentlemen were quickly placed by their seconds, and the horrid signal was given ! Crack, crack ! Two pistols sounded simultaneously, and at the next instant a ball had gone through Mordant's hat (a new one), and he looked opposite him and laughed a hellish laugh ! "Through his left eye !" exclaimed the fiend in human shape. "I aimed for it, and his beauty will not even be spoiled. Famish and I must to the Continent. Well, well, a day sooner or later, what matters ? My debts would have driven me away in a week. Come away, Famish."

During the fatal rencontre a third carriage had driven up, from which two veterans descended. One was a famous General known in our Eastern and Peninsular wars, the other was the Countess's father, Admiral the Earl of Fitzmarlinspike, G.C.B. "Stop !" said the Admiral. "The husband is dead, but the father is alive and demands vengeance !" Mordant turned pale.

...nt and his companion now drove to Wimbledon Common, faithful to his diabolical appointment Mordaunt was duly in waiting, accompanied by his friend Lieutenant Faheigh.

The two Brougham pulled up together: How often had they done so before at the parties of the nobility and gentry! The gentlemen were quickly placed by their seconds, and the word signal...

...given! Crack Crack! Two pistols sounded simultaneously &

at the next instant a ball had gone through Mordaunts hat (a new one) and he looked opposite him & laughed a hellish laugh!.

"Through his left eye! exclaimed the fiend in human shape "I aimed for it, and his beauty will not even be spoiled." Faheigh and I went to the Continent. Well well, a day sooner or later, what matters? My debts would have driven me away in a week. Come away Faheigh.

...ing the fatal encounter a third carriage had driven up from wh two veterans descended. One was a famous General known in our Eastern & Peninsular wars, the other was the Countess's father Admiral the Earl of Fitzmarlinspike GCB.

Stop! said the Admiral. The husband is dead but the father is alive and demands vengeance!. Mordaunt turned pale.

Again the dreadful signal to fire was given, and the intrepid Marlinspike delivered his shot at the instant. Mordant's pistol went off as it fell to the ground.

As it fell to the ground and as he sprang six feet into the air with the Admiral's ball through his wicked and remorseless heart! Gentles! the rest of our afflicting prologue is quickly told. The body of Lord Lancelot was laid at Castle Guinever; that of the fiendish Mordant carried back to his apartments in the Albany, of which the bailiffs had already taken possession. The Fitzmarlinspike family, 'tis known, profess the ancient faith. In the convent of Taunton is a lady, who has doffed the Countess's coronet for the black veil and white cap of the nun. Among the barefooted friars at Puddleswood is one who is old and grey-bearded, and has a wooden leg. But few know that old Brother Barnabas is Fitzmarlinspike's Earl. Rigolette and Couleuvre, the domestics whose betrayal caused all this tragedy, fled, and were apprehended with the spoons. Messieurs Famish and Ragg are both in the Bench; and the General who acted as Lord Fitzmarlinspike's second is now an altered man. And Arabella? the lovely and innocent? how, how is Arabella? Who can tell how much she suffered, how bitterly she wept?

She, of course, never married. She was appointed guardian to the little Lady Emmeline, who is now eighteen years of age, has ninety-six thousand a year, is as lovely as an angel, and called THE HEIRESS OF PIMLICO.

in the dreadful signal to fire was given, and the enraged Mordaunt fuled went off as it fell to the ground

Mordaunt fuled went off as it fell to the ground

As it fell to the ground and as he sprang six feet into the air, with the adequate ball through his wicked and remorseless heart! –

Gentle! the rest of our afflicting prologue is quickly told. The body of Lord Lancelot was laid at Castle Guinever; that of the fiendish Mordaunt carried back to his apartments in the Albany, of wh the bailiffs had already taken possession. The Fitzmarlinspike family 'tis known profess the ancient faith. In the Convent at Taunton is a lady, who has doffed the Countess's coronet for the black veil & white cap of the Nun. Among the bare-footed friars at Puddleswood, is one who is old and grey bearded, and has a wooden leg. But few know that old brother Barnabas is Fitzmarlinspikes Earl. Rizletta and Courlewose, the domestics whose betrayal caused all this tragedy fled, and were apprehended with the spoons. Messieurs Famish and Ragg are both in the Bench; and the General who acted as Lord Fitzmarlinspikes second is now an altered man. And Arabella? the lovely & innocent? how, how is Arabella? who can tell how much she suffered, how bitterly she wept? She of course never married. She was appointed guardian to the little lady Gwendoline; who is now 18 years of age: has ninety six thousand a year: is as lovely as an angel, and called **THE HEIRESS OF PIMLICO**.

THE LIFE OF W. M. THACKERAY

To Leslie Stephen, my brother-in-law, I owe a brother's help and advice. In his biography of my father, reprinted from the " Dictionary of National Biography," the whole framework of the life is given : the story he purposely left for me to tell.

A. I. R.

THE LIFE OF W. M. THACKERAY

THE following is a reprint, with some corrections, of the life of Thackeray in the "Dictionary of National Biography." In conformity with the principles of that work, it is little more than a condensed statement of facts; and, indeed, for certain reasons, even less devoted than usual to critical or other comment. It will, perhaps, be the better suited to fulfil its present purpose of serving as a Table of Contents to the Introductions prefixed to volumes in this edition of Thackeray's works. References are given to the various introductions at the periods which they mainly illustrate.

William Makepeace Thackeray, born at Calcutta on July 18, 1811, was the only child of Richmond and Anne Thackeray. The Thackerays descended from a family of yeomen who had been settled for several generations at Hampsthwaite, a hamlet on the Nidd, in the West Riding of Yorkshire. Thomas Thackeray (1693–1760) was admitted a King's Scholar at Eton in January 1705–6. He was Scholar (1712) and Fellow (1715) of King's College, Cambridge, and was afterwards an Assistant Master at Eton. In 1746 he was appointed Headmaster of Harrow, where Dr. Parr was one of his pupils. In 1748 he was made Chaplain to Frederick, Prince of Wales, and in 1753 Archdeacon of Surrey. He died at Harrow in 1760. By his wife Anne, daughter of John Woodward, he had sixteen children. The fourth son, Thomas (1736–1806), became a surgeon at Cambridge, and had fifteen children, one of whom, William Make-peace (1770–1849), was a well-known physician at Chester; another, Elias (1771–1854), mentioned in the "Irish Sketch Book," became Vicar of Dundalk; and a third, Jane Townley (1788–1871), married in 1813 George Pryme, the political economist. The Archdeacon's fifth son, a physician at Windsor, was father of George Thackeray (1777–1850), Provost of King's College, Cambridge. The Archdeacon's youngest child, William Makepeace (1749–1813), entered the service of the East India

Company in 1766.   He was patronised by Cartier, Governor of
Bengal, was made "factor" at Dacca in 1771, and first collector
of Sylhet in 1772.   There, besides reducing the province to
order, he became known as a hunter of elephants, and made
money by supplying them to the Company.   In 1774 he returned to Dacca, and on January 31, 1776, he married, at Calcutta, Amelia Richmond, third daughter of Colonel Richmond
Webb.   Webb was related to General John Richmond Webb,
whose victory at Wynendael is described in "Esmond."   Another daughter of Colonel Webb married Peter Moore (1753–
1828), who supported Burke and Francis in the impeachment
of Warren Hastings, and was afterwards an active though obscure politician.   He was a guardian of the novelist.   W. M.
Thackeray had made a fortune by his elephants and other trad-
ing speculations then allowed to the Company's servants, when
in 1776 he returned to England.   In 1786 he bought a property
at Hadley, near Barnet, where Peter Moore had also settled.
W. M. Thackeray had twelve children: Emily, third child
(1780–1824), married John Talbot Shakspear, and was mother
of Sir Richmond Campbell Shakspear; Charlotte Sarah, the
sixth child (1786–1854), married John Ritchie, and was mother
of William Ritchie (1817–1862), legal Member of Council in
India; and Francis, tenth child and sixth son (1793–1842),
took orders, and is best known as the author of a Life of
Chatham (1827).   Francis's two sons, the Rev. Francis St.
John Thackeray and Colonel Sir Edward Talbot Thackeray,
V.C., K.C.B., are still living.   Of the six elder sons of W. M.
Thackeray four were in the Civil Service in India, one in the
Indian army, and a sixth at the Calcutta bar.   All had died,
two in action, by 1825.   William, the eldest (1778–1823), was
intimate with Sir Thomas Munro, and had an important part in
the administration and land settlement of Madras.   Richmond,
fourth child of William Makepeace and Amelia Thackeray, was
born at South Mimms on September 1, 1781, and in 1798 went
to India in the Company's service.   In 1807 he became Secretary to the Board of Revenue at Calcutta, and on October 13,
1810, married Anne, daughter of John Harman Becher, a
"reigning beauty" at Calcutta.   William Makepeace, their
only child, was named after his grandfather, the name "Makepeace" being derived, according to a family tradition, from
some ancestor who had been a Protestant martyr in the days
of Queen Mary.   Richmond Thackeray was appointed to the
collectorship of the twenty-four Pergunnahs, then considered to
be "one of the prizes of the Bengal service," at the end of

1811. He died at Calcutta on September 13, 1816. He seems, like his son, to have been a man of artistic tastes and was a collector of pictures, musical instruments, and horses. A portrait in possession of his grand-daughter, Mrs. Ritchie, shows a refined and handsome face.*

His son, William Makepeace Thackeray, was sent to England in 1817 in a ship which touched at St. Helena. There a black servant took the child to look at Napoleon, who was then at Bowood, eating three sheep a day and all the little children he could catch. The boy found all England in mourning for the Princess Charlotte (died November 6, 1817). He was placed under the care of his aunt, Mrs. Ritchie. She was alarmed by discovering that the child could wear his uncle's hat, till she was assured by a physician that the big head had a good deal in it. The child's precocity appeared especially in an early taste for drawing. Thackeray was sent to a school in Hampshire, and then to one kept by Dr. Turner at Chiswick, in the neighbourhood of the imaginary Miss Pinkerton of "Vanity Fair." Thackeray's mother in 1818 married Major Henry William Carmichael-Smyth (died 1861) of the Bengal Engineers, author of a Hindoostanee dictionary (1800), a "Hindoostanee Jest-book," and a history of the royal family of Lahore (1847). The Smyths returned to England in 1821, and settled at Addiscombe, where for two years, from August 1822, Major Smyth was superintendent of the Company's military college. From 1822 to 1828 Thackeray was at the Charterhouse. Frequent references in his writings show that he was deeply impressed by the brutality of English public school life, although, as was natural, he came to look back with more tenderness, as the years went on, upon the scenes of his boyish life. The headmaster was John Russell (1787–1863), who for a time raised the numbers of the school. Russell had been trying the then popular system of Dr. Bell, which, after attracting pupils, ended in failure. The number of boys in 1825 was 480, but afterwards fell off. A description of the school in Thackeray's time is in Mozley's "Reminiscences." George Stovin Venables (a man who devoted to law and journalism powers which might have won a great literary reputation) was a schoolfellow and a lifelong friend. Venables broke Thackeray's

* Very full information as to the above-mentioned Thackerays, and others less connected with his personal history, is given in "Memorials of the Thackeray Family," by Mrs Pryme and her daughter, Mrs Bayne, privately printed in 1879. A very interesting account of some of them is in Sir W. W. Hunter's "Thackerays in India" (1897). For references to the Becher family, see Introduction to "The Newcomes"; and for references to "Grandfathers and Grandmothers," see Introduction to "Ballads and Miscellanies."

nose in a fight, causing permanent disfigurement. He remembered Thackeray as a " pretty, gentle boy," who did not distinguish himself either at lessons or in the playground, but was much liked by a few friends. He rose to the first class in time, and was a monitor, but showed no special promise as a scholar. Towards the end of his school-time he became famous as a writer of humorous verses. Latterly he lived at a boarding-house in Charterhouse Square, and as a " day boy" saw less of his school fellows. In February 1828 he wrote to his mother, saying that he had become "terribly industrious," but "could not get Russell to think so." There were then 370 boys in the school, and he wishes that there were only 369. Russell, as these letters show, had reproached him pretty much as the master of " Greyfriars" reproaches young Pendennis, and a year after leaving the school he says that as a child he had been " licked into indolence," and when older " abused into sulkiness " and " bullied into despair." He left school in May 1828.* Thackeray now went to live with the Smyths, who had left Addiscombe, and about 1825 taken a house called Larkbeare, a mile and a half from Ottery St. Mary.† His recollections were used in " Pendennis," where Clavering St. Mary, Chatteris, and Baymouth stand for Ottery St. Mary, Exeter, and Sidmouth. Dr. Cornish, then vicar of Ottery St. Mary, lent Thackeray books, among others Cary's version of the " Birds" of Aristophanes, which the lad illustrated with three humorous watercolour drawings. Cornish reports that Thackeray, like Pendennis, contributed to the poet's corner of the county paper, and gives a parody of Moore's " Minstrel Boy " (cited in " Thackeray Memorials ") ridiculing an intended speech of Richard Lalor Shiel. This was probably the author's first appearance in print. Thackeray read, it seems, for a time with his stepfather, who was proud of the lad's cleverness, but probably an incompetent " coach." Thackeray was entered at Trinity College, Cambridge.‡ His college tutor was the omniscient William Whewell, with whom, apparently, he had no further relations. He began residence in February 1829. He was thus a " by-term man," which, as the great majority of his year had a term's start of him, was perhaps some disadvantage. This, however, was really of little importance, especially as he had the option of "degrading"—that is, joining the junior year. Thackeray

---

* For notices of Thackeray's infancy and schooldays, see the Introductions to " Vanity Fair," " Pendennis," and " The Newcomes."

† For descriptions of Larkbeare, see Introduction to "Pendennis."

‡ For Cambridge career, see Introduction to " Pendennis."

had little taste for mathematics, though he is said to have shown quickness in Euclid; nor had he taken to the classical training of his school in such a way as to qualify himself for success in examinations. In the May examination (1829) he was in the fourth class, where "clever non-reading men were put as in a limbo." He had expected to be in the fifth. He read some classical authors and elementary mathematics, but his main interests were of a different kind. He saw something of his Cambridge cousins, two of whom were Fellows of King's College; and formed lasting friendships with some of his most promising contemporaries. He was very sociable; he formed an Essay club in his second term, and afterwards a small club of which John Allen (afterwards Archdeacon) and William Hepworth Thompson (afterwards Master of Trinity) were members. Other lifelong friendships formed during or through his college career were with William Henry Brookfield, Edward FitzGerald, John Mitchell Kemble, A. W. Kinglake, Monckton Milnes, Spedding, and Tennyson. The intimacy with FitzGerald was especially close for many years, and the friendship remained when in after life intercourse became less frequent.* He was fond of literary talk, expatiated upon the merits of Fielding, read poetry, and could sing a good song. He also contributed to the "Snob: a literary and scientific journal not conducted by members of the University," which lasted through the May term of 1829. "Snob" appears to have been the cant phrase for townsmen as opposed to gownsmen. In this appeared "Timbuctoo," a mock poem upon the subject of that year, for which Tennyson won the prize; "Genevieve," and other trifles. Thackeray was bound to attend the lectures of Pryme, his cousin's husband, upon political economy, and is said to have admired them. He certainly adorned the syllabus with pen-and-ink drawings. He spoke at the Union with little success, and was much interested in Shelley, who seems to have been then a frequent topic of discussion. Thackeray was attracted by Shelley's poetry, but repelled by his principles. He was at this time an ardent opponent of Catholic emancipation.

He found Cambridge more agreeable but not more profitable than the Charterhouse. He had learnt "expensive habits," and in his second year appears to have anticipated some of the errors of Pendennis. He spent part of the long vacation of 1829 in Paris studying French and German, and left at the end of the Easter term 1830. His rooms were on the ground floor of

---

* For FitzGerald, see especially Introduction to "Christmas Books."

the staircase between the chapel and the gateway of the great court, where, as he remarks to his mother, it will be said hereafter that Newton and Thackeray both lived. He left, as he said at the time, because he felt that he was wasting time upon studies which, without more success than was possible to him, would be of no use in later life. He inherited from his father a fortune which appears to have been about £20,000.* His relations wished him to go to the bar; but he disliked the profession from the first, and resolved to finish his education by travelling. In 1830 he went by Godesberg and Cologne, where he made some stay, to Weimar.† There he spent some months. He was delighted by the homely and friendly ways of the little German court, which afterwards suggested "Pumpernickel," and was made welcome in all the socialities of the place. He had never been in a society "more simple, charitable, courteous, gentlemanlike." He was introduced to Goethe, whom he long afterwards described in a letter published in Lewes's "Life of Goethe." He delighted then, as afterwards, in drawing caricatures to amuse children, and was flattered by hearing that the great man had looked at them. He seems to have preferred the poetry of Schiller, whose "religion and morals," as he observes, "were unexceptionable," and who was "by far the favourite" at Weimar. He translated some of Schiller's and other German poems, and thought of making a book about German manners and customs. He did not, however, become a profound student of the literature. His studies at Weimar had been carried on by "lying on a sofa, reading novels, and dreaming"; but he began to think of the future, and, after some thoughts of diplomacy, resolved to be called to the bar. He read a little civil law, which he did not find "much to his taste." He returned to England in 1831, entered the Middle Temple, and in November was settled in chambers in Hare Court.‡

The "preparatory education" of lawyers struck him as "one of the most cold-blooded, prejudiced pieces of invention that ever a man was slave to." He read with Mr. Taprell, studied his Chitty, and relieved himself by occasional visits to the theatres and a trip to his old friends at Cambridge. He became intimate with Charles Buller, who, though he had graduated a little before, was known to the later Cambridge set; and, after the passage of the Reform Bill, went to Liskeard to

* See Introduction to "Philip," p. xv.
† See Introduction to "Vanity Fair."
‡ For the following period until Thackeray's marriage, see Introduction to "Yellowplush Papers."

help in Buller's canvass for the following election. He then spent some time in Paris, which he was frequently visiting at this period; and soon after his return finally gave up a profession which seems to have been always distasteful. He had formed an acquaintance with Maginn in 1832. F. S. Mahony ("Father Prout") told Blanchard Jerrold that he had given the introduction, a statement which seems to be irreconcilable with the dates of Mahony's life in London. Mahony further said that Thackeray paid £500 to Maginn to edit a new magazine. This is probably an erroneous version of some real transaction.* Thackeray was certainly mixing in literary circles and trying to get publishers for his caricatures. A paper had been started on January 5, 1833, called the *National Standard and Journal of Literature, Science, Music, Theatricals, and the Fine Arts.* Thackeray is said to have bought this from F. W. N. Bayley, a journalist who was afterwards the first editor of the *Illustrated London News.* At any rate he became editor and proprietor. He went to Paris, whence he wrote letters to the *Standard* (end of June to August) and collected materials for articles. He returned to look after the paper a little later, and at the end of the year reports that he has lost about £200 upon it, and that at this rate he will be ruined before it has made a success. Thackeray tells his mother at the same time that he ought to "thank Heaven" for making him a poor man, as he will be "much happier"—presumably as having to work harder. The last number of the *Standard* appeared on February 1, 1834. The loss to Thackeray was clearly not sufficient to explain a change in his position which happened about this time, nor are the circumstances now ascertainable. A good deal of money was lost at one time by the failure of an Indian bank, and probably by other investments for which his stepfather was more or less responsible. Thackeray had spent too much at Cambridge, and was led into occasional gambling. He told Sir Theodore Martin that his story of Deuceace (in the "Yellow-plush Papers") represented an adventure of his own. "I have not seen that man," he said, pointing to a gambler at Spa, "since he drove me down in his cabriolet to my bankers in the city, where I sold out my patrimony and handed it over to him." He added that the sum was lost at écarté, and amounted to £1500. This story, which is reported on trustworthy authority, must refer to this period. In any case, Thackeray had now to work for his bread. He made up his mind that he could draw

---

* B. Jerrold's "Father Prout" in *Belgravia* for July 1868.

better than he could do anything else, and determined to qualify himself as an artist and to study in Paris. "Three years' apprenticeship" would be necessary. He accordingly settled at Paris in 1834. His aunt (Mrs. Ritchie) was living there, and his maternal grandmother accompanied him thither in October and made a home for him. The Smyths about the same time left Devonshire for London. He worked in the atelier of Brine and perhaps Gros,* and copied pictures industriously at the Louvre. He never acquired any great technical skill as a draughtsman, but he always delighted in the art. The effort of preparing his drawings for engraving wearied him, and partly accounts for the inferiority of his illustrations to the original sketches. As it is, they have the rare interest of being interpretations by an author of his own conceptions, though interpretations in an imperfectly known language.

It is pretty certain that Thackeray was at the same time making some literary experiments. In January 1835 he appears as one of the "Fraserians" in the picture by Maclise issued with the *Fraser* of that month. The only article before that time which has been conjecturally assigned to him is the story of "Elizabeth Brownrigge," a burlesque of Bulwer's "Eugene Aram," in the numbers for August and September 1832. If really by him, as is most probable, it shows that his skill in the art of burlesquing was as yet very imperfectly developed. He was for some years desirous of an artistic career, and in 1836 he applied to Dickens (as he said in a speech at the Academy dinner of 1858) to be employed in illustrating the "Pickwick Papers," as successor to Robert Seymour, who died April 20, 1836. Henry Reeve speaks of him in January 1836 as editing an English paper at Paris in opposition to *Galignani's Messenger*, but of this nothing more is known. In the same year came out his first publication, "Flore et Zéphyr," a collection of eight satirical drawings, published at London and Paris. In 1836 a company was formed, of which Major Smyth was chairman, in order to start an Ultra-Liberal newspaper. The price of the stamp upon newspapers was lowered in the session of 1836, and the change gave encouragement for a new start in journalism. All the Radicals—Grote, Molesworth, Buller, and their friends— promised support. The old *Public Ledger* was bought, and, with the new title, *The Constitutional*, prefixed, began to appear on September 15 (the day on which the duty was lowered).

* Introduction to "Yellowplush Papers," p. xxxv. *Cf.* "Thackeray's Haunts and Homes," p. 9.

Samuel Laman Blanchard was editor, and Thackeray the Paris correspondent. He writes that his stepfather had behaved "nobly," and refused to take any remuneration as "director," desiring only this appointment for his stepson. Thackeray acted in that capacity for some time, and wrote letters strongly attacking Louis-Philippe as the representative of retrograde tendencies. *The Constitutional*, however, failed, and after July 1, 1837, the name disappeared and the *Public Ledger* revived in its place. The company had raised over £40,000, and the loss is stated at £6000 or £7000—probably a low estimate.*

Meanwhile Thackeray had taken advantage of his temporary position. He married, as he told his friend Synge, "with £400" (the exact sum seems to have been eight guineas a week), "paid by a newspaper which failed six months afterwards," referring presumably to his salary from *The Constitutional*. He was engaged early in the year to Isabella Gethin Creagh Shawe of Doneraile, co. Cork. She was daughter of Colonel Shawe, who had been military secretary, it is said, to the Marquis of Wellesley in India. The marriage took place at the British Embassy at Paris on August 20, 1836.†

The marriage was so timed that Thackeray could take up his duties as soon as *The Constitutional* started. The failure of the paper left him to find support by his pen. He speaks in a later letter of having written for *Galignani* at ten francs a day, apparently at this time. He returned, however, to England in 1837. The Smyths had left Larkbeare some time before, and were now living at 18 Albion Street, where Thackeray joined them, and where his first daughter was born. Major Smyth resembled Colonel Newcome in various qualities, including a weakness for rash speculations. He wasted money in various directions, and the liabilities incurred by *The Constitutional* were for a long time a source of anxiety. The Smyths now went to live at Paris, while Thackeray took a house at 13 Great Coram Street, and laboured energetically at a variety of hackwork.‡ He reviewed Carlyle's "French Revolution" in the *Times* (August 3, 1837). The author, as Carlyle reports, "is one Thackeray, a half-monstrous Cornish giant, kind of painter, Cambridge man, and Paris newspaper correspondent, who is now writing for his life in London. I have seen him at the Bullers' and at Sterling's."

* Fox Bourne, "English Newspapers," ii. 96–100; Andrews, "British Journalism," p. 237.
† See Marzials and Merivale, p. 107, for the official entry, first made known by Mr. Marzials in the *Athenæum*.
‡ For this period, see Introduction to "Barry Lyndon."

In 1838, and apparently for some time later, he worked for the *Times*. He wrote an article upon Fielding in 1840. He occasionally visited Paris upon journalistic business. He had some connection with the *Morning Chronicle*. He contributed stories to the *New Monthly* and to some of George Cruikshank's publications. He also illustrated Douglas Jerrold's " Men of Character " in 1838; and in 1840 was recommended by Mr., afterwards Sir, Henry Cole for employment both as writer and artist by the anti-corn-law agitators. His drawings for this purpose are reproduced in Sir Henry Cole's " Fifty Years of Public Work." His most important connection, however, was with *Fraser's Magazine*. In 1838 he contributed to it "The Yellowplush Correspondence," containing the forcible incarnation of his old friend Deuceace, and in 1839–1840 the " Catherine : by Ikey Solomons," following apparently the precedent of his favourite Fielding's " Jonathan Wild." The original was the real murderess Catherine Hayes (1690–1726), whose name was unfortunately identical with that of the popular Irish vocalist Catherine Hayes (1825–1861). A later reference to his old heroine in " Pendennis " (the passage is in vol. ii. chap. vii. of the serial form, afterwards suppressed) produced some indignant remarks in Irish papers, which took it for an insult to the singer. Thackeray explained the facts on April 12, 1850, in a letter to the *Morning Chronicle* on " Capers and Anchovies " (dated " Garrick Club, April 11, 1850 "). A compatriot of Miss Hayes took lodgings about the same time opposite Thackeray's house in Young Street in order to inflict vengeance. Thackeray first sent for a policeman ; but finally called upon the avenger, and succeeded in making him hear reason.*

For some time Thackeray wrote annual articles upon the Exhibitions, the first of which appeared in *Fraser* in 1838. According to FitzGerald, they annoyed one at least of the persons criticised, a circumstance not unparalleled, even when criticism, as this seems to have been, is both just and good-natured. In another respect, unfortunately, he conformed too much to a practice common to the literary class of the time. He ridiculed the favourite butts of his allies with a personality which he afterwards regretted. In a preface to the *Punch* papers, published in America in 1853, he confesses to his sins against Bulwer, and afterwards apologised to Bulwer himself. " I suppose we all begin by being too savage," he wrote to Hannay in 1849 ; " I

---

* For an account of this, see Introduction to " Barry Lyndon," p. xix., and Thackeray's " Haunts and Homes," p. 51.

know one who did." A private letter of 1840 shows that he considered his satire to be " good-natured."

Three daughters were born about this time. The death of
the second in infancy (1839) suggested a pathetic chapter in
the " Hoggarty Diamond." After the birth of the third (May
28, 1840) Thackeray took a trip to Belgium, having arranged
for the publication of a short book of travels. He had left his
wife " nearly well," but returned to find her in a strange state
of languor and mental inactivity, which became gradually more
pronounced.* For a long time there were gleams of hope.
Thackeray himself attended to her exclusively for a time. He
took her to her mother's in Ireland and afterwards to Paris.
There she had to be placed in a *maison de santé*, Thackeray
taking lodgings close by, and seeing her as frequently as he
could. A year later, as he wrote to FitzGerald, then his
most intimate friend, he thought her " all but well." He was
staying with her at a hydropathic establishment in Germany,
where she seemed to be improving for a short time. The case,
however, had become almost hopeless when in 1842 he went to
Ireland. Yet he continued to write letters to her as late as 1844,
hoping that she might understand them. She had finally to be
placed with a trustworthy attendant. She was placid and gentle,
though unfitted for any active duty, and with little knowledge
of anything around her, and survived till 1892. The children
had to be sent to the grandparents at Paris ; the house at Great
Coram Street was finally given up in 1843, and Thackeray for
some time lived as a bachelor at 27 Jermyn Street, 88 St. James's
Street, and probably elsewhere.

His short married life had been perfectly happy. "Though
my marriage was a wreck," he wrote in 1852 to his friend Synge,
" I would do it over again, for behold love is the crown and
completion of all earthly good." In spite of the agony of sus-
pense he regained cheerfulness, and could write playful letters,
although the frequent melancholy of this period may be traced
in some of his works. Part of " Vanity Fair " was written in
1841. He found relief from care in the society of his friends,
and was a member of many clubs of various kinds. He had
been a member of the Garrick Club from 1833, and in March,
1840, was elected to the Reform Club. He was a frequenter of
" Evans's," described in many of his works, and belonged at
this and later periods to various sociable clubs of the old-
fashioned style, such as the Shakespeare, the Fielding (of which

* For the following period, see Introduction to " Sketch Books."

3 o

33

he was a founder), and "Our Club." There in the evenings he met literary comrades, and gradually became known as an eminent member of the fraternity. Meanwhile, as he said, although he could suit the magazines, he could not hit the public.

In 1840, just before his wife's illness, he had published the "Paris Sketch Book," using some of his old material; and in 1841 he published a collection called "Comic Tales and Sketches," which had previously appeared in *Fraser* and elsewhere. It does not seem to have attracted much notice. In September of the same year the "History of Samuel Titmarsh," and the "Great Hoggarty Diamond," which had been refused by *Blackwood*, began to appear in *Fraser*. His friend Sterling read the first two numbers "with extreme delight," and asked what there was better in Fielding or Goldsmith. Thackeray, he added, with leisure might produce masterpieces. The opinion, however, remained esoteric, and the "Hoggarty Diamond" is said to have been cut short at the editor's request. He was contemplating a Life of Talleyrand about this time, which, however, came to nothing. His next book records a tour made in Ireland in the later half of 1842. He there made Lever's acquaintance, and advised his new friend to try his fortunes in London. Lever declared Thackeray to be the "most good-natured of men," but, though grateful, could not take help offered by a man who was himself struggling to keep his head above water. The "Irish Sketch Book" (1843), in which his experiences are recorded, is a quiet narrative of some interest as giving a straightforward account of Ireland as it appeared to an intelligent traveller just before the famine. A preface in which Thackeray pronounced himself decidedly against the English government of Ireland was suppressed, presumably in deference to the fears of the publisher. Thackeray would no doubt have been a Home Ruler. In 1840 he tells his mother that he is "not a Chartist, only a Republican," and speaks strongly against aristocratic government. "Cornhill to Cairo" (1846), which in a literary sense is decidedly superior, records a two months' tour made in the autumn of 1844, during which he visited Athens, Constantinople, Jerusalem, and Cairo.* The directors of the "Peninsular and Oriental Company," as he gratefully records, gave him a free passage. During the same year the "Luck of Barry Lyndon," which probably owed something to his Irish experiences, was coming out in *Fraser*. All later critics have recognised in this book one of his most powerful perform-

---

* A diary during this tour is given in Introduction to "Sketch Books."

ances. In directness and vigour he never surpassed it. At the time, however, it was still unsuccessful, the popular reader of the day not liking the company of even an imaginary blackguard. Thackeray was to obtain his first recognition in a different capacity.

Punch had been started with comparatively little success on July 17, 1841.* Among the first contributors were Douglas Jerrold and Thackeray's schoolfellow, John Leech, both his friends, and he naturally tried to turn the new opening to account. FitzGerald apparently feared that employment in a comic paper would involve a lowering of his literary status. He began to contribute in June 1842, his first article being the " Legend of Jawbrahim Heraudee." His first series, " Miss Tickletoby's Lectures on English History," began in June 1842. They ran for ten numbers, but failed to attract notice or to give satisfaction to the proprietors. Thackeray, however, persevered, and gradually became an invaluable contributor, having in particular the unique advantage of being skilful both with pen and pencil. In the course of his connection with *Punch* he contributed 380 sketches. One of his drawings is famous because nobody has ever been able to see the point of it, though a rival paper ironically offered £500 for an explanation.† This, however, is a singular exception. His comic power was soon appreciated, and at Christmas 1843 he became an attendant at the regular dinner parties which formed *Punch's* cabinet council. The first marked success was " Jeames's Diary," which began in November 1845, and satirised the railway mania of the time. The " Snobs of England, by One of Themselves," succeeded, beginning on February 28, 1846, and continued for a year; and after the completion of this series the " Prize Novelists," inimitably playful burlesques, began in April and continued till October 1847. The " Snob Papers " were collected as the " Book of Snobs " (issued from the *Punch* office). Seven, chiefly political, were omitted, but have been added to the last volume of the collected works.

The " Snob Papers " had a very marked effect, and may be said to have made Thackeray famous. He had at last found out how to reach the public ear. The style was admirable, and the freshness and vigour of the portrait painting undeniable. It has been stated that Thackeray got leave to examine the complaint books of several clubs, in order to obtain materials for his

* See for this connection Introduction to " Contributions to *Punch*."

† Some explanation is now given in Introduction to " Contributions to *Punch*," p. xxvi.

description of club snobs. He was speaking, in any case, upon a very familiar topic, and the vivacity of his sketches naturally suggested identification with particular individuals. These must be generally doubtful, and the practice was against Thackeray's artistic principles. Several of his Indian relatives are mentioned as partly originals of Colonel Newcome. He says himself that his Amelia represented his wife, his mother, and Mrs. Brook-field, and he describes to the same correspondent a self-styled Blanche Amory. Foker, in "Pendennis," is said to have been in some degree a portrait—according to Mr. Jeaffreson, a flatter-ing portrait—of an acquaintance. The resemblances can only be taken as generic, but a good cap fits many particular heads.

The success of the "Snob Papers" perhaps led Thackeray to insist a little too frequently upon a particular variety of social infirmity. He was occasionally accused of sharing the weakness which he satirised, and would playfully admit that the charge was not altogether groundless. It is much easier to make such statements than to test their truth. They indicate, however, one point which requires notice. Thackeray was at this time, as he remarks in "Philip," an inhabitant of "Bohemia," and en-joyed the humours and unconventional ways of the region. But he was a native of his own "Tyburnia," forced into "Bohemia" by distress, and there meeting many men of the Bludyer type, who were his inferiors in refinement and cultivation. Such peo-ple were apt to show their "unconventionality" by real coarse-ness, and liked to detect "snobbishness" in any taste for good society. To wear a dress-coat was to truckle to rank and fash-ion. Thackeray, an intellectual aristocrat, though politically a Liberal, was naturally an object of some suspicion to the rougher among his companions. If he appreciated refinement too keenly, no accusation of anything like meanness has ever been made against him. Meanwhile it was characteristic of his humour that he saw more strongly than any one the bad side of the society which held out to him the strongest temptations, and emphasised, possibly too much, its "mean admiration of mean things."

Thackeray in 1848 received one proof of his growing fame by the presentation of a silver inkstand in the shape of "Punch" from eighty admirers at Edinburgh, headed by Dr. John Brown, author of "Rab and his Friends," afterwards a warm friend and appreciative critic. His reputation was spreading by other works which distracted his energies from *Punch*. He contin-ued to contribute occasionally. The characteristic "Bow Street Ballads" in 1848 commemorate, among other things, his friendship for Matthew James Higgin, famous as "Jacob Omnium," one of whose articles, "A Plea for Plush," was erroneously included in the last volume of Thackeray's works. Some final contributions appeared in 1854; but his regular connection ceased after 1851, in which year he contributed forty-one articles and twelve cuts. Thackeray had by this time other occupations which made him unwilling to devote much time to journalism. He wrote a letter in 1855 to one of the proprietors, explaining the reasons of his retirement. He was annoyed by the political line taken by *Punch* in 1851, especially by denunciations of Napoleon III., which seemed to him unpatriotic and dangerous to peace. He remained, however, on good terms with his old colleagues, and occasionally attended their dinners. A sentence in his eulogy upon Leech (1854) appeared to disparage the relative merits of other contributors. Thackeray gave an "atonement dinner" at his own house, and obtained full forgiveness.* The advantages had been reciprocal, and were cordially admitted on both sides. "It was a good day for himself, the journal, and the world when Thackeray joined *Punch*," said Shirley Brooks, afterwards editor; and Thackeray himself admitted that he "owed the good chances which had lately befallen him to his connection with *Punch*."

From 1846 to 1850 he published yearly a "Christmas Book," the last of which, "The Kickleburys on the Rhine," was attacked in the *Times*. Thackeray's reply to this in a preface to the second edition is characteristic of his own view of the common tone of criticism at the time. Thackeray's "May Day Ode" on the opening of the Exhibition of 1851 appeared in the *Times* of April 30, and probably implied a reconciliation with the "Thunderer."

Thackeray had meanwhile made his mark in a higher department of literature. His improving position had now enabled him to make a home for himself. In 1846 he took a house at 13 Young Street, whither he brought his daughters, and where he afterwards received long visits from the Smyths. There he wrote "Vanity Fair." Dickens's success had given popularity to the system of publishing novels in monthly numbers. The first number of "Vanity Fair" appeared in January 1847, and the last (a double number) in July 1848. Thackeray says that he offered it to "three or four publishers."† There are reasons for doubting whether this was not a slip of the pen. It was

* See letter referring to this in Introduction to "Contributions to *Punch*," p. xxxiv.

† Introduction to "Philip," p. xxxiii.

certainly published by Bradbury and Evans, to whom his connection with *Punch* would naturally lead him in the first place. He is said to have received fifty guineas a number, including the illustrations.* The first numbers were comparatively unsuccessful, and the book for a time brought more fame than profit. The success is said to have been stimulated by the popularity of his Christmas book, "Mrs. Perkins's Ball." In any case it gradually became popular, and before it was ended his position as one of the first of English novelists was generally recognised. On September 16, 1847, Mrs. Carlyle wrote to her husband that the last four numbers were "very good indeed"—he "beats Dickens out of the world."

Abraham Hayward, an old friend, had recommended Thackeray to Macvey Napier in 1845 as a promising recruit for the *Edinburgh Review*. Thackeray had accordingly written an article upon N. P. Willis's "Dashes at Life," which Napier mangled and Jeffrey condemned. Hayward now reviewed the early numbers of "Vanity Fair" in the *Edinburgh* for January 1848. It is warmly praised as "immeasurably superior" to all his known works, and the review no doubt helped the success, though it did little more than confirm the general opinion. Edward Fitz-Gerald speaks of its success a little later, and says that Thackeray has become a great man and goes to Holland House. Monckton Milnes writes (May 19) that Thackeray is "winning great social success, dining at the Academy with Sir Robert Peel," and so forth. Milnes was through life a very close friend; he had been with Thackeray to see the second funeral of Napoleon, and had accompanied him "to see a man hanged" (an expedition described by Thackeray in *Fraser's Magazine*, August 1840). He tried to obtain a London magistracy for Thackeray in 1849. It was probably with a view to such an appointment, in which he would have succeeded Fielding, that Thackeray was called to the bar at the Middle Temple on May 26, 1848. As, however, a magistrate had to be a barrister of seven years' standing, the suggestion came to nothing. Trollope says that in 1848 Lord Clanricarde, then Postmaster-General, proposed to make him Assistant Secretary at the Post Office, but had to withdraw an offer which would have been unjust to the regular staff. Thackeray, in any case, had become famous outside of fashionable circles. In those days youthful critics divided themselves into two camps of Dickens and Thackeray worshippers. Both were popular authors of periodical publications, but otherwise a "com-

---

* See Vizetelly's "Glances Back through Seventy Years," i. 281, &c.

parison" was as absurd as most comparisons of disparate qualities. As a matter of fact, Dickens had an incomparably larger
circulation, as was natural to one who appealed to a wider audience. Thackeray had as many or possibly more adherents
among the more cultivated critics; but for some years the two
reigned supreme among novelists. Among Thackeray's warmest admirers was Miss Brontë, who had published "Jane Eyre"
anonymously. The second edition was dedicated in very enthusiastic terms to the "Satirist of Vanity Fair." He was compared to a Hebrew prophet, and said to "resemble Fielding as an
eagle does a vulture." An absurd story to the effect that Miss
Brontë was represented by Becky Sharp and Thackeray by Mr.
Rochester became current, and was mentioned seriously in a
review of "Vanity Fair" in the *Quarterly* for January 1849.
Miss Brontë came to London in June 1850, and was introduced
to her hero. She met him at her publisher's house, and dined
at his house on June 12. Miss Brontë's genius did not include
a sense of humour, and she rebuked Thackeray for some "errors
of doctrine," which he defended by "worse excuses." They
were, however, on excellent terms, though the dinner to which
he invited her turned out to be so oppressively dull that Thackeray sneaked off to his club prematurely.* She attended one
of his lectures in 1851, and, though a little scandalised by some
of his views, cordially admired his great qualities.

"Vanity Fair" was succeeded by "Pendennis," the first number of which appeared in November 1848. The book has more
autobiography than any of the novels, and clearly embodies the
experience of Thackeray's early life so fully that it must be also
pointed out that no stress must be laid upon particular facts.
Nor is it safe to identify any of the characters with originals,
though Captain Shandon has been generally taken to represent
Maginn; and Mrs. Carlyle gives a lively account in January
1851 of a young lady whom she supposed to be the original of
Blanche Amory.† When accused of "fostering a baneful
prejudice against literary men," Thackeray defended himself in
a letter to the *Morning Chronicle* of January 12, 1850, and
stated that he had seen the bookseller from whom Bludyer
robbed and had taken money "from a noble brother man of
letters to some one not unlike Captain Shandon in prison."
Hannay says that it is "certain" that he gave Maginn £500.
The state of Thackeray's finances up to Maginn's death (1842)

---

* See Mrs. R. Ritchie's "Chapters from Some Memoirs," p. 62.
† "Memorials of Janet Welsh Carlyle," ii. 141, 147.

seems to make this impossible, though the statement (see above) made by Father Prout suggests that on some pretext Maginn may have obtained such a sum from Thackeray. Anyway, the book is a transcript from real life, and shows perhaps as much power as "Vanity Fair," with less satirical intensity. A severe illness at the end of 1849 interrupted the appearance of "Pendennis," which was not concluded till December 1850. The book is dedicated to Dr. John Elliotson, who would "take no other fee but thanks," and to whose attendance he ascribed his recovery.

On February 25, 1851, Thackeray was elected member of the Athenæum Club by the committee. An attempt to elect him in 1850 had been defeated by the opposition of one member. Macaulay, Croker, Dean Milman, and Lord Mahon had supported his claims. He was never, as has been said, "blackballed." He was henceforward a familiar figure at the club. The illness of 1849 appears to have left permanent effects. He was afterwards liable to attacks which caused much suffering. Meanwhile, although he was now making a good income, he was anxious to provide for his children and recover what he had lost in his youth.* He resolved to try his hand at lecturing, following a precedent already set by such predecessors as Coleridge, Hazlitt, and Carlyle. He gave a course of six lectures upon the "English Humourists" at Willis's Rooms from May 22 to July 3, 1851. The first (on Swift), though attended by many friends, including Carlyle, Kinglake, Hallam, Macaulay, and Milman, seemed to him to be a failure. The lectures soon became popular, as they deserved to be. Thackeray, though he read widely in a desultory fashion, was not given to systematic antiquarian research, and his facts and dates require some correction. But his delicate appreciation of the congenial writers and the finish of his style give the lectures a permanent place in criticism. His "light-in-hand manner," as Motley remarked of a later course, "suits well the delicate hovering rather than superficial style of his composition." Without the slightest attempt at rhetorical effect his delivery did full justice to the peculiar merits of his own writing. The lectures had apparently been prepared with a view to an engagement in America. Before starting he published "Esmond," of which FitzGerald says (June 2, 1852) that "it was finished last Saturday." The book shows even more than the lectures how thoroughly he had

* For the following period, see Introduction to "Esmond" and the "Lectures."

imbibed the spirit of the Queen Anne writers. His style had reached its highest perfection, and the tenderness of the feeling has won perhaps more admirers for this book than for the more powerful and sterner performances of the earlier period. The manuscript, now in the library of Trinity College, Cambridge, shows that it was written with very few corrections, and in great part dictated to his eldest daughter and Mr. Crowe. Earlier manuscripts show much more alteration, and he clearly obtained a completer mastery of his art by long practice. He took much pains to get correct statements of fact, and read for that purpose at the libraries of the British Museum and the Athenæum.* The book had a good sale from the first, although the contrary has been stated. For the first edition of " Esmond " Thackeray received £1200. It was published by Messrs. Smith and Elder, and the arrangement was made with him by Mr. George Smith of that firm, who became a warm friend for the rest of his life. The acquaintance had already begun in 1850, when the same firm had published the " Kickleburys on the Rhine."

On October 30, 1852, Thackeray sailed for Boston, U.S.A., in company with Clough and J. R. Lowell. He lectured at Boston, New York, Philadelphia (where he formed a friendship with W. B. Reed, who has described their intercourse), Baltimore, Richmond, Charleston, and Savannah.† He was received with the characteristic hospitality of Americans, and was thoroughly pleased with the people, making many friends in the Southern as well as in the Northern States—a circumstance which probably affected his sympathies during the subsequent Civil War. He returned in the spring of 1853 with about £2500. Soon after his return he stayed three weeks in London, and after spending a month with the Smyths, went with his children to Switzerland.‡ There, as he says, he strayed into a wood near Berne, where the story of " The Newcomes " was " revealed to him somehow." The story, like those of his other longer novels, is rather a wide section of family history than the development of a definite " plot." Colonel Newcome, no doubt drawn in part from his stepfather, may be taken as embodying the Anglo-Indian traditions in which the family was so rich. For " The Newcomes " he apparently received £4000. It was again published in numbers, and was illustrated by his friend Richard Doyle, who had also illustrated " Rebecca and

---

* See " With Thackeray in America," pp. 1–6.

† For letters written during this tour, see Introduction to " Esmond " and the " Lectures."

‡ See Introduction to " The Newcomes."

Rowena" (1850). At Christmas, 1853, Thackeray went with his daughters to Rome. There, to amuse some children, he made the drawings which gradually expanded into the delightful burlesque of "The Rose and the Ring," published with great success in 1854.* He sueffred also from a Roman fever, from which, if not from the previous illness of 1849, dated a series of attacks causing much suffering and depression. In 1854 he moved from Young Street to 36 Onslow Square. The last number of "The Newcomes" appeared in August 1855, and in October Thackeray started for a second lecturing tour in the United States. Sixty of his friends gave him a farewell dinner (October 11), at which Dickens took the chair. The subject of this new series was "The Four Georges."† Over-scrupulous Britons complained of him for laying bare the weaknesses of our monarchs to Americans, who were already not predisposed in their favour. The Georges, however, had been dead for some time. On this occasion his tour extended as far as New Orleans.‡ An attempt on his return journey to reproduce the "English Humourists" in Philadelphia failed, owing to the lateness of the season. Thackeray said that he could not bear to see the "sad, pale-faced young man" who had lost money by undertaking the speculation, and left behind him a sum to replace what had been lost. He returned to England in April 1856. The lectures upon the Georges were repeated at various places in England and Scotland. He received from thirty to fifty guineas a lecture. Although they have hardly the charm of the more sympathetic accounts of the "Humourists," they show the same qualities of style, and obtained general if not equal popularity.

Thackeray's hard struggle, which had brought fame and social success, had also enabled him to form a happier home. His children had lived with him from 1846 ; but while they were in infancy, the house without a mistress was naturally grave and quiet. Thackeray had the strongest love for all children, and was a most affectionate father to his own. He did all that he could to make their lives bright. He took them to plays and concerts, or for long drives into the country, or children's parties at the Dickenses' and elsewhere. They became known to his friends, grew up to be on the most easy terms with him, and gave him a happy domestic circle. About 1853 he received as

---

* See Introductions to "The Newcomes" and to "Christmas Books."

† For passages from Thackeray's notebooks for "The Four Georges," see Introduction to "Ballads and Miscellanies."

‡ For letters during this tour, see Introduction to "The Virginians."

an inmate of his household Amy Crowe, daughter of Eyre Evans Crowe, who had been a warm friend at Paris. She became a sister to his daughters, and in 1862 married his cousin, now Sir Edward Talbot Thackeray, V.C. His old college friend Brookfield was settled as a clergyman in London, and had married a very charming wife. The published correspondence shows how much value Thackeray attached to this intimacy. Another dear friend was John Leech, to whom he was specially attached. He was also intimate with Richard Doyle * and other distinguished artists, including Landseer and Mr. G. F. Watts. Another friend was Henry Thoby Prinsep, who lived in later years at Little Holland House, which became the centre of a delightful social circle. Herman Merivale and his family, the Theodore Martins, the Coles and the Synges, were other friends of whose relation to him some notice is given in the last chapter of Mr. Merivale's memoir. Thackeray was specially kind to the younger members of his friends' families. He considered it to be a duty to "tip" schoolboys, and delighted in giving them holidays at the play. His old friendships with Monckton Milnes (Lord Houghton), Venables, Kinglake, and many other well-known men were kept up both at his clubs and at various social meetings. The Carlyles were always friendly, in spite of Carlyle's severe views of a novelist's vocation. Thackeray's time, however, was much taken up by lecturing and by frequent trips to the Continent or various country places in search of relaxation. His health was far from strong. On November 11, 1854, he wrote to Reed that he had been prevented from finishing "The Newcomes" by a severe fit of "spasms," of which he had had about a dozen in the year. This decline of health is probably to be traced in the comparative want of vigour of his next writings.

In July, 1857, Thackeray stood for the city of Oxford, the member, Charles Neate (1806–1879), having been unseated on petition.† Thackeray was always a decided Liberal in politics, though never much interested in active agitation. He promised to vote for the ballot in extension of the suffrage, and was ready to accept triennial parliaments. His opponent was Mr. Edward (afterwards Viscount) Cardwell, who had lost the seat at the previous election for opposing Palmerston on the Chinese question. Thackeray seems to have done better as a speaker than might have been expected, and Cardwell only won (July 21) by a narrow

---

* For some notices of Doyle, see Introduction to "Christmas Books," p. li., &c.
† See Introduction to "The Virginians," p. xxx.

majority—1085 to 1018. Thackeray had fought the contest with good temper and courtesy. " I will retire," he said in a farewell speech, "and take my place at my desk, and leave to Mr. Cardwell a business which I am sure he understands better than I do." " The Virginians," the first-fruits of this resolution, came out in monthly numbers from November 1857 to October 1859.* It embodied a few of his American recollections, and continued with less than the old force the history of the Esmond family.† Thackeray told Motley that he contemplated a grand novel of the period of Henry V., in which the ancestors of all his imaginary families should be assembled. He mentions this scheme in a letter to FitzGerald in 1841. He had read many of the chronicles of the period, though it may be doubted whether he would have been as much at home with Henry V. as with Queen Anne.

In June 1858 Edmund Yates published in a paper called Town Talk a personal description of Thackeray, marked, as the author afterwards allowed, by " silliness and bad taste." Thackeray considered it to be also " slanderous and untrue," and wrote to Yates, saying so in the plainest terms. Yates, in answer, refused to accept Thackeray's account of the article, or to make any apology. Thackeray then laid the matter before the committee of the Garrick Club, of which both he and Yates were members, on the ground that Yates's knowledge was only derived from meetings at the Club. A general meeting of the Club in July passed resolutions calling upon Yates to apologise under penalty of further action. Dickens warmly took Yates's part. Yates afterwards disputed the legality of the Club's action, and counsel's opinion was taken on both sides. In November Dickens offered to act as Yates's friend in a conference with a representative of Thackeray with a view to arranging " some quiet accommodation." Thackeray replied that he had left the matter in the hands of the committee. Nothing came of this. Yates had to leave the club, and he afterwards dropped the legal proceedings on the ground of their costliness.

Thackeray's disgust will be intelligible to every one who holds that journalism is degraded by such personalities. He would have been fully justified in breaking off intercourse with a man who had violated the tacit code under which gentlemen associate. He was, however, stung by his excessive sensibility into

---

* See Introduction to " The Virginians," p. xxxiii., &c.

† A careful account of the genealogies in Thackeray's novels is given by Mr. E. C. K. Gonner in Time for 1889.

injudicious action. Yates, in a letter suppressed by Dickens's advice, had at first retorted that Thackeray in his youth had been equally impertinent to Bulwer and Lardner, and had caricatured members of the Club in some of his fictitious characters. Thackeray's regrettable freedoms did not really constitute a parallel offence. But a recollection of his own errors might have suggested less vehement action. There was clearly much ground for Dickens's argument that the Club had properly no right to interfere in the matter. The most unfortunate result was an alienation between the two great novelists. Thackeray was no doubt irritated at Dickens's support of Yates, though it is impossible to accept Mr. Jefferson's view that jealousy of Dickens was at the bottom of this miserable affair. An alienation between the two lasted till they accidentally met at the Athenæum a few days before Thackeray's death and spontaneously shook hands. Though they had always been on terms of courtesy, they were never much attracted by each other personally. Dickens could not really sympathise with Thackeray's modes of thought. Thackeray, on the other hand, though making certain reserves, expressed the highest admiration of Dickens's work both in private and public, and recognised ungrudgingly the great merits which justified Dickens's wider popularity.

Thackeray's established reputation was soon afterwards recognised by a new position. Messrs. Smith and Elder started the *Cornhill Magazine* in January 1860.* With *Macmillan's Magazine*, begun in the previous month, it set the new fashion of shilling magazines. The *Cornhill* was illustrated, and attracted many of the rising artists of the day. Thackeray's editorship gave it prestige, and the first numbers had a sale of over a hundred thousand. His acquaintance with all men of literary mark enabled him to enlist some distinguished contributors; Tennyson among others, whose "Tithonus" first appeared in the second number. One of the first contributors was Anthony Trollope, to whom Thackeray had made early application. "Justice compelled" Trollope to say that Thackeray was "not a good editor." One reason was that, as he admitted in his "Thorns in a Cushion," he was too tender-hearted. He was pained by the necessity of rejecting articles from poor authors who had no claim but poverty, and by having to refuse his friends—such as Mrs. Browning and Trollope himself—from deference to absurd public prejudices. An editor no doubt requires on occasion thickness of skin if not hardness of heart. Trollope, however,

* See Introduction to "Philip" for this period.

makes the more serious complaint that Thackeray was unme-
thodical and given to procrastination.   As a criticism of Thackeray's methods of writing, this of course tells chiefly against the
critic.   Trollope's amusing belief in the virtues of what he calls
" elbow-grease" is too characteristic of his own methods of production.   But an editor is certainly bound to be business-like,
and Thackeray no doubt had shortcomings in that direction.
Manuscripts were not considered with all desirable punctuality
and despatch.   His health made the labour trying ; and in April
1862 he retired from the editorship, though continuing to contribute up to the last.   His last novels appeared in the magazine.
" Lovel the Widower" came out from January to June 1860,
and was a rewriting of a play called " The Wolves and the
Lamb," which had been written in 1854 and refused at a theatre.   The " Adventures of Philip" followed from January 1861
till August 1862, continuing the early " Shabby Genteel Story,"
and again containing much autobiographical material.   In these,
as in " The Virginians," it is generally thought that the vigour
shown in their predecessors has declined, and that the tendency
to discursive moralising has been too much indulged.   It was
illustrated by Frederick Walker, then beginning his brilliant
career.*   " Denis Duval," on the other hand, of which only a
part had been written at his death, gave great promise of a return to the old standard.   His most characteristic contributions,
however, were the " Roundabout Papers," which began in the
first number, and are written with the ease of consummate mastery
of style.   They are models of the essay which, without aiming
at profundity, gives the charm of playful and tender conversation of a great writer.†

In 1861 Thackeray built a house at 2 Palace Green, Kensington, upon which is now placed the commemorative tablet of the
Society of Arts.‡   It is a red-brick house in the style of the
Queen Anne period, to which he was so much attached ; and
was then, as he told an American friend, the " only one of its
kind " in London.   The " house-warming " took place on February 24 and 25, 1862, when " The Wolves and the Lamb " was
performed by amateurs.   Thackeray himself only appeared at
the end as a clerical father to say in pantomime, " Bless you,
my children !"   His friends thought that the house was too
large for his means ; but he explained that it would be, as in

---

* See Introduction to " Philip," p. xlii., &c.
† See Introduction to " Roundabout Papers" and "Denis Duval."
‡ See Introduction to " Philip," p. xxxiv., &c.

fact it turned out to be, a good investment for his children. His income from the *Cornhill Magazine* alone was about £4000 a year. Thackeray had appeared for some time to be older than he really was, an effect partly due perhaps to his hair, originally black, having become perfectly white. His friends, however, had seen a change, and various passages in his letters show that he thought of himself as an old man, and considered his life to be precarious. In December 1863 he was unwell, but attended the funeral of a relative, Lady Rodd, on the 21st. Feeling ill on the 23rd with one of his old attacks, he retired at an early hour, and next morning was found dead, the final cause being an effusion into the brain. Few deaths were received with more general expressions of sorrow. He was buried at Kensal Green on December 30, where his mother, who died a year later, is also buried. A subscription, first suggested by Shirley Brooks, provided for a bust by Marochetti in Westminster Abbey. Thackeray left two daughters: Anne Isabella, now Mrs. Richmond Ritchie; and Harriet Marian, who in 1867 became Mrs. Leslie Stephen, and who died November 28, 1875.

Nothing need be said here of Thackeray's place in English literature, which is discussed by all the critics. In any case, he is one of the most characteristic writers of the first half of the Victorian period. His personal character is indicated by his life. "He had many fine qualities," wrote Carlyle to Monckton Milnes upon his death; "no guile or malice against any mortal; a big mass of a soul, but not strong in proportion; a beautiful vein of genius lay struggling about him.—Poor Thackeray, adieu, adieu!" Thackeray's want of "strength" meant the excess of sensibility of a strongly artistic temperament, which in his youth led him into extravagance and too easy compliance with the follies of young men of his class. In later years it produced some foibles, the more visible to his contemporaries because he seems to have been at once singularly frank in revealing his feelings to congenial friends, and reticent or sarcastic to less congenial strangers. His constitutional indolence and the ironical view of life which made him a humourist disqualified him from being a prophet after the fashion of Carlyle. The author of "A Novel Without a Hero" was not a "hero-worshipper." But the estimate of his moral and intellectual force will be increased by a fair view of his life. If naturally indolent, he worked most energetically and under most trying conditions through many years full of sorrow and discouragement. The loss of his fortune and the ruin of his domestic happiness stimulated him to sustained and vigorous efforts. He worked, as he was bound to work, for money, and took his place frankly as a literary drudge. He slowly forced his way to the front, helping his comrades liberally whenever occasion offered. Trollope only confirms the general testimony by a story of the ready generosity with which he would assist a friend in distress. He kept all his old friends; he was most affectionate to his mother, and made a home for her in later years; and he was the tenderest and most devoted of fathers. His "social success" never distracted him from his home duties, and he found his chief happiness in his domestic affections. The superficial weakness might appear in society, and a man with so keen an eye for the weaknesses of others naturally roused some resentment. But the moral upon which Thackeray loved to insist in his writings gives also the secret which ennobled his life. A contemplation of the ordinary ambitions led him to emphasise the " vanity of vanities," and his keen perception of human weaknesses showed him the seamy side of much that passes for heroic. But to him the really valuable element of life was in the simple and tender affections which do not flourish in the world. During his gallant struggle against difficulties, he emphasised the satirical vein which is embodied with his greatest power in " Barry Lyndon " and " Vanity Fair." As success came he could give freer play to the gentler emotions which animate " Esmond," " The Newcomes," and the " Round-about Papers," and in which he found the chief happiness of his own career.

Thackeray was 6 feet 3 inches in height. His head was very massive, and it is stated that the brain weighed 58½ ounces. His appearance was made familiar by many caricatures introduced by himself as illustrations of his own works and in *Punch*. Portraits are as follows : A plaster bust from a cast taken from life about 1825, by J. Devile (Mrs. Ritchie : replica in National Portrait Gallery). Two drawings by Maclise dated 1832 and 1833 (Garrick Club). Another drawing by Maclise of about 1840 was engraved from a copy made by Thackeray himself for the "Orphan of Pimlico." Painting by Frank Stone about 1836 (Mrs. Ritchie). Two chalk drawings by Samuel Laurence, the first in 1853, a full face, engraved in 1854 by Francis Hall, and a profile, reading. Laurence made several replicas of the last after Thackeray's death, one of which is in the National Portrait Gallery. Laurence also painted a posthumous portrait for the Reform Club. Portrait of Thackeray, in his study at Onslow Square in 1854, by E. M. Ward (Mr. R. Hurst). Portrait by Sir John Gilbert, posthumous, of Thackeray in the smoking-

room of the Garrick Club (Garrick Club; this is engraved in
" Maclise's Portrait Gallery," where is also the portrait of Thackeray among the " Frasereans "). A sketch from memory by
Millais and a drawing by F. Walker—a back view of Thackeray,
done to show the capacity of the then unknown artist to illustrate for the *Cornhill*—belong to Mrs. Ritchie. The bust by
Marochetti in Westminster Abbey is not thought to be satisfactory as a likeness. A statuette by Edgar Boehm was begun
in 1860 from two short sittings. It was finished after Thackeray's death, and is considered to be an excellent likeness.
Many copies were sold, and two were presented to the Garrick
Club and the Athenæum. A bust by Joseph Durham was presented to the Garrick Club by the artist in 1864 ; and a terra-
cotta replica from the original plaster mould is in the National
Portrait Gallery. A bust by J. B. Williamson was exhibited at
the Royal Academy in 1864 ; and another, by Nevill Northey
Burnard, is in the National Portrait Gallery. For further details
see article by F. G. Kitton in the *Magazine of Art* for July 1891.

The following is a list of Thackeray's works in the order of
their independent publication, with references to the places in
which they first appeared, and to the volume in this edition in
which they are now arranged :—

1. " Flore et Zéphyr : Ballet Mythologique, par Théophile
Wagstaff " (eight plates, lithographed by E. Morton from
sketches by Thackeray), fol. 1836 (vol. ix.). 2. " The Paris
Sketch Book, by Mr. Titmarsh," 2 vols. 12mo, 1840, includes
" The Devil's Wager," from the *National Standard*, " Mary
Ancel," from the *New Monthly* (1838), " Cartouche," " The
Little Poinsinet," and the " French School of Painting," from
Fraser, 1839, and " An Invasion of France," " Mme. Sand, &c.,"
and the " Fêtes of July," from *The Corsair*, a New York paper,
1839 (vol. v.). " The Student's Quarter," published by J. C.
Hotten, professes to be from " papers not included in the col-
lected writings," but is made up of this and one other letter in
The Corsair (see *Athenæum* 7 and 14 August 1886). 3. " Essay
on the Genius of George Cruikshank, with numerous illustra-
tions of his works," 1840 — reprinted from the *Westminster
Review*—(vol. xiii.). 4. Sketches by Spec. No. 1 : " Britannia
Protecting the Drama " (1840) ; Facsimile by Autotype Com-
pany from unique copy belonging to Mr. C. P. Johnson. 5.
" Comic Tales and Sketches, edited and illustrated by Mr.
Michael Angelo Titmarsh," 2 vols. 8vo, 1841, contains the " Yel-
lowplush Papers," from *Fraser*, 1838 and 1840 (vol. iii.);
" Some Passages in the Life of Major Gahagan," from *New*

Monthly, 1838–9 (vol. iii.); "The Professor," from *Bentley's Miscellany*, 1837 (vol. xiii.); "The Bedford Row Conspiracy," from the *New Monthly*, 1840 (vol. iii.); and "The Fatal Boots," from Cruikshank's *Comic Almanack* for 1839 (vol. iii.).   6. "The Second Funeral of Napoleon, in Three Letters to Miss Smith, of London "—reprinted in *Cornhill Magazine* for January 1866—(vol. iv.), and "The Chronicle of the Drum," 16mo, 1841 (vol. xiii.).   7. "The Irish Sketch Book," 2 vols. 12mo, 1843 (vol. v.).   8. "Notes of a Journey from Cornhill to Cairo by Way of Lisbon, Athens, Constantinople, and Jerusalem, by Mr. M. A. Titmarsh," 12mo, 1846 (vol. v.).   9. "Mrs. Perkins's Ball, by Mr. M. A. Titmarsh," 4to, 1847—(*i.e.* Christmas, 1846) —(vol. ix.).   10. "Vanity Fair: a Novel Without a Hero, with Illustrations by the Author," 1 vol. 8vo, 1848—monthly numbers from January 1847 to July 1848; last number double—(vol. i.). 11. "The Book of Snobs," 8vo, 1848; reprinted from "The Snobs of England, by One of Themselves," in *Punch*, 1846–7— omitting 7 numbers—(vol. vi.).   12. "Our Street, by Mr. M. A. Titmarsh," 4to, 1848—Christmas, 1847—(vol. ix.).   13. "The History of Pendennis, his Fortunes and Misfortunes, his Friends and his Greatest Enemy, with Illustrations by the Author," 2 vols. 8vo, 1849–50—in monthly numbers from November 1848 to December 1850, last number double; suspended, owing to the author's illness, for the three months after September 1849— (vol. ii.).   14. "Dr. Birch and his Young Friends, by Mr. M. A. Titmarsh," 16mo, 1849 (*i.e.* Christmas, 1848)—(vol. ix.).   15. "The History of Samuel Titmarsh and the Great Hoggarty Diamond," from *Fraser's Magazine* of 1841, 8vo, 1849 (vol. iii.). 16. "Rebecca and Rowena: a Romance upon Romance," illustrated by R. Doyle, 8vo, 1850 (*i.e.* Christmas, 1849)—(vol. ix.); enlarged from "Proposals for a Continuation of 'Ivanhoe'" in *Fraser*, August and September, 1846.   17. "Sketches after English Landscape Painters, by S. Marvy, with Short Notices by W. M. Thackeray," fol. 1850.   18. "The Kickleburys on the Rhine, by Mr. M. A. Titmarsh," 4to, 1850; Second Edition with Preface (January 5, 1851), being an "Essay on Thunder and Small Beer," 1851 (vol. ix.).   19. "The History of Henry Esmond, Esq., a Colonel in the Service of Her Majesty Queen Anne, Written by Himself," 3 vols. 8vo, 1852 (vol. vii.).   20. "The English Humourists of the Eighteenth Century: a Series of Lectures Delivered in England, Scotland, and the United States of America," 8vo, 1853 (vol. vii.).   The notes were written by James Hannay (see his "Characters," &c., p. 55 *n.*). 21. "Preface to a Collection of Papers from *Punch*," printed at New York, 1852. 22. "The Newcomes: Memoirs of a Most Respectable Family, Edited by Arthur Pendennis, Esq.," 2 vols. 8vo, 1854–5, illustrated by R. Doyle—twenty-four monthly numbers from October 1853 to August 1855—(vol. viii.). 23. "The Rose and the Ring; or, The History of Prince Giglio and Prince Bulbo: a Fireside Pantomime for Great and Small Children, by Mr. M. A. Titmarsh," 8vo, 1855, illustrated by the author (vol. ix.). 24. "Miscellanies in Prose and Verse," 4 vols. 8vo, 1855, contains all the "Comic Tales and Sketches" (except "The Professor"), "The Book of Snobs" (1848), "The Hoggarty Diamond" (1849), and "Rebecca and Rowena" (1850). It also contains the first reprints of "Ballads" (vol. xiii.); "Cox's Diary," from the *Comic Almanack* of 1840 (vol. iii.); the "Diary of Jeames de la Pluche," from *Punch*, 1845–6 (vol. iii.); "Sketches and Travels in London," from *Punch*, 1847 (vol. vi.), and "Going to See a Man Hanged," from *Fraser*, August 1840 (vol. iii.); "Novels by Eminent Hands," from *Punch*, 1847 (vol. vi.); "Character Sketches," from "Heads of the People," drawn by Kenny Meadows, 1840–1 (vol. iii.); "Barry Lyndon," from *Fraser*, 1844 (vol. iv.); "Legend of the Rhine," from Cruikshank's "Tablebook," 1845 (vol. iii.); "A Little Dinner at Timmins's," from *Punch*, 1848 (vol. vi.); the "Fitzboodle Papers," from *Fraser*, 1842–3 (vol. iv.); "Men's Wives," from *Fraser*, 1843 (vol. iv.); and "A Shabby Genteel Story," from *Fraser*, 1840 (vol. xi.). 25. "The Virginians: a Tale of the Last Century" (illustrated by the author), 2 vols. 8vo, 1858–9—monthly numbers from November 1857 to October 1859—(vol. x.). 26. "Lovel the Widower," 8vo, 1861, from the *Cornhill Magazine*, 1860—illustrated by the author—(vol. xii.). 27. "The Four Georges," 1861, from *Cornhill Magazine*, 1860 (vol. vii.: notebook extracts in vol. xiii.). 28. "The Adventures of Philip on his Way through the World; showing who Robbed him, who Helped him, and who Passed him by," 3 vols. 8vo, 1862, from *Cornhill Magazine*, 1861–2 (vol. xi.). 29. "Roundabout Papers," 8vo, 1863, from *Cornhill Magazine*, 1860–3 (vol. xii.). 30. "Denis Duval," 8vo, 1867, from *Cornhill Magazine*, 1864 (vol. xii.). 31. "The Orphan of Pimlico, and Other Sketches, Fragments, and Drawings, by W. M. Thackeray, with some Notes by A. T. Thackeray," 4to, 1876. 32. "Etchings by the Late W. M. Thackeray while at Cambridge," 1878. 33. "A Collection of Letters by W. M. Thackeray, 1847–1855" (with introduction by Mrs. Brookfield), 8vo, 1887; first published in *Scribner's Magazine*. 34. "Sultan Stork," from *Ainsworth's Magazine*, 1842 (vol. v.), and "other stories now first collected "—includes " Dickens in France," from *Fraser's Magazine*, 1842 (vol. v.), to which is added the bibliography of Thackeray " (by R. H. Shepherd), "revised and considerably enlarged," 8vo, 1887.   35. "Loose Sketches.   An Eastern Adventure," &c. (contributions to *The Britannia* in 1841, and to *Punch's Pocket-Book* for 1847), London, 1894 (vol. xiii.).

The first collective or "library " edition of the works appeared in 22 vols. 8vo, 1867–9 ; the "popular" edition in 12 vols. crown 8vo, 1871–2 ; the "cheaper illustrated edition " in 24 vols. 8vo, 1877–9 ; the *édition de luxe* in 24 vols. imp. 8vo, 1878–9 ; and the "standard" edition in 26 vols. 8vo, 1883–5.   All the collective editions include the works (Nos. 1–30) mentioned above (except Nos. 4 and 17), and add "The History of the Next French Revolution," from *Punch*, 1844 (vol. vi.) ; "Catherine," from *Fraser*, 1839–40 (vol. iv.) ; "Little Travels and Roadside Sketches," from *Fraser*, 1844–5 (vol. vi.) ; "John Leech," from *Quarterly Review*, December 1854 (vol. xiii.) ; and "The Wolves and the Lamb "—first printed—(vol. xii.). "Little Billee" first appeared as the "Three Sailors " in Bevan's "Sand and Canvas," 1849 (vol. xiii.).   A facsimile from the autograph of these lines sent to Bevan is in the *Autographic Mirror*, December 1, 1864, and another from Shirley Brooks's album in the *Editor's Box*, 1880.

The last two volumes of the "standard" edition contain additional matter.   Vol. xxv. supplies most of the previously uncollected *Fraser* articles and a lecture upon "Charity and Humour," given at New York in 1852 (vol. vii.) ; the letter describing Goethe; "Timbuctoo," from the *Snob;* and a few trifles. Vol. xxvi. contains previously uncollected papers from *Punch*, including the suppressed "Snob" papers, chiefly political. These additions are also contained in vols. xxv. and xxvi. added to the *édition de luxe* in 1886.   Two volumes, with the same contents, were added at the same time to the "library " and the "cheaper illustrated," and one to the "popular " edition.   The "pocket " edition, 1886–8, has a few additions, including "Sultan Stork " (see No. 34 above), and some omissions.   Vol. xiii. of this edition contains these miscellanea (except the contributions to *Punch* printed in vol. vi., and "Charity and Humour," printed in vol. vii.), and the contributions to *The Britannia* in 1841 and *Punch's Pocket-Book* for 1847, first reprinted in 1894 (see No. 35 above).

The "Yellowplush Correspondence " was reprinted from *Fraser* at Philadelphia in 1838.   Some other collections were also published in America in 1852 and 1853, one volume including for the first time the "Prize Novelists," the "Fat Contributor," and "Travels in London," and another, "Mr. Brown's Letters," &c., having a preface by Thackeray (see above). "Early and Late Papers" (1867) is a collection by J. T. Fields. "L'Abbaye de Penmarch" has been erroneously attributed to W. M. Thackeray from confusion with a namesake.

The above includes all such writings of Thackeray as he thought worth preservation; and the last two volumes, as the publishers state, were intended to prevent the publication of more trifles. The "Sultan Stork" (1887) includes the doubtful "Mrs. Brownrigge" from *Fraser* of 1832. For further details see the bibliography appended to "Sultan Stork." See also the earlier bibliography by R. H. Shepherd (1880), the bibliography appended to Merivale and Marzials, and Mr. C. P. Johnson's "Hints to Collectors of First Editions of Thackeray's Works."

L. S.

A BIBLIOGRAPHY

OF THE WORKS OF

WILLIAM MAKEPEACE THACKERAY

BIOGRAPHICAL EDITION

ARRANGED IN THE ORDER OF THEIR FIRST
APPEARANCE IN BOOK-FORM

BIBLIOGRAPHY

OF THE WORKS OF W. M. THACKERAY *

1836.

FLORE ET ZÉPHYR: Ballet Mythologique dedié à (Sketch of Flore), par Théophile Wagstaff (Autograph). London, published March 1st, 1836, by J. Mitchell, Library, 33 Old Bond St.; à Paris, chez Rittner & Goupil, Boulevard Montmartre. Printed by Graf & Soret. Folio. Nine plates including title, all except title on India paper, lithographed by Edward Morton.

VIGNETTE TITLE.
1. La Danse fait ses offrandes sur l'autel de l'Harmonie.
2. Jeux Innocens de Zéphyr et Flore.
3. Flore deplore l'absence de Zéphyr.
4. Dans un pas-seul il exprime son extrême desespoir.
5. Triste et abattu, les séductions des Nymphes le tentent en vain.
6. Reconciliation de Flore & Zéphyr.
7. La Retraite de Flore.
8. Les Delassements de Zéphyr.

1838.

THE YELLOWPLUSH CORRESPONDENCE. Philadelphia: E. L. Carey & A. Hart. 1838. 12mo, pp. 238.

No. I. Fashnable Fax and Polite Annygoats.
„ II. Miss Shum's Husband.
„ III. Dimond cut Dimond.
„ IV. Skimmings from "The Dairy of George IV."
„ V. Foring Parts.
„ VI. Mr. Deuceace at Paris (Chaps. i.-iv.).
„ VII. „ „ (Chaps. v.-vii.).
„ VIII. The End of Mr. Deuceace's History (Chaps. viii.-x.).

Fraser's Magazine.

Nov. 1837, Jan. to July 1838 (Vol. 16, pp. 644-9; Vol. 17, pp. 39-49, 243-50, 353-9, 404-8, 616-27, 734-41; Vol. 18, pp. 59-71).
See also "Comic Tales and Sketches," Vol. 1, 1841.

---

* This Bibliography, with the Index following, is due to Mr. W. J. Williams.

1840.

AN ESSAY ON THE GENIUS OF GEORGE CRUIKSHANK, with numerous illustrations of his works (from the *Westminster Review*, No. LXVI.), with additional etchings. Henry Hooper, 13 Pall Mall East. MDCCCXL. 8vo, pp. ii–59.

Westminster Review.

June 1840 (No. LXVI., Vol. xxxiv. pp. 1-60). London : Henry Hooper, 13 Pall Mall East. 1841.

1840.

THE PARIS SKETCH BOOK. By Mr. Titmarsh, with numerous designs by the author on copper and wood. 2 vols. London : John Macrone, 1, St. Martin's Place, Trafalgar Square. 1840. 12mo.

CONTENTS OF VOL. 1, pp. viii-304.

An Invasion of France.
  The Corsair, New York, 1839.
A Caution to Travellers.
The Fêtes of July.
  The Corsair, New York, 1839.
On the French School of Painting.
  Fraser's Magazine, Dec. 1839 (Vol. 20, pp. 679-88).
The Painter's Bargain.

Cartouche.
  Fraser's Magazine, Oct. 1839 (Vol. 20, pp. 447-53).
On some French Fashionable Novels.
A Gambler's Death.
Napoleon and his System.
The Story of Mary Ancel.
  The New Monthly Magazine, Oct. 1838 (Vol. 54, pp. 185-97).
Beatrice Merger.

CONTENTS OF VOL. 2, pp. iv-298.

Caricatures and Lithography in Paris.
Little Poinsinet.
  Fraser's Magazine, Oct. 1839 (Vol. 20, pp. 453-9).
The Devil's Wager.
  The National Standard, Aug. 10 and 24, 1833 (Vol. 2, pp. 85-6, 121-2).

Madame Sand and the New Apocalypse.
  The Corsair, New York, 1839.
The Case of Peytel.
Imitations of Béranger—The King of Brentford.
  Fraser's Magazine, May 1834 (Vol. 9, pp. 617-18).
French Dramas and Melodramas.
Meditations at Versailles.

1841.

COMIC TALES AND SKETCHES. Edited and Illustrated by Mr. Michael Angelo Titmarsh, author of " The Paris Sketch Book," etc. In two volumes. London : Hugh Cunningham, St. Martin's Place, Trafalgar Square. 1841. 12mo.

CONTENTS OF VOL. 1, pp. viii–299, and six plates.

THE YELLOWPLUSH PAPERS :—

1. Miss Shum's Husband.
2. The Amours of Mr. Deuceace: Dimond cut Dimond.
3. Skimmings from the "Dairy of George IV."
4. Foring Parts.
5. Mr. Deuceace at Paris (in ten chapters).
6. Mr. Yellowplush's Ajew.
7. Epistles to the Literati.

Fraser's Magazine.

Nos. 1 to 5 first reprinted in "The Yellowplush Correspondence." 1838.
Nos. 6 and 7, Aug. 1838, Jan. 1840 (Vol. 18, pp. 195–200 ; Vol. 21, pp. 71–80).

CONTENTS OF VOL. 2, pp. iv–370, and six plates.

SOME PASSAGES IN THE LIFE OF MAJOR GAHAGAN :—
The New Monthly Magazine (London : Colburn), Feb., March, Nov., Dec. 1838, and Feb. 1839 (Vol. 52, pp. 174–82, 374–8 ; Vol. 54, pp. 319–28, 543–52 ; Vol. 55, pp. 266–81).

THE PROFESSOR :—
Bentley's Miscellany, Sept. 1837 (Vol. 2, pp. 277–88).

THE BEDFORD ROW CONSPIRACY :—
The New Monthly Magazine, Jan., March, and April 1840 (Vol. 58, pp. 99–111, 416–25, 547–57).

STUBBS'S CALENDAR ; OR, THE FATAL BOOTS :—
The Comic Almanack for 1839. London : Charles Tilt.

1841.

THE SECOND FUNERAL OF NAPOLEON : In three Letters to Miss Smith of London, and THE CHRONICLE OF THE DRUM, by Mr. M. A. Titmarsh. London : Hugh Cunningham. 1841. 16mo, pp. 122.

Reprinted (with prefatory note) in *The Cornhill Magazine.* London : Smith, Elder & Co., Jan. 1866 (Vol. 13, pp. 48–80).

A portion of the original manuscript is facsimiled in *The Autographic Mirror*, Feb. 20, 1864 (Vol. 1, p. 6).

1843.

THE IRISH SKETCH-BOOK. By Mr. M. A. Titmarsh, with numerous engravings on wood, drawn by the author. 2 vols. 12mo. London : Chapman and Hall, 186 Strand. MDCCCXLIII. Vol. 1, pp. vi–311 ; Vol. 2, pp. vi–327.

1846.

Notes of a Journey from Cornhill to Grand Cairo, by way of Lisbon, Athens, Constantinople, and Jerusalem : Performed in the Steamers of the Peninsular and Oriental Company. By Mr. M. A. Titmarsh, Author of " The Irish Sketch Book," &c. London : Chapman and Hall, 186 Strand. MDCCCXLVI. 12mo, pp. xiv–301, and Frontispiece.

1847.

Mrs. Perkins's Ball. By [Mr. M. A. Titmarsh, Mrs. Perkins At Home, Friday Evening, 19 Decr Pocklington Square.] London : Chapman & Hall, 186 Strand. MDCCCXLVII. 4to, pp. ii–46.

1848.

" Our Street." By Mr. M. A. Titmarsh. London : Chapman and Hall, 186 Strand. MDCCCXLVIII. 8vo, pp. 54, and 15 Full-page Illustrations.

1848.

Vanity Fair : A Novel without a Hero. By William Make-peace Thackeray. With Illustrations on Steel and Wood by the Author. London : Bradbury and Evans, 11, Bouverie Street. 1848. 8vo, pp. xvi–624, and 40 Full-page Plates.

First published in twenty numbers, with yellow wrappers, monthly, under the title :—" Vanity Fair : Pen and Pencil Sketches of English Society. By W. M. Thackeray." Number 1, Jan. 1847 ; Numbers 19 and 20 (double number), July 1848.

1848.

The Book of Snobs. By W. M. Thackeray, Author of " A Journey from Cornhill to Grand Cairo," of " Jeames's Diary," in *Punch*, " Our Street," " Vanity Fair," &c. &c. London : *Punch* Office, 85 Fleet Street. MDCCCXLVIII. pp. vi–180.

First published as " The Snobs of England, by One of Themselves."

Punch.

1849.

DOCTOR BIRCH AND HIS YOUNG FRIENDS. By Mr. M. A. Titmarsh. London : Chapman and Hall, 186 Strand. 1849. 8vo, pp. vi–49, and 16 Full-page Illustrations.

1849.

THE HISTORY OF SAMUEL TITMARSH AND THE GREAT HOGGARTY
DIAMOND. By W. M. Thackeray, Author of "Pendennis,"
"Vanity Fair," &c. &c. London: Bradbury & Evans, 11,
Bouverie Street. MDCCCXLIX. 8vo, pp. xii–189, and 9
Full-page Plates.

> *Fraser's Magazine*, Sept., Oct., Nov., and Dec. 1841 (Vol.
> 24, pp. 324–43, 389–99, 594–611, 717–34), where it
> appeared under the title:—The History of Samuel
> Titmarsh and The Great Hoggarty Diamond. Edited
> and Illustrated by Sam's Cousin, Michael Angelo.

1849–50.

THE HISTORY OF PENDENNIS: HIS FORTUNES AND MISFORTUNES,
HIS FRIENDS AND HIS GREATEST ENEMY. By William
Makepeace Thackeray. With Illustrations on Steel and Wood
by the Author. 2 Vols., 8vo. London! Bradbury and
Evans, 11, Bouverie Street. Vol. 1, 1849, pp. viii–384, and
24 Full-page Plates; Vol. 2, 1850, pp. xii–372, and 24 Full-
page Plates.

> First published in twenty-four numbers, with yellow
> wrappers, monthly. Numbers 1 to 11, Nov. 1848
> to Sept. 1849; Numbers 12 to 23 and 24 (double
> number), Jan. to Dec. 1850.

1850.

REBECCA AND ROWENA: A ROMANCE UPON ROMANCE. By Mr.
M. A. Titmarsh. With Illustrations by Richard Doyle.
London: Chapman and Hall, 186 Strand. 1850. 8vo, pp.
viii–102, and 8 Full-page Illustrations.

> Reprinted from *Fraser's Magazine*, where the substance of
> it appeared, Aug. and Sept. 1846 (Vol. 34, pp.
> 237–45, 359–67), under the title:—Proposals for a
> Continuation of Ivanhoe. In a Letter to Monsieur
> Alexander Dumas, by Monsieur Michael Angelo
> Titmarsh.

1850.

THE KICKLEBURYS ON THE RHINE. By Mr. M. A. Titmarsh.
London: Smith, Elder, & Co., 65 Cornhill. MDCCCL. 4to,
pp. vi–87, and 15 Full-page Illustrations.

Second Edition, with Preface, being an Essay on Thunder and
Small Beer. London : Smith, Elder & Co. 1851. 4to,
pp. xv–87.

1852.

THE HISTORY OF HENRY ESMOND, Esq., A Colonel in the service
of Her Majesty Q. Anne. Written by Himself. Servetur
ad imum Qualis ab incepto processerit, et sibi constet. In
three volumes. London : Printed for Smith, Elder & Company, over against St. Peter's Church in Cornhill. 1852.
Vol. 1, pp. 344 ; Vol. 2, pp. vi–319 ; Vol. 3, pp. vi–324.

1852–3.

THE LUCK OF BARRY LYNDON : A ROMANCE OF THE LAST
CENTURY. By William M. Thackeray, Author of "Vanity
Fair," "Pendennis," "Men's Wives," "Book of Snobs,"
"Yellowplush Papers," etc. etc. New York : D. Appleton
& Company, 200 Broadway. Vol. 1, 1852, pp. 267 ; Vol. 2,
1853, pp. 260. 16mo. (Appleton's Popular Library of the
Best Authors.)

Fraser's Magazine.

Jan. to Sept., Nov., Dec. 1844 (Vol. 29, pp. 35–51, 187–202, 318–30,
391–410, 548–63, 723–38 ; Vol. 30, pp. 93–108, 227–42, 353–64,
584–97, 666–83).

1853.

THE CONFESSIONS OF FITZBOODLE AND SOME PASSAGES IN THE
LIFE OF MAJOR GAHAGAN. By W. M. Thackeray, Author
of "Pendennis," "The Luck of Barry Lyndon," "The Book of
Snobs," "Men's Wives," etc. New York : D. Appleton &
Company, 200 Broadway. MDCCCLIII. pp. 276. (Appleton's
Popular Library of the Best Authors.)

Fraser's Magazine.

CONFESSIONS OF FITZBOODLE :—
Preface	} June 1842.	Vol. 25, pp. 707–21	
Fitzboodle's Confessions			
Professions by George Fitzboodle	. July ,,	Vol. 26,	43–60
Miss Löwe	. Oct. ,,	,,	395–405
Dorothea	. Jan. 1843.	Vol. 27,	76–84
Ottilia	. Feb. ,,	,,	214–24

SOME PASSAGES IN THE LIFE OF MAJOR GAHAGAN :—
See "Comic Tales and Sketches," Vol. 2, 1841.

1853.

MEN'S WIVES. By William M. Thackeray. New York: D.
Appleton & Company, 200 Broadway. 1853. pp. 274. 16mo.
(Appleton's Popular Library of the Best Authors.)

Fraser's Magazine.

Mr. and Mrs. Frank Berry, two chapters, Mar. 1843 (Vol. 27, pp. 349–61).
The Ravenswing, eight chapters, April to June, Aug. and Sept. 1843
   (Vol. 27, pp. 465–75, 597–608, 723–33 ; Vol. 28, 188–205, 321–37).
Dennis Haggarty's Wife, Oct. 1843 (Vol. 28, pp. 494–504).

. . . .

1853.

A SHABBY-GENTEEL STORY AND OTHER TALES. By William M.
Thackeray. New York: D. Appleton & Company, 200
Broadway. 1853. pp. 283. (Appleton's Popular Library
of the Best Authors.)

A SHABBY-GENTEEL STORY :—
   Fraser's Magazine, June to Aug., Oct. 1840 (Vol. 21, pp. 677–89 ; Vol.
      22, pp. 90–101, 226–37, 399–414).
   Reprinted in *The Miscellanies* (Vol. 4, 1857, with a note added at the
      end).
THE PROFESSOR :—
   See "Comic Tales and Sketches" (Vol. 2, 1841).
THE BEDFORD ROW CONSPIRACY :—
   See "Comic Tales and Sketches" (Vol. 2, 1841).
A LITTLE DINNER AT TIMMINS'S :—
   Punch, May 27, June 17, 24, July 1, 8, 22, and 29, 1848 (Vol. 14, pp.
      219–23, 247, 258–9 ; Vol. 15, pp. 5, 13, 33–4, 43).

1853.

JEAMES'S DIARY, A LEGEND OF THE RHINE, AND REBECCA AND
ROWENA. By W. M. Thackeray, Author of "Vanity Fair,"
"MR. BROWN'S LETTERS TO A YOUNG MAN ABOUT TOWN,"
etc. New York: D. Appleton & Company, 200 Broadway.
1853. pp. 295. (Appleton's Popular Library of the Best
Authors.)

Punch.

JEAMES'S DIARY :—
   A Lucky Speculator,   ⎫ Aug. 2, 1845 (Vol. 9, p. 59).
   Jeames of Buckley Square, ⎭
   A Letter from "Jeames of Buckley Square," Aug. 16, 1845 (Vol. 9, p. 76).
   The Diary, Nov. 8–29, Dec. 6, 13, 27, 1845 ; Jan. 3, 10, 17, 31, Feb. 7,
      1846 (Vol. 9, 207–8, 210, 227, 233, 242–3, 251 ; Vol. 10, 10–11, 13,·
      30–1, 35, 54–5, 72–3).

A LEGEND OF THE RHINE :—
George Cruikshank's "Table-Book,"—London : *Punch* Office, 92 Fleet
Street, 1845—(Parts 6–12) pp. 119–25, 144–52, 167–75, 193–200, 224–8,
241–5, 267–70.
REBECCA AND ROWENA—See 1850.

1853.

MR. BROWN'S LETTERS TO A YOUNG MAN ABOUT TOWN ; with
the " Proser " and other papers. By W. M. Thackeray, Author
of " Vanity Fair," " Jeames's Diary," " The Prize Novelists,"
" The Book of Snobs," etc. etc. New York : D. Appleton &
Company, 200 Broadway. MDCCCLIII. pp. 256. (Appleton's
Popular Library of the Best Authors.) With Preface by the
author, dated New York, December 1852.

Punch.

MR. BROWN'S LETTERS TO A YOUNG MAN ABOUT TOWN :—

Introductory	Mar. 24, 1849.	Vol. 16, p.	115
On Tailoring—and Toilettes in General	„ 31, „	„	125
The Influence of Lovely Woman upon Society	April 7, „	„	135–6
Some more Words about the Ladies	„ 14, „	„	145–6
On Friendship	„ 28, May 5, } „	„	{ 165–6, 184–5
Mr. Brown the Elder takes Mr. Brown the Younger to a Club	May 12–26, „	„	{ 187–8, 197–8, 207–8
A Word about Balls in Season	June 9, „	„	229–30
A Word about Dinners	„ 16, „	„	239–40
On some Old Customs of the Dinner Table	„ 23, „	„	249–50
Great and Little Dinners	July 7, „	Vol. 17,	1–2
On Love, Marriage, Men, and Women	July 14,21, Aug. 4, } „	„	{ 13–14, 23, 43
Out of Town	Aug. 11–18, „	„	53, 66–9

THE PROSER :—

On a Lady in an Opera Box	1850.	Vol. 18, pp.	151–2
On the Pleasures of being a Fogey	„	„	173
On the Benefits of being a Fogey	„	„	197–8

MISCELLANIES :—

Child's Parties and a Remonstrance Concerning them	{ Jan. 13, 27, Vol. 16,	1849.	{ pp. 13–14, 35–6
Science at Cambridge	Nov. 11, 1848.	Vol. 15,	201
Irish Gems	April, „	Vol. 14,	153
The Charles the Second Ball	May, 1851.	Vol. 20,	221
The Georges	Oct. 11, 1845.	Vol. 9,	159

1853.

PUNCH'S PRIZE NOVELISTS, THE FAT CONTRIBUTOR, and TRAVELS
IN LONDON.   By W. M. Thackeray, Author of "Vanity Fair,"
"Mr. Brown's Letters to a Young Man about Town," etc.
New York : D. Appleton & Company, 200 Broadway.   1853.
pp. 306.   (Appleton's Popular Library of the Best Authors.)

Punch.

PUNCH'S PRIZE NOVELISTS :—

George de Barnwell . . .	{ Ap. 3–17, 1847. Vol. 12, {	pp. 136–7 146–7, 155
Phil Fogarty	Aug. 7–21, ,, Vol. 13, {	49–50, 56–7, 67–8
Barbazure	July 10–24, , ,, {	2, 12–13, 21–2
Lords and Liveries . . .	June 12–26, ,, Vol. 12, {	237–8, 247, 257
Codlingsby	{ April 24, May 15–29, } 1847. ,,	{ 166,198–9, 213–14, 223

See also " Burlesques," 1869.

THE FAT CONTRIBUTOR :—

Brighton	Oct. 11, ,,	Vol. 9,	p. 158
Meditations over Brighton . .	,, 25, ,,	,,	187
A Brighton Night Entertainment	,, 18, ,,	,,	168
Brighton in 1847 (in two chapters)	Oct. 23, 30, 1847.	Vol. 13, {	153, 157–8

Travelling Notes :—

1. By our Fat Contributor .	Nov. 30, 1844.	Vol. 7,	237
2. The Ship at Sea—Dolores .	Dec. 7, ,,	,,	256–7
3. From my Log-book at Sea .	,, 14, ,,	,,	265–6

Punch in the East :—

1. From our Fat Contributor .	Jan. 11, 1845.	Vol. 8,	31–2
2. On the Prospects of *Punch* in the East . . . }	,, 18, ,,	,,	35–6
3. Athens	,, 25, ,,	,,	45
4. *Punch* at the Pyramids .	Feb. 1, ,,	,,	61
5. ,, ,, concluded	,, 8, ,,	,,	75

TRAVELS IN LONDON :—

The Curate's Walk (in two parts)	{ Nov. 27, Dec. 4, } 1847.	Vol. 13, {	pp. 201–2, 211–12
A Dinner in the City (in three parts)	{ Dec. 11, 25, 31, } ,,	,, {	223–4, 247–8, 251
A Club in an Uproar . . .	Mar. 11, 1848.	Vol. 14,	95–6
Waiting at the Station .	Mar. 9, 1850.	Vol. 18,	92–3
A Night's Pleasure (in six parts) .	{ Jan. 8, 15, 22, 29 ; Feb. 12, 19, 1848. }	Vol. 14, {	11, 19, 29, 35–6,61–2, 65–6

GOING TO SEE A MAN HANGED :—

Fraser's Magazine .. . . Aug. 1840. Vol. 22, pp. 150–8

1853.

THE ENGLISH HUMOURISTS OF THE EIGHTEENTH CENTURY : A Series of Lectures delivered in England, Scotland, and the United States of America. By W. M. Thackeray, Author of " Esmond," "Vanity Fair," &c. London: Smith, Elder & Co., 65 Cornhill. Bombay : Smith, Taylor & Co. 1853. [The Author of this work reserves to himself the right of authorising a translation of it.] Pp. ii–322.

An American edition published in the same year by Messrs. Harper and Bros., New York, contains in addition the lecture on " Charity and Humour," which was first delivered in New York on behalf of a charity.

1854–5.

THE NEWCOMES : Memoirs of a most respectable Family. Edited by Arthur Pendennis, Esq. With illustrations on steel and wood by Richard Doyle. 2 vols. London: Bradbury and Evans, 11, Bouverie Street. Vol. 1, 1854, pp. viii–380, and 24 Plates ; Vol. 2, 1855, pp. viii–375, and 24 Plates.

First published in twenty-four numbers, with yellow wrappers, monthly. Number 1, Oct. 1853; Numbers 23 and 24 (double number), Aug. 1855.

1855.

THE ROSE AND THE RING ; OR, THE HISTORY OF PRINCE GIGLIO AND PRINCE BULBO. A Fire-side Pantomime for Great and Small Children. By Mr. M. A. Titmarsh, Author of " The Kickleburys on the Rhine," " Mrs. Perkins's Ball," &c. &c. London : Smith, Elder and Co., 65, Cornhill. 1855. pp. iv– 128, and 8 Full-page Illustrations.

1855–7.

MISCELLANIES : Prose and Verse. By W. M. Thackeray, Author of " Vanity Fair," " The Newcomes," &c. London : Bradbury & Evans, 11, Bouverie Street. Vol. 1, 1855 ; Vols. 2 and 3, 1856 ; Vol. 4, 1857.

CONTENTS OF VOL. 1, 1855, pp. viii–510.

BALLADS :—

The Chronicle of the Drum—" Second Funeral of Napoleon," 1841.

The King of Brentford's Testament—George Cruikshank's *Omnibus*, December 1841, No. 8, pp. 244–6.

The White Squall—" Cornhill to Cairo," Chap. 9, 1846.

Peg of Limavaddy—" Irish Sketch Book," Chap. 30, 1843.

BALLADS, *continued :—*

    May-Day Ode—*Times,* April 30, 1851, p. 5, col. 3, dated April 29.

    The Ballad of Bouillabaisse—*Punch,* Feb. 17, 1849 (Vol. 16, p. 67).

    The Mahogany Tree—*Punch,* Jan. 9, 1847 (Vol. 12, p. 13).

    The Yankee Volunteers—*Punch,* Jan. 1, 1851 (Vol. 20, p. 2).

    The Pen and the Album—*Keepsake,* 1853, pp. 48-50.

    Lucy's Birthday—*Keepsake,* 1854, p. 18, dated New York, April 15.

    The Cane-bottom'd Chair—*Punch,* March 27, 1847 (Vol. 12, p. 125).

   *Piscator and Piscatrix.

    Ronsard to his Mistress—*Fraser's Magazine,* Jan. 1846 (Vol. 33, p. 120).

    At the Church Gate—" Pendennis," Chap. 31, 1849-50.

    The Age of Wisdom—" Rebecca and Rowena," Chap. 4, 1850.

   *Sorrows of Werther.

   *The Last of May.

LOVE SONGS MADE EASY :—

    What makes my Heart to Thrill and Glow ?—*Punch,* March 6, 1847
       (Vol. 12, p. 101).

    The Ghazul, or Oriental Love-Song :—

       The Rocks—*Punch,* June 5, 1847 (Vol. 12, p. 227).

       The Merry Bard ,,   ,,   ,,

       The Caïque ,,   ,,   ,,

*FOUR GERMAN DITTIES :—

    A Tragic Story.

    The Chaplet.

    The King on the Tower.

    To a very Old Woman

IMITATION OF HORACE :—

    To his Serving Boy—*administram*—"Memorials of Gormandising,"1841.

AN OLD FRIEND WITH A NEW FACE :—

   *The Knightly Guerdon.

   *The Almack's Adieu.

    The Legend of St. Sophia of Kioff—*Fraser's Magazine,* Dec. 1839 (Vol.
       20, pp. 715-27).

    Titmarsh's Carmen Lilliense—*Fraser's Magazine,* March 1844 (Vol. 29
       pp. 361-3).

LYRA HIBERNICA :—

    The Pimlico Pavilion—*Punch,* Aug. 9, 1845 (Vol. 9, p. 66).

    The Crystal Palace—1851.

    Molony's Lament—*Punch,* 1850 (Vol. 18, p. 113), under the title " Mr.
       Finigan's Lament."

    Mr. Molony's Account of the Ball—*Punch,* Aug. 3, 1850 (Vol. 19, p. 53).

    The Battle of Limerick—*Punch,* May 13, 1848 (Vol. 14, p. 195).

THE BALLADS OF POLICEMAN X :—

    The Wofle new Ballad of Jane Roney and Mary Brown—*Punch,* May 25,
       1850 (Vol. 18, p. 209).

    The Three Christmas Waits—*Punch,* Dec. 23, 1848 (Vol. 15, p. 265).

    Lines on a Late Hospicious Ewent—*Punch,* May 18, 1850 (Vol. 18,
       p. 189).

---

   * These do not appear to have been published anywhere previously.

THE BALLADS OF POLICEMAN X, *continued :—*
  The Ballad of Eliza Davis—*Punch*, Feb. 9, 1850 (Vol. 18, p. 53).
  Damages, Two Hundred Pounds—*Punch*, Aug. 24, 1850 (Vol. 19,
      p. 88).
  The Knight and the Lady—*Punch*, Nov. 25, 1848 (Vol. 15, p. 229),
      under the title " A Bow Street Ballad."
  Jacob Homnium's Hoss—*Punch*, Dec. 9, 1848 (Vol. 15, p. 251).
  *The Speculators.

THE LAMENTABLE BALLAD OF THE FOUNDLING OF SHOREDITCH—From
    the *Times* of Feb. 14 :—
  Punch, Feb. 23, 1850 (Vol. 18, p. 73).

THE END OF THE PLAY—Dr. Birch and his Young Friends, 1849.

THE BOOK OF SNOBS—See 1848.

THE TREMENDOUS ADVENTURES OF MAJOR GAHAGAN :—
  See "Comic Tales and Sketches," Vol. 2, 1841.

THE FATAL BOOTS :—
  See "Comic Tales and Sketches," Vol. 2, 1841.

COX'S DIARY :—
  The *Comic Almanack*, 1840, under the title "Barber Cox, and the
    Cutting of his Comb."

1855–7.

CONTENTS OF VOL. 2, 1856, pp. iv–494.

The following appear in book form for the first time :—
CHARACTER SKETCHES :—
  Captain Rook and Mr. Pigeon.
  The Fashionable Authoress.
  The Artists.
  Heads of the People; or, Portraits of the English :—
  Drawn by Kenny Meadows. With Original Essays by Distinguished
    Writers. London : Robert Tyas, 50 Cheapside. 1840, pp. 305–20 ;
    1841, pp. 73–84, 161–76.

1858–9.

THE VIRGINIANS : a Tale of the Last Century. By W. M.
Thackeray, Author of "Esmond," "Vanity Fair," "The
Newcomes," &c. &c. With Illustrations on Steel and Wood
by the Author. 2 Vols. London : Bradbury & Evans, 11,
Bouverie Street. Vol. 1, 1858, pp. viii–382, Vignette Title
and 23 Plates ; Vol. 2, 1859, pp. viii.–376, Vignette Title
and 23 Plates.
    First published in twenty-four numbers, with yellow wrappers,
    monthly. Nov. 1857 to Oct. 1859.

1861.

THE FOUR GEORGES. By W. M. Thackeray, Author of "Lectures
on the English Humourists," etc. etc. With Illustrations.
London: Smith, Elder and Co., 65 Cornhill. MDCCCLXI. [The
right of translation is reserved.] Pp. iv–226, and 2 Full-
page Illustrations.

The Cornhill Magazine.

George the First—July   1860, Vol. 2, pp. 1–20
George the Second—Aug.   „   „   175–91
George the Third—Sept.   „   „   257–77
George the Fourth—Oct.   „   „   385–406

1861.

LOVEL THE WIDOWER. By W. M. Thackeray. With Illustrations.
London: Smith, Elder and Co., 65, Cornhill. MDCCCLXI. [The
right of translation is reserved.] Pp. iv–258, and 6 Full-
page Plates.

The Cornhill Magazine.

Jan. to June 1860 (Vol. 1, pp. 44–60, 233–47, 330–45, 385–402, 583–97,
    652–68).
See also 1869. Thackeray's Works, Library Edition, Vol. 22.

1862.

THE ADVENTURES OF PHILIP ON HIS WAY THROUGH THE WORLD :
Shewing who Robbed him, who Helped him, and who Passed
him by. By W. M. Thackeray, Author of "Esmond," "Vanity
Fair," "Virginians," etc. In three volumes. London : Smith,
Elder and Co., 65, Cornhill. MDCCCLXII. Vol. 1, pp. viii–
329 ; Vol. 2, pp. iv–304 ; Vol. 3, pp. iv–301.

The Cornhill Magazine.

Jan. 1861 to Aug. 1862 (Vol. 3, pp. 1–24, 166–89, 270–93, 385–408,
    556–83, 641–65 ; Vol. 4, pp. 1–24, 129–52, 257–80, 385–408, 513–36,
    641–64 ; Vol. 5, pp. 1–25, 129–52, 257–80, 385–408, 513–36, 641–64 ;
    Vol. 6, pp. 121–44, 217–40).

1863.

ROUNDABOUT PAPERS. Reprinted from *The Cornhill Magazine.*
With Illustrations by W. M. Thackeray, Author of "Esmond,"
"The Four Georges," "Adventures of Philip," etc. London :
Smith, Elder and Co., 65, Cornhill. MDCCCLXIII. [The right
of translation is reserved.] Pp. iv–352, and 5 Full-page
Illustrations.

The Cornhill Magazine.

On a Lazy, Idle Boy—Jan. 1860 (i. 124–8).
On Two Children in Black—March 1860 (i. 380–4).
On Ribbons—May 1860 (i. 631–40).
On Some Late Great Victories—June 1860 (i. 755–60).
Thorns in the Cushion—July 1860 (ii. 122–8).
On Screens in Dining-rooms—Aug. 1860 (ii. 252–6).
Tunbridge Toys—Sept. 1860 (ii. 380–4).
De Juventute—Oct. 1860 (ii. 501–12).
On a Joke I once Heard from the late Thomas Hood—Dec. 1860 (ii. 752–60).
Round about the Christmas Tree—Feb. 1861 (iii. 250–6).
On a Chalk-mark on the Door—April 1861 (iii. 504–12).
On being Found Out—May 1861 (iii. 636–40).
On a Hundred Years hence—June 1861 (iii. 755–60).
Small-beer Chronicle—July 1861 (iv. 122–8).
Ogres—Aug. 1861 (iv. 251–6).
On two Roundabout Papers which I intended to Write—Sept. 1861 (iv. 377–84).
A Mississippi Bubble—Dec. 1861 (iv. 754–60).
On Letts's Diary—Jan. 1862 (v. 122–8).
Notes of a Week's Holiday—Nov. 1860 (ii. 623–40).
Nil Nisi Bonum—Feb. 1860 (i. 129–34).

See also " Roundabout Papers," 1869.

1867.

DENIS DUVAL. By W. M. Thackeray, Author of "Vanity Fair," "The Adventures of Philip," etc. London : Smith, Elder and Co., 65, Cornhill. 1867. pp. iv–275.

The Cornhill Magazine.

March, April, May, and June 1864 (Vol. ix., pp. 257–91, 385–409, 513–36, 641–65). The notes at the end are by Frederick Greenwood, at that time editor of the magazine.

1867.

EARLY AND LATE PAPERS, Hitherto Uncollected. By William Makepeace Thackeray. Boston : Ticknor and Fields. 1867. Crown 8vo, pp. viii–407.

MEMORIALS OF GORMANDISING :—
Fraser's Magazine, June 1841 (Vol. 23, pp. 710–25).
MEN AND COATS :—
Fraser's Magazine, Aug. 1841 (Vol. 24, pp. 208–17).
BLUEBEARD'S GHOST :—
Fraser's Magazine, Oct. 1843 (Vol. 28, pp. 413–25).

3A

DICKENS IN FRANCE :—
 Fraser's Magazine, March 1842 (Vol. 25, pp. 342-52).

JOHN LEECH'S PICTURES OF LIFE AND CHARACTER :—
 The Quarterly Review, Dec. 1854 (Vol. 96, pp. 75-86).

LITTLE TRAVELS AND ROADSIDE SKETCHES :—
 No. 1. From Richmond in Surrey to Brussels in Belgium. *Fraser's Magazine*, May 1844 (Vol. 29, pp. 517-28).
 No. 2. Ghent—Bruges. *Fraser's Magazine*, Oct. 1844 (Vol. 30, pp. 465-71).
 No. 3. Waterloo. *Fraser's Magazine*, Jan. 1845 (Vol. 31, pp. 94-6).

ON MEN AND PICTURES :—
 Fraser's Magazine, July 1841 (Vol. 24, pp. 98-111).

PICTURE GOSSIP :—
 Fraser's Magazine, June 1845 (Vol. 31, pp. 713-24).

· · · · · · · · · ·

GOETHE :—
 A letter written by Thackeray in answer to a request from G. H. Lewes for some account of his recollections of Goethe. Dated London, 28th April 1855. Printed in Lewes's " Life and Works of Goethe." London : David Nutt. 1855. Vol. 2, pp. 442-6.

A LEAF OUT OF A SKETCH BOOK :—
 The Victoria Regia, a Volume of Original Contributions in Poetry and Prose. Edited by Adelaide A. Procter. London : Emily Faithfull and Co., Great Coram Street, W.C. 1861. pp. 118-25.

THE LAST SKETCH :—
 Cornhill Magazine, April 1860 (Vol. 1, pp. 485-7).

"STRANGE TO SAY ON CLUB PAPER" :—
 Cornhill Magazine, Nov. 1863 (Vol. 8, pp. 636-40).

AUTOUR DE MON CHAPEAU :—
 Cornhill Magazine, Feb. 1863 (Vol. 7, pp. 260-7).

ON A PEAL OF BELLS :—
 Cornhill Magazine, Sept. 1862 (Vol. 6, pp. 425-32).

ON SOME CARP AT SANS SOUCI :—
 Cornhill Magazine, Jan. 1863 (Vol. 7, pp. 126-31).

DESSEIN'S :—
 Cornhill Magazine, Dec. 1862 (Vol. 6, pp. 771-9).

ON A PEAR TREE :—
 Cornhill Magazine, Nov. 1862 (Vol. 6, pp. 715-20).

ON A MEDAL OF GEORGE THE FOURTH :—
 Cornhill Magazine, Aug. 1863 (Vol. 8, pp. 250-6).

ON ALEXANDRINES :—
 Cornhill Magazine, April 1863 (Vol. 7, pp. 546-52).

THE NOTCH ON THE AXE :—
 Cornhill Magazine, April, May, June 1862 (Vol. 5, pp. 508-12, 634-40, 754-60).

DE FINIBUS :—
 Cornhill Magazine, Aug. 1862 (Vol. 6, pp. 282-8).

1869.

Thackeray's Works, Library Edition.   24 Vols. (1867-9).

Vol. 16. BURLESQUES; NOVELS BY EMINENT HANDS; JEAMES'S
   DIARY; ADVENTURES OF MAJOR GAHAGAN; A LEGEND
   OF THE RHINE; REBECCA AND ROWENA; THE HISTORY
   OF THE NEXT FRENCH REVOLUTION; COX'S DIARY.   By
   W. M. Thackeray.   With Illustrations by the Author and
   by Richard Doyle.   London: Smith, Elder & Co., 15
   Waterloo Place, S.W.   1869.   pp. viii-448.

The following appear for the first time in book form :—

NOVELS BY EMINENT HANDS :—
   Crinoline—*Punch*, Aug. 28, Sept. 4, 11, 1847 (Vol. 13, pp. 72-3, 82-3,
      97-8).
   The Stars and Stripes—*Punch*, Sept. 25, Oct. 9, 1847.
   A Plan for a Prize Novel—*Punch* (Vol. 20, p. 75).
      See also *Punch's* " Prize Novelists," 1853.

THE DIARY OF C. JEAMES DE LA PLUCHE, ESQ., WITH HIS LETTERS :—
   Jeames on Time Bargings—*Punch*, Nov. 1, 1845 (Vol. 9, p. 195).
   Jeames on the Gauge Question—*Punch*, May 16, 1846 (Vol. 10, p. 223).
   Mr. Jeames again—*Punch*, June 13, 1846 (Vol. 10, p. 267).
      See also 1853.

THE HISTORY OF THE NEXT FRENCH REVOLUTION — (from a forthcoming
   History of England) :—
   Punch, Feb. 24, March 2-30, April 6-20, 1844 (Vol. 6, pp. 90-3, 98-9,
      113-14, 117, 127-8, 137-9, 147-8, 157, 167-8).

1869.

Vol. 18. BALLADS AND TALES.   By W. M. Thackeray.   London:
   Smith, Elder and Co., 15 Waterloo Place.   1869.   pp.
   viii-413.

The following ballads appear in a collected form for the first
time :—

   Abd-el-Kader at Toulon; or, The Caged Hawk—*Punch*, Jan. 1848
      (Vol. 14, p. 14).
   Mrs. Katherine's Lantern (written by Thackeray in a lady's album)—
      Cornhill Magazine, Jan. 1867 (Vol. 15, pp. 117-18).   The lady
      referred to in the poem is Mrs. Perugini, younger daughter of
      Charles Dickens.
   The Rose upon my Balcony—" Vanity Fair," Chapter 51, 1848.
   A Doe in the City—*Punch*, Nov. 1, 1845 (Vol. 9, p. 191).
   " Ah, Bleak and Barren was the Moor "—" Vanity Fair," Chap. 4, 1848.
   Song of the Violet—" A Shabby-Genteel Story," Chapter 5, 1840.
   Fairy Days—" Fitzboodle Papers "—Ottilia, Chapter 2, 1843.
   Pocahontas—" Virginians," Chapter 80, 1859.
   From Pocahontas—" Virginians," Chapter 80, 1859.

LOVE SONGS MADE EASY:—

My Nora—"Fitzboodle Papers"—Fitzboodle's Third Profession, 1842.

To Mary—"Book of Snobs" (Club Snobs, No. 4), 1847.

Serenade—"Paris Sketch Book," Vol. 2—The Devil's Wager, 1833.

The Minaret Bells—"Men's Wives"—Ravenswing, Chapter 1, 1843.

Come to the Greenwood Tree—"Men's Wives"—Ravenswing, Chapter 2, 1843.

GERMAN DITTY:—

A Credo—"Philip," Chapter 7, 1861.

FOUR IMITATIONS OF BÉRANGER:—

Le Roi d'Yvetot.
The King of Yvetot.
The King of Brentford.
Le Grenier.   "Paris Sketch Book," Vol. 2, 1840.
The Garret.
Roger Bontemps.
Jolly Jack.

OLD FRIENDS WITH NEW FACES:—

When the Gloom is on the Glen   "Sketches and Travels"—A Night's
The Red Flag   Pleasure, Chapter 5, 1848.

Dear Jack—"Novels by Eminent Hands"—"Phil Fogarty," 1847.

Commanders of the Faithful—"Rebecca and Rowena," 1846.

When Moonlike ore the Hazure Seas—"Jeames's Diary," 1845.

King Canute—"Miss Tickletoby's Lectures," 1842, and "Rebecca and Rowena," 1849.

Friar's Song—"Paris Sketch Book," Vol. 2—The Devil's Wager, 1833.

Atra Cura—"Rebecca and Rowena," 1849.

Requiescat—"Rebecca and Rowena," 1849.

Lines upon my Sister's Portrait—"Jeames's Diary," 1845.

The Willow-Tree—"Fitzboodle Papers"—Ottilia, 1843.

The Willow-Tree (another version)—"Fitzboodle Papers"—Ottilia, 1843.

LYRA HIBERNICA:—

Larry O'Toole—"Novels by Eminent Hands"—"Phil Fogarty," 1847.

The Rose of Flora—"Barry Lyndon," Chap. 1, 1844.

The Last Irish Grievance—*Punch*, Nov. 22, 1851 (Vol. 21, p. 223).

THE BALLADS OF POLICEMAN X:—

A Woeful new Ballad of the Protestant Conspiracy to take the Pope's Life—*Punch*, Mar. 15, 1851 (Vol. 20, p. 113).

The Organ Boy's Appeal—*Punch*, Oct. 1853 (Vol. 25, p. 141).

Little Billee—*North British Review*, Feb. 1864 (Vol. 40, p. 254). Originally published as "The Three Sailors" in Bevan's "Sand and Canvas," 1849, pp. 336–42.

Vanitas Vanitatum—*Cornhill Magazine*, July 1860 (Vol. 2, pp. 59–60). See also "Miscellanies," Vol. 1, 1855.

Vol. 20. ROUNDABOUT PAPERS (from *The Cornhill Magazine*), to which is added THE SECOND FUNERAL OF NAPOLEON. By W. M. Thackeray. With Illustrations by the Author. London: Smith, Elder and Co., 15 Waterloo Place. 1869. pp. vi–428.

The following Roundabout Paper from *The Cornhill Magazine* appears in book form with the others for the first time :—

On Half a Loaf—A Letter to Messrs. Broadway, Battery and Co., of New York, Bankers, Feb. 1862 (Vol. 5, 250–6).

See also " Roundabout Papers," 1863.

1869.

Vol. 22. CATHERINE: A STORY; LITTLE TRAVELS; THE FITZBOODLE PAPERS, ETC. ETC. By W. M. Thackeray. With Illustrations by the Author, and a Portrait. London: Smith, Elder & Co., 15 Waterloo Place. 1869. pp. viii–390.

The following appear for the first time in book form :—

CATHERINE: A STORY:—
Fraser's Magazine, May to Aug., Nov. 1839; Jan., Feb. 1840 (Vol. 19, pp. 604–17, 694–709; Vol. 20, pp. 98–112, 224–32, 531–48; Vol. 21, pp. 106–15, 200–12).

THE WOLVES AND THE LAMB:—
Written for the stage about 1854. It is the original of the story of "Lovel the Widower." See 1861.

1876.

THE ORPHAN OF PIMLICO AND OTHER SKETCHES, FRAGMENTS, AND DRAWINGS. By William Makepeace Thackeray. With some Notes by Anne Isabella Thackeray. London: Smith, Elder & Co., 15 Waterloo Place. 1876. Royal 4to.

1877–9.

Thackeray's Works, Cheaper Illustrated Edition, 26 Vols.

Vol. 14. THE BOOK OF SNOBS and SKETCHES AND TRAVELS IN LONDON. By William Makepeace Thackeray. With Illustrations by the Author. London: Smith, Elder, & Co., 15 Waterloo Place. 1878. pp. xii–396.

The following appear for the first time in book form :—

On a Good-looking Young Lady—*Punch*, 1850 (Vol. 18, pp. 223–4).
On the Press and the Public—*Punch*, 1850 (Vol. 19, p. 59).

Vol. 21. BALLADS and THE ROSE AND THE RING. By William
  Makepeace Thackeray. With Illustrations by the Author,
  Mrs. Butler (Miss Elizabeth Thompson), George du Maurier,
  John Collier, H. Furniss, G. G. Kilburne, Mr. FitzGerald,
  and J. P. Atkinson. London : Smith, Elder, & Co., 15
  Waterloo Place. 1879. pp. xii–410.

The under-mentioned is included here among the other Ballads
for the first time :—

> Jeames of Buckley Square : A Helegy—See " Jeames's Diary," 1853.

1885.

Thackeray's Works, Standard Edition, 26 vols. (1883–6).

Vol. 25. MISCELLANEOUS ESSAYS, SKETCHES, AND REVIEWS. By
  William Makepeace Thackeray. With Illustrations by the
  Author. London : Smith, Elder & Co., 15 Waterloo Place.
  1885. pp. x–485.

Critical Reviews.

Fashnable Fax and Polite Annygoats—See "The Yellowplush Cor-
  respondence," 1838.
Jerome Paturot ; with Considerations on Novels in General—*Fraser's
  Magazine*, Sept. 1843 (Vol. 28, pp. 349-62).

A Box of Novels—*Fraser's Magazine*, Feb. 1844 (Vol. 29, pp. 153-69).

A Brother of the Press on the History of a Literary Man, Laman
  Blanchard, and the Chances of the Literary Profession—*Fraser's
  Magazine*, March 1846 (Vol. 33, pp. 332-42).
Strictures on Pictures—*Fraser's Magazine*, June 1838 (Vol. 17, pp.
  758-64).
A Second Lecture on the Fine Arts—*Fraser's Magazine*, June 1839
  (Vol. 19, pp. 743-50).
A Pictorial Rhapsody—*Fraser's Magazine*, June 1840 (Vol. 21, pp.
  720-32).
A Pictorial Rhapsody concluded—*Fraser's Magazine*, July 1840 (Vol. 22,
  pp. 112-26).
On Men and Pictures—"See Early and Late Papers," 1867.
May Gambols—*Fraser's Magazine*, June 1844 (Vol. 29, pp. 700-16).
Picture Gossip—See " Early and Late Papers," 1867.

Tales.

The Professor—See " Comic Tales and Sketches " (Vol. 2, 1841).
Miss Löwe—See " The Confessions of Fitzboodle," &c., 1853.
Bluebeard's Ghost—See " Early and Late Papers," 1867.

Lecture.

Charity and Humour—See " The English Humourists," 1853.

Various Essays, Letters, Sketches, &c.

Memorials of Gormandising—See "Early and Late Papers," 1867.

Men and Coats—See "Early and Late Papers," 1867.

Greenwich—Whitebait—*New Monthly Magazine*, July 1844 (Vol. 71, pp. 416–21).

A Leaf out of a Sketch Book—See "Early and Late Papers," 1867.

The Dignity of Literature—Letter, dated Reform Club, Jan. 8—*The Morning Chronicle*, Jan. 12, 1850 (p. 4, cols. 1–2).

Mr. Thackeray in the United States—*Fraser's Magazine*, Jan. 1853 (Vol. 47, pp. 100-3).

Goethe in his Old Age—See "Early and Late Papers," 1867.

Timbuctoo—*The Snob* (Cambridge 1829, 12mo), No. 4, April 30, 1829.

Dr. Johnson and Goldsmith—*The North British Review*, Feb. 1864 (Vol. 40, p. 256), in an article on Thackeray by Dr. John Brown.

The History of Dionysius Diddler—First published in *The Autographic Mirror*, 1864, Feb. 20 to June 1 (Vol. 1, pp. 6, 15, 28, 39, 40, 60, 68, 76). The drawings were made about 1838 for *The Whitey-Brown Paper Magazine*, suggested to be issued in 1838-9 as a weekly publication.

1886.

Thackeray's Works, Standard Edition, 26 vols. (1883–6).

Vol. 26. CONTRIBUTIONS TO "PUNCH" (not previously reprinted). By William Makepeace Thackeray. With Illustrations by the Author. London : Smith, Elder & Co., 15 Waterloo Place. 1886. pp. xii–431.

MISS TICKLETOBY'S LECTURES ON ENGLISH HISTORY: A Character (to Introduce another Character). Lectures 1–10. 1842 (Vol. 3, pp. 8–9, 12–13, 28–30, 58–9, 70–2, 84–5, 91–2, 116–17, 121–2, 131–3, 142–3).

PAPERS BY THE FAT CONTRIBUTOR :—

1. Wanderings of our Fat Contributor—Aug. 3 (Vol. 7, pp. 61–2).
2. The Sea—Aug. 10, 17 (Vol. 7, pp. 66–7, 83–4).

MISCELLANEOUS CONTRIBUTIONS TO "PUNCH" :—

Mr. Spec's Remonstrance—Feb. 1843 (Vol. 4, pp. 69–70).

Singular Letter from the Regent of Spain—Dec. 1843 (Vol. 5, pp. 267–8).

The Georges—See "Mr. Brown's Letters," &c., 1853.

Titmarsh *v.* Tait—Mar. 14, 1846 (Vol. 10, p. 124).

Royal Academy—May 1846 (Vol. 10, p. 214).

Professor Byle's Opinion of the Westminster Hall Exhibition—July 1847 (Vol. 13, pp. 8–9).

Punch and the Influenza—Dec. 1847 (Vol. 13, p. 238).

The Persecution of British Footmen (in two parts)—April 1 and 8, 1848 (Vol. 14, pp. 131, 143–4).

Irish Gems—See "Mr. Brown's Letters," &c., 1853.

Mr. Snob's Remonstrance with Mr. Smith—May 27, 1848 (Vol. 14, p. 217).

Yesterday : A Tale of the Polish Ball—June 1848 (Vol. 14, p. 237).

1887.

SULTAN STORK AND OTHER STORIES AND SKETCHES. By William
Makepeace Thackeray (1829–1844). Now first collected, to
which is added The Bibliography of Thackeray, revised and
considerably enlarged. London : George Redway, York Street,
Covent Garden. 1887.

SULTAN STORK : Being the one thousand and second Night, translated
from the Persian, by Major G. O'G. Gahagan, H.E.I.C.S.—*Ainsworth's
Magazine*, Feb. and May 1842 (Vol. 1, pp. 33–8, 233–37).

DICKENS IN FRANCE :—
See "Early and Late Papers," 1867.

CARLYLE'S "FRENCH REVOLUTION":—
Times, Aug. 3, 1837 (folio 6, col. 4–6).

1891.

READING A POEM. By Wm. Makepeace Thackeray, communicated
by Brother Charles Plumtre Johnson to the sette, at a meeting
holden at Limmer's Hotel, on Friday the 1st of May, 1891.
Imprinted at the Chiswick Press, Tooks Court, Chancery Lane,
London. MDCCCXCI. pp. xii–66.

(No. xxvii. The Sette of Odd Volumes—Privately printed.)
The Britannia, a weekly journal, May 1 and 8, 1841.

1894.

LOOSE SKETCHES, AN EASTERN ADVENTURE, &c. By W. M.
Thackeray. With a Frontispiece by John Leech. London :
Frank T. Sabin. MDCCCXCIV. pp. xii–113.

Reprinted from *The Britannia*, a weekly journal :—
Reading a Poem—See 1891.
A St. Philip's Day at Paris—May 15 and 22, 1841.
Shrove Tuesday in Paris—June 5, 1841.

Reprinted from *Punch's Pocket Book* for 1847 (London : *Punch* Office, 85 Fleet
Street, pp. 148–56, with plate by Leech) :—
An Eastern Adventure of the Fat Contributor.

1899.

"The Ballad of Catherine Hayes" is included among the other
Ballads for the first time in this volume. See the Introductions to Vol. 4, p. xix., and Vol. 13, p. xxii.

INDEX

TO THE WORKS OF

W. M. THACKERAY: BIOGRAPHICAL EDITION

The two first numbers indicate the volume and page in which the works will be found, while the last number gives the page of the Bibliography in Volume XXV., in which each work is mentioned.

THE END